THE OXFORD HAND

EVANGELICAL THEOLOGY

THE OXFORD HANDBOOK OF

EVANGELICAL THEOLOGY

Edited by

GERALD R. MCDERMOTT

OXFORD
UNIVERSITY PRESS

OXFORD
UNIVERSITY PRESS

Oxford University Press is a department of the University of Oxford.
It furthers the University's objective of excellence in research, scholarship,
and education by publishing worldwide.

Oxford New York
Auckland Cape Town Dar es Salaam Hong Kong Karachi
Kuala Lumpur Madrid Melbourne Mexico City Nairobi
New Delhi Shanghai Taipei Toronto

With offices in
Argentina Austria Brazil Chile Czech Republic France Greece
Guatemala Hungary Italy Japan Poland Portugal Singapore
South Korea Switzerland Thailand Turkey Ukraine Vietnam

Published in the United States of America by
Oxford University Press
198 Madison Avenue, New York, NY 10016

First issued as an Oxford University Press paperback, 2013.

Library of Congress Cataloging-in-Publication Data
The Oxford handbook of evangelical theology / edited by Gerald R. McDermott.
p. cm.
ISBN 978-0-19-536944-1 (hardcover); 978-0-19-933599-2 (paperback)
1. Evangelicalism. 2. Theology, Doctrinal. I. McDermott, Gerald R. (Gerald Robert)
BR1640.O83 2010
230'.04624--dc22 2009047953

9 8 7 6 5 4 3 2 1

Printed in the United States of America
on acid-free paper

Acknowledgments

I am indebted to a good number of people for their help with this project during the last few years. My editor, Theo Calderara, first approached me with the idea, and then provided excellent guidance at many steps along the way. John Stackhouse helped me formulate the initial outline of topics and writers, and kept offering wise advice as the project proceeded. Robert Benne was a continual source of editorial insight and friendly encouragement. Doug Sweeney and Paul Hinlicky made valuable recommendations. I could not have completed this volume without indispensable summer and sabbatical support from Roanoke College and the Institute for Studies of Religion at Baylor University. The Institute's director, Byron Johnson, has been especially helpful and encouraging. One could not ask for a more cheerful and efficient secretary than Judith Pinckney. Finally, I could not have finished this volume without the love and counsel of my dear wife, Jean.

Contents

Part III. Theology of Salvation

Part IV. Theology of Church

Part V. Theology of Mission

Contributors

William J. Abraham is the Albert Cook Outler Professor of Theology and Wesley Studies and Altshuler Distinguished Teaching Professor at Perkins School of Theology, Southern Methodist University, Dallas, Texas. He is the co-editor (with James E. Kirby) of *The Oxford Handbook of Methodist Studies*. His most recent publications include *Crossing the Threshold of Divine Revelation* and *Athens and Aldersgate: John Wesley and the Foundations of Christian Belief*.

Henri A. G. Blocher has taught theology at the Faculté Libre de Théologie Evangélique (Vaux-sur-Seine, France) since its foundation in 1965, and held the Gunther Knoedler chair of Systematic Theology at the Wheaton College Graduate School from 2003 to 2008. From 2002 to 2008 he was president of the Fellowship of European Evangelical Theologians (2002–2008). His last book in English was *Original Sin: Illuminating the Riddle.*

Donald G. Bloesch is Professor of Theology Emeritus at Dubuque (Iowa) Theological Seminary. He is the author of numerous books including *The Struggle of Prayer, Spirituality Old & New, Freedom for Obedience, Essentials of Evangelical Theology*, the now completed seven-volume *Christian Foundations* series, and his ongoing spiritual journal, *Theological Notebook* (four volumes thus far). He has been widely recognized as a prophetic voice in evangelicalism. He received the PhD degree in theology from the University of Chicago and has done postdoctoral study at the universities of Oxford, Basel, and Tübingen. He is a past president of the Midwest Division of the American Theological Society.

Darrell L. Bock is Research Professor of New Testament Studies at Dallas Theological Seminary in Dallas, Texas. His special fields of study involve hermeneutics, Jesus, the gospels, and the relationship of culture to Christianity. He is a graduate of the University of Aberdeen (PhD). He engaged in postdoctoral study at the University of Tübingen as an Alexander von Humboldt scholar, where he authored *Blasphemy and Exaltation in Judaism and the Final Examination of Jesus*. He is editor at large for *Christianity Today* and served as president of the Evangelical Theological Society for the year 2000–2001.

M. Daniel Carroll R. (Rodas) (PhD, University of Sheffield) is Distinguished Professor of Old Testament at Denver Seminary. Prior to his appointment, he was professor of Old Testament and ethics and director of graduate studies at El

Seminario Teológico Centroamericano in Guatemala City, Guatemala, where he remains an adjunct professor. Dr. Carroll is the founder of IDEAL, an Hispanic training program at Denver Seminary. He publishes in English and Spanish-language journals, has authored two books on Amos, and edited several books on Old Testament ethics. His latest book is *Christians at the Border: Immigration, the Church and the Bible.*

Simon Chan (PhD, Cambridge) is an ordained minister of the Assemblies of God and Earnest Lau Professor of Systematic Theology at Trinity Theological College in Singapore. His professional interest has been in the relationship of theology, spirituality and the liturgy. His publications include *Spiritual Theology: A Systematic Study of the Christian Life*, and *Liturgical Theology: The Church as Worshipping Community*. He is currently a consulting editor of the *Dictionary of Christian Spirituality*.

Sung Wook Chung (DPhil, Oxford University) is Associate Professor of Theology at Denver Seminary, Colorado. He earned a DPhil from the University of Oxford and an MDiv from Harvard University. He has authored *Admiration and Challenge: Karl Barth's Theological Relationship with John Calvin*, and edited *Alister McGrath and Evangelical Theology: A Dynamic Engagement; Christ the One and Only: A Global Affirmation of the Uniqueness of Jesus Christ; Karl Barth and Evangelical Theology: Convergences and Divergences; John Calvin and Evangelical Theology: Legacy and Prospect*; and with Dr. Craig Blomberg, *A Case for Historic Premillennialism.*

Oliver Crisp is Reader in Theology at the University of Bristol, UK. He specializes in philosophical theology. His recent publications include *Divinity and Humanity: The Incarnation Reconsidered; Analytic Theology: New Essays in the Philosophy of Theology*, co-edited with Michael Rea; and *God Incarnate: Explorations in Christology.*

Robert A. J. Gagnon is Associate Professor of New Testament at Pittsburgh Theological Seminary. He has a BA degree from Dartmouth College, an MTS from Harvard Divinity School, and a PhD from Princeton Theological Seminary. He is the author of *The Bible and Homosexual Practice: Texts and Hermeneutics*; co-author (with Dan O. Via) of *Homosexuality and the Bible: Two Views*; and, as a service to the church, provides a large amount of free material on the Web dealing with Scripture and homosexuality at http://www.robgagnon.net/. In addition, he has published scholarly articles in such journals as *Journal of Biblical Literature, New Testament Studies,* and *Novum Testamentum.*

Eric Gregory is Professor of Religion at Princeton University. He is author of *Politics & The Order of Love: An Augustinian Ethic of Democratic Citizenship*, and various essays on topics in theology, moral and political philosophy, bioethics, and the role of religion in public life. A graduate of Harvard College, he did graduate studies in theology at Oxford as a Rhodes Scholar, and received his doctorate in religious studies from Yale University. In 2007, he was awarded Princeton's President's Award for Distinguished Teaching.

Trevor A. Hart is Professor of Divinity at the University of St. Andrews. He teaches and publishes in Christian doctrine and systematic theology, and is the author of a number of books, including *The Waiting Father: Thomas Erskine of Linlathen; Justice the True and Only Mercy: Essays on the Life and Theology of Peter Taylor Forsyth; Faith Thinking: The Dynamics of Christian Theology; Hope against Hope: Christian Eschatology in Contemporary Context* (with Richard Bauckham); and *Regarding Karl Barth: Toward a Reading of His Theology.*

Craig S. Keener (PhD, Duke University) is Professor of New Testament at Palmer Theological Seminary of Eastern University. He has authored many articles and fourteen books, including three commentaries that have won awards, one of which has sold half a million copies. His works include major academic commentaries on Matthew, John, other commentaries on Romans, 1–2 Corinthians, Revelation, and New Testament background. Among his other works are *The Spirit in the Gospels and Acts* and *Gift & Giver.* He is married to Dr. Medine Moussounga Keener, from Congo, Central Africa.

Robert Letham (PhD, University of Aberdeen) is Senior Tutor in systematic and historical theology at the Wales Evangelical School of Theology. A Presbyterian minister—senior minister for seventeen years in Wilmington, Delaware—he has taught at London School of Theology, Westminster Theological Seminary, Philadelphia, and Reformed Theological Seminary, Washington, D.C. He has written the following books: *The Holy Trinity: In Scripture, History, Theology, and Worship* (winner of the Evangelical Christian Publishers Association's Gold Medallion Award), *The Work of Christ; Reformed Dogmatics 1523–1619; Through Western Eyes; The Lord's Supper;* and *The Westminster Assembly: Reading Its Theology in Historical Context.*

Roger Lundin is the Blanchard Professor of English at Wheaton College (Illinois). He has written and edited ten books, including *Believing Again: Doubt and Faith in A Secular Age; Invisible Conversations: Religion in the Literature of America;* and *Emily Dickinson and the Art of Belief.* He has been a visiting professor at Calvin College, Regent College, and the University of Notre Dame, and has received major research fellowships from the Erasmus Institute, the Pew Charitable Trusts, and the Evangelical Scholarship Initiative. Lundin has an MA in Theological Studies from Gordon-Conwell Theological Seminary and earned his MA and PhD in English at the University of Connecticut.

John Lunn is the Robert W. Haack Professor of Economics at Hope College in Holland, Michigan. He taught previously at Louisiana State University, and Miami

University (Ohio). He earned his doctorate at UCLA, specializing in industrial organization. Currently, he is studying the causes of the recent economic crisis. He is also working on a book-length manuscript of why many theologians do not like market systems. He has published in a number of scholarly journals, including *European Economic Review, Southern Economic Journal, Journal of Legal Studies, Journal of Industrial Economics, Christian Scholars' Review*, and *Journal of Religious Ethics.*

Michael McClymond, Associate Professor of Theological Studies at Saint Louis University, was educated at Northwestern, Yale, and the University of Chicago. He has held teaching and research appointments at Wheaton and Westmont Colleges, U.C. San Diego, and Emory University. His books include *Encounters with God: An Approach to the Theology of Jonathan Edward; Familiar Stranger: An Introduction to Jesus of Nazareth*; the *Encyclopedia of Religious Revivals in America*; and *Embodying the Spirit: New Perspectives on North American Revivalism.*

Gerald McDermott is the Jordan-Trexler Professor of Religion at Roanoke College. He has written, co-written, or edited thirteen books, including *A Trinitarian Theology of Religions* (forthcoming from OUP), *The Theology of Jonathan Edwards* (OUP 2008), *Jonathan Edwards Confronts the Gods* (OUP 2000); *One Holy and Happy Society; God's Rivals; Can Evangelicals Learn from World Religions?; Cancer: A Medical and Spiritual Guide; Evangelicals and Mormons; World Religions;* and *The Great Theologians: A Brief Guide.*

Scot McKnight is the Karl A. Olsson Professor in Religious Studies at North Park University. His publications include *Turning to Jesus, Finding Faith, Losing Faith,* and *A Community Called Atonement.* This award-winning author maintains a full speaking and lecturing schedule at both the national and international levels.

Alister McGrath is Professor of Theology, Ministry and Education at King's College, London, and Director of its Centre for Theology, Religion and Culture. He served for many years as Oxford University's Professor of Historical Theology before moving to London, and also as Principal of Wycliffe Hall, Oxford, one of British evangelicalism's premier institutions of theological education. His recent books include *The Open Secret: A New Vision for Natural Theology; A Fine-Tuned Universe: The Quest for God in Science and Theology*; and *Heresy: A History of Defending the Faith,* as well as numerous widely used theological textbooks.

C. Ben Mitchell is Graves Professor of Moral Philosophy at Union University in Tennessee and editor of *Ethics & Medicine: An International Journal of Bioethics.* He taught bioethics and contemporary culture for a decade at Trinity Evangelical Divinity School in Deerfield, Illinois, where he was also director of the Center for Bioethics & Human Dignity from 2006–2008. He received his doctorate in philosophy with a concentration in medical ethics (with honors) from the University of Tennessee, Knoxville, including a year-long clinical residency at the University of Tennessee Medical Center at Knoxville, Vanderbilt Medical Center, and the East Tennessee Mental Health Institute.

Mark Noll is the Francis A. McAnaney Professor of History at the University of Notre Dame. He is the co-editor of *Evangelicalism: Comparative Studies of Popular Protestantism in North America, the British Isles, and Beyond, 1700–1990*, as well as author of *American Evangelical Christianity: An Introduction*, and *The Scandal of the Evangelical Mind.*

Cherith Fee Nordling is a North American who loves the Church around the world and through the ages. She has taught on the theology faculty of Wheaton College, Regent College, Kuyper College, Calvin College, and Calvin Theological Seminary. She holds graduate degrees in counseling psychology from Notre Dame de Namur (Belmont, Cal.) and in theology from Regent College (Vancouver, B.C.). She wrote her doctorate in systematic theology under Alan Torrance at the University of St. Andrews (Scotland). Her theological areas of interest include early and contemporary Trinitarian theology, theological anthropology, the Holy Spirit in the Church, and worship.

Ephraim Radner (PhD, Yale University) is Professor of Historical Theology at Wycliffe College, Toronto, an evangelical seminary of the Anglican tradition at the University of Toronto. He is the author and editor of several books on ecclesiology and on Bible, including *The End of the Church, Spirit and Nature, Hope Among the Fragments, Leviticus*, and *The World in the Shadow of God.* A former church worker in Burundi, he has been active in the affairs of the global Anglican Communion.

Gordon T. Smith is the president of reSource Leadership International, an agency fostering excellence in theological education in the developing world. He is also an adjunct faculty member of Regent College, Vancouver, Canada. He is the author of a number of publications, including *Beginning Well: Christian Conversion and Authentic Transformation; The Voice of Jesus: Discernment, Prayer and the Witness of the Spirit*; and *Transforming Conversion: ReThinking the Language and Contours of Christian Initiation.*

Howard A. Snyder serves as professor in the Chair of Wesley Studies at Tyndale Seminary in Toronto, Ontario, Canada. Previously he served for ten years as professor of the history and theology of mission in the E. Stanley Jones School of World Mission and Evangelism at Asbury Theological Seminary in Kentucky. Howard and his family were missionaries in Brazil with the Free Methodist Church, 1968–1975, and he has taught and pastored in Detroit and Chicago. He was professor of church revitalization at United Seminary in Dayton, Ohio, 1988–1996.

Professor Snyder's books include *The Problem of Wineskins, The Community of the King, Liberating the Church*, and *Models of the Kingdom.*

John Stackhouse (PhD, Chicago) holds the Sangwoo Youtong Chee Chair of Theology and Culture at Regent College, Vancouver, Canada. He is the author of more than 500 articles and reviews and seven books in the history, philosophy, sociology, and theology of Christianity. He also has edited four volumes of evangelical theology. His most recent books are *Making the Best of It: Following Christ in the Real World*, and *Can God Be Trusted? Faith and the Challenge of Evil.* He is currently at work on a Christian epistemology.

Timothy Tseng is the Executive Director of the Institute for the Study of Asian American Christianity and teaches Asian Religion at the University of San Francisco. Tim has served as faculty at Denver Seminary, Colgate Rochester Crozer Divinity School, and the Graduate Theological Union, where he was Associate Professor of American Religious History. He has written articles for several journals and has contributed chapters to *Realizing the America of Our Hearts: Theological Voices of Asian Americans; Revealing the Sacred in Asian and Pacific America; Women and Twentieth-Century Protestants; The Social Gospel Today*; and *New Spiritual Homes: Religion and Asian Americans.*

Kevin J. Vanhoozer (PhD, Cambridge) is currently Research Professor of Systematic Theology at Trinity Evangelical Divinity School. Previously he was Blanchard Professor of Theology at the Wheaton College Graduate School and Senior Lecturer in Theology and Religious Studies at the University of Edinburgh, Scotland (1990–98). He is the author of five books, including *The Drama of Doctrine: A Canonical-Linguistic Approach to Christian Theology* and *Remythologizing Theology: Divine Action, Passion, and Authorship*, and editor of ten more, including the *Dictionary for the Theological Interpretation of the Bible.*

Rikk Watts (PhD, Cambridge) is Professor of New Testament at Regent College and Chair of the Mark Group at SBL. A regular presenter at academic conferences, he has published several books, including *Isaiah's New Exodus in Mark* and a commentary on the OT in Mark, various essays, journal and dictionary articles, and reviews, some of which have been translated into other languages. His primary interests include biblical intertextuality, Gospels, Isaiah, intertestamental Scriptural interpretation, hermeneutics, and historiography. Current projects include a volume on Jesus' mighty deeds and Christology, a commentary on Mark, and a primer on biblical theology as God's transformational rhetoric.

Loren Wilkinson is Professor of Philosophy and Interdisciplinary Studies at Regent College in Vancouver. Most of his academic and popular publications—most notably *Earthkeeping in the 90's: The Stewardship of Creation*—have been concerned with recovering the Christian doctrine of creation as a resource for our contemporary life. Wilkinson has master's degrees from Johns Hopkins University and Trinity Evangelical Divinity School, and a doctorate in Humanities from Syracuse University.

Dallas Willard is currently a Professor of Philosophy at the University of Southern California, where he has taught since 1965. He received his doctorate in philosophy and the history of science from the University of Wisconsin (Madison) in 1964, and taught there the following year. He has held visiting appointments at UCLA (1969) and the University of Colorado (1984). In addition to work in philosophy, he writes and speaks in the area of Christian thought, and especially as it concerns spiritual formation. His most recent book is *Knowing Christ Today: Why We Can Trust Spiritual Knowledge.* Professor Willard's Web site is www.dwillard.org.

John D. Witvliet is Director of the Calvin Institute of Christian Worship and teaches worship, theology, and music at Calvin College and Calvin Theological Seminary. He is the author of *The Biblical Psalms in Christian Worship, Worship Seeking Understanding*, and co-editor of *Worship in Medieval and Early Modern Europe* and *The Worship Sourcebook.* He holds graduate degrees in theology from Calvin Theological Seminary, in choral music from the University of Illinois, and a PhD in liturgical studies from the University of Notre Dame.

W. Jay Wood (PhD, University of Notre Dame) is Professor of Philosophy, and current Chair, at Wheaton College. His chief areas of academic interest are epistemology and the philosophy of religion. He is the author of *Epistemology: Becoming Intellectually Virtuous* and has recently co-authored, with Robert C. Roberts, *Intellectual Virtues: An Essay in Regulative Epistemology.*

THE OXFORD HANDBOOK OF

EVANGELICAL THEOLOGY

INTRODUCTION

Evangelical theology has come of age. This is not surprising, given the explosion of the movement in recent decades, not only in England and America but especially the Global South. While evangelicals were confused with fundamentalists by most of the academy until recently (and still are by many), the rise to academic prominence of evangelical historians (such as Mark Noll, George Marsden, Nathan Hatch, and Harry Stout), scripture scholars (the likes of N.T. Wright and Richard Bauckham), philosophers (C. Stephen Evans and Keith Yandell, for example), ethicists (led by Richard Hays) and theologians (including Kevin Vanhoozer, Miroslav Volf, and Alister McGrath) has demonstrated the growing maturity of this movement's intellectual leaders.

Evangelical theology has not reached the self-confidence of Roman-Catholic and post-liberal Protestant theology, and some of its strongest thinkers borrow from the two latter schools. But more of them are learning from their own tradition (for example, from Jonathan Edwards's mammoth philosophico-theological project and John Wesley's capacious if diffuse theology), and sounding distinctive voices in the world of Christian theology. The result has been a new profusion of evangelical theologies. Already, at the end of the 1990s, Lutheran theologian Carl Braaten was saying that "the initiative in the writing of dogmatics has been seized by evangelical theologians in America.... [M]ost mainline Protestant and progressive Catholic theology has landed in the graveyard of dogmatics, which is that mode of thinking George Lindbeck calls 'experiential expressivism.' Individuals and groups vent their own religious experience and call it theology."[1] Evangelicals, on the other hand, still believe theology is reflection on what comes from outside their experience as the Word of God. Perhaps for that reason, they have more to say—talking not just about themselves but about a transcendent God. In any event, they have been remarkably productive. In the first decade of this new century, the presses have groaned under the weight of books by evangelicals in systematic theology, historical theology, ethics, hermeneutics, biblical theology, philosophical theology, theology of culture, public theology, theology of science, and a host of other theological subdisciplines.

But this is not the evangelical theology of the 1970s. Back then, evangelical theology had little but contempt for the charismatic movement because of what seemed to be its loosey-goosey attitudes toward doctrine and serious thinking. Now some of the best-known evangelical theologians—Clark Pinnock and Amos Yong, for example—are charismatics and Pentecostals, and few theologians hold tightly to the old theory that charismatic gifts ceased after the apostolic age. In the 1970s, there was a sizable gulf between dispensational and Reformed theology, with neither side talking to the other. Now that respected scholars such as Darrell Bock and Craig Blaising have developed "progressive" dispensationalism, that gap has narrowed.

The questions have also changed. In 1976, which *Newsweek* magazine dubbed "The Year of the Evangelical," evangelical theologians debated inerrancy of the Bible, the timing and existence of a millennium, Karl Barth's neo-orthodoxy, and the threat posed by abortion-on-demand. They agreed that liberal theology was bankrupt, tradition suspect, and universalism (the view that everyone will eventually be saved) impossible. Most evangelical writers were convinced that Roman Catholicism was a religion of works, and apologetics a useful way of showing that Christian faith is reasonable. Other religions were barely on the theological radar—except as proofs that only Christians would be saved.

Almost a half-century later, the assumptions and questions have shifted dramatically. Evangelical theology has accepted the collapse of foundationalism—the notion that there are, or should be, logical or rational grounds for belief. Although most still see a clear line separating Roman Catholic from evangelical theological method, and some still regard Catholicism as sub-Christian, many have learned from the Catholic theological tradition and agree with the Lutheran-Catholic Joint Declaration on Justification (1999) that the Catholic tradition does not teach salvation by works. Basic theological differences between Calvinists and Arminians remain, but today's debates swirl around the role of women in the home and church, what it means to care for creation, whether justification was too narrowly defined by the Reformation, whether God knows our future choices, if non-Christians can be saved and learn religious truth through their traditions, if we need to change our thinking about homosexuality, and whether the damned are destroyed or eventually saved. All assume the Bible is final authority for Christians, but some are saying we ought to learn about the Bible from (mostly Catholic) tradition.

Theologians on both sides of the debate over tradition are divided over the basic task of theology—whether it is to reapply existing evangelical and orthodox tradition to new issues, or to rethink and possibly change the tradition as theologians gain "new light." All evangelical thinkers recognize that revelation in Scripture contains propositions—ideas that can be expressed in words—as well as non-propositional elements such as stories and images that also reveal. Nearly all would agree that the Bible tells one grand story. But while some think revelation is God both acting *and* speaking so that doctrine and experience can never be separated, others say revelation is about God's acts rather than words and that the essence of faith is experience not doctrine.[2] This Introduction will do three things. First, it will discuss the meaning of the word "evangelical" and outline evangelical theology's basic assumptions, while distinguishing it from other kinds of Christian theology. Second, it will highlight the new approaches to evangelical theology that we see in the following thirty-three chapters. Finally, I will make a few projections about the future of evangelical theology.

Definition, Assumptions and Differences

As Mark Noll explains in the next chapter, the word "evangelical" goes back to the Greek noun *euangelion*, which means "glad tidings," "good news" or "gospel," the last of which goes back to an Old English word for "God talk." Three times the New Testament says that someone who proclaims the gospel of Christ dying for our sins is an *euangelistes* (evangelist).[3] Evangelical*ism* has always proclaimed this salvation that comes from Christ's death with a peculiar intensity. Noll shows the origins of the movement in Pietism, the eighteenth-century awakenings, and the Enlightenment. He unpacks David Bebbington's widely accepted fourfold definition—a movement marked by conversionism, biblicism, activism, and cruci-centrism.

Evangelical *theology*, on the other hand, is something of a different animal. While evangelical theologians would not reject any of Bebbington's marks as inaccurate, they typically speak with more theological specificity. Most would endorse Karl Barth's definition of the word (though Barth was not an evangelical in the American or British sense of the word): "*Evangelical* means informed by the gospel of Jesus Christ, as heard afresh in the 16th-century Reformation by a direct return to Holy Scripture." Some important evangelical thinkers such as N.T. Wright and Thomas Oden are now questioning the primacy of the Reformation. But all would agree with the following six evangelical "fundamental convictions," first proposed by Alister McGrath: 1. The majesty of Jesus Christ, both as incarnate God and Lord and as Savior of sinful humanity; 2. The lordship of the Holy Spirit, who is necessary for the application of the presence and work of Christ; 3. The supreme authority of Scripture, recognizing that the language of Scripture is culturally conditioned but that through it God has nevertheless conveyed the eternal, unconditioned Word. Scripture is to be interpreted with the help of reason and the best tools of scholarship, with attention to differing genres; 4. The need for personal conversion. This is not necessarily an emotional experience but at least involves personal repentance and trust in the person and work of Christ, not simply intellectual adherence to doctrine. 5. Commitment to evangelism and missions. 6. The importance of religious community for spiritual nourishment, fellowship, and growth.

Every one of the above six distinctives is shared by most other Christians. What makes this list evangelical, however, is the degree of emphasis which evangelical theology places on the six marks, and the forms which they take. For example, all Christians say evangelism is important at one level or another, but not all regard it with the urgency evangelicals often show. Some regard social service as evangelism, and others do not consider conversion to faith in Christ to be necessary. When Billy Graham conducted his first crusade in New York City, some Protestant mainline leaders ridiculed his efforts—not only because he did not emphasize structural social reform but also because theologians such as Reinhold Niebuhr regarded personal evangelism as theologically wrong-headed. Some of those same churches today speak of personal evangelism as essential to the growth of the church in the world, but they send out fewer missionaries and do less to train their members for the task of evangelism than their evangelical counterparts typically do. While all Christians speak of the need to turn from the world to Christ, evangelicals have placed more emphasis on conversion because of the Puritan and Pietist legacies from which Edwards, Whitefield, and Wesley learned.

Evangelical theology is often regarded, both by the media and much of the academy, as fundamentalism put into writing. But they are really two different ways of thinking, which can be identified in eight ways. Some evangelical theologians might hold some fundamentalist beliefs, and some fundamentalists might share evangelical attitudes. But most evangelical theologians would distinguish their outlook from fundamentalist perspectives in the following ways.

1. *Interpretation of Scripture.* Fundamentalists tend to read Scripture more literalistically, while evangelical theologians look more carefully at genre and literary and historical context. Another way of saying this is that fundamentalists tend to assume that the meaning of Scripture is obvious from a single reading, while evangelicals want to talk about layers of meaning. For example, more fundamentalists will understand the first three chapters of Genesis to contain, among other things, scientific statements about beginnings, while evangelicals will focus more on the theological character of those stories—that the author/editor was more interested in showing that the earth has a Creator, for example, than precisely how the earth was created.

2. *Culture.* Fundamentalists question the value of human culture that is not created by Christians or related to the Bible, whereas evangelicals see God's "common grace" working in and through all human culture. For evangelicals, Mozart may not have been an orthodox Christian and quite possibly was a moral failure as a human being, but his music is a priceless gift of God. Culture is tainted by sin, as are all other human productions, but it nevertheless can reflect God's glory.

3. *Social action.* There was a time when fundamentalists considered efforts to help the poor to be a sign of liberal theology, because proponents of the social gospel during the modernist controversy of the 1920s were theological liberals. Until recently many fundamentalists limited their view of Christian social action to struggles for religious freedom and against abortion. Evangelicals have been more vocal in their declarations that the gospel also calls us to fight racism, sexism, and poverty.

4. *Separatism*. For many decades in this century fundamentalists preached that Christians should separate themselves from liberal Christians (which sometimes meant evangelicals) and even from conservatives who fellowshipped with liberals. This is why some fundamentalists refused to support Billy Graham—Graham asked for help from mainline Protestant and Catholic churches, and sent his converts back to these churches for further nurture. Evangelical theology puts more emphasis on engagement with culture while aiming to transform it, and working with other Christians toward common religious and social goals.

5. *Dialogue with liberals*. Fundamentalists have tended in the past to believe that liberal Christians (those who doubted Jesus' bodily resurrection, the essential sinfulness of humanity, and the importance of blood atonement) were Christian in name only, that there was nothing to learn from them, and there was no use trying to talk to them once they refused to accept the fundamentalist version of the gospel. The evangelical approach has been to talk with those of more liberal persuasions in an effort to persuade and perhaps even learn. John Stott and Clark Pinnock have both engaged in book-length dialogues with liberal theologians.

6. *The ethos of Christian faith*. Although most fundamentalists preach salvation by grace, they also tend to focus so much on rules and restrictions (do's and don'ts) that their church members could get the impression that the heart of Christianity is law governing outward behavior. There is a similar danger in evangelical churches, but evangelical theology focuses more on the person and work of Christ, and personal engagement with that person and work, as the heart of the Christian faith.

7. *Fissiparousness*. Many evangelical groups have fractured and then broken again over what seems to later generations to have been minor issues. But the tendency seems worse among fundamentalists, for whom differences of doctrine, often on rather minor issues, are considered important enough to warrant starting a new congregation or even denomination. Because evangelical theology makes more of the distinction between essentials and non-essentials, evangelicals are more willing to remain in mainline Protestant churches and in evangelical churches whose members disagree on nonessentials.

8. *Support for Israel*. Fundamentalists tend to see the modern state of Israel as a direct fulfillment of biblical prophecies, and say God's blessing of America is contingent on its support for Israel. Evangelicals generally see the creation of Israel in 1948 as at least an indirect fulfillment of prophecy, lacking the complete fulfillment because there has not been the spiritual renewal that the prophets predicted. Evangelicals run the gamut in support for and opposition to Israeli policies. But while many other Christians see Israel as just another nation-state, fundamentalists and evangelicals typically think today's Israel has continuing theological significance.

If evangelical and fundamentalist ways of thinking differ on both content and practice, evangelical theology differs from classical Protestant orthodoxy more on method. Evangelicalism tends to use the principle of *sola scriptura* more radically than the Protestant traditions out of which it grew. That is, when it subscribes to the doctrines of the great creeds of the church (yet some evangelicals and their theologians don't, crying "No creed but the Bible!"), they do so not because the creeds teach the doctrines but because they believe the doctrines have biblical support. Evangelical theologians are not always averse to reading the great fathers and mothers of the church (such as Macrina, Catherine of Siena, Teresa of Avila, and now Mother Teresa) or to learn from the historic confessions, but they typically insist that they do so with critical care. They want to reserve the right to use Scripture as a trump card over tradition when they see conflict between the two. Others, such as "post-conservative" Roger Olson, say they want to be open to further light breaking out from the Word that might compel either a reshaping of doctrine or new doctrine entirely.

Evangelical theologians say they reject liberalism's faith in human experience as a final norm for truth and morality. Against the homogenizing tendency of liberal theology, which would postulate an underlying religiosity common to all faiths, evangelical theology emphasizes the particularity of Christian revelation and the uniqueness of Christian spirituality. While liberals place a premium on personal autonomy and appeal to internal norms (conscience and religious experience), evangelicals have usually stressed human responsibility to God who has given us external norms in Jesus Christ and Scripture.

Some evangelical theologians have learned from the more recent "research program" called postliberalism, which has been inspired by Karl Barth, Hans Frei, and George Lindbeck. This method of theology highlights the primacy of narrative as an interpretive category for Scripture, asserts the hermeneutical primacy of the world created by the biblical narratives over the world of human experience, and claims the primacy of language over experience (the words we have been given about God shape our experience more than our experience shapes our words about God). Some evangelical theologians cheer postliberals' emphasis on the distinctiveness of Christianity, Scripture as the supreme source of ideas and values, the centrality of Jesus Christ, and its stress on Christian community.

But the problem with postliberalism for other evangelical theologians is that the former tends to reduce truth to a matter of internal consistency. Alister McGrath has argued that postliberals have a difficult time answering the question, Why be a Christian and not a Buddhist? Postliberals are also unclear on the nature of revelation. They deny that the Bible is an objective revelation from God, and say instead that the Bible can contain the Word when the Holy Spirit so moves. As a result, they do not clearly determine whether the gospel stories are fictional or real. McGrath and other evangelical theologians put more emphasis on the objective nature of the biblical revelation. With postliberals they emphasize the necessity of the Spirit's illumination to give true understanding of the Person featured in the biblical story, but they assert that the Spirit inspired the writing of the texts in such a way that makes the Bible the Word of God even if no one ever receives it as such. For these evangelicals, the gospels are not merely stories that help us "perform" a Christian life by portraying a Christ who may or may not have been Jesus of Nazareth, but show us the true Jesus who also was the Christ.

New Approaches in Evangelical Theology

This volume illustrates the new approaches which evangelical theologians are taking to a wide range of problems and doctrines. Mark Noll's introductory essay takes on the familiar complaint that evangelicalism is so diffuse as to be unrecognizable; he agrees with George Marsden that while it consists of a congeries of "constituencies," they nevertheless are "overlapping" and share "history and convictions." Those shared convictions can be seen in the Evangelical Alliance's commitments (1846) to the authority of Scripture, the right of private judgment, and belief in the following: Trinity, Fall, incarnation, salvation by the atonement of Christ, justification by faith, the necessity of the work of the Holy Spirit in conversion, resurrection of the dead and final judgment, and ordinances of baptism and the Lord's Supper. Noll also notes what will be a recurring theme in this volume: evangelicalism's "bias against inherited institutions." In their hunger for spiritual authenticity, evangelicals have typically shown a certain wariness toward tradition.

The Bible and Theological Method

Kevin Vanhoozer takes a new approach to biblical hermeneutics. Unlike some "postconservative" evangelicals, Vanhoozer wants to keep the term "inerrancy," but without older presumptions attached to the term. His new, chastened inerrancy rejects the "wooden literalism" that assumed the Bible is a collection of facts and propositions, acknowledges diverse literary conventions used in the Bible, and interprets biblical historical accounts without modern demands for scientific precision. His portrayal of the Bible as "communicative action" by God tries to overcome the dichotomy between the ways propositionalists and pietists have read the text. Vanhoozer aims to recover the "literal" sense of the text, not to be confused with the literalistic or even (merely) literary sense. The Bible, which he says is "less a text than a [divine] vocal chord," is the final but not exclusive authority for the church.

Jay Wood's essay on faith and reason reflects the collapse of classical foundationalism among evangelical thinkers. He rejects the Enlightenment presumption that all reason is of the same sort (he describes a wide range from apriori intuition and inferential reasoning to a body of knowledge) and its insistence that faith be based on certainty. He cites philosophers Alvin Plantinga, Nicholas Wolterstorff, and William Alston, who have argued that belief in God is "properly basic," which means that it is epistemically justified in the absence of argumentative support, just as we commonly accept belief in the world and other minds as so justified. Wood also delineates a range of meanings for "faith"—from Aquinas's assent to propositions about God based on reason and revelation, to Calvin's and Luther's *fiducia* or trust in God's promises.

For Oliver Crisp, faith implies experience for evangelicals, for at the heart of evangelical understanding is that faith must be "affective" to be genuine. It must have content, but it also must involve trust, which necessarily involves religious experience. The precise outworking of this has been seen differently by what we could call evangelicalism's two principal kinship groups—the Wesleyan-Arminian family's "synergism" and the evangelical-Reformed clan's "monergism." Both camps see the writing of Scripture to have involved supernatural experience by its authors, and both agree that while God accommodated himself to speak in accessible ways to ancient cultures, the text is nevertheless God speaking. For liberals, in contrast, Scripture is merely the "codification of religious experience," so that experience is more normative than Scripture itself. Evangelicals regard Scripture as more authoritative than creeds, and at the same time recognize development in interpretation of doctrine and Scripture.

Alister McGrath takes up what has for a long time been an evangelical shibboleth—tradition. He argues that tradition has been needed to interpret many issues in theology because of the church's changing interpretation of those issues, illustrated by debates over usury, the need for missions, the millennium, charismata, baptismal regeneration, and the Lord's Supper. Scripture is not self-interpreting on issues such as these. McGrath reviews three historic Christian approaches to tradition: Anabaptist rejection, the "single-source" theory held by Luther and Calvin that there is a mutual interplay between Scripture and tradition, and the "dual-source" theory promulgated at the Council of Trent (arguing for two independent sources of revelation) but mitigated at Vatican II. Within evangelical theology there is considerable debate between proponents of the first two views.

Theological Foundations

Robert Letham is an evangelical theologian of the Trinity who is sharply critical of evangelical theology's neglect of not only the Trinity but also theological tradition. First Letham reviews the history of differences between East and West on the Trinity, and suggests a way to resolve the divide by using Athanasius and Cyril of Alexandria. But then he argues that while the rest of the Church has usually found the Trinity to be central to its theological vision, evangelicals have shown little interest. He attributes this to evangelicalism's focus on the human agent in conversion, holiness, and mission. Evangelical theology's insistence on the right of private interpretation, Letham charges, ignores the churchly context of the creation of Scripture and the process of its interpretation. He warns that evangelical theologians should think long and hard before they place their interpretations before the historical consensus.

Loren Wilkinson sounds notes on creation that are not typically associated with evangelical theological tones. He observes an "emerging doctrine" among evangelical theologians that the original creation was amazing grace coming from a loving Triune God. Therefore there is new recognition that creation is beautiful though fallen, and every part of it participates in God's goodness. Against deistic notions of a creation once done and now over, Wilkinson argues that creation continues moment by moment, and that evolution might be a means by which God continually creates. He says Jesus' resurrection points to a future for all of creation.

Henri Blocher notes that while evangelicals have been criticized for being preoccupied with sin and guilt, this "preoccupation" has produced remarkable vitality in their movement. The subject itself distinguishes Christian faith from most other religions. Blocher takes a Barthian approach to knowledge of sin, arguing that we become aware of our sin most accurately by looking through the prism of gospel and not just law. He suggests sin is idolatry at its root—but warns that sin has no essence—and distinguishes between sin as condition and sins as variegated acts, with the sinful "disposition" mediating between the two. He also advises that the origin of sin is mysterious and we are wise not to speculate about it. But the Genesis 3 account is "vital," and must be taken seriously as an account of an historical event—if not an historical account precisely—if sin is to be without excuse.

In his chapter on "Jesus Christ," John Stackhouse observes that evangelicals have been recognized for their Christocentric piety and theology. Some (such as Paul Helm) are now suggesting, as have others in the "Great Tradition," that Christ in his preexistence was also incarnate in some sense. Others have taken up Irenaeus's theory of recapitulation (Christ's "re-doing") in which Christ divinizes members of his body by becoming their new head, replacing Adam. Stackhouse uses the kenotic tradition (Christ emptied himself of some of his divine prerogatives during his incarnation) to suggest modifications in philosophical understandings of divine immutability and impassibility. The incarnation suggests there is change in the life of God and that at least one of the three Persons suffers. While some have recently described satisfaction theories of the atonement as "divine child abuse," Stackhouse reminds evangelicals that the doctrine of the Trinity shows us that "it is *God* as Son who hangs on the Cross, as God looks on as Father and Spirit in the added suffering of grief over the Beloved."

Craig Keener suggests that the Christocentric focus of the evangelical movement is a result of the Holy Spirit, whose work is to reveal Jesus. Keener notes the new dominance of Pentecostal and charismatic movements within global evangelicalism (and antipodal anti-supernaturalism in Western philosophy), and intimates that there are biblical reasons for this. Among others, he points to New Testament emphasis on the Spirit as agent of conversion and moral transformation. Luke-Acts sees the Spirit as power for cross-cultural mission. All this means that for evangelical theology doctrine is necessary but not sufficient. Keener argues that cessationist arguments (against the continuing reality of charismata) are weak, but also advises Pentecostals that the baptism of the Holy Spirit is used in the New Testament not only for conversion but also for subsequent experiences. He also warns that evangelical stress on conversion has obscured the Spirit's transformation of character.

Theology of Salvation

Rikk Watts tackles the oft-controverted relationship between Israel and the church in the question of salvation. After describing the many different ways in which supercessionism (the church superceding Israel) and anti-supercessionism have been understood, he calls for both discontinuity and continuity. On the one hand, he argues that the NT authors see Jesus' atoning work transcending the Temple sacrifices and Jesus himself as the new temple, fulfilling all of Israel's feasts. But he also says Torah and Jesus are not in simple opposition in the NT, and that Jesus' "(re-)new(-ed)" covenant fulfills and transforms the Abrahamic covenant. If God can add Torah without replacing the Abrahamic covenant, then he can change the role of Torah without replacing it. Watts' final estimation is that Jesus does not replace but fulfills all the OT covenants. There was no transfer of privileges from Israel to the church because Jesus and his Jewish followers were a reconstitution of true servant Israel.

Scot McKnight says the gospel is the story of God finding completion in the story of Messiah Jesus. It summons listeners to repentance, faith and baptism. This story is what gave birth to the canonical gospels, Eucharist and baptism, creeds, and the church calendar. He advises that the gospel is not only truthful but transforming, is concerned with justification and (social) justice, and in the first century was an implicit protest to empire. He faults evangelical understandings of the gospel that focus largely on conversion and restrict justification to forensic imputation, as is sometimes the case at "seeker-sensitive" churches. They tend to produce Lone Ranger Christians and superficial theology.

Evangelical understanding of conversion itself has undergone a "sea change," according to Gordon Smith. Because recent evangelical theologians are severing their ties with revivalism, they have come to view conversion as a complex process rather than a point in time. They present it no longer as a result of technique or formula (which was the impression given in parts of the revival tradition) but as an encounter with the Risen Christ—not simply with principles or laws (as in Campus Crusade's "Four Spiritual Laws"). Smith wants evangelicals to recall that conversion takes place and develops within community, and that its direction is "missional"—to reach the world.

Donald Bloesch outlines an evangelical understanding of justification along the lines of *sola fide, solus Christus*, and *sola gratia*. Faith is not the ground of justification but the means by which we receive the gift of salvation. Faith is also both sign of being justified and an encounter with the Justifier. Works are illustrative of faith but do not contribute to salvation. Bloesch commends the Christus Victor theory of the atonement as a balance to other theories, but adds that most evangelicals have adopted the Latin juridical model (from Augustine and Anselm) of penal redemption and legal satisfaction. He suggests that evangelicals consider themselves not simply as sinners saved by grace but also as priests and kings working together with Christ for a new world.

Dallas Willard considers what a theology of salvation means for discipleship. He thinks the evangelical slogan that "Christians are not perfect just forgiven" is symptomatic of a wider problem. That conversion is meant to engender transformation, albeit slowly, was assumed in the eighteenth-century awakenings, but was lost in twentieth-century evangelicalism's concern for proper doctrine. Willard blames the "Christian psychology" movement of the 1960s and the charismatic movement's inattention to holiness. He calls for a new theology of discipleship based on rabbi Jesus' training of his disciples.

Simon Chan urges a return to the "ancient wisdom" of spiritual practices. He asserts that worship is what makes church church, and therefore alerts evangelicals to the importance of liturgy. Chan registers increasing evangelical openness to Roman Catholic use of sacraments, liturgy, silence, and retreats. The result is a new ecumenism among evangelicals who have found greater commonality with Catholics than with liberal Protestants.

Trevor Hart unveils a new approach to eschatology. He reminds evangelicals of the imaginative (not literal) nature of eschatological language in Scripture. The New Earth to come will be a redemption not replacement of this world, and the final judgment will have less to do with vengeance than certification of appropriateness for entry into eternity. His chapter's more dramatic features include consideration of annihilationism (the destruction of the wicked) and universal restoration (the salvation of all). The last proposal has never before been seriously considered by mainstream evangelical theology, and Hart reminds readers that ever since the condemnation of Origenism in 553 the universal church has always taught two distinct destinies for human beings.

Theology of Church

The Achilles' heel of evangelicalism is its ecclesiology. Its "ecclesial atomism" (Ephraim Radner) has produced more splits than unions from the eighteenth century to this day. Radner maintains that the history of evangelicalism has been dominated by a view of the church as a free-will association of like-minded believers. This view resists the sense of the Great Tradition that the church is a living body spanning place and time, to which all believers are connected whether they choose or not. Radner thinks the only hope is "common martyrdom" in which members of the persecuted church see one another across ecclesial lines to recognize the objective and material true Church of Christ.

William Abraham reflects further on evangelicalism's "ecclesial ambivalence," and claims that agreement on *sola scriptura*, often thought to be the only source of unity in the movement, has actually multiplied disputes because it spawns differing interpretations. Abraham shows that evangelicals, despite these differences, have ironically played a pivotal role in the history of ecumenism. He makes the intriguing suggestion that orthodox theology's search for agreement on authority and epistemology has been misdirected, and that in fact the early churches reached agreement on theological essentials without agreement on either authority or epistemology.

If unity has been elusive among evangelicals, John Witvliet insists that evangelicals have generally shared a deep resistance to ritualism and ceremonialism in worship, because of their demand for heartfelt ardor. According to Witvliet, evangelical worship has highlighted preaching, congregational singing, classical evangelical hymns, and personal and family devotions. Evangelicals are divided between memorial and participationist views of the Lord's Supper, with similar differences in their attitudes toward baptism. Recently, Witvliet says, some strains of evangelical worship have yielded to sentimentalist and consumerist temptations.

The explosive growth of Pentecostalism and charismatic churches has caused evangelicals to recognize the practical role of all the spiritual gifts (not just the charismatic ones) in the life of a healthy church. So says Howard Snyder. The three lists of gifts in the New Testament, he avers, are illustrative, not comprehensive. Their intent is to suggest a diversity of gifts and the call for every member of the church to engage in ministry. There are no distinctions in gender, social status, or ethnicity for the distribution or use of these gifts. Snyder concludes that fresh outpouring of the gifts has often come during times of church renewal.

Theology of Mission

Michael McClymond provides a historical overview of the confluence of evangelism, revival, and missions. He notes the curious fact that the word "missions" acquired its modern meaning from the sixteenth-century Jesuits, Catholics whom most evangelicals have thought to be indifferent to missions. At the same time that the World Council of Churches was calling for a moratorium on missions (in the 1970s), John Wimber led huge numbers of evangelicals into "power evangelism." Yet an ecumenical paradigm for missions has emerged nonetheless, according to McClymond. It is Trinitarian (God gives of himself through the Son and Spirit), Christological (the cross and resurrection are key), eschatological (mission is the universal culmination of God's promises to Israel), pneumatological (empowered by the Spirit), and ecclesiological (the church is church only when it is on mission). McClymond also describes four patterns of mission—Roman Catholic, charismatic, socio-ethical, and evangelistic.

Sung Wook Chung takes up the question of mission to other religions and their adherents. He explains the recently dominant typology of exclusivism (other religions are demonic and idolatrous through and through), inclusivism (there is overlap of revelation between Christian faith and other faiths), and pluralism (all religions have equal access to Truth). Evangelicals have opted for the first two types, with inclusivists split between those who insist that knowledge of Jesus is necessary for salvation and those who do not. Chung recommends a "missional" approach that sees mission as not merely a function but the essence of the church, and employs points of contact from general revelation for apologetic and missional endeavors. He uses this approach on both Islam and Buddhism, arguing that there are concepts which each religion shares with Christianity, but at the same time important doctrinal differences. At the end of the chapter he considers different ways that evangelicals have understood the fate of the unevangelized.

Theological Approaches to Contemporary Life

Darrell Bock and Daniel Carroll illustrate the new sophistication of evangelical ethics. Their essay on the Bible and ethics points out that the Bible contains both moral teaching and ethical reflection, that evangelicals need to discern which of four levels of moral discourse a passage or story entails, and that this will help them distinguish between the ethics *of* the Bible and ethical instruction *from* the Bible. They would urge readers to see that the ethical move from the Bible to our world is not always direct or simple because of ethical diversity in the Bible (on gender and the role of the state, for example) and the difference in context. They contend that there is tension between absolute (such as the mandate to protect the vulnerable) and progressive (on women and slavery, for example) revelation on ethical issues, as well as consistency across the testaments on certain question (for instance, homosexual practice).

Eric Gregory laments that despite numerous calls for a distinctively evangelical approach to politics, "what curiously unites [evangelical] internal debates over politics is the absence of theology." He recommends an evangelical political theology that discusses shared concepts between political philosophy and theology proper, such as community, obligation, law, virtue, and human nature. He commends reading in Augustine, whose theology "is saturated with politics and its deep undercurrents," and learning from Oliver O'Donovan, Stanley Hauerwas, and Abraham Kuyper's "Christian pluralism." Finally, Gregory suggests evangelicals make their distinctive contribution to political theology by thinking through ecclesiology, Israel and Judaism, Roman Catholic discussions of politics, and the ways character can be formed by civic engagement.

Like Bock and Carrol (above), John Lunn finds problematic a direct move from biblical injunctions, but this time about poverty and wealth to modern contexts. He urges evangelicals to understand the differences between the economy of ancient Israel and Palestine (with a zero-sum mentality) and the modern market system. In these ancient worlds, the "wealthy" were exploiters by definition, in part because the economy was based on personal relationships, and "poor" was a designation more social than economic. Lunn goes on to explain what makes countries poor, how Christians in rich countries should think about poverty, and how the law of unexpected consequences affects such things as the minimum wage.

Roger Lundin surveys the history of Christian engagement with the arts, noting that the Reformation and Romantic movements, which encouraged inwardness and freedom as opposed to the new science of impersonal laws of nature, scuttled medieval contemplation, which had enabled art as mimesis of an enchanted cosmos. Modernists and fundamentalists in the twentieth century ironically shared a common aversion to nature and culture, positing a Manichean divide between the material and spiritual worlds. In the mid-twentieth century, evangelicals began to call for reengagement with culture, but with the exception of Dutch Calvinists were handicapped by shallow theology and limited cultural understanding. Lundin suggests that black church music has been evangelicalism's greatest contribution to the arts, and highlights contemporary evangelical thinkers such as Wolterstorff, Begbie, and Vanhoozer, who in their different ways see art as useful action.

Alister McGrath laments the recent evangelical ambivalence toward science, which he suggests has resulted from the modernist controversy of the 1920s and the culture wars and new atheist challenges of the last two decades. Often the flashpoint has been evolution. But McGrath, who has an Oxford D.Phil. in molecular biology, argues that opposition to evolution is neither essential nor typical of evangelicalism. In the first fifty years of Darwinism, he points out, evangelical theologians such as B. B. Warfield and James Orr were theistic evolutionists, conceding the possibility that God might have created through the mechanism of natural selection. McGrath cites Wesley's teaching that Scripture is not a science text but a disclosure of God's nature and intentions.

Recent ecclesiological conflicts have raged over sexuality, and evangelicals have played no small role. In his attempt to limn a theology of sexuality, Robert Gagnon proposes that Jesus privileged a creation-based ethic to override Mosaic permissiveness and inequity toward women, a strong interior component to sexual ethics, a loving and forgiving approach to sexual violators, marriage's purpose as a school for holiness, and the penultimate significance of sex and marriage. Jesus also emphasized male-female sexual difference as theologically significant, and therefore rejected homosexual practice. Gagnon holds that Scripture indicts all same-sex practice even if in committed relationships, and that the best analogies to the biblical treatment of homosexuality are not Scripture's treatment of women and slavery but its portrayal of incest and polygamy.

Timothy Tseng reports that Christian theological engagements with race have been chequered. For the most part, Christians in history have accommodated the dominant views of human nature, whether the Great Chain of Being rooted in Aristotelian thought or the emancipated self rooted in the Enlightenment. Nevertheless, the church's core affirmations about the *imago dei*, "one blood" origins of humanity, the universality of sin, the universal availability of salvation through Jesus Christ, and eschatological vision of the nations before the throne of God often challenged the racism that accompanied European expansionism. Tseng notes that while evangelical theology did little or nothing to engage race and racism in previous centuries, evangelical awakenings and the Pentecostal movement helped the Church see with greater clarity the transracial implications of the gospel, and helped dispel the mythical character of "race." He urges evangelicals to examine hidden assumptions, use ethnic studies and critical race theory, speak prophetically against racism, and pay attention not only to multiracial but also ethnic congregations.

Ben Mitchell documents evangelical concern for the vulnerable. Although evangelical biblicism and revivalism for some decades minimized attention to social issues, that same biblicism found a scriptural premium placed on human life at every stage and thereby helped make abortion a galvanizing issue for the evangelical movement. Mitchell highlights biblical texts about the *imago dei*, and points to a consensus among the Fathers and the Reformers on abortion. He also asserts that Scripture makes frequent reference to people with disabilities, causing the early church to champion their rights against Greco-Roman contempt for the physically impaired. Mitchell warns of new threats to an evangelical culture of life: assisted suicide, euthanasia, and embryonic stem-cell research.

Finally, Cherith Nordling takes on the question of gender. She suggests that God's self-giving generosity in Christ challenges evangelical traditions and theologies where oppositional dualisms run deep. Authority, hierarchy, and headship have been interpreted, she holds, through assumptions that prioritize men's being and function over that of women. Nordling does not discount sexual differences, but believes gender is more social than natural. She argues for complementarity without hierarchy. Her reasoning rests on her sense of the biblical narrative of God's original and final intention—that the sexes complement each other to remind us that men and women are incomplete without each other. Christ the incarnate Word has reordered things in his emerging kingdom, where no division is to be based on difference, and equal participation in the gospel is based on self-giving love and service.

The Future of Evangelical Theology

Some years ago, evangelical historian Nathan Hatch said "there's no such thing as evangelicalism." By that he probably meant that evangelicalism and its attendant theologies constitute a many-headed monster that regularly transforms itself into new shapes. But historic evangelicalism does have a recognizable character, as this volume will repeatedly demonstrate. William Abraham warns in his essay on ecumenism that "it would be a mistake…to dismiss evangelicalism as a useless category for understanding Christianity; without it we would have to invent a functional equivalent immediately." For it represents a network of Christians "bound together by a loose but identifiable cluster of convictions and practices that have been and continue to be a potent religious force."

But what will be the future shape of evangelicalism? And what of evangelical theology? The recent explosion of evangelicalism in the Global South means that future evangelical theology, which is already beginning to come from Asia and Africa and Latin America, will give more attention to the reality of spiritual powers in history and manifestations of the supernatural such as dreams, visions, healing, and direct messages from the Spirit. Because of the tendency of majority-world Christians to take the Old Testament more seriously, evangelical theology will have more of a Jewish flavor and be less inclined to spiritualize prophetic promises of land and kingdom. It will be far less ready to sever the connection between moral and dogmatic theology, as Northern theologies have done. Therefore future evangelical theology will be less tempted to relax traditional understandings of the meaning of sex and marriage. But it will also deal with new issues, says Mark Noll, such as the destiny of ancestors and what it means for families and large groups to convert en masse.

There will no doubt be more debate over the role of tradition. Historically, evangelicals have prided themselves on the "Scripture principle," whereby they subjected received traditions and creeds to their sense of what Scripture teaches. But more and more evangelical theologians have begun to see that *sola scriptura* in fact has caused more division than unity, and that beyond the central issues of salvation

Scripture is not self-interpreting. These theologians have called for more serious attention to what they call the "Great Tradition," a broad ecumenical consensus around the historic creeds. They urge their fellow theologians to be wary of replacing biblical interpretations found in this consensus with their own private interpretations.

As the mainline Protestant traditions become more of a sideline, and evangelicalism vies with Roman Catholicism for dominance in the Global South—the new center of gravity in world Christianity—evangelical theology may continue to be influenced by Catholic thought. Rivals often come to resemble each other. Catholics and evangelicals have fought abortion together. Evangelical theologians increasingly draw sustenance from Catholic moral and historical theology. Catholics have launched a new evangelization in partial response to evangelical gains in Latin America, and Catholic theology has reshaped its formulation of justification as a result of evangelical and other Protestant theological dialogues. Evangelicals will continue to believe that Catholics submit themselves to a human magisterium rather than the divine Word, and this will be sounded with more vigor in Global South churches. But just as sixteenth-century Protestant and Catholic theology reacted against each other and thereby influenced each other, twenty-first-century evangelical theology may unwittingly find itself to be not only a leavening agent in the broader church catholic but also shaped in part by its principal challenger.

NOTES

1. Carl E. Braaten, "A Harvest of Evangelical Theology," *First Things* 61 (March 1996), 45–48.

2. Of course this begs the question of whether this "faith" is the existential act of believing or the content of what is believed. But while the orthodox tradition has regarded the two as interconnected and generally has not wanted to prioritize experience over doctrine, or vice versa, the group I call "Meliorists" tends to separate the two and favor one over the other.

3. Ac. 21:8; Eph. 4:11; 2 Tim. 4:5.

CHAPTER 1

WHAT IS "EVANGELICAL"?

MARK NOLL

By the start of the twenty-first century, evangelical Christianity had come to constitute the second largest grouping of Christian believers in the world. Only the Roman Catholic church enjoyed more Christian adherents than the evangelical churches. By comparison with other world religions, evangelicals—taken only by themselves—were more numerous than all but Muslims and Hindus.

But what is meant by "evangelicals" or "evangelicalism"? These are by no means easy questions. The terms are even much disputed among those whom others casually lump together as evangelicals. Billy Graham, the American evangelist who was probably the world's most widely known "evangelical" in the twentieth century, was repeatedly chastised throughout much of his public career by self-described "fundamentalists" for abandoning the separatism that they considered a non-negotiable aspect of the Christian faith. Yet most observers class "fundamentalism" as a subcategory overlapping with "evangelicalism." David Yongi Cho, a Pentecostal minister, pastors the Yoido Full Gospel Church in Seoul, Korea. With over 700,000 members, as announced on its Web site, it is the largest single congregation in the world; the same Web site affirms that the church "practices faith, love, and service based on the cross of Christ and the Bible," a strongly evangelical formula.[1] Pastor Cho and his church have, however, been criticized by other self-described evangelicals as pagan for adapting Christianity to ancestral Korean practices (for example, the prayer mountain as replicating aspects of shamanism) and for replacing the Christian gospel with magical formulas that promise health and wealth. Yet most observers have no difficulty recognizing Cho's brand of Pentecostal Christianity as a variety of evangelicalism.

As suggested by this Korean example, problems of definition today have been compounded by the rapid rise of evangelical-like movements in many locations where few Protestant believers of any kind had existed until very recently. In 1900, according to the well-considered estimate of the editors of the *World Christian Encyclopedia*, well over 90 percent of the world's evangelical Christians lived in Europe or North America. (Their definition is resolutely tautological: "A subdivision mainly of Protestants consisting of all affiliated church members calling themselves Evangelicals, or all persons belong to Evangelical congregations, churches or denominations; characterized by commitment to personal religion.")[2] But now—because of Western missionary activity, cooperative efforts at translating the Bible into local languages, the acceleration of worldwide trade and communication, and especially the dedicated efforts of national Christians in many parts of the world—that earlier situation has been dramatically transformed. Today, according to the same reference work, the number of evangelicals in each of Africa, Latin America, and Asia exceeds the total in Europe and North America combined.[3] Moreover, if the editors' closely allied categories of "Pentecostal," "charismatic," and "neo-independent" were amalgamated under a broad "evangelical" rubric, then Brazil claims more evangelicals than the United States, while China, India, South Africa, the Philippines, Congo-Zaire, and Mexico each counts more than any European country.

The result of this demographic revolution is that theological and biblical issues almost unknown among Western evangelicals now loom large in what, by the broadest definitions, must be called the heartland of the evangelical world. These issues include questions about the destiny of ancestors or about what it means for families and large groups to convert en masse (instead of the standard Western picture of individual conversion). The worldwide expansion of evangelical-type movements also means renewed focus on practices once common among Western evangelicals, but not current in the recent past, such as visions, dreams, healings, and direct messages from the Holy Spirit. Since debates over such practices are first-order concerns in much of the world today, they too must be taken into account when looking for a definition of evangelicalism.

Toward a Definition

Throughout history, the designation "evangelical" has been applied to many different movements within broader Christian history. The word itself has several legitimate senses, but all are related to the etymological meaning of "good news." The English word "evangelical" comes from a transliteration of the Greek noun *euangelion*, which was used by the writers of the New Testament to signify the glad tidings—the good news—of Jesus' appearance on earth as the Son of God to accomplish God's plan of salvation for needy humans. Translators of the New Testament into English usually employed the word "gospel" (which meant good news or glad tidings in Old English) for *euangelion*, as in passages like Romans 1:16—"I am not ashamed of the gospel (*euangelion*), because it is the power of God for the salvation of everyone who believes" (NIV). Thus, "evangelical" religion has always been "gospel" religion, or religion focusing on the "good news" of salvation brought to sinners by Jesus Christ. Already in the middle ages the word was applied, for example, to Isaiah as "the evangelical prophet," because of how later Christians read this Old Testament book as describing the work of Christ. It was also applied to the followers of St. Francis, because their abandonment of worldly possessions was regarded as a clear imitation of Jesus' own life.

During the sixteenth century the word "evangelical" began to take on a more specific meaning associated with the Protestant Reformation. In this usage, the evangelicals were those who protested against the corruptions of the late-medieval Western church and who sought a Christ-centered and Bible-centered reform of the church. Because of these efforts, the word became a rough synonym for "Protestant." To this day in many places around the world, Lutheran churches reflect this older sense of the term (for example, the Evangelical Lutheran Church in America or the Evangelical Church of the Lutheran Confession in Brazil). In contemporary Germany, *evangelisch* retains the older meaning attached to the Lutheran churches descended from the Reformation, while *evangelikal* is a new coinage to designate those who are often called "evangelicals" in other parts of the world.

In this book "evangelical" refers not to Protestants in general but to those Protestants who, beginning more than three hundred years ago, strongly emphasized the redeeming work of Christ, personally appropriated, and who stressed spreading the good news of that message, whether to those with only a nominal attachment to Christianity or to those who had never heard the Christian gospel. The British historian David Bebbington developed a fourfold definition for his own study of evangelicals in the British Isles; it has become a very useful touchstone for discussing other groups in the world that are linked to British evangelicalism or that possess characteristics resembling the groups Bebbington describes.[4] For Bebbington, there are four key ingredients of evangelical religion:

- conversion: evangelicals are people who stress the need for a definite turning away from self and sin in order to find God in Jesus Christ;
- the Bible: evangelicals may respect church traditions in varying degrees and may use schooling, reason, and science to assist in explaining Christianity, but the ultimate authority for all matters of faith and religious practice is the Christian Scriptures;
- activism: evangelicals have historically been moved to action—to works of charity, sometimes to works of social reform, but above all to the work of spreading the message of salvation in Christ—because of their own experience of God;
- the cross: evangelicals also have consistently stressed as the heart of Christian faith the death of Christ on the cross and then the resurrection of Christ as a triumphant seal for what was accomplished in that death (evangelicals have regularly emphasized the substitutionary character of this atonement between

God and sinful humans whereby Christ receives the punishment due to human sins and God gives spiritual life to those who stand "in Christ").

Bebbington's definition has caught on because it outlines so well the shared commitments of many groups in many individual Christian movements and in so many locations of the world. It is also popular because of its flexibility. The great variety among evangelical groups can be explained in part by which of the cardinal principles a particular body emphasizes at a particular time.

Yet even solid definitions like David Bebbington's impose order on a lived reality that is anything but orderly, as indicated by a survey of the North American population from the mid-1990s.[5] The late George Rawlyk of Queen's University, Ontario, the key consultant in shaping the survey, designed its religious questions to map the four characteristics of evangelicalism that Bebbington defined. The survey found that not all of those who called themselves "evangelicals" or a related term held to Bebbington's four markers of evangelical identity (although 74 percent in the United States did so, only 51 percent in Canada claimed all four). It also discovered that many people who did embrace these evangelical markers were in the Catholic church (13 percent of the Americans and 25 percent of the Canadians who called themselves "evangelical" were Catholics). And it found that only about half of those in the denominations descended from historical evangelical movements used terms like "evangelical" to describe themselves (44 percent in the United States, 57 percent in Canada). In other words, there is slippage in the use of evangelical terminology.

For the particularly sensitive issue of whether to classify African-American Protestants as evangelicals, there is further complication. The same mid-1990s survey found that more than one-eighth of all Americans who could be identified as evangelicals by the Bebbington characteristics were African Americans. In the United States, white evangelical churchgoers and black Protestant churchgoers affirm just about the same basic convictions concerning religious doctrines and moral practices. But for well-established historical reasons concerning the discriminatory treatment of African Americans, black Protestant political behavior and social attitudes are very different from those of white evangelicals. If, in terms of both historical descent and religious convictions, most black Protestants could also be considered evangelicals, the history of racial attitudes has driven a sharp social wedge between them and white evangelicals.

Yet if common sense prevails, the difficulties are manageable. As the historian George Marsden has pointed out, evangelicalism can be described as a series of overlapping constituencies that vary in their self-consciousness, but that are related at least loosely in their shared history and convictions.[6] Relatively small numbers of individuals and agencies, often active in parachurch voluntary societies or nondenominational mission agencies, self-consciously use the evangelical label. Much larger numbers are associated with churches and other institutions embedded securely in the historical train of evangelical movements. And still larger numbers from throughout the world, who may have only loose connections with Western evangelical organizations, nonetheless share the historic evangelical beliefs and practices and so may be included in wider considerations of evangelicalism as well.

Later chapters in this book will refine questions of definition and explore the question of boundary marking as experienced throughout the world. The most difficulty in such efforts probably comes from assessing the increasing number of non-Western independent churches. In Africa, these groups are sometimes known as *aladura* churches, from a Yoruba word meaning "praying people," or they are called African Initiated Churches (AIC).[7] Examples, from literally thousands of possibilities, include the Zion Christian Church of Southern Africa and the Cherubim and Seraphim society of West Africa. But similar churches and movements have also proliferated in other parts of the world, such as the Universal Church of the Kingdom of God in Brazil, the house church movements in China, and many other rapidly developing church networks in India, the Philippines, Pacific Islands, Africa, and Latin America. As their names suggest, these Christian movements usually exercise a high degree of independence, they are usually well adapted to the religious and social practices of their different regions, and most imitate the supernaturalism of the New Testament. More traditional evangelicals sometimes critique these indigenous groups for exalting the prophetic powers of their leaders or subordinating the work of Christ to the work of the same leaders. And some critics see too much ancestral religion surviving in these groups, as well as a penchant for promoting Christianity as a means to secure health and wealth in this life. Nonetheless, a twenty-first-century conception of evangelicalism must pay considerable attention to such groups, for many of them originated from contact with historic evangelical missionaries, and most of them promote beliefs and practices that overlap with traditional evangelical emphases. Case-by-case analysis is the only way to discern whether such independent movements are best studied as variants of evangelical Christianity or another species altogether.

Refining Definition through History

Sketching the early stages of evangelical historical development offers greater clarity about shared beliefs and practices, illustrates some of the complexity of definition, and provides wider context for the recent world expansion of evangelicalism. The general movement in time of groups usually considered evangelical has passed from an original pan-European phase, through phases dominated first by Britain and then with American leadership coming on, to once again an international phase, but this one taking in the whole world.

European Background

A stellar constellation of books from the English historian W. R. Ward has successfully pushed consideration of evangelical roots back into the seventeenth century and convincingly expanded attention from the British world to Europe as a whole.[8]

The importance of this perspective for the twenty-first century lies in noticing that the beginnings of evangelicalism were as international as contemporary expressions of evangelicalism have become.

In this picture, distinctly evangelical beliefs and practices emerged in response to political pressure from European state-church establishments, especially in the Habsburg Empire. These responses led to widely scattered revivals where state authorities, Catholic and Protestant, tried to enforce religious conformity. Protests against this pattern of assimilation, arising first in central Europe, soon displayed a number of common features in defense of "true Christianity" against formulaic, systematic, or imposed orthodoxies. Protestors often relied on small-group enclaves as the best form for encouraging "true Christianity." They were often led by laypeople and witnessed much activity by children and youth. And they regularly expressed their hard-won faith in newly written songs and hymns.

By pushing the history back into the seventeenth century, a new set of evangelical pioneers comes into focus, including Johann Arndt (1555–1621), whose much-reprinted *True Christianity* (1605–1610) moved Lutheran theology toward stressing Christ *in* his children rather than just Christ *for* his children. A recovery of this European history also shows clearly how the major elements of Lutheran Pietism heralded common evangelical patterns of later centuries. Philip Jakob Spener (1635–1705), whose *Pia Desideria* of 1675 is regarded as the beginning of organized Pietism, promoted small-group conventicles as a way to encourage the personal appropriation of faith. His successor, August Hermann Francke (1663–1723), used a complex of institutions associated with the University of Halle to translate renewed personal religion into cross-cultural missions, active social service (especially the famous Halle orphanage), and entrepreneurial creativity in raising money for Christian causes. Under Count Ludwig Nicholas von Zinzendorf (1700–1760), the Moravians carried Pietist emphases into a partial break with Lutheranism and an even more wholehearted commitment to personal holiness, missions, and joyful worship.

These earliest expressions of reforming, revivalistic, anti-statist, and small-group Protestantism were international from the start. All throughout the seventeenth century, books from spiritual reformers as well as news of their innovations circulated from the outposts of Pietism in Russia to the British Isles and beyond. Puritan literature was read with special avidity on the continent. When the Moravians appeared in the 1720s, they had a particularly strong impact on the English-speaking world. Moravian hymns, Moravian dedication to missionary service, Moravian proclamation of justification by faith as a doctrine to live by—all exerted a great influence, indirectly or directly, on evangelical leaders in Britain, Ireland, and America. As these early leaders moved from spiritual renewal to social reform, they invariably took further guidance from what had gone before in Europe.

The continental background to modern evangelicalism is relevant for the twenty-first century in one final way. Early defenders of "true religion" sustained a complex relationship to the historical Protestantism of the Reformation. On the one hand, leading pietists like Spener found precedents in Martin Luther and his generation for much of their program, especially the early Reformers' stress on the priesthood of all believers and their insistence on the personal appropriation of justification by faith. On the other hand, the continental pietists were surprisingly eager to read the work of Roman Catholic mystics, like Madame Guyon and Francois Fénelon, and to disseminate writings of mystical and spiritual writers from the Catholic Middle Ages. That combination of self-conscious reliance on the Reformation and broad openness to some Catholic influences has been rare in evangelical history, but over the last several decides, since the Second Vatican Council, it has once again become common in some circles.

Eighteenth-Century Britain and America

The public upsurge of piety that became known as the Evangelical Revival in Britain and the Great Awakening in America did not arise out of thin air.[9] Besides the direct influence of continental Pietism, it also benefited from two movements closer to home. First was a powerful international network of dedicated Calvinists who read each others' devotional works and eagerly followed news about Calvinist reforms elsewhere in Europe. This network enjoyed two strongholds in the English-speaking world. The Puritans in England, who had mobilized during the reign of Queen Elizabeth I (1558–1603) in order to push the Protestant Reformation further, were joined by the Calvinists of Scotland, who were led by the indomitable John Knox, in their pursuit of personal godliness combined with national reform. When monarchs James I (1603–1625) and Charles I (1625–1649) frustrated these efforts in England, several thousands Puritans migrated to the wilderness of New England in order to set up a "Godly Commonwealth" of the sort that English circumstances prevented. Scottish Puritans and the Puritans of Old and New England retained a great deal of medievalism, especially an understanding of Christianity as always corporate or even national, as well as personal. But they also promoted innovations (like the personal conversion) and underscored specific teachings of the general Protestant inheritance (like the need for saving grace) that fed directly into later evangelical movements.

The other home-grown influence came from an unlikely source. The High Church party in the Church of England stressed the more Catholic elements in Anglican tradition and also emphasized the necessity of loyalty to the monarch. Later evangelicals drew not so much from these matters of principle as from the practices these Anglicans used to pursue their goals. Beginning in the late seventeenth century, they created voluntary organizations, more or less outside the boundaries of the official state church, and they stressed the need for disciplined personal religion and active social outreach.[10] These self-conscious traditionalists also stressed the "primitive Christianity" of the New Testament and the early church as a corrective to their age's worldliness. They sang the psalms and even a few newly written hymns as a means of encouraging holiness. Most significant, they organized "societies" to promote personal religion and exert an influence for God on society.

Early evangelicals poured a new wine into what they inherited, but the wineskins often came from their High Church Anglican predecessors.

Although it is important to recognize how early evangelicals in Britain and America followed in paths pioneered by Pietists, Puritans, and Anglicans, it is also important to recognize where they broke new ground. While all the major leaders of the evangelical revivals were themselves members of state churches in England, Scotland, Wales, or the American colonies, they critiqued sharply the practices of inherited state-church Christianity. To pursue the goal of "true religion," they embraced distinctly modern means, especially the encouragement of small groups where awakened believers could share the experiences of faith and encourage one another in the gospel. Many of them also became itinerants, so as to proclaim awakened religion to needy sinners wherever possible, despite the fact that itineration was widely viewed as a sure sign of "enthusiasm," the heedless promotion of social disorder and intellectual irresponsibility.

Key leaders were also securely attached to the modern intellectual assumptions of their age. In particular, they shared many traits characteristic of the European Enlightenment.[11] To be sure, evangelicals remained fixed opponents of some aspects of the Enlightenment, such as criticism of the Bible or excessive trust in natural human ability. Yet in other ways, early evangelicals embraced much of the Enlightenment spirit. They too stressed the power of individuals to choose their own destinies, they too read the Bible for themselves without waiting for church officials to guide their interpretations, they too described real religion as a matter of the affections, and they too looked to natural theology for understanding God's work in the world. Most of all, the evangelical stress on the assurance of salvation marked them as figures of their age. Of course earlier believers had worried about their security before God, but the new evangelicals of the eighteenth century went further and made personal assurance the central goal of their labors.

The leaders of the movement exemplified much of what became commonplace in later history. Most came of age as young adults in the 1730s or 1740s, when evangelicalism took off. Forever after, evangelicalism has been a religion driven by the energy and creativity of younger leaders. George Whitefield became a key uniting figure because he was such an effective preacher in his ceaseless travels throughout England, Scotland, Ireland, and the American colonies. Whitefield was traditional in his status as an ordained Anglican clergyman and in his defense of Calvinistic theology. But he was also the Great Innovator, as well as the Grand Itinerant, for how powerfully he focused on the individual's stance before God as *the* issue of supreme existential importance, for how he subordinated all other considerations to the imperative of preaching the New Birth, and for how he communicated the message of salvation with popular techniques borrowed from the rapidly expanding marketplace of eighteenth-century commerce.[12]

Whitefield's friends and sometime allies, John Wesley and Charles Wesley, were derided with him as "Methodists" because they applied systematic practices to promoting individual spiritual life and organizing lay-driven spiritual renewal.[13] Charles Wesley, who built upon the innovations of Isaac Watts to become the first great hymn writer of the evangelical movement, provided sentiments and forms of words that that have defined evangelical spirituality from his day to the present. Hymns such as "Jesus, lover of my soul," and "O, for a thousand tongues to sing my great Redeemer's praise" gave voice to the Christian experiences of countless individuals; they also provided a measure of unity in Bible-centered song for a far-flung and often contentious movement. John Wesley, an organizational genius, empowered laymen and laywomen to guide their own destinies, developed the small-group society meeting into a powerful engine of evangelical nurture, and exemplified the possibilities (and pitfalls) of incessant activity. The Arminian theology of the Wesleys balanced the Calvinism of other early evangelicals and thereby helped to establish a long-lasting agenda for intra-evangelical theological debate.

Whitefield and the Wesleys never acted alone but always worked in harness with other capable leaders, with few as committed to evangelical causes as Selina, Countess of Huntingdon. She was one of the first in what would become a long line of well-placed individuals who gave their money and status to assist evangelical efforts. In Wales, the layman Howell Harris organized societies almost effectively as John Wesley, the sermons of Daniel Rowland made almost as great an impression in Welsh as Whitefield's in English, and the hymn writer William Williams (Pantycelyn) sang the gospel as effectively in his native language as Charles Wesley did in his.[14] Leaders of the Awakening in Scotland were ministers of the established Presbyterian church, like William McCulloch of Cambuslang, who in 1742 oversaw one of the era's great seasons of revival that accompanied a memorable visit by George Whitefield to his parish.

The American colonies were soon experiencing much of the same revival and renewal as the other side of the Atlantic.[15] In New Jersey the Reformed Dutch minister, Theodore Frelinghuysen, was a direct product of the pietist revival on the continent. Frelinghuynsen's awakening preaching, in turn, moved a nearby Presbyterian, Gilbert Tennent, to preach repentance, reform, and New Birth with fresh vigor. Another Presbyterian, Samuel Davies, pushed evangelicalism into Virginia, heretofore closed to all except the Anglican establishment. Davies's impassioned preaching, his deliberate outreach to slaves and native Americans, and his extensive use of hymns (from England and those he wrote himself) marked a momentous beginning for the evangelization of the American South.

Jonathan Edwards of Massachusetts provided evangelicalism with its most extensive theological efforts.[16] Edwards, who could preach effectively and whose report on an early revival in his Northampton community became a much-consulted template for later awakenings, devoted much of his energy to close study of Scripture and contemporary challenges to the faith. His major books defended a Calvinistic picture of divine grace (*Freedom of the Will*), discriminated carefully between true and uncertain faith (*The Religious Affections*), and combined, as few later evangelicals have been able to do, the most recondite philosophical speculations with the most intensely God-honoring interpretations of Scripture (*Two Treatises: The Nature of True Virtue* and *The End for Which God Created the World*).

Within a matter of years, the stress on conversion, holy living, evangelism, and affective public worship that began among awakened Congregationalists and

Presbyterians was taken up by Baptists and many other groups. When missionaries sent by the Wesleys crossed the Atlantic in the late 1760s and early 1770s, the resulting surge of Methodism dramatically expanded the scope and intensity of evangelical religion in America.

Evangelicalism Comes of Age

Evangelicalism became a culture-shaping force in North Atlantic societies because of its compelling power in scenes of social disorder and national distress.[17] The disorder and distress were often the result of political revolutions that wracked the Anglo-American world from the middle of the eighteenth century to past the midpoint of the nineteenth. In the wake of these revolutions, evangelical religion flourished. The details were unique in each case, but the general pattern was clear. Different varieties of evangelical Christianity took hold with great force—in the Scottish Highlands after the Stuart (Catholic) invasions of 1745–1746; in the United States after the Revolutionary War, 1776–1783; in the Canadian Maritimes after *rejecting* the American Revolution; in lowland Scotland in connection with mobilization for war with France in the 1790s; likewise in England in the wake of the threat of war, and of actual warfare, with France; in the north of Ireland after the failed rebellion of the United Irishmen in 1798; in Upper Canada (modern Ontario) after the American invasions of the War of 1812; and in the American South after the devastation of the Civil War. A possible exception to this pattern was the situation in Wales, where the tumult of the French wars did seem to stimulate a turn to evangelicalism, but where the long-standing affinity between preaching in Welsh and practicing evangelical faith was probably more important than any one period of social unrest.

The key in a remarkably diverse range of social, political, and intellectual circumstances was evangelical resilience defined by Christian experience, personally appropriated, and trust in the Bible above all other authorities. Differ as they certainly did in many particulars, the individuals and groups that were recognized as evangelical possessed a core of common characteristics. First, evangelicals throughout the North Atlantic remained firm Protestants who accentuated the historic Protestant attachment to Scripture. They could differ wildly among themselves on the meaning of the Bible, but the Scriptures remained a bedrock of authority. Second, evangelicals shared a conviction that true religion required the active experience of God. Again, evangelicals prescribed myriad norms for that experience and even more ways for accommodating the experience of God with reason, traditions, and hierarchies. But the experience of God remained a sine qua non for the type of religion that many contemporaries and more historians have labeled "evangelical."

Three more characteristics flowed from this biblical experientialism. First was a bias—it could be a slight prejudice, it could be a massive rejection—against inherited institutions. Since no inherited institution could communicate the power of God's presence as adequately as Scripture and personal Christian experience, no inherited institution enjoyed the respect accorded to experience and the Bible. Second, evangelicalism was extraordinarily flexible in relation to principles concerning intellectual, political, social, and economic life. Since such principles possessed primarily instrumental value by comparison with the ultimate realities found in Scripture and the experience of Christ, they could be taken up, modified, discarded, or transformed as local circumstances dictated. Third, evangelicals practiced "discipline," to borrow a well-considered phrase from Daniel Walker Howe. Their experiential biblicism might lead along many different paths, and with contrasting conclusions, to principles of conduct for self and others, but, however derived, those principles embodied a common evangelical conviction that the gospel compelled a search for social healing as well as personal holiness.[18] In subsequent history, evangelicalism has often expanded in outreach and gone deeper in spiritual depth precisely amid similar scenes of disorder and unrest.

For much of the nineteenth century, white evangelical Protestants constituted the largest and most influential body of religious adherents in the United States, as also in Britain and Canada. Methodists, Baptists, Presbyterians, Congregationalists, and some Episcopalians shared broadly evangelical convictions, and evangelical elements were prominent among Lutherans, German and Dutch Reformed, and the Restorationist churches (Churches of Christ, Disciples of Christ) as well. Evangelicals often combated each other aggressively on the details of their convictions, but in 1846 delegates from many churches in Britain and North America, as well as substantial representation from the European continent, met in England to establish the Evangelical Alliance, a voluntary interdenominational organization whose doctrinal basis succinctly summarized major points of mutual evangelical agreement.[19] The founding commitments of the Alliance remain central to evangelical movements around the world today:

1. the divine inspiration, authority, and sufficiency of the Holy Scriptures;
2. the right and privacy of private judgment in the interpretation of the Holy Scriptures;
3. the Unity of the Godhead and the Trinity of the Persons therein;
4. the utter depravity of human nature in consequence of the Fall;
5. the incarnation of the Son of God, His work of atonement for the sins of mankind, and His mediatorial intercession and reign;
6. the justification of the sinner by faith alone;
7. the work of the Holy Spirit in the conversion and sanctification of the sinner;
8. the immortality of the soul, the resurrection of the body, the judgment of the world by our Lord Jesus Christ, with the eternal blessedness of the righteous and the eternal punishment of the wicked;
9. the divine institution of the Christian ministry, and the obligation and perpetuity of the ordinances of Baptism and the Lord's Supper.

Well before 1846, evangelicals had also begun to take a growing interest in spreading Christianity to other parts of the world. In such efforts, English-speaking evangelicals lagged considerably behind their Continental pietist colleagues. Apart from a few efforts to reach native American Indians with the gospel, significant missionary labors by English speakers did not begin until the end of the eighteenth century. The ex-American slave, David George, emigrated from Nova Scotia to Sierra Leone in 1792 as a dedicated preacher of revival just as that West African colony was being opened for outside settlement under the auspices of Anglican evangelicals. The next year, the English Baptist William Carey set out for India. Soon Carey's Baptist Missionary Society was joined by the Anglican Church Missionary Society, the inter-denominational London Missionary Society, and in not too many years by the American Board of Commissioners for Foreign Missions, along with many other evangelical bodies in what would rapidly grow into great efforts of missionary proclamation. The missionary movement was a very important expression of evangelical zeal in English-speaking countries. It became even more important for planting seeds of Christianity in other parts of the world that would grow vigorously into strong indigenous Christian churches.

At the start of the twenty-first century, evangelicals remain important in the broader Christian histories of Britain and North America. But the great story of the recent past has been the flourishing of evangelical churches and movements in other parts of the world.[20] Evangelicals from around the world continue to come to Britain, the United States, and Canada for training, but so now do missionaries from the Two-Thirds World arrive to spread the gospel among fellow immigrants in the West, and also to evangelize among Western pagans. To be sure, the newer evangelical churches of the world also face many difficulties of their own—instability, lack of wise leadership, shortage of educational resources, ethnic violence, numbing poverty, and more. But from these churches insights, practices, songs, and doctrinal emphases have also begun to flow back toward the original evangelical homelands. As one recent commentator has written with a focus on the Pacific: "New Zealand Maori, like other indigenous peoples, valued evangelical Christianity for its acknowledgment of the supernatural. The results may put *pakeha* [New Zealanders of European descent] back into the beginners class of spiritual things."[21] The theological explorations in the chapters that follow reflect wisdom from three centuries of evangelical life, but are also alert to the recent changes that have once again made evangelical Christianity an international and multicultural religion of great, if also complex, vitality.

NOTES

1. english.fgtv.com/yfgc.pdf.

2. David B. Barrett, George T. Kurian, and Todd M. Johnson, *World Christian Encyclopedia*, 2 vols. (2nd ed., New York: Oxford University Press, 2001), 1:13–14.

3. Ibid.

4. D. W. Bebbington, *Evangelicalism in Modern Britain: A History from the 1730s to the 1980s* (London: Unwin Hyman, 1989), 2–17.

5. It was conducted by the Angus Reid Group of Toronto in 1996, with 3,000 respondents each in the United States and Canada. For further examination of its results, see "How Very Different: A poll shows how Canadian and U.S. attitudes vary on family, politics and religion," *Maclean's*, November 4, 1996, 36–40; Mark A. Noll, *American Evangelical Christianity: An Introduction* (Oxford: Blackwell, 2001), 30–38; and Sam Reimer, *Evangelicals and the Continental Divide: The Conservative Protestant Subculture in Canada and the United States* (Montreal: McGill-Queen's University Press, 2003).

6. George M. Marsden, "Introduction," *Evangelicalism and Modern America* (Grand Rapids: Eerdmans, 1984), ix.

7. See especially David B. Barrett, *African Initiatives in Religion* (Nairobi: East African Publishing House, 1971); and Martinus Daneel, *Quest for Belonging: Introduction to a Study of African Independent Churches* (Gwerlu, Zimbabwe: Mambo Press, 1987).

8. See W. R. Ward, *The Protestant Evangelical Awakening* (Cambridge: Cambridge University Press, 1999); Ward, *Faith and Faction* (London: Epworth, 1993); and Ward, *Early Evangelicalism: A Global Intellectual History, 1670–1789* (Cambridge: Cambridge University Press, 2006).

9. This section summarizes Mark A. Noll, *The Rise of Evangelicalism: The Age of Edwards, Whitefield and the Wesleys* (Downers Grove, Ill.: InterVarsity Press, 2003), 50–99.

10. For the Anglican and also Puritan roots of what became evangelicalism, the best short statement is John Walsh, "Origins of the Evangelical Revival," *Essays in Modern English Church History in Memory of Norman Sykes*, ed. G. V. Bennett and J. D. Walsh (New York: Oxford University Press, 1966), 132–162.

11. See especially, Bebbington, *Evangelicalism in Modern Britain*, 42–74.

12. See Harry S. Stout, *The Divine Dramatist: George Whitefield and the Rise of Modern Evangelicalism* (Grand Rapids: Eerdmans, 1991): and Jerome Dean Mahaffey, *Preaching Politics: The Religious Rhetoric of George Whitefield and the Founding of a New Nation* (Waco: Baylor University Press, 2007).

13. See Harry D. Rack, *Reasonable Enthusiast: John Wesley and the Rise of Methodism.* 2nd ed. (London: Epworth, 2002); and Kenneth G. C. Newport and Ted A. Campbell, eds., *Charles Wesley: Life, Literature and Legacy* (London: Epworth, 2006).

14. See David Ceri Jones, *A Glorious Work of God in the World: Welsh Methodism and the International Evangelical Revival, 1735–1750* (Cardiff: University of Wales Press, 2004).

15. See Thomas S. Kidd, *The Great Awakening: The Roots of Evangelical Christianity in Colonial America* (New Haven: Yale University Press, 2007).

16. See George M. Marsden, *Jonathan Edwards: A Life* (New Haven: Yale University Press, 2003).

17. This section follows Mark A. Noll, "Revolution and the Rise of Evangelical Social Influence in North Atlantic Societies," in *Evangelicalism*, ed. Noll, David W. Bebbington, and George A. Rawlyk (New York: Oxford University Press, 1994), 113–136.

18. Daniel Walker Howe, "The Evangelical Movement and Political Culture in the North during the Second Party System," *Journal of American History* 77 (March 1991): 1216–1239. For a similar statement, see also Timothy L. Smith, "Righteousness and Hope: Christian Holiness and the Millennial Vision in America, 1800–1900," *American Quarterly* 31 (1979): 22–45.

19. J. W. Massie, *The Evangelical Alliance; Its Origin and Development* (London: John Snow, 1847).

20. For orientation, see David Martin, *Tongues of Fire: The Explosion of Protestantism in Latin America* (Oxford: Blackwell, 1990); and Martin, *Pentecostalism: The World Their Parish* (Oxford: Blackwell, 2001).

21. John Roxborogh, "Mapping the Evangelical Landscape in New Zealand," in *Mapping the Landscape: Essays in Australian and New Zealand Christianity: Festschrift in Honor of Professor Ian Breward* (New York: Peter Lang, 2000), 327.

BIBLIOGRAPHY

Bebbington, D. W. *Evangelicalism in Modern Britain: Its History from the 1730s to the 1980s*. London: Unwin Hyman, 1989.

Bebbington, David W. *The Dominance of Evangelicalism: The Age of Spurgeon and Moody*. Downers Grove, Ill.: InterVarsity Press; and Leicester, U.K.: Inter-Varsity Press, 2005.

Haykin, Michael A. G., and Kenneth J. Stewart, eds. *The Emergence of Evangelicalism: Exploring Historical Continuities*. Nottingham, U.K.: Inter-Varsity Press, 2008; this volume discusses the influential picture of evangelical identity provided by David Bebbington (see above).

Hindmarsh, D. Bruce. *The Evangelical Conversion Narrative: Spiritual Autobiography in Early Modern England*. Oxford: Oxford University Press, 2005.

Hutchinson, Mark, and Ogbu Kalu, eds. *A Global Faith: Essays on Evangelicalism and Globalization*. Sydney: Center for the Study of Australian Christianity, 1998.

Larsen, Timothy, and Daniel J. Treier, eds. *The Cambridge Companion to Evangelical Theology*. Cambridge: Cambridge University Press, 2007.

Noll, Mark A. *The Rise of Evangelicalism: The Age of Edwards, Whitefield and the Wesleys*. Downers Grove, Ill.: InterVarsity Press; and Leicester, U.K.: Inter-Varsity Press, 2003.

Noll, Mark A., David W. Bebbington, and George A. Rawlyk, eds. *Evangelicalism: Comparative Studies of Popular Protestantism in North America, the British Isles, and Beyond, 1700–1990*. New York: Oxford University Press, 1994.

Ward, W. R. *The Protestant Evangelical Awakening*. Cambridge: Cambridge University Press, 1992.

Wolffe, John R. *The Expansion of Evangelicalism: The Age of Wilberforce, More, Chalmers and Finney* (Downers Grove, Ill.: InterVarsity Press; Nottingham, U.K.: Inter-Varsity Press, 2006).

PART I

THE BIBLE AND THEOLOGICAL METHOD

CHAPTER 2

SCRIPTURE AND HERMENEUTICS

KEVIN J. VANHOOZER

A People of the Book

Evangelicals are a "people of the book" because they are, first and foremost, a people of the gospel (*euangelion*). This chapter thus focuses on the nature (what it is), authority (rightful say-so), and interpretation (how to use it/make it work correctly) of the Bible, the "book" in question.[1] Strictly speaking, evangelicals do not believe "in" the Bible but in the God who authored and speaks authoritatively through it. Yet this God, and the gospel, are "in" the Bible as well, and the purpose of exegesis is to "lead out" (*ex* + *ago*) the message of salvation so that the interpreter-disciple can follow it in faith and obedience. The challenge for an evangelical theory (doctrine) and practice (interpretation) of Scripture is to hold fast to the gospel fixed in writing while engaging the living God who is its author and attending to the great salvation that is its subject matter.

"Biblicism" is one of the most frequently cited defining marks of evangelicalism. Of course, the claim to be people of the good book—the book of good news—is a statement more of aim than achievement. Still, evangelicals take their doctrinal and ethical marching orders from the Scriptures, and the goal is to be a people whose faith, hope, and love—her doctrine, duty, and devotion—centers on the promise of God fulfilled in Jesus Christ, the one about whom the gospel is proclaimed.

It therefore comes as no surprise to learn that evangelicals invest heavily in the Bible: in various translations and editions of the Bible, in Bible study, in composing hymns and praise choruses that set its words to music, in writing and consuming commentaries, in demonstrating doctrines to be biblical and, last but not least, in the doctrine of Scripture itself. Devotional Bible reading, for example, "is more foundational to evangelical piety than the rosary is to Roman Catholic piety."[2] Moreover, the sermon—an exposition of a particular biblical text—was traditionally the place where the Bible was brought to bear or applied to all areas of life. Bible studies among college students are perhaps as central to the dissemination of evangelical tradition to the next generation as Bible translation is to evangelicals in the global South. These foundational practices for forming disciples presuppose doctrinal convictions concerning the nature and authority of the Bible.

Perhaps the best barometer of evangelical thinking about Scripture and hermeneutics is the kind of commentaries they produce. Some commentary series look like their "critical" counterparts, only with conservative results; others are geared toward application and contemporary relevance; others recover the insights of past generations; still others seek to bridge the gap between biblical studies and systematic theology. The latest entry hands over the commentating task from biblical scholars to systematic theologians.

The Bible is God's word, the supreme rule for faith, thought, and practice, the revealed source of the evangelical understanding of grace, faith, and Jesus Christ as well as their respective Reformation *solas: sola gratia, solus Christus, sola fide.* Undergirding it all is *sola scriptura* or the "Scripture principle," namely, the confession that "what the Bible says, God says." Indeed, the consensus that Scripture is the final and authoritative source for Christian life and theology "represents a basic unifying factor through the whole of contemporary evangelicalism."[3] While the future of evangelicalism may well lie in its ability to preserve the principle of *sola scriptura*, the particular character of evangelicalism will lie in its ability to specify the meaning of *sola scriptura.*[4]

Where We've Come from: Heirs of Protestant Orthodoxy and Pietist Revival

Who speaks for God? Evangelicals see themselves as standing with historic Christian orthodoxy in locating the supreme authority for faith, life, and thought with "the Holy Spirit speaking in the Scriptures."[5]

The Nature of the Bible: Inspiration

What sets the sixty-six books apart from and over all other human texts and makes them suitable to "rule" ("canon" = rule) is their being uniquely "of God." Evangelicals concur with the Bible's own claim to be "breathed out" (*theopneustos*) from God (2 Tim. 3:16). Typically translated as "inspiration," this notion speaks directly to the nature of the Bible and its divine origin. Evangelicals concur with the Great Tradition in viewing the Bible to be the product of God's own authorship through the words of human witnesses who nevertheless used their own wits to compose under the Spirit's supernatural supervision.

Evangelicals put great emphasis on the Bible's self-attestation (e.g., Ps. 119; Rom. 3:2; 2 Pet. 1:20–21) and especially on Jesus' attitude toward the Old Testament Scriptures (e.g., Mt. 5:17–19; Mk. 7:6–8; 12:36; Jn. 10:35).[6] If Jesus recognized the Scriptures as God's own word, surely his followers should do no less. That God spoke "by the prophets" (Heb. 1:1) meant by their writings as well, and hence, by extension, the New Testament documents, too. Indeed, most evangelicals came to associate inspiration with the words rather than the authors of Scripture (or their ideas). Inspiration is thus "verbal" and "plenary" because each and every word pulls its weight in communicating God's word.[7]

The inspiration of Scripture is the means whereby God preserves in writing his revelation in the history of Israel and Jesus Christ. The primary emphasis is on God's providential guiding of the process of the texts' composition. B. B. Warfield defines inspiration as "that extraordinary, supernatural influence...exerted by the Holy Ghost on the writers of our Sacred Books, by which their words were rendered also the words of God."[8] Though it is common for outsiders to associate verbal plenary inspiration with the so-called "dictation" theory, such a view fails to do justice to what evangelical theologians actually have said and believe. What matters to evangelicals is the inspired result, not a detailed knowledge or uniform understanding of the process.

The Authority of the Bible: Infallibility (and Eventually Inerrancy)

It is one thing to say elevated things about Scripture, quite another to let Scripture have its say. Evangelicals are not content to admire Scripture. To acknowledge the supreme authority of the Bible is to let it have the final word in matters concerning Christian faith and practice—indeed, in all areas of life to which it speaks. The Bible's authority is the medium by which God exercises his own authority, that is, his rightful power to determine belief or command action and to expect obedient assent.

The Reformers took a decisive step in proclaiming the final authority of Scripture over tradition. *Sola scriptura* means that neither oral traditions, nor the magisterial teaching authority of the Roman Catholic church, nor new Spirit-given revelations can supplement the Bible ("it is written"). On the contrary, Scripture, as the product of God's authorship, is sufficient, authoritative, and infallible—the latter concept signaling its utter trustworthiness in guiding the church to knowledge of God and salvation in Christ.[9]

Since the Reformation, evangelicals have tried to balance the supremacy of Scripture alongside other authoritative sources of theology with varying success, with some favoring church tradition, others personal experience, and still others the leading of the Holy Spirit.[10] In modern times, the most precarious balancing act involved revelation and reason, especially when the Bible became a document of the university and began to be read "like any other book."

Confronted with an academic tide of historical criticism, some evangelicals modified their position on biblical authority, arguing that the Bible speaks reliably only on matters of faith and salvation. As to history, geography, and cosmology, the Bible is as weak as any other human text. Others, such as the Princetonian theologians Charles Hodge and B. B. Warfield, responded by attacking head-on this skeptical attitude towards the Bible's historical reliability. They developed the doctrine of infallibility further, making the Bible's utter truthfulness in matters salvific and scientific alike more explicit by speaking of *inerrancy* and claiming that though "the word [inerrancy] is 19th-century...the belief it expresses is as old as Christianity."[11] Contemporary inerrantists typically acknowledge ancient literary conventions (e.g., nonchronological narration) and phenomenological language (e.g., the sun "rising"), recognizing that the assertion of the Bible's utter truthfulness presupposes right interpretation.

Hermeneutics: The Interpretation of the Bible

If the Bible is God's word, then there is no more important mandate for the people of the book than to understand and respond to what God is saying. The authority of the Bible must be not only professed but lived out. All the treasures of divine wisdom count for nought unless the church knows how to make withdrawals from the deposit of truth in order to formulate its doctrine and apply its life-giving light to new issues and contexts.

Evangelicals have tended to follow the Reformers' principles that, first, the authoritative sense is the literal sense, and second, Scripture interprets Scripture. Debate has centered on the meaning of the literal sense: is the most relevant factor the human author's communicative intention, determined by grammatico-historical exegesis that recovers linguistic meaning by reconstructing the author's historical context—or the divine author's intention, which is best determined in light of the canonical context? The second principle is handy for resolving any ambiguities: read unclear passages in light of those that are more clear. The overall aim is to recover what the authors, as commissioned mouthpieces for God, are saying rather than to read one's own ideas and interests into the text.

Because evangelicals believe that God's message for the church is applicable to every age, there has been a tendency to apply apparently time-bound passages by isolating the universally valid principle behind the text in order to find its equivalent present-day cultural clothing. The same principles thus get applied to new particular cases. Here, too, the main impulse is conservative or, better, *preservative:* namely, preserving divinely revealed truth. Yet evangelicals also want to bring biblical authority to bear on new problems, and some are looking for ways of interpreting the Bible with creative fidelity that go beyond "principlizing."[12]

Where We Are: Modern and Postmodern Challenges

Like other people groups, evangelicals are not immune from changes in the broader social and intellectual culture. Indeed, the story of evangelicalism is perhaps best told in tandem with the story of the rise and fall of the Enlightenment, that is, against the backdrop of the modern and postmodern revolutions. Each upheaval of thought precipitated its own "legitimation crisis" with regard to meaning, authority, and truth, a legitimation crisis that has shaped evangelical attitudes toward Scripture and hermeneutics alike.[13]

External Challenges: Reacting

Speaking in the broadest of terms: the Enlightenment's call for reason rather than tradition and authority to ground belief, combined with its presumption of naturalism and its critical approach to the study of history, challenged the foundations and the framework of the evangelical doctrine of Scripture; the postmodern critique of the modern ideal of detached objectivity and its emphasis on the situatedness of knowing subjects has created problems, and possibilities, for evangelical hermeneutics. The evangelical view of Scripture and hermeneutics is to a great extent a function of its reactions to three centuries of external challenges.

With regard to inspiration, the most important challenge was the modern tendency to deny God's supernatural action in history and the natural world. If science disallowed divine interventions, then the Bible could not be God-breathed. Modern liberal theologians considered the Bible to be an expression of human religious experience, not an instance of divine revelation.

The questioning of the Bible's divinity had a direct impact on its status as authority, too.[14] Scholars challenged the truth of the Bible's accounts of history, for example, by providing evidence for their own critical reconstructions of what actually happened. Advances in scientific knowledge, especially evolutionary theory, led to the Scopes Monkey Trial and to the demoting of the early chapters of Genesis to the status of creation myths comparable to others in the Ancient Near Eastern world. Such developments prompted a conservative corrective, and evangelicals led the charge in arguing both for supernaturalism (i.e., divine providence) in general and for the historical reliability of the biblical accounts (i.e., divine inerrancy) more particularly.

In the twentieth century, evangelicals hammered out their views of Scripture and hermeneutics largely by grappling with Karl Barth. Cornelius Van Til worried that Barth's "neo-orthodoxy" was in fact a "new modernism" that eviscerated the Bible of its authority in deference to "events" of revelation for which the Bible was only an occasion, not a statement.[15] Bernard Ramm, by contrast, argued that Barth's claim that the Bible "becomes" the word of God struck the right balance between criticism and faith, the humanity and the divinity of Scripture, the words and the Word.[16] The key issue is whether Barth imports an unbiblical notion of God's absolute freedom into his view of Scripture.[17] The debate continues.[18]

The 1978 Chicago Statement on Biblical Inerrancy attempted to restate the traditional Scripture Principle and to amplify the meaning of Scripture's truthfulness. The Statement was a reaction to critical attacks on the trustworthiness of Scripture (and to Barth), but even more an attempt to shore up a fragile evangelical consensus. Despite their doctrinal divisions on a host of other doctrines, some three hundred delegates agreed that Scripture is not only infallible (trustworthy in matter of salvation) but, when properly interpreted, inerrant—wholly true—in all that it affirms, including history and science.[19]

As to biblical interpretation, many evangelicals were quick to use modern hermeneutical tools and principles in a faith-based framework, especially when these lent credence to the idea that their interpretations were "objective." Indeed, perhaps the most surprising criticism of evangelicals today is not that they are premodern, mired in primitive mythology, but rather that they are distinctly *modern* in their approach to biblical authority and interpretation. The doctrine of inerrancy, say its postmodern critics, is committed to a wooden literalism that insists upon the "factual" truth of every statement, a typical modern preoccupation that resembles Cartesian rationalism and British evidentialism more than Luther and Calvin.[20] As to interpretation, Stanley Hauerwas decries the emphasis on "private judgment" and maintains that evangelicalism must be liberated from the illusion "that the text of the Scripture makes sense separate from a Church that gives it sense."[21]

Internal Challenges: Rethinking

While some evangelicals continue to react, others have begun to rethink their position in light of the above challenges. What follows is a list of seven talking points that pertain to Scripture and hermeneutics, and hence to the writing of commentaries, over which evangelicals are currently deliberating or divided. The strategies and solutions that emerge in response to these internal challenges may help evangelicals decide what they mean by *sola scriptura* and thus how to define the identity of the movement vis-à-vis other Christian traditions.

1. *How to tell the story of evangelicals and biblical authority (and who gets to narrate it)*

The main issue here is the extent to which evangelicals are misbegotten children of the Enlightenment. Evangelicals typically view themselves as heirs of the Reformation who have stood against the modern liberal tide. Jack Rogers and Donald McKim stood this claim on its head by arguing that the nineteenth-century Princetonians invented the doctrine of inerrancy and, by so doing, exchanged their birthright as children of faith for a mess of empiricist and propositionalist pottage, that is, for the modern scientific method.[22] John Woodbridge wrote a book-length rebuttal arguing that the Princetonian view was fully in line with the historic tradition.[23] Meanwhile, in the global South the Bible is being read through the lenses not of modernity but of premodernity: Philip Jenkins argues that evangelicals in the non-Western world are able to identify with the world of the biblical text much more directly. Many live in agricultural societies marked by social poverty on the one hand and a belief in spiritual powers on the other.[24] The story of evangelicals and the Bible marches on, and it is less likely to stumble when no one faction alone gets to narrate it.[25]

2. *Where to locate the doctrinal "home" of Scripture*

This issue strikes at the very heart of evangelical identity: if evangelicals are a people of the book, it makes a difference whether the book is primarily a handbook of doctrine or a source of spiritual sustenance.[26] Many if not most evangelicals locate the doctrine of Scripture under revelation, the doctrine that stresses the way in which God makes himself known. The Bible, in this view, is the source of true beliefs about God and hence the norm of correct doctrine.[27] Others locate Scripture under pneumatology or, more specifically, sanctification. The emphasis here is on the Bible as a means of spiritual formation, the Holy Spirit's tool for shaping and nurturing Christian identity and for fostering a relationship with God.[28]

3. *How to do justice to the humanity as well as the divinity of Scripture*

Evangelicals have for years debated the extent to which faith is compatible with biblical criticism. Most agree that "believing criticism"—an approach that sees no contradiction between the scholarly study of the human composition of the biblical books and a faith appropriate to saints in their divine origin and inspiration[29]—is not a contradiction in terms. As to how much criticism is permissible, there is continuing debate.[30]

4. *Whether, and how, to speak of inerrancy as well as infallibility*

For many evangelicals, inerrancy is the single most important distinguishing mark of the movement, in part because its proponents believe that to surrender it is to sound the death knell of biblical authority.[31] The so-called "battle for the Bible" was in fact a battle over the importance, and definition, of inerrancy. It is important to note that inerrantists are happy to acknowledge figures of speech, differences of literary genre, and do not insist on modern standards of scientific precision. It is unrealistic to expect of Scripture a kind of accuracy it never promises. Everything depends on the kind of claims the authors are making. Inerrantists insist that, when all the facts are known, there will be neither internal contradictions nor external falsifications of what the authors claimed. Non-inerrantists are often motivated by a concern to deal with the phenomena of Scripture inductively and by the assumption that the main purpose of Scripture is to mediate the message of salvation, not to communicate historical and scientific information.[32] Some in the latter camp are also inclined to side with Barth and see the Bible not as an object with divine attributes but a creaturely means that God in his freedom employs to witness to Jesus Christ.

5. *How to negotiate the disciplinary ditch between biblical studies and systematic theology*

Like other Christian groups who study the Bible in the academy, evangelicals have suffered the effects of the institutional divide between biblical studies and systematic theology. The former focuses on historical investigation ("what it meant"), the latter on conceptual elaboration ("what it means"), though both have to negotiate their respective ways through the labyrinth of faith and criticism. This disciplinary ditch is even uglier for evangelicals inasmuch as neither side is willing to say that it is less biblical than the other. The question thus arises: what does it mean to be biblical and who (i.e., which discipline) is in the best position to be so? Is exegesis without hermeneutical and theological presuppositions possible? I. Howard Marshall reports increasing numbers of graduate students wanting to study "hermeneutics" rather than the New Testament! Marshall himself is less interested in general questions about whether texts have meaning than he is in reading the New Testament "so as to understand it in its own time."[33] The evangelical tide is moving in the other direction, however, as the increasing number of exegetes and systematicians alike expressing interest in the theological interpretation of Scripture amply attests.[34] At issue is whether evangelicals must not only employ exegetical procedures (technique) but undergo the discipline of spiritual formation so as to acquire right habits of reading (interpretive virtue) as well.

6. *Whether, and how, the Spirit illumines individual readers and/or traditions (i.e., ecclesial communities)*

Does being a people of the book preclude being a people of a tradition? The Reformers set their principle of the priesthood of all believers in contrast to the older Roman Catholic notion that only official church officers could authoritatively interpret the Scriptures. Some evangelicals, perhaps under the influence of the modern notion of individual autonomy, misappropriated this principle, claiming "No creed but the Bible," thereby confusing one's personal responsibility to read Scripture with one's right as an individual to say what one thinks it means. In response, some so-called "postconservative" evangelicals have gone postmodern, emphasizing the rationality of community traditions rather than of autonomous knowers, and pointing out that the Bible itself represents "the self-understanding of the community in which it developed."[35] Others, too, in order to avoid collapsing the voice of the Spirit into that of the Bible, acknowledge that the Spirit guides individuals into the truth precisely by guiding the whole church. The open question, then, is whether, and how, evangelicals should affirm the priesthood of all believers, the authority of the Great Tradition or, somehow, both. Stated differently: Is "the Holy Spirit speaking in the Scriptures" functionally equivalent to "the Holy Spirit speaking to the church as she *reads* the Scriptures"? The Spirit's illumination is related to the clarity of Scripture as well: Is the perspicuity of the Bible an objective property of the text or the result of the Spirit's work in readers? At any rate, there is renewed interest in recovering ancient traditions of interpreting Scripture, at least in part because of a recognition that, first, readers' interpretive practices are formed by traditions and, second. such traditions may be the Spirit's work.[36]

7. *Whether, and how, to move "beyond" the Bible*

Evangelicals seek to be biblical, finally, not only in looking back towards past tradition but also in looking forward at the present context. "Contextualization" of the Bible is necessary for at least two reasons: evangelicals want to minister the gospel in new places (or in old places whose contexts have changed); and evangelicals want to bring the Bible to bear on new problems (such as stem cell research and transgender issues). In short, there are good missiological and ethical reasons for wanting not merely to exposit but to *apply* the Bible. The challenge is to preserve the same gospel in different contexts. Many evangelicals rely on "principlizing," that is, abstracting the transcultural principles from their biblical context in order then to clothe these naked principles in cultural garb that is intelligible in the contemporary context. More controversial is the "redemptive-movement" hermeneutic that hearkens not to the letter of Scripture (e.g., on slavery) but to a Spirit-guided trajectory of meaning that points to an "ultimate ethic" (e.g., egalitarianism)—a kind of promised land that lies beyond what even the New Testament church was able to realize.[37]

Quo Vadis? Toward an Evangelical Future

Evangelicals are a people of the book because they believe the good news and trust its author. If evangelicals are to conform their doctrine and interpretation of Scripture to the gospel, then they must do so in light of the God of the gospel. The evangelical approach to biblical authority and interpretation must be of a piece with the substance of evangelical faith, with what God is *doing* in and through his word, namely, renewing all things in Christ through the Spirit. Evangelicals confess that the God who began a "good word" among us will bring it to completion (cf. Phil. 1:6), which is to say, *communion.*

The way forward for those seeking to be biblical is, first, to interpret the Scriptures theologically, with an eye to discerning God's work in the world and his purpose for the church, and second, to think theologically about Scripture itself, remembering that it is the word of the living God and not simply a historical or literary text. Evangelicals must therefore root their doctrine of Scripture in the context of the work of the triune God; the proper dogmatic location of Scripture is in God's economy of communicative action. For the gospel is neither a system of theoretical truths nor morality but an account of what God has said and done: a theodrama. The Bible is in this perspective a vital element in God's great plan of self-communication whose end is covenantal communion.

Theology's task is to understand what God is doing in Christ through the Spirit to renew creation. In order rightly to participate in this good news, evangelicals need both doctrinal direction and spiritual vitality as they read the Bible. A dramatic model which sees the gospel as a divine doing, the Bible as the church's holy script (where Scripture is both epistemic criterion and means of grace), and interpretation as performance offers a conjunctive rather than disjunctive way forward that combines word and spirit, head and heart.

Inspiration: Scripture as Communicative Act of the Covenanting God

The evangelical intuition is correct: the Bible is what it says it is, namely, God's word. The God of Scripture speaks, and Scripture is a result of that divine speaking. The grounding theological insight of an evangelical doctrine of Scripture is that God himself is doing things in and through the human discourse of the Bible in order personally to relate to his people. Indeed, God so invests and identifies himself in his words that to fail to respond to the word of God is to disobey God himself.

The Bible, then, is itself one of God's mighty acts, a form of God's own communicative presence. Without these scriptural acts we would have no reliable means of interpreting God's acts in history. According to the Scriptures, however, God's revelatory words always accompany God's redemptive deeds. We can go further: according to the Scriptures, God often acts in the world by speaking. When God speaks, he is also *doing* things with words (e.g., commanding, promising, warning, etc.). It follows that Scripture is a medium of God's communicative activity, and thus an extension, as it were, of his personal presence.

To view the Bible as composed of diverse divine speech acts is to overcome the long-standing dichotomy in evangelicalism between propositionalists, for whom the Bible is a book of divinely revealed information, and pietists, for whom the Bible is primarily a means of personal address and spiritual sustenance. The way out of this head vs. heart cul-de-sac is to recognize that God relates personally to his people precisely by doing various things with propositions beyond merely informing.

The Bible is the God-ordained means of communicating the terms, and the reality, of the covenant whose content is Jesus Christ. What is God saying/doing in Scripture? He is administering his covenant: promising, commanding, exhorting, comforting, and in general presenting himself (and his Son) while simultaneously soliciting our response.[38] God is relating to his people as Savior and Lord via the medium of written words. God is as free to do this as he was free to relate to the apostles via the medium of the living Word, the humanity of Jesus.

As to the Bible's "humanity," it is fully but not *merely* a human product. Like the church, Scripture is a fully human phenomenon subject to the contingencies of language, culture, and society. There is therefore a place for reason to examine what the authors likely meant given their historical context. Yet the discourse of the Bible is also God's communicative work: God-voiced, God-worded, God-breathed.

The Old Testament prophets were "moved by the Holy Spirit" and "spoke from God" (2 Pet. 1:21). Those who deny verbal inspiration typically have a diluted view of divine providence. But is it harder to move an apostle to write an epistle than to raise a man from the dead? Evangelicals believe that this "moving" is not oppressive but organic, an instance of God's providential ordering and preparation of both author and situation. The human discourse has integrity, but it is ultimately commissioned, enabled, and authorized by the divine playwright who coordinates diverse voices into a rich harmonic canonical whole.[39]

Infallibility/Inerrancy: The Economy of Truth

The Bible is theodramatic discourse: something someone (prophets and apostles; ultimately the Holy Spirit) says (Scripture) about something (the drama of redemption) to someone (the church) at some time (past; present) in some way (a variety of literary forms) for some purpose (faith, hope, and love). The infallibility of the Bible follows from the fact that God is the ultimate authorial agent who is doing things with the words of Scripture. "God has something to say and he is very good at saying it."[40] Specifically, God is speaking truth in many ways: presenting Jesus Christ, the fulfillment of the law and promises, the one through whom all things were created and are being recreated. The words of the covenanting God are trustworthy—utterly reliable—for God cannot deny himself (Heb 6:18; Titus 1:2).[41] Indeed, God's truth is linked to his covenant faithfulness: his words can be relied on absolutely to accomplish the purpose for which they were sent/used (Isa. 55:11). The authority of Scripture derives from the authority of God as he speaks in and through the Scripture.

To emphasize Scripture as the speech action of God, then, is not to forget the question of truth. It is, however, to situate truth among the other "perfections" of Scripture in the economy of communication. Everything that God does in Scripture with words is infallible in the sense that it will not fail to achieve its intended purpose. When God makes assertions, those assertions, when properly interpreted, are true and trustworthy, wholly reliable: they accomplish the authorial purpose for which they were sent. The inerrancy of Scripture is that quality of the biblical text that, as God's communicative act, ensures that what is stated, when interpreted rightly and read in faith, corresponds to the way things in creation and history are.[42] It is important to remember, however, that the Bible is an ingredient in the economy of divine communicative action, not a textual talisman with its own mystical power. It follows that the Bible's truth serves specific communicative purposes, especially bearing witness to the reality of God, human beings, and the great redemptive work accomplished in Jesus Christ. The truth that the Spirit communicates in Scripture is not merely theoretical and historical, then, but practical, transformative, and relational: a truth that sets free, gives life, and promotes wisdom.

It is one thing to say that a statement is true, another to say what it means. Inerrancy offers few interpretive guidelines other than affirming the overall consistency of the Bible's claims.[43] Moreover, to interpret the Bible we need to do more than grasp a few isolated truths. Verbal inspiration is not a license for reading words out of canonical context.[44] We need to be able to grasp the whole, and to situate the parts in the whole. The unity of the Bible is neither that of a philosophical system nor a system of moral truths. On the contrary, the unified sum and substance of the Bible are theodramatic: the gospel recounts the history of what God has said and done with his "two hands" (Son and Spirit), and indicates what we should say and do in response.

What ultimately counts is the God who reveals himself through the language and literature of the Bible, and not simply the detached propositional content. The form of what Scripture says is not merely incidental to its truth. Evangelicals ought to recognize the cognitive significance not only of statements and propositions but also of all the Bible's figures of speech and literary forms. Evangelicals must come to appreciate that the literal sense is the literary, not the literalistic, sense.[45]

Interpretation and Illumination

Affirming the truth of Scripture takes us only so far. We still have to determine what the Bible means ("that about which truth is"). Biblical authority without biblical interpretation is empty, but biblical interpretation without genuine understanding is blind. Given the nature and authority of Scripture as outlined above, we can draw three lessons for biblical hermeneutics.

1. *Evangelicals must develop catholic sensibility, an awareness of how believers at other times, places, and situations have responded to the word of God*

The ancient Rule of Faith specifies what Scripture is ultimately about: the creative and redemptive work of the triune God. The Rule thus serves as a crucial help for right interpretation. Evangelicals must hearken to the *ministerial* authority of the great tradition, attentive to insights from Christians in other times and places, as well as to present-day Christians in other cultural contexts. Catholicity is the antidote to the tribalism and parochialism that infect evangelical thinking that never leaves its ghetto.

2. *Evangelicals must also learn canon sense, that is, the ability to interpret a particular biblical passage in light of the canonical whole and entire drama of redemption*

The "canonic" principle stipulates that theology, regardless of its context, must accord with the Scriptures if it does not want to proclaim and perform some gospel other than that of Jesus Christ. This implies that evangelicals must come to appreciate the synthetic power of the imagination, that cognitive faculty that enables us to discern meaningful patterns in what those without imagination see only as unrelated parts. Where critical reason analyzes, breaking texts up into their constituent parts, the canonical imagination unifies, finding that Jesus Christ is the one in whom all things biblical ultimately hold together (cf. Col. 1:17). By learning imaginatively to indwell the biblical texts, we see through them to reality as it really is "in Christ." Canon sense is the antidote to piecemeal interpretations that abstract "lessons" from the text but that fail to understand the place of particular parts in the whole drama of redemption.

3. *Evangelicals must pray for critical and contextual sensitivity, that is, for the illumination of the Holy Spirit*

Illumination does not make Scripture true but renders its truth intelligible to interpreters whose minds would otherwise be clouded by sin. Academic qualification and exegetical procedures alone are not enough. For interpretation to be more than a Pelagian exercise of human ingenuity, we must see that it too is part of the economy of God's communicative action. Again, the overarching purpose in biblical interpretation is rightly to engage and respond to the prior communicative action of the triune God. The Bible is less a text with "properties" than the vocal cord conveying the words of the living God. The Spirit is the Lord of the authoring and hearing of Scripture alike. Evangelicals must be careful not to short-circuit the economy of communication by simply affirming the objective truth of Scripture and then inviting exegetes to have their way with the text. Rather, evangelicals trust the Spirit to lead them into all biblical truth, penetrating its subject matter (ultimately, the gospel of Jesus Christ) in part by means of believing criticism. Determining "what it meant" is, however, not enough: the truth of Scripture exists to give life, to set free, and to be done in new cultural contexts. It is ultimately the Spirit who ministers the word to the church, cultivating catholic sensibility, canon sense, and cultural sensitivity.

Sola scriptura remains the evangelical watchword: Scripture alone is the authoritative script for right participation in the life and love of the triune God because it alone is the authorized text of the only true God. With regard to interpretation, however, Scripture is not alone but *above* other sources, the final but not the exclusive authority. These other sources (e.g., reason, experience, tradition) exercise a ministerial role in interpreting the Bible, especially when the community has to decide how to bring Scripture to bear on matters of which it speaks only indirectly. In such cases being biblical means not woodenly repeating the text but interpreting it with creative fidelity: improvising with a holy script.[46]

Conclusion: Holy Script and Gospel Theater

Those who read Scripture are called to be "doers of the word, and not merely hearers" (Jas. 1:22). The superiority of divine communicative action—theodrama, for short—as a model for thinking about biblical authority and interpretation consists in its awareness that understanding is a matter not only of cognition but also action, and in its insistence that there are biblical texts whose meanings are only fully "realized" as something is done with them or on their basis. To be a people of the gospel, evangelicals must take up their book and walk.

Only through the Spirit's ministry of the word and sacrament in the context of the community of faith is the authority of Scripture acknowledged as the means of fellowship with the triune God, training in righteousness, and walking in wisdom it was meant to be. Only by interpreting the authoritative words of life by the illumination of the Spirit can interpreters discover the freedom for which Christ has set them free. In the final analysis, evangelicals must be not only a people who profess the book but a people who perform it, publicly exhibiting the strange new world of the Bible and the gospel of Jesus Christ upon whose axis it spins and to whose reality it bears witness.

NOTES

1. These three foci cover the relevant affirmations of the Evangelical Alliance, formulated in 1846: first, the divine inspiration, authority, and sufficiency of the Holy Scriptures; and second, the right and privacy of private judgment in the interpretation of the Holy Scriptures.

2. Timothy Larsen, "Defining and Locating Evangelicalism," in Larsen and Daniel J. Treier, eds., *The Cambridge Companion to Evangelical Theology* (Cambridge: Cambridge University Press, 2007), 7.

3. Kenneth S. Kantzer, "Unity and Diversity in Evangelical Faith," in David F. Wells and John D. Woodbridge, eds., *The Evangelicals: What They Believe, Who They Are, Where They Are Changing*, rev. ed. (Grand Rapids: Baker, 1977), 72.

4. Specifically, will evangelicals interpret the "sola" of Scripture as meaning the Bible *alone*, in which case they will rely solely on exegetical procedures, or the Bible *above* (*prima scriptura*), in which case there is room for incorporating reason, experience, and especially tradition, as well.

5. Westminster Confession of Faith, I, X. See also Bernard Ramm, *The Evangelical Heritage: A Study in Historical Theology* (Grand Rapids: Baker, 2000). Evangelicals are also Nicene Christians to the extent that Nicea too affirmed that God "spoke by the prophets" (*est locutus per prophetas*).

6. On the Bible's testimony to itself, see Wayne Grudem, "Scripture's Self-Attestation and the Problem of Formulating a Doctrine of Scripture," in D. A. Carson and John D. Woodbridge, eds., *Scripture and Truth* (Grand Rapids: Zondervan, 1983), 19–64. On the significance of Jesus' attitude toward the Old Testament, see John W. Wenham, *Christ and the Bible* (Downers Grove, Ill.: InterVarsity Press, 1973).

7. Cf. Charles Hodge: "In saying that the Bible is the word of God, we mean that he is its author, that he says whatever the Bible says"; "Inspiration," *Biblical Repository and Princeton Review* (October 1857), 661–663.

8. B. B. Warfield, *The Inspiration and Authority of the Bible* (Phillipsburg, N.J.: Presbyterian and Reformed Publishing, 1979), 420.

9. On the sufficiency of Scripture, see Timothy Ward, *Word and Supplement: Speech Acts, Biblical Texts, and the Sufficiency of Scripture* (Oxford: Oxford University Press, 2002).

10. Painting in broad strokes, one might say that evangelical Anglicans tend to favor church tradition, Wesleyans Christian experience, and Pentecostals the leading of the Holy Spirit. At their best, however, they all employ reason, tradition, and experience alike as means of interpreting Scripture, thus implicitly recognizing the magisterial authority of the Bible.

11. J. I. Packer, "Infallibility and Inerrancy of the Bible," in Sinclair B. Ferguson, David F. Wright, and J. I. Packer, eds., *New Dictionary of Theology* (Downers Grove, Ill.: InterVarsity Press, 1988), 337.

12. We shall return to this point below, where I shall offer an alternative approach.

13. Studies by James D. Hunter and others, for example, have charted the changing attitudes of evangelical college students in North America to the Bible. See James D. Hunter, *Evangelicalism: The Coming Generation* (Chicago: University of Chicago Press, 1987) and the "response" by James M. Penning and Corwin E. Smidt, *Evangelicalism: The Next Generation* (Grand Rapids: Baker, 2002), 51.

14. The inaugural address of Charles Augustus Briggs, "The Authority of Holy Scripture" (1891) is representative of this challenge.

15. Cornelius Van Til, *Karl Barth and Evangelicalism* (Philadelphia: P&R Publishing, 1964).

16. Bernard Ramm, *After Fundamentalism: The Future of Evangelical Theology* (San Francisco: Harper & Row, 1983).

17. God is not so free as to be able to renege on his word. See Mark D. Thompson, "Witness to the Word: On Barth's Doctrine of Scripture," in David Gibson and Daniel Strange, eds., *Engaging with Barth: Contemporary Evangelical Critiques* (Nottingham, U.K.: Apollos, 2008), 179.

18. See Gibson and Strange, eds., *Engaging with Barth*, and Sung Wook Chung, ed., *Karl Barth and Evangelical Theology: Convergences and Divergences* (Grand Rapids: Baker, 2006).

19. See Paul D. Feinberg's widely cited definition in "The Meaning of Inerrancy," in Norman Geisler, ed., *Inerrancy* (Grand Rapids: Zondervan, 1980), 293–294.

20. So Carl Raschke, *The Next Reformation: Why Evangelicals Must Embrace Postmodernity* (Grand Rapids: Baker, 2004), chap. 5.

21. Stanley Hauerwas, *Unleashing the Scriptures: Freeing the Bible from Captivity to America* (Nashville: Abingdon, 1993), 27.

22. See Jack B. Rogers and Donald K. McKim, *The Authority and Interpretation of the Bible* (New York: Harper & Row, 1979), and Donald W. Dayton, "The Pietist Theological Critique of Biblical Inerrancy," in Vincent Bacote et al., eds., *Evangelicals and Scripture: Tradition, Authority and Hermeneutics* (Downers Grove, Ill.: InterVarsity Press, 2004), 76–89.

23. *Biblical Authority: A Critique of the Rogers/McKim Proposal* (Grand Rapids: Zondervan, 1982). See also Randall H. Balmer, "The Princetonians and Scripture: A Reconsideration," *Westminster Theological Journal* 44 (1982): 352–365; Paul Helseth, "'Re-imagining' the Princeton Mind: Postconservative Evangelicalism, Old Princeton, and the Rise of Neo-Fundamentalism," *Journal of the Evangelical Theological Society* 45 (2002): 427–450.

24. Philip Jenkins, *The New Faces of Christianity: Believing the Bible in the Global South* (New York: Oxford University Press, 2006).

25. Donald W. Dayton proposes what he terms an "alternative historiography" of evangelicalism that views it more in terms of the "history of effects" of Pietism than of the Reformation. See his *Theological Roots of Pentecostalism* (Peabody, Mass.: Hendrickson, 1991).

26. This is Stanley Grenz's way of putting the matter in his "Nurturing the Soul, Informing the Mind: The Genesis of the Evangelical Scripture Principle," in Bacote et al., eds., *Evangelicals and Scripture*, 21–41.

27. See Carl F. H. Henry's magisterial defense of the Bible as propositional revelation in his *God, Revelation, and Authority*, 6 vols. (Waco, Tex.: Word, 1976–1983). See also William J. Abraham's critique of the tendency to treat the Bible as an epistemic norm in his *Canon and Criterion in Christian Theology: From the Fathers to Feminism* (Oxford: Clarendon, 1998).

28. William Abraham argues that inspiration has less to do with speaking than with producing effects on others via speaking or writing; see *The Divine Inspiration of the Holy Scripture* (New York: Oxford University Press, 1981). His argument appeals more to the meaning of the English term "inspiration" than to the Greek term *theopneustos*. For a related argument, see Kern Robert Trembath, *Evangelical Theories of Biblical Inspiration: A Review and Proposal* (New York: Oxford University Press, 1987).

29. See Mark A. Noll, *Between Faith and Criticism: Evangelicals, Scholarship, and the Bible in America* (New York: Harper & Row, 1986).

30. See, for example, the recent controversy over Peter Enns, *Inspiration and Incarnation: Evangelicals and the Problem of the Old Testament* (Grand Rapids: Baker, 2005), and Kenton L. Sparks, *God's Word in Human Words: An Evangelical Appropriation of Critical Biblical Scholarship* (Grand Rapids: Baker, 2008). For a similar proposal about the "humanity" of the process of formation of the New Testament canon, see Craig D. Allert, *A High View of Scripture: The Authority of the Bible and the Formation of the New Testament Canon* (Grand Rapids: Baker, 2007).

31. The Evangelical Theological Society initially required its members to affirm only the doctrine of inerrancy, though more recently it has added a clause on the Trinity.

32. Gabriel Fackre distinguishes three types of inerrancy and three types of infallibility in *The Christian Story*, vol. 2, *Authority: Scripture in the Church for the World* (Grand Rapids: Eerdmans, 1987), 63–73. David Dockery identifies nine different evangelical positions in "Variations in Inerrancy," *SBC Today*, May 1986, 10–11.

33. "Evangelicalism and Biblical Interpretation," in Craig Bartholomew, Robin Parry, and Andrew West, eds., *The Futures of Evangelicalism: Issues and Prospects* (Leicester, U.K.: Inter-Varsity Press, 2003), 101.

34. See, for example, the following publishing ventures: the 8-volume Scripture and Hermeneutics Series (Grand Rapids: Zondervan), the Two Horizons Commentary series (Grand Rapids: Eerdmans), the Brazos Theological Commentary on the Bible series, the Paideia series (Grand Rapids: Baker) that explores how New Testament rhetoric shapes theological convictions and forms moral habits, the *Journal of Theological Interpretation*, and Kevin J. Vanhoozer, ed., *Dictionary of Theological Interpretation of the Bible* (Grand Rapids: Baker, 2005). For an insightful account of these developments in evangelicalism and beyond, see Daniel J. Treier, *Introducing Theological Interpretation of Scripture: Recovering a Christian Practice* (Grand Rapids: Baker, 2008).

35. Stanley Grenz, *Revisioning Evangelical Theology: A Fresh Agenda for the 21st Century* (Downers Grove, Ill.: InterVarsity Press, 1993), 121.

36. See, for example, the Ancient Christian Commentary on Scripture series edited by Thomas C. Oden and published by InterVarsity Press, and the Evangelical *Ressourcement: Ancient Sources for the Church's Future* series, edited by D. H. Williams and published by Baker.

37. See William J. Webb, *Slaves, Women, and Homosexuals: Exploring the Hermeneutics of Cultural Analysis* (Downers Grove, Ill.: InterVarsity, 2001); I. Howard Marshall, *Beyond*

the Bible: Moving from Scripture to Theology (Grand Rapids: Baker, 2004); Gary Meadors, ed., *Four Views on Moving Beyond the Bible to Theology* (Grand Rapids: Zondervan, 2009).

38. See David Gibson, "The God of Promise: Christian Scripture as Covenantal Revelation," *Themelios* 29.3 (Summer 2004): 27–36.

39. Jesus' own testimony is consistent with the present account: "for I have not spoken on my own.... What I speak, therefore, I speak just as the Father has told me" (Jn. 12:49–50).

40. Mark D. Thompson, *A Clear and Present Word: The Clarity of Scripture* (Downers Grove, Ill.: InterVarsity Press, 2006), 170.

41. Cf. the editor's remark in Paul Helm and Carl R. Trueman, *The Trustworthiness of God: Perspectives on the Nature of Scripture* (Grand Rapids: Eerdmans, 2002): "God is towards his people the same as the words he speaks to them" (x).

42. Strictly speaking, therefore, inerrancy is a subset of infallibility: everything that God does with words succeeds, but only assertions "succeed" in bearing truth. At the same time, we should also note that other divine speech acts presuppose, imply, or entail truth claims whose truth is part and parcel of their success.

43. For example, one cannot determine from inerrancy alone whether a given biblical text is intended to be metaphorical, whether it is history or apocalyptic, or what kind of precision it has.

44. Furthermore, speech acts, not individual words, are the basic units of meaning.

45. On the importance of literate reading of the Bible, see my "Lewis and Scripture," in Michael Ward and Rob McSwain, eds., *The Cambridge Companion to C. S. Lewis* (Cambridge: Cambridge University Press, forthcoming).

46. For a discussion of biblical interpretation in terms of dramatic performance, see N. T. Wright, *The Last Word* (San Francisco: Harper, 2005), 121–127; Kevin J. Vanhoozer, *The Drama of Doctrine: A Canonical-Linguistic Approach to Christian Theology* (Louisville, Ky.: Westminster John Knox, 2005), 399–444.

BIBLIOGRAPHY

Bacote, Vincent, Laura C. Miguélez, and Dennis L. Okholm, eds. *Evangelicals and Scripture: Tradition, Authority and Hermeneutics*. Downers Grove, Ill.: InterVarsity Press, 2004.

Meadors, Gary, ed. *Four Views on Moving Beyond the Bible to Theology*. Grand Rapids: Zondervan, 2009.

Packer, J. I. *God Has Spoken: Revelation and the Bible*. 3rd ed. Grand Rapids: Baker, 1994.

Ramm, Bernard. *Special Revelation and the Word of God*. Grand Rapids: Eerdmans, 1961.

Thompson, Mark D. *A Clear and Present Word: The Clarity of Scripture*. Downers Grove, Ill.: InterVarsity Press, 2006.

Treier, Daniel J. *Introducing Theological Interpretation of Scripture: Recovering a Christian Practice*. Grand Rapids: Baker Academic, 2008.

Vanhoozer, Kevin J. *The Drama of Doctrine: A Canonical-Linguistic Approach to Christian Theology*. Louisville, Ky.: Westminster John Knox, 2005.

Ward, Timothy. *Words of Life: Scripture as the Living and Active Word of God*. Downers Grove, Ill.: InterVarsity Press, 2009.

Warfield, B. B. *The Inspiration and Authority of the Bible*. Phillipsburg, N.J.: Presbyterian & Reformed, 1979.

Webster, John. *Holy Scripture: A Dogmatic Sketch*. Cambridge: Cambridge University Press, 2003.

Work, Telford. *Living and Active: Scripture in the Economy of Salvation*. Grand Rapids: Eerdmans, 2002.

Wright, N. T. *The Last Word: Beyond the Bible Wars to a New Understanding of the Authority of Scripture*. San Francisco: Harper, 2005.

CHAPTER 3

FAITH AND REASON

W. JAY WOOD

PERHAPS no two words in the theological lexicon are more crucially ambiguous than "faith" and "reason." Getting clear about these terms will help us to understand the relationship (if any) between them. To see the connections between faith and reason, it will not suffice to offer a few historical snapshots that show how thinkers have viewed these two as compatible or incompatible to varying degrees. This approach fails to get at the underlying notions of faith and reason being considered. Here I offer a rudimentary taxonomy of some of the more common understandings of faith and reason that in turn provides something of a rubric for seeing many different ways they may be related.[1]

REASON

The ancient Greeks sometimes referred to humans as the "rational animal." Our crowning glory and what separates us from the beasts, they thought, is a unique repertoire of cognitive powers, though the complexion of our cognitive powers was then and remains a matter of debate. The following five powers, at any rate, are largely uncontested: perception, memory, introspection, a priori intuition, and inferential reasoning.[2] Even though we share powers of perception and memory with the beasts, we employ them in different ways, owing to the expanded set of intellectual powers to which they are connected. Some animals can remember, but not so as to construct a narrative sense of self or to write a memoir. As is also plain, our cognitive powers are at the same time major sources of knowledge. Typically, knowledge—adequately grounded true belief—comes to us via one of our native cognitive faculties. The

Christian tradition also acknowledges that insofar as our intellectual powers bring knowledge and understanding, they allow us to participate somewhat in the image of God, who is perfect in knowledge and understanding.

Whether humans possess powers in addition to these five is a contested matter. Do we have an independent moral faculty—a conscience—as Jerome taught? Do we, as Thomas Reid thought, have an aesthetic sense to discern true beauty? Do we have a *sensus divinitatus*, a divine sense that orients human reason in a God-ward way, as John Calvin and, more recently, Alvin Plantinga have proposed? And even though most philosophers recognize perception and testimony as significant sources of information, they nevertheless disagree about the degree of positive epistemic status such sources confer. These debates notwithstanding, one common understanding of reason refers to our human cluster of cognitive powers.

Second, reason sometimes refers to a canonical standard or procedure for employing one's cognitive powers if knowledge, understanding, and other intellectual goods are one's goals. In his *Discourse on Method*, Descartes notes that "to be possessed of good mental powers is not sufficient; the principal matter is to apply them well."[3] Having the normal human intellectual endowment is no guarantee that one will employ those powers well, or in such a way as to gain knowledge. Precisely what standards one should observe depends on the kind of positive epistemic status one claims for one's belief. A brief sampling of some of the methods, procedures, rules, and requirements that philosophers have proposed for winning knowledge and/or justified belief might start with Descartes, a strong foundationalist, who embraced the impossibly high standard that one ought to believe only claims that are invincibly certain and that one introspectively knows to be certain. Linda Zagzebski thinks that knowledge is a true belief that arises from acts of intellectual virtue, such as being open-minded or intellectually cautious. Evidentialists, such as W. K. Clifford, argue that one commits gross "intellectual sin" to believe anything before having amassed sufficient evidence for that belief. Coherentists, such as Keith Lehrer, think that a belief is justified if it coheres better than any competing belief in one's overall set of beliefs. Reliabilists, such as Alvin Goldman, promote the view that a belief is justified so long as it is the output of some reliable belief-producing process. A close cousin of this view is Alvin Plantinga's position that a belief is warranted so long as it is produced by properly functioning faculties in an appropriate environment. Needless to say, not all of these standards can be honored—as some are incompatible with each other—and which should be honored is a matter of deep and protracted debate in the philosophical community.

Reason also frequently refers to some body of knowledge, some concrete discoveries or findings uncovered through scientific or other means of intellectual investigation. To be reasonable in this third sense means, at a minimum, that one ought not to believe claims that run contrary to truths we have acquired through successful use of our cognitive powers. On this meaning of "reasonable," we would call someone unreasonable who believes, contrary to biological evidence, that female children develop when an east wind weakens the male sperm, or that being exposed to the night air causes one to catch a cold. Many alleged incompatibilities between faith and reason arise when science forwards claims that appear in conflict with the specific teachings of religion, the clash between creation and evolution being a notorious example.[4]

Sometimes we think of reason as thinking that accords with the dominant worldview or the prevailing "spirit of the age." Someone committed to one of the many viewpoints that make up postmodernity might think medieval Platonists "unreasonable," not because they lacked properly functioning cognitive faculties, not because they failed to observe rigorous standards of belief, and not necessarily because science has conclusively shown Platonism to be false. Rather, the partisan of postmodernity might simply view the medieval mindset as alien, as shaped by assumptions, driven by questions, and attempting to resolve intellectual issues that have not so much been refuted as eclipsed.[5] It is not so much that one worldview has been refuted as that its vocabulary has become passé—no longer useful to address the concerns that matter to us most. So, one can be labeled unreasonable in virtue of occupying what, to one's interlocutor at any rate, is an alien intellectual perspective. This fluidity of intellectual perspectives prompts Richard Rorty to say, along with the Romantics, that "imagination, rather than reason, is the central human faculty," and that "a talent for speaking differently, rather than for arguing well, is the chief instrument of cultural change."[6]

Finally, one might mean by reason "practical reason," the reasoning that helps us to achieve various goals and purposes we deem important, such as finding the best directions to one's destination or the best recipe for cooking a Thanksgiving turkey. Practical rationality depends crucially on theoretical rationality—but is not reducible to it—for the reasoning we do to bring about our goals and purposes depends on its being guided by suitably rational means-end beliefs. To achieve the goal of cooking a tasty turkey, I must form correct beliefs about the weight of the bird, the temperature setting on the oven, and so forth. Some philosophers seek to ground religious belief in practical, not epistemic reason.[7]

Nothing about these five accounts of reason suggests that one cannot have a comprehensive view that appropriately combines all five senses of the term. One might embrace an overall intellectual perspective that contains an account of what our standard-issue cognitive powers are, how they should put to use to win knowledge, as well as how scientific discoveries, a particular worldview, and the concerns of practical reason bear on one's knowledge. And as we ask how reason is related to faith, we must consider just what sense or senses of reason are in play.

Faith

The notion of faith is equally if not more varied than that of reason. Faith has been variously used to mean a contrast to knowledge, a specific set of theological doctrines, the trust we place in God, a theological virtue, or even an attitude one adopts in the face of the unknown. Faith is not unique to traditional monotheisms, nor is it used exclusively in religious contexts; people are sometimes said to have faith in another person, in a political cause, or in some physical object—I have faith that the bridge will bear my weight. In its fullest and most robust sense, faith is a complex quality that, paradigmatically, involves one's intellect, will, and actions, in acts of belief or judgment, trust, and characteristic patterns of obedience. Throughout the narrative of faith in one's life, one or another of these facets of faith may be more prominent.

Affirming propositional beliefs is not the whole of faith—the devils, after all, are said to believe, yet tremble—but it is an element of paradigmatic instances of faith. One way, then, to think of faith is as a body of propositions that articulate the intellectual content of a religion, and by doing so, we can distinguish among the content of the Christian faith, the Buddhist faith, the Muslim faith, and so on.

In what way are faith propositions embraced—as knowledge, as belief, as mere opinion? Aquinas distinguished between what he called "the preambles of the faith" and the "mysteries of the faith." The preambles of faith include propositions such as "God exists," "God is one," and "God created the world," all of which are contained in or implied by the Nicene Creed and can be demonstrated or "seen" to be true through our native intellectual powers. As demonstrated, these claims constitute knowledge (*scientia*) in the classical sense common to most medieval thinkers. To know a proposition, according to this tradition, requires that one be self-reflectively aware of its certainty, as occurs with self-evident truths grasped through understanding (*intellectus*) and with claims inferred from such self-evident starting points (*scientia*). The truth of other propositions in the creed—to wit, "we believe in one Lord, Jesus Christ, the only Son of God, eternally begotten from the Father, God from God, Light from Light, true God from true God, begotten, not made, of one being with the Father..."—are neither evident to reason nor demonstrable. These beliefs, the so-called "mysteries of the faith," come to us chiefly through the testimony of a prophet, apostle, or the Church, all of which ultimately look to God's authoritative acts of self-disclosure.

Because the truths of faith are grounded in God's say-so, one can be fully confident in their truth and embrace them as certain. Though one may be certain that God exists and that Jesus Christ is God Incarnate, the ground of that certainty, says Aquinas, is different; the first is certain because it is evident by the power of creaturely reason; the second certain because it is revealed by a perfect God. For this reason we accept the truths of faith, not by the natural movement of the intellect, but through an act of the will. In faith, says Aquinas, "the intellect assents to something, not through being sufficiently moved by its proper object, but through an act of choice, whereby it turns voluntarily to one side rather than to the other: and if this be accompanied by doubt or fear of the opposite side there will be opinion (*opinio*), while if there be certainty and no fear of the other side, there will be faith"[8] Aquinas was also aware that not all persons have the time, talent, or training to prove the various preambles of faith, and thereby gain knowledge. So God graciously includes the preambles of faith as part of the revelation of himself given to prophets, apostles, and the Church. Together, the preamble and the mysteries of the faith comprise the core of the Christian faith expressed propositionally and professed by the creeds.

John Calvin criticized some medieval Scholastic accounts of faith as overly intellectual, as overemphasizing faith as assent to propositions, as if God were in the business of delivering divine treatises. Calvin himself defines faith as "a sure and firm knowledge of the divine favor toward us, founded on the truth of free promise in Christ, and revealed to our minds, and sealed on our hearts by the Holy Spirit."[9] Since the content of faith surpasses our powers of creaturely intellect, it surpasses understanding, and thus cannot be comprehended. By "sure and firm" Calvin does not mean infallibly certain in the Cartesian sense; rather, he underscores our appropriate confidence and assurance that God will act faithfully to bring about our good. Interestingly, Calvin says that such sure and firm assurance is compatible with episodes of doubt and uncertainty about our faith.[10] Nicholas Wolterstorff explains this apparent tension by saying that persons of firm faith, though assailed by doubt, will be reluctant to doubt their faith and will be steadfast and persevere in it.[11]

Calvin's emphasis on the importance of trust (*fiducia*) underscores one of the central elements of faith in the Christian tradition, and signals a second significant understanding of faith—faith as *trust* in God. Here Calvin follows the lead of Martin Luther who said "it is a further function of faith that it honors him whom it trusts with the most reverent and highest regard, since it considers him truthful and trustworthy. There is no other honor equal to the estimate of truthfulness and righteousness with which we honor him whom we trust."[12] Faith in the sense of trust is marked by a lack of anxiety and a corresponding confidence that the person trusted is able, willing, and can be counted on to act for one's good. Trusting God is obviously linked to believing certain things about God, for instance that he exists, has the power to bring about our good, and will act benevolently toward those who seek him (Hebrews 11:6). The decision to trust another, however, is chiefly the result of the orientation of the will. Faith is also linked to obedience since, as Luther points out, trusting God is our chief act of obedience, from which other good works follow.

Faith as trust is also intertwined with the other theological virtues of hope and love. If faith as trust is looking expectantly and confidently for God to bring about one's ultimate good, then the good is not yet fully realized. The heroes of the faith in Hebrews are all said to have "died in faith, not having received what was promised" (11:13). Hope, then, is faith extended into the future—the reasonable expectation that good of some sort will come to one. Soldiers may reasonably hope, even in the midst of desperate circumstances, that needed reinforcements will arrive in time. Some hope is unreasonable, say, hoping to win the lottery. But hope in God, according to Christian thinking, is grounded inductively in the history of his saving deeds and goodness to his people. Faith is also intimately bound up in love, since to love God is to adore him as the heart's highest quarry, one's highest end and ultimate fulfillment. Christianity teaches that the fulfillment of that love relationship will not happen in this life, but in a new heaven and a new earth. Therefore, those who reciprocate God's love hope that he will bring about their highest good.

The relationships of faith to hope and love point to faith understood in a third sense: faith as a theological virtue. Virtues are acquired dispositions to excellent functioning in some generically human sphere of activity that is difficult and important. Virtues, so defined, range over intellectual, moral, and theological matters, disposing us to right thinking, right emotions and action, and true faith in God, all of which are essential to achieve our flourishing and final end. Faith, as a virtue, is thus a polyconsequential disposition that qualifies the whole person—mind, will, and body—issuing in right actions, emotions, and judgments or beliefs. The virtue of faith cannot be acquired by sheer dint of effort (as some of the Greeks said of the moral virtues), but in addition to a cooperative will requires the work of the Holy Spirit in us. The infusion of grace may then result in one's having faculties—intellectual, volitional, and behavioral—that harmoniously combine, mutually informing and reinforcing each other, in a life routinely directed to kingdom ends.

As noted, the proper orientation of the will is crucial for right understanding and right action in the life of faith. Philosophers divide the faculty of the will into two main parts: the executive and conative will. By the executive will is meant the power of self-directedness whereby we successfully move ourselves toward our desired ends. The conative will refers to the structure of our loves, concerns, cares, and emotions: what we refer to collectively as "the affections." If the executive will moves us toward desired ends, the conative will contains those affections by which we are attracted and moved. Persons with the virtue of faith have wills oriented to God and the things God loves; the structure of their cares, concerns, loves, attachments, and emotions are appropriately ordered to God. Aquinas lists among the gifts of wisdom imparted by the Holy Spirit a sympathetic "attunement" or "connaturality" for moral and divine matters.[13] Similarly, Jonathan Edwards suggests that special grace confers on its recipients a new "sense of the heart" that assists reason to discern the clear evidence of divine activity, giving rise to religious knowledge. A rightly ordered will is important for detecting and assessing aright the probative force of evidence or signs of God's existence. So when Aquinas calls faith an act of the will, he does not mean to suggest that believing in God is subject to our direct voluntary control. Rather, our conative will must rightly dispose us to belief, and our executive will must direct our attention and thinking to the things of God.

Finally, we look at nonpropositional or nondoxastic accounts of faith, which deny that believing claims about God is a necessary requirement for faith. Sometimes persons judge that a fair and impartial examination of evidence fails to support the belief that God exists. Perhaps the prevailing naturalistic worldview makes the truth of theism seem unlikely to them. Despite the lack of positive evidence to underwrite religious faith, one may nevertheless find oneself powerfully attracted to the vision of life a religion offers. Robert Audi admits that while the fullest conception of faith includes beliefs of various sorts, a narrower conception, which he calls "volitional faith," is sufficient for one's having religious faith. Here faith is viewed chiefly as a positive attitude toward or a disposition to orient one's life in a religious way.[14] Clearly, an attitude or positive stance toward God or a religious tradition has an intellectual dimension, since one needs concepts and understanding to supply the propositional content of what one's attitude is about. Moreover, one could not have a positive attitude toward God while steadfastly and categorically denying that God exists. Audi describes nondoxastic faith mainly as a state of the will rather than intellect, a kind of religious resolve to embrace a perspective one takes as appropriate for living one's life.[15]

To embrace a religious framework in this volitional or attitudinal sense is to be inspired by it, to allow it to influence one's life, to frame the way one looks upon the world in terms of the religion, to motivate one's patterns of behavior, and even to be open to the possibility of rational grounds emerging that would allow one to believe the framework to be true.

The Relationship of Faith and Reason

With some of the primary meanings of faith and reason in place, a few of the many possible permutations regarding their relationship can more easily be explored. The first connection between faith and reason to underscore is the faith that we must have *in* reason if we are to avoid skepticism. Virtually no one denies the general reliability or truthfulness of his cognitive powers. (We institutionalize people who, while sitting in a crowded classroom, deny that there are other people in the room.) How do I know that when I seem to see a tree in front of me, or remember having had coffee with my breakfast, that I am not profoundly deceived or mistaken in some way? What *guarantees* do I have that my cognitive faculties do not systematically twist and distort my connection to a mind-independent world? No guarantees at all.

A fundamental starting point for the intellectual life is that we must have faith in the overall reliability of our cognitive powers. How could it be otherwise, since we cannot provide a noncircular vindication of our intellectual powers without using the very powers whose reliability is in question? "We will never be able to get evidence," writes Linda Zagzebski, "that our human faculties in general give us appropriate connections to reality.... That means that the need for self-trust arises at a fundamental level in the life of a rational agent."[16] Faith that our native faculties "give us appropriate connections to reality" requires that we trust our faculties when they tell us there is an external world, that its laws are uniform, that there are other minds, and so on. Most epistemologists now admit that efforts by classical foundationalists, such as Rene Descartes, to use reason to validate reason were failures. Richard Foley sums up the point succinctly: "Significant inquiry requires an equally significant leap of intellectual faith."[17] Hence faith, in the sense of trusting in someone or something else to bring about one's good, is essential for persons seeking true and comprehensive beliefs.

To place some sort of generic faith in the reliability of our intellectual faculties leaves unanswered how, specifically, Christian faith is related to reason. Through two millennia, faith has coexisted uneasily with philosophy, giving rise to the "problem of faith and reason." Tertullian put the question picturesquely: "What has Jerusalem to do with Athens? What concord is there between the Academy and the Church?"[18] Augustine, and many of the medieval thinkers that followed him, were chiefly concerned to identify and demarcate reason's powers, and then to clarify faith's relationship to knowledge (*episteme*). Augustine delineated a middle path between the extremes of the Manichean and Neo-Platonist philosophers, for whom self-reflective certainty was the sole intellectual standard, and Church fathers such as Tertullian, who famously claimed that Christ's resurrection "is by all means to be believed, because it is absurd...the fact is certain because it is impossible."[19] Augustine's elegant solution provided an enduring model: "Understanding is the reward of faith. Therefore, seek not to understand in order to believe, but believe in order to understand."[20] "For faith is understanding's step; and understanding faith's attainment."[21] Certainly this is true in order of time. Children must begin by trusting the testimony of others before they are mature enough to see some truths for themselves. And as we have already noted, reason cannot get off the ground unless one has faith that our cognitive faculties are reliable, that there is an external world to which our faculties direct us, that nature's laws are uniform, that we are not under malign skeptical influence, and so on. For Augustine, the life of faith will one day culminate in faith's reward, knowing God as we have been known, seeing him face to face. This being so, we ought not shrink from what foretastes of this are to be offered in this life. "Therefore, whatever a man of faith does not yet see he ought to believe in such a way as to hope for and love the seeing of it."[22]

Though Augustine and Aquinas were chiefly concerned to mark faith and reason's distinctive boundaries, both were also aware that it is possible to believe foolishly, to misplace trust. Aquinas insists, however, "that to give assent to the truths of faith is not foolishness even though they are above reason."[23] The truths of faith are accompanied, he says, by "fitting" or "likely" arguments that attest to their having come from God. Divine revelation was accompanied by miracles, moral transformation, the rapid spread of the Church, and can be seen as the fulfillment of prophecy, which all serve to authenticate the revelation as coming from God. Aquinas is clear that the signs that attest to the truths of faith as coming from God do not serve as arguments that give us *intellectus* (a priori apprehension of intellectual first principles) or *scientia* (deductions from first principles) of the truths so revealed. So the believer's certainty concerning the matters of faith rests on their having been revealed by God, not on our possessing independent epistemic grounds for their truth.

Aquinas shared the view that philosophy pursues answers to its questions by employing our native cognitive powers. But these powers are limited, and in many cases remain immature, untrained, and liable to error. Yet to achieve salvation and to pursue lives ordered to God and the things of God, we need information our native faculties cannot provide: hence the need for God to reveal knowledge to us, which one accepts on the authority of the proposer. Yet, what if the deliverances of reason should seem to conflict with those received by faith? Faith's directive to seek understanding does not address what believers should do if the content of faith conflicts with the deliverances of reason, or understanding. Does one side always or only sometimes trump the other?

Aquinas maintained the optimistic view that the truths of reason cannot be contrary to those we take on faith. For the same God who designed our intellectual faculties also reveals the knowledge necessary for our salvation. So if our faculties are properly employed, and the revelation rightly understood, there can be no conflict.[24] "Whatever arguments are brought forward against the doctrines of the faith are conclusions incorrectly derived from the first and self-evident principles embedded in our nature. Such conclusions do not have the force of demonstration; they are arguments that are either probable or sophistical, and so there exists the possibility to answer them."[25] Contemporary philosophers, however, largely adopt the view that faith need not be *proven* incorrect to be unreasonable. To show that faith is improbable suffices to show that it is unreasonable.

Post-Cartesian philosophy shifts the focus away from the distinctive spheres of faith and reason to questions about the epistemic rationality of faith, reason in the second sense described above. Locke's epistemology was forged in response to the wars of the Reformation and the social unrest spawned by religious enthusiasts, the strength and confidence of whose religious feelings ran far ahead of good judgment. Knowledge, he maintains, comes in a pretty narrow band width for humans, being restricted to the outputs of a priori intuition and what can be demonstrated from the same, as well as the immediate deliverances of perception; the rest is but faith and opinion. God's existence, in Locke's view, is among the truths we know by "natural deduction." As for mere belief or opinion, Locke requires that we adjust the depth of our assent to reflect the amount and quality of our evidence. In short, "we want probability to direct our assent in matters where we have neither knowledge of our own nor testimony of other men to bottom our reason upon."[26]

Faith, says Locke, "is the assent to any proposition, not thus made out by the deductions of reason, but upon the credit of the proposer, as coming from God, in some extraordinary way of communication. This way of discovering truths to men, we call revelation."[27] Yet Locke thinks even faith, as a deliverance of revelation, must be appropriately regulated by reason. He counsels that we adjust the level of confidence we have in any matter of faith so as not to exceed our evidence that God has indeed revealed it. And the evidence most appropriate to ground a particular claim as coming from a divine source is that it be accompanied by a miracle. So, of God's revelation through Christ, Locke says: "The evidence of Our Saviour's mission from heaven is so great, in the multitude of miracles he did, before all sorts of people, that what he delivered cannot but be received as the oracles of God, and unquestioned verity."[28] But many of us have never seen a miracle, and those beneficiaries to whom the faith was first given with miraculous accompaniment are two millennia gone. It follows from Locke's view, then, that the confidence we place in any item of faith cannot exceed the attenuated historical evidences we now have that any such item was miraculously revealed. Most persons, of course, have never attended to the historical credentials of Christian revelation claims, but depend on the word of authorities that such events transpired. And testimonial evidence cannot underwrite a level of confidence in claims to faith that puts them on a par with knowledge. Locke thus anticipates Lessing's famous "ugly ditch" that divides the probable conclusions afforded by historical study and the certainty demanded by faith.

Anthony Kenny has recently criticized faith commitments on grounds similar to Locke's:

> No doubt it may be reasonably believed that Moses and Jesus did and said many of the things ascribed to them in the Bible; but can it reasonably be believed with a degree of certainty resembling that of knowledge? Unless the relevant story can be as certain as the commitment which faith demands of the believer, the commitment is, so far forth as it is faith, irrational. And if the belief is a commitment that is rationally in proportion to the support given by the history, it is, so far forth as it is rational, something less than faith.[29]

Kenny poses a dilemma to the believer: Since the believer's evidence for something's having been revealed from God falls short of what is needed for knowledge, the believer is irrational to accept it on a par with knowledge. If the believer lowers his confidence in a belief to match his evidence, he fails to embrace it as faith. Kenny thinks that some historical claims can qualify as knowledge. He claims *to know*, for instance, that Charles I was beheaded in London. That Jesus was raised from the dead does not, however, enjoy that level of historical support. He concludes, though, that religious faith is not a virtue but a vice—unless the historical events constituting the divine revelation can be supported with evidence equal to that enjoyed by his belief about Charles I.

One can respond to Kenny's challenge either by trying to meet his demands for evidence or by denying that evidence is necessary to have the degree of warrant needed for knowledge. Richard Swinburne tries to meet the demand for evidence by offering a traditional two-stage approach that begins by offering arguments for God's existence, then moves to establish the historical reliability of the Bible, especially as it depicts the life and work of Christ. Swinburne's probabilistic case for Christian faith requires him to offer independent arguments for God's existence, the possibility of miracles, the reliability of the biblical record, and for the present-day Christian Church as a reliable continuer of the apostles' teachings. By Swinburne's admission, the evidential case for the truth of the Christian revelation claims is, at best, probabilistic. But Swinburne disagrees with Kenny that faith commitments must be epistemically certain from the outset. When Christians speak of faith's certainty, they often have in mind the firmness of faith, rather than epistemic certainty. And when they do speak of the *episteme* of faith, they acknowledge that it is a mark of mature faith, and must be nurtured through ongoing reflection in the company of the faithful, and as aided by the work of the Holy Spirit.

Recently, Reformed epistemologists such as Alvin Plantinga, Nicholas Wolterstorff, and William Alston have argued that belief in God can be properly basic, that is to say, epistemically warranted in the absence of argumentative support, thus denying Kenny's assumption that knowledge claims must be underwritten with propositional evidence. Belief in God, they say, is like belief that there is an external world or that there are other minds. We do not adduce reasons for such beliefs; rather, we simply find ourselves believing them in appropriate experiential circumstances. Clearly, this is an account of warranted belief in what epistemologists call the "externalist" tradition; one need not have reflective access to the grounds of a belief to be warranted in believing it. Plantinga explains that our taking belief in God as basic is the outworking of what John Calvin called the *sensus divinitatis*, a disposition or capacity of reason that disposes us to form beliefs about God and the things of God in appropriate circumstances. Plantinga extends this idea of beliefs arising out of warrant-producing processes to include the central claims of the gospel. In what he calls the "Extended Aquinas-Calvin Model," Plantinga proposes a model to explain how our accepting the central claims of the gospel, such as that Jesus Christ is God Incarnate, are warranted because they are instigated in us by the reliable direction of the Holy Spirit.[30] Critics point out that the same strategy for justifying faith commitments might be employed by devotees of Krishna or some other deity. They too might point to some special cognitive faculty the proper functioning of which leads one to belief in Krishna. Plantinga acknowledges this point, and does not try to provide argument for the truth of his model. He rests content to say that *if* his model is true, then the beliefs comprising Christian faith are warranted.

Pascal famously claimed that our natural powers of creaturely reason are powerless to prove that God exists. "If there is a God, he is infinitely beyond our comprehension, since, having neither parts nor limits, he bears no relation to ourselves. We are therefore incapable of knowing either what he is, or if he is."[31]

Though pure, epistemic reason cannot commend belief to us, practical reason can. It is, says Pascal, in our best practical interests to believe in God since, if he exists, we have everything to gain and nothing to lose, so go ahead and wager on God. Clearly, a belief's conferring practical advantage does not make it true, but might it nevertheless be rational? Gary Gutting argues along Millian lines, that the interests of truth are best served in a free marketplace of ideas, where committed adherents debate opposing points of view on religion. So pragmatic commitment to religious belief can be viewed as in accord with our general obligation to search for evidence that bears on its truth. Gutting cautions, however, that this strategy licenses only an interim, or provisional, assent to the religious beliefs in question, as we must hold them while being constantly open to new evidence that may show the truth of one side or the other. Gutting argues that interim assent is religiously inadequate, and not at all characteristic of the kind of commitment most religions require.[32] One might reply to Gutting by noting that full-blown rather than tentative assent is precisely what is required to serve the interest of finding out the truth. Suppose a doctor informs you that your medical condition gives you a 50/50 chance of recovery. You also know that studies show that those who sincerely believe that they will recover have a stronger likelihood of recovering. In such a case as this, one's full-blown prudential belief serves epistemic interests.

Paul Helm qualifies his evidentialist approach to religious faith to acknowledge the demands of practical reason. Trusting God, he writes, is not different from trusting a bridge to bear one's weight. Both demand evidence if they are to be instances of reasonable faith. All else being equal, he says, the strength with which we trust God should be proportioned to the evidence we have for God's existence and trustworthiness. Helm admits, however, that sometimes all else is not equal. Sometimes our personal needs are so pressing that we have to act in the absence of evidence. Here considerations of prudential rationality outweigh all else. "In faith over the long term, belief ought to be proportioned to evidence, and desire to belief. But in the short term, and where desire is stronger than belief, it may nevertheless be rational to have a belief whose strength is greater than present evidence warrants."[33]

Finally, we examine how thinkers seek to accommodate faith to Richard Rorty's radically antirealist account of reason as so many contingent intellectual paradigms composed in part of ever-evolving systems of linguistic conventions and interpretations. Don Cupitt embraces Rorty's antirealist vision but, unlike Rorty, does not reject religious faith, claiming that faith must be reconceived to accommodate this antirealist position.

> We have reversed the traditional outlook of Christian Platonism. The world above and all the absolutes are gone. The whole of life and all our standards are now inside language and culture. For good or ill *we* make our own history, *we* have shaped our own world, *we* have together evolved all norms to which our life is subject. Religion for us must inevitably be something very different from what it was in the heyday of Platonic realism. It is plain that if I am right, then Christianity must be revolutionized to survive.[34]

Once one realizes that the content and practice of one's faith is due entirely to the contingencies of history and socialization, one is much less inclined, says Cupitt, to trumpet one's own religion as true or superior to other religions. Abandoning the idea that religion offers any sort of transcendental truth turns religious faith into a distinctive kind of attitude that Cupitt describes as "undogmatic," "post-authoritarian," and "without spiritual authority." There is no truth to which religion points us; rather, it allows humans, like artists, "creativity to confront the flux." Religious faith is therefore but one means of coping in an utterly contingent, ever-changing, multicultural world.

How shall we think about the relationship between Christian faith and reason in the antirealist view? Since Cupitt endorses Nietzsche's claim that "there are no facts, only interpretations,"[35] it follows that religious faith cannot run afoul of reason in the sense of being contrary to established scientific facts, since science too fails to establish mind-independent truths. And if, as the quotation above alleges, all standards are inside language and culture, it would appear that faith could not oppose some universal canon of good intellectual conduct, since no such canons exist. Where, then, is the point of friction between traditional Christian faith and antirealism? Just this: that traditional Christian faith thinks it has truths to offer that transcend the local culture and its conventions, and Cupitt thinks neither religion nor science is in a position to make good this boast. But the prevailing view among scientists and most ordinary people is that we are capable of knowledge about the world, and that if any view runs contrary to the culture, it is Cupitt's. Surely religion, not antirealism, more closely accords with traditional accounts of reason.

The varieties of faith and reason admit of many other ways of seeing their interrelationships that must go unmentioned. The views we have treated—ancient, medieval, modern, and postmodern—provide the reader with examples sufficient to trace out further permutations.

NOTES

1. I will focus on faith as articulated in the Christian tradition, though Christianity shares elements of faith with other religious traditions.

2. Perception, memory, and reasoning by logical inference are familiar terms. A priori intuition refers to one's capacity to see self-evident and necessary truths, such as that $A = A$, or $10 > 2$. Introspection refers to our ability to access some of our interior mental, emotional, and physical states, for instance, that I am now thinking about ice cream, or I feel anxious.

3. Rene Descartes, *Discourse on Method*, trans. Elizabeth Haldane and G.R.T Ross (New York: Dover, 1955), 82.

4. Many Christian thinkers do not think their faith conflicts with evolution. See, for example, Francis S. Collins, *The Language of God* (New York: Free Press, 2006).

5. Richard Rorty, *Contingency, Irony, and Solidarity* (Cambridge: Cambridge University Press, 1989), 6.

6. Ibid., 7. Of course Nietzsche said it earlier: "What decides against Christianity now is our taste, not our reasons." Friedrich Nietzsche, *The Gay Science*, trans. Josefine Nauchhoff, ed. Bernard Williams (Cambridge: Cambridge University Press, 2001), 132.

7. Jason Stanley, among others, has challenged the sharp boundary between epistemic and practical reason. See his *Knowledge and Practical Interests* (Oxford: Oxford University Press, 2005).

8. Thomas Aquinas, *Summa Theologiae*, II–II. Q. 1. Art. 4.

9. John Calvin, *Institutes of the Christian Religion*, vol. 1, trans. Henry Beveridge (Grand Rapids: Eerdmans, 1981), 3.2.7.

10. Ibid., 3.2.17, 21.

11. Nicholas Wolterstorff, "The Assurance of Faith," *Faith and Philosophy* (October 1990): 412–413.

12. Martin Luther, *The Freedom of a Christian*, in John Dillenberger, *Martin Luther: Selections from His Writings* (New York: Anchor Doubleday, 1962), 59.

13. Aquinas, *Summa Theologiae*, II–II. 45.2.

14. Robert Audi, "The Dimensions of Faith the Demands of Reason," in *Reasoned Faith*, ed. Eleonore Stump (Ithaca: Cornell University Press: 1993), 70–89.

15. Ibid., 82.

16. Linda Zagzebski, *On Epistemology* (Belmont, Cal.: Wadsworth, 2009), 73.

17. Richard Foley, *Intellectual Trust in Oneself and Others* (Cambridge: Cambridge University Press, 2001), 20. See also Keith Lehrer, *Self-Trust: A Study of Reason, Knowledge, and Autonomy* (Oxford: Oxford University Press, 1997).

18. Tertullian, *The Prescription against the Heretics* 7, in H. T. Kerr, ed., *Readings in Christian Thought* (Nashville, Tenn.: Abingdon, 1966), 39.

19. Tertullian, *On the Flesh of Christ*, in A. Roberts and J. Donaldson, *The Ante-Nicene Fathers*, vol. 3 (Grand Rapids: Eerdmans, 1951), chap. 5.

20. Augustine, *Epistula* 120, in *Letters*, vol. 2 (83–130), in *Fathers of the Church*, trans. W. Parsons (Washington, D.C.: Catholic University Press, 1953).

21. Augustine, *Sermone* 76.1–2, in *The Nicene and Post-Nicene Fathers of the Christian Church*, ed. Philip Schaff, Vol. 6 (Grand Rapids: Eerdmans, 1979), 481.

22. Augustine, *Epistula* 120.

23. Thomas Aquinas, *Summa Contra Gentiles*, trans. Anton Pegis (Notre Dame: University of Notre Dame Press, 1975), bk. 1, chap. 6.

24. See, for instance, Aquinas, *Exposition of De Trinitate*, ii, 3.

25. Aquinas, *Summa Contra Gentiles*, bk. 1, chap. 7, 7.

26. John Locke, *An Essay Concerning Human Understanding* (New York: Dover, 1959), 4.18.1.

27. Ibid., 4.18.2.

28. John Locke, *The Reasonableness of Christianity* (Stanford: Stanford University Press, 1958), 57.

29. Anthony Kenny, *What Is Faith?* (Oxford: Oxford University Press, 1992), 56–57.

30. See Alvin Plantinga, *Warranted Christian Belief* (Oxford: Oxford University Press, 2000).

31. Blaise Pascal, *Pensées*, 45: 680, trans. Honor Levi (Oxford: Oxford University Press: 1995), 153.

32. Gary Gutting, *Religious Belief and Religious Skepticism* (Notre Dame: University of Notre Dame Press, 1982), 174.

33. Paul Helm, *Faith with Reason* (Oxford: Oxford University Press, 2000), 157.

34. Don Cupitt, "Anti Realist Faith," in *Readings in Philosophy of Religion*, ed. Andrew Eshleman Malden, Mass.: Blackwell, 2008), 415.

35. Friedrich Nietzsche, *1880's Notebooks*, quoted in *The Stanford Encyclopedia of Philosophy*, http://stanford.edu/entries/Nietzsche.

BIBLIOGRAPHY

Aquinas, St. Thomas. *Summa Theologiae*, trans. Fathers of the English Dominican Province. Westminster, Md.: Christian Classics, 1981.

———. *Summa Contra Gentiles*, trans. Anton Pegis. Notre Dame: University of Notre Dame Press, 1975.

Audi, Robert. "The Dimensions of Faith the Demands of Reason." In *Reasoned Faith*, ed. Eleonore Stump. Ithaca: Cornell University Press, 1993.

Calvin, John. *Institutes of the Christian Religion*, vol. 1, trans. Henry Beveridge. Grand Rapids: Eerdmans, 1981.

Evans, C. Stephen. *Faith beyond Reason*. Grand Rapids: Eerdmans, 1998).

Gutting, Gary. *Religious Belief and Religious Skepticism*. Notre Dame: University of Notre Dame Press, 1982.

Helm, Paul. *Faith with Reason*. Oxford: Oxford University Press, 2000.

Hoitenga, Dewey. *Faith and Reason from Plato to Plantinga*. Albany: State University of New York Press, 1991.

Kenny, Anthony. *What Is Faith?* Oxford: Oxford University Press, 1992.
Locke, John. *An Essay Concerning Human Understanding*. New York: Dover, 1959.
Luther, Martin. "The Freedom of a Christian." In John Dillenberger, *Martin Luther: Selections from His Writings*. New York: Anchor Doubleday, 1962.
Pascal, Blaise. *Pensées*, trans. Honor Levi. Oxford: Oxford University Press, 1995.
Penelhum, Terence. *Reason and Religious Faith*. Boulder, Col.: Westview, 1995.
Plantinga, Alvin. *Warranted Christian Belief*. Oxford: Oxford University Press, 2000.
Swinburne, Richard. *Faith and Reason*. 2nd edition. Oxford: Oxford University Press, 2005.
Wolterstorff, Nicholas. "The Assurance of Faith." *Faith and Philosophy* (October 1990): 412–413.

CHAPTER 4

FAITH AND EXPERIENCE

OLIVER D. CRISP

Evangelical theology has traditionally had a somewhat ambivalent relationship to the notion of "experience," understood here as some event lived through, of which one is consciously aware. In this chapter we will focus on the role *religious* experience plays in the formation, sustenance, and development of Christian doctrine. We will also consider the relationship between religious experience as a putative source of encounter with the divine, and other sources of testimony appealed to in order to ground theological authority, such as Scripture or tradition. We will see that in evangelical thought there are different, sometimes conflicting, accounts of the relation experience bears to doctrine or to norms of theological authority.

But faith itself is an act that implies religious experience. So, in addition to the question of the relation between faith and religious experience of the sort just mentioned, there is a logically prior question about how faith itself is to be understood qua experience in evangelical theology. The concept of faith admits of numerous different interpretations.[1] But for most evangelicals, faith is an act that involves two components. The first is propositional content, that is, believing that such and such is the case. This we shall call the doxastic component of faith. The second part is trust—what we might call the fiducial component of faith. Some people think faith is essentially nonpropositional or numinous and cannot be expressed in language. I shall have nothing to say about such notions of faith in what follows—not because they are unimportant, but because they do not seem to be typical of mainstream evangelical theology.

It seems clear that faith is something that is normally acquired. For some, faith acquisition comes about through a process of discovery, reflection, careful weighing of evidence, and so on. For others it seems to be a sudden intrusion into their lives, as it was for the apostle Paul. God's presence is somehow impressed upon that person in such an immediate way that he or she cannot deny it; it is overwhelming. Whether faith is acquired through reflection or through dramatic change, it looks as though one important feature of such faith is that one comes to hold certain beliefs in virtue of having faith. It also seems fairly clear that such faith in God also includes a fiducial component. From this it should be clear that reflection on the very concept of faith and the role it plays in evangelical theologies must also include consideration of how faith relates to experience, since to have faith is to undergo some sort of experience.[2]

The Act of Faith in Wesleyan and Edwardsian Theology

Though it is the subject of disagreement between competing parties of evangelicals, the concept of faith in evangelical theology has historically had fairly well-defined boundaries, which is due in large measure to the legacy of the Reformation. The Reformers bequeathed to their theological progeny an understanding of the nature of faith and its central and defining place in Protestant thought, which evangelicals have traditionally taken very seriously. But the issue of what faith consists in—what it is, exactly—should be distinguished from the matter of what function it has in theology, what role it plays. I suggest that these two issues, the conceptual and the functional aspects of faith, correspond to two levels of disagreement among evangelical theologians on the role of faith. It is tempting to think that this question of the role of faith in the life of the believer has been what has most often divided evangelicals. But in fact such differences are the outcome of deeper commitments about the conceptual component of faith.

This was true even when evangelical theology was in its infancy, if the story told in the recent literature by David Bebbington and those who have followed his lead is correct.[3] Assume, for the sake of argument, that Bebbington is right and evangelicalism as a movement began in the 1730s with the revivalism of the John and Charles Wesley, George Whitefield, and Jonathan Edwards, at the onset of what has become known as the Great Awakening. Then it would appear that at the beginning of evangelicalism there was a difference of opinion on the nature of faith, on its role in theology, and on how it is related to religious experience which continues to the present.[4]

To see this, let us turn to consider some of the main points of convergence and divergence over the matter of faith that existed between traditional evangelical Wesleyan Arminianism and evangelical Reformed theology of the sort embraced by stalwarts of evangelical history such as George Whitefield and Jonathan Edwards.[5] We begin with the conceptual level, concerning the nature of faith. Wesleyan evangelicals have traditionally agreed with their Reformed counterparts that it is faith alone that justifies a person before God; that faith is a gift of God; that faith brings about moral and spiritual reorientation; and that (as a consequence of this) faith itself must be experiential. In other words, faith is inherently *affective*. It cannot be a merely notional or intellectual assent to a given statement or proposition, though it normally includes such assent.[6]

Following Jonathan Edwards, we might think of the *affections* as that faculty of the soul which inclines or disinclines a person to do a thing under consideration, and includes the will, the mind, and the heart in such inclination. In this view, religious affections do not admit of a bifurcation between "heart" and "mind." They are more like "reasons of the heart." This means they are not reducible to emotion, passion, or intellectual preference, but involve the interplay of mind, will, and heart, as Edwards suggests.[7] That this affective understanding of faith crosses the Arminian-Calvinist divide in historic evangelical theology can be illustrated from the experience of both John Wesley and Edwards, both of whom give paradigmatic accounts of "affective" faith-acquisition. Wesley's famous report of his "conversion" runs thus:

> In the evening, I went very unwillingly to a society in Aldersgate Street, where one was reading Luther's Preface to the Epistle to the Romans. About a quarter before nine, while he was describing the change which God works in the heart through faith in Christ, I felt my heart strangely warmed. I felt I did trust in Christ, Christ alone for salvation; and an assurance was given me that he had taken away *my* sins, even *mine* and saved me from the law of sin and death.[8]

Edwards's account has striking similarities,

> The first that I remember that ever I found anything of that sort of inward, sweet delight in God and divine things, that I have lived much in since, was on reading those words, I Tim. 1:17. "Now unto the King eternal, immortal, invisible, the only wise God, be honour and glory for ever and ever, Amen." As I read the words, there came into my soul, and was as it were diffused through it, a sense of the glory of the Divine Being; a new sense, quite different from any thing I ever experienced before. Never any words of scripture seemed to me as these words did. I thought with myself, how excellent a Being that was; and how happy I should be, if I might enjoy that God, and be wrapped up to God in heaven, and be as it were swallowed up in him.[9]

But there are also important areas of conceptual disagreement between the two evangelical parties on the question of faith acquisition. The Wesleyans could not agree with the Reformed that salvation is *only* by divine grace through faith—despite protestations to the contrary. Broadly speaking, Arminian theology as a genus, of which evangelical Wesleyans are a species, is committed to a doctrine of synergism, according to which there is both a human and a divine contribution to be made to the process by which faith is acquired.[10] We might say that for the synergist, humans have the freedom to embrace or reject prevenient divine grace by, or with, faith. By contrast, most Reformed theologians (though perhaps not all) assert a doctrine of monergism.[11] This, very roughly, is the doctrine according to which no human contribution can be made to the process by which faith is acquired. That is, for the monergist humans are *utterly incapable* of responding to God's suasions with faith. The work of salvation is entirely a work of grace; the human decision in regeneration follows in the wake of a prior (and absolutely singular) divine act.[12]

This leads us to note, more briefly, the second level of disagreement between Wesleyan and Reformed evangelicals on the matter of the role faith plays in their respective theologies. We have seen that evangelicals have tended to converge on the centrality of faith for the Christian life and on the importance of the idea that one is saved only through faith, despite wranglings over what salvation *sola fide* entails. But they have disagreed among themselves about the practical consequences of this commitment in the *ordo salutis* and the life of faith. Here the different theological characters of the two evangelical traditions come into play more obviously. Consider, for example, how faith is deployed in, say, the doctrine of regeneration or perseverance. Arminian evangelicals have traditionally thought that in both regeneration and perseverance, the human subject contributes to the process involved, which the Reformed have denied. This is one important reason for the different accounts of the order of salvation and of perseverance that one finds in these two traditions.

However, it is also true to say that in the past century (and for a variety of reasons) the conceptual boundaries thought to circumscribe what is doctrinally permissible in discussion of the nature of faith in the evangelical constituency have broadened out. This means that there is now a greater range of options on the nature of faith and its function in evangelical thought than was true at the close of the nineteenth century. For instance, there are evangelical biblical scholars for whom Pauline faith is as much a matter of belonging to the covenant community as it is a question of having some alien righteousness imputed to the believer by God (e.g., N. T. Wright and the so-called "New Perspective" on Paul).

Thus far, we have seen that the relationship between faith and experience is an intimate one. For evangelical theologians, faith depends on experience; it is affective. It is practically impossible to have faith without such experience, even if, as a matter of fact, for some people faith in God begins at the same moment experience of God occurs.[13] But a lively, affective faith is not enough. One can have the sort of evangelical understanding of faith just outlined, and yet live a wicked life (cf. Rom. 6:1). Such antinomianism is a real problem for evangelicals who take seriously the experiential dimension to faith, as expounded by evangelical leaders of the past like Wesley and Edwards. In the recent literature, Richard Swinburne has taken the view that the best way to avoid antinomianism is to adopt a pragmatic model of faith. Whereas a number of theologians in the Western tradition such as St. Thomas Aquinas or Martin Luther have emphasized both the doxastic and fiducial elements of faith, Swinburne wants to make a case for acting-as-if certain things were the case. The fiducial pragmatist (as we shall call him) need not believe that there is a God, but he must act as if there is a God, living a life consistent with that belief, informed by certain moral commitments and actions. Swinburne comments, "On the Pragmatist view, a man S has faith if he acts on the assumptions that there is a God who has the properties which Christians ascribe to him and has provided for me the means of salvation and the prospect of glory, and that he will do for S what he knows that S needs or wants—so long also as S has good purposes."[14]

What is potentially lacking in the Lutheran account of faith, where one believes that there is a God and trusts that through Christ's work he or she will be saved, is *good purpose*. It is this that leaves the door open to antinomianism. In short, the Lutheran view (as Swinburne characterizes it) cannot exclude the scoundrel from being a person of faith. This is precisely why Swinburne thinks the pragmatic account of faith is superior to the Lutheran. The fiducial pragmatist must have a good purpose in view, which the Lutheran view cannot guarantee.

But Swinburne clearly has a rather different conception of faith than that of evangelicals attracted to the affective account of theologians like Edwards. Swinburne thinks belief is not praiseworthy because it is not voluntary: one cannot simply bring oneself to believe a particular proposition. The mind believes a given proposition on the basis of the evidence. But trust occurs where there is an evidential gap. It is what stands "in" that gap. Thus, I trust God despite the lack of overwhelming evidence for his existence. However, as Paul Helm has pointed out, this means there is a paradox at the heart of Swinburne's account of pragmatic faith. For, according to Swinburne,

> to the extent that the existence of God is evidentially established it is more reasonable to believe that he exists than not, but for that very reason there is less opportunity for faith in him, for trust. Merit comes only from trust, but trust can only occur when there is evidential deficiency... to the extent that you have good grounds for a belief about God you at the same time reduce opportunities for trusting God, for acting on an assumption while having a good purpose, and so you reduce the opportunities for faith in God, and so lessen your chances of gaining merit by exercising such faith.[15]

The upshot of this is that for the Swinburnian fiducial pragmatist, ignorance about intellectual arguments concerning God is better for one's faith!

But, assuming that the evangelical does have a conception of faith like the Lutheran, how can he or she exclude the possibility of antinomianism? An affective faith might still issue in a lack of good purpose. In fact, it looks as if one cannot prevent antinomianism, even if it is part and parcel of faith to be experiential, as it is on the Wesleyan and Edwardsian accounts. However, something is surely awry with the person who thinks faith is affective and yet that such faith need not issue in good purpose. Similarly, one cannot exclude the possibility that one's spouse does not reciprocate conjugal love, but simulates it from purely selfish motives. But this does not in and of itself nullify conjugal love, or the trust one places in one's spouse. The misuse of a thing does not invalidate its right use.

Experience and Doctrine

From consideration of faith as experience, we turn to wider concerns about faith, experience, and doctrine. Recall the distinction made at the beginning of this chapter concerning the role religious experience plays in the formation, sustenance, and development of Christian doctrine, as well as in the relationship between religious experience as a putative source of encounter with the divine, and other sources of testimony appealed to in order to ground theological authority. We shall consider each of these issues in turn.

Indisputably, religious experience plays an important role in the genesis of doctrine, as well as in its sustenance and development. This holds true irrespective of one's particular theological proclivities. But it is not clear that an evangelical account of the genesis of doctrine requires that in every instance the human authors of Scripture underwent some supernatural experience of which they were conscious, as a necessary condition for the genesis of biblical doctrine. For instance, reading Luke-Acts one gets the impression that the author did not write either because he believed he had a specific experience to communicate, or because he believed he was "under the influence" of the Holy Spirit, but because he thought it important to leave a record of the events described. The same is not true of, say, Paul or Jeremiah, for whom particular religious experience was a fundamental motivation for their writings.

This is consistent with the claim that Luke-Acts was written under the inspiration of the Holy Spirit, because divine ministrations need not be something of which we are conscious. (I am not conscious of God upholding me at every moment of my existence. Yet the doctrine of providence suggests this is just what he does.) This has the strange consequence that a specific revelatory *experience* of God, understood as an event lived through of which the subject is conscious, is not a necessary condition for the formation of Scripture. Yet I think this must be embraced, given that some of the human authors of Scripture appear not to have been aware of the fact that their writings were divine revelation (or, perhaps, the vehicle for divine revelation).[16] But then, what role does experience play in the formation of doctrine? One way of becoming clearer on this question involves distinguishing different levels of experience in relation to the formation of Scripture. At the *mundane level*, there are those experiences which are necessary for the author to be in a position to write the sort of material he does. So the author of Luke-Acts has the experience of growing up in a literate community, being shaped by that community, becoming a physician, meeting Paul, deciding to write Luke-Acts (or being the author substantially responsible for this document), and so on. Without these particular mundane experiences, Luke-Acts would not exist as we have it. And it is surely plausible to think that God ensures that the author of Luke-Acts has these experiences in order to bring about the writing of the portion of Scripture he writes.

But then there is another level of *supernatural experience*, where authors live through an event of which they are conscious, and which they report in terms of a divine encounter of some kind. This is also an important feature of Scripture, and happens at key moments in the biblical narrative, for example, Moses on Sinai, Isaiah in the Temple, Ezekiel in his vision of the Valley of Dry Bones, the Mount of Transfiguration, and Paul's conversion. But it is not clear that all biblical authors are consciously aware of having had such experiences—or even that every author reports having had, or having heard about, such experiences (for example, the books of Ruth, Esther, and Proverbs).

So it seems that experience is very important in the formation of Scripture, and that the right concatenation of mundane experience is used by God to bring about the writing of Scripture. But in some cases this does not appear to include the notion of a consciously apprehended religious experience informing the output, in addition to such mundane experience. In such cases I presume God works secretly by his Holy Spirit, providentially ensuring that the mundane experience that informs the writing of a particular author of Scripture enables that author, by the inspiration of the Holy Spirit, to write the Word of God. But importantly, such divine workings may be hidden from the person writing, who may not be conscious of this secret divine work.[17]

Note that this evangelical understanding of divine revelation and the process of inscripturation need not be flat-footed about how the particular canonical form of the text came about. What is important is the claim that through these different sorts of literature, in diverse ways, using the texture and voice of particular authors, in texts brought together and edited over time, we find God speaking. These are not merely the words of human beings that, through reflection upon the divine, came to hold particular views and transmitted them, or came to have particular experiences and wrote them down for posterity. These are the very words of God communicated through the feeble, fragile, fallible medium of human beings. God so fashions and shapes these humans that all the idiosyncrasies and traits a particular author has are used by the divine author to convey exactly what he intends to say. For the evangelical theologian there can be nothing implausible in thinking that God accommodates himself in such a complex manner as to ensure, through this process of experience, writing, and transmission, that what results is what he intended to convey to his people. As the Old Princeton theologian Benjamin Warfield memorably put it, the different biblical authors are like the colored panes in a stained glass window. The same light shines through them all, but it is refracted in many different and beautiful ways corresponding to the color, shape, and transparency of the glass through which it passes.[18]

But more important than this, the Christian theologian has a theological reason for thinking that it is characteristic of God to accommodate himself in such complex ways to his creatures. This can be seen preeminently in the Incarnation, the supreme instance of divine accommodation. Christology cannot be an afterthought in an evangelical account of divine revelation and its relation to faith and experience. It must be foundational. For Christ, as the Word of God Incarnate, is divine revelation incarnate. We know God has revealed himself to the extent that we know Christ is God—not because revelation only includes those places in Scripture where Christ is reported as speaking, but because the Second Person of the Trinity is the Word of God. He is, as it were, the speech of God, who brings forth creation and who inspires the prophets and apostles by his Spirit. So, divine revelation is in a way guaranteed by the role played by Christ as God Incarnate, as well as by the work performed by Christ qua Word of God who by his Spirit communicates to the prophets before Christ and the apostles after his ascension. The upshot of this is that as one aspect of the *opus dei*, revelation is a triune work. Although it terminates upon the Word of God in a particular manner, it also involves the Father in its instigation and the Spirit in its communication.

This also gives some indication of how an evangelical account of the relation between experience and the formation of biblical doctrine may differ from that of classical liberal theology. Liberal theologians thought that Scripture is the codification of religious experiences. But they denied that these religious experiences constitute a divine revelation. They conceived of religious experience as what generates doctrine, including the doctrine in Scripture. But they thought doctrine was inherently revisable on the basis of new experiences of God. There is, in this way, a constant process of experiencing God, checking this with Scripture and the tradition, and using such experience to correct or adjust the testimony of the Christian faith in line with the "God consciousness" or "sense of absolute dependence" the theologian perceives in and through the person and work of Christ. Hence, according to liberal theologians, experience is normative in Christian theology in a way that Scripture is not. This picture of the relation between faith and experience is beguiling because it captures an important truth about how doctrine is often generated through religious experience. The problem with liberal theology does not lie in its placing experience of God at center stage, but rather in its decoupling such experience from a robust concept of divine revelation along with an insistence upon a particular conception of religious experience as fundamental to the formation of doctrine. It is this move that enabled the liberal theologians to invert the traditional Reformation idea of Scripture as final norm in matters of doctrine, replacing it with contemporary religious experience.

So much for the role of experience in the genesis of doctrine; what of the role it plays in its sustenance and development? Like most evangelical thinkers, I take it that doctrine is propositional, or can be expressed in propositional form. Scripture contains propositions. It also contains lots of other sorts of things like commands, imprecations, and tropes that are not propositions. But this is not to deny that we find doctrine in Scripture. Similarly, we find doctrine in the catholic creeds and in the confessional symbols of particular ecclesial communities (e.g., the Westminster Confession, the Augsburg Confession, the Bapist Confession of 1689, and so on). Here, there is a way in which experience plays a role in bearing witness to Scripture in the doctrine confessed by the Church. As the contemporary Anglican evangelical theologian John Webster puts it, "a creed or confessional formula is a public and binding indication of the gospel set before us in the scriptural witness, through which the church affirms its allegiance to God, repudiates the falsehood by which the church is threatened, and assembles around the judgement and consolation of the gospel."[19]

I suggest that this is a right understanding of the role of the creeds and confessions of Christendom. The ecumenical symbols of the Church were authorized by councils that were moved by the Holy Spirit (whether or not they were conscious of this and "experienced" the work of the Holy Ghost) and that witnessed to Scripture in the canons forged thereby. To the extent that these canons are extrapolations of Scripture's explicit and implicit message, they are to be upheld. But only thus far. Scripture is normative in a way that not even the catholic creeds are. The same goes for particular confessions that are also witnesses, in the first instance to Scripture, but also as echoing those ideas found in previous creedal documents which the framers of such confessions recognized as other, more ancient witnesses to the same truth.

This, or something very like it, has been the traditional understanding of most evangelicals with respect to the creeds and confessions of the Church, in common with many other orthodox Christians. The extent to which a given creed or confession effectively witnesses to Scripture is, of course, an important theological consideration, but here is not the place to explore that. It is sufficient for present purposes to understand that the authority of the creeds and confessions is derivative. The experience of those framing these documents is not normative for Christian faith, as the experience of the apostles and prophets as authors of Scripture was. The Fathers who worked on the great symbols of the Church were certainly guided by the same Holy Spirit that inspired the authors of Holy Writ. But the sort of guidance needed was more by way of recognizing what to say about Scripture, what to leave out, and how to express it in language that would preserve the Church and communicate to the generation to which they addressed themselves, in thought-forms and ideas inevitably somewhat removed from those of the Bible. Such guidance is very different from divine revelation. It is like the difference between writing *Jane Eyre*, and writing a study guide to *Jane Eyre. Jane Eyre* would exist without the study guide. But the study guide would never have been conceived without *Jane Eyre*. Just so with respect to the two sorts of literature that make up Scripture and the creeds and confessions, respectively, and the different sorts of experience each required.

This is not to deny that there is doctrinal development of a sort: the more Christians have reflected on Scripture, and listened to theologians from the past, the clearer certain issues have become (although this is not always the case and this does not imply a sort of Hegelian unfolding of the true nature of doctrine through history). But an evangelical account of faith and experience cannot countenance the prospect that something might be added to Scripture, or stand alongside Scripture as an equivalent source of authority. In this way evangelicals are heirs to the Reformation *sola scriptura*. Scripture has a final authority that no other source of creaturely testimony does (bar Christ). It is alone in that sense. But of course Scripture is never alone in another sense. It is always read and understood within the community of faith in a tradition stretching back to the Apostles, under the guidance of the Holy Spirit.

Conclusion

It does not seem likely that there will be a convergence of differing evangelical conceptions of the relation between faith and experience any time soon. Some writers worry that the doctrinal plurality currently tolerated on a number of doctrinal loci, including issues that are part of the Bebbington Quadrilateral, is a cause for grave concern about the integrity of evangelicalism and its future as a coherent theological movement. Increasingly, theologians who are evangelicals identify themselves with one or other subgroup by adding a particular prefix to the noun "evangelical," such as "postconservative evangelical," "progressive evangelical," "catholic evangelical," "liberal evangelical," and so on. It may be that in due course the doctrinal nuances that pick out these differing subgroups will lead them in such different directions that the term "evangelical" becomes more like its German equivalent *evangelische* (roughly: Protestant) than the name for a coherent theological movement, or homogeneous group of beliefs held by particular theological communities.

This is a real concern. But I have argued that the two main evangelical genera that emerged from the Great Awakening, namely, Wesleyan Arminianism and the evangelical Reformed thought of theologians like Jonathan Edwards, share enough in common concerning the notion of faith, especially of faith as affective experience, for them to be considered part of one family of Christian theology that has its roots in the Reformation. I have also outlined one account of the role experience plays in the formation of doctrine in Scripture, which (I submit) is consistent with an evangelical way of thinking.[20] Finally, I have given some indication of how this differs from the way in which subsequent generations have reflected on Scripture, which has been codified in the bodies of doctrine comprising the creeds and confessions. There is more to be said about how evangelicals view their own private religious experiences with respect to faith, and about the relationship between faith and what is often called Christian practice. But enough has been said here to indicate how discussion of such matters might begin.[21]

NOTES

1. See William Lad Sessions, *The Concept of Faith* (Ithaca: Cornell University Press, 1994).

2. Note that here and in what follows, "experience" is not equivalent to "feelings."

3. See David Bebbington, *Evangelicalism in Modern Britain: A History from the 1730s to the 1980s* (London: Routledge, 1989). Bebbington argues that there are four distinctive features of theologies that are evangelical: biblicism (a high view of Scripture in all matters touching Christian faith and practice); cruciocentrism (the centrality of the atonement); conversionism (that fallen human beings need to hear and respond to the gospel); and activism (the dominical imperative to evangelize). This characterization of evangelicalism has become known as the Bebbington Quadrilateral.

4. Garry Williams has recently argued that the elements of the Bebbington Quadrilateral are already present in Reformation and Puritan theology. If that is right, then evangelicalism was aboriginally Augustinian in its understanding of faith and experience, and only subsequently fissured along "Calvinistic" and "Arminian" lines. This would mean there was originally much more convergence on the concept of faith and on how to understand religious experience in light of faith among evangelicals than Bebbington's

thesis would allow for. But even if Williams is right (and I think there is much to be said for his argument) it is still the case that there are those in the evangelical constituency who align themselves with an evangelical Arminianism, as well as those who stand within Augustinianism broadly construed. That is all I am assuming here. See Garry J. Williams, "Enlightenment Epistemology and Evangelical Doctrines of Assurance," in Michael A. G. Haykin and Kenneth J. Stewart, eds., *The Advent of Evangelicalism: Exploring Historical Continuities* (Nashville: B&H Publishing, 2008), 345–374.

5. I pick these two strains of evangelical theology because they have clear historical precedent in the literature, and entail distinct theological positions. But one could just as easily speak in denomination-specific terms of evangelical Baptists, some of whom have historically been Reformed (such as Andrew Fuller, Charles Spurgeon, John Piper) and some of whom have been more Arminian in their theology (such as the late Stanley Grenz or Roger Olsen). Or one could speak of evangelical Anglicans who are Arminian or Reformed, or free Evangelicals, Disciples of Christ, charismatic, Pentecostal, and so on. The relevant issues here can be transposed without much change to these particular denominational contexts.

6. Does this mean one must have a consciously affective experience in order for a given experience to count as genuinely "religious"? Not necessarily. One can profit from reading Scripture without being conscious of simultaneously enjoying a particular experience of God over and above the reading. The Holy Spirit may be at work in the believer without that believer being conscious of him, and so on. But from an evangelical perspective, the affective component to faith is vital.

7. Jonathan Edwards, *Religious Affections: The Works of Jonathan Edwards, Vol. 2*, ed. John E. Smith (New Haven: Yale University Press, 1959), 96–97. Edwards admits that "it must be confessed, that language here is somewhat imperfect" in defining religious affections (Ibid., 97).

8. From *John Wesley*, ed. Albert Outler (New York: Oxford University Press, 1964), 66.

9. From Jonathan Edwards, "Personal Narrative" in *A Jonathan Edwards Reader*, ed. John E. Smith, Harry S. Stout, and Kenneth P. Minkema (New Haven: Yale University Press, 1995), 283–284. The fact that the precise date and morphology of the conversions of Wesley and Edwards have been disputed need not detain us here.

10. There are important doctrinal differences between the Arminianism espoused by Jacob Arminius and his immediate disciples, such as Episcopius, and later Wesleyan Arminianism. Arminian theology is a rich and variegated genus, just as Reformed theology (its theological parent) is. Both Arminianism and Reformed Christianity belong to what, to borrow another zoological term, we might call the *family* of evangelical theology. Recent work in historical theology has helped clarify some of the differences between species of Arminian theology. See, for example, Richard Muller, *God, Creation and Providence in the Theology of Jacob Arminius* (Grand Rapids: Baker, 1991). Cf. Roger Olson, *Arminian Theology: Myths and Realities* (Downers Grove, Ill.: Intervarsity Press, 2006).

11. Reformed theologians are typically theological determinists, but some have advocated theological libertarianism, like the Arminians. An excellent example of Calvinistic libertarianism can be found in William Cunningham's essay "Calvinism and the Doctrine of Philosophical Necessity" in *The Reformers and the Theology of the Reformation* (Edinburgh: Banner of Truth, 1989 [1862]), 471–599. But it is very difficult to see how a libertarian Calvinist can uphold monergism with respect to the acquisition of faith.

12. The reason for such incapacity is moot. Many Reformed theologians argue that the noetic effects of sin are such that human beings are incapable of turning to God without divine grace. But the Amyraldians and, later, followers of Jonathan Edwards in New England, argued that there is no natural impediment to fallen human beings trusting in

God by faith, but there is a moral inability to do so. See, for example, Jonathan Edwards, *Freedom of the Will: The Works of Jonathan Edwards, Vol. 1*, ed. John E. Smith (New Haven: Yale University Press, 1957), 156–162, 362–363.

13. Experience of God need not generate faith. James 2:19 tells us "You believe that God is one; you do well. Even the demons believe—and shudder." But clearly the demons believe that there is a God without trusting in God. They have known God, have experience of God, but have no faith in God. The same is true of many human beings—which is why it is possible to commit the unforgivable sin by rejecting the susurrations of the Holy Spirit (Mk. 3:29).

14. Richard Swinburne, *Faith and Reason* (Oxford: Oxford University Press, 1981), 116.

15. Paul Helm, *Faith with Reason* (Oxford: Oxford University Press, 2000), 146.

16. Experience of God is not a sufficient condition for the formation of the canon because other conditions are necessary, such as the process of inscripturation, which in the case of many biblical books included a period of oral transmission of the purported experience, being written down, preserved, and redacted by a given ecclesial community, and being accepted by the Church as of divine origin. None of these things necessarily undermines the status of Scripture as divine revelation, any more than the recording of an interview with the prime minister, and its being written down and edited at some later date for publication and dissemination, necessarily undermines the status of the words on the page of the published form of the interview as being those uttered by the prime minister.

17. Compare the Puritan theologian William Ames, who writes, "Divine inspiration was present among these writers in different ways. Some things were utterly unknown to the writer in advance, as appears in the history of creation or in the foretelling of things to come. But some things were previously known to the writers.... Some things were known by a natural knowledge and some by a supernatural. In those things that were hidden and unknown, divine inspiration was at work." *The Marrow of Theology*, trans. John D. Eusden (Boston: Beacon Hill, 1968), 186. See also Kenneth J. Stewart, "The Evangelical Doctrine of Scripture, 1650–1850: A Re-examination of David Bebbington's Theory" in *The Advent of Evangelicalism*, 398–413.

18. Benjamin B. Warfield, "Inspiration" in *International Standard Bible Encyclopedia, Vol. 3*, ed. James Orr (Chicago: Howard Severance, 1915), 1473–1483.

19. John Webster, *Confessing God: Essays in Christian Dogmatics II* (Edinburgh: T & T Clark, 2005), 73–74.

20. It would be anachronistic to claim that the Church Fathers who recognized the canon of Scripture were evangelicals in the Bebbington sense of that term. The account set forth here may be thought of as a Reformed perspective on the relationship between religious experience and the formation of doctrine consistent with evangelicalism—a sort of Reformed evangelical gloss on how the Fathers came to canonize the creeds.

21. My thanks to Gavin D'Costa, Paul Helm, Gerald McDermott, Benjamin Myers, and Douglas Sweeney for their comments on a previous draft of this chapter.

BIBLIOGRAPHY

Bebbington, David. *Evangelicalism in Modern Britain: A History from the 1730s to the 1980s*. London: Routledge, 1989.

Edwards, Jonathan. *Religious Affections: The Works of Jonathan Edwards, Vol. 2*, ed. John E. Smith. New Haven: Yale University Press, 1959.

Haykin, Michael A. G., and Kenneth J. Stewart, eds. *The Advent of Evangelicalism: Exploring Historical Continuities*. Nashville: B&H Academic, 2008.
Helm, Paul. *Faith with Reason*. Oxford: Oxford University Press, 2003.
Larson, Timothy, and Daniel J. Treier, eds. *The Cambridge Companion to Evangelical Theology*. Cambridge: Cambridge University Press, 2007.
Sessions, William Lad. *The Concept of Faith*. Ithaca: Cornell University Press, 1994.
Stackhouse, John G., Jr. ed. *Evangelical Futures: A Conversation on Theological Method*. Grand Rapids: Baker, 2000.
Swinburne, Richard. *Faith and Reason*. Oxford: Oxford University Press, 1981.
Webster, John. *Confessing God: Essays in Christian Dogmatics II*. Edinburgh: T & T Clark, 2005.
Wolterstorff, Nicholas. *Divine Discourse*. Cambridge: Cambridge University Press, 1995.

CHAPTER 5

FAITH AND TRADITION

ALISTER E. MCGRATH

EVANGELICALISM, by common consent, is a form of Christianity that celebrates and proclaims the supreme spiritual, moral, and theological authority of the Bible. At the Diet of Worms (April 18, 1521), Martin Luther famously declared: "My conscience is captive to the word of God." Inspired and instructed by Luther's example, evangelicalism has seen itself as captive to that same word of God. The principle of the sufficiency of Scripture is of central importance to evangelicalism. The declaration of the Westminster Confession summarizes the evangelical consensus on this major issue:

> The whole counsel of God, concerning all things necessary for his own glory, man's salvation, faith and life, is either expressly set down in Scripture, or by good and necessary consequence may be deduced from Scripture; to which nothing at any time is to be added, whether by new revelations of the Spirit, or traditions of men.

Evangelicalism has, on the whole, agreed with this statement, and by doing so has indicated its theological and spiritual continuity with the Reformation. The life and thought of the Christian community is grounded in, and must continually be reevaluated in the light of, Scripture.

Yet evangelicals have long recognized that an emphasis upon the authority of Scripture needs to be supplemented by attentiveness to the question of its proper interpretation. Events within the early Lutheran Reformation made the importance of this point painfully clear. In 1521, Andreas Bodenstein von Karlstadt, Luther's close colleague, proclaimed that Scripture clearly taught that infant baptism, all forms of church music, and any kind of religious image, were forbidden. Martin Luther hastily blocked Karlstadt's reform, and declared that Scripture was firmly supportive of all three.

The issue here is familiar, and is often cited as the Achilles' heel of contemporary evangelicalism. How can the validity of competing interpretations of Scripture be determined without appealing to some ground of authority which ultimately lies beyond Scripture itself? Evangelicalism, having affirmed the supreme authority of Scripture, finds itself without any meta-authority by which the correct interpretation of Scripture could be determined. This difficulty concerning the authority and interpretation of Scripture is not solved through an appeal to the principle that Scripture interprets itself (*scriptura sui ipsius interpres*). This still requires adjudication of the issue of which of a range of interpretations of Scripture is to be regarded as the most biblical—and this requires agreement on the authority by which this issue of biblical interpretation is to be resolved.

Tradition and the Interpretation of Scripture

Evangelicalism stands within the traditions of Christian thought and devotion that developed as a result of the Protestant Reformation of the sixteenth century. In many ways, evangelicalism must be considered to have inherited both the benefits and challenges that this rich heritage has conveyed. Even the briefest account of Protestant biblical interpretation during the first five hundred years of its existence, to which evangelicalism is heir, shows shifting understandings of what the Bible says, and how it is to be read, which are laden with significance for the identity of the movement. If Protestantism—and hence evangelicalism—is held to be defined by both its emphasis upon the authority of Scripture and a set of specific interpretations of the Bible, then, in addition to being pluriform from the outset, it has undergone significant changes since its emergence.

Four examples of shifting Protestant understandings of the meaning of the Bible may be noted to illustrate this point. In each case, the settled interpretation of earlier generations underwent significant modification, as opinion shifted decisively toward significantly different views.

1. *Is usury allowed?* The consensus throughout the first age of Protestantism, on the basis of the unconditional Old Testament prohibition of the practice, was that this was not permissible. Yet Calvin's creative and highly original argument of 1545 that this specific biblical mandate could be overlooked in order to fulfil more fundamental biblical principles introduced a new way of thinking. It took more than a century for Protestantism as a whole to come around to this new way of thinking. Yet such is the widespread acceptance of the practice today that most contemporary evangelicals would be surprised to learn that this was ever an issue for their forebears.

2. *Are Christians meant to evangelize?* The predominant interpretation of the gospel imperative to "make disciples of all nations" (Matthew 28:19) in the sixteenth century was that this command was addressed to the apostles, not to subsequent generations. It was not until the late eighteenth century that this view began to be

challenged successfully, particularly through the growing influence of missionary societies in England. By the end of the nineteenth century, most evangelicals considered that the obvious and clear meaning of the passage was that all Christians were called to evangelize, and support the work of missions.

3. *Will there be a millennium at the end of time?* The belief that there would be a period of a thousand years—the millennium—during which Christ will reign on earth immediately before the end of history was widespread in the early church. Writers such as Irenaeus and Tertullian regarded this as the clear and obvious meaning of Revelation 20:2. Yet from the time of Augustine onward, this way of reading this text was abandoned, in favor of an "amillennial" view, which held that Christ presently reigns from heaven. Following the influence of Puritan writers, particularly Jonathan Edwards, a "postmillennial" view was upheld by most evangelicals until the middle of the nineteenth century, when a "premillennial" reading of the text began to gain a significant following. Today, premillennialism is the numerically predominant way of reading the text, espoused by Pentecostals and many American evangelicals.

4. *Do charismatic phenomena happen today?* While all Protestants agreed that such phenomena as "speaking in tongues" took place in the early church, as recorded in the New Testament, there was a consensus that these ceased with the ending of the apostolic age. Although occasionally raised as a possibility by some marginal groups, this "cessationist" view was totally predominant within Protestantism for the first four hundred years of its existence. Today, it is the minority view. Pentecostalism's insistence that such phenomena happen today is now numerically dominant within global evangelicalism.

Alongside these significant shifts in patterns of biblical interpretation over the last five hundred years, a number of debates have continued, repeating the debates of past years with occasional extensions. An obvious example is the long-standing debate over how to interpret the words of Jesus of Nazareth at the last supper: "This is my body" (Matthew 26:26). Here, the main positions taken in the first age of the Reformation remain contested within evangelicalism to this day, with Protestant debates still circling well-established landmarks and authorities. For example, Lutheran evangelicals continue to insist upon a doctrine of baptismal regeneration, to the puzzlement of some evangelicals in other traditions. No evangelical now expects these debates to be resolved to the satisfaction of all; indeed, many now regard them as lying beyond resolution, having become so deeply ingrained within the traditions that make up contemporary evangelicalism that they cannot be disentangled from those traditions' sense of identity and historical rootedness.

It will be clear that this difficulty associated with biblical interpretation is not a new problem, nor one that is unique to evangelicalism. It has been an endemic problem for the Protestant theological tradition as a whole. How can conflict over biblical interpretation be resolved, without acknowledging criteria or agencies above Scripture? To place any means of adjudication above Scripture is to compromise its unique authority. The early disputes between Luther and Karlstadt illustrate how a shared commitment to the authority of Scripture does not entail agreement on the outcome of the interpretative process.

The issue became of pressing importance during the 1520s in Zurich. Having agreed in principle that the religious and civil affairs of the city would be governed in strict accordance with Scripture, the question of which interpretations of Scripture should be adopted became acutely pressing. Frustrated at the inability of theologians to offer definitive interpretations, the city council of Zurich decided it would judge the matter for itself. Biblical interpretation thus became a matter of political debate, settled by the vote of the city council. It was not a sustainable solution; nevertheless, it indicated the vulnerability and impracticability of the notion of a "self-interpreting Scripture."

This point was made forcefully by the English poet John Dryden in his satirical poem *Religio Laici* (1682). Dryden invited his readers to imagine an evangelical, convinced that the Bible clearly teaches the divinity of Christ yet disturbingly confronted with another Protestant who interprets those same passages purely in terms of Christ's humanity—the Socinian heresy, a subtle reworking of Arianism.

> We hold, and say we prove from Scripture plain,
> That Christ is *God;* the bold Socinian
> From the same Scripture urges he's but *man.*
> Now what appeal can end th'important suit;
> Both parts talk loudly, but the Rule is mute?

Dryden's point is that Scripture did itself not disclose, clearly and unambiguously, the rule by which it was to be interpreted. And as there was no authority higher than Scripture, how could evangelicalism discriminate between orthodoxy and heresy?

Some evangelicals have responded to such challenges by reasserting the clarity of Scripture, insisting that heresies can be avoided simply by maintaining the clear meaning of the Bible. Others, especially those who have studied the history of interpretation of the Bible, are more cautious, recognizing that serious historical and hermeneutical issues make this a more complex matter than might at first seem to be the case. This realization has led to a growing appreciation of the role that tradition might play in contemporary evangelical biblical interpretation and systematic theology.

Concepts of Tradition

The word "tradition" comes from the Latin term *traditio*, which bears such senses as "handing over," "handing down," or "handing on." Understood in this sense, it is a thoroughly biblical idea. Paul reminded his readers that he was handing on to them core teachings of the Christian faith which he had received from others (1 Corinthians 15:1–4). The term "tradition" possesses two related senses, as it can refer to both the action of passing teachings on to others—something which Paul insists that must be done within the church—and to teachings which are passed on in this manner. Tradition can thus be understood as a process as well as a body of teaching. The

Pastoral Epistles in particular stress the importance of "guarding the good deposit which was entrusted to you" (2 Timothy 1:14).

Yet the New Testament also uses the notion of "tradition" in a negative sense, meaning something like "human ideas and practices which are not grounded in Scripture." Jesus Christ, for example, was openly critical of certain human traditions within Judaism (e.g., see Matthew 15:1–6; Mark 7:13) which he held to be in conflict with the word of God.

The importance of the idea of tradition first became obvious in a controversy that broke out during the second century. The "Gnostic controversy" centred on a number of questions, including how salvation was to be achieved. (The word "Gnostic" derives from the Greek word *gnosis*, "knowledge," and reflects the movement's distinctive belief in certain arcane ideas that had to be known in order to secure salvation.) Christian writers found themselves having to deal with some highly unusual and creative interpretations of the Bible. How were they to deal with these? If the Bible was to be regarded as authoritative, was every interpretation of the Bible to be regarded as of equal value?

Irenaeus of Lyons (c. 130–c. 200), one of the early church's greatest theologians, was quite clear that it did not. The question of how the Bible was to be interpreted was of the greatest importance. Heretics, he argued, interpreted the Bible according to their own taste. Orthodox believers, in contrast, interpreted the Bible in ways that their apostolic authors would have approved. What had been handed down from the apostles through the church was not merely the biblical texts themselves but also a certain way of reading and understanding those texts. For Irenaeus, tradition is a guarantor of faithfulness to the original apostolic teaching, a safeguard against the innovations and misrepresentations of biblical texts on the part of the Gnostics. Apostolic tradition safeguarded apostolic teaching.

This argument remains of importance to any discussion of the role of tradition within biblical interpretation. Can one interpret Scripture without reference to what Christians have believed in the past? Or is the tradition of Christian biblical interpretation at the very least a resource, if not an authority in itself, for contemporary evangelical biblical interpretation?

Evangelicalism's attitude to tradition has been shaped by the great debates of the sixteenth-century Reformation, which can be understood as marking an attempt to renew and reform the life and thought of the church in the light of Scripture. Three distinct approaches to the notion of tradition crystallized during the debates of that era, which can be summarised as follows.

1. The Rejection of Tradition as a Legitimate Theological Resource

The movement known as the "Radical Reformation" or "Anabaptism" was strongly critical of allowing any role to tradition. For radical theologians of the sixteenth century, such as Thomas Muntzer and Caspar Schwenkfeld, every individual believer had the right to interpret Scripture as he or she pleased, subject to the guidance of the Holy Spirit. For the radical Sebastian Franck, the Bible "is a book sealed with seven seals which none can open unless he has the key of David, which is the illumination of the Spirit." The way was thus opened for individualism, with the private judgment of the individual raised above the corporate judgment of the church. Thus the radicals rejected the practice of infant baptism (to which the magisterial Reformation remained committed) as nonscriptural, in that there is no *explicit* reference to the practice in the New Testament. Similarly, doctrines such as the Trinity and the divinity of Christ were rejected as resting upon inadequate scriptural foundations.

2. A Single-Source Theory of Tradition

As noted earlier, second-century patristic theologians such as Irenaeus of Lyons began to develop the idea of an authorized way of interpreting certain texts of Scripture, which he argued went back to the time of the Apostles themselves. Scripture could not be allowed to be interpreted in any arbitrary or self-serving way: it had to be interpreted within the context of the historical continuity of the Christian church. The parameters of its interpretation were historically fixed and "given." "Tradition" here means simply "a traditional way of interpreting Scripture within the community of faith." This is a single-source theory of theology: Theology is based upon Scripture; and "tradition" designates a "traditional way of interpreting Scripture."

Most theologians of the mainstream Reformation, including both Martin Luther and John Calvin, adopted this approach, insisting that traditional interpretations of Scripture—such as the doctrine of the Trinity or the practice of infant baptism—could be retained, provided they could be shown to be consistent with Scripture. The mainline reformers believed that the Bible had been honored, interpreted and applied faithfully in the past, and that Protestant theologians were under an obligation to take their reflections into account as they interpreted the Bible today. Luther insisted that tradition—understood as ideas inherited from the past—operated in a ministerial, not magisterial, mode—serving, not directing, the church. On the basis of this observation, it will be clear that it is incorrect to suggest that the magisterial reformers elevated private judgment above the corporate judgment of the church, or that they descended into some form of individualism.

This also explains the very high view of Augustine of Hippo held by both Luther and Calvin. Yet most interesting of all is the very high esteem in which the mainline reformers held the patristic writers in general. Luther once styled his reforming program at Wittenberg as a return to "the Bible and Augustine," and regarded Augustine as a theological lodestar. Luther's Wittenberg colleague Philip Melanchthon developed similar arguments, most notably that the Reformation could be seen as a return to the consensus of the early church, especially as found in the writings of Augustine and Ambrose.

A similarly high evaluation of the earlier Christian tradition can be found in the writings of Calvin. Although especially concerned to maintain fidelity to Augustine as a reliable interpreter of Scripture, Calvin also had a positive evaluation of the thought of John Chrysostom. This positive evaluation of the teachings and practices of the early church became of critical importance in the debate between Calvin and Sadoleto over the nature of the true church, and was especially significant in relation to the Lausanne Disputation of October 1536. At this important disputation, which took place shortly after Calvin's arrival at Geneva, a Catholic critic of the evangelical reformers suggested that evangelicals despised patristic writers, regarding them as possessing no authority in matters of doctrine. Calvin declared that this was simply not true: not merely did the evangelicals respect the Fathers more than did their Catholic opponents; they also knew them better than they did.

While Calvin was not prepared to endorse the theological opinions of the fathers uncritically, he emphasized their stabilizing and ministerial role for evangelical theology: "We do not exalt their authority in such a way as to debase the dignity of the word of our Lord, to which alone total obedience is due within the church of Christ." Having made it clear in his *Reply to Sadoleto* that the patristic testimony is subordinate to Scripture, Calvin proceeded to establish the ministerial role of tradition for evangelical theology: "Although we hold that the Word of God alone lies beyond the sphere of our judgment, and that the fathers and councils are of authority only to the extent that they concur with the rule of the Word, we still give to those fathers and councils such rank and authority as it is proper for them to hold under Christ."

3. A Dual-Source Theory of Tradition

In the fourteenth and fifteenth centuries an understanding of tradition developed which held it to be a separate and distinct source of revelation, in addition to Scripture. Since Scripture, it was argued, was silent on a number of points, God had providentially arranged for a second source of revelation to supplement this deficiency: a stream of unwritten tradition, going back to the Apostles themselves. This tradition was passed down from one generation to another within the church. Theology is thus held to be based upon two quite distinct sources, Scripture and unwritten tradition (hence the idea of "dual sources"). A belief that is not to be found in Scripture may thus, on the basis of this dual-source theory, be justified by an appeal to an unwritten tradition.

This position was defended strongly at the Council of Trent, which was charged with stating and defending the Roman Catholic position against the threat posed by the Reformation. Trent ruled that Scripture could not be regarded as the only source of revelation. Scripture and tradition alike were to be regarded as inspired by the same Holy Spirit, and safeguarded and handed down by the same Catholic Church.

Evangelical theologians, committed to the supremacy of Scripture, found the third of these approaches unacceptable, at least in the form stated at the Council of

Trent. (The Second Vatican Council, it should be noted, is often thought to have given Scripture a more significant place than Trent.) The Council of Trent thus seemed to place tradition on the same level as Scripture, and thus undermined and subverted its supreme authority. So which of the two rival approaches was to be preferred? The total rejection of tradition, or the recognition of a potentially positive and constructive—yet carefully circumscribed—role for traditional interpretations of Scripture?

In dealing with this question, an important historical point needs to be noted. Evangelicalism is a movement with a complex historical pedigree and provenance, containing within itself elements which are either directly influenced by or sympathetic to both the mainline and radical Reformations. Tensions whose origins lie within the Reformation—the role of tradition being an excellent example—may therefore be expected to be encountered in contemporary evangelicalism. The tension may be less than in the past and it may well be modulated by the spirit of graciousness and longing to understand one another which is characteristic of evangelicalism at its best. Yet it remains. Evangelical attitudes to tradition continue to be shaped, at least to some extent, by the location of individual evangelicals in relation to the options mapped out and explored by the Reformation.

The evidence is complex, and open to several interpretations. In general terms, however, it seems that evangelical theologians who worked within mainline denominations historically linked to the magisterial Reformation—such as Anglicans, Lutherans, and Presbyterians—tend to adopt, or at least be sympathetic to, a "single-source" approach to tradition, seeing it as a distillation of faithful biblical witness and reflection from the past. Baptist evangelicals, who often stand in direct theological lineage with the Radical Reformation, tend to regard Scripture as being sufficiently perspicuous in its own right that no appeal to tradition or additional hermeneutical aids is necessary.

Tradition and the Authority of Scripture

So what of the *sola Scriptura* principle, central to both the Protestant Reformation of the sixteenth century, and to contemporary evangelicalism? Does not this emphatic affirmation of "the Bible alone" by definition exclude other sources of theological authority? That was certainly the view taken by Radical theologians of the sixteenth and early seventeenth centuries, who held that the Bible alone was to be revered, interpreted, and applied, without the false interposition of rival authorities or agencies. Luther and Calvin's respect for Augustine was regarded as totally unnecessary on the one hand, and misguided on the other. Some Radical theologians—such as Sebastian Franck—argued that the true church had ceased to exist on earth, and had been displaced by an apostate body. It was therefore meaningless to speak of the "reformation" of the church, as there was no church to reform. What was required was a restoration of something which had ceased to exist since the time of the apostles. Why bother engaging with people like Augustine and other patristic writers, who were not even (at least, by Franck's criteria) Christians, and might even be apostles of the anti-Christ? For Franck, true Christianity ended with the apostles, and was born again in the sixteenth century. To engage with people like Augustine was to become contaminated with the ideas of an apostate body which falsely claimed to be Christian. Christians should therefore engage directly with the Bible, rather than pay attention to the views of those who went before them.

Luther and Calvin, on the other hand, argued that their high regard for such writers did not in any way compromise the unique authority of Scripture. They were simply respecting the insights of able and gifted biblical teachers from previous generations, and always regarded them as servants of the Word, not its masters. To affirm the supreme authority of Scripture in matters of doctrine does not prevent us from paying attention to what others who have gone before us have found in their engagement with Scripture.

There is a growing recognition within contemporary evangelicalism, especially on the part of evangelicals within historic denominations, that to affirm the supreme authority of Scripture in matters of doctrine does not prevent us from paying attention to what others who have gone before us have found in their engagement with Scripture. Indeed, many now argue that the fundamental evangelical theme of obedient attentiveness to Scripture makes it all the more important to listen respectfully to the views of our forebears in the walk of faith, who paid such respectful attention to the biblical materials before us. A willingness to listen and reflect is seen as being of considerable importance in securing the stability of evangelical theological reflection. Such an approach can be found in the writings of many evangelical writers who see themselves as standing within the "great tradition," such as James Orr and J. I. Packer.

The Ministerial Role of Tradition within Evangelicalism

As J. I. Packer pointed out in his earliest major writing, *Fundamentalism and the Word of God* (1958), the Christian past provides a resource for the evangelical present. As we seek to interpret Scripture and unfold its many treasures, we can learn from the wisdom of the past.

> The Spirit has been active in the Church from the first, doing the work he was sent to do—guiding God's people into an understanding of revealed truth. The history of the Church's labour to understand the Bible forms a commentary on

> the Bible which we cannot despise or ignore without dishonouring the Holy Spirit. To treat the principle of biblical authority as a prohibition against reading and learning from the book of church history is not an evangelical, but an Anabaptist mistake. (1958, 48)

Packer stresses the importance of being aware of the historic and corporate nature of the Christian faith, while insisting the tradition plays a ministerial, not a magisterial, role in theological reflection. Everything must constantly be checked out against Scripture, following Paul's command to "test everything" and "hold on to the good" (1 Thessalonians 5:21). As Packer himself notes, "Scripture must have the last word on all human attempts to state its meaning, and tradition, viewed as a series of such human attempts, has a ministerial rather than a magisterial role" (1958, 48).

In practice, even evangelical theologians standing in more radical traditions acknowledge at least some role, however circumscribed, for tradition. This can be seen, for example, in the evangelical tendency to cite the interpretations of earlier evangelical writers in weighing up how a given biblical passage is to be interpreted. This was given classic expression in the debate during the 1980s and 1990s over the "new perspective" on Paul, championed by writers such as E. P. Sanders, which criticized traditional Lutheran understandings of justification by faith, especially its dialectic between law and gospel. The ensuing evangelical response suggested that many evangelical biblical scholars found any criticism of Luther distressing, perhaps even unacceptable. The evangelical response to Saunders suggests that many were committed to reading Paul through Lutheran spectacles—in effect, exemplifying the "single source" approach to tradition, noted earlier.

The debate over the "new perspective" on Paul within evangelicalism points to a widespread, but not universal, tacit understanding within the movement that traditional Reformation understandings of Paul's doctrine of justification by faith are in the first place correct, and in the second are essential to evangelicalism's self-identity. The disquiet over the approach to Paul's theology by the leading New Testament scholar N. T. Wright is a significant indication of a deep intuition within many evangelical groups that the Reformation heritage is sacrosanct at this point. It is therefore interesting, perhaps even surprising, to note how little attention has been paid in this debate to the significant degree of diversity of the theologies of justification that emerged within the first phase of the Reformation. A critical comparison of the views of Martin Luther, John Calvin, and Martin Bucer gives much cause for thought on this point. On this point, at least, much of evangelicalism appears firmly committed in practice to a "single source" theory of tradition, even if this is not always made explicit.

As noted earlier, the concept of tradition—both as a process of "passing down" and as a specific set of teachings that are passed on in this way—plays a significant role in the New Testament. The Pastoral Epistles, for example, stress the importance of "guarding the good deposit which was entrusted to you" (1 Timothy 6:20; 2 Timothy 1:14). At first sight, then, evangelicals should not have any a priori difficulties with the notion of tradition, at least in the positive New Testament sense of the term. Yet there are anxieties within the evangelical community over this matter, and it is important to identify and explore these. Three are of especial importance.

First, there is a concern that tradition can be seen as a human invention or fabrication, in opposition to the word of God. The New Testament certainly notes this type of tradition, and is vigorously critical of both the notion itself and its consequences. Developing this idea further, some evangelicals point out that the Council of Trent appears to give equal weight to human traditions and Scripture, which is irreconcilable with the Reformation emphasis upon the priority of Scripture. This is a major concern, and needs to be taken with the greatest seriousness. Yet it is fundamentally a criticism of the "two-source" theory of tradition, developed by the Council of Trent, not the rival approach associated with Luther and Calvin.

Second, tradition carries with it the sense of "traditionalist"—the dead hand of previous generations, which demands that we continue to think and act in precisely the same manner as earlier generations, thus locking evangelicalism into a sixteenth-, eighteenth-, or nineteenth-century worldview. To give authority of any kind to "tradition" might therefore seem to run the risk of condemning evangelicalism to sleepwalking with the dead. In an age that is acutely aware of the importance of public perceptions of Christianity—witness the growth of "seeker-sensitive" worship services—a concern or tradition seems totally out of place. Tradition is thus directly opposed to contemporanity.

Yet this concern can be met. Jaroslav Pelikan makes a defensible and helpful distinction between "tradition" and "traditionalism," which enables the point at issue to be identified: "Tradition is the living faith of the dead, traditionalism is the dead faith of the living. And, I suppose I should add, it is traditionalism that gives tradition such a bad name" (1984, 65).

Third, twentieth-century evangelicalism, especially in North America, has been deeply shaped by many of the leading themes of the Enlightenment. This is illustrated by the influence of the "common sense" philosophy of Thomas Reid and others on nineteenth-century evangelicalism, especially at Princeton, and the "propositionalist" approach to revelation adopted by more recent writers such as Carl Henry. Yet the Enlightenment's strident critique of tradition helped shape modern American evangelicalism's attitude toward the Christian past, encouraging the emergence of an attitude of suspicion toward patristic writers. The weakening of the Enlightenment influence on evangelicalism in recent years has thus opened the way to the theological reappropriation of tradition within the movement.

Tradition and Recent Developments within Evangelicalism

The growing importance of discussions concerning the place of tradition within evangelicalism can be illustrated from many developments, of which four will be singled out for discussion in the remainder of this chapter.

First, many evangelicals, especially in the United States, express concern over the historical shallowness of their faith, and a sense of longing for deep historical roots. A lack of any sense of historical rootedness is known to be a significant consideration in prompting many evangelicals, especially in North America, to convert to Catholicism or Orthodoxy. Obvious examples of this trend include Peter Gillquist, the former leader of the evangelical organization Campus Crusade, and Frank Schaeffer, son of the noted Calvinist apologist and polemicist Francis Schaeffer. In 1987, Gillquist led something like 1,700 of his followers into the Antiochian Orthodox Church. Schaeffer converted to Greek Orthodoxy in 1990, citing its capacity to "embrace paradox and mystery" and rootedness in tradition as attractors. More recently, Francis Beckwith, Baylor University professor of church-state relations, resigned as president of the Evangelical Theological Society in 2007 to join the Catholic Church, offering an explanation that again pointed to a belief that evangelicalism did not take tradition with sufficient seriousness.

This trend has raised a number of important questions, both cultural and theological. For example, what weaknesses does this development expose within evangelicalism's attitude to history and tradition? The most often quoted answer is that it points to evangelicalism as having a lack of historical depth. It is significant that evangelicals within long-established churches—such as the Church of England—do not feel this pressure. It is within the North American scene that evangelical groupings have emerged which have ignored or excoriated an engagement with the past; these, it would seem, are the most vulnerable to this kind of defection.

A second development of importance, primarily associated with evangelicalism in North America, is the emergence of the so-called "Paleo-Orthodox" movement. This is especially associated with the Methodist theologian Thomas C. Oden, a former theological modernist who underwent a major intellectual realignment in the 1980s. In his landmark *After Modernity... What?* (1990a), Oden emphasized the theological importance of historical reconnection with the patristic era on the part of Protestant denominations. He called upon the churches "to begin to prepare the postmodern Christian community for its third millennium by returning again to the careful study and respectful following of the central tradition of classical Christianity." Oden coined the phrase "Paleo-Orthodoxy" to distinguish his approach from the "Neo-Orthodoxy" of Karl Barth.

Oden's growing influence within evangelicalism in the 1990s led many of its younger thinkers to explore how the dynamism and fundamentally Protestant character of evangelicalism could be preserved, without being trapped in historical superficiality. The most significant outcome of this theological program within evangelicalism has been the *Ancient Christian Commentary on Scripture*, edited by Oden. This twenty-eight-volume work, which began to appear in 1998, aims to make available the exegetical insights of the first eight centuries of biblical exposition to the contemporary church. A series of works appearing around the same time emphasized the importance of reading and understanding Scripture in the light of its past exegesis, especially during the patristic age. The long-term impact of such developments on evangelical theological method could be considerable.

A third development is the Deep Church movement, initially associated with the United Kingdom, although now increasingly influential within North American evangelicalism. The phrase "deep church" was coined by C. S. Lewis in 1952, as a way of pointing to the deep rootedness of the church in history. The Deep Church movement has sought to bring new theological and cultural depth to contemporary evangelicalism and Pentecostalism by emphasizing the importance of tradition as a resource and guide. The slogan "remembering our past to face our future" summarizes the movement's commitment to immersion in the past as a tool for developing theological and spiritual depth, and recovering ministerial practices and wisdom that have been marginalized through the rise of modernity. This approach encourages evangelicals to reconnect with the faith and practice of the early church as they seek resources to live as disciples in a postmodern world. While there are clear parallels with "Paleo-Orthodoxy," the Deep Church movement has set an agenda that is broader than issues of biblical interpretation and theological reflection, extending to spirituality, apologetics, and social engagement.

A fourth area of development has taken place in response to the critique of modernity and the attitudes to rationality characteristic of the Enlightenment by writers such as Alasdair MacIntyre and Louis Dupré. The relationship between evangelicalism and the Enlightenment has been complex, with many evangelicals assuming that evangelicalism in some sense entails a modern worldview. This has led to some severe, and occasionally unwise, critiques of evangelicals who have drawn attention to the difficulties now facing anyone wishing to defend the core epistemological assumptions of modernity.

This has led to a group of recent evangelical writers, including Stanley Grenz and John Franke, to argue for an increased recognition of the role of tradition in shaping notions of theological rationality. On this approach, "rationality" is not a universal notion, but is shaped and constituted by traditions. The Enlightenment is thus to be seen as one among many traditions of rationality, rather than as a universal, tradition-transcending, approach. This has important—though strongly contested—implications for the notions of theological objectivity, and especially the extent to which truth is to be recognized as at least a partially "constructed" notion.

Conclusion

Evangelicalism's multifaceted evaluation and use of the notion of "tradition" reflects its complex historical and ideological relationship with the sixteenth-century Reformation on the one hand, and the eighteenth-century Enlightenment on the other. Both are the subject of ongoing negotiation and dispute within evangelicalism, suggesting that the question of evangelicalism's future attitudes toward tradition remains open. Yet the evidence suggests that evangelical theology is coming to view the theological heritage of the past as a resource and stimulus for its own reflections. The potential significance of this development for the stabilization and enrichment of evangelicalism seems to be enormous.

REFERENCES

Adam, A.K.M. 2006. *Reading Scripture with the Church: Toward a Hermeneutic for Theological Interpretation*. Grand Rapids: Baker Academic.

Bacote, Vincent, Laura C. Miguélez, and Dennis L. Okholm, eds. 2004. *Evangelicals and Scripture: Tradition, Authority, and Hermeneutics*. Downers Grove, Ill.: InterVarsity Press).

Beam, Craig Allen. 1998. "Gadamer and MacIntyre: Tradition as a Resource of Rationality." *Kinesis* 25: 15–35.

Davies, Rupert E. 1946. *The Problem of Authority in the Continental Reformers: A Study in Luther, Zwingli, and Calvin*. London: Epworth Press.

Dulles, Avery. 1988. "Vatican II and the Recovery of Tradition." In Dulles, *The Reshaping of Catholicism*. San Francisco: Harper & Row, 75–92.

Dupré, Louis K. 2004. *The Enlightenment and the Intellectual Foundations of Modern Culture*. New Haven: Yale University Press.

Erickson, Millard J., Paul Kjoss Helseth, and Justin Taylor, eds. 2004. *Reclaiming the Center : Confronting Evangelical Accommodation in Postmodern Times*. Wheaton, Ill.: Crossway Books.

Fraenkel, Peter. 1961. *Testimonia Patrum: The Function of the Patristic Argument in the Theology of Philip Melanchthon*. Geneva: Droz.

Grenz, Stanley J., and John R. Franke. 2001. *Beyond Foundationalism: Shaping Theology in a Postmodern Context*. Louisville, Ky.: Westminster John Knox Press.

Hall, Christopher A. 1998. *Reading Scripture with the Church Fathers*. Downers Grove, Ill.: InterVarsity Press.

Hanson, R.P.C. 1962. *Tradition in the Early Church*. London: SCM Press.

Holmes, Stephen R. 2002. *Listening to the Past: The Place of Tradition in Theology* (Grand Rapids: Baker Academic.

Lane, A.N.S. 1999. *John Calvin: Student of the Church Fathers*. Edinburgh: T & T Clark.

McGrath, Alister E. 2007. *Christianity's Dangerous Idea: The Protestant Revolution*. San Francisco: HarperOne.

MacIntyre, Alasdair. 1988. *Whose Justice? Which Rationality?* London: Duckworth.

Newman, Carey C., ed. 1999. *Jesus and the Restoration of Israel: A Critical Assessment of N. T. Wright's Jesus and the Victory of God*. Downers Grove, Ill.: InterVarsity Press.

Oden, Thomas C. 1990a. *After Modernity... What? Agenda for Theology*. Grand Rapids: Zondervan.

———. 1990b. "Then and Now: The Recovery of Patristic Wisdom." *Christian Century*, December 13, 1164–1169.

———, ed. 1998–2008. *Ancient Christian Commentary on Scripture*. 28 vols. Downers Grove, Ill.: InterVarsity Press.

Packer, J. I. 1958. *Fundamentalism and the Word of God*. London: Inter-Varsity Press.

Pelikan, Jaroslav. 1984. *The Vindication of Tradition*. New Haven: Yale University Press.

Schüssler, Hermann. 1977. *Der Primät der heiligen Schrift als theologisches und kanonistisches Problem im Spätmittelalter*. Wiesbaden: Steiner.
Steinmetz, David C. 1986. "Luther and Calvin on Church and Tradition." In Steinmetz, *Luther in Context*. Bloomington: Indiana University Press, 85–97.
Vanhoozer, Kevin J. 2005. *The Drama of Doctrine: A Canonical-Linguistic Approach to Christian Theology*. Louisville, Ky.: Westminster John Knox Press.
Walker, Andrew, and Luke Bretherton, eds. 2007. *Remembering Our Future: Explorations in Deep Church*. London: Paternoster.
Williams, Daniel H. 2005. *Evangelicals and Tradition: The Formative Influence of the Early Church*. Grand Rapids: Baker Academic.

PART II

THEOLOGICAL FOUNDATIONS

CHAPTER 6

THE TRIUNE GOD

ROBERT LETHAM

The State of the Question from the Classical Christian Tradition

In considering the connection between evangelicalism and the doctrine of the Trinity, we must concentrate on the tradition in relation to which evangelicalism is to be located. The Trinitarian crisis of the fourth century was precipitated by the views of Arius. From what we can gather, Arius held that the Son was not co-eternal with the Father, since "there was when he was not"—he was another being, the agent employed in the creation but himself created. This meant he could be neither the revelation of God nor the savior of the church. The Council of Nicaea (325 C.E.) decisively rejected these arguments. It did not resolve the question, however, for it lacked the precise terminology to distinguish the way God is three from the way he is one.

In the resulting confusion, with Athanasius asserting that the Son was the same identical being (*homoousios*) as the Father, and Eunomius adopting arguments akin to those of Arius, it required the Cappadocians—Basil, Gregory of Nyssa, and Gregory of Nazianzus—to clear the way for a resolution of the problem. Basil was the first to suggest that *ousia* be reserved for the one being of God and *hypostasis* for the three. As such, both the Son and the Holy Spirit were seen—with the Father—as fully God, the creator, the one object of worship. God is one being, three persons; each person is the whole God, equal in power and glory, mutually indwelling one another. The Council of Constantinople (381 C.E.) declared this so.

A generation later, in the West, Augustine unfolded his understanding of the Trinity, expressing his agreement and solidarity with the church's doctrine in *De Trinitate* and various other writings, especially his *Tractates on John*. He stressed the indivisibility of the works of the Trinity, that the Father and the Son are of the same identical substance, and that the sending of the Son refers not to the essence of God but to the relations of the persons.

In the second half of *De Trinitate*, Augustine introduced some analogies for the Trinity, hesitantly and aware of their serious limitations.[1] However, these analogies—or illustrations—have had a great impact over the years. The unity of God was Augustine's starting point. He sought reflections of the Trinity in the human mind, but seems to have found difficulty doing justice to the full personal distinctions of the three. He described the Trinity in terms of a lover, the beloved, and the love existing between them. In particular, there appears something of a quandary concerning the Holy Spirit. Does Augustine reduce the Spirit to an attribute? The lover and the one loved are clearly capable of being understood as distinct persons—but love is a quality, not a personal entity.

Until recently, it was considered almost axiomatic that Augustine was influenced by Neoplatonism. From this, it is claimed, comes his overwhelming stress on the one divine essence and his great difficulties recognizing real distinctions for the three. In turn, this has left a legacy for the Western church: a modalistic tendency that blurs the distinctness of the persons. Colin Gunton has attacked Augustine's Trinitarianism along these lines.[2] G. L. Prestige recognized that his "attention [is] firmly riveted on the essential unity," so he has an "essentially different" doctrine from that of the Greeks.[3] In contrast, Basil Studer is more positive,[4] while M. R. Barnes has carefully undermined the received idea of Neoplatonic influence. Read in context, Barnes argues, Nicene theology underlies Augustine's Trinitarianism. He calls the received view "dead wrong." Augustine has been read piecemeal, with bits and pieces extracted from his writings without regard to the historical and theological contexts. It fails to reflect the doctrinal content of the texts.[5]

Studer is correct when he says that Augustine gives "a dogmatic description of what is believed about the Trinity as this emerges from the traditional understanding of the biblical passages in question. In any case, it is the Nicene faith in the identical essence of the Father, Son, and Spirit and in their common action that Augustine makes his starting point."[6] After all, Augustine was simply seeking to illustrate how three things separately exhibited work inseparably; thus the three persons are revealed distinctly yet their operation is inseparable.

East and West on the Trinity

With this, one might have thought that the issue was definitively settled and that agreement would reign unchallenged. However, over the years differences of outlook on the Trinity have bedevilled relations between the Eastern and Western churches. What reasons exist for such divergence?

Theodore De Régnon argued for a significant distinction between Eastern and Western Trinitarianism, a position criticised in recent decades, spearheaded by

M. R. Barnes.[7] How far is such a distinction valid? Lewis Ayres, for one, argues that it is inapplicable to the fourth century, stresses continuity between Augustine and the Cappadocians, and dismisses its application to later developments.[8]

The acid test with the Eastern church is the liturgy, which is at the heart of Orthodox belief and practice, rather than the writings of individual theologians, which are considered simply as *theologomena*, theological opinions. Contrary to the West, for which originality refers to something new, in the East originality means faithfulness to the originals.[9] The Eastern liturgy—whether of St. Basil or St. Chrysostom—is strikingly different from its Western counterparts. Throughout there is a profusion of Trinitarianism; prayers and doxologies abound, saturated in a repeated recognition of the three persons in indivisible union. Worship and theology are inseparable; the liturgy is the heart of its belief. In contrast is the well known separation of the Trinity from the doctrine of God in Western theology since Aquinas, and its relegation to a virtual appendage until the middle of the last century. While to Eastern Christians Trinitarian worship is axiomatic, to the vast majority of Westerners the Trinity is little more than an abstruse mathematical conundrum.

Moreover, the claim that East and West diverged was not new with De Régnon. It was firmly held over a millennium earlier by the Patriarch of Constantinople, Photios. In his treatise on the Holy Spirit he denounced Augustine and his Latin followers as effective heretics by their modalistic blurring of the distinctions between the Father and the Son. The later Eastern developments that arose with Gregory Palamas, such as the distinction between God's essence and his energies, were not shared in the West, nor is it readily apparent how they could be. The apophatic theology of the East radically differs from its Western apophatic counterpart, being at root a negation of rational thought and an exercise in prayer and mystical contemplation. Additionally, converts to Orthodoxy from Rome or Protestantism have been required to renounce, inter alia, the *filioque* clause before their chrismation. Together, these features demonstrate that East and West do not see the Trinity identically, and that such differences have been and are matters of significant disagreement, affecting worship, thought, life, and ecclesial relations.

However, it is also true that this distinction can be overplayed. The West has had a strong focus on the simplicity of God—in a very strong form in Aquinas—but the Cappadocians also maintained it. Augustine may have proposed psychological illustrations to help in grasping aspects of the Trinity—while Gregory of Nazianzus ruled out attempts to seek created analogies—but Augustine's purpose was to affirm his agreement with the Trinitarian settlement reached in the East, not to distance himself from it.

In What Ways Have East and West Differed?

Communion was ruptured between the Eastern and Western churches in 1054 and confirmed after the collapse of the Byzantine Empire in 1453. A number of serious disagreements had developed. On the Trinity, the Eastern and Western churches faced different tendencies to imbalance. The East, with the Father held to be the source of the personal subsistence of the Son and the Holy Spirit and the guarantor of unity in the Trinity, faced the danger of viewing the Son and the Spirit as somehow derivative. The West, for its part, has fallen more toward modalism, with the blurring or eclipsing of the eternal personal distinctions.

In the West, Aquinas separated discussion of *de deo uno* (the one God) from *de deo trino* (the triune God). In his *Summa contra Gentiles* he holds back discussion of the Trinity until book 4, after considering the doctrine of God in detail in book 1. In the *Summa Theologiae* he discusses the existence and attributes of God in Part One, qq. 1–25, turning to the Trinity only in qq. 27–43. This pattern became standard in Western theological textbooks and was exacerbated by the pressures of the Enlightenment. Revelation and the supernatural were problematic in the Kantian framework. As a symptom of the malaise, Friedrich Schleiermacher restricted his treatment of the Trinity to an appendix in his book, *The Christian Faith*. The focus of attention from the eighteenth century shifted from God to this world. Alexander Pope's famous lines sum it up: "Know then thyself, presume not God to scan, the proper study of mankind is man."[10] A batch of new academic disciplines emerged in the nineteenth century devoted to the study of humanity—with psychology, sociology, and anthropology the most prominent. Biblical theology, pressured by the Kantian world to prescind from eternity and ontology, tended to restrict and limit the reference of biblical statements about the Father and the Son to the historical dimension only. The problem with this line of thought is that, if the referent of biblical statements is exclusively this-worldly and restricted to human history, then God as he has revealed himself does not necessarily reveal God as he is eternally in himself.

Colin Gunton argued that the Western tendency toward modalism lies at the root of the atheism and agnosticism that have confronted the Western church in a way that they have not done in the East. Whatever the validity of his claim, Western Trinitarianism has found it difficult to break this mold. Both Barth and Rahner, to cite but two examples, were strongly biased in that direction. In particular, Barth's statement on the as "God reveals himself as the Lord" and his triad of revealer, revelation, and revealedness has the flavor of unipersonality, although in fairness we must recognize that, like Rahner, he opposed modalism as such.[11]

The *filioque* Clause

By far the most serious area of disagreement between East and West concerned the *filioque* clause added by the West to the Niceno-Constantinopolitan creed (C). C states that the Holy Spirit "proceeds from the Father." The trouble started in sixth-century Spain where, due to the threat of a continued Arianism, local liturgies added *a patre filioque*, "from the Father *and the Son*." This addition spread and was adopted by local councils, particularly the Council of Toledo (589),[12] was accepted by the French church in the late eighth century, but was not inserted into the Creed by Rome until 1014 under Pope Benedict VIII. The fourth Lateran Council of 1215 mentioned it, and the Council of Lyons in 1274 proclaimed it as dogma.

The East objected to this development on ecclesiastical grounds. Such a change should have required an ecumenical council akin to Nicaea, Constantinople, and Chalcedon, it maintained.

The East also objected on theological grounds. We shall examine the reasons for this in a moment. The dominant influences in Eastern Trinitarianism, the Cappadocians and John of Damascus, placed primary stress on the Father as the source of the personal subsistence of the Son and the Holy Spirit. Since they said the Father is the guarantor of unity in the Godhead—the sole principle, source, and cause of the Son and the Holy Spirit—the Spirit proceeds from the Father. But, Eastern theologians argued, the *filioque* suggests that the Son is a source, origin, or cause of the Holy Spirit and therefore compromises the monarchy of the Father. The Greek Fathers had said instead that the Holy Spirit is the treasure and the Son is the treasurer—the Son receives and manifests the Spirit but does not cause the Spirit's existence as such.

Another related problem in Eastern eyes is that the clause confuses the Father and the Son. The Father is not the Son. Thus, the relation between the Spirit and the Father differs from the relation between the Spirit and the Son. Therefore to talk of the Spirit proceeding from the Father *and* the Son without differentiation is to confuse the two. This is underlined by Augustine's teaching that the Spirit proceeds from both as from a common source.

According to the West, the Eastern repudiation of the *filioque* leaves no clear relation between the Son and the Holy Spirit, in odd contrast to the patristic teaching of *perichōrēsis*, whereby the persons of the Trinity indwell and interpenetrate one another. The West holds that this exhibits subordinationist tendencies reaching back as far as Origen, for in the East the Son and the Holy Spirit are commonly said to receive their deity from the Father, and so both seem to be derivative.

This argument is not sustainable. The claim that the East holds apart the Son and the Holy Spirit is simply wrong. Throughout, the Eastern church has accepted expressions such as "from the Father through the Son" as validly conveying the intent of C. It maintains a mediating role for the Son in the procession of the Spirit. It argues the Holy Spirit rests on the Son (as at Jesus' baptism), is received by the Son, and in turn is sent by him. In saying that the Spirit proceeds from the Father, the East presupposes the relation between the Father and the Son, for the Father is the Father *of the Son*, the Son is eternally in and with the Father, and the Father is never apart from the Son.[13] The Cappadocian teaching on mutual indwelling underlies this—it represents a crowning affirmation of the close relations of the Son and the Holy Spirit. Besides, C is not silent on the relation of the Holy Spirit and the Son, for it says the Spirit is worshiped and glorified together with the Father and the Son, and is the author and giver of life together with the Father and the Son, "by whom [the Father] made the worlds." In short, the East consistently affirms that the Son participates in the Holy Spirit's procession from the Father both immanently and economically.

Second, while the *filioque* affirms the intimate relation between the Son and the Spirit, the West claims its rejection has led to a gulf in the East between theology and piety. Speculative theology, grounded on the Logos, has been separated from worship, mediated by the Holy Spirit. Thus Eastern piety, so Western observers like Bavinck claim, is unduly dominated by mysticism.[14] However, one of the most famous elements of Eastern piety, the Jesus prayer, is thoroughly Christocentric—"Lord Jesus Christ, Son of God, have mercy on me a sinner"—and can hardly be more evangelical or Christological in tone. That the East has no monopoly on unbridled mysticism was made evident by the "Toronto blessing" and other similar phenomena in the West.

A third objection carries greater weight. Following John of Damascus, the East generally considers the essence of God to be unknowable, and that only God's energies or operations are revealed in the things around him.[15] This dichotomy is used to offset some of the biblical evidence for the joint and coordinate involvement of the Son in relation to the Holy Spirit. As a sympathetic critic like T. F. Torrance argues, this drives a wedge between the inner life of God and his saving activity in history, ruling out any real access to knowing God in himself.[16] It also departs from earlier Greek patristic thought, which rejected this distinction.[17] Besides opening a yawning chasm between the economic Trinity and the immanent Trinity, the tendency seems to be toward a quaternity—the unknowable divine essence plus the three revealed persons—rather than a Trinity.

Possibilities for Agreement

1. The Eastern split between God's essence and his energies, after John of Damascus, poses problems—Eastern apologists argue that references to the Son sending the Spirit apply only to the energies, and therefore the purely economic. Jürgen Moltmann answers this by saying we can speak of only one Trinity, so "the divine cannot appear in the economy of salvation as something other than it is in itself. Therefore one cannot posit temporal Trinitarian relations within the economy of salvation which are not grounded in the primal Trinitarian relations." Thus, Moltmann continues, this relation between the Son and the Holy Spirit cannot be restricted to the temporal sending. If this were so, there would be a contradiction in God. This cannot be, for God remains true to himself. What holds true in his revelation must also be true in his being.[18]

2. In the West, the danger of modalism is very real. If we start with the divine unity, the persons become problematic as real, personal, permanent, irreducible, and eternal ontological distinctions.

3. The *filioque* clause is misleading for three possible reasons. First, if the Spirit proceeds from the Father and the Son as a single source, the distinction between the Father and the Son is blurred. Second, there appears some evidence of a tendency to subordinate the Holy Spirit if the *filioque* is needed to support the consubstantiality of the Son. If the deity of the Son requires him to be the spirating source of the Holy Spirit, where does that leave the Spirit, who is the source of no other hypostasis? Third, a basic principle of Trinitarian theology is flouted by the West: the attributes of the divine nature are shared by all three persons, while the divine properties are held by one person. But in the *filioque* a property (spiration) is shared by two persons, while the third is excluded.[19]

4. For a resolution of this problem, the East must recognize that the *filioque* was used in support of teaching the East fully accepts—the consubstantial unity of the Trinity, the deity of the Son, and the intimacy between the Son and the Holy Spirit. For its part, the West must recognize that Augustine's teaching that the Father and the Son are the common cause of the eternal being of the Holy Spirit unintentionally compromises the monarchy of the Father in the eyes of the East.

5. Help can be found by turning to Alexandria. In his *Letters to Serapion on the Holy Spirit*, Athanasius dealt at length with the Trinitarian relations. There he said the Son is consubstantial with the Father, out of the being of the Father. Whatever the Father has, the Son has.[20] But more important, the Trinity is indivisible, so that wherever the Father is mentioned the Son should also be understood, and where the Son is the Holy Spirit is in him.[21] The Spirit is never apart from the Word, the Son, a point Athanasius repeated time and again.[22] The Son is the image of the Father, but so also the Holy Spirit is the image of the Son.[23] The Son is in the Father and the Father is in the Son and so also the Holy Spirit is in the Son and the Son is in the Holy Spirit. Thus, the Spirit cannot be divided from the Word.[24] As the Son comes in the name of the Father, so the Holy Spirit comes in the name of the Son.[25] Nothing could be clearer than the intimate, unbreakable relation between the Son and the Holy Spirit in Athanasius's thought. The three persons indwell one another, and are in each other. This applies as much to the Son and the Spirit as to the Son and the Father, or the Father and the Spirit.

Similar lines of thought are evident in Cyril's *Dialogus II de SS. trinitate*[26] and *Thesaurus de sancta et consubstantiali trinitate*.[27] The Spirit is not alien from the divine essence, for he is of the essence, since he *inexists* (*enhypostatos*), proceeding from it and remaining in it.[28] So the Spirit is from the Father *and* the Son, since he is of the divine being, proceeding *in* it and *from* it.[29] Hence, the Spirit is from the being of the Son as well as the being of the Father.[30] While he naturally proceeds from the Father,[31] because of his enhypostatic relations he is *in* the Son and *from* the Son[32] and so can be said to proceed from the Father *in* the Son.[33] Cyril also says that the Son is sent from the Father *through* the Son (citing both John 15:26 and 14:26!)[34] and that he proceeds from the Father *and* the Son.[35]

Recent Developments

Moltmann attempts to bridge the divide by proposing that the Spirit proceeds *from the Father of the Son*. He points to the Son's conception by the Spirit and baptism by the Spirit. Here the Spirit precedes the Son. Moltmann stresses the reciprocal relations of the persons, preserving the procession of the Spirit from the Father while recognizing the Son's participation. He seems to concede the case to the East, and from the West's perspective does not adequately express the role of the Son.[36] Pannenberg rejects the *filioque* on the grounds that it implies the subordination of the Holy Spirit and also because Scripture says the Son receives the Spirit from the Father. He says it undermines the idea that the relations of the Trinitarian persons are reciprocal.[37]

On the other hand, the evangelical Anglican Gerald Bray defends the *filioque*. Different positions here, he argues, indicate differing views of salvation. The East's rejection of the clause is directly related to its soteriology, in which deification by the Spirit is at the heart, while for the West the work of Christ is central—the cross and resurrection, applied by the Holy Spirit.[38] Under Western eyes, the East undermines the gospel by failing to place the atoning work of Christ in center stage and integrate it with the work of the Spirit. For the East, death is the great enemy. Sin is subordinate to death. Christ's resurrection defeats death. Salvation is a conquest of mortality, the risen Christ bringing life in its place. The cross is not ignored, but is seen from the standpoint of the resurrection. The idea of sin as a transgression of the law of God, for which Christ on the cross makes atonement, is hardly found.

For the West, however, salvation is at root moral and ethical, whereas for the East it is cosmic. For the West, a holy God delivers his people from sin; for the East the risen Christ delivers the human race from death.[39] The gulf between East and West, according to Bray, is wider than the *filioque*. Referring to Calvin, he suggests that "the work of the Holy Spirit is to remake us in the image of Christ, so that we might enjoy the benefits of Christ's relationship to the Father" and so "He is remaking us in the image of Christ's *person*...to do which He [the Spirit] must share in the hypostasis of the Son, and therefore proceed from Him." The clause is integral and necessary to Reformed and evangelical Christianity. In the absence of the *filioque*, it is hard to see how the evangelical view of salvation could be maintained.[40]

Clearly, both atonement for sin and conquest of death should feature in any evangelical theology, and so the entail of the *filioque* cannot be discarded.[41] Discussions must extend further afield. However, Bray overlooks the rich reflection in the East on the baptism of Jesus. Here the Spirit descends from the Father in heaven and rests upon the Son, who breathes him out on his disciples. The West needs to advance beyond the *filioque* to take cognisance of these other dimensions.

The 1991 "Agreement between Orthodox and Reformed Churches"[42] is historic but limited in scope. The Western representatives were from the World Alliance of Reformed Churches. There was neither representation of other Protestant bodies or Rome, nor adequate representation of Augustinian Trinitarianism; the Reformed participants were already sympathetic—not uncritically—to the East. Yet with agreement on *from the Father through the Son* progress was made. However, the Cyrilline phrase *from the Father in the Son* (cf. Jn. 14:17–20, 17:21–23) maintains both sides' intent as well as the perichoresis[43] of the persons.

Revival of Interest in the West

A resurgence of interest in the Trinity developed from the middle of the twentieth century, spearheaded by Karl Barth and Karl Rahner. Most notably, Rahner proposed that "the economic Trinity is the immanent Trinity and the immanent Trinity is the economic Trinity," a suggestion known as "Rahner's axiom." Insofar as it is used to affirm that the revelation of the Trinity in human history is congruent with the Trinity in itself, the axiom has value; in fact, it is necessary for any Trinitarian doctrine, since it affirms that God's self-revelation is true to himself. However, it has more often been employed to undermine or deny the immanent Trinity in the interests of the panentheistic idea that God and the cosmos are codependent. It has been developed in this way by, inter alia, Moltmann, Catherine Mowry La Cugna, and Elizabeth Johnson. God is then simply part of the cosmic process, in the world and the world in him, in a relationship of mutual dependency. This line of thought has been heavily criticized by Paul Molnar as abandoning the freedom of God. He includes Wolfhart Pannenberg and Robert Jenson in such criticisms, too.[44]

At the same time, and often in connection with the above trend, there has developed a focus on a social Trinity, in which the three persons are compared to a family or a reciprocal association of friends. This has in part been a necessary corrective to the Western imbalance we noted. However, at times it has verged close to tritheism. Moltmann has been heavily criticised on this account by Molnar, George Hunsinger, and myself.[45] Sometimes, the idea has served the interests of a feminist agenda.

There are any number of ways in which a biblical and informed theological doctrine of the Trinity can, and should, affect both church and world. In this sense, the resurgent interest in the Trinity is welcome. A clearly Trinitarian liturgy can only enhance the worship, prayers, and mission of the church. Here the Eastern church has an advantage, for its liturgy—unchanged since the fourth century—is replete with Trinitarian prayers and doxologies, while for the vast majority of Western Christians it is an irrelevant mathematical conundrum. Since God has impressed his glory on his creation, the Trinity should enable us to see the unity-in-diversity in the world around us; a unitary monad would not and could not have made such a universe. Where the Trinity is not acknowledged, has a society the capacity to recognize unity-in-diversity and diversity-in-unity? If not, can it possibly operate in accordance with the reality of things as God has made them? Is not the inevitable tendency to relapse into undifferentiated unity, as in the Islamic world, or atomistic diversity, as in postmodernism? Is not either possibility an impediment to human well-being?

The State of the Question from the Evangelical Tradition

Protestant reflection on the Trinity in the sixteenth and seventeenth centuries took place firmly within the bounds of the Western tradition. Richard Muller has demonstrated this in his exhaustive discussions of post-Reformation Reformed dogmatics.[46] However, its most significant contributions were from John Calvin (1509–1564) and John Owen (1616–1683), both of whom devoted much greater attention to the three persons than the West had previously done, Richard of St. Victor apart. Calvin's doctrine of the Trinity in his *Institutes* is effectively his doctrine of God. He considers the deity of the Son and the Holy Spirit consecutively, marshaling extensive biblical evidence and support from the Fathers and medievals. Most noticeable is his absence of reflection on the essence of God. Nor does Calvin proceed from the doctrine of God to the Trinity as in Aquinas; in this he is closer to Peter Lombard.[47]

Owen's work, *Of Communion with God the Father, Son, and Holy Ghost, each person distinctly, in love, grace, and consolation* (1657) is without parallel. He discusses in great detail how our communion with the three comes to expression by considering communion with the Father, the Son, and the Holy Spirit consecutively. So pronounced is his tri-personal focus that he has to be careful at one point to distinguish his argument from tritheism.[48] Recent renewed interest in Owen's Trinitarianism offers possibilities for narrowing the divisions we discussed above.[49]

Jonathan Edwards (1703–1758) also broke in significant ways from the Western tradition. He combined aspects of Augustine's psychological model with the social model of a family or a communion of friends. His focus was on the three persons. However, his discussion of the putative covenant of redemption in eternity between the Father and the Son followed the generally adopted description, in which the Spirit was absent. An attempt to connect the economic Trinity and immanent Trinity, it was a construction with obvious subordinationist and tritheist elements, although Edwards managed to compensate for it by a remarkable emphasis on the Holy Spirit elsewhere.[50] Pauw concludes that Edwards was innovative but his Trinitarianism lacked stability. However, Edwards's distinctive Trinitarianism impacted the whole of his theology and ethics. William Danaher has also noted the impact of the social model of the Trinity in Edwards and its connection with his ethics, something until recently rarely developed in Western thought. Like Owen, Edwards's Trinitarianism offers prospects for extensive reflection.[51]

Paucity of Interest in the Trinity in Evangelicalism

Since the eighteenth century, evangelicalism has demonstrated a paucity of interest in the Trinity, in stark contrast to the tradition of the church. The Apostles' Creed and the Niceno-Constantinopolitan Creed—confessed in East and West down the centuries—both center on the Trinity, the church, and sacraments.

> *We believe in one God the Father Almighty*, maker of heaven and earth and of all things visible and invisible;
>
> *And in one Lord Jesus Christ the Son of God...And in the Holy Spirit*, the Lord and life-giver, who proceeds from the Father, who is worshiped and glorified together with the Father and the Son, who spoke by the prophets; *And in one holy, catholic and apostolic Church;* We confess one baptism for the forgiveness of sins... Amen.

Calvin followed this basic pattern, by structuring the *Institutes* in similar fashion. Book 1 is on "God the Creator," Book 2 on "God the Redeemer in Christ," and Book 3 on the way we receive the grace of Christ, which is "by the secret energy of the Spirit,"[52] while Book 4 concerns the church and sacraments, "the external means or aids by which God invites us into the society of Christ and holds us therein."

The Westminster Confession of Faith and *The Westminster Larger Catechism* adopted a similar structure. The Confession considered God the Trinity in chapter 2, and the decrees of God in chapter 3, then proceeding to the mediation of Christ, the covenant of grace, and the order of salvation to the church and sacraments in chapters 25–31.

However, the foci of post-eighteenth century evangelicalism have centered on the human agent in conversion, holiness, and world mission. How far is this a reaction to the Enlightenment and its restriction of knowledge to this-worldly phenomena? To what extent does this resonate with the burgeoning historical consciousness and the development of intellectual pursuits devoted to the study of humanity rather than God, where religious experience features with great prominence? Kindred movements to evangelicalism were existentialism, pietism, Cartesian inwardness, and the attention to spiritual experience in theologians such as Schleiermacher. As I have written elsewhere, "The ultimate focus of that movement [evangelicalism] was the individual," in contrast to the unity-in-diversity of the Trinity.[53]

In this concentration on human experience, evangelicalism has shown itself to be at variance from the historic church. I have argued that

> evangelicalism as such, by pushing the central and time-honoured realities to the side and declaring some of them non-essential, has created an imbalance of momentous proportions.... Evangelicalism *at its best* has marched off at a tangent from the trajectory of the historic church.... It has rarely stopped to ask whether the movement itself was a capitulation to philosophical voices from outside the church. In reality, evangelicalism is a variant form of Christianity and one that, due to the dangerously loose lines that connected it to the heritage of the wider, historic faith, could now be in danger of losing its grasp of the faith it seemingly holds dear. To repeat [David] Wells' comment: "What, then, is the essence of being an evangelical today? Well, that all depends."[54]

Evangelicalism's insistence on the right of private interpretation—not a principle evident in the confessional age of Protestantism, and one opposed by Westminster[55]—has spawned independent churches and denominations by the thousands. It ignores the churchly context of the giving of Scripture and the ongoing process of the interpretation of Scripture in the church. There can be little possibility of concord or coherent constructive thought on the Trinity with that foundation. Where legislative authority is restricted to local congregations, any pronouncement on a wider basis—such as a confession of faith—can have merely a consultative or advisory function.

Moreover, with a proliferation of independent churches and para-church groups comes a haphazard approach to theology. Evangelicalism lacks a coherent theology. The best to be hoped for are piecemeal reactions on isolated and particular doctrines. The Bible, the atonement, justification, creation, and soteriological inclusivism are calculated to set the evangelical's pulse racing—but as discrete topics. In the United States, this is clear in the doctrinal basis of the Evangelical Theological Society, limited to two brief statements on the Trinity and biblical inerrancy, which could exclude many who confess the Niceno-Constantinopolitan creed and include many who do not. This partly explains the uneasy relationship of people like B. B. Warfield (1851–1921) and J. Gresham Machen (1889–1937) with other conservative groups; with their confessional theology, they were never entirely comfortable with the obsession of fundamentalists with particular doctrines, such as creation.[56]

These factors may help explain why evangelicalism has produced little to date on the Trinity, for it is effectively a series of splinter groups hived away from the central tradition of the church, in which the Trinity was central. It is hard to envisage evangelicalism as such, apart from individual evangelical theologians, contributing to discussion without overcoming these problems. A systematic theology such as Wayne Grudem's cannot command universal assent due to its baptistic ecclesiology, its position on charismatic gifts, women, and even the Trinity.[57] A confessional commitment to the historic Christian tradition would be necessary. Yet that can hardly be attained in the current situation.

Sadly, in keeping with this neglect, the Trinity means little or nothing to the average evangelical churchgoer. Attention over the years has been strongly directed to the life and ministry of the incarnate Son, especially his death and resurrection. The cross has been identified as one of the central themes of the movement.[58] In more recent decades, the charismatic movement has drawn attention to the Holy Spirit. However, commonly in evangelicalism people talk of "God" or "the Lord," in stark contrast to Gregory of Nazianzus, who wrote of "my Trinity," and "when I say 'God,' I mean the Father, the Son, and the Holy Spirit."

A Future Direction for Evangelical Thinking

In Contrast to Orthodox Liturgy and Belief

The Eastern church has remained virtually unchanged down the centuries. Its liturgy has roots in the fourth century.[59] In contrast, evangelicalism has a history of adaptation, like a chameleon, to its surrounding culture. The perennial tension between the faith once delivered and the contextualization needed to reach the world with the gospel is acute; Bruce Nicholls calls these respective poles dogmatic contextualization and existential contextualization.[60] Evangelicalism has struggled with this tension. This may be a good sign, for real tension inevitably produces a struggle. However, its focus on individual doctrines at the expense of the historic Christian confession bespeaks a diminished central focus and a propensity to be shaped by the social context. One may ask if evangelicalism has not lost something along the way.

Reconnect with the Great Tradition

Hence, for evangelicalism to lay claim to share the Trinitarian confession of the early church it cannot avoid the attempt to reconnect to the Great Tradition. As Colin Gunton wrote, "If we can no longer in any way appropriate for ourselves the language of the past—for example, the affirmations of the Nicene Creed—then on what grounds are we able to judge whether we share the faith of the Fathers who formulated the Creed? How can we be sure that we are doing Christian theology at all?"[61]

If evangelicalism is a valid part of the Christian church, it will seek to be rooted to the historic teaching of the church. While it will maintain the supremacy of Scripture in all matters of faith and conduct, with priority over all church councils, it will think very carefully and long before placing its own interpretation of the Bible above that of the historic consensus of the church. By this, it will have adopted a clear Trinitarian basis for its theology, life, and mission. Its worship and mission activity, theology, and cultural engagement will seek to glean the best from both West and East. In other words, the best service evangelicalism can render the Christian church is to cease to be evangelical in the independent and atomistic sense to which we have referred.

NOTES

1. Augustine, *De Trinitate*, 8-15. *The Works of Saint Augustine: A Translation for the 21st Century: The Trinity*, trans. Edmund Hill, ed. J. E. Rotelle (Hyde Park, N.Y.: New City Press, 1991), 237-443.

2. Colin Gunton, "Augustine, the Trinity, and the Theological Crisis of the West," *Scottish Journal of Theology* 43 (1990): 33–58.

3. G. L. Prestige, *God in Patristic Thought* (London: SPCK, 1952), 237.

4. Basil Studer, *Trinity and Incarnation: The Faith of the Early Church*, trans. Matthias Westerhoff, ed. Andrew Louth (Collegeville, Minn.: Liturgical Press, 1993), 167–85; Studer, *The Grace of Christ and the Grace of God in Augustine of Hippo: Christocentrism or Theocentrism?* (Collegeville, Minn.: Liturgical Press, 1997); Studer, "Augustin et la foi de Nicée," *Recherches Augustiniennes* 19 (1984): 133–154.

5. Michel René Barnes, "Rereading Augustine on the Trinity," in Stephen T. Davis, Daniel Kendall, S.J., and Gerald O'Collins, S.J., eds., *The Trinity: An Interdisciplinary Symposium on the Trinity* (Oxford: Oxford University Press, 1999), 145–153.

6. Studer, *Grace of Christ*, 106.

7. Theodore De Régnon, *Études de théologie positive sur la Sainté Trinité* (Paris: Retaux, 1898); Michel René Barnes, "De Régnon Reconsidered," *Augustinian Studies* 26 (1995): 51–79; Barnes, "Rereading Augustine on the Trinity," in Stephen T. Davis, et al., eds., *The Trinity*, 143–176.

8. Lewis Ayres, *Nicaea and Its Legacy: An Approach to Fourth-Century Trinitarian Theology* (Oxford: Oxford University Press, 2004).

9. See Robert Letham, *Through Western Eyes: Eastern Orthodoxy: A Reformed Perspective* (Fearn, Ross-shire, Scotland: Mentor, 2007).

10. Alexander Pope, *An Essay on Man*, II:1. *The Works of Alexander Pope* (London: Printed for B. Lintot et al., 1736), 2:20. http://collections.chadwyck.co.uk/searchFulltext.do?id=Z000463804&divLevel=0&queryId=&area=e_poetry&forward=textsFT&pageSize=&print=No&size=882Kb&warn=Yes.

11. Karl Barth, *Church Dogmatics*, I/1, ed. G. W. Bromiley and T. F. Torrance (Edinburgh: T & T Clark, 1975), 295ff.

12. But see R. M. Haugh, *Photius and the Carolingians: The Trinitarian Controversy* (Belmont, Mass.: Norland, 1975), 160–161, who questions this explanation and argues that it "first entered the Ecumenical Creed in the Latin West by a simple method of transposition and not by any willful act of interpolation in conscious violation of the Ecumenical decrees." Sergei Bulgakov rightly argues that the phrase was unnecessary, for Arianism could have been rebutted quite readily without it; "pour rejeter l'arianisme et reconnaître l'équi-divinité et la consubstantialité du Fils au Père, on n'a nul besoin de cette surérogation." Sergei Nikolaevich Bulgakov, *Le Paraclet*, ed. Constantin Andronikof (Paris: Aubier, 1946), 125.

13. See the references to Athanasius below. Jürgen Moltmann's proposal that the Spirit proceeds "from the Father of the Son" assumes that a consensus would form in the East in support of this, which is far from certain; see his volume *The Trinity and the Kingdom: The Doctrine of God* (London: SCM, 1991), 185–187.

14. Herman Bavinck, *The Doctrine of God* (repr. Edinburgh: Banner of Truth, 1977), 313–317; Bavinck, *Reformed Dogmatics: Volume 2: God and Creation*, ed. John Bolt, trans. John Vriend (Grand Rapids: Baker Academic, 2004), 314–318.

15. John of Damascus, *The Orthodox Faith*, 1:4. *A Select Library of Nicene and Post-Nicene Fathers of the Christian Church*, second series, ed. Philip Schaff and Henry Wace (repr. Edinburgh: T & T Clark, 1989), 9/2:3–4.

16. Thomas F. Torrance, *The Christian Doctrine of God: One Being, Three Persons* (Edinburgh: T & T Clark, 1996), 187.

17. Athanasius, *On the Decrees of the Synod of Nicea*, 22. Athanasius, *De decretis or Defence of the Nicene Definition*, 22; *A Select Library of Nicene and Post-Nicene Fathers of the Christian Church*, second series, ed. Philip Schaff and Henry Wace (repr. Grand Rapids: Eerdmans, 1980), 4:164–165.

18. Jürgen Moltmann, "Theological Proposals Towards the Resolution of the Filioque Controversy," in *Spirit of God, Spirit of Christ: Ecumenical Reflections on the Filioque Controversy*, ed. Lukas Vischer (London: SPCK, 1981), 165–166.

19. Photios argues that "everything not said about the whole, omnipotent, consubstantial, and supersubstantial is said about one of the three persons. The procession of the Spirit is not said to be common to the three, consequently it must belong to one of the three." Photios, *On the Mystagogy of the Holy Spirit* (n.p.: Studion, 1983), 36.

20. Athanasius, *Letters to Serapion on the Holy Spirit*, 2: 5, *Patrologia graeca* [*PG*] 26: 616. Ed. J. P. Migne et al. (Paris: 1857–1866), 26:616.

21. Ibid., 1: 14, *PG* 26: 566.

22. Ibid., 1: 14, 17, 20, 31, 3: 5, 4: 4; *PG* 26: 565–566, 572, 576–577, 601, 632–633, 641.

23. Ibid., 4: 3, *PG* 26 :640–641.
24. Ibid., 1: 20–21, *PG* 26: 580.
25. Ibid., 1: 20, *PG* 26: 580.
26. Cyril of Alexandria, *Dialogue on the Most Holy*, PG 75: 721–723.
27. Cyril of Alexandria, *Thesaurus on the Holy and Consubstantial*, PG 75: 565.
28. Ibid., *PG* 75: 577.
29. Ibid., *PG* 75: 585.
30. Ibid., *PG* 75: 587, 589.
31. Ibid., *PG* 75: 597.
32. Ibid., *PG* 75: 581.
33. Ibid., *PG* 75: 577.
34. Ibid., *PG* 75: 581.
35. Ibid., *PG* 75: 585.
36. Moltmann, *The Trinity and the Kingdom*, 178–190.
37. Wolfhart Pannenberg, *Systematic Theology*, trans. G. W. Bromiley (Grand Rapids: Eerdmans, 1991), 1:319–321.
38. Gerald Bray, "The *filioque* Clause in History and Theology," *Tyndale Bulletin* 34 (1983): 139–144.
39. Timothy Ware, *The Orthodox Church* (London: Penguin, 1969), 230–234; John Meyendorff, *Byzantine Theology: Historical Trends and Doctrinal Themes* (New York: Fordham University Press, 1979), 159–165.
40. Bray, "The *filioque* Clause," 142–143.
41. See Robert Letham, *The Work of Christ* (Leicester: Inter-Varsity Press, 1993), especially chap. 7.
42. For the official text, see Thomas F. Torrance, *Theological Dialogue between Orthodox and Reformed Churches*, vol. 2 (Edinburgh: Scottish Academic Press, 1993), 219–232; or "Agreed Statement on the Holy Trinity between the Orthodox Church and the World Alliance of Reformed Churches," *Touchstone* 5, no. 1 (Winter 1992): 22–23. For commentary on the agreement, see Thomas F. Torrance, *Trinitarian Perspectives: Toward Doctrinal Agreement* (Edinburgh: T & T Clark, 1994), 110–143.
43. The mutual indwelling of the three persons.
44. Paul D. Molnar, *Divine Freedom and the Doctrine of the Immanent Trinity: in Dialogue with Karl Barth and Contemporary Theology* (London: T & T Clark, 2002).
45. Ibid., 201–202; Letham, *The Holy Trinity: In Scripture, History, Theology and Worship* (Phillipsburg, N.J.: Presbyterian & Reformed, 2004), 298–312; George Hunsinger, review of Moltmann, *The Trinity and the Kingdom* in *The Thomist* 47 (1983): 129–139.
46. Richard A. Muller, *Post-Reformation Reformed Dogmatics: The Rise and Development of Reformed Orthodoxy, ca. 1520 to ca. 1725*. Vol. 4: *The Triunity of God* (Grand Rapids: Baler Academic, 2003).
47. P. Lombard, *Sententiae in IV Libris Distinctae* (Rome: Editiones Collegii S. Bonaventurae ad Claras Aquas Grottaffearati, 1971), bk. 1.
48. W. H. Goold, ed., *The Works of John Owen* (London: Banner of Truth Trust, 1965–1968), 2: 15–19.
49. Carl R. Trueman, *The Claims of Truth: John Owen's Trinitarian Theology* (Carlisle: Paternoster, 1998); Trueman, *John Owen: Reformed Catholic, Renaissance Man* (Aldershot: Ashgate, 2007); Kelly M. Kapic, *Communion with God: The Divine and the Human in the Theology of John Owen* (Grand Rapids: Baker Academic, 2007).
50. Amy Plantinga Pauw, *"The Supreme Harmony of All." The Trinitarian Theology of Jonathan Edwards* (Grand Rapids: Eerdmans, 2002).

51. William J. Danaher, Jr., *The Trinitarian Ethics of Jonathan Edwards* (Louisville, Ky.: Westminster John Knox Press, 2004).

52. John Calvin, *Institutes of the Christian Religion*, 3:1:1. *Library of Christian Classics Volume XX: Calvin: Institutes of the Christian Religion in two volumes (Vol. XX: Books I.i to III.xix)*, ed. John T. McNeill, trans. Ford Lewis Battles (Philadelphia: Westminster Press, 1960), 537–538.

53. Robert Letham and Donald MacLeod, "Is Evangelicalism Christian?" *Evangelical Quarterly* 67 (1995): 32.

54. Ibid., 15–16.

55. See Robert Letham, *The Theology of the Westminster Assembly* (Phillipsburg, N.J.: Presbyterian and Reformed / Philadelphia: Craig Center for the Study of the Westminster Standards, 2009).

56. D. G. Hart, *Defending the Faith: J. Gresham Machen and the Crisis of Conservative Protestantism in Modern America* (Baltimore: Johns Hopkins University Press, 1994).

57. Wayne Grudem, *Systematic Theology* (Grand Rapids: Zondervan, 1995); see Kevin Giles, "The Evangelical Theological Society and the Doctrine of the Trinity," *Evangelical Quarterly* 80 (2008): 323–338. Grudem's teaching on "the eternal subordination of the Son" to the Father is open to considerable misunderstanding and has aroused the opposition of many inside and outside evangelicalism.

58. David W. Bebbington, *Evangelicalism in Modern Britain: A History from the 1730s to the 1908s* (London: Unwin Hyman, 1989), 2–17.

59. See Letham, *Through Western Eyes*.

60. Bruce J. Nicholls, *Contextualization: A Theology of Gospel and Culture* (Exeter: Paternoster Press, 1979).

61. Colin E. Gunton, *Yesterday & Today: A Study of Continuities in Christology* (Grand Rapids: Eerdmans, 1983), 4–5.

BIBLIOGRAPHY

Ayres, Lewis. *Nicaea and Its Legacy: An Approach to Fourth-Century Trinitarian Theology*. Oxford: Oxford University Press, 2004.

Barth, Karl. *Church Dogmatics*, I/1, ed. G. W. Bromiley and T. F. Torrance. Edinburgh: T & T Clark, 1975.

Bray, Gerald. "The *Filioque* Clause in History and Theology." *Tyndale Bulletin* 34 (1983): 139–144.

Danaher, William J., Jr. *The Trinitarian Ethics of Jonathan Edwards*. Louisville, Ky.: Westminster John Knox, 2004.

Goold, William H., ed. *The Works of John Owen*. Repr. London: Banner of Truth, 1966, 2:1–454.

Hanson, R.P.C. *The Search for the Christian Doctrine of God: The Arian Controversy 318–381*. Edinburgh: T & T Clark, 1988.

Letham, Robert. *The Holy Trinity: In Scripture, History, Theology, and Worship*. Phillipsburg, N.J.: Presbyterian & Reformed, 2004.

Molnar, Paul D. *Divine Freedom and the Doctrine of the Immanent Trinity: In Dialogue with Karl Barth and Contemporary Theology*. London: T & T Clark, 2002.

Moltmann, Jürgen. *The Trinity and the Kingdom: The Doctrine of God*. Minneapolis: Fortress, 1993.

Needham, Nick. "The *Filioque* Clause: East or West?" *Scottish Bulletin of Evangelical Theology* 15 (1997): 142–162.

Pauw, Amy Plantinga. *"The Supreme Harmony of All": The Trinitarian Theology of Jonathan Edwards*. Grand Rapids: Eerdmans, 2002.

Rahner, Karl, *The Trinity*, trans. Joseph Donceel. New York: Crossroad, 1997.

Rostelle, John E., ed. *The Works of Saint Augustine: The Trinity*. Trans. Edmund Hill. Hyde Park, N.Y: New City Press, 1991.

Wickham, Lionel, and Frederick Williams, trans. *St. Gregory of Nazianzus: On God and Christ; The Five Theological Orations and Two Letters to Cledonius*. Crestwood, N.Y.: St. Vladimir's Seminary Press, 2002.

CHAPTER 7

CREATION

LOREN WILKINSON

THE doctrine of creation is foundational to Christian faith; yet, till very recently, it has played a minor role in evangelical thought. Perhaps the first reason for this neglect is, ironically, the inescapable nature of creation itself. People become blasé about the continual miracle of the existence of anything at all (including ourselves) and the even stranger fact of our awareness of that miracle. Evangelicals have often tended to demote creation to the unbiblical idea of "nature" and neglected its theological significance.

So it has been left mainly to European philosophers to ask, "Why is there something, rather than nothing?" But as Colin Gunton puts it in the introduction to *The Triune Creator* (an important resource for evangelical retrieval of the doctrine), there are only "two possible answers to the question...: that the universe is the result of creation by a free personal agency, and that in some way or other it creates itself."[1] The first answer points to theism, the second to atheism. Both of these answers are unavoidably theological.

Despite the theological implications of those answers, evangelicals have resisted basing their theology on creation. Whereas "nature" is a universal experience, "creation" is not, but is rather an item of faith, and must be understood in the context of revelation. Thus evangelicals have rarely built their theology on a foundation of "natural revelation" (common as those attempts were a century ago). In reaction against such attempts, Karl Barth said a decisive "No" to Emil Brunner's argument for an apologetic "common ground" in our experience of creation, and developed instead his massive argument that we can only understand creation in light of the story of the Covenant that is opened to us in Christ. As Barth's influence on evangelical thought continues to grow, so also does this rather ambivalent attitude toward a theology of creation.

However, our rapidly increasing knowledge of the "new story of creation" as told by science (in cosmology, ecology, evolutionary biology, genetics, neurochemistry, quantum physics, and so on) increasingly invites evangelical thinkers to bring that scientific knowledge together with the "old story" of the Gospel. But this evangelical engagement with the story told by science is often an uncomfortable one. This discomfort is shown by the fact that in contemporary public discourse references to "creation" most often appear in one of two quite different contexts.

The most common context is argument about "creation or evolution," and is signaled by words like "creationist" and "creationism." The other context is discussion of the worsening environmental situation where "the Creation" is used, often by non-Christian environmentalists, as a kind of value-laden synonym for "the earth." For example, in 2006 the prominent Harvard biologist E. O. Wilson published a book called *The Creation: An Appeal to Save Life on Earth*, which is written as an open letter to an evangelical pastor, pleading with him to act on what Wilson feels any Christian's faith should call him to affirm: the value of life on the planet.

Both the origins and environmental debates are ideological minefields, obscuring serious theological thought. Gradually, however, as the tensions lessen, a much richer understanding of creation is beginning to take shape. That emerging doctrine of creation increasingly tells the old story of biblical revelation in the light of the new story of the universe which is being told by science—but without giving up a robust belief in the reality of what the doctrine affirms. As we shall see, an insufficiently Trinitarian doctrine of creation has probably encouraged our culture's drift towards "practical atheism." But a more Trinitarian doctrine of creation might help reverse that drift.

Some principal features of that recent evangelical engagement with the doctrine of creation are summarized below in the form of ten theses. The positions outlined in these theses are not inventions but recoveries: large truths that have always been close to the center of the gospel, but that now appear in a new light. Often, as we shall see, the resources to articulate this larger view have been found by evangelicals in older Catholic, Orthodox, and patristic sources. Important areas of disagreement and mystery remain, and almost all of the theses that follow also imply agendas for further thought. But increasingly, creation is no longer a marginal theme for evangelicals, in large part because they are recovering (in a retrieval that goes all the way back to Irenaeus) a Trinitarian doctrine of creation.

1. Though "creation out of nothing" remains a foundational belief, increasingly evangelicals speak of "creation out of love"—an affirmation which takes seriously that the Creator God is the triune God.

Irenaeus, following Scripture, described an intimacy between God and creation which later theological language of "immanence," "transcendence" and "providence" tended to obscure. His Trinitarian language of God creating by Word and Spirit preserves both the otherness of God and his loving care. Today, it enables evangelicals to steer an orthodox path between the paradoxical affirmations of (on the one hand) the infinite gap between God and creation and (on the other) the closeness of God to each creature. Various postmodern religious movements (neopaganism, ecofeminism, deep ecology) haves sensed this closeness, but speak of it in pantheistic terms (all is God; God is all).[2] Increasingly evangelicals are able to speak of that divine closeness to creation in personal and triune terms—as the action, through Christ and the Spirit, of the God of love. Clark Pinnock, for example, suggests the idea in a chapter of *Flame of Love* titled "Spirit in Creation": "Something of the why of creation is revealed by the nature of God. He creates in a way that is consistent with his loving nature as a relational being. . . . Creation arises from loving relationships in the divine nature. God creates out of his own abundant interpersonal love—it is the expression of his generosity."[3]

"Creation out of love" by the triune God, immanent and transcendent, is a rediscovered foundation for contemporary Christian thought and action.

2. Creation is the original "amazing grace," to which the appropriate human responses are wonder, thanks, and worship. It is the writers and artists who have been pioneers in restoring this attitude.

The clearest voices in articulating this response to creation as a gift of love have come not from the theologians but the artists. Most prominent here are C. S. Lewis and J.R.R. Tolkien. Tolkien's "Essay on Fairy Stories" lays out the theology behind his vastly better known *Lord of the Rings.* In the essay he speaks of the human imagination as a response in kind to the gift of creation through divine imagination: "We make still by the law in which we're made."[4]

Standing behind both Lewis and Tolkien is the nineteenth-century George MacDonald, whose deep sense of the Godward-pointing goodness of the ordinary "baptized the imagination" of C. S. Lewis. Lewis says of MacDonald, "That quality which had enchanted me in his imaginative works turned out to be the quality of the real universe, the divine, terrifying, and ecstatic reality in which we all live."[5] And one of the most enduring of these Christian guides to discovering the astonishment of creation is G. K. Chesterton. In *Orthodoxy*, the story of his conversion, he describes the fascination children have with "fairy tales," which "echo an almost pre-natal leap of interest and amazement. These tales say that apples were golden only to refresh the forgotten moment when we found they were green. They make rivers run with wine only to make us remember, for one wild moment, that they run with water."[6] Chesterton never lost sight of the fact that creation is a gift and a surprise, and his writing has helped recent generations of Christians—including evangelicals—find a deeper theology of creation.

Another Victorian writer who has nourished evangelical thought about creation is the poet Gerard Manley Hopkins. A convert to Catholicism and a Jesuit priest, his writing is informed by the incarnational thought of the medieval Franciscan Duns Scotus. Not read widely till the twentieth century, evangelicals have increasingly adopted Hopkins as one of their own. They have learned a great deal from his understanding that "Christ Plays in Ten Thousand Places" and that the "Bent World" is nevertheless "Under the Bright Wings." These phrases from Hopkins poems have all become titles of recent books by evangelicals.

3. Creation is both an original event and a continuing process.

The evangelical doctrine of creation has suffered from a sort of modalism in which creation has come to be seen mainly as the past action of the transcendent Father; redemption as the historical and accomplished work of the incarnate Son;

and sanctification—and other "spiritual gifts"—as the concern of the indwelling and immanent Spirit. This divine division of labor—encouraged by the wording of the Christian creeds[7]—has the effect of making creation seem to be only an act in the distant past, with a distancing of God quite similar to deism, except (depending on one's theology) for occasional but rare "super-natural" interventions, either for special creative acts (as in the creation of life, or the human soul) and the answering of prayer. Otherwise creation chugs along "naturally."

Seeing creation as a gift of the creator has enabled evangelicals to understand more clearly that whatever they may believe about the timing of the beginning of creation, creation is not something God did and then stopped doing, Rather, as in the words of Kallistos Ware (an Orthodox thinker who has gained an increasing hearing among evangelicals): "We should say, not 'God made the world and me in it,' but God is *making* the world, and me in it, here and now, at this moment and always.' Creation is not an event in the past, but a relationship in the present."[8]

There is abundant biblical witness of the immediate and continuing nature of God's relationship to creation, most extensively in Psalm 104, which recasts the Genesis 1 story of creation into God's present and continuing action ("You send forth your Spirit and they are created," v. 30). Setting "creation" over against "evolution" tends rather to treat creation more as a noun—the static result of a past action—rather than a verb—a continuing process as a result of God's upholding immanence.

4. Creation is contingent, which means that as an act of God's love it surpasses our reason, so we can know only from experience—not by thought—what God is doing. At the same time it is ordered, and hence capable of being described by human language and mathematics. Recognition that these two beliefs are essential preconditions for science is leading many evangelicals to an increasing ease with science.

An important development in contemporary evangelical theology of creation is a reversal of the widespread idea that creation is in necessary opposition to science. Rather, it has come to be more and more widely acknowledged that the Christian doctrine of creation was an important, perhaps even necessary, component in the rise of modern science. An important source of this retrieval is the work of Oxford philosopher Michael Foster. In 1934 he published the first of three articles in the journal *Mind* with the overall title, "The Christian Doctrine of Creation and the Rise of Modern Natural Science."[9] Foster's thesis, meticulously argued, rests on three simple points. First, modern science is fundamentally empirical—that is, it investigates the natural world in a process of discovery, not as illustration of what could be concluded by reason alone. This method assumes the contingency of creation—that it could be other than it is. Thus the things in creation cannot be known simply by thought: they must be experienced. Such a contingent creation is the work of a Creator who does what he wills rather than what is rationally necessary. This is a picture far more consistent with the God of Scripture than with the rational God of Greek philosophy, and only when this more biblical understanding of creation prevailed did modern science begin.

What such a creation requires from those who would know it is not an infallible method of knowing, but faith, commitment, passion. Here an important ally for evangelical thinkers has been the philosopher of science Michael Polanyi, and particularly his magisterial 1958 work *Personal Knowledge.* Polanyi was fond of citing Anselm's declaration as fundamental to the nature of science: "I do not seek to understand in order that I may believe, but I believe in order to understand." He argues that the knowledge which science seeks to establish is always tentative, humble, and personal, based on a belief that the creation which is being investigated is both knowable and surprising. But the essential subjectivity of knowing does not make what is known any less real: "Such knowing is indeed *objective* in the sense of establishing contact with a hidden reality."[10]

Such a way of knowing has come to be called "critical realism," and informs many important influences on evangelical thought. Lesslie Newbigin, for example, in his book *The Gospel in a Pluralist Society*, draws heavily on Polanyi's conviction that creation is something which can be known only by being believed. N. T. Wright, in the introductory chapters of his foundational *The New Testament and the People of God*, cites Polanyi in defense of his method of getting at the historical truth of the gospels: "This is a way of knowing that acknowledges the *reality of the thing known, as something other than the knower*... while also fully acknowledging that the only access we have to this reality lies along the spiraling path of *appropriate dialogue or conversation between the knower and the thing known.*"[11] And John Polkinghorne, physicist turned theologian, draws often on Polanyi in tracing the similarities between the faith which leads to knowledge of the Creator and that which leads to knowledge of the creation.[12]

Paralleling this belief in the contingency of creation is the recognition that the creation which science knows is nevertheless ordered, harmonious, and beautiful. Yet we cannot encounter this beauty through rational contemplation; we must experience it in the world which God has created. Like the love of God itself, it is beyond our ability to imagine or anticipate; creation must first of all be experienced to be known. But it *can* be experienced, known, and described. This ability of the human mind—in particular, of mathematics—to accurately describe creation is strange. As one physicist has put it, "The enormous usefulness of mathematics in the natural sciences is something bordering on the mysterious.... The miracle of the appropriateness of the language of mathematics for the formulation of the laws of physics is a wonderful gift which we neither understand nor deserve."[13]

Such language of "gift," "mystery," and "miracle" about creation, coming from one who is simply describing the practice of physics, is the sort of thing that has nourished among evangelicals a more positive view both of creation and our knowledge of it. There is a danger, though, that the language of order and intelligibility can lure Christian thinkers back into the kind of Platonism which is insufficiently appreciative of the contingent. This may be the case with a recent Cambridge-centered movement called Radical Orthodoxy. It takes the position that the recovery of contingency which Foster describes—with its corollary of a God whose actions are more explicable in terms of will than of reason—has had the effect of cutting off belief that creation participates in God. The result of this conviction of nonparticipation, it is argued, is a sort of flattening of all creatures which leads ultimately to modernity and nihilism.

"Intelligent Design" is a movement more closely allied with evangelicalism than is radical orthodoxy. Nevertheless, it is similar in its argument for a detectable presence of the Creator in the created as a kind of hedge against secularism. Defenders of intelligent design (ID) argue that there is an "irreducible complexity" in living things which is evidence of divine design, but which modern science refuses to acknowledge. Some ID proponents suggest that we are on the verge of a breakdown in the prevailing scientific paradigm which does not recognize intelligent design in nature. Other evangelicals, however, argue that the movement appeals to the old "God of the gaps" idea, in which our inability to explain a phenomenon is seen as evidence of God's presence. At its best, the ID movement is an important gadfly for the scientific establishment, reminding us that science must remain humble before the inexhaustible gift and mystery of the cosmos which it studies; at its worst, the questions raised by ID proponents have been used by some evangelicals as an excuse to cast doubt on the whole scientific enterprise rather than as an impetus to do better science.

Despite very large differences in culture and appeal, both Radical Orthodoxy (a sophisticated Anglo-Catholic movement) and Intelligent Design (a more populist American movement) are deeply suspicious of a kind of "methodological atheism": the exclusion of God from scientific explanation.

The larger evangelical discussion says that to take creation seriously as the sole source of information about itself neither "flattens it" (as accused by Radical Orthodoxy), nor is "methodologically atheistic" (as accused by Intelligent Design). Rather, this new appreciation for the contingency of creation is an affirmation of its genuine freedom. Creation depends neither on divine "participation" nor "intervention" but rather on a loving God who, through the Spirit and Word, upholds things in genuine otherness from himself. This basic congruence between science and theology, reinforced (via Polanyi) by an appreciation of all knowledge as a belief-based dialogue with a contingent and intelligible reality has helped to break down barriers between science and Christian faith, and is opening a whole generation of evangelical thinkers to a greater ease with science.

5. Creation is genuinely free. Increasingly evangelicals understand that creation is a network of relationships among creatures upheld in their uniqueness and freedom by the Creator. The climax of that free relatedness is human personhood.

The growing evangelical openness to science is rooted in a recognition that creaturely reality can and must be known in its integrity, uniqueness, and freedom. The ultimate instance of this free relatedness is human personhood. This recognition of the centrality of personal relationship is rooted in a deepening understanding of the intrinsically relational nature of the triune God. Colin Gunton has led the way here in two important studies: *The One, the Three, and the Many* and *The Triune Creator*. In the first book, Gunton argues that an understanding of the triune God enables us to affirm genuine otherness (without individualism) and genuine relatedness (without homogeneity). Gunton argues: "Of the universe as a whole we should conclude that it is marked by relationality.... [A]ll things are what they are by being particulars constituted by many and various forms of relation.... [A]ll created people and things are marked by their coming from and returning to the God who is himself, in his essential and inmost being, a being in relation."[14]

In *The Triune Creator* Gunton traces the many ways in which the Christian theological tradition has overlooked this essential relationality of creation. Creatures do not participate in God. Rather, in their God-upheld otherness they are in *communion* with God and each other. Particularly in the Protestant world, the sovereignty of God has been so elevated that the reality of creaturely freedom is eclipsed. Jeremy Begbie points out that running through the Neo-Calvinist tradition is a deep dualism between creation and redemption.[15] Creation is seen there as the work of God's power, but redemption as the work of his grace and love. There is little sense in this tradition (which informs much of evangelicalism) of creation itself as grace, of *being* as a gift of love.

Something of this understanding of the love of God underlying the freedom of the creature is evident in the "openness of God" debate. One not need agree with every aspect of this approach to see the wisdom in Clark Pinnock's words about the creating Spirit, which both differentiates and brings unity:

> The triune nature helps us to think about the relative autonomy of the world and its relatedness to God. The world is created in distinction from the Father, to be able to relate and respond freely to God. It is a distinct though dependent reality, made for relationship, and a world in which the Son can become incarnate, both as the fulfillment of God's desire to disclose himself and as redemptive sacrifice (if required).[16]

Implicit in Pinnock's words is a minority view of the incarnation with profound implications for the way Christians view creation: that the incarnation, which has become our redemption, was intended by God from the beginning. Creation was as much for the sake of the incarnation as the incarnation was for the sake of the creation. The very possibility of such a God elevates creation. And it gives an added urgency to two questions: What is the human task in creation? And how is that creation restored in Christ?

6. Creation is not complete without human beings, who have a unique and central role to play: to "image God" to creation, and in turn to speak praise from creation back to the Creator. In the Old Testament account, the Sabbath is a reminder both of the gift of creation and the human relationship to it.

In the carefully structured Genesis 1 creation account, human beings are created on the sixth day (significantly, sharing that day of creation with the animals) "in the image of God." Sustained criticism from the environmental movement of the special place which this account seems to give humans has required a good deal of careful evangelical thought on the human role in creation. Many critics point out that in the Christian world the perception that we humans are made in the image of God has encouraged a "species-ism" damaging to creation. Evangelicals have responded mainly by defending the special place of people in creation in terms of the idea of "stewardship," based especially on the Genesis 2 picture of Adam placed in Eden to serve and protect it. However, the concept of stewardship has ironically sometimes been used by Christians to justify a "wise use" reduction of creation to "natural resources" for the human project. Not surprisingly, radical environmentalists have criticized stewardship as being too anthropocentric (the wolf of "dominion" in shepherd's clothing).

This recent debate has encouraged further thinking on the meaning of "image of God," and an important product of that thinking has been the recognition that the language is drawn from the tradition of temple construction in the ancient Near East. Creation is God's temple, and the last thing placed in the temple is the image of the god.[17] This understanding of what God's "image" means suggests that it is functional and relational, rather than some unique trait (like rationality, conscience, or morality). Humanity's task and privilege is both to model God's care and love to creation, and to articulate creation's praise and worship to the Creator. Creation is not complete without this articulate, conscious human presence; but that presence is flawed if it does not recognize both responsibility to creation, on the one hand, and to the Creator, on the other. (Even nontheistic proponents of the "new story" of creation being told in modern cosmology often recognize the uniqueness of human consciousness, and the mystery that, so far as we know, only on this planet has matter come to be conscious and conscientious, developing an impetus not only to survive but also to care.)

One of the ways that evangelicals are recovering an understanding of the significance for creation of the human presence in it is through a fuller thinking on the meaning of Sabbath. In the numerically significant creation account, completion and rest come not on the sixth day with man, but on the seventh, when God rests in delight at "all the work that he had done in creation." The commandment to observe the Sabbath is thus placed in the context of the finished work of creation. Evangelicals are discovering—with the help of Jewish thinkers like Abraham Heschel—that the Sabbath invites the discipline of recognizing creation as a gift, to be offered back in thankfulness to the creator. Sometimes this uniquely human action of articulated thanks and praise is expressed in terms of the action of a priest (as in Alexander Schmemann's *For the Life of the World*, or Robert Farrar Capon's *An Offering of Uncles: The Priesthood of Adam and the Shape of the World*). It has also produced a good deal of thoughtful writing on the place of the Sabbath in the life of the Christian. Jürgen Moltmann has led the way here in the concluding section of *God in Creation*, but it has been an important theme in many other works (the "Sabbath" poems of Wendell Berry, for example, or *The Sabbath* by Norman Wirzba.). We will consider below (see #9) how the Sabbath celebration of "the old creation" might relate to the eighth-day Christian celebration of the "New Creation." But first we must consider changing evangelical attitudes toward "the fall," and its effect on Creation.

7. Human failure to be the "image of God" is the primary way that creation is fallen; this relational understanding of a "fallen creation" implies that much which Christians have called "natural evil" is nevertheless a part of God's good creation.

A growing awareness that the "image of God" is relational—having to do with how persons relate to God on the one hand and to creation on the other—has prompted new evangelical thinking about the nature of the fallenness of creation.

One of the reasons why the doctrine of creation has languished in evangelical thought may well be belief that creation itself is fallen, and only humanity will be redeemed. The rest of creation is in some sense "expendable" in God's story. This is no longer a tenable position among most thoughtful evangelicals (though it continues as a major influence in dispensationalism, with its picture of a "rapture" in which Christians are lifted out of a world doomed to destruction).

The marginalization of material creation *because it is material* is a Platonic mistake. Nevertheless, there certainly is biblical support for the idea of a fallen creation. Genesis 3 describes a changed relationship; Romans 8 speaks of creation groaning. The frequent promise of "new creation" certainly implies a serious flaw in the *old* creation.

Throughout much of Christian history, biblical passages like these have been taken to mean that an ontological and moral change came upon creation with Adam's sin. Creation was no longer "very good." No longer a garden to be tended, creation became instead a wilderness to be tamed and made humanly useful. Such a view assumes a very different meaning of "image of God," one that stresses power and dominion, not care. But an even greater difficulty with this older idea of a fallen nature—in which death, pain, and carniverosity are all consequences of Adam's sin—is its implication that much of the intricacy and beauty of creation is the result of sin. Scripture gives us a different picture. The lion's strength enables him to kill the antelope; the antelope's speed enables him (sometimes) to escape; nevertheless the young lions, say the Psalmist, "seek their food from God." This wild and risky creation where death plays an important role seems to be God's intention. That this is a mystery with which we are not very comfortable seems to be one of the points of God's answer to Job, which amounts to a guided tour of creation in its wildness and unfathomability.

The gift of creation entails the risk of freedom. To call creation the work of love is to recognize that God does not manipulate creatures, but allows them to be free. But the creator is not aloof from this world of pain. Creation opens up the possibility of the cross; God suffers with his creatures.

8. In recognizing that Jesus on the cross is "the lamb slain before the foundation of the world," evangelicals are beginning to recognize the radical nature of God's love for the whole creation—and to understand what it might mean for human beings to image God for creation.

To take seriously the crucified Jesus as the word in whom all things hold together suggests that vulnerability, as much as power, characterizes God's relationship to creation. In *Love's Endeavour, Love's Expense*, W. H. Vanstone describes all love, including God's love, as "limitless . . . precarious, and . . . vulnerable."[18] In a hymn that sums up his argument, Vanstone writes:

> Thou art God; no monarch Thou
> Thron'd in easy state to reign;
> Thou art God, Whose arms of love
> Aching, bent, the world sustain.

Vanstone's argument was instrumental in the publication of a collection of essays called *The Work of Love: Creation as Kenosis*, in which a variety of scientists and theologians consider the idea of creation through the costly freedom which God gives creatures.[19] Jürgen Moltmann argues in that collection that "it is not God's power that is almighty. What is almighty is his love." Holmes Rolston III, founder and long-time editor of the *Journal of Environmental Ethics*, argues that creation is permeated by self-giving love, evident in cellular and sexual life. He turns the common way of thinking about evolution on its head. Instead of "the selfish gene," he argues, we need to speak of "the giving gene." In the cross, suggests Rolston, we are given a clue to the sacrifice at the heart of creation: "The aura of the cross is cast backwards across the whole global story, and it forever outlines the future."[20]

The idea that God creates by emptying himself, upholding creatures in their freedom but taking upon himself the ultimate consequences of that freedom, is not a widely held view among evangelicals. But it will certainly come to be discussed more thoughtfully in the years ahead, particularly as evangelicals come to terms with the rich but violent history of prehuman life on the earth, and consider the possibility that what we call "evolution" might be God's means of creation. Such a reflection will inevitably cause evangelicals to think more carefully as well about the significance of Jesus' resurrection for creation.

9. The resurrection of Jesus points to a future not just for humanity but also for the whole creation.

One of the most important developments in evangelical thinking about creation is the recovery and reappropriation of the understanding (kept alive and well in the Eastern Orthodox tradition) that the resurrection is good news not only for people but also for all creation. Christians are beginning to consider the possibility that violence and death have been a part of the creation story from the beginning. The cross reveals something crucial about the nature of the Creator, and sheds light on the mystery of suffering. But the resurrection speaks to an even grimmer aspect of the "new story" of creation. Science points to the destruction of creation—on the earthly and solar level, the likelihood that the sun may die the death of a nova, and take the scorched earth with it; on the universe level, the likelihood that entropy will continue to an ultimate cooling off of the cosmos to absolute zero. The fact that such ends might be billions or trillions of years in the future does not obviate the fact that creation too will die. But the resurrection is the evangelical promise that "the last enemy to be destroyed is death." It is good news not just for humanity but also for the whole created order.

That Jesus' resurrection is the beginning of a new creation is hinted in the numerical symbolism that "the first day of the week" is also "the eighth day"—the day after the Sabbath, the celebration of the old creation, and the beginning of the new creation. Moltmann explores the relation of old and new, Sabbath and Sunday in *God in Creation*, where he suggests, "It would be a useful practical step...if the *eve* of Sunday were allowed to flow into a Sabbath stillness....[A]fter the week's work one comes to rest in God's presence, sensing on this evening something of the divine "completion" of creation. Worship on Sunday morning can then be set wholly in the liberty of Christ's resurrection for the new creation."[21]

As John Updike put it in a famous poem, "If the cells' dissolution did not re-knit, the amino acids rekindle, the church will fall." The resurrection, the foundation of evangelical belief, puts not only the church on the strongest possible foundation but the whole material universe as well. Wright puts this powerfully in *Surprised by Hope*. In commenting on 1 Corinthians 15, Wright argues,

> If evolutionary optimism is squelched by, among other things, the sober estimates of the scientists that the universe as we know it today is running out of steam and cannot last forever, the gospel of Jesus Christ announces that what God did for Jesus at Easter he will do not only for all those who are "in Christ" but also for the entire cosmos. It will be an act of new creation, parallel to and derived from the act of new creation when God raised Jesus from the dead.[22]

This understanding that the resurrection is good news for creation is having an important influence on how evangelicals are living out their belief.

10. Evangelicals increasingly are living out their renewed belief that the Christian Gospel is good news for the whole creation.

One of the most visible ways that creation has become an evangelical concern is through a recognition that the oft-used term "the environment" is an inadequate name for the creation, which is recognized repeatedly as good in Genesis 1. It is the creation with which God makes the first recorded covenant (in Genesis 9, at the end of the flood story), and it is creation's "all things" that hold together and are reconciled to God in Christ (Col. 1). The generally anti-Christian tone of the environmental movement has driven Christian thinkers back to the riches of Scripture and tradition to recover and restate many of the ideas summarized in these theses. A very early (1970) contribution was Francis Schaeffer's *Pollution and the Death of Man*, in which he argued that the church and Christian communities ought to be "pilot plants" for the new creation. Today there are at least half a dozen books whose title is some variation on the phrase "Caring for Creation," most of them by writers of evangelical persuasion.

A growing number of Christian organizations see that the care of creation is an essential part of the Gospel—for example, the "Evangelical Environmental Network," which has issued a widely circulated "Evangelical Declaration on the Care of Creation." Beginning in the early 1980s, the AuSable center in Michigan began hosting a series of forums on the care of creation. Those forums brought scientists and theologians together, produced many important publications, and conducted ongoing education in "creation care" for students in evangelical colleges. Even more widespread is A Rocha International, with some presence in over twenty countries. It began as a mission in Portugal whose founders Peter (an Anglican minister) and Miranda Harris saw the scientific study and preservation of birds and their migratory habitat as parts of Christian mission. Peter's books *Under the Bright Wings* and *Kingfisher's Fire* tell the story of the growing embodiment of that theological vision.

All such Christian "creation care" programs live in theological tension between their own committed work and a recognition that ultimately "the earth is the Lord's," and it is God who cares for and saves creation, not human persons. But it is a tension shared by the increasing number of Christians who see their work in the world—whether in science, politics, agriculture, the arts, homemaking, or education—as a kind of sharing in the kingdom of God. (The practical creational implications of that phrase from the Lord's Prayer, "Your kingdom come, on earth, as in heaven" have been noted by many). Here the Reformed tradition, with roots via Abraham Kuyper back into Calvin's recognition that the whole creation is a theater for the mighty works of God, has been an important resource (as, for example, in Al Wolters' influential little book *Creation Regained: A Transforming View of the World*).[23]

But what is the continuity between evangelical work and God's work? In some way that question is being answered by recovery of the insight that Christ as the new Adam invites a perfected humanity into the work of the Trinity. Though there is much mystery here, the principle is put clearly in *Voicing Creation's Praise*, a foundational work on theology and art by Jeremy Begbie. In his conclusion to a succinct summary of the twofold movement—of God in Christ toward creation, and of creation in Christ (Col. 1:17 and Acts 17:27–28) toward God—Begbie proposes a Trinitarian summary of the doctrine of creation which evangelicals are retrieving: "In Christ, our broken and distorted humanity has been reestablished in its proper orientation toward the Creator . . . through the Holy Spirit we are invited to share in the renewed humanity of Christ . . . to be drawn in the Spirit through Christ into God's own life will inevitably carry with it an obligation towards the created order, to bring creation to praise its maker."[24]

NOTES

1. Colin Gunton, *The Triune Creator: A Historical and Systematic Study* (Grand Rapids: Eerdmans, 1998), 3.

2. Evangelicals reject pantheism, but are a little more ambivalent about a similar-sounding term, "pan-entheism," a word that means not "all is God" (pantheism), but all things are *in* God. Though it has been colored by its association with process theology, Jürgen Moltmann, among others, has suggested that there is a fully orthodox "panentheism"—as suggested in Col. 1: 17 and Acts 17:27–28.

3. Clark H. Pinnock, *Flame of Love: A Theology of the Holy Spirit* (Downers Grove, Ill.: InterVarsity Press, 1996), 55.

4. J.R.R. Tolkien, "On Fairy Stories" in C. S. Lewis, ed. *Essays Presented to Charles Williams* (Grand Rapids: Eerdmans, 1966), 72.

5. C. S. Lewis, *George MacDonald: An Anthology* (New York: Macmillan, 1960), 21.

6. G. K. Chesterton, *Orthodoxy* (Vancouver: Regent College Publishing, 2004), 62.

7. The Christian creeds were formulated in response to other needs; they are not at all in tension with the triune involvement in creation being described here.

8. Kallistos Ware, *The Orthodox Way* (Crestwood, N.Y.: St. Vladimir's Seminary Press, 1990), 57.

9. M. B. Foster, "The Christian Doctrine of Creation and the Rise of Modern Natural Science," *Mind* 43, 1934.

10. Michael Polanyi, *Personal Knowledge: Towards a Post-Critical Philosophy* (Chicago: University of Chicago Press, 1958).

11. N. T. Wright, *The New Testament and the People of God* (Minneapolis: Fortress, 1992), 35.

12. See, for example, John Polkinghorne, *Quantum Physics and Theology: An Unexpected Kinship.* (New Haven: Yale University Press, 2007).

13. Cited in E. O. Wilson, *Consilience: The Unity of Knowledge* (New York: Random House, 1998), 53.

14. Colin Gunton, *The One, the Three, and the Many: God, Creation, and the Culture of Modernity* (Cambridge: Cambridge University Press, 1993), 229.

15. Jeremy Begbie, *Voicing Creation's Praise: Towards a Theology of the Arts* (London: T & T Clark, 1991). See esp. 142 ff., "Calvinism, Christ and Art."

16. Pinnock, *Flame of Love*, 56.

17. Rikki Watts, "On the Edge of the Millennium: Making Sense of Genesis 1," in *Living in the Lamblight*, ed. Hans Boersma (Vancouver: Regent College, 2001), 129–151. See also John Walton, *The Lost World of Genesis One* (Downer's Grove, Ill.: IVP Academic, 2009).

18. W. H. Vanstone, *Love's Endeavour, Love's Expense: The Response of Being to the Love of God* (London: Darton, Longman and Todd, 1977), 53.

19. John Polkinghorne, ed. *The Work of Love: Creation as Kenosis* (Grand Rapids: Eerdmans, 2001).

20. Holmes Rolston III, "Kenosis and Nature," in Polkinghorne, *The Work of Love*, 60.

21. Jürgen Moltmann, *God in Creation* (New York: Harper Collins, 1991), 296.

22. N. T. Wright, *Surprised by Hope* (New York, Harper, 2008), 99.

23. Al Wolters, *Creation Regained: A Transforming View of the World* (Grand Rapids: Eerdmans, 1986).

24. Jeremy Begbie, *Voicing Creation's Praise*, 178.

BIBLIOGRAPHY

Begbie, Jeremy. *Voicing Creation's Praise.* London: T & T Clark, 1991.

Gunton, Colin, *The One, the Three and the Many: God, Creation and the Culture of Modernity.* Cambridge: Cambridge University Press, 1993.

———. *Christ and Creation.* Carlisle, Paternoster Press, 1992.

———. *The Triune Creator.* Grand Rapids: Eerdmans, 1998.

Moltmann, Jürgen, *God in Creation.* San Francisco: Harper, 1985.

Lamoreux, Denis O. *Evolutionary Creation: A Christian Approach to Evolution.* Eugene, Ore.: Wipf and Stock, 2008.

Pinnock, Clark. *Flame of Love: A Theology of the Holy Spirit.* Downers Grove, Ill.: InterVarsity Press, 1996.

Polkinghorne, John. *Science and the Trinity: The Christian Encounter with Reality.* New Haven: Yale University Press, 2004.

———, ed. *The Work of Love: Creation as Kenosis.* Grand Rapids: Eerdmans, 2001.

Vanstone, W. H. *Love's Endeavour, Love's Expense: The Response of Being to the Love of God.* London: Darton, Longman and Todd, 1977.

Wright, N. T. *Surprised by Hope.* New York: Harpers, 2008.

CHAPTER 8

SIN

HENRI A. G. BLOCHER

EVANGELICAL theology focuses on sin as the key aspect of the human predicament, and so do evangelical preaching and piety. Barr highlighted the trait in sarcastic tones: for the targets of his critique, "sin is a fearful horror, ever-present and all-embracing." Its doctrine functions as *the* presupposition of the rest.[1] Many Bible readers, not all of them happy with this presupposition, grant that it nevertheless reflects the mind of the biblical authors. The theme is at least implicit everywhere, and dominates characteristic biblical genres. "The prophetic literature," Geoffrey Bromiley observes, "is one long protest against the various forms of sin both against God and against neighbor."[2] Important psalms are devoted to confession, and many denounce the sinful behavior of enemies. Strikingly, the "redemption" Israel needs is from "iniquities" or guilt (Ps. 130). The Gospel proclaims the remission of sins (Luke 1:77 and 24:47, a significant *inclusio* in the arrangement of the Gospel), with the cross of Jesus as the source (which truth is revealed in the resurrection): this death, according to God's plan, was *for our sins* (1 Cor. 15:3; Rom. 4:25, etc.). Doing away with sin was Christ's mission (1 John 3:5; Heb. 9:26): he repeatedly stated that he had come for sinners, precisely to shed his blood as the ransom-price that could secure their forgiveness (Matt. 9:13; 20:28; 26:28). The angel explained his name with reference to sins (Matt. 1:21) and John the Baptist hailed him as the Lamb of God who takes away (and bears—double meaning of *airôn*) the sin of the world (John 1:29). Cornelius Plantinga forcefully reminds us that "speaking of grace without sin... is to trivialize the cross of Jesus Christ, to skate past all the struggling by good people down the ages to forgive, accept, and rehabilitate sinners, including themselves, and therefore to cheapen the grace of God that always comes to us with blood on it."[3]

Preoccupation with sin is no monopoly of evangelicals. Its insistence distinguishes Christianity from other main religions. It characterizes the Western form as compared with Eastern Orthodoxy, with dramatic emphasis in areas of Augustinian influence. The Protestant Reformers thought they were restoring the Augustinian sense and charged the late Middle Ages with a watered-down doctrine of human sinfulness. The Anabaptists themselves, though no friends of Augustine, shared in a convergent accentuation—in the form of a pessimistic view of the "world" as Satan's realm from which they had to separate.[4] Pietism and Puritanism, the proximate sources of the evangelical movement, and the revivals that followed in their train, concentrated on personal sin and guilt, and the sanctification struggle against them. In the nineteenth century, this was often combined by evangelicals with a negative appraisal of cultural changes, buttressed by the expectation of an imminent Apostasy and Great Tribulation thought to be foretold in biblical prophecy. Orthodoxy was losing its former hold on social life, while Liberalism was espousing modernistic optimism at the price of tenets essential to Christian truth. Not all of this was healthy: "The unspoken maxim," Ted Peters suggests, had become "the guiltier I feel, the closer to God I am."[5] It is difficult to ignore a neurotic climate, and the manipulation of guilt feelings.

But not all of this was unhealthy. The magnitude of achievements in relief work, education, charitable institutions, and the growth of the missionary movement attest a remarkable vitality among "sin-obsessed" evangelicals. Liberal theologies lack a unified focus; when they do not revel in the dissolution of meaning and dance with nihilistic wolves, they spend most of their energy in fighting social evils and structural sin.

This may be true also of a number of evangelicals, who have worked hard at recovering a sociopolitical conscience.[6] A significant minority, the new band of "emergent" postconservatives, who could fast evolve into postevangelicals, tones down the traditional accent on guilt.[7] Nevertheless, a consistent majority of theologians—a massive majority if one looks beyond the borders of the English-speaking world—feels constrained by the Word of God to abide by the former insistence on sin and guilt: it remains an evangelical distinction.

Gaining a True Knowledge of Sin

The doctrine of sin requires specific *prolegomena*. How can one speak responsibly on the topic? Three questions call for consideration. May we listen to universal experience, and especially the voice of "conscience"? If "law" is to play a major role, how should we distinguish among natural law, positive law, laws of nature, and the law of special revelation? Does the true light on sin ultimately fall from the law or the gospel? Though not all theologians have dealt with all three, it is possible to sketch answers.

Herman Bavinck is confident that the Christian message "has already the conscience of all on its side.... All human beings have a notion of good and evil, a conscience which excuses and accuses[;] they are aware of guilt and impurity, they fear punishment and long for redemption."[8]

The role of conscience is highlighted by both biblical and pagan authors. Paul appeals to its witness in his demonstration of universal sinfulness (Rom. 2:15). Stoics emphasized this inner tribunal, and the New Testament concurs: not only Paul (nineteen occurrences of *suneidèsis* in his epistles, plus two in his addresses in Acts, and one as a verb) but also Hebrews (five occurrences). The Old Testament assigned conscience's probative function to the "heart," as can be seen in some passages (1 Sam. 24:6 and 25:31; Job 27:6). Oliver O'Donovan reminds us that the ancient meaning is *self-consciousness*, "especially that uneasy awareness that one has of oneself when one knows one has done something wrong," and deplores the medieval and modern usage that has shifted the meaning to make conscience "the whole faculty of moral understanding and self-direction."[9] Yet this leaves to conscience an important role nonetheless—to show us our sin.

But can conscience be trusted? Is experience a reliable guide to reality? The biblical witness suggests that conscience may be "weak" and generate an "uneasy awareness" even when an act is not truly wrong (1 Cor. 8:7, 10, 12; cf. 10:29); it can be sullied and made insensitive when it ought to accuse more sharply (Titus 1:15); its witness may lull even an apostle into deceptive feelings of peace (1 Cor. 4:4).[10] The human heart is supremely tortuous (Jer. 17:9), callous, and vain; its analytic powers have been plunged into darkness (Eph. 4:18); experience—the selective ways humans perceive, represent, and interpret the world—constantly distorts the truth of reality. Sinners mutilate, misconstrue, and reverse the objective testimony of their own lives. Conscience as human experience, therefore, can function as the symptom that something has gone wrong (Paul's interest in Rom. 2), but is unable to go further. It warns of the presence of sin, but is unable to give sure knowledge. Common grace—or the divine preservation of created substance and order—ensures that sinners keep a vague, deformed, and partial awareness of their alienation as can still be used as a substratum, but nothing more. Something else is required.[11]

The apostle associates debates within the conscience with the "work of the law" written on the hearts of Gentiles who "do not have the law" and yet "are law unto themselves" (Rom. 2:14–15). Most evangelical scholars follow Calvin here, rather than Augustine and Barth, by arguing that non-Christian Gentiles are in view, and that the "work of the law" is the work prescribed by the law, which even Gentiles happen to do at times (rather than the condemnation the law brings about, or its pedagogical work leading to Christ). Since Paul concludes his development with the statement that "through the law sin is recognized/accurately known (*epignôsis*)" (Rom. 3:20b), readers have wondered ever since which law he means.

Romans 2:14–15 is the proof-text for the view prevalent in Catholic tradition: Paul meant the moral law, comprising permanent standards of right and wrong, and a reflection of the eternal law of God's holiness, which is engraved on the spiritual creature's conscience, and has been part of human nature since creation. Evangelicals generally accept the idea of such a *natural* law, whereby sin would be defined negatively (telling us what we are not to do or be), but they doubt the actual accessibility of its knowledge. For, they say, the same deficiencies that make the witness of conscience uncertain also hinder access to God's eternal law. For similar reasons, evangelicals do not share the confidence in "reason" shown by John Paul II's *Veritatis Splendor.* Some insist that directions built into our constitution were never supposed to be the only guide of behavior: even in Eden, they were "interpreted" by the Word of special revelation (Gen. 2:16–17; cf. 1:28–30).[12] Evangelicals concede that because of common grace, remnants of the natural engraving retain a measure of efficacy: though indecisive, the reasonings they inspire may assist in persuading sinners about their sins. And also because of common grace, "positive law" plays a role, either positive moral law embedded in culture or enacted in positive law. Yet immorality and crime do not always coincide with sin—they only overlap![13]

A symbol of this relationship could be the positive legislation God instituted for Israel: it was adapted to the sinful state of the people (Matt. 19:8), can be compared with the codes of neighboring nations, and yet it also defined sin in the true God's sight. The law given to Israel was part of special revelation. Once freed from the trappings that belonged to preparation and come to its own in the economy of fulfilment, this law became the law of God for all humankind, through which sin can be identified and known.

Since the law of God republishes the natural law in a purified version—it is both ancient and new (1 John 2:7–8), just as the Redeemer is the Creator—it recapitulates previous forms and provides the necessary and sufficient standard by which to interpret those forms.

A fourth kind of law is the set of laws of nature that God imposed on cosmic phenomena, to regulate their sequence, to bind consequence B to cause A, to establish ordered patterns for the movements of his creatures (e.g. Jer. 31:35–36). It is not labelled "moral," for one does not incur guilt if one tries to escape its grip, and in a sense it is physically unbreakable. It is no sin if one defies the law of gravity and soars above the clouds on one's ultra-light. In that case, the law of gravity still applies, but other laws are used to offset its effects.

But the relationship between sin and the laws of nature is not so simple. Human behavior is part of the cosmic nexus. It interferes with the patterns God established in his wisdom. If a man foolishly disregards elements of the physical law—if he rolls onto a bridge twice the weight the bridge can bear, if he despises the alternation of night and day, if he meddles in the DNA material of some bacteria and new diseases spread—is there no sinful note in his attitude toward this fourth kind of law? Deeper still: the law of effect B following A applies to human behavior itself, inwardly or intrinsically. Psychology and sociology are able to predict, on the basis of A entailing B, acts that are commonly categorized as "sins." How relevant are they to the knowledge of sin?

The question opens largely uncharted territory to theologians. Resistance against a deterministic outlook—which is a reckless extrapolation from the (limited) predictive power of the social sciences—appears to be both possible and necessary. Yet psychological and sociological competence does indeed help us assess the acts of sinners, and one discovers biblical hints pointing in the same direction. The task that lies ahead for evangelicals is that of thinking through theologically how that help is fruitfully received. The task has been undertaken in promising fashion, mostly by Christian psychologists,[14] but there is still much digging and building, maybe pulling down and clearing, to do.

Taking their cue from Romans 3:20, most theologians look to the law to gain knowledge of sin. Some, however, question this orientation and rather go to the gospel. Gerrit Cornelis Berkouwer excoriates an "abstract" use of the law, of which Pietism put forth an extreme example with the *Busskampf* (repentance-struggle) law, and only law was to be preached first, to bring about repentance, and when repentance had been achieved grace could be announced.[15]

Berkouwer contends that the law made sin manifest through its historical role: Israel misunderstood the divine intention, and used the law as an instrument of self-justification, the most odious of all sins.[16] For him, "there remains no formal 'mirror'-idea of the law with the correlative of a sheerly intellectual knowledge of the law's legal [*sic*] demands."[17] Sin is seen for what it is only in the forgiveness of sins, at the foot of the cross.[18] Berkouwer's polemic against "a legal order anticipating, or giving way to, the order of God's grace"[19] may reflect Barthian influence on his thought: Karl Barth fearlessly smashed to pieces the binary pattern of law and gospel, covenant "of works" and covenant of grace. He insisted on one covenant in Christ—and in fact called the law "the form of the Gospel," logically subsequent to the Gospel.[20] In bold obedience to his "Christological concentration," Barth drew the doctrine of sin from the heart of the Gospel: the person of Jesus Christ. The analysis elaborated in the *Church Dogmatics IV/1* starts from a Chalcedonian confession: Christ as God humbled himself, and therefore sin should be seen as pride; Christ as man was raised to heights of glory, and therefore sin should be seen as sloth, sluggishness, inertia, *akèdia;* Christ as the God-man is the warrant and witness of the union of God and humanity, and therefore sin should be seen as the lie. Indeed, for Barth, the knowledge of sin comes through the gospel!

Evangelicals, for the most part, have closed their ears to the song of Barth's sirens. Together with many Lutheran critics, they have maintained the distinction of the two phases, and the order—not to be reversed—of law and gospel; they have questioned the way Barth understands and practices Christological concentration and denied that every individual be "in Christ" (the incarnate Christ) by virtue of the first creation.[21] They have suspected Barth's inferences from Christology to be rather arbitrary, covertly guided by preconceived ideas. But Berkouwer's stance, which is less radical and revolutionary, should not escape attention.

Berkouwer's account of the role of the law is hardly convincing; his interpretation of Romans 3:20 resembles special pleading (not exploring a way but explaining away!). Nowhere does Paul suggest that the failure of the law derives from the intolerable impiety of justification by works: this is a Bultmannian misunderstanding rather than Barthian, at the opposite pole from the New Perspective on Paul and Judaism.

The weakness of the law was the inability of the flesh to meet its righteous demands (Rom. 8:3–4), and the apostle frankly admitted that righteousness would be reached by the law *if* the law provided the life-power of obedience (Gal. 3:21). Leviticus 18:5 does define a God-instituted way of justification in Paul's reading (Rom. 10:5; Gal. 3:12),[22] though it was intended to fail and thus to lead beyond itself to Christ (Gal. 3:22–24). If it fails for all, it is due to transgression by humans unable to obey. But then their refusal to acknowledge this fact, and their insistence they can provide "enough" satisfaction, using the law to foster this illusion—this pattern becomes another pernicious form of sin.

When this is clarified, one should heed Berkouwer's warnings. Though the Word of special revelation is less easy to circumvent than the message of the created order, the tortuous heart of sinners will always invent ways to misconstrue divine precepts. Subjectively, the encounter of darkened and distorted powers of understanding with the law alone will result in grievous misapprehension. The healing light of grace is required to restore spiritual eyesight. Romans 3:20, then, is to be understood as speaking of the objective identification of sin: sin can be named by reference to the law, while true self-knowledge comes to sinners only when they receive forgiveness. Furthermore, the distinction (Luther's *discrimen*) between law and gospel should not become a simplistic disjunction. The gospel, as it presupposes the law, also implies a kind of republication: God's will for the walk of his children comes out in exact detail, and its deeper intentions are better perceived. It sharpens the knowledge of sin. The gospel reveals how God in his mysterious, baffling, transcendent, wisdom (1 Cor. 2:7–9) used the most heinous of all human sins to overcome sin for ever, to wipe off the guilt and break the tyranny for ever. The cross supremely reveals human sin. Knowledge of sin comes through the law, through the gospel, and through the cross—none of these in isolation.

Searching for a Definition of Sin

In this light, what is sin? "It is," Bromiley answers, "disobedience, unbelief, ignorance, the positive assertion of usurped autonomy, and the wicked deviation, or violation of God's righteous will and law."[23] This is definition by condensed description (often the most helpful kind). However, many seek a more analytical definition.

Many evangelicals suggest a negative statement similar to Strong's: "Sin is lack of conformity to the moral law of God, either in act, disposition or state."[24] Strong quotes from an older divine, whom he mistakenly identifies as Calvin, with the Latin equivalent: *Illegalitas, seu difformitas a lege.*[25] The text commonly appealed to is 1 John 3:4, "Sin is lawlessness." The Greek word for "lawlessness," *anomia*, comes from the privative prefix and *nomos*, the law. But a more scientific philology suggests a different translation: in Judaism and in the New Testament, the connotation of *anomia* is that of end-time rebellion, paroxystic opposition to God, in league with the Devil.[26] Plantinga widens the negative reference by considering *shalom* and covenant: "Sin is not only the breaking of the law but also the breaking of covenant with one's savior."[27] He recalls the interpersonal dimension by citing "any act—any thought, desire, emotion, word or deed—or its particular absence, that displeases God and deserves blame." He also describes sin as a "disposition."[28] This is a welcome amplification but not a departure from the usual position. The negative definition and the primary reference to law agree with the tenor of Scripture generally.

One advantage to this extended definition is that it fits the privative, and therefore parasitic, character of evil. As introduced by Origen and refined by Augustine, the insight that evil (and the human evil of sin) has no positive being has been appropriated by evangelical theology. Creation by the only God who is absolute Goodness rules out any substantial view of sin. Being belongs to God and derivatively to his creatures, which are good inasmuch as they are his creatures (1 Tim. 4:4). Biblical vocabulary (most evangelical treatments review the main terms, as space limitations do not allow this one to do) and the network of metaphors and symbols bear out this thesis: words abound with a negative element (equivalent to *un*righteousness, *dis*obedience, *im*piety...), linked to roots implying inconsistency, emptiness, vanity, with images of darkness, chaos, destruction, and disease. Berkouwer aptly refutes suggestions that the negative understanding (more accurately, privative: the lack or deprivation of something that ought to be there) entails a minimizing of its noxiousness.[29] The metaphors to tell how detrimental sin proves to be, though it has no being, are those of *corruption* and *perversion*. Evil is the corruption of some good (Gen. 6:11–12 onward) and so relative or "secondary."[30] Yet it wields enormous destructive, dehumanizing power: "Sin is fruitful just because, like a virus, it attaches the life force and dynamics of its host."[31] Comparison with viruses is enlightening: "Corruption is spiritual AIDS—the mysterious, infectious, and progressive attack on our spiritual immune system that eventually breaks it down and opens the way for hordes of opportunistic sins."[32] One muses over the possible correspondence of specific pathologies and the form of corruption that prevails in a given epoch: in biblical times, leprosy was typical, with the stigma of uncleanness; triumphant modernity could discern the image of its sin in cancer (the map of our mega-cities resembles the picture of a cancerous cell); our decaying modernity, with all defense mechanisms vilified, reveals an AIDS-stricken spirit! "Viruses are the ultimate parasites,"[33] and sin as corruption may be said to be a parasitic affection, as many have perceived.[34] Its symbiosis with goodness explains why it is so difficult to eradicate: "Sin has dug in, and, like a tick, burrows deeper when we try to remove it."[35]

Perversion means displacing or disturbing hierarchies, spoiling beneficial order or harmony. Augustine famously interpreted sin as turning the order of love upside down: using (*uti*) what we should enjoy (*frui*, enjoy for itself, as the ultimate end, with goodness desired for its own sake) and enjoying what we should only use. In other words, we try to use God, while we make false gods out of creatures. We think we can find in them our final beatitude and sacrifice to them our lives, while we should only see them as means in the service of God. Evangelicals readily adopt this insight, in line with the prophets' unrelenting denunciation of idolatry, and Paul's in the New Testament (remembering that greed is one form of idolatry, Col. 3:5).

Calvin charged the human spirit with being "at all times a perpetual workshop to forge idols" (*Institutes of the Christian Religion* I.xi.8). Ted Peters recalls Luther's existential definition, "That to which your heart clings and entrusts itself is, I say, your God" (*The Large Catechism*), and, with a splendid quotation from Martin Luther King, Jr., analyzes idolatry in a thoroughly evangelical fashion.[36]

The major importance of idolatry as the perversion lying deep in human sin draws attention to the religious status of sin: it is committed, or happens, *coram Deo* (in the sight of God), and therefore differs from the common conception of immorality as simply the violation of a rule.[37] This is why the biblical outlook rules out autonomous ethics and celebrates the coincidence of holiness and morality in God.

Many inquire about the "essence" of sin, its first principle. The ancient church emphasized concupiscence, Augustine pride, the Reformers unbelief, many moderns (Strong included) selfishness or lovelessness. Berkouwer settles for this last proposal ("Man's sin is *lovelessness*"), since sin is lawlessness and the law is summed up in the love-command. He wisely adds, "Nevertheless, it is wrong to ignore the other descriptions of sin and to have an open eye for only this central, all-inclusive meaning of God's law."[38]

But starting from the command does not guarantee reaching unambiguous conclusions. How do we most disobey? When we love ourselves? When we hate God and neighbor? When we remain indifferent? When we love things beyond measure? Close association with nonbiblical worldviews casts suspicion on some interpretations: when Platonic influence makes us obsessively suspicious of the senses, or when modern idealism tends to accuse particularity as such, or when evolutionary ideologies locate the cause of sin in obsolete biological impulses. But the difficulty in choosing among other proposals on biblical and other grounds suggests that the quest cannot succeed. The essence eludes our grasp. After all, "essence" only belongs to being. Reason was made to appreciate the harmony of God's creation, and sin is the *other.* "Sin," Plantinga discerns, "is finally unknown, irrational, alien."[39] We approach sin through negative and formal definitions, and, obliquely through metaphors (corruption, etc.). Or as Plato said of the "receptacle," only "through a bastard kind of reasoning" (*Timaeus* 52B).

One more feature belongs to the notion of sin: its ascription to the will. It comes under the exercise of freedom. Augustine brilliantly defended the point in his early treatise on free will, *De libero arbitrio* (book I, but also II.i.1 or III.xvii.49). He maintained this conviction, and in his late *Retractationes* protested against the Pelagian misuse of his formulas (I.ix.3–4). His beautiful witness to the nature of sin still stands: "I have not found a substance, but the perversity of a will that turns away from the supreme substance, from Thee, O God, and turns to inferior things—rejecting its own innermost interests and inflates itself outwardly" (*Confessiones* VII. xvi.22). This has been professed by the tradition. Calvin, for instance, explains that sin remains sinful and the sinner remains responsible even though it involves a spiritual slavery, because it remains willful and uncoerced. It is not nonwilling (*noluntas*) but still a case of willing (*voluntas*) (*Institutes* II.iv.1). Scripture supports this proposition. Various passages make sin both a matter of choice (Prov. 1:29; Is. 42:24; John 3:19) and a disposition of the will (Eph. 2:3; 1 Pet. 4:3). Perhaps more telling, the source of sin is the heart, according to the sweeping statement of Genesis 6:5 and to our Lord's indictment (Matt. 15:18–20). The heart is the seat of reason and will, the latter two always intertwined.

We must not be blind to difficulties that arise. Separately from the theme of sin's slavery, Scripture speaks of *involuntary* sins. This is the usual Septuagint translation for the sins of "error" (Lev. 4, four times; Nbs. 15:24–29, eight); they are also called sins "of ignorance" (Lev. 5:18; 22:14), a word used in Hebrews (9:7). The choice of the word *hamartia* for human evil in the Septuagint (ratified by the New Testament) gives pause to thought: Aristotle gives no prominence to the term, but uses it for semivoluntary faults, half-way between "unrighteousness" and "bad luck, blunder" (*atuchèma*) (*Nicomachean Ethics* V.10.1135b). Modern awareness of determinisms—social, psychological, biological, and genetic—that weigh upon the "willing" of humans, compounds the problem: Is "free will" more than an illusion? The question appears to be a challenge for evangelical theologians.

Differentiating between degrees and levels of freedom, with "threshold effects," cannot be avoided. How can it be *thought* in depth? The suggestion is offered here that a radical distinction must be made between created causalities and the divine Causality (if the word is to be used) which is unique, wholly other—for in Him we live, we move and we *are* (everything we are). "Incompatibilism" is valid for the former, but not for God.[40]

Only the all-embracing Causality of God can "redeem" the partial causalities (determinisms) of created agents or factors and safeguard a significant level of freedom among human beings. Dependence on the Father, which uniquely grounds created freedom, since He controls all determinations and plays with them in infinite tactfulness (they are his "hands"), protects his sons and daughters from the stifling effects of worldly determinations by themselves.

Mapping the Diversity of Sin and Its Consequences

Scripture and tradition speak of *sin* and of *sins*. Evangelicals do well to keep the balance between the two: attention to sin "singular" only turns it into an abstract force, a kind of metaphysical determinant of the human condition. But a focus on sin*s* only, specific and particular, minimizes their interrelatedness, ignores the soil from which they spring—or, to take Jesus' other metaphor, the tree which bears the fruit—and forgets the constitution of a "world of iniquity," framework for the sinful life.

The combination of singular and plural can be explored through several distinctions. A rather unproblematic one is that of *commission* and *omission*

(Jas. 4:17). It already suggests that deliberate "acts" are not the only category. The distinctions among act, disposition and state are traditional, and are accepted by most evangelical scholars. Among them, the emphasis on states prevails with Augustinians, especially Reformed, whereas Arminians concentrate on discrete sinful acts and tend to qualify the sinful character of the corruption of "nature" (which they do not deny). One pleads that the distinction should not be hardened into separation: acts belong to the tissue of moral life, their causes and motives make them part of the state from which they stem, and which they, in turn, modify by their consequences; conversely, states are dynamic processes which involve at every moment the decision (usually implicit decision) to confirm or to change the status quo. An act is a state expressed, and a state is an act maintained and renewed through time.

Disposition, as mediating between act and state, provides a useful concept. Strong explains, "besides substance and acts, there are habits, tendencies, proclivities, some of them native and some of them acquired. They are voluntary, and have moral character."[41] In a way reminiscent of Nietzsche, he speaks of the moral and spiritual taste of the person: "By taste we mean the direction of man's love, the bent of his affections, the trend of his will."[42] It could translate Paul's *phronema* in Romans 8:5–7 as "affection, outlook, mindset, desire, interests." Evangelicals should welcome McFadyen's elaboration of the theme when he highlights the dynamics of personal identity and life-orientation: "Distortions in willing evidence distortions at the core of personal identity, in the basic trajectory and pattern of intentionality."[43]

Sins differ in degree. Some are lighter and some graver (Ps. 19:13; John 19:11; Luke 12:47–48), though the Lord's appreciation for this distinction may surprise us (lenient in Gen. 12:10–20, severe in Nbs. 20:6–12). Evangelicals have little use, however, for categorical classifications, which had an enormous impact on Catholic spirituality. Most would not object to the selection of the seven "capital sins" (which should not be confused with "mortal sins"): since Gregory the Great (*Moralia* XXXI), the "capital sins," *head-sins*, are those which generate others, irrespective of their intrinsic seriousness. Evangelicals reject the idea of "venial sins," that is, sins forgivable by virtue of their lack of importance. These are sins so light that they do not count for destiny, and are compensated by good works—or for those which carry a little more weight, by purgatory sufferings.[44] Evangelicals reply that breaking a minor article of the law renders one guilty of the whole (Jas. 2:10), and a few dead flies spoil the whole bottle of perfume (Eccles. 10:1). They agree with Michel du Bay, who was later condemned by the Roman Church, that all sins are, of themselves, mortal. 1 John 5:16–17 is to be understood of the difference between sins committed by a brother, which will be forgiven through faith in Christ, and the sin of the antichrists (2:18–23; 4:1–6; 5:10), which ruins the truth of the gospel and therefore leads to death.

One recognizes that Catholic spiritual directors have not condoned lighthearted sinning and have demanded serious self-examination; they have labeled "venial sin" what Protestants may have considered mere temptation, with no guilt incurred. The Protestant and evangelical mind is drawn to dramatic simplification (either/or), whereas Roman Catholic logic delights in comparisons of all shades of gray, provided they lead to teachable reverence for the Mother Church. Plantinga brings together the recognition of degrees and evangelical radicality: "All sin is equally wrong, but not all sin is equally bad."[45] On the unforgivable "blasphemy against the Spirit," Matt. 12:31–32, torrents of ink have flown. Berkouwer's treatment attracts followers: there is no mystery left, the rejection of God's offer of grace brought to the soul by the Spirit seals off the only access to forgiveness. So it is unforgivable by virtue of its own working.[46]

Since it corrupts the rich variety of created beings and all their relations, sin can show an almost infinite diversity. In general, it introduces itself under the guise of some good (cf. Gen. 3:6): this is why temptation is seductive. One should hesitate, however, before making this a universal rule, with the presupposition that humans always choose what looks good in their eyes. Plantinga admits that sin "tries to bag a good of some kind" but makes the shrewd observation: "As human life degenerates, as people explore deeper and deeper recesses of evil, they begin to seek pleasure not in such created goods as sex or material plenty or the exercise of dominion. They seek it instead in the very dynamics of sin"; they rebel "for the hell of it."[47] If the motive becomes evident at the end of sin's logic, it must have been there from the start—together with the desire for pleasurable experiences, a deep suicidal hatred of being and beauty, because being and beauty are of God.

Other antithetical forms of sin coexist. Barth's analysis in terms of pride *and sloth* is a timely reminder: not only pride but also the reverse deny God's intention. Feminist theologians rightly brand as *akèdia* the false humility and patience, the spurious sacrificial attitude, that so many preachers imposed upon their hearers, especially their female hearers. There is little warrant, however, for the thesis which would specialize forms of sin: pride for males and sloth for females. The latter would then be exhorted to assert themselves, and stand by their own resources. If self-assertion was the trap into which many males have fallen, to their own ruin, it will prove as deadly for women.[48] Scripture warns all against temptations of both the right and the left-hand side (Josh. 1:7)!

With the singular use of "sin" arises the question of its extent. It contaminates all members of the race (from 1 Kgs. 8:46 to 1 John 1:8) from the earliest age (Gen. 8:21)—except Jesus Christ. Evangelicals rule out all other exceptions, with Thomas Aquinas (*Summa theologia* Ia–IIae, qu. 81, art. 3). They reject, as he did, Mary's Immaculate Conception (yet he still thought she benefited from a "prevenient purification" while in her mother's womb, art. 5 ad 3m; cf. IIIa, qu. 27). Sin also extends to the whole of the person's being and faculties (Is. 59:3–11; Rom. 3:13–18; Titus 1:15). This is called "total depravity": it is total extensively, not intensively: there is nothing intact, everything is more or less damaged.[49] Arminians will minimize and speak of propensities that do not carry guilt, but nonetheless acknowledge an evil, corrupt bent. Non-Arminians insist propensities are sinful.

Divergence sharpens on the issue of free will. The Reformed point to slavery and inability (John 8:34; 1 Cor. 2:14): free will is concretely *servum-arbitrium*.

Arminians maintain (supposing a general grace) the will's freedom, in the sense of absolute and autonomous self-determination.[50] Opinions also vary on the noetic effects of sin: the darkening of intelligence. The Kuyperian school, radically Augustinian (one must believe to understand), emphasizes the disorientation of reason also in earthly matters: heart-apostasy (Dooyeweerd) or self-absolutizing presuppositions (Van Til) vitiate all intellectual endeavors.[51] One notes that Aquinas was less optimistic than often represented: he argues that reason is weakened and stupefied (*hebetatur, Summa theol.* Ia–IIae, qu. 85, art. 3 respondeo). He says that natural ability remains (art. 2 ad 3m) but only in the way the faculty of sight remains in the blind man!

The bond of slavery does not consist only in habits, errors, mechanisms, and "creases" no one can iron out. Evangelicals receive the scriptural revelation that spiritual agents, which are quasi-personal, also interfere. Sinners are held captive by the devil (Acts 10:38; Heb. 2:14–15). Evangelicals also realize that sin corrupts the social dimensions of human life: it is transpersonal and embodied in "structures" of injustice (Rauschenbusch's insights have filtered through). The Devil uses them to oppress humankind (the "world"), by using our corrupt nature (the "flesh"), thus constituting the enslaving trinity. Some theologians (especially under Wink's influence) have tried to interpret the "Powers" as a first-century representation of the structures. This cannot be accepted as the original meaning, as Peter O'Brien, after John Stott, has shown.[52] It smacks of underhanded demythologization. But the Powers do play with the structures, and both signal the cosmic magnitude of sin's tyranny.

A sin generates sins: the cancer-like proliferation[53] of sin is one consequence, just as bondage to sin is another. The first consequence distinct from sin itself is guilt. It may be one meaning of the Hebrew word *'àwôn* ("iniquity") and is expressed by "bearing one's sin." "We call guilt," Adolf Schlatter wrote, "the perpetual bond that binds the agent to the act."[54] Theologians (e.g., Charles Hodge) have discerned two facets: the *reatus culpae*, the personal demerit; and the *reatus poenae*, the judicial debt and obligation to satisfy justice by undergoing punishment. John Murray criticized this distinction sharply,[55] and Turretin's formulation is probably superior: *reatus in actu primo* (guilty in its primary aspect) and *in actu secundo* (in its secondary aspect).[56] But the meaning is essentially the same. The distinction helps explain the atonement: the judicial debt was transferred to the sinless Redeemer, but we still remain unworthy.

Guilt calls for punishment. Punishment in Scripture is both the "natural" consequence, the "harvest" one reaps (Gal. 5:7–8), and a judicial infliction (God is involved as the theme of "wrath" demonstrates). The proper punishment is death (Rom. 6:23): the consequence of cutting oneself off from the Giver of life, and the restoration of the just order in the moral universe. Is physical death part of the penalty? A majority of evangelical theologians maintain this reading of Genesis 3—the more natural one. Spiritual death, alienation from God, is obvious. The "second death" of everlasting punishment is a contentious topic. The main rival views are annihilationism, a current interpretation of orthodoxy that imagines the damned as rebels for ever, and a revised understanding of orthodoxy that stresses the fixity of death and "reconciliation" in the sense of Colossians 1.[57] Further discussion belongs to the chapter on eschatology.

Discovering the Origin of Sin?

Whence sin in humankind? Most evangelical believers probably answer: "An Enemy did it" (Matt. 13:28). Satan's fall was the beginning. Several theologians appeal to the Lucifer/Cherub passages of Isaiah 14 and Ezekiel 28, though most biblical scholars have seen that a reference to Satan is unlikely there. A sober account makes three points: biblical logic constrains evangelical theology to hold that angels fell, with the warrant of Jude 6; the subject is shrouded in mystery, and it is wiser to refrain from speculating; it does not solve the enigma, since Adam and Eve had no reason to yield. "Through *one man* sin entered into the world" (Rom. 5:12).

The Genesis 3 story is vital for evangelical theology. It captures the original intention of the text, which thinkers like Emil Brunner and Paul Ricoeur well perceived: the disjunction between the origin of being and the origin of evil is of one piece with ethical monotheism and the prophetic call for repentance. Sin is without excuse because it enters the scene later, historically. The evangelicals' distinction today is that they argue in favor of *real* historicity: if one lets it go, the profit of meaning (which Paul Ricoeur wishes to keep) is altered, and thus dissolves. This does not commit them to literalism. The issue is not whether we have an historical account of the Fall, but whether we have the account of an historical Fall. "I do not enter into the question," wrote James Orr, "of how we are to interpret the third chapter of Genesis—whether as history or allegory or myth, or most probably of all, as old tradition clothed in oriental allegorical dress,—but the truth embodied in that narration, viz. the fall of man from an original state of purity, I take to be vital to the Christian view."[58] Though correspondence with the present state of palaeo-anthropology is hard to clarify, one can maintain the thesis responsibly. Even John Goldingay finds the "usefulness" of Genesis 3 "in its assertion that at the beginning of the human story something happened that brought about a once-for-all negative change to humanity's situation."[59]

Most theologians in the Reformed tradition affirm the imputation of Adam's "alien" sin. The "seat" of the doctrine, however can be read otherwise: Romans 5 shows that *our* sins can be imputed to us on the basis of Adam's headship—the springboard for Paul's a fortiori argument. The common distinction between a sin "of nature" (or sinful nature) and "actual" sins is also questionable. A Platonic hypostatisation of "nature" is lurking. It is possible to argue that sin as wilful disposition is germinally, and therefore actually, present even in infants.[60]

Sin's universality almost irresistibly suggests a metaphysical determinant of humanity; only the historical break after the beginning compensates and safeguards the ethical and interpersonal character of sin, as the alien, introduced by the misuse of created freedom. On that basis, sin is the scandal, entailing guilt. On that basis also, it can be redeemed, historically.

NOTES

1. James Barr, *Fundamentalism* (London: S.C.M., 1977), 25 and 177. Barr claims that there is no understanding of sin among those he calls fundamentalists.

2. G. W. Bromiley, "Sin," *International Standard Bible Encyclopaedia*, revised, ed. Geoffrey W. Bromiley (Grand Rapids: Eerdmans, 1988), 4: 519.

3. Cornelius Plantinga, Jr., *Not the Way It's Supposed to Be: A Breviary of Sin* (Grand Rapids/Leicester: Eerdmans/Apollos, paperback 1996), 199. Brilliant, finely balanced, and nuanced.

4. Paradoxically, Anabaptist Balthasar Hubmaier rebuked U. Zwingli for diluting the dogma of original sin: H. Wayne Pipkin and John H. Yoder, eds., *Balthasar Hubmaier: Theologian of Anabaptism* (Scottdale, Pa.: Herald, 1989), 285 with n. 41.

5. Ted Peters, *Sin: Radical Evil in Soul and Society* (Grand Rapids: Eerdmans, 1994), 285. Peters wraps liberals in "the mantle of unhappy consciousness" for their social criticism; I doubt the depth of their *self*-criticism.

6. Recovery triggered by Carl F. H. Henry's *The Uneasy Conscience of Modern Fundamentalism* (Grand Rapids: Eerdmans, 1947).

7. Scot McKnight, *A Community Called Atonement* (Nashville, Tenn.: Abingdon, 2007) offers an interesting example, since he is one of the most competent, still evangelical, "emergent Church" thinkers.

8. H. Bavinck, *Wijsbegeerte der Openbaring* (Kampen: J. H. Kok, 1908), 195.

9. Oliver O'Donovan, *Resurrection and Moral Order: An Outline for Evangelical Ethics* (Leicester/Grand Rapids: Inter-Varsity Press/Eerdmans, 1986), 114.

10. Helmut Burkhardt, *Einführung in die Ethik, I: Grund und Norm sittlichen Handelns* (Basel: Brunnen, 1996), 81–83, classifies the deficiencies of conscience: error, oversensitivity, numbness, formalization (indifference to contents, values).

11. Along similar lines, see Gerrit C. Berkouwer, *Sin*, transl. Philip C. Holtrop (Grand Rapids: Eerdmans, 1971), 152–155. A classic.

12. A cherished theme of Cornelius Van Til's! See, for example, *A Christian Theory of Knowledge* (Philadelphia: Presbyterian & Reformed, 1968, 29–30; *Common Grace and the Gospel* (Nutley, N.J.: Presbyterian & Reformed, 1974), 69.

13. In some countries conversion to Christianity is a crime, and in others positive law legitimizes abortion.

14. See S. L. Jones, ed., *Psychology and the Christian Faith* (Grand Rapids: Baker, 1986); on the present topic, Terry D. Cooper, "Pride and Self-Contempt: A Controversial Issue in Psychology and Theology," *Edification: Journal of the Society for Christian Psychology* 1/1 (2007): 49–56.

15. On the *Busskampf*, see Berkouwer, *Sin*, 189–190.

16. Ibid., 167–185.

17. Ibid., 183.

18. Ibid., 199.

19. Ibid., 184.

20. Years before *Church Dogmatics II/2*, he launched his thesis in *Evangelium und Gesetz* (Munich: Chr. Kaiser, 1935).

21. They stress 2 Cor. 5:17: if anyone is in Christ—not all are—it is the *new* creation, with the things past, the things of the first creation, left behind. Cf. Rom. 16:7: Andronikos and Junia received the "in Christ" qualification before Paul did.

22. Denied by Berkouwer, *Sin*, 208.

23. Bromiley, "Sin," 518.

24. Augustus H. Strong, *Systematic Theology* (repr. Philadelphia: Judson, 1958), 549. Wayne Grudem, *Systematic Theology: An Introduction to Biblical Doctrine* (Grand Rapids/Leicester: Zondervan/Inter-Varsity Press, 1994), 490, offers a parallel wording. Grudem is widely used as *the* textbook in many schools.

25. Ibid., 558. The quote is ascribed to Calvin (no reference); it fails to appear in Calvin: it comes from Calov!

26. Colin G. Kruse, "Sin and Perfection in 1 John," *Southern Baptist Journal of Theology* 10/3 (Fall 2006): 63–64, following Ignace de La Potterie's treatment.

27. Plantinga, *Not the Way*, 12.

28. Ibid., 13.

29. Berkouwer, *Sin*, 256–266.

30. Bromiley, "Sin," 519: "Its positive reality is paradoxical and secondary."

31. Plantinga, *Not the Way*, 90.

32. Ibid., 32–33.

33. Ibid., 90 n. 28, quoting Geoffrey Cowley, precisely on AIDS.

34. Ibid., 89 and the whole chapter, "Parasite" (78–95).

35. Ibid., 88.

36. "There is so much frustration in the world because we have relied on gods rather than God. We have genuflected before the god of science only to find that it has given the atomic bomb, producing fears and anxieties that science can never mitigate. We have worshipped the god of pleasure only to discover that thrills play out and sensations are short-lived. We have bowed before the god of money only to learn that there are such things as love and friendship that money cannot buy and that in a world of possible depressions, stock market crashes, and bad business investments, money is a rather uncertain deity. These transitory gods are not able to save or bring happiness to the human heart. Only God is able. It is faith in Him that we must rediscover." *The Words of Martin Luther King, Jr.*, ed. Coretta Scott King (New York: Newmarket Press, 1958), 63; quoted in Peters, *Sin: Radical Evil*, 87–90.

37. Plantinga, *Not the Way*, 18–19.

38. Berkouwer, *Sin*, 254.

39. Plantinga, *Not the Way*, 88.

40. Inasmuch as a worldly, creaturely, agency determines my act, this act is no longer free (such determination is incompatible with true freedom); but if God determines my act, owing to the unique relationship that binds all creatures and especially humans to him, he grounds my true freedom. Plantinga, ibid., 24 n. 29, fails to distinguish between the two.

41. Strong, *Systematic Theology*, 826. John Murray, *Collected Writings II: Select Lectures in Systematic Theology* (Edinburgh: Banner of Truth Trust, 1977), 170, sees it corresponding to the scholastics' *habitus*.

42. Strong, *Systematic Theology*, 825.

43. Alistair McFadyen, *Bound to Sin: Abuse, Holocaust and the Christian Doctrine of Sin* (Cambridge: Cambridge University Press, 2000), 127. Remarkably lucid on parallels between child abuse and Holocaust; also on Augustine.

44. For example, Grudem, *Systematic Theology*, 503–504.

45. Plantinga, *Not the Way*, 21.

46. Berkouwer, *Sin*, 323–353 (particularly referred to, 343, 345). Cf. Grudem, *Systematic Theology*, 506–509.

47. Plantinga, *Not the Way*, 50. He quotes, 51, from Livy, *History of Rome* I,1, who confesses that Romans have been brought "in love with death," agreeing with Prov. 8:35–36.

48. Ibid., 143, and the whole section 141–144, answering Charlotte Davis Kash with sensitivity and finesse.

49. For example, Grudem, *Systematic Theology*, 497.

50. Norman Geisler, *Systematic Theology* (Minneapolis: Bethany House, 2004), 3: 84–87.

51. For Herman Dooyeweerd, see *A New Critique of Theoretical Thought*, trans. from the Dutch by David H. Freeman and William S. Young (Phillipsburg, N.J.: Presbyterian and Reformed, 1969), 1: 61. For Cornelius Van Til, see Greg L. Bahnsen, *Van Til's Apologetic: Readings and Analysis* (Phillipsburg, N.J.: Presbyterian and Reformed, 1998), 461–476.

52. Peter T. O'Brien, "Principalities and Powers: Opponents of the Church," in *Biblical Interpretation and the Church: Text and Context*, D. A. Carson, ed. (Exeter: Paternoster, 1984), 110–150; John R. W. Stott, *God's New Society: The Message of Ephesians* (Leicester: Inter-Varsity Press, 1979), 267–275.

53. Plantinga, *Not the Way*, 55.

54. Adolf Schlatter, *Das christliche Dogma* (Stuttgart: Vereinsbuchhandlung, 1911), 252.

55. John Murray, *The Imputation of Adam's Sin* (Nutley, N.J.: Presbyterian & Reformed, 1977), 73–85.

56. Franciscus Turretinus, *Institutio theologiae elencticae* (repr., New York: Robert Carter, 1847), 1: 538 (locus IX, qu. 3).

57. Frederick F. Bruce, *The Epistles to the Colossians, to Philemon and to the Ephesians* (repr. Grand Rapids: Eerdmans, 1993), 74–76, shows that "reconciliation" in that passage does not mean salvation but the restoration of the right relationship: "This reconciliation of the universe includes what would otherwise be distinguished as pacification" (76). Important symposium: Nigel M. de S. Cameron, ed., *Universalism and the Doctrine of Hell* (Carlisle/Grand Rapids: Paternoster/Baker Book House, 1992).

58. James Orr, *The Christian View of God and the World* (repr., Grand Rapids: Eerdmans, 1960), 185.

59. John Goldingay, *Old Testament Theology, I: Israel's Gospel* (Downers Grove, Ill.: InterVarsity Press, 2003), 145.

60. Thomas F. Torrance kindly gave me his *The Soul and Person of the Unborn Child* (Edinburgh: Handsel Press, 1999) as our minds met on the subject.

BIBLIOGRAPHY

Barth, Karl. *Church Dogmatics IV/1*. Trans. G. W. Bromiley. Edinburgh: T & T Clark, 1956.

Berkouwer, Gerrit C. *Sin*. Trans. Philip C. Holtrop. Grand Rapids: Eerdmans, 1971.

Blocher, Henri. *Original Sin: Illuminating the Riddle.* Leicester: Apollos, 1997.

Grudem, Wayne. *Systematic Theology: An Introduction to Biblical Doctrine.* Grand Rapids/Leicester: Zondervan/Inter-Varsity Press, 1994.

McFadyen, Alistair. *Bound to Sin: Abuse, Holocaust and the Christian Doctrine of Sin.* Cambridge: Cambridge University Press, 2000.

Murray, John. *The Imputation of Adam's Sin.* Nutley, N.J.: Presbyterian & Reformed, 1977.
Peters, Ted. *Sin: Radical Evil in Soul and Society.* Grand Rapids: Eerdmans, 1994.
Plantinga, Cornelius Jr. *Not the Way It's Supposed to Be: A Breviary of Sin.* Grand Rapids/ Leicester: Eerdmans/Apollos, paperback 1996.
Ramm, Bernard. *Offense to Reason.* San Francisco: Harper & Row, 1985.
Smith, David L. *With Willful Intent: A Theology of Sin.* Wheaton: Victor Books, 1994.

CHAPTER 9

JESUS CHRIST

JOHN G. STACKHOUSE, JR.

One might fairly assume that, whatever else evangelicals disagree about in theology, they share a common understanding of the person and work of Jesus Christ. Alas, one would be wrong in that assumption.

To be sure, evangelicals continue to be Christocentric in their theology just as much as they are in their piety. And evangelical theologians generally continue to aver a basic creedal orthodoxy—even those who represent traditions that maintain a stout anti-creedal biblicism. The current generation of evangelical theologians, however, has discussed a wide range of questions about the received traditions of Christology. And the answers supplied to those questions have excited further explorations in the doctrine of Christ—even as they have also prompted some evangelicals to denounce others as heretics.

At the heart of the gospel testimony to Jesus is a narrative, however, not a creed or some other theological summary. So let us consider an evangelical theology of Christ by way of key passages in the life of Jesus. And in what follows, unless the text specifies otherwise, references to "evangelicals" will mean "evangelical theologians," not evangelicals in toto.

Pre-Existence. Evangelicals are Trinitarians, and so they believe that before there was an earthly Jesus, there was the Son of God, the Logos, the second member of the Trinity who would become human in the economy of salvation sometime around 4 B.C.E.

Some evangelicals have been influenced by the likes of Colin Gunton to speak of "Jesus" before the actual incarnation, in order to symbolize the identity of the Son of God with the (later) figure of Jesus of Nazareth.[1] Others, such as Paul Helm, believe that God is eternally changeless and thus the second person of the Trinity is, in a sense unimaginable to us, *always* incarnate.[2]

Most evangelicals, however, regardless of their views of God and time (and perhaps in some tension with, or even contradiction of, those views, since many confess, when they are dealing with theology proper, an immutable God), believe that the Word of God always existed as a co-equal, co-eternal member of the Godhead and at a particular point in time descended into Mary's womb to be born. At this time his parents obeyed the Lord's command to name him Jesus—"Yahweh saves"—"for he shall save his people from their sins" (Matt. 1:21).

Incarnation. This key term means that God literally became not just human but "flesh" (*carne*, in Latin). There is a kind of shock intended here—as if God became *meat*—in order to affirm the genuine materiality of Christ's coming over against any attempt to spiritualize it or mythologize it away. Indeed, while Christians do not pretend to understand all of what is meant by this stupendous claim, they have tried to clarify what they mean partly by ruling out what they do *not* mean.

Jesus was not, first, a ghost or hologram or other apparition. He was fully human physiologically: he ate, slept, walked, talked, and—ultimately—died. Jesus' mother Mary became pregnant through God's miraculous power, but otherwise Jesus was born in the normal way, raised in the normal way, and lived in the normal way. He was a human being.

Second, Jesus was more than a human being. Christians insist that the only way to make sense of the whole career of Jesus of Nazareth—his life, death, later appearances, and final, abrupt disappearance—is to go well beyond respecting or even revering Jesus to actually worshiping him. Now, the first Christians were staunch Jews and thus staunch monotheists who worshiped only one God. Thus they concluded that if Jesus were to be worshiped, as they believed he must be, then Jesus had to be more than a prophet, or wonder-worker, or even an angel. Jesus of Nazareth had to be God. In this way, Christians came to understand that God had two aspects or personalities or ego-centers or *somethings* (Christians have never been able to agree on the exact nature of God's plurality-in-unity): God was at least two-in-one. And quite quickly Christians came to understand that God is actually three-in-one, a Trinity, as they determined that the Holy Spirit of God constituted the third member of what theologians call the Godhead.[3]

The bottom line, in any case, is that in Jesus of Nazareth, we have God. We have not only a messenger from God, a representative of God, an example of devotion to God, a teacher of God's truth, a conveyor of God's power—*we have God.* How this can be—how God's being and human being, how God's psyche and a human psyche, can be one individual—is something no reasonable Christian claims to understand. To be fair, however, we believe that human beings have psyches not because we can fully describe and explain them, but because we have such strong evidence of their presence and activity. It is by similar logic that the early Christians concluded that in Jesus Christ they confronted the very presence and activity of God in a truly human person.

Recent evangelical theology has lifted up two main themes in regard to the incarnation: recapitulation and kenōsis.

Recapitulation. The motif of Christ "redo-ing" shows up in two important agendas of evangelical theology. The former of these is the project of N. T. Wright, who follows in the train of Ed Sanders and James D. G. Dunn to emphasize the

"Jewishness" of Jesus, over against other portrayals of him as a Cynic sage, wonder-worker, moralist, or whatever. In this frame of reference, the incarnation fundamentally is about Jesus taking on the identity of the nation of Israel, living in obedience to the covenant (versus Israel's long record of disobedience) and fulfilling the Law (versus Israel's failure to do so). Simultaneously, Jesus does the work of Yhwh. also, bringing divine salvation to his people. Furthermore, Jesus not only brings salvation to Israel, but—according to God's ancient plan to bless all nations through the seed of Abraham—also to the whole world.[4]

The latter version of "recapitulation" emerges particularly among those scholars—such as Terrence Tiessen and Hans Boersma—who exposit Irenaeus of Lyon.[5] Irenaeus, in turn, follows the apostle Paul's teaching that Christ substitutes for Adam—indeed, that Christ becomes the new, perfect, and thus salvific head of the human race. As Jesus lives a holy life, entirely pleasing to God, he undoes what Adam did to himself and his progeny and brings blessing instead.

Both of these versions of recapitulation seem at least a little like versions of (Eastern) Orthodoxy's doctrine of *theōsis*, the process of "deification" by which humanity is progressively infused with the divine life via the bridge established between the transcendent and the immanent, between God and his creation, in the incarnation of the Son of God. Thus it appears that the incarnation itself is salvific. And indeed some evangelical theologians have explored this idea through fresh study of the Church Fathers.

Just as Orthodoxy does not stop there, however, and forget the later events of Christ's career, so do those who champion recapitulation maintain the ancient affirmation of the cross and resurrection of Jesus. Whatever recapitulation means, it includes the Jewish Messiah and the new Adam "making peace through the blood of his cross" (Col. 1:20).[6]

Before we leave this episode in Christ's life, however, we might pause to remark that a site of contention in previous generations of evangelical theology, namely, the Virgin Birth, is generally taken for granted today. Evangelical attention instead has been devoted to understanding just what sort of child was produced by the power of God in Mary's womb.

Thus, along with recapitulation, has come a second zone of inquiry, namely, *kenōsis*.[7]

Evangelicals stand with all other orthodox Christians in affirming the parameters set out at Chalcedon in 451: Jesus was truly divine and truly human, one person in two natures. Evangelicals also affirm that Christians do not and cannot comprehend just *how* the Second Person of the Trinity became human. Recent evangelical theology, however, has returned to the category of kenōsis to see if it can render at least a little more coherent this paradox of the Incarnation.

The paradox is posed by the very affirmations of Chalcedon that seem so contradictory. How can the Logos of the world sleep as an infant in his mother's arms? How can the light of the world not know some things (Mk. 13:32)? How can the Son who is co-eternal with the Father "grow in wisdom" (Lk. 2:52)? How can he who created and sustains the cosmos suffer, die, and be buried?

Christmas crèche scenes to the contrary, the Bible does not report that the infant Jesus glowed in his manger. He looked and acted like every other newborn. Furthermore, despite some fanciful stories in certain ancient quasi-Christian literature about a young wonderworking Jesus, the authoritative Gospels give us only glimpses of his birth and growing-up years, with no hint that he wrought any prodigies.

The traditional Christian answer, followed by most evangelicals, is that the Son of God *took on* humanity, adding to his divinity the reality of human being. In some way we do not understand, the respective traits and experiences of Christ's divinity and humanity were shared in his person, in the so-called *communicatio idiomatum*.

Several related problems have always been implied by this rendering of the Incarnation, problems that kenotic theology—best known as a nineteenth-century movement generally resisted by orthodox Christians but taking on new life nowadays—recognizes and seeks to solve.

The first problem is a textual one. The Bible itself says that Christ *emptied* himself—from which word's Greek root we derive *kenōsis* (Php. 2:7). That passage, however, is not obviously clear as to what "emptying" means. Other passages clarify the issue, as they speak of Jesus "growing in wisdom and stature" and not knowing the time of the end (Lk. 2:52; Mk. 13:32). One says that Jesus learned obedience through suffering—two mysteries in a single phrase (Heb. 5:8)! So as Christians who take their theological cues particularly from the Bible, evangelicals are willing to consider these verses as they seem to imply that not only did God add to himself humanity, but also in some way subtracted something from himself in order to do so.

The second problem is a theologico-practical one. If Jesus did not experience life as a human being in the same way that we do—most significantly, as a truly limited human being who trusted and obeyed God the Father (Jn. 5:19) and who depended on and was led by God the Holy Spirit (Mk. 1:12)—then Jesus cannot serve as an example to us (so much for *imitatio Christi*), cannot live and die for us as a genuinely human representative (so much for atonement), and cannot represent us as our sympathetic advocate (so much for his high priestly ministry).

The third problem is a theologico-philosophical one. The event of the Incarnation seems to be an obvious change in the life of God—indeed, the most drastic change we can see in Scripture. It also is an event fraught with suffering. Therefore, the traditional views of God as both immutable and impassible must be revised, and kenotic theory helps us do that.

Evangelical kenotic theology is kenotic theology that retains full allegiance to Chalcedon, unlike some of the nineteenth-century experiments in kenotic theology that gave the whole enterprise a bad name among orthodox theologians because the divinity of Christ seemed much too compromised. This evangelical theology suggests that God the Son somehow (we don't know how) freely relinquishes his powers and roles as equal member of the Trinity, handing them over to the Father and the Spirit, as it were (most of what follows is "as it were"), to undergo a genuinely human experience of limitation and consequent dependence—on God, yes, and on his parents, his society, and the planet, just as we also must depend on this matrix of life. He really does learn as we learn, eventually coming to awareness of his divine-human identity and role—doubtless through his parents' recollections of angelic testimony, the teaching of the Torah available in Nazareth, his own precocious learning of it (Lk. 2:49), and perhaps direct revelations, all of which are guided by the Holy Spirit.

Thus when Jesus enters his public ministry, he does so with awareness of who he is and what he is to do, while depending all along on the Father and the Spirit, as we must do, rather than exerting his own divine powers on his own, as it were.

Several objections immediately spring to mind, of course. What happens to the universe with the divine Logos temporarily out of office? Nothing bad: the Father and the Spirit handle things quite competently. If God is omnipotent by definition, how can he be less than omnipotent as Christ and still be divine? God is better defined as being omnipotent such that his power includes the power for one member of the Trinity to temporarily relinquish that power in order to accomplish the great good of salvation—while God in his Trinity never ceases being omnipotent. How can God change and even suffer? Well, judging from the Scriptural testimony, apparently God can.

There is much more to be said about all of these issues, of course, and evangelical theology will be engaging them. Open Theists can see kenotic theology as vindicating their overall perspective—that is, that God exists in time as we do, and thus does not see the future with absolute and certain clarity, as orthodoxy has traditionally affirmed he does.[8] Alas, those who reject Open Theism might be inclined therefore to reject kenotic theology by association. But many evangelical theologians already are working with kenotic categories without recourse to Open Theism, and it remains to be seen what progress on this front will be made in the generation to come.

Inauguration. Christianity looks back on its Jewish/Israelite heritage, and sees God select a man and a woman, Abraham and Sarah, from whom a chosen nation descends. This nation's history will serve as an object lesson to all nations: God is good and wants to bless; those who respond with gratitude and cooperation reap blessing after blessing; those who respond with disdain and rejection reap curse after curse.

God nonetheless preserves Israel even in the face of Israel's frequent betrayals. More than this, God promises through a long line of prophets to lift Israel to a position of spiritual, moral, economic, and political health such as Israel has never known. In fact, Israel will be at the heart of a universal kingdom of peace in which all nations will be subdued and in which members of all nations will enjoy God's reign from Jerusalem.

God promises to do this through a specially appointed person, one who will combine the offices of prophet, priest, and king (some of whom were recognized in ancient Israel by the rite of anointing with oil, and thus were *messiahs*) into the office of Messiah—the Anointed.

Jesus did not have the career that Jews of first-century Palestine expected Messiah to have. Yes, he worked wonders, miracles that showed supernatural power at work in his life. Yes, he aligned himself with the Scriptures and taught as a respected, if uncredentialed, rabbi. Yes, he seemed to have considerable personal charisma, speaking with an extraordinary individual authority. But Jesus failed to accomplish the most basic task of Messiah: He did not free his people from their bondage to imperial Rome. He did not set up an independent kingdom to recall the glories of David and Solomon. He had virtually nothing to do with politics until his own trial and execution. And he was executed by that oppressive state. Some Messiah!

In the public career of Jesus, however, as he touched people with gentleness and healing, as he spoke with unparalleled authority and aptness, as he moved with steadfast purpose toward his final confrontation with the powers of his day, we see flashes of God's pure shalom amid the swirling murk of our world.

This is what Jesus meant when he proclaimed that "the kingdom of God is at hand" (Mk. 1:15). Jesus' life inaugurated God's direct and uncompromised rule on earth, a rule (or "kingdom") that was realized fully only in Jesus' own obedience to God—as he thus represented both Israel and, thus, the whole world. But from this beginning the invitation to enter the Kingdom would extend outward to Jesus' faithful disciples and, through their own lives and testimony, to individuals and nations across the globe.

Evangelicals—again, notably N. T. Wright—have thus emphasized the Jewishness of Jesus' mission, even as they wisely keep in mind also John's transmutation of the Jewish message of entering the Kingdom into the global invitation to receive new birth for life of the age to come (= "eternal life").

Jesus' life was more than preaching and showing the Kingdom of God, to be sure. It serves as a model for authentic human life in and under God. As such, the question arises about the reality of temptation for Jesus. Kenotic Christology helps here as well, for in positing a Jesus who could not simply "turn on" his divinity like a lamp to banish sin, this theology upholds a truly useful example for us of a man who did not yield, ever, to sin as he prayed, recalled Scripture, and otherwise resisted temptation. Whether Jesus *could* have sinned—which would be impossible not only according to his divine nature but also according to the holy human character he had, such that he could no more sin than a loyal husband could surrender to a temptress—no longer governs this question of his temptation. The temptation nonetheless is real—as a trying experience that both demonstrates and confirms character is real—so long as we see that *as far as Jesus knew*, it was real. Thus he experienced genuine testing, and thus he provides a genuine example to follow.

Anabaptist ethics have captured evangelical attention as they articulate a compelling form of the age-old tradition of the imitation of Christ. John Howard Yoder is the main figure in this movement, with evangelicals also following the lead of Yoder's epigone Stanley Hauerwas.[9] Indeed, evangelicals have put this ethic into practice notably in the so-called "new monasticism" that includes married couples as it seeks to live out a disciplined communal life of service to Christ and the world he loves.[10]

Evangelical feminism is also inspired by Jesus' message of the Kingdom of God being present "already" if "not yet" fully, even as that movement has yet to follow through its championing of female pastors to a comprehensive reading of Scripture and doctrine that benefits from a feminist Christian perspective. And this message of Christ the messianic King coming to liberate the oppressed finds resonances also in the Pentecostal/charismatic communities of evangelicals who expand the evangelical frame of reference to spiritual warfare, especially in areas of the world in which reports of such conflict are common and where the church is booming: Africa, China, Korea, Latin America, and elsewhere.

Crucifixion. In the last events of Jesus' earthly career, evangelicals see the decisive events in God's work of reclaiming and restoring the world. The Cross of Jesus does not disqualify him as Messiah. It is the event above all that *entitles* Jesus to be called the Christos, God's true servant. In three of the four Gospels, Jesus explicitly ties together his Messiahship with his death and resurrection (Matt. 16:16–21; Mk. 8:29–31; Lk. 9:20–22). The Cross is part of Christ's saving work on our behalf. It is at once both his greatest humiliation and greatest glory.

In the Crucifixion, evangelicals agree with the Christian tradition that there are several subjective benefits to the Crucifixion. In the Cross we have an example of dedication to a cause, a martyr willing even to suffer and die in obedience to the Father's will (Mk. 14:36; Heb. 12:1–4). We have a display of God's love, as in the brutal pinioning of wrists to wood, God flings his arms wide to embrace the world. We have an assurance of God's sympathy with our affliction, as we see beyond doubt that God knows what it is like to suffer, and to suffer unfairly.

Beyond these benefits, furthermore, evangelicals rejoice in the objective benefits of the Cross. Mysterious as it remains even to the wisest minds, the fundamental Christian affirmation is that the Cross of Jesus does not just show us things, it did something once for all. That is why it was necessary: not merely as a symbol pointing to something else (the love and sympathy of God in the face of the enormity of human sin) but as in itself a world-changing event that did indeed direct the love and sympathy of God to deal effectively with the enormity of human sin.

Two principal images have been used by Christians to explain what Jesus accomplished on the Cross: Christ as Sacrifice, and Christ as Victor. The former harks back to the extensive symbolism of Israelite temple worship, in which animals were killed and offered to God as substitutes for the human sinners who gave them up. "Life for life" was the basic principle, because sin at its root is the repudiation of life. The Hebrew prophets themselves made clear that these rituals together formed an elaborate picture of both God's holiness (God views sin as mortally serious, and therefore the most graphic symbolism of life and death was necessary to portray its cost and its redemption) and God's mercy (God was willing to accept animal substitutes, although it makes no logical or moral sense to do so: how can the blood of bulls or goats possibly make up for human sin?). The ultimate payment for, the ultimate cost of, human sin had to be borne by human beings.

For God could hardly say, "Okay, you seem sorry, so let's just forget about it." Convenient as that might seem to us, such a scenario fails to take sin seriously.

Evangelicals often refer to the language of financial transactions to make this point. I owe you a thousand dollars. I cannot pay you. You can take me to court and try to make me pay you, but let's say that I truly have no resources to do so. So (in some legal systems) you can press charges and have me punished in prison for failing to pay my debt. But you aren't any richer for doing so, are you? My going to prison might quench your thirst for vengeance, but it doesn't deal with the debt.

Your other choice, however, is to forgive the loan. What this means, strictly speaking, is that you pay yourself the thousand dollars on my behalf. Of course, you will always have a net loss of a thousand dollars. What you have done, though, is remove my name from the list of debtors and taken the loss yourself.

In any situation of forgiveness, that is, there are actually four elements in play. Three are obvious: the offender, the offended, and their relationship. But a fourth must be borne in mind, else the Cross makes no objective sense as Sacrifice. Let us consider another example.

Little Darrell has been told many times by his mother not to touch her fine linen tablecloth. But Darrell loves to crawl up on one of the dining room chairs to gaze down at this vacant canvas. One day, he succumbs to its allure and begins to improve it with his crayons.

An hour later, his horrified mother shrieks as she enters the dining room to see Darrell's ornamentation extending from one end to the other of the family heirloom.

Darrell, recognizing at once that he has disobeyed and upset his mother, whom he loves, bursts into tears and cries out, "I'm sorry, Mommy! I'm sorry! I'm sorry!" He runs toward her and buries his head in her legs, sobbing out his repentance.

Darrell's mother is an unusually good person and immediately drops to her knees to hug him. "That's okay, honey," she whispers. "I forgive you."

So the offender, Darrell, has repented. His mother, the offended, has forgiven him. And their relationship is mended in mutual love.

But the fourth element, the tablecloth itself, remains ruined regardless of her forgiving him.

The Bible speaks of sin this way: not just as a rupture in a relationship, but as an objective state of affairs that requires reparation. There is a debt still to be paid, a ruined tablecloth still to be restored. Here is the ancient concept of guilt, a consequence of any action that strays from goodness, whether intentional evil or not. The Old Testament law provided a ritual to atone for actions that deviated from goodness even as the perpetrator of them had no intention of committing evil (Lev. 4). Figures in the Bible are depicted as transgressing God's rules and suffering for it even when they had no idea they were doing wrong (Gen. 20:9). We can't just clap each other on the back, or shake hands, or hug, and walk away, as crucial as it is also to restore good relations between us.

Jesus repairs it. Jesus pays it. Jesus bears it. Jesus absorbs it. Jesus, somehow, and whatever "it" is, makes things right by his sacrifice of himself. Some evangelicals have been repelled by "satisfaction" or "substitutionary" theories of the atonement, but most retain them as approximations of this crucial idea at the heart of the Bible's portrayal of sin, its effects, and its remedy.

We can now see one important reason why the doctrine of the Trinity is vital to the Christian understanding of things. If God and Jesus are different beings, then

Jesus on the Cross looks like just one more scapegoat being punished for the sake of other humans' sins. Indeed, now we would have Christianity championing human sacrifice. And we would have the same conundrum we had before: how can punishing someone else possibly suffice for my offenses? Some feminist theologians have gone even further to accuse the idea of Sacrifice as sanctioning child abuse: God the Father victimizes his Son. If the doctrine of the Trinity is stoutly affirmed, however, then it is *God* as Son who hangs on the Cross, as God looks on as Father and Spirit in the added suffering of grief over the Beloved.

Does God the Father, however, not turn away from the Son? Some evangelicals, along with Christians of other stripes, have affirmed that he does as Christ becomes "sin for us" (2 Cor. 5:21). All point to Christ's famous cry from the cross—"My God, my God, why has thou forsaken me?"—as a cry of dereliction (Mk. 15:34).

What sort of Trinitarianism, however, can be coherently held with the idea of one member of the Trinity turning away from another? Two considerations might help here.

The first suggestion is that, from the kenotic angle, God the Father does not turn away in any metaphysical, "Trinity-splitting" way, but God the Son so identifies with fallen humanity that, for a time, he *experiences* the forsakenness that is our due as he suffers in our stead.

A second, bolder approach, is consistent with both kenotic and more traditional Christologies and avoids the serious problem of viewing Christ even for a brief while as somehow losing fellowship with his Father and suffering instead on his own. Indeed, what happens then to the Holy Spirit? Does he withdraw from Jesus, too? How, then, does Jesus endure atoning for the whole world? Does he "switch on" his divinity for *that* episode?

This second approach begins by noting that Jesus demonstrates his lifelong relationship with the Father at the beginning and at the end of the Crucifixion. He prays for the Father to forgive the soldiers killing him and he commends his spirit to his Father at the end of his life. So whatever separation is supposed to happen must occur in a quite small window of time.

Then we note that Jesus' cry of dereliction is a direct quotation of Psalm 22. Thus it actually puts Christ in the place of David, God's favorite, who is surrounded and victimized by Gentile enemies, and who is ultimately confident of God's vindication! He is the one, to recall Isaiah 53, who looks to us as if he were stricken by God, but instead is doing God's perfect will as his suffering servant (Isa. 53:3–4). There is no separation in the Godhead. Instead, God the Father and God the Holy Spirit bless God the Son as he bears the penalty of the sins of the world away from all of us who deserve it.

Along with the image of Sacrifice, then, evangelicals have recently reappropriated the image of Christ as Victor. Following Gustav Aulén's *Christus Victor* (1931), a number of evangelicals have highlighted the language of the Bible and of the Church Fathers that speaks of the Cross of Jesus as a decisive battle in God's ongoing war with sin, evil, suffering, death, hell and the devil.[11]

To be sure, even Aulén allows that Christus Victor is not a theory, not even a coherent narrative, but an "idea" or "motif." Moreover, it has paradoxes (some would say contradictions) at its heart. For example, the omnipotent God is supposed to be conquering enemies (sin, evil, suffering, death, hell, the devil) that exist only by his sufferance anyway, and several of which are themselves the executors of his judgment on sin and evil. For another, the motif posits God's love as triumphing over what is in fact God's wrath, versus the satisfaction/penal substitution/sacrifice theories that show God consistently dealing with his wrath and his love.

Aulén's rejection of the "Latin" theory of Sacrifice seems to rest on what he sees to be its emphasis upon the human side of Jesus rendering something up to God, rather than seeing God involved in every dimension of the Atonement. And his latter-day evangelical champions share this same worry. But, as we have seen, they need not worry, for a firm Trinitarianism prevents the idea of Sacrifice from becoming anything other than God's self-giving on our behalf.

Perhaps it is better, then, for evangelical theology to retain all of these vital and biblical depictions of atonement. And perhaps we can understand something of the mystery of Christ's Sacrifice and his Victory like this.

A warrior is expected to defeat his opponent by inflicting a wound so severe that it renders response impossible. A warrior could defeat his opponent in at least one other way, however. Instead of hammering his opponent into submission, a warrior could choose to stand still and take his enemy's best blow—indeed, to absorb all of his blows, one after the other, until the enemy literally exhausts his power and collapses, spent. To take it to the extreme, the warrior himself could expire from this suffering. But if he gets up, he wins. This is what Jesus did on the Cross and in his subsequent resurrection.

Resurrection. The concept and event of resurrection is the key to the Christian hope, and evangelicals affirm it in a traditional way. Indeed, it continues to be a focus of evangelical apologetics as what it was in the apostolic preaching: the vindication of Jesus by God, the proof that his teaching was true and that his work was efficacious (Acts 2; Rom. 8:11; 1 Cor. 15). As Israel was told always to find hope in God because of what he had done in the Exodus, so Christians have found hope in God because of what he did in the resurrection of Jesus.

For evangelicals, as for all orthodox Christians, resurrection does not mean "reincarnation" or "resuscitation." It means that Jesus' whole self, physical and psychospiritual, was transformed into a new mode of existence. The old body was transformed into the new body; therefore witnesses reported that Jesus' tomb was empty. Indeed, the grave clothes were still lying there as if Jesus' body had metamorphosed and disappeared right through them. What happened to Jesus, Christians believe, also will happen to all who love and trust him. Some day after their death, when Christ returns in the final stage of the cosmic drama, the blessed dead will rise, fit for the enjoyment of the new life God has prepared for them.

The resurrection is not a site of much evangelical theological work at present. But it connects with the Crucifixion, a traditional locus of attention, and with the ascension, an event typically underplayed in evangelical theology and piety.

Ascension. Following his resurrection, Jesus appeared among his now-delighted (if also astonished and fearful) disciples for short periods of teaching and encouragement. And after a few weeks, he met them on the Mount of Olives, just outside the ancient city of Jerusalem, to bid them good-bye.

He commissioned them to go out as his messengers ("apostles" means "ones who are sent"), bringing the good news of God's saving power offered to everyone who would believe. He promised to return someday, to wrap up this stage of human history in the final judgment of evil and the rescue of his people. In the meanwhile, he said, the project of redemption would continue through spiritual and human extensions of himself. The Holy Spirit would soon come upon the disciples and unite them into the Church, God's main agent of proclamation and healing in the world. As God had reached the world through the spirit and body of Jesus of Nazareth, now God would continue to draw the world out of evil and toward fellowship with God through the Holy Spirit empowering Christ's Body on earth, the Christian Church.

Following this stupendous promise (particularly astonishing given the small, motley collection of disciples to whom it was given on a Judean hilltop), Jesus symbolized his return to heavenly authority and power by literally rising straight up into the air, as if he were going "up" to heaven, until a cloud finally obscured him from sight. This ascension, then, was the final visible act of God in Jesus, an act that drove home to the disciples the status of their Lord and the solemn importance of their assignment. It also impressed upon them his bodily absence and their need to look forward to the reception of the Holy Spirit, as the God who once dwelt in a tabernacle or temple with Israel and then had "tabernacled among us" (Jn. 1:14) in the person of Jesus would now come closer still, literally inhabiting his people as temples of the Holy Spirit (1 Cor. 6:19).

So what of Christ since then? One can gather from some evangelicals the idea of Christ taking an extended sabbatical, a well-deserved rest from his strenuous labors. He has handed the baton, as it were, to the Holy Spirit—a quasi-modalist image reminiscent of Joachim of Fiore (c. 1130–c. 1201) and perpetuated particularly in some Pentecostal circles today—and now waits to come back at the end of the age. (It is not simply modalism, as three divine persons are affirmed. But the progressive focus on first the Father, or "God-in-general," then the Son, and then the Spirit is implicitly anti-Trinitarian, as modalism is explicitly.)

Yet "Jesus is Lord" is the earliest confession of the Christian church, and Jesus is Lord *now*. He rules the church, yes, and he rules the whole world. His place at the right hand of the Majesty on high (Heb. 1:3) is an executive position from which Jesus performs his particular work of redemption especially through the church and from which he performs also his general work of governance as Logos of all creation.

Furthermore, the New Testament and particularly the book of Hebrews testify to God's abiding love for us in the picture of Jesus interceding for us as High Priest. Hebrews 10:11–13 exemplifies that book's main concern to demonstrate that the Way of Christ fulfills Judaism, as Christ's ministry fulfills and transcends the work of priest, sacrifice, and temple: "And every priest stands day after day at his service, offering again and again the same sacrifices that can never take away sins. But when Christ [Gk: *this one*] had offered for all time a single sacrifice for sins, 'he sat down at the right hand of God,' and since then has been waiting 'until his enemies would be made a footstool for his feet.'"[12]

This same book, however, declares that Jesus not only accomplished salvation as a once-for-all act in his earthly career, but that he continues to convert, to sanctify, to save his people:

"Jesus has also become the guarantee of a better covenant. Furthermore, the former priests were many in number, because they were prevented by death from continuing in office; but he holds his priesthood permanently, because he continues forever. Consequently he is able for all time to save those who approach God through him, since he always lives to make intercession for them" (Heb. 7:22–25).

These two teachings—that Jesus has accomplished our salvation through his life, death, and resurrection and that Jesus now is accomplishing our salvation through his ongoing care for his people, depicted by his interceding for us with God the Father—come together in one passage that combines throne room and tabernacle: "We have such a high priest, one who is seated at the right hand of the throne of the Majesty in the heavens, a minister in the sanctuary and the true tent that the Lord, and not any mortal, has set up" (Heb. 8:1–2). What saves this picture from tritheism (with one God interceding with another) or, even worse, from the implication that God the Father does not love us himself (and thus is constantly placated by the Son) is Trinitarianism, as the three persons of the Trinity are in truth one God who loves us with sympathy that is both human and divine, as Christ is.

As for Jesus' return, we shall leave full consideration of that to other chapters in this volume. But evangelicals join with the church of all places and times to affirm that Jesus' return will be literal, physical, triumphant, and soon. In the meanwhile, evangelical theologians will continue to explore the depths of the incomprehensible fact of the Incarnation and to emerge from their studies not only with fresh ideas, but with fresh praise to God "for his inexpressible gift" (2 Cor. 9:15).

NOTES

1. Colin E. Gunton, *The Triune Creator: A Historical and Systematic Study* (Grand Rapids: Eerdmans, 1998).

2. See Helm's essay, along with others, in *God and Time*, ed. Gregory E. Ganssle (Downers Grove, Ill.: InterVarsity, 2001).

3. Larry W. Hurtado, *Lord Jesus Christ: Devotion to Jesus in Earliest Christianity* (Grand Rapids: Eerdmans, 2003).

4. See Wright's series beginning with *The New Testament and the People of God* (Minneapolis: Fortress, 1992). See also Scot McKnight, *A Community Called Atonement* (Nashville, Tenn.: Abingdon, 2007).

✓ 5. Hans Boersma, *Violence, Hospitality, and the Cross: Reappropriating the Atonement Tradition* (Grand Rapids: Baker Academic, 2004); Terrance L. Tiessen, *Irenaeus on the Salvation of the Unevangelized* (Lanham, Md.: Scarecrow, 1993).

6. See also McKnight, *A Community Called Atonement.*

7. C. Stephen Evans, ed., *Exploring Kenotic Christology: The Self-Emptying of God* (Oxford: Oxford University Press, 2006).

8. Clark Pinnock et al., *The Openness of God: A Biblical Challenge to the Traditional Understanding of God* (Downers Grove, Ill.: InterVarsity, 1994).

9. Douglas Harink, *Paul among the Postliberals* (Grand Rapids: Brazos, 2003).

10. John R. Stock et al., *Inhabiting the Church: Biblical Wisdom for a New Monasticism* (Eugene, Ore.: Wipf & Stock, 2006).

11. Gustaf Aulén, *Christus Victor: An Historical Study of the Three Main Types of the Idea of the Atonement,* trans. Jaroslav Pelikan (New York: Macmillan, 1969);Gregory A. Boyd, *God at War: The Bible and Spiritual Conflict* (Downers Grove, Ill.: InterVarsity, 1997); Joel B. Green and Mark D. Baker, *Recovering the Scandal of the Cross: Atonement in New Testament and Contemporary Contexts* (Downers Grove, Ill.: InterVarsity, 2000).

12. To affirm these teachings of the New Testament is not to affirm that God has abandoned his covenant with the Jews—a topic over which evangelical theologians continue to deliberate.

BIBLIOGRAPHY

Bockmuehl, Markus. *This Jesus: Martyr, Lord, Messiah.* Downers Grove, Ill.: InterVarsity, 1994.

Davis, Stephen, Daniel Kendall, and Gerald O'Collins, eds. *The Resurrection: An Interdisciplinary Symposium on the Resurrection of Jesus.* Oxford: Oxford University Press, 1997.

Evans, C. Stephen. *The Historical Christ and the Jesus of Faith: The Incarnational Narrative as History.* Oxford: Clarendon Press, 1996.

Gunton, Colin E. *The Actuality of Atonement: A Study of Metaphor, Rationality and the Christian Tradition.* Grand Rapids: Eerdmans, 1989.

Habermas, Gary R., and Michael R. Licona. *The Case for the Resurrection of Jesus.* Grand Rapids: Kregel, 2004.

Hurtado, Larry W. *Lord Jesus Christ: Devotion to Jesus in Earliest Christianity.* Grand Rapids: Eerdmans, 2003.

McClymond, Michael J. *Familiar Stranger: An Introduction to Jesus of Nazareth.* Grand Rapids: Eerdmans, 2004.

McKnight, Scot, and Joel B. Green, eds. *Dictionary of Jesus and the Gospels.* Downers Grove, Ill.: InterVarsity, 1992.

Wilson, Jonathan R. *God So Loved the World: A Christology for Disciples.* Grand Rapids: Baker, 2001.

Wright, N. T. *Jesus and the Victory of God.* Minneapolis: Fortress, 1997.

———. *The Resurrection of the Son of God.* Minneapolis: Fortress, 2003.

CHAPTER 10

THE HOLY SPIRIT

CRAIG KEENER

Although the Spirit has always been important in Trinitarian theology, Pentecostal and charismatic movements (as well as Vatican II in the Roman Catholic Church) have invited renewed attention to the work of the Holy Spirit. This change includes evangelicalism, where the voices of the global South and parts of Asia (now numerically the majority of evangelicals) tend to be charismatic by Western standards. This chapter seeks to emphasize elements of pneumatology that are most significant in light of both NT sources and these global concerns.

Contemporary Pneumatologies

In keeping with the growing charismatic emphasis in Christianity, theologians such as Karl Rahner and Jürgen Moltmann have emphasized the ideally charismatic nature of the church that values the giftings and participation of each member. Likewise, many (including Moltmann and Clark Pinnock) seek to articulate the value of glossolalia in Spirit-experience. Against charismatic subjectivity and modern individualism, many resist the modern urge to privatize and subjectivize faith, including spiritual experience; thus some insist on a wider role for the Spirit than theology has typically emphasized. Some (like Wolfhart Pannenberg and Moltmann) develop the biblical perspective of the Spirit's role in creation and sustenance (e.g., Ps 104:30), reemphasizing the Spirit's immanent cosmic role. Many also emphasize the Spirit's activity in all humanity, not just among believers in Christ. Feminist theologians often emphasize feminine aspects of the Spirit (a feminine noun in Hebrew, though neuter in Greek).

Evangelical theology has tended to focus on a narrower range of concerns, although it does not always exclude such wider discussions. Thus, for example, Pinnock and Amos Yong have explored the Spirit's work among people of other faiths in addition to that among Christians; the strong majority of evangelicals, however, continue to focus on the Christocentric experience of the Spirit dominant in the NT. Many (such as Donald Bloesch) seek to bring word and Spirit together. While evangelicals currently hold diverse views regarding gender, many Pentecostal and charismatic theologies expect the Spirit to empower all believers for ministry regardless of gender.

Evangelicals have historically emphasized especially the objective word (Scripture and Christ), and today often wrestle to connect both the objective word (emphasized, for example, by the magisterial Reformers) and the subjective Spirit (emphasized, for example, by Pentecostals or early Friends). Evangelical theology's emphasis on Scripture influences the focus on biblical themes in most of this chapter. Likewise, the new dominance of Pentecostal and charismatic movements (as broadly defined) in global evangelicalism, which is increasingly influencing global evangelical theology, shapes considerations about which issues this chapter must emphasize.

The Spirit as a Person

Reasoning from the baptismal formula in Matt 28:19, Athanasius (c. 295–373) concluded that the Spirit was a divine person like the Father and the Son. The Cappadocian fathers emphasized the Trinity; one of these, Gregory of Nazianzus (329–389), noted that while the OT revealed especially the Father and the NT more fully the Son, believers in the age of the Spirit increasingly understood the distinct person of the Spirit. The Council of Constantinople in 381 declared that the Father, Son, and Spirit share the same glory and are due the same worship.[1]

Like other Christians, evangelicals are Trinitarian and regard the Spirit as a divine person distinguishable from the Father and the Son. (Because modalists are few and usually isolated from the Christian theological mainstream, I omit discussion of them here.) Although the biblical evidence does not always emphasize the distinct personality of the Spirit, the distinction sometimes appears. This is clearest in Trinitarian formulas (Matt 28:19; 2 Cor 13:13 [14 in some versions]; Gal 4:6), and in John 14–16, where Jesus sends another advocate like himself (Jn 14:16), who acts in very personal ways (14:17, 26; 15:26; 16:7, 13–15). Although the masculine pronouns there simply reflect the corresponding noun *paraklētos* ("advocate," "intercessor," "helper"), like the usual neuter pronouns fitting *pneuma* ("Spirit"), the activities parallel those of Jesus himself elsewhere in the Fourth Gospel.[2]

Because affirmation of the Spirit as a person is rarely a matter of controversy among Christians, I focus below more on activities of the Spirit emphasized in the

NT. In the NT the Spirit is the indispensable element of power for the believer's life with God, whether in becoming a new person in Christ, living the Christian life, empowerment for worship and sharing Christ with others, or various gifting for ministry to others.

The Spirit and God's Activity

I have categorized the biblical evidence somewhat arbitrarily; all of it involves the Spirit's person, power, and presence. In this section, I survey the Spirit as the foretaste of the coming age, as the revealer of Jesus, as God's active presence, and as the power for worship acceptable to God.

The Spirit of the Coming Age

In many eras and parts of the world, evangelicalism has been associated with eschatological interest, although evangelicals have varied widely in their views (for example, from amillennial to postmillennial to premillenial). Nevertheless, evangelicals, like other Christians, have often neglected a central aspect of early Christian pneumatology: the NT's frequent portrayal of the experience of the Spirit as a foretaste of the coming age.

The prophets often spoke of God pouring out his Spirit in the future time of Israel's restoration (Isa 44:3; 59:21; 61:1; Ezek 36:27; 37:14; 39:29; Joel 2:28–29). With some exceptions (like the Qumran sectarians), most Jewish groups in Jesus' era believed that the Spirit was no longer active to the degree experienced by the OT prophets, effectively relegating the most dramatic activity of the Spirit to a future time. On the feast of tabernacles (Jn 7:2, 37) Jerusalemites listened to passages about the eschatological rivers of water from Jerusalem or its temple (Ezek 47:1–7; Zech 14:8). Jesus fulfills this expectation by promising the Spirit (Jn 7:37–39).

Early Christians associated the Spirit with Jesus' resurrection (Rom 1:4; 8:11; 1 Tim 3:16; 1 Pet 3:18) and their own coming resurrection (Rom 8:10–11; 1 Pet 4:6; cf. Rev 11:11). When Jesus spoke of both the Spirit and his coming kingdom, his disciples asked what they regarded as the obvious question: was Jesus about to restore the kingdom to Israel (Acts 1:4–6)? Jesus answered by distinguishing the time of his kingdom's consummation from the present eschatological era between his comings: Spirit-empowered witness to the nations was part of the prophetic promise (Acts 1:7–8; see Isa 43:10, 12; 44:3, 8). After recognizing theophanic signs that could be associated with the end-time, such as wind (Acts 2:2; cf. Ezek 37:5–10, 14) and fire (Acts 2:3; cf. Isa 66:15; Lk 3:9, 16–17), Peter declares that the Spirit associated with Israel's restoration was already being poured out "in the last days" (Acts 2:16–18).

Other sources also recognized that the eschatological era of the Spirit had already dawned: thus believers already had the "first fruits" (beginning of the harvest) of the Spirit, guaranteeing their resurrection (Rom 8:23), and experienced a foretaste of the future restoration by the Spirit (1 Cor 2:9–10; cf. Heb 6:4–5). The Spirit was the "down payment" of their future inheritance (2 Cor 1:22; 5:5; Eph 1:13–14), marked them for future redemption (Eph 4:30), and enabled them to await future vindication (Gal 5:5). The Spirit in effect actualized God's kingdom in the present (Rom 14:17).

Because other Jewish groups may have criticized early Christians for claiming a Messiah without Israel's visible restoration, one of the key elements of early Christian apologetic was the Spirit's dramatic activity in Jesus and in his followers. In their view, the messianic ("kingdom") era, while not yet consummated, had already begun; the Spirit's activity confirmed Jesus as God's anointed and themselves as his followers. Living in eschatological expectation, recognizing their continuity with the biblical prophets, early Christians expected the Spirit to make a discernible difference in believers' lives, a foretaste of the kingdom. The Spirit involved a lived experience rather than a doctrine to be acknowledged yet dissociated from life. The best of evangelical religion, like the best of Christian faith more generally, reflects this confidence, although theologically evangelical faith is as capable as any other of becoming experientially nominal.

The Spirit Reveals Jesus

Trinitarian theology historically emphasizes the relationship among members of the Trinity, often even describing the Spirit in terms of the love between the Father and the Son (Augustine). The Christocentric focus that evangelicalism shares with much of Christendom fits not only the NT gospel message but also the promised activity of the Spirit. The divine Spirit in the NT is the Spirit of Christ (Jn 16:14–15; Acts 2:33, 38; 16:7; Rom 8:9).

In keeping with the philosophic milieu of their era, the Eastern church fathers emphasized transformation by vision of the divine; the NT model for divine vision was Moses, who was transformed by his encounter with God's glory (2 Cor 3:7–18). But whereas philosophers sought to contemplate a deity of pure intellect, and Jewish mystics sought visions of God's throne, early Christians found the locus of the vision and knowledge of God where God had revealed himself, in Christ (Jn 1:18; 14:7–9; 2 Cor 4:4; Col 1:15; 3:1–2).

The Spirit, often associated with prophecy in the OT and early Jewish sources, continues this Christocentric revelation of God. When the Spirit comes, he recalls what Jesus already taught (Jn 14:26); testifies about Jesus (15:26); glorifies him (16:14); reveals the things of Jesus (16:15); and speaks what he hears from Jesus (16:13) as Jesus shared what he heard from his Father (15:15). Probably in conflict with the synagogue authorities' epistemology, John believes that the Spirit will enable Jesus' followers to continue to experience him (14:17, 23). Prophets offered many claims to speak by the Spirit; the only secure claims, however, were those that concurred with the standard of the Jesus who came in the flesh, described in the Fourth Gospel

(1 Jn 4:1–6). That is, the true Spirit of God would always be in accordance with the canonical Jesus.

In some sense, the Spirit continues to reveal Jesus even to the world. *Paraklētos*, "helper" (Jn 14:16, 26; 15:26; 16:7) sometimes meant "intercessor" or, in a forensic context, even "advocate." The Spirit is also a "witness" (15:26). Yet the Spirit also "prosecutes" the world concerning sin, righteousness, and judgment (16:8–11), presumably through believers, to whom he comes (16:7). The description of the Spirit's activity in 16:8–11 parallels activities of Jesus elsewhere in John's Gospel (3:20; 5:30; 8:21, 46; 12:31; 14:30; 15:22–24), suggesting that the Spirit continues the active ministry of Jesus to the world.

The Spirit's Christocentric revelation appears often in the NT. The Spirit also empowers testimony for Jesus (Rev 19:10; Acts 1:8) or guides their witness (Acts 8:29; 10:19). The Spirit reminds believers that they are God's children (Rom 8:16) and of God's love for them in Christ (Rom 5:5–8). Many Majority World evangelicals may also find special interest in the Spirit's power to face conflict and suffering (e.g., Mk 1:7–13; 13:11; Acts 13:51–52).

God's Presence

Historically, Christians have understood the Spirit as uniting the church to God. The OT spoke of God's Spirit with his people both in the past (Neh 9:20; Isa 63:10–11, 14) and future (Ezek 39:29; Hag 2:5). In the NT, as well, the Spirit actualizes God's presence among his people. Jesus promised to bring his followers into the Father's presence (Jn 14:2–6); the Spirit who had been with them in Jesus' ministry would now reside in them (14:16–17; Rom 8:9, 11), along with the Father and Son (Jn 14:23; cf. 1 Jn 3:24; 4:13). Believers should thus recognize God's presence with them continually.

The Spirit and Worship

Evangelicals vary widely in worship styles, reflecting both denominational and cultural distinctions. In the NT, one mark of true believers is that they "worship by the Spirit," in contrast to dependence on a holy place or an outward ritual rooted merely in specific ethnic traditions (Jn 4:20–24; Phil 3:3). Just as the NT contrasts the inadequacy of the flesh with the power of the Spirit in the moral sphere (Gal 5:16–23; Rom 8:2–11, esp. 8:8), so the only worship appropriate to an infinitely holy God would be worship inspired by God's Spirit.

OT narratives about prophetic or charismatic worship probably offer the primary background for the NT "worship by the Spirit" (cf. e.g., 1 Sam 10:5–6). This includes priests and Levites in the temple "prophesying" in worshiping God (1 Chron 25:1–5), the setting that generated many of the psalms (2 Chron 29:30). (God inspired both prophecy and praise, and some psalms moved between them, e.g., Ps 46:1, 10.) We should not of course read these narratives through modern lenses of what "charismatic" worship must or must not include: for example, prophetic worship in the temple was supremely orderly and organized (1 Chron 25:1–8). The essential point is that God is so holy that God's own presence and power are needed so that people can worship him adequately. It is God's inspiration that distinguishes between mere music about God and worship to him.

The Spirit and Transformation

The Spirit's empowerment extends even to becoming a believer and living the Christian life. Because evangelicals agree on most of these details but debate especially one aspect of this empowerment (namely, whether "baptism in the Spirit" involves conversion or a subsequent event), I start with that debate. Then I turn to the Spirit and conversion, moral fruit, and mental transformation.

At Conversion or after Conversion?

Evangelicals divide concerning definitions of "baptism in the Spirit" and the nature of experiences subsequent to conversion. I briefly summarize here the current debate before turning to an approach that I believe can synthesize some of the best insights of various approaches.

Although Puritan and Reformed "sealers" (like Richard Baxter) believed in a subsequent work, most Reformed thinkers emphasize the reception of the Spirit at conversion, viewing this experience as "baptism in the Spirit." Most Holiness and Pentecostal movements emphasize a baptism in the Spirit subsequent to conversion; sacramental traditions that affirm baptismal regeneration usually claim, in a similar way, a second work of the Spirit at confirmation. (Sacramental traditions also can envision an experiential "release" of the Spirit already imparted at baptism, as often in charismatic Catholic and sacramental Protestant theologies.) John Wesley had emphasized a second work of grace producing greater inward purity; some of his followers began to call this experience "baptism in the Holy Spirit." In the late nineteenth and early twentieth centuries, some other evangelicals, including some in the Reformed tradition, also spoke of a second work, "baptism in the Spirit," often for empowerment for service (D. L. Moody; A. J. Gordon; R. A. Torrey; Andrew Murray; F. B. Meyer; earlier Charles Finney).

Such expectations influenced the early twentieth-century Pentecostal movement; some evangelicals, reacting against Pentecostals, then became more vocal against this position. The twentieth-century shift to Pentecostalism constituting a major face (in many places even the primary face) of evangelicalism in the Majority World today (although Pentecostals and especially charismatics do not share a single, unified view) makes dialogue all the more important. Whereas some Western evangelical academics were once dismissive of Pentecostal perspectives, the tone of today's discussion has become much more respectful and often welcomes diverse perspectives.

The debate proves less serious once its contenders get past semantics: virtually all participants agree that the Spirit is somehow received (normally in the most important way) at conversion; nearly all likewise concur that believers can have experiences with the Spirit subsequent to conversion (indeed, not just a single one). A significant part of the debate involves the labels given to the different experiences. (Many who argue for a subsequent experience also allow that the experience they emphasize can sometimes occur simultaneously with conversion.)

Some of the difficulty in the debate is that the biblical evidence supports both positions, in that "baptism in the Spirit" is used broadly and sometimes differently by different biblical authors. Thus when John the Baptist announced that Jesus would baptize in the Spirit and in fire (Matt 3:11//Lk 3:16), he contrasted how Jesus would deal with the repentant (the Spirit) and with the unrepentant (fire; cf. Matt 3:10, 12). While all the repentant would be baptized in the Spirit, John summarizes here all Jesus' eschatological activity by the Spirit, not dividing it into various aspects. (Although John envisions a gift to all the righteous, he knew that this end-time outpouring would include prophetic empowerment; Joel 2:28–29.) When Jesus speaks of being "born from the water of the Spirit" (as Calvin and many other exegetes translate the Greek construction in Jn 3:5), he may play on the traditional Jewish image of proselyte baptism to refer to a *spiritual* proselyte baptism, an immersion in the Spirit. In such passages, baptism in the Spirit would seem to involve conversion, whatever other nuances may be present (see most clearly 1 Cor 12:13).

By contrast, Luke seems to focus on a particular aspect of the Spirit. While the Spirit may be received at conversion (Acts 2:38–39; cf. Lk 3:16), Luke does not usually emphasize the regenerative activity of the Spirit. Instead, he focuses on power for witness (Acts 1:8), expressed in terms of speaking by divine inspiration (2:17–18; cf. 2:4). What is more, the particular aspect of the Spirit he emphasizes, while implicitly provided in conversion, sometimes appears to be experienced subsequent to conversion. Some (notably Dunn) have argued that the Samaritans, who received the gospel with joy and were baptized, were not yet converted before the apostles laid hands on them to impart the Spirit (Acts 8:12–17). Most Acts scholars, however, while appreciating Dunn's treatment of the Spirit in Paul, question his approach in Acts 8. Likewise, some see in Pentecost a subsequent empowerment for Jesus' disciples (though Pentecost might be a special case); many think Paul already "converted" before he was filled with the Spirit (Acts 9:5–17); and certainly other fillings occur subsequent to initial experiences in Acts (e.g., 4:8, 31; 13:9).

Luke ties together the promise to the first disciples with the promise to all believers with various designations: being "baptized" in the Spirit (Acts 1:5, addressing the "apostles") involves the "promise" (1:4; 2:33, 39), hence the "gift" (2:38), a promise to all believers (2:38–39). This constitutes "receiving" the Spirit (1:8; 2:38; 10:47; 19:2), but at least in 8:15, 17, can happen after conversion. (Indeed, "filling" with the Spirit in 2:4 can happen multiple times; 4:8, 31; 9:17; 13:9.) Thus, while Luke concurs theologically with other NT voices that believers receive access to every aspect of the Spirit at conversion, he also seems to allow (whatever the ideal) that believers can embrace or experience some aspects of this empowerment subsequently. This claim should not be controversial: just as most acknowledge that various discoveries or experiences of, or obedience to, biblical truth have revolutionized lives of some who were already believers, there is no reason to deny that believers can experience empowerment subsequent to conversion even if that grace was already implicit beforehand. Because Luke is the one NT witness narrating how early Christians experienced the Spirit, we should take his evidence seriously. Both theological traditions we have noted thus have some claim to represent Scripture's witness.

The Spirit Purifies and Makes New

Christian theology has always noted the role of the Spirit in salvation. Seeking to counter merely nominal faith as well as to missionize non-Christian areas, evangelicals have particularly stressed the Spirit's role in conversion. German Pietism and the British evangelical awakening emphasized being born again supernaturally, an emphasis that pervades global evangelicalism today. The biblical basis for such an emphasis involves not so much an emotional experience (although in much of evangelicalism it has been understandably emotional) as a supernatural transformation (Jn 1:12; 3:3–8; Gal 4:29; 1 Pet 1:3, 23; 1 Jn 2:29; 5:1, 4). Following the metaphor of birth, however, such an initial transformation is the beginning of eternal life. It imparts the character of the begetter (Jn 3:6; 1 Jn 3:9; cf. 2 Pet 1:4)—moral aspects of God's nature (we discuss this further below as the "fruit of the Spirit").

Although early Judaism developed especially the OT association of the Spirit with the activity of the prophets, some sources also associated the Spirit with purification (following Ezek 36:25–27). John's Gospel develops this association, contrasting traditional religious associations of water. Jesus relativizes the value of ritual purification (John 2:6–10), is greater than the Samaritan holy site of Jacob's well (4:10–14), and offers healing that sacred Jerusalem's pools could not provide (5:5–9; 9:6–7). More critically, Jesus' baptism in the Spirit is greater than John's baptism (1:31–33). In Jn 3:3–5, Jesus may speak of a spiritual proselyte baptism, a baptism in the Spirit (implicitly greater than traditional proselyte baptism with water).[3] Purifying "water" in 3:5 and 4:14 is probably symbolic for the purifying Spirit (7:39).

The Fruit of God's Presence and Character

The Eastern church has historically emphasized the Spirit's role in transforming believers to share the divine life and character. Theologians such as Moltmann have lamented the sometimes exclusive association of the Spirit with redemption; some, like Pinnock, have sought to reappropriate the Eastern church's emphasis on union with God. Although many evangelicals (for example, in the Holiness tradition) have shared this emphasis, the evangelical emphasis on conversion has obscured this emphasis on spiritual character for some. Some Western evangelicals have tended to define their faith theologically, and some Pentecostals and charismatics have tended to define it in terms of spiritual power for ministry. Because it has not been a controversial distinctive, the "fruit of the Spirit" has generated less discussion, although some (like Wesley or the early Indian Pentecostal Pandita Ramabai) have spoken of love as the greatest sign of the Spirit. Edwards, who is sometimes called the premier evangelical theologian, said love is "the sum of all virtue" because it *is* the Holy Spirit. William Seymour, an African-American at the heart of the early Pentecostal revival, emphasized Spirit-empowered love to cross ethnic barriers, exemplified symbolically by the geographically diverse crowds on the day of Pentecost (Acts 2:5–11).

In Scripture, the Spirit not only initially transformed those who transferred their allegiance to Christ but also caused them to share God's moral character. Some of Paul's detractors insisted that Gentile Christians must obey the law to be true members of God's people; Paul countered that the law of the Spirit was what produced the righteousness taught by the law (Rom 7:6; 8:2–4; 2 Cor 3:3, 6–8, 17–18); those who obeyed the Spirit would fulfill the real moral point of the law without depending on its external (and specifically Israelite) form (Gal 5:16, 22–23). Although Greeks also spoke of righteous character not needing external laws, Paul alludes especially to Ezekiel's promise that God would put his Spirit in the hearts of his people so they would obey him from the heart (Ezek 36:27; cf. Jer 31:33). Paul insists that believers must depend on the Spirit (and God's work in them) rather than flesh (mere human ability) to perform righteousness.

Paul contrasts the works of the flesh with the fruit that comes naturally from depending on God's Spirit, who lives in believers (Gal 5:19–23). Love fulfills the law (5:14); those led by the Spirit are not "under" the law (5:18), for the Spirit causes them to love (5:22), and the law will not oppose such a lifestyle (5:23). Paul is no antinomian: the issue is that the law is now internalized rather than merely an external standard; because the Messiah had come, the promised new covenant meant that the Spirit wrote God's law in the hearts of his people (see Jer 31:31–34; Ezek 36:25–27, noted above). Jewish people spoke of "walking" according to God's commandments; Paul encourages those who have life by the Spirit to "walk" by the Spirit (5:16, 25). The life of the Spirit should not exhibit pride and competition, but loving, humble service (5:13–15; 6:1–3).

Fruit such as love and peace have corporate implications. In a context of ethnic division between Jew and Gentile, Paul emphasizes that the Spirit provides unity for believers (Eph 4:3), who together become a united temple for God's worship by the Spirit (Eph 2:18–22). The Spirit generates "fellowship" (2 Cor 13:14; Phil 2:1–2) and love (Col 1:8).

The Mind of the Spirit

Whereas some segments of evangelicalism have highlighted the mind (and even been accused of embracing rationalism), others, particularly with backgrounds in U.S. revivalism or groups socially marginalized from the mainstream, emerged with a suspicion of education and reason. As the academy has grown less hostile toward the latter groups and their own opportunities for education have increased, the dichotomy has diminished, but it persists in some circles.

One helpful approach to such conflicts may be Paul's teaching about the Spirit inspiring the mind and perspectives. Whereas some charismatics have emphasized only the Spirit's witness to the human spirit (Rom 8:16), Paul seems interested in the mind as well as the spirit, the rational as well as the affective aspect of the human personality (1 Cor 14:14–15). The "renewed" mind reflects the new era in Christ, not the present age (Rom 12:2), hence considers how to serve others (12:3–8). The Spirit provides a mindset involving life and peace, contrasted with that of flesh (8:5–7; cf. Is 26:3). Just as only the person knows their own heart, so only God's Spirit knows God's heart and can reveal it to believers (1 Cor 2:10–12). Paul declares that believers have the mind of Christ by the Spirit (1 Cor 2:16). (He echoes here Is 40:13, which has "Spirit" in the Hebrew and "mind" in the Greek version.)[4]

The Spirit and Empowerment to Serve Others

I briefly survey here gifts and cross-cultural evangelism. Reports of charismatic phenomena pervade the church's history, albeit more in some periods than in others.[5] When the Montanists claimed to revive prophecy in the late second century, more traditional church leaders countered by appealing to the continuance of "orthodox" prophecy. Firsthand and secondhand accounts of healings and exorcisms abound in the church fathers (and other surviving documents from antiquity). Augustine initially believed that miracles had ceased, but later retracted that view. He admitted that the sick were not always healed nor did the baptized always speak in tongues, as he thought characteristic of an earlier era; nevertheless, he knew of many miracles. In just two years of record-keeping, his diocese documented over seventy miracles, and he was aware of many not included.

By the fifth century such phenomena apparently declined, especially in the West, but they never died out, as stories of saints and mystics (e.g., Hildegard of Bingen) testify. Miracle claims abound especially in the East (e.g., Constantinople and Ethiopia), though many medieval reports are shrouded in hagiography. Many sought healings through saints' relics, perhaps as a point of contact for faith with the apostolic past (cf. 2 Kgs 13:21).

Charismatic phenomena appeared at various points in modern evangelicalism, including in the First Great Awakening (1740–1742, reported by Jonathan Edwards). They were even more prominent in the ministry of John Wesley (1703–1791) and the early Methodists, spilling over into the Second Great Awakening in the early nineteenth-century United States. While the value of suffering predominated in much of nineteenth-century evangelical theology, reports of healing ministries in Britain, Germany, and Switzerland combined with the spirit of faith missions to generate increased emphasis on divine healing by the late nineteenth century. Healing claims were a hallmark of late nineteenth-century radical evangelicals and were adopted by early Pentecostalism.

Biblical evidence regarding the Spirit's empowerment is not limited to such activities, but that it includes them challenges the sterility of some Western Enlightenment assumptions, assumptions rejected by most Christians in the Majority World. Indeed, some Western evangelicals who have charged some movements in the global South with elements of syncretism (sometimes accurately, sometimes not) have rarely reckoned with how deeply the worldview of deism may have shaped their own syncretism.

The Spirit Gifts Believers for Service

Three NT passages connect the image of the body with diverse gifts (Rom 12:4–8; 1 Cor 12:8–30; Eph 4:4–13), developing an image of diversity and unity familiar in current political and philosophic discourse. Divine grace (*charis*) empowers these gifts (*charismata*; Rom 12:6; 1 Pet 4:10; cf. Eph 4:7), and God grants individuals the faith to serve in these different functions (Rom 12:3, 6). More to the point here, God's Spirit energizes and empowers these gifts (1 Cor 12:4, 7–11). Just as the believer's moral life depends on God's power, so does the believer's service to other believers.

Because another chapter in this volume treats the gifts more specifically, we merely survey some of them here.[6] Christ's gift grants various sorts of leaders to the church (Eph 4:7, 11); their role (implemented in various ways) is to equip all believers for the work of ministry, until the entire body comes to maturity in Christ (Eph 4:11–13). In Rom 12:6–8, the various functions include not only what we consider "supernatural" gifts like prophecy but also "natural" ones like support for the needy; our modern dichotomy between "natural" and "supernatural" obscures the point that God empowers us for all these works. In 1 Cor 12, where Paul expressly attributes gifts to the Spirit, his first list begins with wise and knowledgeable speech, highly prized in Corinth, and ends with tongues and interpretation, excessively exalted in Corinth (12:8–10). Both sorts of gifts are open to abuse (e.g., 1 Cor 8:1). That Paul offers other lists of gifts even in the same context (12:28, 29–30; 13:1–2, 8, 9; 14:26) shows that he intends these lists to be ad hoc rather than comprehensive, simply examples of the sorts of ways God empowers believers to serve one another.

Because of problems in Corinth, Paul contrasts two of these gifts at greater length. In 1 Cor 14, Paul prefers prophecy to tongues in the public assembly because all profit from intelligible speech. Prayer in tongues was profitable publicly if interpreted; otherwise its value was especially for private prayer. Apparently Paul understood tongues as prayer with one's spirit, or the affective aspect of the personality, yet able to be interpreted in an intelligible form (14:14–15).

Using arguments from some Reformers (but most widespread in some dispensational circles), some evangelicals believe that particular gifts ceased either around the end of the first century or in following centuries. This position seems problematic, however, in that the same gifts, with the same evidences as in Scripture, have resurfaced periodically throughout history. It is also problematic to divide the gifts on the list: why should prophecy and tongues cease, for example, yet faith and knowledge continue? (One might respond that Paul refers only to a supernatural quantity of faith or means of knowledge, but "knowledge" does not normally bear that meaning elsewhere in 1 Corinthians.) Most exegetes find this approach to this letter unconvincing: the only text that mentions the passing of gifts (prophecy, tongues, and knowledge, 13:8–9) also designates the timing: when believers see Jesus face to face (13:10–12). Most exegetes assign that time to Jesus' return. (Other cessationists have appealed to apostles and prophets belonging only to a foundational era based on Eph 2:20, but this seems to press too much chronology into a building metaphor. Contrast, for example, Eph 4:11–13; Rev 11:10; 18:20.)

Other factors historically facilitated skepticism in the continuance of the gifts. One was the prevalence of an antisupernatural prejudice in Western philosophy since the radical Enlightenment.[7] Another was some Reformers' reaction against irrational and unsubstantiated claims dominant in their era (both those associated with relics and those associated with some prophets who stirred political unrest). Careless claims today often invite the same reactions, yielding the same range of opinions.

In general, cessationism is stronger (though still a minority) among evangelicals in the West; the most abundant miracle claims dominate in much of the global South and parts of Asia.[8] Most evangelical scholars today believe that the gifts continue, but do not believe that every believer must pray in tongues (the classical Pentecostal position). Nevertheless, both those who believe that some gifts have ceased and classical Pentecostals constitute sizeable numbers of evangelicals. (Indeed, although the numbers can be calculated differently depending on definitions, and views among them vary, many observers estimate over half a billion Pentecostals and charismatics today.) Whether or not employing the evangelical label, however, most of them also recognize the others as fellow members of the broad evangelical movement, because they emphasize the same gospel message.

The Spirit Empowers for Evangelism

Evangelicals emphasize evangelism and missions; biblically, dependence on the Spirit is central to this concern. Luke's first volume speaks of the Spirit empowering Jesus both to proclaim and to meet needs (Lk 4:18–19; cf. Acts 10:38), an interest also continued in his second volume, Acts. Acts, however, emphasizes the empowerment of Jesus' followers to continue his mission. Although Luke focuses on key figures like Peter and Paul, he recognizes that the Spirit is for all believers (Acts 2:38–39).

Developing an important biblical emphasis, early Judaism associated the Spirit most often with prophecy and the sorts of activities associated with prophets.[9] This is also Luke's primary emphasis, reiterated by his Joel quotation in Acts 2:17–18: "your sons and daughters will prophesy." But while Luke clearly believes in literal prophets and prophetesses (e.g., Lk 2:36; Acts 11:27–28; 21:9–11), his own interest is especially the "word of the Lord" in the gospel (e.g., Acts 8:25; 12:24). Echoing language from Isaiah, in what many regard as the "thesis statement" or program for Acts, Luke indicates that the Spirit will empower witness to the ends of the earth (1:8; cf. Lk 24:47–49). The rest of Acts illustrates this expectation. Dependence on God's power for proclamation and often for signs confirming that proclamation characterizes the rest of Acts.

When the Spirit first comes in Acts 2, the immediate sign that Peter identifies with prophetic empowerment (2:17–18) is worship in "other tongues" (2:4), apparently languages unknown to the speakers. Although this phenomenon is not mentioned in every instance of initial receiving the Spirit in Acts (hence is debated, for example, in Acts 8:17), Luke mentions it also in connection with two other outpourings of the Spirit (10:46; 19:6). Luke does note other fruits of the Spirit's coming, such as boldness (4:31; 13:9–10) and economic sharing (2:44–45; 4:31–35), but why does he mention tongues three times?

Given Luke's emphasis on the Spirit's power to proclaim Christ cross-culturally (1:8), tongues provided a useful confirmation of a primary *purpose* of the Spirit's coming. If God's Spirit could inspire believers to worship God in other people's languages, how much more could he inspire them to proclaim him to other people in languages shared by both? Many scholars find an allusion to the scattering of languages at Babel in Acts 2:5–11; now the Lord disperses his own followers to proclaim him throughout the world. The Spirit also empowers subsequent groups for the same task (10:46; 19:6). Ultimately, believers in all cultures share the same Spirit, hence become partners in the same global mission.

Late nineteenth-century radical evangelicals understood Acts 2 as referring to "missionary tongues" that would enable them to evangelize the world without needing to learn other languages. People prayed for such tongues, and early Pentecostals believed that the prayer had been answered. In the vast majority of cases, missionaries discovered that they still had to learn local languages to share the gospel, but missions remained a central emphasis in Pentecostalism. Some Pentecostals (like some other evangelicals) believed that the Spirit could also empower newer, indigenous churches (cf. Acts 8:15–17; 10:44–47; 19:6); this emphasis on Spirit-empowered partnership in the gospel has contributed to the growth of global Christianity. Evangelicals today claim a range of views, as noted above, between Pentecostal and cessationist. All can agree, however, about the common mission to which tongues in the Book of Acts points. The Spirit empowers God's people to sensitively share the good news about Christ across all cultural barriers, and to partner respectfully with believers in other cultures for the common mission of the church.

Conclusion

We have surveyed here only some of what evangelicals believe about the Spirit, and only some of the biblical evidence to which they appeal. Nevertheless, a common pattern emerges throughout this material. Whether the issue is salvation, moral behavior, mission or ministry to one another in Christ's body, God's own Spirit is the only sufficient empowerment. That is, important as beliefs are, doctrine by itself is not enough. Those who truly believe in God through Christ must depend on him, trusting the power of the Spirit he provides.

NOTES

1. For one detailed survey of historical and contemporary pneumatology, see Veli-Matti Karkkainen, *Pneumatology* (Grand Rapids: Baker, 2002), 37–177.

2. See sources and discussion in Craig S. Keener, *The Gospel of John: A Commentary.* 2 vols. (Peabody, Mass.: Hendrickson, 2003), 953–969.

3. For this interpretation, see ibid., 537–555; also Craig Keener, *The Spirit in the Gospels and Acts: Divine Purity and Power* (Peabody, Mass.: Hendrickson, 2010), 135–189.

4. For more details, see Craig Keener, "'Fleshly' versus Spirit Perspectives in Romans 8:5–8," 211–229 in *Paul: Jew, Greek and Roman*, ed. Stanley Porter (Leiden: Brill, 2008); Keener, *1–2 Corinthians* (New York: Cambridge University Press, 2005), 39–40.

5. See, for example, Morton T. Kelsey, *Healing and Christianity in Ancient Thought and Modern Times* (New York: Harper & Row, 1973); Robert Bruce Mullin, *Miracles and the Modern Religious Imagination* (New Haven: Yale University Press, 1996); Amanda Porterfield, *Healing in the History of Christianity* (New York: Oxford University Press, 2005).

6. Among many useful studies of these gifts in the New Testament, see for example, D. A. Carson, *Showing the Spirit: A Theological Exposition of 1 Corinthians 12–14* (Grand Rapids: Baker, 1987); Max Turner, *The Holy Spirit and Spiritual Gifts in the New Testament Church and Today*, rev. ed. (Peabody, Mass.: Hendrickson, 1998).

7. See Jon Ruthven, *On the Cessation of the Charismata: The Protestant Polemic on Postbiblical Miracles* (Sheffield: Sheffield Academic Press, 1993), esp. 35–40, 71.

8. See, for example, Philip Jenkins, *The Next Christendom: The Coming of Global Christianity* (New York: Oxford University Press, 2002), 107; cf. also, for example, Christiaan Rudolph De Wet, "Signs and Wonders in Church Growth" (M.A. missiology thesis, Fuller Theological Seminary, 1981); Tony Lambert, *China's Christian Millions: The Costly Revival* (Grand Rapids: Monarch Books, 1999); *Asian and Pentecostal: The Charismatic Face of Christianity in Asia*, ed. Allan Anderson and Edmond Tang (Oxford: Regnum; Baguio City, Philippines: APTS Press, 2005).

9. Robert P. Menzies, *Empowered for Witness: The Spirit in Luke-Acts* (New York: T & T Clark International, 2004), 49–101; Max Turner, *Power from on High: The Spirit in Israel's Restoration and Witness in Luke-Acts* (Sheffield: Sheffield Academic Press, 1996), 86–104; Keener, *Spirit*, 10–13, 31–33.

BIBLIOGRAPHY

Cho, Youngmo. *Spirit and Kingdom in the Writings of Luke and Paul: An Attempt to Reconcile These Concepts.* Foreword by R. P. Menzies. Waynesboro, Ga.: Paternoster, 2005.

Dunn, James D. G. *Baptism in the Holy Spirit: A Re-examination of the New Testament Teaching on the Gift of the Spirit in Relation to Pentecostalism Today.* Studies in Biblical Theology, 2d ser., 15. London: SCM, 1970.

Fee, Gordon D. *God's Empowering Presence: The Holy Spirit in the Letters of Paul.* Peabody, Mass.: Hendrickson, 1994.

———. *Paul, the Spirit, and the People of God.* Peabody, Mass.: Hendrickson, 1996.

Kärkkäinen, Veli-Matti. *Pneumatology: The Holy Spirit in Ecumenical, International, and Contextual Perspective.* Grand Rapids: Baker, 2002.

Keener, Craig S. *Gift and Giver: The Holy Spirit for Today.* Grand Rapids: Baker, 2001.

Menzies, Robert P. *Empowered for Witness: The Spirit in Luke-Acts.* London: T & T Clark International, 2004.

Philip, Finny. *The Origins of Pauline Pneumatology: The Eschatological Bestowal of the Spirit upon Gentiles in Judaism and in the Early Development of Paul's Theology.* Tübingen: Mohr Siebeck, 2005.

Turner, Max. *The Holy Spirit and Spiritual Gifts in the New Testament Church and Today.* Rev. ed. Peabody, Mass.: Hendrickson, 1998.

Turner, Max. *Power from on High: The Spirit in Israel's Restoration and Witness in Luke-Acts.* Sheffield: Sheffield Academic Press, 1996.

Yong, Amos. *The Spirit Poured Out on All Flesh: Pentecostalism and the Possibility of Global Theology.* Grand Rapids: Baker, 2005.

PART III

THEOLOGY OF SALVATION

CHAPTER 11

ISRAEL AND SALVATION

RIKK WATTS

THE New Testament is surprisingly reticent when it comes to direct statements on Israel's future. Jesus speaks of the Twelve judging Israel (Matt 19:28; *par.* Luke 22:30) and warns a soon-to-be desolate Jerusalem they will not see him again until he is welcomed (Matt 23:39). But when pressed on the timing of Israel's kingdom, he deflects the question (Acts 1:6–8). And if the plethora of interpretations are any indication, Paul's "all Israel will be saved" (Rom 11:25–26) remains almost as mysterious as the mystery it was meant to reveal.

Nevertheless, from the beginning texts such as Hebrews 8:13, which was generally taken to mean that the entire old covenant was obsolete, and Galatians 3:6–9, where only believers, whether Jew or Gentile, were genuine descendents of Abraham, were suggestive. These, along with the increasingly Gentile character of early Christianity, the Jewish disasters of 70 and 135 C.E., and heightened tensions between Jews and Christians, led several second-century Christian writers to declare that in rejecting Christ the Jews as a nation had forfeited the covenant and its promised salvation, and both now belonged to the Christians (*Barn.* 4, 6–8) who were the real people of God (Justin, *Dial.* 11:5; Melito of Sardis, *Peri Pascha* 39–45).

But this was not the whole story. Augustine, for example, could see God's providence in the ongoing existence of unbelieving Jews, since their prophecies by their very antiquity authenticated Christian demolition of pagan images and temples (*De civitate Dei*, 4.34). As to Paul's clarification of "this mystery" (Rom 11:25–26), the early Fathers found it as confusing as does recent scholarship, offering a similar variety of interpretations (Cohen 2005). Several understood "all Israel" to include believing Jews and Gentiles (Irenaeus, *Adv. ha.* 4.2.7; Clement of Alexandria, *Exc. Theod.* 56.4–5; Theodore of Mopsuestia, *In ep. ad. Rom.* 11.26, and Augustine,

Ep. Rom. 149.19). However, sometimes Origen and Augustine took it to mean ethnic Israel as whole (e.g., *Comm. Rom.* 8.11; *Gen. hom.* 5.5; *Lev. hom.* 3.5; 5.11; and *Quaest. Hept.* 2.154; 5.56; *Quest. ev.* 2.33; *Enarrat. Psa.* 45.15; 138.8), as did the majority of subsequent commentators until the twelfth century, but on other occasions only the remnant was meant (Origen, *Comm. Rom.* 8.11; *Jerem. Hom.* 5.4; *Comm. Matt.* 17.5; and *Ep. Rom.* 149.19; cf. Chrysostom, *Hom. Rom.* 19.7). For Pelagius, instead of the church replacing Israel, God had leveled them so that "all Israel" (that is, without distinction) applied, strikingly, to the present salvation of Jews but, as with Gentiles, only by faith (*Expos. Rom.* 11.1, 11, 26). Aquinas hoped for the reintegration of "all Israel" (though not every individual) in the third age of the church (*Expos. Sup. Ep. Rom.* II.2). While for Luther the text was too obscure to permit comment (*Lect. Rom.* 315), Calvin expected that not only would a remnant of Israel be ingathered (*Comm.*, "Isaiah," 8.269) but they would obtain the first place (*Comm.*, "Romans," 19.434–440).

In the modern period, the Holocaust as a partial consequence of "Christian" Europe's centuries of anti-Semitism, the dramatic emergence in 1948 of the State of Israel, the demise of foundationalism and cultural metanarratives, and the rise of violent fundamentalisms—all these have forced scholars to reconsider the moral implications of their exegesis. Simultaneously, Historical Jesus studies and the New Perspective on Paul (NPP) in affirming the ineluctable Jewishness of Jesus, Paul, and the earliest "Christians," along with the NPP's emphasis on national salvation, have also sharpened sharpened the question of Israel's status.

Gabriel Fackre (1993: 147–167) is thus able to list five varieties of "supersessionism": 1) retributive: God has permanently judged Israel and replaced it with the church; 2) nonretributive: the new covenant is inaugurated in Christ but Israel's future remains unspecified; 3) modified: while only Christ brings salvation, Jews must have the right to live as Jews; 4) messianic: while Jews must convert to Christ, they completely retain their customs; and 5) Christological election: just as predestination has two sides, so too have the people of God, and thus Israel's eternal election cannot be separated from Christ (Karl Barth).[1] In some of these views, though certainly not all, Israel's entire history is reduced to a transitory earthly type destined to pass away before its overwhelming antitype, the eternal spiritual reality of Christ and the church ("economic" supersessionism). In its most deeply embedded form, the Bible is read as a generalized universal narrative from creation to redemption, to which the distinctively Jewish elements are mere background ("structural" supersessionism; so Soulen 1996).

Fackre then describes eight forms of antisupersessionism: 1) Dispensationalism: Israel's rejection of Christ was an interruption to God's plan for the nation and, because prophecies to a literal people require a literal fulfillment, with the church removed from the earth Christ will reign over a converted Jewish nation in Palestine for a thousand years; 2) One People: Israel remains humanity's representative people with Christians naturalized citizens thereof; having no need for conversion, they should be free to establish a state predicated on peace and righteousness (Marcus Barth 1978); 3) Paradoxical: Israel's covenant remains in full force but the church is still to summon all, including Jews, to Christ (cf. now also, for example, Kinzer 2005 and Nanos 2002, 2009, where Jewish Yeshua believers, who are still obligated to observe Torah, stand in a bilateral ecclesial relationship with Torah-free Gentile believers, thereby linking the latter to historic Israel and its covenantal promises); 4) Eschatological: in the end all faithful Jews will encounter Jesus and be saved; 5) Two Covenant: Israel is saved under its own covenant and only Gentiles under the new (Gaston 1979; Stendahl 1976); 6) Midrashic: since all Scripture must conform to the OT revelation of God, classical statements as to Jesus' deity, the Trinity, and salvation through faith in Christ are inappropriately supercessionist even for Christians (Van Buren 1980, 1988); 7) moral pluralism: a variety of religious perspectives can be "true" and so neither Jew nor Christian can make absolute claims about the other, and 8) cultural-linguistic: all doctrinal statements are merely linguistic constructs within which a given community operates and, as such, Israel's understanding of its future salvation is not subject to Christian beliefs. Options 6–8 would appear to be nonstarters for evangelicals (on option 5, see below).

There is also confusion over several terms. Some identify "supersessionism" with "replacement"—God's covenant with the Church has replaced his covenant with the Jews (Soulen 1996). Others, advocating a temporal supersessionism, deny that the church ultimately replaces Israel (Longenecker 1989) and anticipate a future conversion of the majority of Jews (whether within an amillennial or premillennial schema), though they are less clear about the future of Israel as a nation. Some also equate Two Covenant—Israel and Christian Gentiles are saved under the terms of their separate covenants—with *Sonderweg* (special way). However, some proponents of the latter view strenuously deny such an identification. For them "all Israel" is presently under God's judicial hardening, and will not and cannot be converted by the church. This will happen in a "special way" only at Christ's victorious *parousia*, when they will finally respond in faith to him (Mussner 1976; Hofius 1990).

Several critical questions emerge. What do we mean by "Israel" and the "church," and what is the nature of their relationship? What is the status of God's covenants with and prophetic promises to Israel? How do they relate to Jesus and his "new covenant" (Luke 22:20; 2 Cor 3:6)? And who is the "all Israel" of Romans 11:26, and when and how is it to be saved?

The term "Israel," in contrast to the outsider descriptor "the Jews," is a self-designation employed across the NT of a people defined by three basic ideas: God's gracious election of Jacob and his descendents, their obligation of ongoing faithfulness to the divine covenants and in particular circumcision, and the theocratic ideal that emerged from their history, notably the Davidic Golden Age. Never merely ethnic, it is a nevertheless a social term of self-dignity, pertaining to the religious identity and purity of the people. It implies privilege even when regularly employed of those who rejected their Messiah. Leaving aside for the moment Galatians 6:16 and Romans 11:26 (see below), it is always used in this traditional sense and is never applied to the church.

However, as demonstrated by M. A. Elliott (2000), there were already serious divisions over Israel's constitution within first-century Judaism. Various sectarian groups maintained that since many in Israel, including their leaders, had effectively abandoned the covenant, they would suffer judgment and only the faithful remnant would be saved. For some, whereas apostate Israel, guilty of an eternal sin, had been given over to evil spirits, the remnant would enjoy the gift of the Spirit as its confirmatory seal. Although commonly understood as anticipating an other-worldly "apocalyptic" vindication, these groups clearly expected salvation within history (Rowland 1982: 160–176, Wright 1992: 280–338), which salvation often included Gentiles, though always with the remnant at the center. Obviously each group was convinced that it alone was faithful to the covenant. It was for them that "Messiah(s)," however understood, would come. Occasionally they claimed that both the covenant and the name Israel applied only to them. In the main, though, these terms retained their regular referents and a hope for the restoration of Israel in some larger sense was expressed. The famous Mishnaic dictum—"all Israel has a share in the world to come"—reflects a similar ambiguity when it goes on to detail an extensive list of exceptions (*Sanh.* 10:1).

There was a similar diversity of views as to what this future salvation entailed. Most anticipated the restoration of the dispersed tribes, often after a period of intense suffering, to a prosperous, sometimes nearly paradisiacal, land, to each other, and to their God. To varying degrees and in different combinations this might involve a messianic agent, the imagery of a great feast, a renewed covenant with a greater level of obedience to Torah and the outpouring of God's spirit, the removal of uncleanness and disabilities (either through a generalized notion of healing or sometimes exclusion), the building of a new Temple, and the return of Yahweh to Zion. The status of the nations was more problematic, with some expecting only their destruction, while others envisaged their pilgrimage to Jerusalem to offer tribute and even worship. Sometimes Israel's inheritance included the whole earth, which itself might even undergo destruction and new creation, while Satan, his agents, and evil itself were finally annihilated. Commonly this involved a day of judgment, and particularly of the Gentiles by Israel. Central to all of this was the idea, held by several groups, of a future resurrection.

It should be clear from the foregoing, along with the thoroughgoing Jewishness of Jesus and early "Christianity" and the pervasive influence of Israel's Scriptures, that the NT belongs squarely within this milieu. That the pre-Christian Paul regarded Stephen and other followers of "The Way" as under Jewish jurisdiction confirms as much (cf. the later Paul's repeated submission to Synagogue discipline; 2 Cor 11:24). Hence the many similarities, for example, between the Synoptics' presentation of Jesus and the messianic salvation envisaged in *Psalms of Solomon* 17.[2] Even though John's Jesus utters some of the more provocative statements concerning "the Jews," he is equally adamant that salvation is only "from the Jews" (John 4:22; cf. Rom 9:4–5).

The central bone of contention for first-century Jews was the significance of Jesus, who for the NT is Israel's Messianic Son of God, Danielic Son of Man, and ruler over God's Messianic Kingdom. In his casting out of unclean spirits, healing the blind, deaf, mute, and lame, his gift of the promised indwelling Spirit, and his feedings in the desert and commanding the sea, he alone inaugurates the long-awaited new creational/new exodus restoration of creation and of humanity as the image of God, first in Israel and then among the nations (Watts 2002; Wright 1996). Strikingly, although Jewish sectarian groups fundamentally defined themselves in terms of fidelity to Torah, Jesus in calling the Twelve, redefining both his family and God's will around his teaching (Mark 3:33–35), and summoning people to faith in himself reconstitutes (but does not replace) Israel around his very person. To be a faithful Israelite is to believe in him. As the baptism-temptation sequence demonstrates, with its "beloved son" designation (cf. Exod 4:22), descent of the Spirit (cf. Isa 63:11), passing through the water, and a "forty-" day desert sojourn, Israel's foundational exodus moment is recapitulated in Jesus, though now in full obedience. He is Isaiah's true servant-Israel (Isa 42:1 in Mark 1:11 *par.;* cf. Isa 53 in Mark 8:31; 10:45), and thus the true vine (John 15; cf. Ps 80:8–9).

That Jesus answers prayers, purifies lepers (Mark 1:40–44; Luke 17:12–14), heals the sick ("and they came *to him* in the Temple," Matt 21:14), and eschatologically forgives sins (Mark 2:1–12; Luke 7:48), indicates that his realization of salvation transcends the Temple's supplicatory sacrifices in that he now effects what they sought (cf. Heb; also Marshall 1999: 355). It also implies that the present condemned Temple (Jer 7:11 in Mark 11:17; cf. Mark 13) will be replaced by one centered on him, the new chief stone (Mark 12:10, citing Ps 118:22 which, while referring to David, was also related to the restoration of the Temple and understood in some Jewish traditions to mean the stone that completed Solomon's temple, *T. Sol.* 22:7; 23:4; cf. *Tg.* Zech 4:7). Stephen's speech likewise suggests that for Luke, although the Temple is an acceptable place for various traditional activities (Acts 2:46; 3:1; 5:20, 42; 21:26; cf. Matt 17:27), it is no longer the true locus of God's presence (Acts 7:48–53). In John it is Jesus who is the new Temple (e.g., 2:19–21) and thus in Revelation it is the Lord God and the Lamb who constitute the Temple in the New Jerusalem (21:22).

Jesus also fulfills Israel's feasts: not only Passover—by initiating in his death Israel's long-awaited new exodus—but also (for John) Sabbath, Tabernacles, and Dedication. For Hebrews, Jesus, patterned after the Melchizedekian priesthood, does this so completely—whether of past revelation, Moses, Joshua, Aaron, the Levitical priesthood, its sacrifices, the Tabernacle, and Sinai—that he far transcends these earlier shadows, which will soon vanish (8:5–13; cf. 9:9–15). Moreover, those gathered around Jesus and filled with his Holy Spirit now constitute a living Temple (2 Cor 6:16; Eph 2:21; 1 Pet 2:5; John 2:21–22; 7:37–39; Coloe 2001).

But Jesus' presence is also "greater" than the Temple (Matt 12:6). Enigmatic to be sure, the neuter adjective seems to refer to the very presence of God (vv. 18, 28). Paul, however, clearly identifies Jesus with God, most notably in his introducing the Lord Jesus into the Shema (1 Cor 8:6), his characteristic use for Jesus of the indefinite Lord (*kyrios*) derived from the LXX's rendering of the personal name Yahweh, his attribution of divine prerogatives to Jesus, and his thoroughgoing Christ-Devotion (Fee 2007; Hurtado 2003). That he betrays no apology suggests that his high Christology was both uncontentious and early. This being so, the common tendency to read the later Synoptics primarily through a messianic (low Christology) lens is no longer tenable.

Consequently, since the concern of both Isaiah 40:3 and Malachi 3:1 is the coming of Yahweh's very presence, as in the first Exodus, their invocation in the Synoptics suggests that Jesus himself is to be identified with the very presence of Yahweh (e.g., Mark 1:1–3). If so, it is unsurprising that Jesus calmly forgives sins (explicitly identified as God's sole prerogative, 2:7) and at a word subdues and tramples the sea (4:35–41; 6:47–52). The subsequent drowning of Israel's demonic enemies therein (5:1–13) and associated feedings (e.g., 6:32–44, *par.;* John 6) only underline the fact of God's personal exodus/new exodus presence (Isa 63:9). The Baptism's rent heavens therefore answers to Isaiah's last great petitionary lament (63:7–64:12): God has indeed come down and done fearful things which "we" did not expect (64:1–3).[3] Considering the shaping of the Transfiguration to resemble a new Sinai replete with glory-cloud, tabernacles, and Yahweh's voice, it is significant that Moses and Elijah talk not with God but with Jesus, and instead of a command to keep Torah, the participants are instructed to hear Jesus' words (Mark 9:7). There is also Jesus' demand for total unquestioning loyalty, even to employing the language of slaves (Matt 10:24–25; Luke 17:9; John 13:16; 15:15, 20). Unparalleled among other teachers and their disciples, might we see here a reflection of Israel's call to utter submission to God (cf. Luke 1:38; 2:29)? Thus Jesus' final procession to the Temple resembles the very coming of God himself (Wright 1996): having just affirmed that "the Lord our God is One" what does it imply for Jesus then to ask what it means for the Messiah to be David's "Lord" (Mark 12:35–37), if not that in himself the very Lord of the Temple had come to his house, as Malachi 3 had warned? John might be more explicit with his prologue, where Jesus is the Exodus shekinah-glory tabernacled in human form and with several of his "I am" sayings, but it is not obvious that he has moved beyond what is already in the Synoptics. From the perspective of the NT, Jesus embodies the very presence which as its raison d'être the second Temple was intended to house but whose visible residence, unlike Solomon's Temple, had remained pointedly absent. It is now in him that humanity encounters the presence of God and where true worship takes place (John 4:21–23).

If Jesus' presence radically decenters the Jerusalem Temple, what of Torah? The first thing to be noted is that when questioned on the heart of the Law, Jesus' twofold answer won him a ringing endorsement (Mark 12:32; Luke 10:39) which is hardly surprising, given his assertion that his teaching was its fulfillment (Matt 5:17). Whatever else may be true, the Law and Jesus cannot be set in mere stark opposition. But there is more to the picture. Admittedly difficult, Habakkuk 1:4 already suggests that Torah was ineffective in combating evil (Watts 1999: 5–6). Jeremiah's new covenant implies something similar: it needed to be written on the heart through the Spirit (Jer 31:31–34; Ezek 36:27–28). The Gospels have little to say here. Certainly Jesus holds his reading of Torah to be absolute (Matt 5–7, even if his teaching and actions initially strike his hearers as abolishing it; 5:17). For Mark, given that Jesus is in some mysterious way the very presence of Yahweh who speaks with Yahweh's own authority (e.g., 2:7; 4:41), this extends even to rescinding the food laws. Whereas Yahweh had in the first exodus set certain foods apart to be unclean "for you" (Lev 20:25) Jesus in the second exodus implies to his reconstituted Jewish

Israel that all foods are now to be regarded as clean (Mark 7:19b, perhaps reflected in Peter's later experience in Acts 10 where, although the primary object is people, nevertheless if people are not to be considered unclean how much less so, on the principle of *qal vahomer*, is food), thus signaling a sea-change in Torah's role. Similarly in Paul's response to concerns over food and days (presumably at least Sabbath), the locus of authority is no longer Torah but the individual's conscience in the context of mutual love (Rom 14:5, 14, 22–23). This is not to denigrate Torah (Matt 5:17–20; cf. Rom 7:12) but only to recognize its fulfillment lies in the cosmically authoritative Words of Jesus (Matt 24:35; 28:18; cf. Gal 3:23–28; 4:9). For John, Torah was a gracious gift; but Jesus is more so (1:16). For while the Law came through Moses, the grace and truth of God's glorious exodus presence (v. 14) came through Jesus (v. 17; cf. 5:39). Jesus, then, although identified with the Logos (1:1) is apparently not to be so identified with Torah. He alone has seen the Father and made him known—in ways greater and fuller than Torah, it is implied.

For many in the first century, Israel's eschatological hopes included resurrection life and the coming of the Spirit. The Baptist proclaims that the latter lies within Jesus' gift (Matt 3:11), and for John, appealing to various images used of Torah, Jesus alone is the living water, the bread from heaven, and the light of the world who brings sight (understanding) and eternal life. This too is Paul's thinking. In the resurrected Jesus the eschaton had arrived. Although Torah was holy, just, spiritual, and good (Rom 7:12–14) and he, Paul, blameless according to its demand (Phil 3:6), he nevertheless found himself opposing God. That is, his zealous devotion to the traditions of the Fathers led him to attack the church and so to persecute Jesus, God's son (Gal 1:13–14; Acts 9:4).[4] For Paul, whoever was of the works of the Law, presumably including Paul himself, was under a "curse" (Gal 3:10, 13). As was well known, over most, including most in Israel's less-than-glorious history, Torah pronounced a curse because they did not keep it, indwelling sin using it to bring exile and death (Gal 3:10; Rom 7:5–14). But Paul, himself righteous under the Law (Phil 3:6), surprisingly argues he too was effectively under a curse ("we know" Gal 2:16; "us" 3:13) precisely because he could "do" it (3:11–12). The Law's demand and attendant curse had placed the emphasis on "doing" its requirements (3:12) whereas God's promised salvation had now been revealed through Christ-faith (2:16). It was Christ-faith as the goal of Torah (cf. Rom 8:4; 10:4) not Torah-obedience that sealed Paul as eschatologically justified through the gift of the Spirit (2 Cor 1:22: Eph 1:13; cf. Acts 2:38). In this sense, Sanders (1977: 550–552) is right. Torah's problem was that it was not Christ. It did not bring Spirit, nor was it resurrected in Sinai-glory, which glory is now seen in the face of God's Christ (2 Cor 3:12–18). Although having died to Torah (Gal 2:19) and being no longer under its guardianship (3:24–25), which Paul now sees as belonging to the old age of slavery (4:8–10), he is nevertheless adamant that his gospel upholds Torah (Rom 3:31) since through the Spirit it now fulfills Torah's demands for righteousness (8:4).

Given, then, Jesus' centrality to God's eschatological salvation, to reject him is ultimately to blaspheme the Holy Spirit and to repeat the rebellion of the exodus (Mark 3:28–29; Isa 63:10). It necessarily excludes any hope of forgiveness, since one rejects the very one through whom forgiveness comes (Matt 23:39; cf. Rom 11:26). A house so divided cannot stand. Jesus' prophetic cursing of the fig-tree and his announcement of the Temple's destruction, even applying against it judgments previously made against Babylon and Edom (Isa 13 and 34 in Matt 24:29), means that "your house"—is it no longer God's?—is left "to you" desolate (Matt 23:38; Mark 13:1–2; Jerusalem, Luke 19:41–44; cf. also Matt 11:20–24). At the climax of his hearing before Caiaphas, Jesus' dual invocation of Daniel 7's son of man and of Psalm 110 implies that official Israel has become Daniel's fourth beast—is Caiaphas himself the little horn?—and that God will put them under Jesus' feet, replacing the present order with Jesus' own Melchizedekian priesthood (cf. Heb 7). Here only the leadership is specifically disinherited (Mark 12:9–12). But elsewhere in the Gospels and Acts, the rejection of Jesus and his message sees Isa 6:9–10 invoked upon all (Mark 4:11–12; Matt 13:14–15; Acts 28:25–27; cf. 13:40–41). Because the gospel is God's eschatological offer of salvation to all without distinction, to persecute its messengers is to be hostile to humanity (1 Thess 2:15–16). But these are historical statements, and even though reflecting a theological principle—salvation is only through Jesus' name—they are not historical absolutes. Judgment on one "generation" does not necessarily determine the future for all—regardless of the presumption of some (Matt 27:25)—as the faithfulness of Paul himself and Jesus' many Jewish followers demonstrates (Acts 6:7; 21:20).

Only from this perspective can one begin to explain the extraordinary claims of the NT's deeply committed Jewish authors. Rosemary Ruether is right: the central issue is Christology (1974: 246–251). However, to claim that the NT is anti-Semitic prejudiciously privileges one view of Judaism, ignoring that this was an intra-Jewish debate. According to Acts, early followers of Jesus engaged with the synagogue, a relationship that continued, however troubled, for some time, and this long after Paul's communities had begun a separate existence (Dunn 2006; Stark 2006: 136–139). But this remarkable thing Israel's God had done—attested by resurrection and Spirit—could not be forced into old wineskins (Luke 5:36–38). The old has gone, everything has become new (2 Cor 5:17; cf. Gal 3–5). If in Jesus Torah, Temple, and even Israel's conception of deity—now manifest as a crucified God (Bauckham 1998)—have been radicalized, we ought not be surprised if the same applies to notions of Israel, especially when according to the Gospels it is now reconstituted around Jesus and defined by loyalty to him.

It should be obvious from the above, however, that one cannot simply say that "the church" replaces Israel. There is clearly a deep and abiding continuity affirmed not only by Matthew's extended genealogy featuring Abraham, David, and the coming of Messiah but also by Jesus, the twelve, and his first Jewish followers being reconstituted Israel, marked by the authenticating eschatological Spirit. John, also echoing Exodus 4:22, understands that only through belief in his "Name" can humanity regardless of genealogy (4:7–42; 8:31–59; 12:20–21) become God's children (1:11–12; cf. Matt 8:10–11; 28:18–20). Even so, it is only when grafted into a Jesus-defined-Israel that his fellow Jews can bear the fruit God requires (John 15:5; cf. Isa 5:1–7; Ps 80:8–9; Jer 2:21). Branches that do not abide in him—fruit-bearing apart from him is inconceivable (John 6:29)—are cut off (15:6; cf. Paul's olive tree where the same also applies to Gentiles, Rom 11:13–24). It is Jesus' absolute significance that explains John's ambiguous use of an outsider term like "the Jews." Devout Jews believe (John 8:31; 11:45); others do not (5:18; 9:22). "Brothers" though they are (Acts 7:2; 13:26) they must believe in "the Name" of the Lord (Jesus) if they are to be saved (John 2:21, 38; 4:11–12)—and in Luke many do (Luke 2:41; Acts 6:7). To remain under Torah is to be "blinded" from the life-giving but potentially lethal Shekinah glory (cf. Exod 33:20) as by a veil that is only removed in Christ, whose glory transforms from glory to glory into the full image of God in him (2 Cor 3:7–17).

Paul's constant summoning of his mixed membership churches—the first exodus similarly involved a mixed multitude (Exod 12:38)—to holiness is nothing if not what is expected of God's people who, having been redeemed in this new exodus (1 Cor 5:7), are to be "Holy as I AM holy" (Lev 11:45 LXX; cf. 1 Pet 2:9). True circumcision, and by implication, the true Jew regardless of outward condition (Rom 2:27–29), is of the heart and entails belief in Christ (Phil 3:3; Col. 2:11–12). Grafted into the Jesus-reconstituted-Israel-olive-tree (Rom 11:17–24) and with the dividing wall of Torah abolished (Eph 2:15; *pace* Marcus Barth 1974: 264) they are all, believing Jew and Gentile together, children of Abraham (Gal 3; Rom 4), a kingdom of priests (1 Pet 2:9; Rev 1:6), and heirs and co-heirs with Christ (Rom 8:17) their brother (Heb 2:11) reigning "in the heavenly places" with him (Eph 2:6). Revelation concludes, then, with the twenty-four elders bowing to the Lamb (5:8), the full number of the "twelve" tribes (144,000) interpreted as a numberless multitude from every tribe and race (7:3–17) whose robes are washed in the blood of the Lamb, and a New Jerusalem—the one bride of Christ—whose twelve gates bear Israel's names, and whose foundations those of the twelve apostles (21:12–14) and in the midst of which is the presence of God and the Davidic Lion-Lamb. Such is the merging of Israel's traditional imagery with Jesus and his followers that it is exceedingly difficult to see two ways, or even two peoples here.

What then of the Jesus' movement's self-designations? The term "Christian" occurs only three times in the NT, and in each case appears to be an outsider label (Acts 11:26; 26:28; 1 Pet 4:16). The earliest designation is "The Way," an apparently Jewish term (Isa 40:3; cf. 1QS 8:13–16; 9:16–21) and thus confined to particularly Jewish settings (Acts 9:2; 19:9, 23; 22:4; 24:14, 22). But it soon falls into disuse. Far more common is *ekklēsia.* Employed by Matthew's Jesus (16:18; 18:17), it apparently derives from *qahal* which, given Matthew's new Moses/new Exodus/New Torah Deuteronomic pattern, seems intended to characterize Jesus' followers as a reconstituted congregation of Israel (Deut 5:22; 9:10; 33:4). But it is instructive that *qahal's* first three occurrences in Israel's Scriptures concern God's promise to Jacob (Israel) that he would become an "assembly" of nations (*ethnōn;* Gen 28:3; 35:11; 48:4; cf. Matt 1:1; 28:18–20). That the LXX uses *sunagōgē* suggests the translators have Diaspora Synagogues in mind (cf. Acts 15:21). However, when "Christianity" began to take root in the larger Graeco-Roman world, *ekklēsia* as the alternative LXX rendering of *qahal* would have been an ideal designation for this "assembly of nations"—comprising both Jew and Gentile—as the fulfillment of Yahweh's promise to Jacob/Israel (cf. Matt 8:11–12;

28:18–20; John 10:16). This seems to be behind Paul's unique expression "Israel of God" (Gal 6:16) which, in fulfillment of God's promises to Abraham is now defined, in the light of Christ-faith, the Spirit, and being "without distinction" (Rom 10:12; Gal 3:28), as those "who keep *this* rule" as opposed to the works of Torah (2:15–21; 5:25; 6:16) and thus enjoy the long-awaited Isaianic blessings of peace and mercy (Köstenberger 2001; cf. Isa 54:10; Gal 1:8–9).

What then of the covenants? As we have seen, the Exodus covenant with Israel is already fulfilled in believers (Exod 19:5–6; e.g., 1 Pet 2:9). For Paul, Matthew, Luke, and John, Jesus is the fulfillment of the Abrahamic (thus Patriarchal; Gen 12:2–3) and Davidic (2 Sam 7) covenants (Gal 3; Rom 1:1–4; Matt 1:1; Luke 1:55; Acts 3:13–26; John 8:31–59; 7:42). Central, however, is the "(re-)new(-ed) covenant" (Jer 31:31–34; Ezek 36:24–27) instituted in the Lord's supper (e.g., Luke 22:20; cf. 1 Cor 11:25; 2 Cor 3:6; Heb 8:8; 9:15; 12:24). Clearly recalling the Passover, and while in one sense clearly a renewal, this is surely more than a mere renewal (cf. Josh 24; *pace* Dunn 2001). Not only are Jesus and his death now the focus, but he changes the menu and, in applying the language of Israel's founding moment at Sinai to his death, its fundamental orientation (Exod 24:8 in Mark 14:24)—and this in an entirely Jewish setting. Presumably as with Torah, this (re-)new(-ed) covenant in faithfully "full-filling" these earlier covenants eschatologically takes them up into itself *and* transforms them via the person of Jesus (Heb 8:13; cf. John 6:52–58). This, it seems, is why Matthew, that most Jewish of the gospels, when speaking of the as-yet-to-be-realized kingdom declares that faith in Jesus is alone what enables one to sit at table with Abraham, Isaac, and Jacob. Tragically, by refusing to believe in him, the children of the promised and future kingdom will be cast out (8:11–12). If so, then Jesus' declaration to the twelve that they will judge Israel probably reflects not a future independent identity for the nation but the disciples' sharing in the Son of Man's eschatological judgment of the nations, now understood as including faithless Israel (cf. the application of Ps 2:1–2 to Israel in Acts 4:25–27), and this on the sole basis of their allegiance or not to Jesus (Acts 4:12; cf. 1 Cor 6:3; 1 Enoch 62:1–14; Matt 25:31–46). Similarly, Jesus' warning that you will not see me again until you say, "Blessed is the one who comes in the name of the Lord" (Matt 23:39) is not intended to imply either a future for an Israel whose identity is independent of Jesus' reconstitution or a special later coming. Instead, it declares that there is no hope of salvation for Jerusalem until it reverses its earlier rejection of his messianic entry (Matt 21:9; cf. "blasphemy against the Spirit," in Matt 12:31).

As to the land, there is a long tradition of seeing the restoration of traditional territory and Jerusalem to ethnic Israel as essential to the fulfillment of the covenants and prophetic promises. But again, if the role of the Temple and Torah and even the constitution of Israel itself can be reinterpreted, we ought not be surprised if this happens to the land also. Indeed, the promise of the restored land is expanded, as it was in some Jewish traditions, such that Abraham is the heir of the entire "world" (Rom 4:13). Jerusalem itself, according to Jesus, is no longer spiritually significant (John 4:21), since the eschatological waters of new creation salvation will flow instead from every believer's "navel" (7:38; Ezek 47). Henceforth, the new

Jerusalem, now an entire Holy of Holies of itself and marked by the God's indwelling Spirit, will be the size of the whole earth (Rev 21:16; cf. Isa 54:11–17). The prophecies are likewise transformed (e.g., 1 Pet 1:10). Strikingly, in spite of the scores of references in which Israel's prophecies are declared or implied to be fulfilled in Jesus and his people (cf. Beale and Carson 2007), not once does the NT unambiguously declare that there is any residue to be fulfilled outside of him in all whom *all* of God's promises are "yes and amen" (2 Cor 1:20). The idea that there must yet be a literal fulfillment for "national" Israel whether independent of Christ or even in him seems at odds with the thoroughgoing hermeneutic of the NT and Jesus himself.

What, then, of Jewish customs? For both Paul and Luke it appears that Jewish believers were welcome to celebrate their traditional customs such as rites of purification and sacrifice (Acts 21:24–26), circumcision (16:3), and food laws and Sabbath observance (1 Cor 9:19–20; Rom 14:2–23; cf. Matt 24:20). But the critical issue is the theological warrant for such. As noted earlier, this is no longer a matter of the universal demand of Torah upon all Jewish Christians—for Paul himself all foods were clean—but instead the state of the individual's conscience and faith before God (14:5, 14, 22–23; *pace* Kinzer 2005, Nanos 2009). Even so, these matters can never be at the expense of the gospel's vision of a single unified new humanity (Gal 2:11–13; Rom 14:17–21), and in any case they were of no eschatological significance (Rom 14:17; cf. Heb).

Thus far the united witness of the NT is that Jesus, as the fulfillment of Israel's narrative, symbols, and praxis, sums up and reconstitutes Israel, its mission, and its future in himself (Wright 1996; cf. 1992). There is, then, only one new humanity consisting of believing Jew and Gentile together. But the continuity of the Abrahamic people of God old and new lies not in Torah-obedience but in Christ-faith. It is important to recognize, however, that God having reconstituted Israel around Jesus and changed its marks does not equate to what is commonly known as "replacement" theology, which is often seen as setting Israel and the church, the Torah and Spirit in stark opposition. By the same token, to affirm continuity does not mean that Christ-faith simply assumes the status of a mere addition to an otherwise unchanged situation. If in the interests of safeguarding his covenant with Abraham—which for Paul is apparently the foundation of all—God can add Torah without thereby implying the former's utter "replacement," there seems no reason why he cannot later change the role of Torah (e.g., rescind food laws, circumcision, and the observance of days and feasts) in the interests of his fulfilling that same covenant and again without implying "replacement" theology (cf. Gal 3). In other words, as Paul notes in Galatians, Jesus' *ekklēsia* of the nations is God's Israel as he had promised Abraham. The only thing that has changed concerns the later secondary addition, namely, the role and the scope of Torah. But even here the righteousness it demanded is established. This, then, is not so much opposition or "replacement" as commonly conceived but a generic trajectory of fulfillment.

This brings us finally to the notoriously difficult Romans 11:25b–26: "a hardening has come upon part of Israel, until the full number of the Gentiles has come in. And so all Israel will be saved as it is written, 'Out of Zion will come the Deliverer;

he will banish ungodliness from Jacob' " (NRSV). The questions here concern what is meant by hardening "in part" and "all Israel" and when and how does "all" Israel's salvation occur? Although there is a range of subtle variations the four main alternatives are as follows (cf. Zoccali 2008).

The most popular view today is that Paul envisages the future salvation of national Israel, probably at the *parousia* (Käsemann 1980: 307, Dunn 2006; cf. *m. Sanh* 10:1). With the full number of Gentiles ingathered, the nation's "partial hardening"—either a less-than-complete hardening of the entire nation, or as seems more likely a hardening of part of the nation (cf. 11:7)—will be removed when, in analogy with Paul's Damascus Road experience, Israel will have a revelation of Christ (thus the following reference to Isa 59:20–21 and 27:9 in vv. 26b–27). It is "in this way" (adv. *houtōs*) that all Israel will be saved; "all Israel" generally being understood in contrast to the remnant of 11:5 but in keeping with OT usage meaning the nation as a whole and not necessarily every individual. Others, however, envisage either every faithful Jew (Fitzmyer 1993: 623; Mussner 1976; Hofius 1990), or even every Jew (Bell 1994: 137–140) that ever lived. From this perspective, the twofold mystery is that Israel's hardening is only for a time and that the nation's salvation follows instead of precedes that of the Gentiles. But there are significant problems. That ethnic Israel will receive a distinctive revelation: a) fails to recognize that Paul's vision was uniquely missional and individual in character; b) effectively reintroduces a distinction whereby on purely ethnic grounds some receive an especially compelling revelation (cf. John 20:29); c) is a conversion based on power as opposed to the weakness and folly of the cross which is so fundamental to Paul's gospel (1 Cor 1:18–2:15); d) reverses the sequence where Israel's confession is the precondition for, not the result of, seeing Jesus as deliverer (Matt 23:39); and e) creates the problem of how "all" (depending on how it is defined) can be justified when a significant number of ethnic Israel throughout history are not so blessed.

The Two Covenant interpretation (Stendahl 1976: 1–5; Gaston 1987: 135–150; Stowers 1994: 285–316; Gager 2000: 128–142) seems highly unlikely. Not only does it render Paul's silence on the then-current reality of Gentile Proselytism and his willingness to be "accursed" for Israel inexplicable but, in keeping with the rest of the NT, he elsewhere knows of only one people of God, one covenant community, one saving faith ("to the Jew first and also to the Greek"), and one olive tree (Rom 11:17–24) into which broken-off Jewish branches can be restored provided they believe (11:23). That the object of this belief, and the solution to Israel's failure, is Christ is clear enough (3:21–26; 10:3–4).

For the remaining two alternatives, Paul's "in this way" (Rom 11:26) refers to the ongoing consequences of Christ's initial redeeming work. Far from God having abandoned his historic people (11:1, 11), the eschatological "now" means mercy for both Jew and Gentile. Just as hardened (partial) Israel's present disobedience results in mercy for the Gentiles, so too mercy to the Gentiles results in the elect in Israel being shown mercy (11:5, 7). "All Israel" is now being saved "in this way," that is, through the jealousy-provoking salvation of the Gentiles. But whereas one view holds "all Israel" to mean the complete number of the elect from ethnic/empirical

Israel (Lenski 1945: 723–728; Ridderbos 1975: 354–361; Hendrikson 1981: 379–382; Merkle 2000: 711–721; Zoccali 2008), the other understands "all Israel" to mean all faithful Jews *and* Gentiles, that is, the Israel of God (Gal 6:16; e.g., Calvin 1961: 254–256; Barth 1968: 412–417; Wright 2001: 687–693). The difficulty with the latter is the rhetorical incongruence of introducing Gentiles into a discussion that concerns reaffirming Israel's place in God's plan.

In order to resolve these matters, we need recall that the fundamental issue in Romans is how Paul's claim that his Christ-gospel is the revelation of God's righteousness can be trusted when its rejection by most of ethnic/empirical Israel seriously calls God's faithfulness, in particular his promises to save them, into question. Having spent considerable time justifying his gospel, Paul finally turns in Romans 9–11 to the looming question of Israel's hostile response. First, in spite of appearances, he argues that God's dealings with his people have been consistent and faithful. From the beginning their very existence as bearers of the promise was predicated solely on his electing mercy (9:9–13), not least following their apostasy during the Exodus when he could have justly hardened and judged them as he did idolatrous Pharaoh (Exod 33:19 in Rom 9:15, 18). How then, in this new exodus, can a yet again "idolatrous" and self-reliant Israel, having rejected his Christ (9:33) and thus once more a pot in Yahweh's judicial hands (Isa 29:16 in Rom 9:20–22), complain when God chooses this time to put the sandal on the other foot and harden some of Israel while showing mercy to others including idolatrous Gentiles (9:23–24)?

Second, even so, God has not abandoned his people (Rom 11:2–6). Paul himself is a case in point (11:1). And lest believing Gentiles boast against the very (Jesus-reconstituted) olive tree into which they themselves are grafted (11:17–18), God is more than capable of regrafting the removed branches if they repent of their unbelief (11:23–24). Indeed, Paul magnifies his work among the Gentiles precisely to facilitate this process in the hope that in being provoked to jealousy some Jews might turn and be saved (11:13).

Paul now turns to this "mystery" (Rom 11:25) which characteristically in his writings refers to present fulfillment of God's promised work, albeit in a most unexpected manner (e.g., Rom 16:25; 1 Cor 2:7; 1 Tim 3:16; cf. Eph 1:9; 3:3). An ongoing present reality (cf. *achri ou* in 1 Cor 11:26), it is probably at least contemporaneous with his own "provoking" glorying in his Gentile ministry. It also involves "hardening" (Rom 11:26), which typically in the OT and in apocalyptic settings is God's response to those whom having refused his offer of mercy he now "strengthens" in their rebellion on the path to their final just judgment (Wright 1991). This is consistent with the Gospels where, in response to hard-hearted hostility (Matt 12:22–50; Mark 3:22–35) Jesus' parables, as did Isaiah's preaching, confirm his opponents in their opposition (Matt 13:13–15; Mark 4:11–12). But that hardening too is partial, upon only some of Israel, in that many respond (Matt 13:16; Mark 3:34–35).

The mystery, then, arises from Israel's unexpected rejection of God's Christ and God's astonishing reponse. Whereas the prophets expected a restored Israel to be a glorious light to the Gentiles, the nation's rejection of Jesus threatened to forestall that plan. But God in his surpassing wisdom was able to use even his people's rebellion, particularly of their leaders, to fulfill his Abrahamic promise of blessing the nations. Through the judicial and righteous hardening of the rebels God further increased their hostility to the point where Philip, Paul, and others were forced to go to the Gentiles. God was able to accomplish his purposes in spite of, and even by means of, Israel's rebellion. But God has not abandoned his people. The glorious outcome of the Gospel among the Gentiles was intended to provoke an as-yet-unknown number of unbelieving Israel to respond—Paul hopes to save "some"—which will continue until the fullness of the Gentiles have come in. The dynamic is again the same as in the Gospels. Although Jesus' parables harden "outsiders," it is a category and not a fixed number. Hence the general warnings to listen carefully and the parable of the soils: how one hears will determine one's final destiny (Mark 4:23–25). When some unbelieving Jews are thus provoked to hear aright, then in repenting they will no longer be judicially hardened and instead will welcome their Messianic deliver (Isa 59:20–21; 27:9 in Rom 11:26–27; cf. Matt 23:39).

Taking *houtōs* in its usual modal sense of "in this way," it is through this provocation that "all Israel" will finally be saved. If in his day Jesus' parables caused some to change their mind, so also might Paul's announcement of the Gentiles' turning to God through his proclamation of Jesus. The combined Isaiah citation (59:20–21; 27:9), as do such Isaiah texts elsewhere in Paul and the NT, refers to what God has already inaugurated in Christ: it is "in this way"—a repentance borne of jealousy (Rom 10:19–21)—that God banishes their sins.

It is sometimes objected that "all" must mean more than a remnant of Israel (Rom 11:5). But the question concerns God's faithfulness to the elect, not the entire nation (cf. 9:6), as Isaiah, Paul's key scriptural resource in these chapters, well understood. True, God would remove iniquity from Zion (59:20–21). But the subsequent promises that "all" would possess the land (60:21–22) and of a new heavens and earth meant not the indiscriminate salvation of the nation but God's final judicial division between faithless and faithful Israelites (65–66). In the jarring image of the final utterance of the book, only the latter would enter the new Jerusalem outside of which lay the bodies of the rebels (66:24). While the New Perspective is right to note the national dimensions of Israel's salvation, the individual element must not be downplayed. As far, then, as Paul's "all" is concerned, to Isaiah's "my servants" must also be added the numerous ancient saints such as the Patriarchs, David, and so on (cf. Matt 8:11–12). The actual number is known only to God, but unless Paul rejects Isaiah's final word, the point is that none of *faithful* Israel will be missing (cf. 144,000 in Rev 7).

One more word on the expression "all Israel." Its very uniqueness ought to occasion pause (cf. Rom 9:6). Already in Romans 9:7–8, Paul noted the principle, even before Christ, that it is promise not flesh that marks out true Israel. His Israel *kata sarka* (1 Cor 10:18) suggests that he knows an Israel *kata pneuma* (cf. Rom 8). Given that *kata pneuma* is how one ought now to know Christ (cf. 2 Cor 5:16) and given the prominence of the promised Spirit in Paul, the expression "all Israel" most likely means new creational Israel as it, too, ought to be known, that is eschatologically, *kata pneuma*, the Israel of God according to his promise (Gal 6:16), which as such includes believing Jew and Gentile who together call on the name of the Lord

(Rom 10:11; Wright 1991: 231–257). It is regularly contended, however, that Paul could not change the meaning of Israel in one sentence, and that doing so would shift his focus from ethnic Israel. But why then add "all" if Israel is Israel *simpliciter?* And a shift to the Israel of God would be consonant with Paul's overall objective and particularly his strong emphasis on equality in Christ without distinction (e.g., 10:12). That is, although he begins by reminding the Gentiles of Israel's historical priority, Paul does not seek to balance the ledger by now emphasizing Jewishness as much as noting how integrally Jew and Gentile are related. Rhetorically speaking, this would then lead perfectly to the strong emphasis on the equality of Jew and Gentile that characterizes the remaining chapters and his theology elsewhere.

Whatever else, given the complexities of this text it seems a risky business, as Luther implied, to build an entire theology of national Israel's salvation thereupon. It seems to this author that today's popular position—a massive final turning to Christ at the eschaton—is more problematic theologically than most recognize. If pressed, then either of the final two minority views appears more likely, and I would probably go with the last: Gentiles are saved due to the hardening of rebellious national Israel, some of whom in return are provoked to repentance by the salvation of those very Gentiles. God indeed will have mercy on both and in this way all the Israel of God will be saved.

In conclusion, as Israel's Scriptures, first-century Jews, and the NT together recognize, Israel and its salvation are defined by (re-)new(-ed) covenant loyalty. For the Jewish authors of the NT, this relationship has now been fulfilled and redefined in that utterly transforming cosmic event inaugurated in the glorious person of God's Christ, his Son. It seems mistaken then to speak of a transfer of Israel's privileges to the church since Jesus and his Jewish followers are in fact the reconstitution of true servant Israel. Even the term *ekklēsia* appears grounded in God's promise to Jacob that he would become a company of nations. Just as some Gentiles were included under the terms of the old covenant, so too *mutatis mutandis* under the terms of the (re-)new(-ed) covenant though now in astonishing numbers. What have changed are the marks of this reconstituted people: Christ-faith, Jesus' teaching, baptism, the reception of the Spirit, and the Lord's "new" covenant meal. Thus the promises to Abraham and the privileges of his offspring are realized in Jesus and enjoyed by any who through Christ-faith enter into the "new" covenant which itself is the climax and realization of all those previous. The righteousness of God has indeed been revealed from heaven in the gospel of his Son, through whom he has mercy on all, Jew and Gentile alike.

NOTES

1. See Mark R. Lindsay, *Barth, Israel, and Jesus* (Aldershot: Ashgate, 2007).

2. For example, Jesus, too, effects the rule of God (cf. *Pss. Sol.* 17:1, 46), is fundamentally concerned with the purity of Jerusalem and the Temple (vv. 22–36), exposes

corrupt officials by his strong word (v. 36), expels defiling sinners (vv. 22–25, 27–28; albeit redefined), is empowered by the Spirit and mighty in deed (vv. 36–40), instructs Israel in righteousness (vv. 10–18, 32), faithfully shepherds them in holiness and freedom from oppression (vv. 40–41; though from unclean spirits), and shows compassion to those of the nations who honor him (v. 34b). See Rikk Watts, "The Lord's House and David's Lord," *Biblical Interpretation* 15 (2007): 311–312.

3. On the assimilation of Jesus' miracles to those of Yahweh see Barry Blackburn, *Theios Aner and the Markan Miracle Traditions* (Tübingen: Mohr Siebeck, 1991).

4. Cf. the LXX where "persecution" is regularly attributed to enemies. Further, it is hard to see Paul taking a different view from those leaders from Jerusalem whose rejection of Jesus was equated with blaspheming the Spirit thus making God their enemy (cf. Isa 63:10). Paul's later "the foremost of sinners" (1 Tim 1:15) should not be dismissed as empty rhetoric.

REFERENCES

Barth, Karl. 1968. *The Epistle to the Romans*. Trans. Edwyn C. Hoskyns. Oxford: Oxford University Press.

Barth, Markus. 1974. *Ephesians 1-3*. AB 34. New York: Doubleday.

———. 1978. *Jesus the Jew*. Trans. Fredrick Prussner. Atlanta: John Knox.

Bauckham, Richard. 1998. *God Crucified: Monotheism and Christology in the New Testament*. Grand Rapids: Eerdmans.

Beale, Greg, and Don Carson, eds. 2007. *Commentary on the NT Use of the OT*. Grand Rapids: Baker.

Bell, Richard H. *Provoked to Jealousy: The Origin and Purpose of the Jealousy Motif in Romans 9–11*. Tübingen: J.C.B. Mohr.

Calvin, John. 1961. *The Epistles of Paul to the Romans and to the Thessalonians*. Trans. Ross Mckenzie. Ed. David W. Torrance and Thomas F. Torrance. London: Oliver & Boyd.

Cohen, Jeremy. 2005. "The Mystery of Israel's Salvation: Romans 11:25–26 in Patristic and Medieval Exegesis." *Harvard Theological Review* 98: 247–281.

Coloe, Mary L. 2001. *God Dwells with Us: Temple Symbolism in the Fourth Gospel*. Collegeville, Minn.: Liturgical Press.

Dunn, James D. G. 2001. "Judaism and Christianity: One Covenant or Two?" In *Covenant Theology: Contemporary Approaches*, ed. Mark J. Cartledge, and David Mills. Carlisle, Cumbria: Paternoster, 33–55.

———. 2006. *The Partings of the Ways between Christianity and Judaism and Their Significance for the Character of Christianity*. 2nd. ed. London: SCM.

Elliott, M. A. 2000. *The Survivors of Israel*. Grand Rapids: Eerdmans.

Fackre, Gabriel J. 1993. *Ecumenical Faith in Evangelical Perspective*. Grand Rapids: Eerdmans, 147–167.

Fee, Gordon D. 2007. *Pauline Christology*. Peabody, Mass.: Hendrickson.

Fitzmyer, Joseph. 1993. *Romans*. AB 33. New York: Doubleday.

Gager, John G. *Reinventing Paul*. New York: Oxford University Press.

Gaston, Lloyd. 1979. "Paul and the Torah." In Alan T. Davies, ed., *Antisemitism and the Foundations of Christianity*. New York: Paulist Press, 48–71.

———. 1987. *Paul and the Torah*. Vancouver: University of British Columbia Press.

Hendrikson, William. 1981. *Exposition of Paul's Epistle to the Romans*. 2 vols. Grand Rapids: Eerdmans.
Hofius, Otfried. 1990. "'All Israel will be Saved': Divine Salvation and Israel's Deliverance in Romans 9–11." *PSBSup* 1: 19–39.
Hurtado, Larry. 2003. *Lord Jesus Christ*. Grand Rapids: Eerdmans.
Käsemann, Ernst. 1980. *A Commentary on Romans*. Trans. and ed. Geoffrey W. Bromily. Grand Rapids: Eerdmans.
Kinzer, Mark. 2005. *Postmissionary Messianic Judaism: Redefining Christian Engagement with the Jewish People*. Grand Rapids: Brazos.
Köstenberger, Andreas J. 2001. "The Identity of the '*ISRA L TOU THEOU* (Israel of God) in Galatians 6:16." *Faith and Mission* 19: 3–24.
Lenski, R.C.H. 1945. *The Interpretation of Paul's Epistle to the Romans*. Columbus, Oh.: Wartburg.
Longenecker, Bruce W. 1989. "Different Answers to Different Issues: Israel, the Gentiles, and Salvation History in Romans 9–11." *Journal for the Study of the New Testament* 36: 95–123.
Marshall, I. Howard. 1999. "'Israel' and the Story of Salvation: One Theme in Two Parts," in *Jesus and the Heritage of Israel*. Harrisburg, Penn.: Trinity Press International.
Merkle, Ben L. 2000. "Romans 11 and the Future of Ethnic Israel." *Journal of the Evangelical Theological Society* 43: 709–721.
Mussner, Franz. 1976. "'Ganz Israel wird getrettet werden' (Röm 11,26): Versuch einer Auglegung." *Kairos* 18: 241–255.
Nanos, Mark D. 2009. "The Myth of the 'Law-Free' Paul Standing between Christians and Jews," *Studies in Jewish-Christian Relations* 4: 1–21.
Nanos, Mark D. 2002. *The Irony of Galatians*. Minneapolis: Fortress.
Ruether, Rosemary. 1974. *Faith and Fratricide*. New York: Seabury.
Ridderbos, Herman. 1975. *Paul: An Outline of His Theology*. Trans. John Richard DeWitt. Grand Rapids: Eerdmanns.
Rowland, Christopher. 1982. *The Open Heaven*. London: SPCK.
Sanders, E. P. 1977. *Paul and Palestinian Judaism*. Philadelphia: Fortress.
Soulen, R. Kendall. 1996. *The God of Israel and Christian Theology*. Minneapolis: Fortress.
Stark, Rodney. 2006. *Cities of God*. New York: HarperCollins.
Stendahl, Krister. 1976. *Paul among Jews and Gentiles, and Other Essays*. Philadelphia: Fortress.
Stowers, Stanley K. *A Rereading of Romans: Justice, Jews, Gentiles*. New Haven: Yale University Press.
Van Buren, Paul. 1980. *Discerning the Way*. New York: Seabury.
———. 1988. *Christ and Context*. San Francisco: Harper & Row.
Watts, Rikk E. 1999. "'For I Am Not Ashamed of the Gospel': Romans 1:16-17 and Habakkuk 2:4." In *Romans and the People of God: Festschrift for Gordon D. Fee*, ed. Sven Soderlund and N. T. Wright. Grand Rapids: Eerdmans, 3–25.
———. 2002. "The New Exodus/New Creational Restoration of the Image of God." In *What Does it Mean to be Saved?*, ed. John J. Stackhouse, Jr. Grand Rapids: Baker: 15–41.
Wright, N. T. 1991. *The Climax of the Covenant*. Edinburgh: T & T Clark.
———. 1992. *The New Testament and the People of God*. Minneapolis: Fortress.
———. 1996. *Jesus and the Victory of God*. Minneapolis: Fortress.
———. 2001. *The Letter to the Romans*. Nashville: Abingdon Press.
Zoccali, Christopher. 2008. "'And so all Israel will be Saved': Competing Interpretations of Romans 11.26 in Pauline Scholarship." *Journal for the Study of the New Testament* 30: 289–318.

BIBLIOGRAPHY (IN ADDITION TO REFERENCES)

Blaising, Craig A., and Darrell L. Bock, eds., *Dispensationalism, Israel and the Church: The Search for Definition*. Grand Rapids: Zondervan, 1992.

Diprose, Ronald E. *Israel and the Church: The Origins and Effects of Replacement Theology*. Waynesboro, Ga.: Authentic Media, 2004.

Donaldson, Terence L. "Jewish Christianity, Israel's Stumbling and the *Sonderweg* Reading of Paul." *Journal for the Study of the New Testament* 29 (2006): 27–54.

Guelich, Robert A., ed. "The Church and Israel: Romans 9–11." *Ex Auditu* 4 (1988): 1–123.

Holwerda, David E. *Jesus and Israel: One Covenant or Two?* Grand Rapids: Eerdmans, 1995.

Wilson, Stephen G., ed. *Anti-Judaism in Early Christianity*. Vol. 2, *Separation and Polemic*. Waterloo: Wilfrid Laurier University Press, 1986.

CHAPTER 12

THE GOSPEL

SCOT MCKNIGHT

"EVANGELICAL" and "gospel" are words joined at the hip. The word "evangelical" transliterates the Greek term *euaggelion* and the word "gospel" is its translation. It is not without significance that an English, Anglican Calvinist evangelical theologian, J. I. Packer, and an American Wesleyan evangelical theologian, Thomas Oden, teamed up to form an evangelical consensus statement called *One Faith*, and began with "The Good News: The Heart of the Gospel."[1] But what is the gospel and how may it be defined?

The Gospel and the Bible

The quest for the precise background to the word "gospel" has been discussed intensely of late, but the most significant context remains the Old Testament. In particular, a text like Isaiah 40–66 was surely at work for Jesus in framing God's saving plan. Thus, from Isaiah 40:9:

> Get you up to a high mountain,
> O Zion, *herald of good tidings*;
> lift up your voice with strength,
> O Jerusalem, *herald of good tidings*,
> lift it up, do not fear;
> say to the cities of Judah,
> "Here is your God!"

And from 52:7:
How beautiful upon the mountains
are the feet of the messenger who announces peace,
who brings *good news*,
who announces salvation,
who says to Zion, "Your God reigns."

The good news here is a declaration that God is king and that YHWH reigns supreme. This good news brings in its wake potent consequences, including salvation and peace and love and joy and justice for Israel.

Jesus, in what is called his inaugural sermon, explicitly draws from Isaiah 61 not only to announce his gospel:

"The Spirit of the Lord is upon me,
because he has anointed me
to bring good news to the poor.
He has sent me to proclaim release to the captives
and recovery of sight to the blind,
to let the oppressed go free,
to proclaim the year of the Lord's favor"
(Luke 4:18–19).

Jesus' vision here does not disappear when the apostles began to preach. But, there is a notable shift from the gospel *of* Jesus to the gospel *about* Jesus. The evangelical New Testament scholar Klyne Snodgrass observes: "The gospel of Jesus, i.e., the gospel Jesus preached, is quite different from the gospel about Jesus which the early church preached. The church's gospel is rightly summarized as the proclamation of the death and resurrection of Jesus." For those committed to the sweep of biblical theology, however, Snodgrass continues: "But as crucial as that [early church] focus is, *it makes little sense apart from the gospel Jesus proclaimed*."[2]

In fact, the kingdom gospel continued by embracing the cross and resurrection. Philip preached "the good news about the kingdom of God and the name of Jesus Christ" (Acts 8:12), and Paul spent three months in Ephesus arguing "persuasively about the kingdom of God" (19:8; cf. 20:25; 28:23). If the emphasis shifts with the apostles, the substance of Jesus' eschatologically shifting kingdom vision remains present (1 Cor 4:20; Col 1:13; 4:11; James 2:5; Rev 1:6, 9).

Whether we look to the preaching of Peter (Acts 2:14–41; 10:34–43) or to Paul (13:16–41; 17:22–31) or to the clearly creedal language of Paul in 1 Cor 15:1–8 (perhaps 15:20–28 as well), the gospel of the earliest apostolic witness was a uniform structuring of the story of God that finds its completion in the story of the Messiah.[3] Gospeling was telling the story of Jesus. The gospel of the apostles, built as it was on Jesus' vision of the historic fulfillment of God's plan in the kingdom of God, was a revelatory narrative of what God had done for the salvation of his people Israel in and through the saving events of Jesus Christ. Hence, as with Isaiah, the benefits of the kingdom are sometimes announced as well: forgiveness of sins (Acts 10:43), salvation (Rom 1:16), or peace (Eph 2:14–18). This gospel, the early church learned, was for all. The theme of blessing from Genesis 12:2–3 onward made this clear, even if it involved a struggle for the apostles.[4]

One further element is the response to gospeling: it summoned listeners to repentance and faith and baptism. Whether we look to Jesus' message (Mark 1:14–20), to Peter's preaching (Acts 2:38), to Paul's preaching (Acts 13:38–39), or to John's framing of the fundamental response through believing/faith (John 1:12), the condition for entrance is to repent from one's sins, to believe/trust in Jesus Christ, and to be baptized in the name of Jesus Christ (cf. Gal 3:27; Rom 6:1–12; Tit 3:5; 1 Pet 3:20).

This gospel that narrates the story of Jesus Christ led to three inexorable developments. The basic narrative develops, first, into the canonical Gospels. The Gospels themselves—Matthew, Mark, Luke, and John—are in and of themselves gospeling. In addition, that story of Jesus also developed into the Christian Eucharist. The apostle Paul, at the end of his presentation of the words of institution, says this: "For whenever you eat this bread and drink this cup, you proclaim the Lord's death until he comes" (1 Cor 11:26). Eucharist is also gospeling, according to the apostle Paul. It is not beyond the pale of biblical exegesis to think that baptism also is gospeling.[5] Baptism is both death and resurrection in Romans 6:1–14, and one can infer that the rite itself is a gospeling event. A third development is creed or ongoing theological articulation, and we will devote most of the rest of this chapter to this feature of gospeling. (There is insufficient space here to develop two other results of primitive gospeling: the formation of the Church calendar, which gets its backbone from the narrative life of Jesus, and the liturgy connected both to the daily or weekly service and to the Eucharist. Each of these is gospel-shaped once we recognize that gospel refers to the narrative shape of the redemptive acts of God in the life of Jesus.)[6]

The Gospel and the Church

The reductive realities at work in much of today's populist gospeling, to the extent that it can be reduced at times to "Jesus came to die for sins so humans can go to heaven when they die," are put to a shivering, revealing test when they face the robust and profound articulations of the gospel in the history of the Church. In particular, as Ted Campbell sketches that history, the narrative of the gospel at work in a text like 1 Cor 15:1–8 developed into the early Christian orthodox creeds.[7] The creeds, and one thinks here of the Nicene Creed and the Chalcedonian Definition, bring to expression the dynamic significance of what lies behind and under a proper understanding of the gospel. The Nicene Creed and its later developments were not exercises simply in sophisticated theology but also in the exploration of what had always been at work in the gospel (tradition) itself (see 1 Cor 15:1 [*parelabete* or "received"; see also Luke 1:2; 1 Cor 11:23; 2 Thess 2:15]). It is justifiable to say that the creeds are instances of gospeling. Christian orthodoxy, the formation of Christian faith in the first few centuries after Christ and singularly expressed in the Nicene Creed, shaped the evangelicalism of both the Reformers and the eighteenth century.[8] Accordingly, one needs to emphasize that ancient orthodoxy is evangelical in the proper senses of the word.[9]

Alongside the creeds there developed a profound catechesis that prepared a person for baptism. Two of the more noteworthy instances of such a catechesis can be found in Cyril of Jerusalem, *Catechetical Lectures*, and in his younger contemporary John Chrysostom's *Baptismal Instructions*. It is sometimes missed how significant catechesis is [was?] for comprehending the gospel for premoderns, and one reason certainly is the informality both of conversion and entrance into church in contemporary evangelicalism. This liturgical [and catechetical?] process is inherent to almost all understandings of the gospel in the history of the Church.

In the sketch that follows, we focus on how seminal theologians articulated the gospel that was expressed in the praxis of Gospel reading and preaching, Eucharistic participation, and creedal confessions.[10]

From Ignatius to Augustine

Ignatius (ca. 35 or 50 to 98 or 117), who had a robust sense both of Eucharist and tradition, understands gospel in terms of the salvation-historical shift that occurred in Christ and, at the same time, he reveals the subtle shift that took place in articulating that gospel in terms of mortality and immortality, death and life: "But the Gospel possesses something transcendent [above the former dispensation], viz., the appearance of our Lord Jesus Christ, His passion and resurrection. For the beloved prophets announced Him. But the Gospel is the perfection of immortality" (Ign., *To the Philadelphians* 9).

Irenaeus (2nd century C.E.–ca. 202), who understands the word "gospel" as the New Testament, the Gospels, the new covenant, and the *regula fidei*, says this of Marcion for his rejection of the Gospel of Luke: "Now if any man set Luke aside, as one who did not know the truth, he will, [by so acting,] manifestly reject that Gospel of which he claims to be a disciple" (*Against Heresies* 14.3). For Irenaeus, the gospel message and the four Gospels are tied together. This gospel, witnessed to by the one God who spoke both the Testaments (cf. 12.3), gets a characteristically early Christian shape in terms of ransom and recapitulation when Irenaeus speaks of its saving benefits: "For this cause, too, did Christ die, that the Gospel covenant being manifested and known to the whole world, might in the first place set free His slaves; and then afterwards, as I have already shown, might constitute them heirs of His property, when the Spirit possesses them by inheritance" (9.4).

The African Tertullian (ca. 160–ca. 220 C.E.) claims there is but one gospel: "They accordingly even gave him 'the right hand of fellowship,' as a sign of their agreement with him, and arranged amongst themselves a distribution of office, not a diversity of gospel, so that they should severally preach not a different gospel, but (the same), to different persons, Peter to the circumcision, Paul to the Gentiles" (*Against Heresies*, 23). Importantly, the gospel and the Trinity go hand in hand.

> What need would there be of the *gospel, which is the substance of the New Covenant*, laying down (as it does) that the Law and the Prophets lasted until John the Baptist, if thenceforward the Father, the Son, and the Spirit are not both believed in as Three, and as making One Only God? God was pleased to renew His covenant with man *in such a way as that His Unity might be believed in, after a new manner, through the Son and the Spirit*, in order that God might now be known openly, in His proper Names and Persons, who in ancient times was not plainly understood, though declared through the Son and the Spirit. Away, then, with those "Antichrists who deny the Father and the Son." (*Against Praxeas* 31; emphasis added)

One cannot fail to see how important theological verities were to someone like Tertullian for understanding the heart of the gospel.

The true gospel is apostolic tradition, and here we enter into an issue that shapes modern evangelicalism but that, because there is no mechanism by which it can be sustained, causes it troubles, namely, some sense of an ecclesial authority. Notice how Tertullian expresses the authority of the apostolic, ecclesial gospel:

> Now, what that was which they preached—in other words, what it was which Christ revealed to them—can... properly be proved in no other way than by those very churches which the apostles founded in person, by declaring the gospel to them directly themselves, both *vivâ voce*, as the phrase is, and subsequently by their epistles. If, then, these things are so, it is in the same degree manifest that all doctrine which agrees with the apostolic churches... must be reckoned for truth, as undoubtedly containing that which the (said) churches received from the apostles, the apostles from Christ, Christ from God. (*Against Heresies*, 21)[11]

We come now to a person of momentous significance for his wise articulations of orthodoxy: Athanasius (ca. 293—May 2, 373). Hounded into five exiles by the Arians, Athanasius penned his famous *On the Incarnation of the Word of God* in his mid-twenties, became bishop of Alexandria at the young age of thirty-three, and spent his life preaching and teaching the orthodox unfolding of that gospel. For Athanasius the only way to read Scripture aright is to do so in light of Scripture's context and the "ecclesiastical scope" (*Against Arius*, 3.58). The entire narrative of Jesus, which might be called the backbone of his *regula fidei*, is summed up in his famous line: "God became humans so that humans might become like God" (*On the Incarnation* 54.3).

The narrated life of Jesus (the gospel) formed the structure for how Athanasius understood the Christian faith. Here are some definitive words of Athanasius's famous *Statement of Faith*, which articulates the Christological backbone for the gospel of orthodoxy:

> We believe in one Unbegotten God, Father Almighty, maker of all things both visible and invisible, that hath His being from Himself. And in one Only-begotten Word, Wisdom, Son, begotten of the Father without beginning and eternally... Who, when at the consummation of the ages (Heb. 9. 26), He had

> descended from the bosom of the Father, took from the undefiled Virgin Mary our humanity, Christ Jesus, whom He delivered of His own will to suffer for us, as the Lord saith: 'No man taketh My life from Me. I have power to lay it down, and have power to take it again' (Joh. 10. 18). In which humanity He was crucified and died for us, and rose from the dead, and was taken up into the heavens, having been created as the beginning of ways for us (Prov. 8. 22), when on earth He showed us light from out of darkness, salvation from error, life from the dead, an entrance to paradise, from which Adam was cast out, and into which he again entered by means of the thief, as the Lord said, 'This day shalt thou be with Me in paradise' (Luke 23. 43), into which Paul also once entered. [He showed us] also a way up to the heavens, whither the humanity of the Lord, in which He will judge the quick and the dead, entered as precursor for us.

Evangelicalism will make a colossal mistake if it reduces "gospel" to the message of salvation that prompts faith and ignore the substantial ideas logically entailed in that gospel message. And not only is orthodoxy itself the unfolding of gospel, so also does that orthodox gospel transform (*theosis*) humans into saints. His famous *The Life of Anthony* illustrates a gospel life of holiness. Athanasius connected the apostolic preaching of the gospel with the witness of the apostolic life, and he then urges the same upon all Christians in light of final accountability. Here are his words from his *Easter Letter* in 330 C.E.: "For not only were they entrusted with the charge of preaching the Gospel, but, if we enquire, we shall see, as it is written, that its power was displayed in them. 'Be ye therefore followers of me,'" he wrote to the Corinthians (see 2.1, 2).

This focus on a life that witnesses to the gospel was sometimes called the "gospel life," and more often than not was connected to the rigors of asceticism (cf. Basil, *Letters* 173, 184).

We have then among the earliest architects of orthodoxy this dual emphasis: the gospel as the unfolding of the "gospel mystery," that is the mystery of the incarnation and redemption (see Gregory of Nyssa, *Great Catechism* 24), and the new life of love and purity that such a gospel demands and creates. John Chrysostom, for whom everything is Eucharistic, speaks for the whole church when he says this:

> What then is this? "The gospel." For the sum of the gospels hath its original hence, from God having become man and having been crucified and having risen again.

The gospel for this mighty preacher is the incarnation, the crucifixion, and the resurrection, and this gospel is what the angels reveal and the prophets glimpsed. This gospel came to embodied reality in the Eucharist, which ingestion was designed by God to lead to transformation.[12]

Some today continue to commit the error Augustine (354–430 C.E.) attributed to Faustus, who reduced the word "gospel" to the moral teachings or precepts of Jesus. Augustine, whose *Confessions* and various theological treatises make abundantly clear his perception of the fallenness of humans—that they are dead in their sins apart from the awakening that comes from the gospel of God's grace—affirms an orthodox, robust, narratival, and early-preaching-of-Acts understanding of the gospel in his reply to Faustus:

> The name evangelist ["gospeler"] is properly given to the narrators of the birth, the actions, the words, the sufferings of our Lord Jesus Christ. The word gospel means good news, and might be used of any good news, but is properly applied to the narrative of the Saviour. (*Reply to Faustus the Manichaean* 2.2)

Augustine, too, connects gospel to life in a passage that contemplates the games the mind plays with itself as it ponders its choices. Then he lays down a Romans 6–like observation that completes his observation that the gospel is a (Eucharistic and baptismal) narrative about Jesus Christ's life and death and resurrection: only "by dying a gospel-death we may live a gospel-life" (*Letters* 95, to Paulinus and Therasia). Thus, the gospel is an appeal to enter into that narrative of Jesus.

From Aquinas to Wesley

Thomas Aquinas (1225–1274), starting in an entirely different place from Augustine and approaching theology through the lens of an Aristotelian method, entertained questions about both eschatology (preterism, to be precise) and gospel preaching. In response to the accusation that the gospel of the kingdom has run its limit and that the church is now to preach the gospel of Christ (in the power of the Holy Spirit), Thomas responds with this:

> Since Christ said at the very outset of the preaching of the Gospel: "The kingdom of heaven is at hand" (Mat. 4:17), it is most absurd to say that the Gospel of Christ is not the Gospel of the kingdom. But the preaching of the Gospel of Christ may be understood in two ways. First, as denoting the spreading abroad of the knowledge of Christ. . . . Secondly, the preaching of the Gospel may be understood as extending throughout the world and producing its full effect, so that, to wit, the Church would be founded in every nation. (*Summa Theologica*, Treatise on Law, Q. 106. Art 4)

Here we find a robust connection of gospel to church, but what is notable about Thomas is that gospeling means spreading the "knowledge of Christ," and one would have to think that he implies both the Gospels' telling of the story of Jesus and the orthodox articulations of the gospel (as known in the Western church). Aquinas' gospel would have emerged out of a Eucharistic and creedal context, with the Eucharistic element gaining in centrality during his days.

Following in the line of Augustine and responding in some important ways to Thomas and the developments in the Roman church from the thirteenth and fourteenth centuries, Martin Luther (1483–1546) famously sets in contrast in more than salvation-historical ways the Law and the Gospel (cf. *The Twofold Use of the Law*, 1–3). The former brings guilt and the latter creates grace and forgiveness and an alien righteousness. It was Luther's exposition of Romans that brought home to him the gospel of justification by faith, apart from works, and the role that Law was to play in awakening faith in Christ's righteousness alone. We will content ourselves with a telling example of how Luther put the gospel into focus. It concerns the famous hermit in *Vitae Patrum* (Lives of the Fathers):

> For over seventy years this hermit had led a life of utmost austerity.... When the hour of death came he began to tremble, and for three days was in a state of agony. His disciples came to comfort him.... But he replied: "Alas, I truly have all my life served Christ and lived austerely; but God's judgment greatly differs from that of men." Note, this worthy man, despite the holiness of his life, has no acquaintance with any article but that of the divine judgment according to the Law. He knows not the comfort of Christ's Gospel. After a long life spent in the attempt to keep God's commandments and secure salvation, the Law now slays him through his own works. He is compelled to exclaim: "Alas, who knows how God will look upon my efforts? Who may stand before him?" That means, to forfeit heaven through the verdict of his own conscience. The work he has wrought and his holiness of life avail nothing. They merely push him deeper into death, since he is without the solace of the Gospel, while others, such as the thief on the cross and the publican, grasp the comfort of the Gospel, the forgiveness of sins in Christ. Thus sin is conquered; they escape the sentence of the Law, and pass through death into life eternal. (*Twofold Use*, 39–40)

For Luther, the gospel is a power that transforms a person from terror before the judgment of God and grants that person confidence and healing: the gospel "is a message of healing and salvation" (*Twofold Use*, 41–44).

Luther, too, connects gospel to the orthodox creeds. For him, the entire gospel is contained in the Second Article, which he also connects to the Christian church. Hence, in his *Larger Catechism*, he writes:

> If now you are asked, What do you believe in the Second Article of Jesus Christ? answer briefly: I believe that Jesus Christ, true Son of God, has become my Lord. But what is it to become Lord? It is this, that He has redeemed me from sin, from the devil, from death, and all evil. For before I had no Lord nor King, but was captive under the power of the devil, condemned to death, enmeshed in sin and blindness.

And again on the Third Article:

> We further believe that in this Christian Church we have forgiveness of sin, which is wrought through the holy Sacraments and Absolution, moreover, through all manner of consolatory promises of the entire Gospel.

The brilliance of Luther, as is the case with the magisterial Reformers, was that redemption, justification, and confidence before God can only be had *by faith* and only *by grace*. The gift of forgiveness comes only because of the merited righteousness of Christ that is imputed to the believer. The gospel for Luther summons humans to an intensely personal relationship with Christ, and it is the intensity of focus on this that marks off a distinctive element of the Reformation.

The Reformers upped the ante when it came to conceptualizing the gospel as the personal experience of salvation. Accordingly, they articulated the gospel to effect conversion (just as the early Christians used the church calendar to "preach the gospel" annually). One finds the same demand for personal faith in the entire history of the church, but few would dispute that there was a renewed focus on personal regeneration in the Reformers with their crystallization of the gospel in the radical cleavage between God's utter holiness and human sinfulness.

In Calvin's wake flowed the greatest of American theologians, Jonathan Edwards (1703–1758). Creedal substance mattered in the gospel Edwards preached: one must believe, in a personal way, certain things to be certainly true. Edwards:

> Thus in order to a profession of Christianity, we must profess that we believe that Jesus is the Messiah; for this reason, because such a belief is essential to Christianity. And so we must profess, either expressly or implicitly, that Jesus satisfied for our sins, and other essential doctrines of the gospel, because a belief of these things also are essential to Christianity. But there are other things as essential to religion, as an orthodox belief; which it is therefore as necessary that we should profess, in order to our being truly said to profess Christianity. Thus it is essential to Christianity that we repent of our sins, that we be convinced of our own sinfulness, that we are sensible we have justly exposed ourselves to God's wrath; that our hearts renounce all sin, that we do with our whole hearts embrace Christ as our only Saviour, that we love him above all, are willing for his sake to forsake all, and that we give up ourselves to be entirely and for ever his, &c. Such things as these as much belong to the essence of Christianity, as the belief of any of the doctrines of the gospel; and therefore the profession of them as much belongs to a Christian profession. (*Religious Affections*, 3.13)

In this Edwards is a classical, Protestant, and Reformed gospeler: the emphasis is on God's holiness and love, human sinfulness and God's wrath, and the utter need for humans to cry out to God for his grace.

If many evangelicals today anchor their understanding of gospel in the Reformers, one voice often ignored by all but the Wesleyans and Methodists is John Wesley (1703–1791), who may be said to represent another side of the reforming, reviving gospel. Wesley both experienced the travails of personal conversion and devoted his life relentlessly to spreading the gospel and summoning Great Britain to holiness. Wesley's gospel was the preaching of the good news of Jesus Christ—the narrative of his life, death, and resurrection—for the purpose of personal redemption and moral transformation. Here are his own words, reflecting as they do the turn of the ages that occurred after the death and resurrection of Christ:

> And herein does it [Christian faith] differ from that faith which the Apostles themselves had while our Lord was on earth, that it acknowledges the necessity and merit of his death, and the power of his resurrection. It acknowledges his death as the only sufficient means of redeeming man from death eternal, and his resurrection as the restoration of us all to life and immortality; inasmuch as he "was delivered for our sins, and rose again for our justification." Christian faith is then, not only an assent to the whole gospel of Christ, but also a full reliance on the blood of Christ; a trust in the merits of his life, death, and resurrection; a recumbency upon him as our atonement and our life, as given for us, and living in us; and, in consequence hereof, a closing with him, and cleaving to him, as our "wisdom, righteousness, sanctification, and redemption," or, in one word, our salvation.

We find here again that Protestant gospel emphasis: not just the narration of the story of Christ but the necessity of personal participation through faith in Christ. Any gospel that does not summon to personal repentance and faith is not properly Protestant.

The story of the formulation of the contemporary gospel of evangelicalism would not be complete without including something about Dwight L. Moody (1837–1899), who led evangelistic campaigns in both Great Britain and the United States in the 1870s, formulating an emotional message that was fit to convert sinners. Moody's entire evangelistic approach was shaped around the Three R's: "Ruin by sin, Redemption by Christ, and Regeneration by the Holy Ghost."[13] Another way Moody put this was to focus on the timeless points in the narrative about Jesus Christ, and in this Moody shows himself an orthodox Christian: "The Gospel preached by the apostles rested upon four pillars: the atoning death of Christ, His burial and resurrection, His ascension, His coming again. These four doctrines were preached by all the apostles, and by them the Gospel must stand or fall."[14]

The Gospel and Contemporary Evangelicalism

Contemporary evangelicalism has these three streams flowing into its gospel: the primacy of Scripture, adherence to the orthodox creeds (though sometimes not perceived as gospeling), and the Protestant Reformation's emphatic summoning to the personal experience of faith. For much of evangelicalism, the Eucharist plays little role in how the gospel is perceived. The diminution of creed and Eucharist in large pockets of evangelicalism illustrates that evangelicalism is shaped deeply by the revivalism of the nineteenth century. In other words, evangelicalism (today) is not so much simply a species of Calvinism as it is the flourishing of convertive piety and the adjustments that occurred in gospeling as a result of revivalism. This is where the work of David Bebbington brings us into sharper focus for understanding the gospel: evangelicalism is a convergence of Biblicism, crucicentrism, conversionism, and activism in piety and service.[15]

The gospel of contemporary evangelicalism emerges from this mixture of voices and puts before us the major evangelical gospeler of the twentieth century: the southern American Billy Graham.

In the 1950s and 1960s, Billy Graham (b. 1918) swept the world with his crusades. At the heart of his crusades was evangelism, and at the heart of his evangelism was his understanding of the gospel. In his own autobiography, aptly named after the invitation hymn he so often used, *Just As I Am*, Billy Graham describes the gospel he has always preached.[16] It begins, first, with a "message about God" as creator of humans as the image of God: "He created us and loves us so that we may live in harmony and fellowship with Him [and] our lives are never fulfilled and complete until His purpose becomes the foundation and center of our lives." Second, the message is about the "human race, and about each one of us." To quote his constant source of authority: "The Bible says that we have been separated and alienated from God because we have willfully turned our backs on Him and are determined to run our lives without Him." But, third, God still loves us and seeks for us to dwell with him eternally.

Now to the heart of his gospel: "In God's plan, by His death on the Cross, Jesus Christ paid the penalty for our sins, taking the judgment of God that we deserve upon Himself when He died on the Cross. Now, by His resurrection from the dead, Christ has broken the bonds of death and opened the way to eternal life for us." Finally, "this message is about our response." How do we respond and accept this message? By confession of sin, repentance, and commitment of our lives to Christ.

For Billy Graham and for the many who follow him, this is the evangelical gospel: God loves you, you are a sinner, God still loves you, Jesus paid the price for your reconciliation with God. You must accept this message, confess your sinfulness and repent, and commit your life to Christ. God does the saving but humans [in the power of the Spirit] do the responding.

John Stott (b. 1921), the expositor who evangelized, in many ways complemented Billy Graham, the evangelist who began with exposition. In Stott's own articulation of the gospel, seen perhaps most maturely in his *The Contemporary Christian*, Stott's central themes are not unlike those of Billy Graham: the tragedy that humans are sinful (dignity and depravity); the appeal of genuine freedom from (guilt, self, fear) and for (being our true selves as God meant us to be); the centrality of the atoning and substitutionary death of Jesus Christ on the cross; the power of the Spirit, the relevance of the resurrection, and the Lordship of Jesus Christ.[17] This message—and it has a more robust character than what is seen in Billy Graham—summons everyone to a radical commitment: intellectually, morally, vocationally, socially, politically, and globally.[18] The pointed climax of the gospel—in the Lordship of Christ—produces a gospel that outstrips the all-too-typical reductionism finding fertile, if shallow, soil in populist evangelism in the West.

The Gospel and Evangelicalism Today

The biblical message about the meaning of "gospel" as the recital of the (Eucharistic, baptismal) saving events in the life of Jesus Christ, along with the connection the Church has always made to the ecclesial orthodox creeds and to a transformed life, as well as to an impact on the whole of life under the Lordship of Christ, challenges the shallow gospel often proclaimed and reduced to tract-size sound bites today. The gospel is nothing less than a bold declaration of God's salvation by narrating the central events in Jesus' life: his incarnation, his death, his burial, his resurrection, his glorification, and his coming again. Anything less is neither the gospel of the Bible nor that of the Church.

One has to observe that evangelicalism has sometimes tempted evangelists and preachers to create an evangelistic style and message that too easily generate an experience. A particular form of this "experiencing of the gospel" in the United States is the seeker-sensitive approach. But a seeker-sensitive model for evangelism too easily leads to a seeker-friendly approach to theology that leads to a superficial theology. The combination of an experience-shaped gospeling and a seeker-friendly theology can be fatal for individuals, local churches, and the health of Western evangelicalism.

Alongside this reshaping of the gospel toward an experience is the tragic, one-sided emphasis one finds in the Western evangelical rejection of anything social in the core of the gospel. But, a genuinely biblical gospel embraces Jesus' kingdom vision for justice as inherent to what God's redemptive work in this world means. The gospel aims at kingdom, the society in which God's will is done.

The gospel for some is teamed up with modernity's rabid focus on the individual as the source of meaning and can lead at times to a near absence of "church" in the gospel of much of evangelicalism. The biblical gospel loses its structural teleology when church is not the context for and the direction of all gospeling. Radical individualism can flow from a gospel that focuses on personal decision, while a properly balanced robust gospel keeps both the individual and the church in view at all times.

Contemporary discoveries and discussions in biblical studies, like the New Perspective on Paul,[19] have put the evangelical understanding of the gospel to the test. This view, which has a number of varieties within it, offers a more subtle understanding of Judaism, the interaction of both Jesus and the apostles with that Judaism, and a framing of the message of redemption in that context. It sometimes leads to less emphasis on an Augustinian anthropology as the ontic grounds for gospeling, a greater emphasis on the sociological framework in which all gospeling occurred, a challenge to a perceived obsession with forensic imputation and justification, and a complete reworking of the older Protestant-Catholic divide of whether justification is an imputation or impartation or both.

In addition, recent scholarship on "gospel" has uncovered possible anti-imperial strains in the term "gospel." In particular, since the Roman emperor used the word "good news" to describe his announcements and connected such news to *pax Romana* and the divine sonship and saviorhood of the emperor, when we see the early Christians using these terms to define their message and Savior, we need to consider whether the Christians were claiming something about the idolatry of the imperial cult.[20]

Another issue at work is the so-called "rediscovery" of Jesus' kingdom vision for understanding gospel. The one-sided emphasis in the evangelical gospel on Pauline theology has led many to experience the message of Jesus as nothing less than a discovery. One need not choose between Jesus and Paul. Any gospel that does not contain both Jesus' kingdom vision and Paul's gospel of justification is to run a new course of history that somehow escapes how we got to the creeds, to the Reformation, and to the evangelicalism we now know.

NOTES

I am grateful to Chris Ridgeway, Bradley Nassif, Mary Veeneman, and William Andrew Tooley for discussions about this article.

1. *One Faith: The Evangelical Consensus* (Downers Grove, Ill: InterVarsity Press, 2004), 35–38.

2. K. Snodgrass, "The Gospel of Jesus," in *The Written Gospel*, ed. M. Bockmuehl and D. A. Hagner (Cambridge: Cambridge University Press, 2005), 31–44, here p. 31, emphasis added.

3. See C. H. Dodd, *The Apostolic Preaching and Its Developments* (New York: Harper & Row, 1964); M. Green, *Evangelism in the Early Church* (Grand Rapids: Eerdmans, 1970).

4. See esp. R. Bauckham, *The Bible and Mission* (Grand Rapids: Eerdmans, 2003), 27–54; C.J.H. Wright, *The Mission of God* (Downers Grove, Ill.: InterVarsity Press, 2005), 191–221.

5. See Ambrose, "The Baptismal Rite," in H. Bettenson, *The Later Christian Fathers* (New York: Oxford University Press, 1970), 182–186.

6. See A. Kreider, *Worship and Evangelism in Pre-Christendom* (Cambridge: Grove Books, 1995).

7. Ted A. Campbell, *The Gospel in Christian Traditions* (New York: Oxford University Press, 2009). In citing original sources in what follows, whenever possible I have used the translations in the "Christian Classics Ethereal Library" (www.ccel.org).

8. See S. R. Holmes, *Listening to the Past* (Grand Rapids: Baker Academic, 2002); D. H. Williams, *Evangelicals and Tradition* (Grand Rapids: Baker Academic, 2005).

9. See here B. Nassif, "The Evangelical Theology of the Eastern Orthodox Church," in *Three Views on Eastern Orthodoxy and Evangelicalism*, ed. J. J. Stamoolis (Grand Rapids: Zondervan, 2004), 25–87.

10. See *The Epistle to Diognetus* for an example of an evangelistic text.

11. At *Against Marcion* 3.8, Tertullian affirms the humanity of Christ as the gospel.

12. There is not space here to develop the ongoing development of these very same themes in Cyril of Alexandria, Maximos the Confessor, Simeon the New Theologian (who focused on the need for the personal experience of the gospel), or in the Iconclastic controversy that put into bold relief the artistic significance of the Incarnation.

13. W. H. Daniels, ed., *Moody: His Words, Work, and Workers* (New York: Nelson and Phillips, 1877), 256.

14. D. L. Moody, "Shall We Meet Our Loved Ones Again?" http://www.jesus-is-savior.com/Books,%20Tracts%20&%20Preaching/Printed%20Sermons/DL_Moody/loved_ones.htm.

15. See D. Bebbington, *Evangelicalism in Modern Britain: A History from the 1730s to the 1980s* (London: Unwin Hyman, 1989), 1–17; Bebbington, *The Dominance of Evangelicalism: The Age of Spurgeon and Moody* (Downers Grove, Ill.: InterVarsity Press, 2005), 21–51. See also D. Dayton, *Discovering an Evangelical Heritage* (Peabody, Mass.: Hendrickson, 1976).

16. Billy Graham, *Just As I Am: The Autobiography of Billy Graham* (San Francisco: HarperSanFrancisco/Zondervan, 1997), 726–729. All quotations are from these pages.

17. See J.R.W. Stott, *The Contemporary Christian* (Downers Grove, Ill.: InterVarsity Press, 1992), 31–98.

18. See also *The Lausanne Covenant*, perhaps the finest statement in the history of the Church on evangelism. I have used *Let the Earth Hear His Voice: International Congress on*

World Evangelization, Lausanne, Switzerland, ed. J. D. Douglas (Minneapolis: World Wide Publications, 1975), 2–9.

19. The major theses have been shaped by E. P. Sanders, James D. G. Dunn, and N. T. Wright.

20. See here G. N. Stanton, *Jesus and the Gospel* (Cambridge: Cambridge University Press, 2004), 9–62; N. T. Wright, *Paul in Fresh Perspective* (Minneapolis: Fortress, 2005), 59–79.

BIBLIOGRAPHY

Campbell, Ted A. *The Gospel in Christian Traditions*. New York: Oxford University Press, 2009.
Dodd, C. H. *The Apostolic Preaching and Its Developments*. New York: Harper & Row, 1964.
Douglas, J. D., ed. "The Lausanne Covenant.," In *Let the Earth Hear His Voice*, 2–9. Minneapolis: World Wide Publications, 1975.
Green, M. *Evangelism in the Early Church*. (Grand Rapids: Eerdmans, 1970.
Nassif, B. "The Evangelical Theology of the Eastern Orthodox Church." In *Three Views on Eastern Orthodoxy and Evangelicalism*, ed. J. J. Stamoolis, 25–87. Grand Rapids: Zondervan, 2004.
Packer, J. I., and T. C. Oden. *One Faith: The Evangelical Consensus* (Downers Grove, Ill.: InterVarsity Press, 2004).
Snodgrass, K. "The Gospel of Jesus." In *The Written Gospel*, ed. M. Bockmuehl and D. A. Hagner, 31–44. Cambridge: Cambridge University Press, 2005.
Stanton, G. N. *Jesus and Gospel*. Cambridge: Cambridge University Press, 2004.
Tuttle, Robert G., Jr. *The Story of Evangelism: A History of the Witness to the Gospel*. Nashville, Tenn.: Abingdon, 2006.
Wright, C.J.H. *The Mission of God*, Downers Grove: InterVarsity Press, 2006.

CHAPTER 13

CONVERSION AND REDEMPTION

GORDON T. SMITH

A Sea Change in Understanding

It is not be an overstatement to say that evangelicals are experiencing a "sea change"—a paradigm shift—in their understanding of conversion and redemption, a shift that includes the way in which they think about the salvation of God, the nature and mission of the church, and the character of religious experience. Although there is no one word to capture where evangelicals are going in this regard, there is a word that captures what they are leaving behind: revivalism.

Revivalism is a religious movement heir to both the seventeenth-century Puritans and the renewal movements of the eighteenth century, but one that largely emerged in the nineteenth century. It was broadly institutionalized in the twentieth century in the conservative denominations in North America as well as in para-church and mission agencies that then in turn spread the movement within North America and globally. For evangelicals up until at least a generation ago, the language of conversion *was* the language of revivalism; it shaped and in many ways determined their approach to worship, evangelism, and spiritual formation.

Evangelicalism is certainly not monolithic; the points at which evangelicals differ among themselves is significant—both Baptists and Pentecostals see themselves as coming under this umbrella, along with Mennonites, and then also Calvinists and Wesleyans. But for all their diversity, the way in which they spoke of conversion and redemption was remarkably similar. Evangelicals took for granted that the language and categories of revivalism were the language and categories of the New Testament.

Conversion was viewed to be a punctiliar experience: persons could specify with confidence and assurance the time and place of their conversion, by reference, as often as not, to the moment when they prayed what was typically called "the sinner's prayer."

The focus of conversion was the afterlife: one sought salvation so that one could "go to heaven" after death, and the assumption was that "salvation" would lead to disengagement from the world. Once converted, the central focus of one's life would be church or religious activities, particularly those that helped others come to this understanding of salvation that assured them of "eternal life" after death. Life in the world was thought to hold minimal significance. What counted was the afterlife. And if one had "received Christ," one could be confident of one's eternity with God. Conversion was isolated from the experience of the church. Indeed, it was generally assumed that a person would come to faith outside of the church and then be encouraged, after conversion, to join a church community.

Typically evangelicals approached evangelism through the use of techniques or formulas by which a person would be introduced to spiritual principles or "laws" on the assumption that if these principles were accepted as "true," a person would offer an appropriate prayer and thus "become" a Christian.

Baptism, it was insisted, was subsequent to conversion and essentially optional. For although baptism was thought to be perhaps important, true spiritual experience was considered a personal, interior, subjective experience and thus not sacramental. Evangelicals have typically had a deep distrust in sacramental actions, insisting that they do not have redemptive significance.

Further, the church was often defined as in the business of making conversions happen; its life and mission were oriented toward getting more people converted through whatever means possible. Successful congregations were characterized by numerical "conversion growth."

Significantly, conversion was viewed as something distinct from "disciple-making." The making of disciples was thought to be subsequent to conversions. Thus evangelicals would speak of "making converts into disciples"; evangelism and disciple-making were distinguished, and typically the approach to evangelism was distinct from the approach to spiritual formation.[1]

On each of these points, evangelicals are moving toward a thorough reenvisioning of the nature of conversion and redemption. Increasingly, there is appreciation that conversion is a complex experience by which a person is initiated into a common life with the people of God who together seek the in-breaking of the kingdom, both in this life and in the world to come. This experience is mediated by the church and thus necessarily includes baptism as a rite of initiation. The power or energy of this experience is one of immediate encounter with the risen Christ—rather than principles or laws—and this experience is choreographed by the Spirit rather than evangelistic techniques. Evangelicals are reappropriating the heritage of the Reformation with its emphasis on the means of grace, and thereby affirming the priority of the Spirit's work in religious experience.

The fundamental categories and assumptions of revivalism are thus being questioned as never before. There were voices in the past that questioned revivalism:

C. S. Lewis, always adored by evangelicals, was seemingly oblivious to the language and categories of revivalism. A. W. Tozer, J. I. Packer, and John R. W. Stott, while obviously evangelicals, nevertheless seemed to be able to articulate the Christian faith in other than the language and categories of revivalism, as did many others. But the difference of the past generation of theological reflection is that we can genuinely speak of a sea change, so much so that the language and categories of revivalism are simply no longer viable. However much this vision powerfully shaped the life of the church and its mission and, indeed, influenced more than a generation of evangelical missionaries to spread around the globe, the church has over the past generation sought new linguistic wineskins and new theological categories by which to understand conversion and redemption.

A number of factors have brought about this thorough rethinking and thus the challenge to revivalism.

1. *Biblical studies.* Evangelicals are indebted to both Old and New Testament scholars, including James Dunn, Gordon Fee, N. T Wright, Christopher Wright, and others, who have called for a biblical theology of conversion and redemption that is more deeply rooted in the Scriptures and that takes account of the full scope of God's purposes in Christ. These scholars are drawing more fully on the vision of God's righteousness that emerges in the Old Testament and finds expression in the Gospels, as well as the letters of Paul—and not just a verse here or there, but rather the grand sweep of Pauline theology. As this vision of God's salvation permeates the language and thought of evangelicals, they are being weaned from their propensity to make a one-to-one correlation between conversion and "getting saved." More and more evangelicals appreciate that God's salvation has both a past and future dimension, is about not merely conversion but lifelong transformation, and has both a corporate and cosmic dimension.

2. *The nature of religious experience.* Theologians within the evangelical tradition are learning from interdisciplinary contributions to the study of the nature of religious experience, and thus by implication the experience of conversion. Philosophers (such as Charles Taylor and Louis Dupre), behavioral scientists (notably Lewis Rambo, but also developmental theorists such as James Fowler and Erik Erickson, as well as anthropologists such as Paul Hiebert) have broadened the evangelical appreciation of the phenomenon of religious experience. This consideration of the nature of religious experience has also been informed by critical reflection on a postmodern awareness of the spiritual dimension of life, and of the nature of Christian religious experience in a post-Christian social environment (see especially Brad Kallenberg and Robert Webber on this). Further, as evangelical witness has led to the conversion of Hindus and Muslims, there has been an increasing willingness to ask, for example, not "how *should* a Muslim become a Christian" but how *does* it actually happen: What is the character of their experience and how can we appreciate this without having to superimpose the categories of revivalism on their faith journey?

3. *Cross-pollination from other Christian traditions.* For more than a generation, evangelical theologians have become increasingly open to critical theological engagement with Christians of other theological traditions. The evangelical understanding

of conversion and redemption is now informed by Orthodox voices (including Alexander Schmemmann and John Zizioulas), Roman Catholics (such as Yves Conger, Karl Rahner, Hans Urs Balthasar, Bernard Lonergan, Bernard Haring, and Rosemary Haughton), and mainline Protestant theologians (including Karl Barth, Dietrich Bonhoeffer, George Lindbeck, and many others). This exchange and learning across theological traditions has deeply enriched the evangelical understanding of conversion and redemption.

4. *The global character of evangelicalism and the impact of Pentecostalism.* The majority of evangelical Christians now live outside of the West and to a great extent are either self-identified Pentecostals or significantly influenced by the Pentecostal and charismatic movement of the past century. Theologians sympathetic to this development, such as Clark Pinnock, insist that emphasis on the ministry of the Spirit is not incidental but central to the life and witness of the church—and therefore to the church's understanding of conversion. This global experience has also forced evangelicals into a deeper appreciation of the social, economic, and ecological implications of conversion, as the voices of the emerging churches of the global church insist that these factors much be taken into account in seeking a biblical theology of genuine religious experience. The global church has reinforced the growing recognition that authentic religious experience is not merely personal and subjective; it also does and must find expression in the tangible including the pursuit of peace and justice, and an identification with the poor.

5. *A recovery of both the evangelical and the ancient Christian heritage.* The challenge to revivalism has come, as much as anything, from historians. While evangelicals have actively sought to recover their full Christian heritage—including the breadth of medieval and sixteenth-century Spanish mysticism—the most notable rethinking of revivalism has come from two sources. Some historians (notably Richard Lovelace, Mark Noll, and Bruce Hindmarsh) have called for a deeper appreciation of the evangelical heritage itself, especially its prerevivalism roots in the great renewal movements of the eighteenth century. Others have profiled the "ancient" Christian heritage, urging evangelicals to draw on the wisdom of the church fathers and the liturgical and catechetical practices of the early church (Thomas Oden and Robert Webber).

Taken together, these five factors have profoundly affected the way that evangelicals think about conversion and redemption. One voice more than any other is sounded in this conversation—that of Lesslie Newbigin, whose theology was shaped by experience in both West and East, as a missioner and then bishop in India. Newbigin argued that conversion is a matter of understanding, ethics, and community—that there is no conversion without conversion of the mind, identification with the reign of Christ, and incorporation into a faith community that is marked by and sustained by its sacramental actions—baptism and the Lord's Supper. Newbigin's fundamental observation and conviction is that the church is not a provider of religious products and services but rather that the church is a people in mission. The church, collectively, is through an active discipleship a living embodiment of the kingdom to which the church witnesses. Thus the church is not obsessed with its own growth but with the kingdom, as it seeks to live the Gospel within particular social and cultural contexts. This perspective is reinforced by Newbigen's recognition and reminder to his readers that all reasoning arises from a particular rational tradition which is embodied within a living community.

Marks of an Emerging Understanding of Conversion and Redemption

There is emerging in the conversation around the nature of conversion and redemption, and its implications for the church and its mission, a language that has some distinctive elements.

The Complexity of the Conversion Experience

Evangelicals increasingly understand conversion to be a complex experience. Therefore it cannot be reduced to a single moment or "crisis" in one's life, or to the event of having prayed a particular prayer. Conversion is more complex than "receiving Jesus into one's heart"; it is a process, a series of events and often a season of quiet or waiting that is as significant as any specific event or action by the person coming to faith. Evangelicals still recognize that conversion is a beginning; but while they believe the Christian journey in one sense is a continuous conversion, they recognize nonetheless that it is not the whole of the Christian life. While it is a beginning, conversion is a process that may well take a number of years.

In the late 1980s and early 1990s, a British study of conversion experiences came to the following remarkable conclusion and observation: "The gradual process is the way in which the majority of people discover God and the average time taken is about four years: models of evangelism which can help people along the pathway are needed."[2] While in the early 1990s this was viewed as a remarkable observation, within fifteen years it was virtually taken for granted that this is how we need to think of conversion in the post-Christian West. In the East, studies of the nature of conversion—including, but not limited to, that of Muslims—has led to a broad and widely accepted appreciation of the gradual and extended process of conversion.

This gradual process has profound implications for models of evangelism and pastoral care. It means that congregations and parachurch groups can no longer assume that they need to target a particular "decision" or moment when someone crosses the line and now can be assured of "eternal life." If conversion is more complex and a more extended process, the church needs to rethink its ministry to enquirers who are on the way to faith in Christ.

The Priority of God and the Work of the Spirit.

Evangelicals have always affirmed the priority of God: the sovereignty of God and the work of the Spirit. But one of the features of revivalism was its rather heavy emphasis on human volition, on the one hand, and "technique" for effecting conversions, on the other. Converts were taught that God was in a waiting mode, eager to save but waiting for the potential Christian to kick-start the process with the appropriate prayer. Further, evangelicals were taught that they could learn how to "win souls," and that through the appropriate methods—whether in public evangelistic preaching or personal "witnessing"—one could "lead people to Christ."

As evangelicals recover their full Christian heritage, they discover a deepening appreciation for both the timing and means of the Spirit, who is the only true "soul winner." Conversion is choreographed by God and God alone, and God is neither rushed nor hurried. This also means that Spirit is active in the life of a potential converts long before they come to conscious faith in Christ, so much so that conversion is a response to the saving initiative of God. It is not so much that God responds to the sinner's prayer as that the sinner in life and prayer responds to the initiative of God.

Here is where it is urgent that evangelicals get past the older Calvinist-Arminian debates and come to a nuanced appreciation for the interplay between God and human response—a theology of religious experience that is grounded in the sovereign priority of God's grace and yet takes human volition seriously as Spirit-inspired response to God's initiative. Then evangelical approaches to evangelism will reflect trust in both the timing and means of the Spirit's work; and evangelicals will learn to be more attentive to the Spirit's work in individuals, communities, and other religious traditions.

Conversion Not to the Church but to Christ and Christ's Kingdom

Evangelicals are increasingly insistent that conversion is not ultimately to the church but to Christ and his kingdom, and that therefore the kingdom and not the church is the focus of mission. The church is only a means to the end. Lesslie Newbigen was one of many voices insisting on this distinction between church and kingdom and offering the language of "sign" to speak of the way in which the church witnesses to the kingdom.

The significance of this distinction can hardly be overstated; what it implies is that mission is not about church growth but kingdom growth; mission is not about getting people to join the church but rather it means inviting women and men to come under the authority of the reign of Christ and inviting them to participate in the kingdom purposes of the ascended Lord. Therefore it frees the church to be about its calling: rather than focusing on the potential convert, primary attention is to Christ (in worship) and Christ's kingdom (in mission). The potential convert is invited into this worship and mission. But worship is not "dumbed down" to accommodate the seeker; instead, in radical hospitality the seeker is invited to learn the language of Christian worship. Mission is not about selling people on the Christian religion so they will join the club; rather, it is about the kingdom and Christ's call to the nations to recognize the in-breaking of his reign. This kingdom orientation means the church does not minimize the demands of the gospel or the implications of the cross for radical discipleship

The Church Mediates the Process of Conversion

The church is a means, not an end. And yet, it is the God-ordained means by which God, by the Holy Spirit, is bringing people, communities, and nations to faith in Christ. With full acknowledgment that the work of the Spirit is not limited to the church or by the church, evangelicals are actively seeking to articulate an ecclesiology that is Trinitarian and kingdom oriented. This has included a growing appreciation of how the church mediates the experience of conversion and the salvation of God.

While historically ill at ease with such statements as "you cannot have God as your father unless you have the church as your mother," evangelicals are now coming to a deeper appreciation of the ecclesial character of the God's mission in the world and the ecclesial nature of authentic religious experience.

On the one hand, this means that one is not truly converted to Christ until and unless one is incorporated into Christian community—as was noted above with reference to the epistle to the Ephesians. To be a Christian and united with Christ is to be in communion with the people of God who are the body of Christ and the fellowship of the Spirit. This perspective arises out of an appreciation of the very nature of the mission of God: that God is forming for himself a people. This conviction means that while religious experience is located in the individual human heart, it is never purely personal and subjective. The experience of the individual is always housed and husbanded by the experience of the faith community. What William Abraham, Thomas Oden, and others have stressed is that the church is not just any gathering of Christians, but rather the contemporary church in deep continuity with the ancient church and the creedal faith of that church. It is the church as a community that confesses the Triune God and the Christ who is witnessed to through the Apostles' and Nicene Creeds.

But more, evangelicals are drawing on both their evangelical heritage and the witness of the Puritans and John Wesley and others, and they are learning from the experience of the early church (see Alan Kreider in this regard) to appreciate how it is appropriate to speak of conversion as a process of first *belonging* before one believes. This suggests that not only is incorporation into the church an essential element or dimension of conversion—incorporation into the church is also the very means by which one comes to faith in Christ. It is not that one comes to Christ and then joins the church but rather that one comes to Christ through the embodied witness of the church—one belongs and, likely in time, comes to believe. One belongs in order to learn the language of faith. The enquirer joins a community that worships the Triune God and, over time, comes to recognize the presence of the One who is the focus of attention for the faith community. Then also, the seeker is a learner who joins a community of learners, who then in turn allow their learning to shape and empower them for mission in the world. The enquirer is both an observer and participant, entering into the mission of God while in a process of coming to know who is this God who has reached out in Christ and who is at work in the human heart through the gracious presence of the Spirit.

This of course means that hospitality is a vital element in Christian witness. But, always, as noted above, hospitality is offered in a way that insists that the church remains the church. The most effective witness of the church in the world is to be, precisely, the church. This understanding has also led to a greater awareness of the vital need for rites of initiation into Christian faith—rites that are located within and linked to the liturgical life and rhythms of the church.

With this vision of the church as midwife to the process of conversion, evangelicals are learning that this process needs to be articulated: it is a journey with specific and intentional markers along the way. For some evangelicals, this will mean learning from the post-Vatican II Roman Catholic Rite for the Christian Initiation of Adults (RCIA) wherein enquirers come to faith in Christ through an intentional catechetical process. Robert Webber has advocated something similar in his *Journey to Jesus*.

With a process in place, *within* the life and worship of a congregation, along which a person can journey to faith in Christ, the "evangelist" is seen not so much as someone who sells an idea or religious brand, but rather as one who comes alongside, as a moral or spiritual companion (a docent, as some have suggested)[3] to respond to questions, raise possibilities, suggest next steps and wait patiently as people come to faith in their own time—and God's time, which may not be the timing of the evangelist.

Baptism Integral to the Experience of Conversion

Evangelicals have tended to separate baptism from conversion and assume that conversion comes before baptism or, in the case of infant baptism, that it is only a witness to a conversion that is yet to come. While baptism certainly is an act of "witness," evangelicals are seeking to recover the close affinity between baptism and conversion in a way that reflects the deep assumptions and language of the New Testament, including but not limited to such texts as "repent and be baptized for the forgiveness of your sins" (Acts 2:38). The call for baptism as an integral element of conversion is not intended to challenge the critical and indeed central place of faith and repentance in the journey to Christian faith, but rather as a way to appreciate that faith and repentance need to be embodied in symbolic action (that is, ritual).

As evangelicals, along with other Christians, appropriate the wisdom of the ancient church, baptism will increasingly be viewed as not only integral to conversion but the actual focal point of the journey to faith in Christ. Conversion itself is a process, a series of events—a journey or pilgrimage to Christ. Baptism is the essential and animating benchmark on that road to faith. It is not synonymous with conversion, but we cannot speak of Christian conversion without it. This means, according to Abraham, that the church must "find a way to reunite conversion and baptism in a coherent, unified process of initiation."[4] By integrating baptism and conversion, evangelicals will recover the New Testament doctrine which Richard Longnecker describes as "the indissoluble connection between conversion, water baptism, and the baptism of the Holy Spirit."[5] We must then also speak of the connection between conversion and baptism in the Holy Spirit. But first, an additional comment regarding water baptism.

The whole question of baptism and conversion has created a stimulating conversation among theologians who serve in Hindu, Jewish, and Muslim contexts where baptism is such a boundary between previous religious affiliations and the emerging new life in Christ—where baptism effectively breaks off all contact with one's previous identity, and the family and social systems that sustained that identity. The question is asked: To become a Christian, must one utterly forsake, for example, one's Muslim identity and thus sever all ties with the very ones who most need to know this new faith? Should baptism be done in secret? Or should it be delayed to accommodate the long-term intentions of God within a particular community? These questions do not diminish the importance of baptism and Christian community, but suggest that it is whole families and social systems that God seeks and not merely individual conversions. Perhaps the church needs to keep the long view in mind as it struggles to grow in cross-cultural contexts.

The Gift of the Spirit Integral to the Experience of Conversion

By the end of the twentieth century, evangelicals seemed to fit clearly into two camps: those who were comfortable in speaking of the baptism of the Spirit and those who were not. The latter assumed they were baptized in the Spirit at conversion or baptism, so that there was no need for a specific reference to the gift or baptism of the Spirit at a baptism. In contrast, those of the holiness and Pentecostal traditions believed the Christian could expect the baptism of the Spirit, and assumed that this would occur subsequent to conversion as a second, crisis experience.

One of the most vital aspects of the emerging understanding of conversion and redemption for evangelicals will be the ways they connect the baptism of the Spirit to faith in Christ: how it relates to their conversion and how it is symbolized or ritually articulated.[6]

Through conversion one is initiated into a life that is thoroughly immersed in the Spirit. Evangelical New Testament exegetes are rightly insisting both that we cannot speak of Christian experience without explicit reference to the Spirit, and also that we cannot speak of this baptism of the Spirit as purely something subsequent to conversion (see James Dunn on this). Thus evangelicals need to resist their propensity to marginalize Pentecostal Christians because of a fear of "enthusiasm." Pentecostal Christians need to recover the ancient Trinitarian and Christocentric faith that is the necessary theological anchor to their experience of the Spirit. With all Christians, we need to see that conversion means receiving the gift of the Spirit (again, Acts 2:38: "and you will receive the gift of the Spirit").

For the ancient church, this was symbolized through ritual action. Baptism included *chrismation*: the anointing of the baptismal candidate with oil and prayer for receiving the Spirit. Many evangelicals are now saying that some variation of this practice needs to be incorporated into evangelical approaches to baptism and initiation. Might this be a way in which Charismatic and evangelical Christians can find common ground? Locate the baptism of the Spirit clearly and explicitly in the experience of water baptism, through a clear ritual action. In so doing, evangelicals would affirm the Charismatic insight that the whole purpose of Christ's coming and water baptism is precisely that Christians would be filled with the Spirit; Charismatics could affirm that the experience of the Spirit is Christological—known in and grounded in the work of Christ, as testified to by water baptism.

Conversion Leads to Transformation

Heirs to revivalism often distinguish conversion from discipleship and imply that conversion guarantees eternity with God "in heaven." This was diagnosed by Richard F. Lovelace in his seminal *Dynamics of Spiritual Life* as a "sanctification gap." Evangelicals had, he observed, placed such a stress on initial conversion that they had neglected the fuller New Testament call to spiritual growth toward spiritual maturity.[7]

Much of this "gap" has to be attributed to the revivalistic propensity to make conversion as easy as possible, and to disconnect it from the processes of spiritual formation by which a Christian grows and matures in their faith.

Lovelace proposed a biblical model for the spiritual life that reflects continuity between conversion and spiritual formation. It speaks of conversion as, at best, a good beginning, and requires a theology of "sainthood." This means a clear articulation of the sanctified Christian life—what it will look like when a person is mature in Christ. Conversion is seen as only part of a whole—the whole of the Christian life into which one is initiated.

This model requires that we draw on the wisdom of those who, within the evangelical heritage, have insisted on sanctification as the goal of Christian experience: Wesleyans, holiness preachers and others. But we must do so in a way that is anchored not in moralistic legalism but deep union with Christ—and in a way that sees the whole Christian life flowing out of that union.

This will be possible, as Lovelace suggests, only when we recover the essential unity among the three human faculties of intellect, will, and emotion.[8] Evangelicals need to turn from their "scandalous"[9] failure to affirm the Christian mind, actively seek the proper ordering of the affections, and embrace together the costliness of authentic Christian discipleship. This unity of mind, heart, and will begins with the process of evangelism and catechesis for enquirers. From the start, evangelism should engage the mind, connect the heart (to truth), and call forth the engagement of the will. In this way, it leads naturally to a process of spiritual formation and maturity. A convert joins a community that is growing up in Christ (Ephesians 3:15).

Conversion Is for Mission

Newbigen rightly insisted that the church needed to recover an authentic biblical notion of election: that in the ancient and then Pauline sense, election is not for privilege but service. The elect are not so much conscious of their own salvation as that they are called to participate in the saving purposes of God in the world.

This suggests that we do not speak of conversion in escapist terms, as a means by which one gets on the life raft before the ship goes down. Instead, conversion is the radical transformation of an individual life toward generous service in the world. It is an act of joining the church that is "in mission." The church is a people who in the name of Christ are called to make a difference for the kingdom, in the world. The strength of a congregation is not its size or rate of growth, but, first, the degree to which its members are equipped to fulfill their vocations, and, second, the degree to which the congregation as a whole participates in the work of God in and for the world.

Therefore conversion equips and empowers converts to be in but not of the world. They are not called out of the world, but very intentionally called to take their newfound faith into the world and to live out that faith in the marketplace—the marketplace of ideas in education and the arts, as well as the marketplace of business and commerce. But they are also called as aliens from their own culture because their values, mores, and vision of life are those of the reign of Christ. This means that the focus of the church is not new converts but the Triune God and reign of Christ. And potential converts are invited to join in worship and service. By these means new converts and older disciples together witness to the world.

Conclusion

Evangelical Christians are deeply concerned for those who do not know God and have yet to experience conversion, through faith and repentance, to Christ Jesus. Nothing in this chapter's "sea change" has altered this vision and commitment. And yet, at their best, evangelicals have always recognized that people are converted not because they have come to terms with "spiritual laws" or questions they might be asked when they "get to heaven," or even "evidence that demands a verdict"—but because they experience the transforming grace of God through an encounter with the risen and ascended Christ.

The only question that remains, then, is whether evangelicals will trust these instincts and devote themselves to Christ-centered worship and kingdom-oriented mission. Will this be evident in deep trust that God will do God's work in God's time? To trust the work of God is to trust the Spirit and this necessarily means that the church trusts the Word—the Scriptures preached—as the essential means of grace and conversion.

This begs the question of what it means to be the church. The evangelical tradition is at a fork in the road and, given this sea change in the understanding of conversion and redemption, the most crucial issue at stake is what it means to be a congregation. Evangelicals will only be able to navigate these waters if they can formulate a dynamic theology of the church that reflects the Triune character of God, the means of grace—Spirit and Word—and a radical orientation in mission toward the kingdom of God.

NOTES

1. For more on this, see Dallas Willard's chapter on "discipleship" in this volume.
2. John Finney, *Finding Faith Today: How Does It Happen?* (Swindon: British and Foreign Bible Society, 1992), 25.
3. George R. Hunsberger borrows this image from David Lowes Watson, in "The Newbigen Gauntlet: Developing a Domestic Missiology for North America," in *The Church between Gospel and Culture: The Emerging Mission in North America*, ed. George R. Hunsberger and Craig Van Gelder (Grand Rapids: Eerdmans, 1996), 23.
4. William J. Abraham, *The Logic of Evangelism* (Grand Rapids: Eerdmans, 1989), 133.
5. Richard N. Longenecker. *The Acts of the Apostles* (Grand Rapids: Zondervan, 1981), 284.
6. See more on this in Craig Keener's chapter in this volume, "Holy Spirit."
7. Richard F. Lovelace, *Dynamics of Spirit Life* (Downers Grove, Ill.: InterVarsity Press, 1979), 232.
8. Ibid.
9. Mark Noll, *The Scandal of the Evangelical Mind* (Grand Rapids: Eerdmans, 1994).

BIBLIOGRAPHY

Abraham, William J. *The Logic of Evangelism*. Grand Rapids: Eerdmans, 1989.

Dunn, James. *Baptism in the Holy Spirit: A Re-examination of the New Testament Teaching on the Gift of the Spirit in Relation to Pentecostalism Today*. Philadelphia: Westminster, 1970.

Hindmarsh, D. Bruce. *The Evangelical Conversion Narrative: Spiritual Autobiography in Early Modern England*. Oxford: Oxford University Press, 2005.

Hunsberger, George R. *Bearing the Witness of the Spirit: Lesslie Newbigen's Theology of Cultural Plurality*. Grand Rapids: Eerdmans, 1998. See particularly chapter 5 on Conversion.

Kallenberg, Brad J. *Live to Tell: Evangelism in a Postmodern World*. Grand Rapids: Brazos, 2002.

Kreider, Alan. *The Change of Conversion and the Origin of Christendom*. Harrisburg, Pa.: Trinity Press, 1999.

Newbigen, Leslie. *The Household of God: Lectures on the Nature of the Church*. London: SCM Press, 1953.

Roberts Gaventa, Beverly. *From Darkness to Light: Aspects of Conversion in the New Testament*. Philadelphia: Fortress, 1986.

Smith, Gordon T. *Beginning Well: Christian Conversion and Authentic Transformation*. Downers Grove, InterVarsity Press, 2001.

Smith, Gordon T. *Transforming Conversion: Rethinking the Language and Contours of Christian Initiation* Grand Rapids: BakerAcademic, 2010.

Webber, Robert E. *Journey to Jesus: The Worship, Evangelism and Nurture Mission of the Church*. Nashville, Tenn.: Abingdon, 2001.

CHAPTER 14

JUSTIFICATION AND ATONEMENT

DONALD G. BLOESCH

He has appeared once for all at the end of the age to put away sin by the sacrifice of himself.

—Hebrews 9:26

He does not give grace so freely that He has demanded no satisfaction, but rather He has given Christ as the one who makes satisfaction for us.

—Martin Luther

Without the doctrine of justification ... there never can be any true Christian church.

—Karl Barth

Revisiting Old Truths

While the doctrine of forensic justification only slowly emerged as an enduring formal principle in the theology of the church, the idea of justification (*dikaiosynē*) as well as that of atonement had deep roots in the early history of Israel and could be said to be a salient theme in Old Testament theology. It was commonly believed that every misdemeanor in both faith and conduct requires a compensation or reparation for the wrong done. For some, this reparation may take the form of animal sacrifice and for others acts of asceticism, such as prolonged fasting. When people turn away from the living God and bow down before idols, they will not do so with impunity. As the New Testament scholar John Knox phrased it: "A price must be paid; a penalty must be suffered, a sacrifice must be offered.... Paul... undoubtedly finds in the life and death of Christ the indispensable atoning sacrifice."[1]

In the dispensation of grace, evident most clearly in the New Testament, animal sacrifices are no longer demanded—only the sacrifice of a broken heart. In New Testament religion justification by outward rituals is now called into question. The law of God must still be obeyed, but following the law is not sufficient for the renewal of the human spirit. What is demanded now in the light of the coming of Christ is the confession of Christ as the liberator from the curse of the law as well as the fulfillment of the spirit of the law. And the key to such fulfillment is not works of obedience but the solitary act of faith—simply believing in loving gratitude for what God has done for us in Jesus Christ. Faith has its validation in fruits of the Spirit, which necessarily follow a faith commitment.

It was not until the stirrings of the Protestant Reformation that we have an unequivocal affirmation that the efficacy of Christ's atonement rests on faith alone (*sola fide*).[2] This conviction also implies Christ alone (*solus Christus*), for apart from outward ceremonies and sacrifices, he makes us worthy of receiving God's forgiving mercy. It also entails grace alone (*sola gratia*), for every good thing comes from the hand of God. Many of the church fathers and doctors of the medieval church acknowledged the priority of grace over works in the plan of salvation, but they were reluctant to envisage faith as an act of the redeemed that could by itself bring about atonement for sin. Of course, they allowed for the work of the Spirit in bringing illumination to seekers after righteousness, but for medieval churchmen the impartation of the Spirit was often conditional on the rituals that the church performs in order to make atonement for sin concrete and effective. Justifying faith was often recognized as a factor, even a significant factor in a person's coming to salvation, but it was not then celebrated as the doctrine "by which the church stands or falls" (the Reformation position).[3]

In classical Reformed theology, faith is not so much the ground of justification as the means by which we receive justification. The ground of justification is the reconciling work of God in Jesus Christ, which takes place apart from us, but justification is realized subjectively when Christ's saving work is applied to the repentant sinner in the act of faith. We are justified by faith *for* works but not apart from works. Calvin spoke of a double justification in which our works also need to be justified.

Contrary to popular understanding, the Reformers did not harbor a monolithic view of the relative importance of faith and works in the plan of salvation. Luther vigorously held that faith alone justifies; yet it is not faith as intellectual assent but faith as personal decision and encounter. Calvin's stress was on the grace of God prior to faith but also active in faith, bringing about faith. Both theologians asserted that faith is necessary for the assimilation of grace into the life of the Christian; yet this is not faith as a meritorious work but as an undeserved gift of the

Spirit. The mainstream Reformers were united in holding to the substance of faith but differed in their emphases, sometimes quite profoundly—as in the case of the sacraments. On the doctrines of atonement and justification, however, they were quite close.

A large part of the church, including some evangelically oriented Catholics, affirm the role of good works in manifesting the redeeming work of Christ on the cross. At the same time they rightly resist the idea that works contribute in any substantial way to the efficacy of our justification in the divine counsel. Works are important to show us the way we must live as people set free from bondage to sin, but our good works do not play a positive role in liberating us from the power of sin. The Reformers followed Paul in affirming the justification of the ungodly (Rom. 5:4–11). We are justified not because of our righteousness, for we have none; we are justified because of God's eternal decision for humanity, which can be attributed only to God's unfathomable generosity. We do not have to be perfected before we are justified; we are justified while we are yet in our sins provided we believe in Christ's redemption.

In the Reformation perspective, faith is the incontrovertible sign that we are already justified by virtue of God's grace. Justification is a gift that ensures our acceptance by a loving and merciful God. Justification is the ground of our faith rather than vice versa. It is also the goal of our faith in that it liberates the will for service to others.

The Reformers and their followers also made a prominent place for the subjective dimension of salvation, which they located first of all in the person and work of Jesus Christ, the eternal Son of God. This subjective reordering is often called in church tradition regeneration or sanctification. God gives us in Jesus Christ a twofold grace: justification and sanctification (Calvin). The miracle of grace is a verdict of acquittal pronounced on us from on high and also a transformative presence that mitigates the power of sin to enslave us. John Wesley envisaged sanctification as a second work of grace that fulfills the work of justification. For the mainstream Reformers, sanctification and justification are two sides of the one redeeming work of grace, which results in an ontological change in a person's inner being. While the Reformers proclaimed the message of the justification of the ungodly, Pietists and Wesleyans have celebrated the sanctification of the righteous. Both aspects of our salvation are rooted in the free grace of God. Justification constitutes the foundation of our salvation; sanctification relates to the apex or goal of salvation. The Reformers regarded justification as the enduring basis of the Christian life; sanctification is the core and heart of the Christian life. Wesley could even describe the latter as "a still higher salvation." For the magisterial Reformers (Luther and Calvin and their followers), justification is the ultimate as opposed to the preliminary work of the Spirit in human life.

From the perspective of many of the church fathers, the human dilemma rests on the invasion of God's good creation by the demonic powers of darkness.[4] The grace procured for us by Christ's atoning work opens the doorway to freedom in the spirit. For Anselm on the other hand (d. 1109), the core of the human problem lies in the infringement of God's honor by sin.[5] In the first position, the chief adversary of the Christian faith is the devil, the bastion of iniquity. In the second, it is the abasing of God's honor or the breaking of God's law. Among the mystics, the human predicament is rooted in isolation from God and from our fellow humanity. This isolation can be overcome only by fellowship with the living God—"leaning on the everlasting arms."[6]

Theories of the Atonement

One should recognize that there are various theories of the atonement of Christ, just as there are divergent ways of laying hold of the mystery of justification. The brilliant Swedish Lutheran scholar Gustaf Aulén in his provocative *Christus Victor* has given the church a valuable resource by which to grasp the tensions between the principal approaches to understanding Christ's atonement.[7] In this discussion we shall go beyond Aulén by including views he does not consider. We salute him for paving the way toward an understanding of the atonement that is both ecumenical and evangelical, reflecting the mind of the church through the ages as well as the testimony of holy Scripture.

What Aulén calls the classic or Christus Victor view is prone to depict the cross of Christ as a ransom paid to the principalities and powers of the world. Yet this payment paradoxically overthrows these powers because they cannot withstand the force and severity of God's love. This is mythological language, to be sure, but it points to literal realities! The atonement means liberating the captives to sin by furnishing them with the capacity to overcome the powers of darkness—sin, death, and the devil. Luther added the law of God and the wrath of God to the "tyrants" that have been cast down by Christ's resurrection and the outpouring of the Holy Spirit. In the classic view, it is God who provides the sacrifice for sin, and it is God who sets us free from bondage to the demonic powers. This theory dominated the early church scene and has resurfaced in various theologians in church history, including Martin Luther and Karl Barth.

A second theory (entertained by Peter Abelard, Faustus Socinus, and Laelius Socinus of the radical Reformation) stresses the exemplary side of the sacrifice of Christ. This approach is often called the moral influence theory of the atonement. Christ fulfills his atoning work by showing people the pathway to personal victory over the powers that afflict us. By his sacrificial suffering Christ guides us toward value judgments that are rich and enduring.

For the nineteenth-century German Lutheran theologian Albrecht Ritschl (d. 1889), Jesus was the bearer of a religio-ethical ideal. His sacrifice was one of obedience, not a penal sacrifice. Jesus made justification accessible to the human creation by revealing it. Justification is effective only in reconciliation, which is a human work. In this theology reconciliation is a realized ideal in human life. The kingdom of God signifies "the moral unification of the human race" by works of love.[8]

Also wielding considerable influence in Christian history is the mystical theory, which we find already in the early church. Atonement is becoming at one with the Savior through prayer, meditation, and contemplation. Salvation lies in a return to the undivided unity between creature and Creator by which we are lifted above worldly desires to a direct encounter with the ground of all being. Justification becomes an unfolding process of inner transformation by the indwelling Spirit of God. A monistic and Platonic orientation endemic to mysticism had the baneful effect of countering the moral dualism of the biblical prophets and some of the church fathers. Platonism and Neoplatonism were especially pronounced in Dionysius the pseudo-Areopagite, John Cassian, Gregory Palamas, John of the Cross, Meister Eckhart, and John Tauler.

The view that is embraced by most evangelicals today and also by traditionalist Catholics is the so-called Latin theory associated with Augustine (d. 430) and Anselm in particular. Here the dominant metaphor is penal redemption. The imagery is that of a law court. Christ takes upon himself the penalty that falls on a broken humanity because of its sin. In the sacrifice of atonement Jesus bears the burden of our sin and guilt by dying in our place. Aulén labels this the Latin or juridical theory of the atonement, since it reduces the atonement to a legal transaction: here sinners are set free by Jesus Christ, who fulfills the requirements of the law and thus restores humanity to divine favor. This position is firmly rooted in Christian tradition but is especially associated with Protestant orthodoxy. The sacrifice on the cross is made by Jesus in his humanity in contradistinction to the classic theory, where it is God himself who provides the sacrifice for sin, thereby satisfying the demands of a moral universe.

A middle way between the Christus Victor and Latin theories is what some have called the governmental theory, which we see in Hugo Grotius (d. 1645) and John Miley, among others.[9] Here God is depicted as the moral ruler and sin as an offense against God's holy law. The cross of Christ signifies the relaxation of the law of God rather than a satisfaction of the demands of the law. God relaxes the rigor of his law out of pity for a humanity weakened by sin. The cross of Christ is a moral beacon in the world of sin rather than a propitiation of the wrath of God or a dethroning of the powers of the world.

Finally, we need to consider the theory of vicarious identification or vicarious repentance, which is reflected in J. McLeod Campbell, Vincent Taylor, Malcolm Furness, P. T. Forsyth, and to a lesser degree Karl Barth.[10] Here the Son of God identifies himself with the sin and guilt of humanity and confesses this guilt to the holy Father. The cross is a demonstration of "the creative sympathy of the holy" (Forsyth) rather than the elevation of the human creature through acts of discipline and devotion (as in certain strands of mysticism and asceticism). According to Forsyth, God gave a public demonstration of his mercy by the crucifixion of Christ on the cross. We are saved solely by grace, not by a pilgrimage of faith, nor by a cooperative endeavor that includes both divine and human activity. In Forsyth's view, the satisfaction is offered not to a distributive justice, not to a legal claim, but to a holy person. "It is an offering, primarily, not of pity but of sanctity, and neither by God to man nor by man to God but by God to God, the self-sacrifice of the perfectly holy Son to the perfect holiness of the Father."[11] To make atonement for sin is to rectify the human situation of estrangement from both God and fellow humanity, to tear down the walls of distrust that undermine humanity. In this context the sacrifice of Christ is more properly described as a love offering than a sin offering.

In all these theories the theme of substitutionary atonement is prominent, though this is more evident in some positions than in others. In the ransom or classic theory, Christ is the sacrificial lamb that proves to be the lion of Judah that cannot be defeated. In the Latin theory, Christ receives the penalty for human sin in our place by suffering and dying on the cross. In the subjectivistic theories of the atonement, Christ is the transforming agent of the new life, which fundamentally alters the human disposition. Christ becomes the new eyes that enable us to penetrate the darkness that envelops us. For many of these scholars, Christ is our Representative more than our Substitute.

Nearly every carefully crafted theory of the atonement will include a discourse on justification and reconciliation; yet the atoning act of our salvation as expounded in the Bible represents much more than the forgiveness of sins. It entails liberation, acquittal, regeneration, satisfaction, expiation, propitiation, and certainly also sanctification. The sacrifice of Christ on the cross effects not only pardon for sin but also release from the power of sin. It involves not only the propitiation of God but also the liberation of the sinner. It removes not simply the sense of guilt but also the very stain of guilt. It acknowledges the need for the Christian life as well as personal faith in the redemptive efficacy of Christ's atoning work on the cross.

The cross reveals not only the suffering of Jesus as a man of God but also the suffering of God in the person of his Son. God has taken pity on our sad condition and has acted decisively to save us. But before the cross in history there is a cross in the heart of God (cf. Mat 26:39; 27:46). God vicariously identifies with our pain and misery, but he does so voluntarily. He suffers not by necessity or compulsion, but in his sovereign freedom.

The atonement is made by Jesus Christ as the God-Man, who turns away God's wrath because he embodies God's righteousness and love. It should be understood as both a royal victory and a priestly sacrifice. In the cross both God's holiness and his mercy are made manifest. Aulén has done the Christian world a signal service by reclaiming the vision of the church fathers in describing the atonement as God's act of deliverance in Jesus Christ. Yet he could have given a fuller exploration of the decisive role of penal redemption and satisfaction in the atoning sacrifice of Christ. These notions are certainly found in Luther, Calvin, and Barth among others, and surely also in holy Scripture. Aulén could have reminded us that salvation involves the satisfaction of the law of God as well as the overthrow of the law as the catalyst for sin. By pitting the law of God and reason against the claims of faith, he tends to break the continuity in the plan of salvation, which begins in God's gracious election in Jesus Christ and culminates in the incarnation of Christ in human form.

Martin Luther sagaciously referred to the "happy exchange" in describing the drama of human redemption. Christ's righteousness is imputed to us as forgiven sinners; our sin is imputed to him in the act of faith. His righteousness covers our sin; our sin is hidden in his righteousness. Our justification is grounded in his sacrifice; his sacrifice is the altar on which our sins are laid.

Issues Today

Among the issues that continue to grip theology in our day is the imponderable relationship between justification and sanctification, already broached in the preceding section. Despite efforts to fuse the two together, evangelical theology generally insists that neither is subordinate to the other. The two actions are complementary rather than contradictory. Justification provides the ground of our salvation; sanctification leads us toward the goal. Justification is not dependent on sanctification for its efficacy, but it gives sanctification its purpose and direction.

A closely related issue in contemporary theology is coming to terms with the legacy of mysticism, apparent in the discussion of both justification and sanctification. In an age when the great mystics of Christendom are being rediscovered, it is pertinent to ask whether justification is exclusively a forensic judgment, or does it not also include a mystical thrust? In my opinion, as an evangelical theologian standing in the tradition of the Protestant Reformation, justification links the believer concretely with the life and death of Christ, just as sanctification informs the believer of a change of status in the sight of God as well as a change in being. In faith we are now adopted sons and daughters of Christ summoned to do battle for the cause of the gospel. Justification and sanctification can take the form of both crisis and process. These two aspects of salvation are not to be identified, for this would blur the juridical dimension of the atonement, which must remain central though never separate from the mystical wellsprings of the faith.

The paradoxical relation of justification to experience is also an abiding concern in theology today. Here we see the continuing influence of Friedrich Schleiermacher (d. 1834) on the academic theological scene.[12] With the rise of the so-called empirical theology associated with Henry Nelson Wieman, Bernard E. Meland, Daniel Day Williams, and John Cobb, Jr., among others,[13] and the perduring impact of revivalistic Christianity upon the mainstream of church and culture, we are led to inquire whether either justification or the atonement can take place apart from experience. Experience is not the content of theology, but it may be considered the earthen vessel in which the truth of theology comes to us. It is profoundly biblical to affirm that we as believers in Christ are saved *by* grace *through* faith and *in* experience. A theology that seeks to be both catholic and evangelical will make a prominent place for "the evangelical experience," as Forsyth and his followers sometimes described it. The experience itself does not save, but it witnesses to the grace that alone saves—yet not without the disciplines of faith and devotion animated by the outpouring of the Holy Spirit.

Modern theology, both conservative and liberal, tends to elevate faith as an efficient cause of salvation and justification. Some theologians hold that the believer can contribute in some small way to the unfolding of salvation. Yet this position serves to undercut the catholic and evangelical vision of a life liberated by grace alone. As Bernard of Clairvaux put it, we contribute to our salvific identity only the wages of our sin, which is promptly covered by the grace of God manifested in Jesus Christ. This is to say we contribute nothing positive but only the negativity of a sinful being. Through grace we are led to acknowledge the miracle of justification that has taken place in our lives, but there is no synergism involved. We do not cooperate in the gaining of our salvation, but we do cooperate with the Spirit of God in manifesting the fruits of our salvation to the world.

In the wider ecumenical dialogue, which brings together Catholics, Protestants, and Eastern Orthodox, the question arises whether believers can be co-redeemers with Christ in the plan of salvation. A current debate in Catholic circles is whether Mary can be named as Co-Redemptrix, implying that she has a salvific role in our salvation in addition to Jesus Christ—the one Mediator between God and humanity (1 Tim. 2:5). Theology across the ecumenical spectrum has thus far shown wise resistance to the further elevation of Mary as exemplifying a partnership with Christ in effecting salvation. Yet as our Catholic and Orthodox friends remind us, there is a Mary minimalism that sees Mary as only a servant of grace and not also a means of grace. Such a stance constitutes an ongoing threat to Christian unity and integrity. We must not close our eyes to the wisdom of the church through the ages by underplaying or devaluing the unique role of Mary in the incarnation of Christ in history.

In an era when liberation theology remains a live option for many Christians, it is necessary to explore the relationship between justification and justice—in the sense of social action. While we are passive in receiving justification by the one Redeemer the Lord Jesus Christ, we are made active by the Spirit in working for justice in society that points to the kingdom of God, though it does not duplicate this higher righteousness. The mission of the church is still primarily to win souls for Christ, not to build a utopian society that is thought capable of meeting all the physical and material needs of humanity. We are summoned by our Creator and Redeemer to strive for a greater degree of justice in society, and this work itself constitutes a valiant witness to God's justification in Jesus Christ. Yet we must never identify our feeble attempts at social reform with the coming kingdom of God. Such efforts manifest a sanctified Eros rather than a selfless Agape, which can only be a product of the Holy Spirit.

Mother Teresa of Calcutta rightly discerned that the soul of the care of the poor is the care of the poor soul.[14] In this perspective the goal of our social endeavor is the rehabilitation of the sinner before the throne of God's grace. The search for justice does not warrant a break between divine justification and social amelioration.

Whatever we can do in building a more humane social order is ultimately done to glorify Christ and serve his kingdom, which originates in the realm of the Spirit.

The church's social witness must continue to uphold Jesus as the very Son of God—true God and true man in one person. He is the one mediator between God and sinful humanity. Jesus is not a martyr to the cause of social righteousness but a Savior who implants within humanity a new heart, new aspirations and new goals.

Theologians on the left frequently speak of the need for constructing a nonviolent conception of the atonement. Rational persuasion is deemed more efficacious in shaping a new social order than the shedding of blood for the remission of sins. Sharon Baker avers that "God's forgiveness gives expression to the anti-violent nature of God who seeks to save those who are trapped in strictures and structures of injustice often justified by mistaken notions of God and the atonement." She suggests that we reinterpret the Jesus event "into a theory of at-one-ment that deconstructs notions of a violent God bent on retributive justice."[15] This fanciful interpretation blurs the distinction between kingdom righteousness and social justice and thereby loses sight of the gospel truth that God's love is much more than nonviolent resistance. It is the nonresistance of selfless love, which can only be approximated by sinful mortals, and then only for a time (Reinhold Niebuhr).[16] God's kingdom contravenes the pacifist strategy just as much as that of the social revolutionary. In the more authentically biblical perspective, Christ came to set up a kingdom that operates not on the basis of technical skill but on the basis of spiritual conversion. The Christian conquers not simply by the demonstration of vicarious love but by the proclamation of the gospel, which tells us that God justifies the ungodly (Rom. 5:6–11).

Today with the resurgence of orthodox Calvinism in various circles, the idea is reintroduced that the atonement is limited, that Christ came only to call his own, not to save the whole of humanity. A universalism associated with Karl Barth and neo-orthodoxy is being challenged by a new wave of particularism, which limits the efficacy and outreach of the gospel in its confrontation with the gods of the culture. John Howard Yoder and other Anabaptists sometimes create the impression that the blessing of salvation extends only to the realm of radical obedience. We are justified only to the extent that we take up our own cross and follow Christ into the darkness of the world. For Karl Barth, God's justification goes out to all, but only those benefit who accept this verdict and seek to live according to it. At the same time, we are not really equipped to live the Christian life in its fullness until we are born again in the Spirit.

In the Barthian schema, justification by God's grace saves us from both sin and temptation; these evils are counteracted by grace, which does not abide in coexistence with sin but on the contrary expels sin, replacing the old nature with a new nature. God's triumph over evil is universal, but this fact remains hidden until the awakening to faith through the power of the Spirit. In Barth's theology baptism is not the means by which we receive salvation (as in Catholicism), but the sign of our commitment to bring the good news of this salvation to a lost and dying humanity.[17]

Barth, like Aulén, sees the atonement of Christ as a royal victory over the powers of sin and death, a victory that is manifested and celebrated in the Christian life—a life restored to the favor of God through repentance and forgiveness. We are called not to heroism but to faithfulness to our Lord and his gospel. Nevertheless, when people of faith resolutely take up their cross and follow Christ, they often commit acts that can be deemed heroic and that merit the acclaim of the wider culture.

The Road Ahead

Further questions deserve to be raised in a discussion of this magnitude. Is reconciliation with God mutual or unilateral? Is the human nature of Christ alone affected by God's reconciling work on the cross (as in the Latin view), or is God himself reconciled in addition to the human subject? Here we see the relevance of the doctrine of divine impassibility. Is God incapable of suffering (as in the classical view), or does God freely enter into our afflictions bringing about the fulfillment of the law, sowing the seeds of a new humanity? The traditional position, in both Catholic and Protestant orbits, is that God in himself does not suffer but God in Christ experiences human suffering, though it is now converted into something creative and redemptive.

Those who are attracted to process theology and humanistic psychology are only too ready to acknowledge suffering in God, for this connotes a need within God that humans can help satisfy through education and enlightenment. The openness of God theology (open theism) also makes a place for divine suffering in the panorama of salvation. The notion of grace is not extinguished in this theology but is dangerously compromised, since it leaves a God who is only in partial control.

The pivotal role of the incarnation of Christ in bringing about atonement for sin can be discerned in many of the new theologies. Indeed, it is asserted that the incarnation prepares the way for the atonement of Christ and thereby belongs to the plan of salvation. Christ was able to help us because he came to us in human garb, meeting us on the plane of humanity, showing us how to live in a world reclaimed by the grace of God. Justification is the outcome of predestination and the foundation for a life of sanctification (Rom. 8:28–30). Christ came to us in our sin in order to save us from our sin. He provides divine pardon for sin as well as release from the power of sin by the action of the Holy Spirit.

In articulating anew the atoning work of Christ on the cross we would do well to acknowledge both the objective and subjective dimensions of our salvation. Salvation has occurred outside of us in the atoning work of Christ on the cross. Through the shedding of his blood our sins are forgiven, and a new righteousness wells up within us. Yet this redemptive work does little good if it lies entirely outside our experience. We as forgiven sinners need to appropriate this salvation. We need to be justified in fact (de facto) as well as in principle (de jure). And for the faith of the Reformation and the Great Awakenings as well as for the luminaries of neo-orthodoxy, justification as a concrete experience is offered to us by the Spirit of God, and we are empowered to respond to the Spirit in faith, hope, and love.

Karl Barth has sometimes been criticized for overplaying the objective ground of our salvation and deemphasizing the subjective appropriation of grace. Evangelical theology affirms both *sola gratia* and *sola fide*. We are justified by grace through faith and to the honor and glory of the living God as he has related himself to us in Jesus Christ. But even before we taste of the glory of regeneration and justification, we can be assured that God is both with us and for us, since he has already opened the doorway to our salvation by rising from the dead in the person of his Son Jesus Christ and sending forth his Spirit to renew the world. Our decision for Christ is a manifestation of the redeeming work of the Spirit within us. It is a compelling testimony to an invisible grace, which has its roots in the eternal love of God in Christ. Our mission as recipients of divine grace is to live under the cross as the servants of Christ and to testify to the glory of the cross as his ambassadors.

In this age of ecumenicity it is also appropriate to explore the role of the sacraments in our justification and redemption. In orthodox Catholic theology as articulated at the Council of Trent (1545–1563), our justification is effected in the rite of baptism and continues as a purifying process throughout life. In evangelical Protestantism our justification was already decreed in the mind of God before all creation; our task is to tell others the good news of redemption and reconciliation and live in such a way that glory and honor are given to the living God, not to a rapacious, egocentric self. We should not expend our energies in tapping into our supposed infinite possibilities, but we should strive to make our calling sure by following Christ into the darkness of the world with the light of the gospel as both our guide and the content of our message. We should pray to be anointed by the Spirit of God to a missional vocation—bearing witness to the once-for-all sacrifice of Christ on the cross and his glorious resurrection from the grave. We are not asked to duplicate Christ's righteousness; our mandate is to celebrate his righteousness by walking in his steps and exulting in his name. When this happens, atonement for sin is now finalized and confirmed. We can then claim to be saved within as well as without. If we are justified we can be certain of this fact through the illumination of the Spirit, who always works in accord with the message of justification expounded in holy Scripture. As born-again Christians we have not only the gift of salvation but also the assurance of our salvation through faith in Jesus Christ. We not only assent to the truth of divine revelation, but we are also confronted by the inbreaking of this revelation in the experience of faith, sometimes misleadingly referred to as the inner light.[18]

For the churches of the Reformation, the rites of baptism and the Lord's Supper further attest the outpouring and revivification of the Holy Spirit (in addition to preaching and prayer). Yet these rites are powerless when separated from the decision of faith and the obedience of love. The motto of the Reformation on this matter was "no sacrament without faith" (*nullum sacramentum sine fide*).[19] In fairness to our Catholic and Orthodox brethren, this idea appears in these communions as well, but not necessarily as a determining principle.

Faith and obedience exist in correlation. In faith we venture onto the path of obedience, giving glory to God through the witness of our lives. We are justified by faith when this faith is animated by the Spirit working and living within us. The ultimate source of our justification is neither our faith nor our obedience, but Christ's work of reparation made on our behalf through the life-giving power of the Holy Spirit. Jesus has come, and he is coming again to incorporate us in his mystical body, the holy catholic church, and to empower us to share the light of the gospel with all those who are seeking his redemption by virtue of an eternal calling—to be the sons and daughters of the most high God. In the tradition of revivalistic Protestantism it is commonly asserted that we are only sinners saved by grace. But in the fuller evangelical vision we must also affirm that we are priests and kings working together with Christ for a new world (1 Pet. 2:5; Rev. 1:5–6). We shall never become gods (deification), but through faith we will be made resolute witnesses to God's saving acts in biblical history, especially the glorious incarnation of God in Jesus Christ.

One final observation: as Christians we are called not only to responsible citizenship in society (Mat. 22:15–22), not only to service in discipleship, but also to sainthood—not in the sense of being revered more than others but in the sense of the imitation of Jesus Christ—being baptized into his death and rejuvenated by his resurrection. We are called to be saints of the most high God, and this sainthood is paradoxically realized in our role as servants of the Lord Jesus Christ. May we walk the road of eternal life through the power of the Holy Spirit and to the glory and honor of the God who justifies and sanctifies lost sinners!

NOTES

1. *Interpreter's Bible*, vol. 9 (Nashville, Tenn.: Abingdon, 1954), 433–434.

2. See Richard A. Muller, "Justification," in Donald K. McKim, ed., *Encyclopedia of the Reformed Faith* (Louisville, Ky.: Westminster/John Knox Press 1992).

3. Note that Karl Barth sees the article by which the church stands or falls as the confession of Jesus Christ "in whom are hidden all the treasures of wisdom and knowledge" (Col. 2:3). See Eberhard Busch, *Barth* (Nashville, Tenn.: Abingdon, 2008), 65.

4. Among the church fathers who assigned a special role to the devil in our salvation and who are cited by Aulén are Irenaeus, Origen, Gregory of Nyssa, Athanasius, John Chrysostom, and Augustine.

5. St. Anselm, *Cur Deus Homo*. See bibliography.

6. See Elisha A. Hoffman, "What a Fellowship," in *Hymns for the Living Church*, ed. Donald P. Hustad (Carol Stream, Ill.: Hope Publishing, 1974), no. 417.

7. Gustaf Aulén, *Christus Victor*, trans. A. G. Hebert (New York: Macmillan, 1951).

8. H. R. Mackintosh, *Types of Modern Theology* (London: Nisbet, 1937), 151.

9. See John Miley, *The Atonement in Christ* (New York: Hunt & Eaton, 1889).

10. There is no one theologian who fully exemplifies this theory, which remains an ideal type. It represents the remarkable convergence of various streams of theology.

11. P. T. Forsyth, *The Christian Ethic of War* (London: Longmans, Green, 1916), 93–94.

12. For Schleiermacher's relevance to the contemporary theological discussion, see Najeeb George Awad, "Should We Dispense with *Sola Scriptura?* Scripture, Tradition and Postmodern Theology," in *Dialog* 47:1 (Spring 2008), 64–79.

13. See Bernard E. Meland, ed., *The Future of Empirical Theology* (Chicago: University of Chicago Press, 1969).

14. I cannot locate the exact reference, but it is academically correct to regard this remark as being attributed to Mother Teresa. Cf. Edward LeJoly, *Servant of Love* (San Francisco: Harper & Row, 1977), 139–140.

15. Sharon L. Baker, "Justice, Mercy and Forgiveness: Jesus' Cross to Bare," in *The Princeton Theological Review* 13:2 (Fall 2007), 34.

16. See Reinhold Niebuhr, *An Interpretation of Christian Ethics* (New York: Harper & Bros., 1935).

17. See Karl Barth, *Church Dogmatics*, ed. G. W. Bromiley and T. F. Torrance (Edinburgh: T & T Clark, 1969), 4:4. Also see Donald G. Bloesch, *Jesus Is Victor! Karl Barth's Doctrine of Salvation* (Nashville, Tenn.: Abingdon, 1976).

18. When I use the phrase "the inner light" in a positive sense, I am not referring to the inner light as the core of the human soul (as in Quakerism) but to the indwelling Holy Spirit, the bestower of faith and renewal.

19. See Emil Brunner, *Truth as Encounter* (Philadelphia: Westminster, 1964), 182.

BIBLIOGRAPHY

Anderson, H. George, T. Austin Murphy, and Joseph A. Burgess. *Justification by Faith.* Minneapolis: Augsburg, 1985.

St. Anselm. *Why God Became Man* (*Cur Deus Homo*), ed. and trans. Jasper Hopkins and Herbert W. Richardson. Lewiston, N.Y.: E. Mellen Press, 1974.

Aulén, Gustaf. *Christus Victor*, trans. A. G. Hebert. New York: Macmillan, 1951.

Baillie, Donald. *God Was in Christ.* New York: Charles Scribner's Sons, 1948.

Barth, Karl. *Church Dogmatics*, trans. G. W. Bromiley. Edinburgh: T & T Clark, 1969, 4:1.

Berkouwer, G. C. *Faith and Justification*, trans. Lewis B. Smedes. Grand Rapids: Eerdmans, 1954.

Bloesch, Donald G. *Essentials of Evangelical Theology.* 2 vols. San Francisco: Harper & Row, 1978.

———. *Jesus Christ: Savior and Lord.* Downers Grove, Ill.: InterVarsity Press, 1997.

Brunner, Emil. *The Mediator*, trans. Olive Wyon. Philadelphia: Westminster, 1947.

Clifford, Alan C. *Atonement and Justification.* Oxford: Clarendon, 1990.

Crabtree, Arthur. *The Restored Relationship.* Valley Forge, Pa.: Judson, 1963.

Forsyth, Peter T. *The Justification of God.* London: Independent Press, 1948.

———. *The Work of Christ.* London: Independent Press, 1948.

Hengel, Martin. *The Atonement*, trans. John Bowden. Philadelphia: Fortress, 1981.

Husbands, Mark, and Daniel J. Treier, eds. *Justification: What's at Stake in the Current Debates.* Downers Grove, Ill.: InterVarsity Press, 2004.

Küng, Hans. *Justification*, trans. Thomas Collins, Edmund Tolk, and David Granskou. Philadelphia: Westminster, 1964.

Mattes, Mark C. *The Role of Justification in Contemporary Theology.* Grand Rapids: Eerdmans, 2004.

McDermott, Gerald R. "Jonathan Edwards on Justification by Faith—More Protestant or Catholic?" *Pro Ecclesia* 17:1 (Winter 2008): 92–111.

McGrath, Alister E. *Iustitia Dei: A History of the Christian Doctrine of Justification*. Cambridge: Cambridge University Press, 2005.

Packer, J. I. "Justification." In Walter A. Elwell, ed., *Evangelical Dictionary of Theology*, 2nd ed., 643–647. Grand Rapids: Baker, 2001.

Paul, Robert S. *The Atonement and the Sacraments*. New York: Abingdon, 1960.

Ritschl, Albrecht, *The Christian Doctrine of Justification and Reconciliation*. Clifton, N.J.: Reference Book Publishers, 1966.

Stuhlmacher, Peter. *Revisiting Paul's Doctrine of Justification*. Downers Grove, Ill.: InterVarsity Press, 2001.

Vainio, Olli-Pekka. *Justification and Participation in Christ*. Leiden: Brill, 2008.

CHAPTER 15

DISCIPLESHIP

DALLAS WILLARD

How one thinks of discipleship within evangelicalism depends upon how one draws the line around that movement. If one draws the line, as is now common, to include only the "evangelicalism" that emerged from the conservative-to-fundamentalist churches of North America after World War II, then there is very little to say about discipleship there except what is anecdotal—and there is not a lot of that. There has simply been no consistent general teaching or practice under the heading of discipleship among evangelicals of this period: none that would be recognizable as discipleship in terms of biblical teaching or of the Christian past.

In the post-WWII period, the strongest association of evangelicalism was with *evangelism*, and for many citizens of North America the only thing they knew of evangelicals was that they were evangelistic. And indeed they were. They were intent upon proclaiming a gospel of "salvation" and upon winning converts to Christ. The most visible evangelical of the period was the world-renowned evangelist, Billy Graham. And the subgroup of evangelicals most associated with programs of discipleship, the Navigators, was focused upon winning converts—converts who were explicitly recognized by them as *not* being disciples until an optional further stage in commitment. Being a disciple was, for them, to be in training to become a soul winner, and discipleship was the process of training you underwent (under the direction of "workers," people of a third stage of commitment and development) to enable you to win converts.[1] The slogan of the Navigators was "To know Christ and to make Him known." Their aim, as they said, was "to produce reproducers."

This vision was firmly tied to the version of the Gospel and of salvation that dominated evangelicalism during the period. It was strictly a gospel of forgiveness of sins and assurance of heaven after death upon profession of faith in Jesus Christ—or, minimally, profession of faith in his having suffered the penalty for our sins upon the cross. If you believed in his death as your substitute, you were a

Christian, even though you never became a disciple. Many of the Navigators were certainly among the finest followers of Christ from any period of Christian history. Their founder, Dawson Trotman, was an ardent disciple of Jesus by any sane standard and one of the greatest of twentieth-century Christ followers.[2] But as disciples, Navigators were far better than their theology and their program. They have blessed and continue to bless the earth with their lives and testimonies. Nevertheless, in them the essential disconnection between post-WWII evangelicalism and discipleship prevailed and still prevails today.

Relying on Correct Beliefs Alone

During the mid to late twentieth century, evangelicalism came to define itself in terms of the profession of correct belief alone. Holding correct doctrine was as a rule presented as the condition of forgiveness of sins. Obsessed with threats from modernism and liberal theology, on the one hand, and from the looming presence of an allegedly "scientific" worldview on the other, evangelicalism undertook to "contend earnestly for the faith which was once for all delivered to the saints" (Jude verse 3). This meant to defend the truth of doctrines taken to be essential to a "saving" faith in Christ. Ironically, this phase of evangelicalism developed—as a social form—into a particular version of "nominal Christianity." It had traditionally defined itself in opposition to nominal Christianity, emphasizing as it did an individualized "birth from above" and an ongoing personal experience of God. But its actual "nominal" status is the reality back of the statistics often quoted at the beginning of the twenty-first century, which show little or no behavioral difference between the lives of contemporary evangelicals on the whole and the lives of those outside its circles. Being a Christian in evangelical terms came to be a matter of professing belief in time-honored tenets of traditional Christianity, with a few additional points about the nature and authority of the Bible and about eschatology.[3]

Called to a Closer Walk

But that left a deficiency which came to be deeply felt—especially among evangelicals most seriously devoted to Christ. This felt need for experience of God, for a life in God, expressed itself in various ways—ways always in some tension with the prevailing theology and with the most prominent evangelical leaders and teachers of the time. This tension has been an enduring problem within modern evangelicalism. It has expressed itself in various ways: for example, through interest in what was viewed as "higher life" or "deeper life" teachings. The Keswick movement (associated with the

Keswick Convention, running from 1875 to the present)[4] was centered on these teachings, and interest in them was cultivated by such authors as Andrew Murray (1828–1917) and F. B. Meyer (1847–1929). A slightly older work by Hannah Whitall Smith, *The Christian's Secret of a Happy Life* (1875), was very influential in this vein, along with numerous similar writings, and more contemporary works such as Rosalind Rinker's book, *Prayer: Conversing with God* (1959), which presented prayer as a lively conversation with God. These and similar works revitalized the "devotional life" of many evangelicals, often taken by them to be "discipleship" itself. Still older Catholic writers such as Thomas à Kempis (*The Imitation of Christ*) and Brother Lawrence (*The Practice of the Presence of* God) stoked the hidden fires of evangelical devotion—simultaneously confirming the grim suspicions of many leaders and teachers that the "deeper life" seekers and teachers were not properly evangelical. They were not satisfied with just believing the essentials or with "the pure milk of the word."

The Charismatic movement—breaking out in the early twentieth century in its "Holiness" form, and reviving in the post-WWII period *without* the emphasis on holiness—was yet another challenge to the adequacy of this most recent "official" form of evangelical Christianity. Many evangelical leaders simply rejected the charismatic experience, and taught (some still teach) that charismatics are misled and dangerous to the faith. This was largely for fear that their "experiences" were not biblical and would undermine the authority of the Bible. But the hunger for and reality of an interactive life with God (the Holy Spirit) was not to be denied to people generally, and today the most effectual carriers of "evangelical truths" to the world are in fact charismatics. However, the focus upon spiritual gifts that characterizes the charismatic groups and teachers still does not include a realistic and theologically coherent teaching and practice of discipleship. It is still true of them that to be a Christian—even a "Spirit-filled" Christian—does not require that you be a disciple of Jesus Christ, or that you, through the course of discipleship, take on the character of Jesus Christ in your life as a whole.

The widely felt inadequacy of the official twentieth-century evangelical teachings to life (however effectual they might be for death and judgment) also expressed itself by the emergence of "Christian Psychology" among evangelicals in the 1960s. This movement was a tacit acknowledgement that teaching the truth, and eliciting profession of the central doctrines, did not solve the problems of Christian living. As a result it was strongly resisted across a broad range of evangelical life. By the twenty-first century, however, it had burgeoned into a vast profession, with extensive training and higher academic degrees available from the most prominent evangelical educational institutions. It clearly intersects in its aims and some of its methods with what would have counted as discipleship or training in following Christ at other times and places. Many of the larger evangelical churches and groups now provide psychological counseling as a major part of their ministry.

Currently, Christian psychology is interacting with yet another significant tendency in evangelical life. The emergence of "spiritual formation" among evangelicals toward the end of the twentieth century was also a response to the felt need of many for a spiritual life, in addition to correct beliefs and outward practices. This need was associated with the increasing failure of "denominational distinctives" to constitute a spiritual existence or a life for the individual. It is rare to find evangelicals within these churches who could make a life of being a Presbyterian, Baptist, Catholic, Lutheran, Pentecostal, and so on. By contrast, "spiritual formation," like discipleship itself during some periods of the past, was associated with learning to live a remarkably different kind of life: one of pervading spiritual reality and transformed character. In its quest, spiritual formation among evangelicals reached out to learn from the Church and from Christians across the ages, on the one hand, and it also turned the individual's focus toward redemption of their life as a whole.[5] "Spiritual formation" edged—however obscurely or unintentionally—toward thinking of salvation, the essence of Christian deliverance, in more comprehensive terms than the afterlife alone. Once again, prominent evangelical spokespersons were uneasy. But how one understands salvation turns out to be the key to what one makes of discipleship, as well as to any possible renewal of evangelicalism as a redemptive force for the future. Post-WWII evangelicalism simply had no essential place for discipleship in its view of salvation.

Evangelicalism from Wesley to Finney

We must draw the line around evangelicalism beyond post-WWII America if we are to see any close connection between its vital core and discipleship to Jesus Christ. It is sometimes said that evangelical Christianity began in the eighteenth century, with people who were willing to preach out of doors at a time when that was a very radical step. The reference to "preaching out of doors" picks out the ministries of George Whitefield (1714–1770) and John Wesley (1703–1791), but also those of many preachers who followed after them in the settlements and frontiers of America. Jonathan Edwards (1703–1758), though he did not regularly "preach out of doors," is often regarded as historic evangelicalism's most competent theologian (we must not forget his overlap with Puritanism). Some have even thought of evangelicals as an American brand of Protestant Christianity. This unfortunately results in seeing contemporary evangelicalism as having a greater continuity with the evangelical past than it actually has. The "revivalism" of George Whitefield, John Wesley, Jonathan Edwards, and even Charles Finney (in the first half of the nineteenth century), was a very different kind of phenomenon from the "revivals" of the twentieth century, which were almost entirely focused upon converting the lost. The revivals of the 1900s gradually transmuted into evangelistic campaigns or "outreach." The earlier evangelical "revivalists," by contrast, focused upon "stirring up" Christians or church members, and urging them on to overall holiness of life and devotion to God.[6] That is why the word "revival" was used by them. What they did naturally led into a process of learning and growing in holiness and power, as the New Testament clearly presupposes. Evangelizing was a natural side effect of the revival of slumbering Christians, and the evangelizing of this earlier period easily saw discipleship to Jesus as a natural development from conversion and confidence in Jesus Christ as Lord, and therefore Master and Teacher.

New Testament language fits well with this earlier phase of evangelicalism, as compared to today's: "Work out your salvation with fear and trembling; for it is God who is at work in you, both to will and to work for His good pleasure. Do all things without grumbling or disputing; that you may turn out to be blameless and innocent, children of God above reproach in the midst of a crooked and perverse generation, among whom you appear as lights in the world" (Phil. 2:12–15). This calling and reality was not thought by earlier evangelicals to be for a special group of Christians—perhaps "full-time Christian workers"—but as the opportunity and obligation of everyone who placed their hope in Christ. It was a shift away from this viewpoint that opened the way for twentieth-century evangelicalism, dominated by a particular version of Calvinist theology and its peculiar soteriology.

Eighteenth- and nineteenth-century evangelicalism made an essential place for holiness and wholeness, for transformation of character and for ordinary occupations as divine calling. An excellent place to see this at its best is in the sermons and writings of Phillips Brooks (1835–1893). It was entirely natural to the underlying theology of the earlier period that Wesley and Finney, both "revivalist" in the earlier sense, developed and applied elaborate, scripturally based accounts of Christian perfection as something continuous in its nature with Christian salvation. Their theology was essentially Arminian, and thus their understanding of grace and salvation was quite different from that of their twentieth-century counterparts. While discipleship could be seen as a natural part of salvation as they understood it, the later evangelicals have been more careful to avoid "perfectionism" than to avoid sin. They favor bumper stickers that say, "Christians are not perfect, just forgiven." *Just* forgiven. There lies the problem for contemporary evangelicalism with respect to discipleship. What does discipleship have to do with forgiveness? With saving faith?

The Sources of Evangelicalism in Luther

To respond to these questions adequately we must push the time line further back, to the point in Western history where the terminology "evangelical" enters the stream of Christianity. The language originates in sixteenth-century Germany, amid the turmoil and violence of the Protestant Reformation. People became known as "evangelicals" because of their appeal to the Gospels, the "Evangels," of the New Testament, against the authority and power of traditional institutions and sources. It was at Martin Luther's (1483–1546) suggestion that the new churches emerging out of the turmoil called themselves "evangelical" (*evangelische*). Philip Melanchthon (1497–1560) drew up a standard form of "evangelical" worship service, with Luther's approval; and Luther himself wrote out his "Shorter Catechism" in 1529. Preaching became the centerpiece of the public meeting, and church architecture changed to accommodate that and make it easier for the attendees to hear the sermon. Congregational singing was introduced, and Luther became a writer of great hymns. For many people throughout Europe even today, "evangelical" simply means "Protestant."

What lay at the heart of evangelical religion at its origin? Two things: devotion to the Bible as the ultimate source of authority and divine life, and personal experience of conversion to and practical communion with God. These, with the fundamental tensions built into them and with all of the blessings and problems they present, are the bedrock of evangelical religion, today as in the past. They, in fact, are what have sustained and driven evangelical religion, for individuals and for groups, up to its latest surges of charismata and "spiritual formation." The followers of Luther soon drifted from these two basic elements in various ways, into splintering "orthodoxies," institutional deadness, and social conformity. The landscape of history is littered with the skeletons of these "orthodoxies," and even with the skeletons of further movements that arose to revive those skeletons. Pietism (seventeenth century) soon arose to counteract or revive the Lutheran orthodoxy that settled over much of Europe within a century or so after Luther. There is a current of continuity running from the radical faith of Luther himself, though the great Pietist teachers, Philipp Spener (1635–1705) and August Hermann Francke (1663–1727), to the Moravians, on to Wesley, and to the holiness, "Deeper Life," and charismatic streams running through or alongside the later evangelical churches, right up to the "spiritual formation" impulses of the present times.

Basic evangelicalism is a *theologia cordi*, "a religion of the heart," joined in an unstable relationship to the exclusive authority of Scripture. The influence of this basic evangelicalism on other social formations and denominations of the Christian Church remains constant and irrepressible. Its ever-present insistence that being a Christian is a matter of a life one lives—founded in biblical teachings and consisting in personal interaction with God and the various facets of his kingdom—connects with deep hungers of the human soul. The effort to force the basic genius of evangelicalism into the armor of a more particular orthodoxy—a recurring tendency running rampant on the heels of Luther and painfully oppressive at later times, including post-WWII America—is perpetually resisted by the stream of spiritual life flowing from Scripture and from the intermingling of human life with the Trinitarian presence.

The New Testament Picture of Discipleship

Evangelicalism always looks to the Bible as the point of reference from which concepts are defined, practices legitimated, and principles adopted. So we must ask what can be made of discipleship and of the disciple of Jesus as seen in the life of the

New Testament. Indeed, as it turns out, the New Testament "disciple" is by no means a peculiarly "Christian" innovation.[7] The disciple is one aspect of the progressive and massive decentralization of Judaism that began with the destruction of the first Temple (588 B.C.E.) and the Babylonian exile, and proceeds through the dispersal of the Jewish people among the nations that followed the destruction of Jerusalem in 70 C.E. During this period, the synagogue emerges as the center of the local Jewish communities, devotion to the Torah becomes the focus of the synagogue, and the rabbi or "great one" stood forth in the role of interpreter of Torah: "By degrees, attachment to the law sank deeper and deeper into the national character.... Hence the law became a deep and intricate study. Certain men rose to acknowledged eminence for their ingenuity in explaining, their readiness in applying, their facility in quoting, and their clearness in offering solutions of, the difficult passages of the written statutes."[8] The rabbi with his coterie of special students was a familiar feature of Jewish religious practice by the time of Jesus.

There was no one way in which to become a rabbi in the Jewish society of Jesus' day. It is true that most of those who became rabbis did so by studying under a rabbi, and having a "formal" training had some obvious advantages. But there was no "licensing" process, and an element of the Old Testament prophet carried over to the role of rabbi. A rabbi could, like the prophet, be "from nowhere." His was a performance-based status, and public recognition *as* a rabbi was a response to the power of the individual's words and deeds, not to their "credentials." The usual path of advancement seems to have been through the schools for young people around the synagogue. Some students did very well, memorizing huge portions of scripture and listening to interpretations by teachers. Then, if they wished, they might approach a rabbi requesting him to take them as their disciple. If accepted, there would follow a lengthy period of close association with their rabbi—hearing, observing, and imitating. They were simply *with* their rabbi, serving him and becoming like him in thought, character, and abilities. Jesus' observation that "a disciple does not rise above his teacher; but everyone after he has been fully trained will reach his teacher's level" (Luke 6:40), was both a commonplace observation about the nature of the rabbi/disciple relation and—as the context makes clear—a warning about the limitations and dangers of that arrangement. ("Can a blind person guide a blind person? Will not both fall into a pit?" Luke 6:39).

Jesus and His Disciples

Jesus, however, did not simply fit himself into the more or less standard model of the rabbi. He had no "formal" education beyond the synagogue schools and did not become a disciple of a rabbi. He did receive a (*very* unorthodox) stamp of approval from John the Baptizer, but not as his disciple. He was known to the people around him as uneducated. Amazed at the depth and power of his words, they exclaimed: "How does this man have such learning, when he has never been taught?" (John 7:15) Also, Jesus did not accept disciples upon application, testing them to see if they were "worthy." He personally selected—though not from "the best and the brightest" in his community—those he would especially train. There was a larger outer circle of people who seem to have just showed up in his presence and received training of various degrees (the "other seventy" of Luke 10:1, for example, and the group in the "upper room" of Acts 1:13). Often would-be disciples were subjected to severe discouragement by him (Matt. 8:18–22, Luke 9:57–62 and 14:26–33). He also leveled scalding criticisms at the proud practitioners of the law in his day (Matt. 23:13–33, Luke 11:39–52), and prohibited his followers from being called "rabbi" and using other "respectful greetings" exchanged among those who took themselves to be highly qualified as teachers (Matt. 23:1–12). He was not "one of the boys," nor were his disciples to be.

Nevertheless, the basic nature of the rabbi/disciple relationship of his day was retained by Jesus and his disciples and, arguably, remains normative to this day. That relationship is very simple in description. His disciples were *with him, learning to be like him.* "With him" meant in that day that they were literally where he was and were progressively engaged in doing what he was doing. Jesus moved about the Jewish villages and towns, primarily around the Sea of Galilee, with occasional forays beyond that, and especially to Jerusalem. His main disciples ("apostles") were with him in all of this, and no doubt at considerable hardship to themselves and their families. Peter on one occasion plaintively remarks: "We have left everything to follow you" (Matt. 19:27). It was no doubt a thought that often occurred to his disciples.

As they traveled about he did three things in the synagogues, homes, and public areas: He *announced* the availability of life in the kingdom of God, he *taught* about how things were done in the kingdom of God, and he *manifested* the present power of the kingdom by amazing deeds (Matt. 4:23, 9:35, Luke 4:18–44). Then, after a period of training, he set his disciples to doing the things they had heard and seen in him—continuing all the while to evaluate their work and to teach them as they progressed. This continued through his trial and death, and during his post-resurrection presence with them when he trained them in how he would be *with them* after his ascension, without visible presence. His instruction as he left was for his disciples to make *disciples* of all "nations"—of all types of people—and his promise was that he would be *with them* always until the end of the age (Matt. 28:19–20).

The Method of "Being with" Passed on through Disciples

While the charge was to make disciples of Jesus and *not* of the disciples, the basic method—teaching, example, and imitation—remained the same, as his immediate followers proceeded to do what he had told them to do. The method was: to gather a group of people by telling the story of Jesus, featuring his resurrection and pending return; to show by example what it meant to live *with him* now, already beyond death; and to lead others into such a life of being "with Jesus, learning to be like him." No New Testament text better fills out what this life of learning was than Colossians 3:1–17.

The role of example and imitation in the learning community of disciples is often stressed in the New Testament. Numerous statements from the Apostle Paul concisely state the strategy of being and making disciples. In one of his earliest letters to groups of disciples he reminds the readers of how "Our gospel [proclamation] did not come to you in word only, but also in power and in the Holy Spirit and with full conviction; just as you know what kind of men we proved to be among you for your sake. You also became imitators of us and of the Lord, having received the word in much tribulation with the Joy of the Holy Spirit, so that you became an example to all believers in Macedonia and in Achaia" (1 Thess. 1:5–7).

Paul proceeds in this letter to spell out how he and his fellow workers lived "pure, upright, and blameless" in their conduct toward the believers, and to encourage them to "lead a life worthy of God, who calls you into his own kingdom and glory" (1 Thess. 2:10–12). In 1 Corinthians he exhorts the believers to imitate him, to be "reminded of my ways which are in Christ" (1 Thess. 4:16–17), and to "be imitators of me, just as I also am of Christ" (11:1). In 2 Thessalonians he indicates that the readers "know how you ought to imitate us." He reminds them of how he led a disciplined life and worked hard to support himself, "not because we do not have that right [to support from them], but in order to offer ourselves as a model for you that you might imitate us" (2 Thess. 3:7–9). To the Philippians he said: "Keep on doing the things you have learned and received and heard and seen in me, and the God of peace will be with you" (Phil. 4:9). He elsewhere reminds Timothy that he had "observed my teaching, my conduct, my aim in life, my faith, my patience, my love, my steadfastness, my persecutions and suffering the things that happened to me in Antioch, Iconium, and Lystra" (2 Tim. 3:10–11). And in an earlier letter he directed him to "show himself an example to those who believe" (1 Tim. 4:12). The writer of the letter to the Hebrews counsels his readers not to be sluggish, "but imitators of those who through faith and patience inherit the promises" (Heb. 6:17). They should "remember your leaders, those who spoke the word of God to you; consider the outcome of their way of life, and imitate their faith" (13:7). As it was for "your leaders," the writer assures them, it will also be for you, and that is because "Jesus Christ is the same, yesterday and today and forever" (13:8–9). The point of this much misapplied verse is, as the context makes clear, that the nature of discipleship to Jesus and its outcomes does not change.

Transformation through This Kind of Discipleship

Now this practice of discipleship in the communities of Christ followers—being with Christ learning to be like him, in part by being with those who are further along on that same path—is what lends realism and hope to the glowing pictures of his people that stand out from the pages of the New Testament. Such passages as Matthew chapters 5–7, John 14–17, Romans 12, 1 Corinthians 13, Ephesians 4–5, and

Colossians 3 readily come to mind. These are not just passages stating required behaviors, as *laws* might do—"Turn the other cheek" and so forth—not a new and sterner legalism. Rather, as expressing what lies "beyond the righteousness of the scribes and Pharisees" (Matt. 5:20), they are indications of *what life becomes* for those who are devoted disciples of Jesus Christ within the fellowship of disciples and under the administration of the Word and of the Holy Spirit. A life of this quality is the "output" of disciples of Jesus who make disciples wherever they go, gather them in Trinitarian reality, and teach them in such a way that they come to do all that Jesus told us to do out of transformed personalities. What is now generally regarded as "normal Christianity" drops away with the "cleaning of the inside of the cup" (Matt. 23:25–26). Discipleship is the status or position within which spiritual (trans)formation occurs.

As we have noted, post-WWII evangelicalism does not naturally conduct its converts and adherents into a life of discipleship, nor into pervasive Christlikeness of character—with the routine, easy obedience that it entails. What this most recent version of evangelicalism lacks is a *theology of discipleship*. Specifically, it lacks a clear teaching on how what happens at conversion continues on without break into an ever fuller life in the Kingdom of God. How, to cite Paul's language, does "the grace of God that brings salvation" discipline us, train us, in such a way that we turn from "ungodliness and worldly lust" to live lives that are "sensible, righteous, and godly in the present world"? (Titus 2:11–14; cf. Phil. 2:12–15). How is it, exactly, that he who gave himself for us also "redeems us from all iniquity and purifies for himself a people of his own who are zealous for good deeds"? (Titus 14; cf. Eph. 2:10) To such questions contemporary evangelicalism has no answer. Its doctrine of grace and salvation prevents it from developing an understanding of discipleship that makes discipleship ("being with Jesus learning to be like him") a natural part of salvation. The basic genius of evangelicalism as such, however, is never content to leave the matter there.

NOTES

1. This threefold scheme is laid out in LeRoy Eims, *The Lost Art of Disciple-making* (Grand Rapids: Zondervan, 1978), which long served as an unofficial guide for the work of Navigators.

2. See *Daws: A Man Who Trusted God* (Colorado Springs: Navpress, 1974).

3. There are, of course, many individuals among evangelicals today who would not accept this. Charismatics and heirs of the various "holiness" traditions would find it hard to swallow. But then what is emphasized by them is still not *discipleship*.

4. Keswick is a town in the district of Allerdale, Cumbria, in the Lake District of England, a center of tourism for centuries. Keswick became the venue for an annual Christian Convention that began in 1875 and continues today. It was a well-known source of "higher life" teachings for more than a century, and has been influential around the world.

5. The work of Richard Foster and his *Renovåre* ministry was highly influential in this direction.

6. On this, consult Charles Finney's lectures on *Revivals of Religion* (Old Tappan, N.J.: Fleming H. Revell, n.d.; many editions) along with the works of Jonathan Edwards.

7. See the careful study of the history of the "disciple" in the world of the New Testament provided by Michael J. Wilkins, *The Concept of Disciple in Matthew's Gospel, as Reflected in the Use of the Term Μαθητής* (Leiden: E. J. Brill, 1988).

8. John M'Clintock and James Strong, eds., *Cyclopaedia of Biblical, Theological, and Ecclesiastical Literature*, vol. 8 (New York: Harper and Brothers, 1894), 870.

BIBLIOGRAPHY

Bonhoeffer, Dietrich. *The Cost of Discipleship*. New York: Macmillan, 1966.

Longenecker, Richard N., ed. *Patterns of Discipleship in the New Testament*. Grand Rapids: Eerdmans, 1996.

Henderson, D. Michael. *A Model for Making Disciples: John Wesley's Class Meeting*. Nappanee, Ind.: Francis Asbury Press, 1997.

Howard-Brook, Wes, and Sharon H. Ringe, eds. *The New Testament—Introducing the Way of Discipleship*. Maryknoll, N.Y.: Orbis Books, 2002.

Hull, Bill. *Choose the Life: Exploring a Faith that Embraces Discipleship*. Grand Rapids: Baker, 2004.

———. *The Disciple-Making Church*. Grand Rapids: Baker, 1998.

Law, William. *A Serious Call to a Devout and Holy Life: Adapted to the State and Condition of All Orders of Christians*. London: Griffith Farran, n.d., many editions.

Wilkins, Michael J. *The Concept of Disciple in Matthew's Gospel*. Leiden: E. J. Brill, 1988.

Wilkins, Michael U. *Following the Master: Discipleship in the Steps of Jesus*. Grand Rapids: Zondervan, 1992.

Willard, Dallas. *The Great Omission*. San Francisco: Harper San Francisco, 2006.

———. *The Spirit of the Disciplines*. San Francisco: Harper and Row, 1988.

CHAPTER 16

SPIRITUAL PRACTICES

SIMON CHAN

Traditional Evangelical Beliefs and Practices

Most evangelicals would agree that certain spiritual disciplines are necessary for the formation of the godly life.[1] A text frequently cited in support is 1 Tim 4:7: "Train yourself in godliness."[2] If asked to list what they regard as the most important spiritual practices, they are not likely to differ very widely in their answers. Topping the list would be the daily personal devotion or the Quiet Time consisting of about twenty to thirty minutes (it used to be longer!) of spiritual exercises of Bible reading, study of and meditation on a passage, and prayers of praise and intercession. Next on the list is regular church attendance (citing Heb 10:25). The third is service, of which evangelism or sharing one's faith with others is considered a top priority, but various forms of social outreach to the disadvantaged are also important. All these practices are concrete expressions of one's surrender and obedience to Christ.[3]

Underlying these practices are certain core convictions about the nature of the Christian life. For evangelicals, the Christian life is essentially a personal relationship with God. If we follow Bebbington's characterizations,[4] the evangelical convictions could be roughly structured in the following way:

- The Christian life begins with a decision to turn from sin and, to use a popular phrase, "accept Jesus Christ as personal savior" ("conversionism").
- The sole objective basis of conversion is the death of Jesus Christ on the cross ("crucicentrism").
- The Christian can be certain of salvation through the cross because the Bible says so ("biblicism").

- Having received the saving grace of God, the Christian must share the message with others ("activism").

A brief consideration of some of the practices will show how closely they are linked to the evangelical belief system. The Quiet Time grows out of the deep conviction that the Bible is God's word. As one evangelical puts it, "No Spiritual Discipline is more important than the intake of God's Word."[5] Reading the Bible followed by prayer is the way one "hears" from God even in matters of personal guidance. In their practice of prayer, evangelicals have generally preferred extemporaneous or free prayer to set or liturgical prayers. This is because personal relationship is thought to be best expressed in personal conversation rather than using a prepared speech.[6]

Another key concept that shapes evangelical spirituality is the assurance of salvation. Theologically, the basis of assurance is God's acceptance of us in Christ, that is, our justification through faith in Christ.[7] Assurance is but one aspect of evangelical biblicism: God has given sure promises in the Bible concerning one's salvation. One can be saved and *know* it! This "blessed assurance" gives evangelicals the confidence to pursue their activism with vigor, especially in evangelism and mission.[8]

The British evangelical David Gillett notes that unlike the seventeenth-century Puritans who struggled over their assurance,[9] eighteenth-century evangelicals seemed to experience "the free availability of assurance."[10] The source of this was John Wesley's understanding of salvation as an experiential reality and therefore a sure fact. Bebbington calls this Wesley's "optimism of grace."[11] With this optimism comes a holy boldness and joyful freedom unseen in Puritanism and Pietism of the previous century. Unlike the Puritans, evangelicals do not look inward for signs of saving grace but look into the Bible to claim God's sure promise. A different sort of spiritual tool is now used to reinforce personal assurance: While the Puritans scrupulously kept a diary to trace the "workings of grace," modern evangelicals have evolved the habit of underlining and memorizing verses in the Bible that contain divine promises. Passages such as 1 Cor 10:13, Prov 3:6, and Isa 41:10 are probably the most heavily underlined.[12] An added tool for this purpose, popular with evangelicals a generation ago, is the "promise box" containing small cards on which Scripture promises are printed. Overall, compared to the Puritans, the evangelical use of the Bible is less legalistic and rigorous as far as assurance is concerned. As Gillett observes, "The Bible is still the test of all doctrine but it is now used in a far less systematic and analytical way."[13]

In addition, evangelicals have developed an array of tools to enhance their spiritual practices. The Quiet Time may be supported by a wide range of devotional aids in the forms of books, tracts, and magazines, but increasingly by using the latest in electronic storage and delivery systems and the internet. Activism may take the forms of camps, conventions, crusades, and rallies or a rock-style musical concert, "festivals of praise," "prayer walks," and mission-exposure trips. The overriding concern of winning the world to Christ by any means is often translated into finding the most effective strategies and methods of evangelism. This may be the primary explanation for the high degree of cultural adaptability. As Gillett notes, evangelical spirituality tends to draw largely from popular culture. For example, its songs are usually expressed through the idiom of the day.[14]

To summarize, evangelical spirituality understood as a coherent set of practices grows out of a certain framework of belief. That is to say, although many of the evangelical spiritual practices have roots in other Christian spiritual traditions,[15] what makes them distinctive is the way in which they are configured in a distinctively evangelical way.

Enlarging Evangelical Spiritual Practices

For much of its history, evangelicalism has been concerned with the "theology of the Christian life," that is, with how to attain and nurture a personal relationship with Jesus as savior and Lord.[16] But in more recent times there has been greater concern over the larger implications of the gospel whose radical nature, many evangelicals believe, had not been sufficiently grasped in the past. In the landmark document "The Lausanne Covenant" from the International Congress on World Evangelization at Lausanne in 1974, evangelical leaders from more than 150 nations agreed to "affirm that evangelism and sociopolitical involvement are both part of our Christian duty."[17] Since then, works by evangelicals on the social dimension of the gospel have become quite plentiful.[18] Many of these writers are calling on evangelicals to radical social engagement of a more or less direct kind. The specifics may differ from place to place and even among different Christians in the same social context, but what is clear is for Christians to recognize that they are called to live and act out the gospel in the world. The common theme in "radical discipleship" is people committed to take their obedience to Christ seriously enough to resist the pressure of the world and its value systems. This commitment may be expressed in the form of alternative communities (for example, several families pooling their resources together).[19] The aim is not only to be different but also to challenge the unjust status quo in society and address structural problems.[20]

The broadening of the evangelical vision also extends to spiritual practices. In the last three decades evangelicals have opened up to a much wider range of spiritual practices. The popularity of Richard Foster's *Celebration of Discipline* first published in 1978 is indicative of this shift. Many books have since been written covering a vast array of spiritual disciplines.[21] Not only has the range of spiritual practices expanded considerably, but the traditional division between "spiritual" and "material" has also become less conspicuous. Even a "disorderly discipline" like mothering can be no less a spiritual exercise.[22] These shifts are no doubt signs of a maturing spirituality.[23]

A number of developments have contributed to a more comprehensive evangelical spirituality beyond the Quiet Time and evangelism. First, the charismatic renewal in the 1960s has helped to break down many barriers between evangelicals and Pentecostals. The Pentecostal doctrine of Spirit-baptism, even if it is not widely accepted as a doctrine,[24] may have nonetheless given the evangelical doctrine of assurance a new lease on life as an experiential reality.[25] Charismatics have considerably enlivened the traditional evangelical worship; certain practices normally associated with Pentecostals are increasingly playing a significant role in the lives of evangelicals and even among Catholics.[26] In recent years, the rapidly growing churches of the "global south" have attracted much attention. Studies by Walter Hollenweger, Harvey Cox, David Martin, Allan Anderson, and Philip Jenkins[27] have highlighted the predominance of Pentecostal-type Christianity in the Third World so that much of the traditional distinctions between the two movements could no longer be clearly drawn.[28] Among evangelical-charismatics, perhaps the most radical expression is the "signs and wonders" movement associated with John Wimber and Peter Wagner. Sometimes dubbed the "Third Wave," it has not only appropriated Pentecostal practices but gone farther into "strategic level spiritual warfare" as a major strategy for mission.[29] The robust "tarrying meeting" of earlier Holiness and Pentecostal movements is superseded by "prayer walks" involving sometimes tens of thousands in a mass display of force.[30]

It would be strange if the influence went only in one direction. Pentecostals and evangelicals have become more open to certain traditional Catholic practices like silence and Ignatian retreats.[31] Some evangelical Anglicans are calling for greater assimilation of sacramental and liturgical practices.[32] What is perhaps surprising is to see traditionally nonsacramental Baptists making the same call (see below). Still others have moved on to embrace Orthodoxy or Catholicism.[33]

These cross-fertilizations have resulted in a more ecumenically aware evangelicalism. Evangelicals are discovering that there is perhaps more that unites them with Catholics than with their liberal Protestant counterparts.[34] An outcome of these ecumenical exchanges is a more modest appraisal of themselves. The evangelical tradition is seen not as the fullest expression of Christianity but as one of its contributing "streams."[35] Consequently, evangelicals are more willing to appropriate the spiritual practices of other Christian traditions into their own spirituality. In fact, this is seen as a necessity. A self-contained evangelical spirituality, warns Gillett, is a danger to itself:

> As a spirituality of renewal, evangelicalism needs this wider tradition to save it from the excesses of individualism, extravagance and fanaticism, as well as from spiritual bankruptcy, should its own inner dynamic be lost. If a spirituality is not broader than the very essentials of evangelicalism it rarely survives well the transmission from one generation to another. This is probably one of the reasons . . . why so many children of staunch, but somewhat exclusive, evangelical homes seem to reject their evangelicalism in adulthood and turn to other spiritual traditions. It is because they are rejecting a package which was presented as a complete whole rather than as the inner renewing dynamic within a wider tradition of Christian spirituality.[36]

The changes in evangelical practices should also be seen in relation to shifts in spiritual patterns in the wider society. American religion, according to Robert Wuthnow, has moved from the spirituality of "dwelling" to the spirituality of "seeking."[37] The first is a spirituality of settledness stemming from the assurance and certainty of home, tradition, and institutions. The second is a spirituality on the move, a fluid spirituality where identity is not determined by being plugged into a preexisting and stable structure, but forged through negotiation, searching, and selecting. In the spirituality of seeking, religion becomes an "industry" and the faithful "consumers."[38] Both types of spirituality, however, are inadequate:

> Habitation spirituality encourages dependence on communities that are inherently undependable and fosters an idolization of particular places to the point that energies gravitate too much to those places rather than being deployed to the full round of human needs in a complex world. A spirituality of seeking in contrast, is invariably too fluid to provide individuals with the social support they need or to encourage the stability and dedication required to grow spiritually and to mature in character.[39]

The weaknesses in the two types have given rise to a third type: "the ancient wisdom that emphasizes the idea of spiritual practices." Unlike the spirituality of seeking, the spirituality of practice is "inevitably embedded in religious institutions." It "require[s] individuals to engage reflectively in a conversation with their past, examining who they have been, how they have been shaped, and where they are headed."[40] Wuthnow observes that spiritual practitioners draw their resources from institutions, yet often find institutions stifling.[41] However, many were able eventually to find meaning in their religious communities after distancing themselves to practice a spirituality outside of their familiar spaces.[42] The "spiritual disciplines" tradition of Foster, Willard, and others seems to recognize this fact. This is why primary emphasis is placed on personal discipline. As Willard puts it,

> I should sustain [the church] and nourish myself within it and upon it. But how can I succeed in doing this? Concretely, the only place where I can "fight the good fight of faith, lay hold on eternal life" (1 Tim. 6:12), is in and through the management of my body, dealing rigorously and wisely with it and depending on God's help.[43]

From Spiritual Disciplines to Ecclesial Practice

The spirituality of practice, coupled with a growing awareness of the importance of the church,[44] has led many evangelicals to focus on ecclesial practice. There are at least four discernable expressions of this trend. One is the "emerging church" movement comprising mostly people who are dissatisfied with fundamentalist and conservative evangelical forms of Christianity. Its main concern is to relate the church to a postmodern culture, and this accounts for its highly eclectic appropriation of the past.[45] Another is the "Federal Vision" movement coming from within some conservative Reformed churches, such as the Presbyterian Church of America and the Orthodox Presbyterian Church. It represents a more systematic retrieval of the Christian tradition, especially the doctrine of the church. The visible church created by God's covenant with humanity is an objective, spiritual reality and not some kind of façade for the "real" invisible church established from eternity by God's inscrutable decree. Federal vision may be seen partly as an attempt to humanize the harshness of traditional Reformed decretal theology.[46] A third movement comprises Baptists who are seeking to develop a distinctive Baptist vision of catholicity.[47] A fourth movement, the "evangelical catholic," comes from mostly the orthodox elements of mainline denominations.[48] It is probably the most theologically developed of the four. Its goal is no less than the recovery of a truly catholic vision of the church. The discussion on ecclesial practice that follows will therefore be drawn mostly from the last group.

The return to the "ancient wisdom" of communal practice must be understood within the postmodern milieu.[49] With the collapse of the metanarrative and a new emphasis on the concrete and particular, the way is open for reasserting what has always been the central Christian conviction that truth is particularized in Jesus Christ, whose story is embodied in the church, his Body. The "virtue ethics" of Alasdiar MacIntyre has been particularly influential in shaping the evangelical understanding of ecclesial practice.[50] Practice for MacIntyre is not primarily about the acts of individuals aimed at personal formation but is essentially communal or "cooperative."[51] It is cooperative not only in the sense that it engages "contemporary practitioners" but also in the sense that it inevitably engages a tradition: "those who have preceded us in the practice."[52] Christian ethics, *mutatis mutandis*, is the practice of the virtues of the community that indwells and is shaped by the Christian story.

The works of Stanley Hauerwas are perhaps most instrumental in advancing a Christian version of MacIntyrean moral philosophy.[53] The church as a traditioning body has become the new center for thinking about the hermeneutical task and the nature of practice in spiritual formation. Hermeneutically, the idea that one could get at an objective meaning of Scripture through scientific exegesis has given way to a view that sees truth deriving from a symbiotic relation between the text and the interpretive community.[54] The church recognizes Scripture as its foundational document because it contains the gospel which gives the church its distinctive identity. The church actualizes its evangelical identity by indwelling the text—a process which gives rise to ecclesial practices. We may say that ecclesial practices are essentially attempts at becoming church. This strategy is increasingly being employed by evangelicals who are looking for deeper roots. Thus the document "Re-Envisioning Baptist Identity" declares: "*We affirm Bible Study in reading communities* rather than relying on private interpretation or supposed 'scientific' objectivity."[55] The same shift can also be seen in the emerging Pentecostal scholarship in the last decade. Pentecostals have added a pneumatological dimension into interpretation and consequently are much more open to a dynamic view of Scripture compared to older evangelicals. Pentecostal scholars like Kenneth Archer and James K. A. Smith are calling for a reassessment of the traditional evangelical understanding of Scripture and the role of the Holy Spirit in the church in the interpretive process.[56]

In summary, what distinguishes postmodern evangelical practices from earlier forms is the place of the church in relation to Scripture and this, consequently, affects the nature of spiritual practices. Spiritual disciplines are necessary, but they must aim at the recovery of the church as a traditioning community. The failure Willard notices of the church to form the person[57] is not because the community's role is inherently perfunctory; rather, it is because communities that used to play a decisive role in shaping the Christian identity (the family and church) have lost much of their traditioning capacities to secularism. It is the secular "community" of individualism that has become decisive in the modern world.[58] The answer to the secular challenge, therefore, cannot be found in individual self-cultivation alone, but in recovering the traditioning power of the church whose basic identity is being shaped as it indwells the Christian story. In short, it is *for* the church that we engage in ecclesial practice, and it is *through* the church that we can do it well.

This understanding of practice has found its most theologically developed form among the "evangelical catholic" theologians. A central feature in their works is the understanding of worship as the central practice of the church. As Hauerwas puts it,

> In worship Christians meet God in time-honored ways. Worship is where people are conformed to Christ, join in his work, are accepted back into his fellowship, and dance to the beat of his drum. Worship anticipates heaven, where all these things are gloriously fulfilled. But worship is also a training for discipleship on earth. It is the time when Christians learn how to be God's friends by eating with him.[59]

Worship is what makes the church the church and distinguishes it from other communities. The decisiveness of worship for ecclesial formation would explain why word and sacrament are regarded as the two key constitutive elements of worship, since they are historically understood as constitutive of the church. They are what Reinhard Hütter calls the "core practices" of the church. These core practices are not arbitrarily derived but are anchored in the teaching and practice of Jesus (even Free Churches recognize them as binding "ordinances"). Besides the proclamation of the word, baptism, and the Eucharist, there are other core practices. Following Luther's "marks" of the church, Hütter includes the following: office of the keys (discipline); ordination or church offices; prayer, doxology, catechesis; and the way of the cross or discipleship.[60] They attain their status as core practices because they have a long history in the church and are of proven value in shaping the Christian community. Take, for example, the church offices. Their importance can be seen as early as the second century in the church's combat with heresies. The place of the bishop standing in historical succession to the apostles constitutes one of the key arguments of Irenaeus against the Gnostics.[61]

Core practices imply that there are also secondary practices, such as private prayer, social concern, and hospitality. The latter grow out of the core and find their basis in the core. Without their foundation in the core, they cease to be Christian. Personal spiritual discipline becomes another form of self-help, while social concern and hospitality become mere activism, indistinguishable as Christian virtues, unless they are practiced as part of a whole way of life shaped by the Christian story.[62]

The newer evangelicals are coming to the realization that worship concretely expressed in a normative liturgy is essential for ecclesial identity. One example, as noted earlier, can be found among Baptists who have sought to recover their "catholic" identity. Baptist sacramentalist Steven Harmon would agree with Geoffrey Wainwright that "the proper locus of tradition [is] not in texts or a body of propositional truths but in the worship of the Christian community."[63] Perhaps a more telling example has come from the "convergence" movement in the 1990s, which has resulted in the formation of a number of "communions" such as the International Communion of the Charismatic Episcopal Church (1992),[64] the Communion of Evangelical Episcopal Churches (1993),[65] and its sister communion, the Communion of Convergence Churches (2005).[66] The convergence movement seeks to bring together three major spiritual streams: the evangelical with its focus on the gospel; the charismatic with its emphasis on the dynamic work of the Spirit; and the sacramental and episcopal, which brings the other two together within the liturgical celebration. Advocates of convergence believe that charisma and institution are but two aspects of a single reality. To put it in terms of Wuthnow's typology, they believe that the spirituality of ecclesial practice epitomized in the liturgy may yet revitalize the spirituality of dwelling.

An Assessment

From Quiet Time to ecclesial practice—evangelicals have come a long way in thirty years. But this development has also left the movement more fragmented than before. Not all evangelicals are comfortable with this new openness. Some are concerned that the introduction of spiritual practices from other Christian traditions compromises the purity of the faith. Dave Hunt, for example, accuses Richard Foster of encouraging the use of "shamanistic" practices like visualization.[67] Willard has been charged with interpreting biblical texts to promote a range of spiritual disciplines that are not explicitly prescribed in the Bible. For conservative evangelicals, spiritual disciplines are not what we can decide for ourselves but what God determines for us. As one of them puts it, "If we need solitude, God can grant that. He might make it so the only job we can find is being a midnight shift watchman."[68] According to another, genuine evangelical spirituality and practice can only be legitimated within the boundaries set by the principles of *sola scriptura* and *sola fide*.[69]

There will still be the Quiet Time practitioners whose biblicistic interpretation will keep them from embracing the spiritual practices of the larger Christian traditions.

Liturgical prayers will continue to be seen as a threat to a more personal relationship with God. If the advocates of a catholic evangelical Christianity are to be convincing, they will have to show that the older evangelicals' chief concerns, namely, biblical authority and personal relationship, are not compromised or abandoned but preserved and enhanced. Biblical authority is better preserved when the Bible is recognized as the *church's* book rather than an independent source of propositional truths derived from an "objective" reading of the text (which for traditional evangelicals means the grammatical-historical method of interpretation). The church that canonizes the Bible also subjects itself to its authority. Biblical authority comes from the conviction that the ultimate author of the Bible is God and its chief content is Christ. The Bible is not just a collection of books but essentially one book. This is why the church reads the Bible canonically, that is, always as a whole and in terms of the whole. If Christ is its content, then it must be read "spiritually" beyond the literal meaning. If the Old Testament finds its fulfillment in Christ, then its *ultimate* intent could only be teased out by means of "spiritual exegesis." This is the method of the church fathers[70] and also, contrary to what is commonly believed, that of Reformers like John Calvin.[71] When the Bible is read canonically, biblical practices are not just those that the Bible explicitly prescribes, but may come from examples, types, history, events, and stories. What makes any of these genres a source of authoritative teaching is how it is constituted as part of the whole canon. Thus the biblical basis for Christians observing bodily disciplines is not solely because there are specific texts enjoining it (there are, in fact, very few), but because it is part of a larger Christological theme: the imitation of Christ, Jesus' identification with humanity through the incarnation, and salvation that includes the transformation of the body. This is the way Willard seeks to commend the various bodily disciplines as "biblical."[72] Without being explicit about it, Willard was actually reading the Bible canonically.

As for the fear that the liturgy would compromise personal relationship, it could be pointed out that the correlation between personal relationship and free prayer and between evangelical spirituality and Free Church ecclesiology[73] is perhaps more culturally determined than theologically necessary. In Asia or Africa, relationships could be personal and formal at the same time. The Confucian concept of filial relationship is personal and also governed by terms of address indicating honor and respect for parents.[74] In the non-Western world it is not uncommon to find many evangelical churches that are also hierarchical.[75] Furthermore, embracing a liturgical spirituality does not mean neglecting the Quiet Time; rather, it means refocusing it from myself to a new center, the church. It means that whenever I pray, I am not praying by myself but joining in the prayers of all the saints and heavenly hosts. To be sure, it requires a mental paradigm shift, but people who have learned to participate actively in liturgical prayers soon find a new way of expressing a deeply personal faith.[76] In short, the central concerns of traditional evangelicals are not lost but transposed to a different key.

Another concern is whether an ecclesially based ethic might insulate the church from the larger culture. Although many evangelicals tend to equate social responsibility with direct involvement (as seen, for example, in the Lausanne

Document), there is nothing to suggest that radical discipleship expressed in direct social action is the only option. Hauerwas has argued that his theological ethics entails its own way of engaging the world. The ecclesial identity is shaped by the gospel story, which lays claim to universality. The truthfulness of this claim enables the Christian to see the world for what it is—a divided and fragmented world—and gives rise to the conviction both to challenge the world's false claims and offer it hospitality.[77] Thus the way the church challenges and engages the world is primarily by becoming a "community of character," or what Lesslie Newbigin calls the "hermeneutic of the gospel."[78] This understanding of the church seems to find confirmation in some sociological and anthropological studies that show that where people are part of strong traditioning communities, even what appears to be private practices of piety could have unpredictable and far-reaching social and political ramifications.[79]

If evangelical spirituality continues to progress along the trajectory that this study on evangelical spiritual practices has briefly traced, then it augurs well for the future of the movement. It holds promise for a more fruitful form of ecumenism based on a common spiritual heritage as evangelicals discover their deep spiritual affinities with older Christian traditions.

NOTES

1. The phrase "spiritual practices" is here used interchangeably with spiritual disciplines. Their precise referents, as we shall see, change over time. When I refer to "traditional (or conservative) evangelical" I am referring to that which approximates Bebbington's definition, to be distinguished from the newer forms to be discussed below.

2. For example, Donald S. Whitney, *Spiritual Disciplines for the Christian Life* (Colorado Springs: Navpress, 1992), 14.

3. David Parker, "Evangelical Spirituality Reviewed," *Evangelical Quarterly* 63.2 (1991): 123–148, and David K. Gillett, *Trust and Obey: Explorations in Evangelical Spirituality* (London: DLT, 1993), provide, respectively, a succinct and comprehensive description of evangelical practices. Ian Randall, however, points out that this common portrait needs to be qualified, in *Evangelical Experiences: A Study in the Spirituality of English Evangelicalism 1918–1939* (Carlisle, Pa.: Paternoster, 1999), 5–6.

4. David Bebbington, *Evangelicalism in Modern Britain: A History from the 1730s to the 1980s* (London: Unwin Hyman, 1989), 3.

5. Donald S. Whitney, *Spiritual Disciplines*, 24.

6. Gillett, *Trust and Obey*, 34–35.

7. John Cockerton, *Essentials of Evangelical Spirituality* (Bramcote, Notts: Grove Books, 1994), 7–8.

8. Ibid., 10.

9. For an account of the struggle for assurance, see Norman Petit, *The Heart Prepared: Grace and Conversion in Puritan Spiritual Life* (New Haven: Yale University Press, 1966).

10. Cockerton, *Essentials*, 47.

11. *Evangelicalism in Modern Britain*, 60.

12. Cockerton, *Essentials*, 56–57.

13. *Trust and Obey*, 48.

14. Ibid., 19–22.

15. Peter Adams, *Roots of Contemporary Evangelical Spirituality* (Bramcote, Notts: Grove Books, 1988).

16. Cockerton, *Essentials*, 3. Whitney's *Spiritual Disciplines* may be taken as a case in point. It focuses primarily on hearing, reading, studying and memorizing, and meditating upon the word (chaps 2 and 3). For Whitney, as for most conservative evangelicals, hearing the word means hearing a sermon (26).

17. The Lausanne Covenant, Section 5.

18. See, for example, Ronald Sider, *Rich Christians in an Age of Hunger: A Biblical Study* (Downers Grove, Ill.: InterVarsity Press, 1984); Jim Wallis, *The Call to Conversion* (New York: Harper and Row, 1981); Christopher Sugden, *Radical Discipleship* (Basingstoke, Hants: Marshall, Morgan and Scott, 1981).

19. Sugden, *Radical Discipleship*, 8–10.

20. Ibid., 14–16.

21. For example, Dallas Willard, *The Spirit of the Disciplines* (San Francisco: HarperCollins, 1991); Siang-Yang Tan and Douglas H. Gregg, *Disciplines of the Holy Spirit* (Grand Rapids: Zondervan, 1997); Adele Ahlberg Calhoun, *Spiritual Discipline Handbook: Practices That Transform Us* (Downers Grove, Ill.: InterVarsity Press, 2005). Calhoun enumerates sixty-two disciplines organized around the central focus on worship.

22. Jenell Williams Paris, "Disorderly Disciplines," *Christianity Today*, http://www.christianitytoday.com/ct/2007/may/30.48.html,

23. As seen, for example, in various attempts at integrating evangelical theology and spirituality in *For All the Saints: Evangelical Theology and Christian Spirituality*, eds. Timothy George and Alister McGrath (Louisville, Ky.: Westminster John Knox Press, 2003).

24. However, Martin Lloyd-Jones' attempt to recover the Puritan doctrine of assurance as an experience distinct from conversion shows how closely it parallels the Pentecostal doctrine of subsequence. See his *Joy Unspeakable: The Baptism with the Holy Spirit* (Eastbourne: Kingsway, 1984).

25. See Gillett, *Trust and Obey*, 63–64.

26. The Alpha course, produced by the Anglican charismatic church Holy Trinity in Brompton, U.K., is used in both evangelical congregations and Catholic parishes in many parts of the world as a strategy for evangelism and "re-evangelizing" nominal Christians. The course includes a component on the "filling of the Spirit." Joyce Gan, "Try Alpha," http://www.catholic.org.sg/cn/wordpress/?p=1945.

27. Walter Hollenweger, *Pentecostalism: Origins and Developments Worldwide* (Peabody, Mass.: Hendrickson, 1997); Harvey Cox, *Fire from Heaven: The Rise of Pentecostal Spirituality and the Reshaping of Religion in the Twenty-First Century* (Cambridge, Mass.: Da Capco Press, 2001); David Martin, *Pentecostalism: The World Their Parish* (Oxford: Blackwell, 2002); Allan Anderson, *An Introduction to Pentecostalism: Global Charismatic Christianity* (Cambridge: Cambridge University Press, 2004); Philip Jenkins, *The Next Christendom: The Coming of Global Christianity*, rev. ed. (New York: Oxford University Press, 2007).

28. Evangelicalism in the West, too, has been largely "charismaticized." See Dave Tomlinson, *The Post Evangelical* (London: SPCK, 1995), 15–21.

29. C. Peter Wagner, *Warfare Prayer: How to Seek God's Power and Protection in the Battle to Build His Kingdom* (Ventura, Cal.: Regal Books, 1992).

30. For a critical study of this movement in the Singapore context, see Tan-Chow May Ling, *Pentecostal Theology for the Twentieth-First Century* (Aldershot: Ashgate, 2007).

31. Rich Heffern, "The Pentecostals and the Monks," *National Catholic Reporter*, December 15, 2006, 9a, 10a.

32. Philip Seddon, *Gospel and Sacrament: Reclaiming a Holistic Evangelical Spirituality* (Cambridge: Grove Books, 2004); Christopher Cocksworth, *Holding Together: Gospel, Church and Spirit the Essentials of Christian Identity* (London: SCM Canterbury Press, 2008).

33. Dwight Longenecker, "Evangelical Catholics," http://www.holyspiritinteractive.net/columns/.dwightlongenecker/currentevents/06.asp. Thomas Howard, *Evangelical Is Not Enough: Worship of God in Liturgy and Sacrament* (San Francisco: Ignatius Press, 1984); Peter Gilquist, *Becoming Orthodox: A Journey to the Ancient Christian Faith* (Brentwood, Tenn.: Wolgemuth and Hyatt, 1989); Michael Harper, *A Faith Fulfilled: Why Are Christians across Great Britain Embracing Orthodoxy?* (Ben Lomond, Cal.: Conciliar Press, 1999).

34. See, for example, the document "Evangelicals and Catholics Together: The Christian Mission in the Third Millennium" in *First Things* 43 (May 1994): 15–22. For subsequent development of ECT, see *Catholics and Evangelicals: Do They Share a Common Future?*, ed. Thomas P. Rausch (Mahwah, N.J.: Paulist, 2000).

35. For example, Richard Foster, *Streams of Living Water: Celebrating the Great Traditions of the Christian Faith* (Engelwood, Mo.: HarperCollins, 1998).

36. *Trust and Obey*, 31. Gillett simply confirms the assessment of Thomas Howard, the evangelical turned Catholic: evangelical is not enough. See *Evangelical Is Not Enough.*

37. Robert Wuthnow, *After Heaven: Spirituality in America since the 1950s* (Berkeley: University of California Press, 1998). Although the study is on American religion, the phenomenon seems to be found in many other places influenced by popular American religion.

38. Ibid., 11–12.

39. Ibid., 15–16.

40. Ibid., 16.

41. Ibid., 183.

42. Ibid., 197.

43. *The Spirit of the Disciplines*, 125.

44. For example, Stanley Grenz, *Renewing the Center: Evangelical Theology in a Post-theological Era* (Grand Rapids: Baker, 2000); *Evangelical Ecclesiology: Reality or Illusion?*, ed. John G. Stackhouse (Grand Rapids: Baker, 2003); *The Community of the Word: Toward an Evangelical Ecclesiology*, ed. Mark Husbands and Daniel J. Treier (Downers Grove, Ill.: InterVarsity Press, 2005).

45. A good introduction is perhaps *Stories of Emergence: Moving from Absolute to Authentic*, ed. Mike Yaconelli (Grand Rapids: Zondervan, 2003). Its better known representatives are Brian D McLaren, *A Generous Orthodoxy* (Grand Rapids: Zondervan, 2006), and Dan A. Kimball, *The Emerging Church: Vintage Christianity for New Generations* (Grand Rapids: Zondervan, 2003).

46. See, for example, Peter J. Leithart, *Kingdom and the Power: Rediscovering the Centrality of the Church* (Phillipsburg, N.J.: P & R Publishing, 1993); Steve Wilkins, ed., *The Federal Vision* (Los Angeles: Athanasius Press, 2004).

47. For example, D. H. Williams, *Retrieving the Tradition and Renewing Evangelicalism: A Primer for Suspicious Protestants* (Grand Rapids: Eerdmans, 1999); *Baptist Sacramentalism*, ed. Anthony R. Cross and Philip E. Thompson (Carlisle, Cumbria:

Paternoster, 2003); Steven R. Harmon, *Towards Baptist Catholicity* (Eugene, Ore.: Wipf and Stock, 2006). See the landmark document "Re-Envisioning Baptist Identity: A Manifesto for Baptist Communities in North America" put out by some members of the Cooperative Baptist Fellowship. It is reproduced in *Perspectives in Religious Studies* 24.3 (2006): 303–310, and in Harmon, *Towards Baptist Catholicity*, 215–223.

48. For example, Reinhard Hütter, "The Church as Public: Dogma, Practice, and the Holy Spirit," *Pro Ecclesia* 3.3 (Summer 1994): 334–361; *Suffering Divine Things* (Grand Rapids: Eerdmans, 2000); Carl Braaten, *Mother Church: Ecclesiology and Ecumenism* (Minneapolis: Fortress, 1998); Carl Braaten and Robert Jenson, eds., *Marks of the Body of Christ* (Grand Rapids: Eerdmans, 1999); James J. Buckley and David S. Yeago, eds., *Knowing the Triune God: The Work of the Spirit in the Practice of the Church* (Grand Rapids: Eerdmans, 2001).

49. All the four movements enumerated above could be said to represent different ways of addressing the postmodern question. The same could be said about the Radical Orthodoxy of John Milbank, Graham Ward, and Catherine Pickstock. For an introduction to this movement, see James K. A. Smith, *Introducing Radical Orthodoxy: Mapping a Post-Secular Theology* (Grand Rapids: Baker, 2004).

50. Nancey Murphy, Brad J. Kallenberg, and Mark Thiessen Nation, eds., *Virtues and Practices in the Christian Tradition: Christian Ethics after MacIntyre* (Harrisburg, Pa.: Trinity Press, 1997).

51. Alasdair MacIntyre, *After Virtue: A Study in Moral Theory*, 2nd ed. (Notre Dame: University of Notre Dame Press, 1981), 187.

52. Ibid., 194.

53. Stanley Hauerwas, *A Community of Character: Toward a Constructive Christian Social Ethic* (Notre Dame: University of Notre Dame Press, 1986). For an introduction to his thought, see *The Hauerwas Reader*, ed. John Berkman and Michael G. Cartwright (Durham: Duke University Press, 2001).

54. See, for example, Harmon, *Towards Baptist Catholicity*, chap. 3.

55. Harmon, *Towards Baptist Catholicity*, 217. Emphasis in the original.

56. Kenneth Archer, *A Pentecostal Hermeneutic for the Twenty First Century: Spirit, Scripture and Community* (London: T and T Clark, 2004); James K. A. Smith, "The Closing of the Book: Pentecostals, Evangelicals, and the Sacred Writings," *Journal of Pentecostal Theology* 11 (October 1997): 49–71.

57. *Spirit of the Disciplines*, 125. The "spiritual disciplines" tradition of Foster, Willard, and others, perhaps because of the weakness of ecclesial institutions, does not put much emphasis on ecclesial practice.

58. It sounds contradictory that secular individualism should be called a community. But it is a community in the sense that secularists inhabit the secular narrative that gives shape and coherence to the secular way of life.

59. *Blackwell Companion to Christian Ethics*, ed. Stanley Hauerwas and Samuel Wells (Oxford: Blackwell, 2004), 25. Cf. Catherine Pickstock's argument that because human beings are doxologically constituted, that is, oriented to the praise of God, all language finds its consummation in the liturgy. *After Writing: On the Liturgical Consummation of Philosophy* (Oxford: Blackwell, 1998).

60. Reinhard Hütter, "The Church: The Knowledge of the Triune God: Practices, Doctrine, Theology," in James J. Buckley and David S. Yeago, eds., *Knowing the Triune God: The Work of the Spirit in the Practice of the Church* (Grand Rapids: Eerdmans, 2001), 34–35. For a fuller treatment, see his *Suffering Divine Things*, 128–145. For Luther's "marks," see

Martin Luther, "On the Councils and the Church," *Luther's Works*, 41, ed. Eric W. Gritsch (Philadelphia: Fortress, 1966).

61. *Against Heresies*, III.3 cf. III.24.1.

62. Martha Ellen Stortz, "Evangelical Spirituality: Practicing the Marks of the Church," *Word and World* 20.1 (2000): 91, 94–95. http://www.luthersem.edu/word&world/Archives/20-1_20th_Century/20-1_Face_to_Face.pdf.

63. Harmon, *Towards Baptist Catholicity*, 60.

64. http://www.iccec.org/.

65. http://www.theceec.org/history.html.

66. http://www.thecccusa.com/content.cfm?id=2022. The works of the late Robert Webber have been instrumental in the formation of these communions.

67. Dave Hunt, *The Seduction of Christianity: Spiritual Discernment in the Last Days* (Eugene, Ore.: Harvest House Publishers, 1985).

68. Bob DeWaay, "The Dangers of Spiritual Formation and Spiritual Disciplines," *Critical Issues Commentary* 91 (November/December 2005): 6. http://cicministry.org/commentary/issue91.pdf.

69. Donald S. Whitney, "Defining the Boundaries of Evangelical Spirituality." http://bibicalspirituality.org/pdef.html.

70. For example, Robert Louis Wilken, *The Spirit of Early Christian Thought: Seeking the Face of God* (New Haven: Yale University Press, 2003); "How to Read the Bible," *First Things* 181 (March 2008): 24–27.

71. See Kathryn Greene-McCreight, "'We Are Companions of the Patriarchs' or Scripture Absorbs Calvin's World," *Modern Theology* 14.2 (April 1998): 213–224.

72. *Spirit of the Disciplines*, 5–10, 29–36, 100–112 passim.

73. Roger Olson, "Free Church Ecclesiology and Evangelical Spirituality," in *Evangelical Ecclesiology: Reality or Illusion?*, ed. John G. Stackhouse (Grand Rapids: Baker, 2003), 173.

74. See, for example, Julia Ching, *Confucianism and Christianity: A Comparative Study* (New York, Tokyo: Kodansha International, 1977), 97–98.

75. See Allan Anderson, *Zion and Pentecost: The Spirituality and Experience of Pentecostal and Zionist/Apostolic Churches in South Africa* (Pretoria: University of South Africa Press, 2000); *An Introduction to Pentecostalism*.

76. This appears to be what a number of recent Vatican documents on the liturgy are aiming at by their repeated calls to active and "conscious" participation. *Redemptionis Sacramentum* (2004), nn. 36–42. http://www.vatican.va/roman_curia/congregations/ccdds/documents/rc_con_ccdds_doc_20040423_redemptionis-sacramentum_en.html. See also *Sacramentum Caritatis* (2007), n. 55; cf. n. 63. http://www.vatican.va/holy_father/benedict_xvi/apost_exhortations/documents/hf_ben-xvi_exh_20070222_sacramentum-caritatis_en.html#top.

77. *A Community of Character*, 89–94.

78. *The Gospel in a Pluralist Society* (Grand Rapids: Eerdmans, 1989), 222–233.

79. For example, Elizabeth E. Brusco, *The Reformation of Machismo: Evangelical Conversion and Gender in Colombia* (Austin: University of Texas Press, 1995); Richard Shaull and Waldo Cesar, *Pentecostalism and the Future of the Christian Churches: Promises, Limitations, Challenges* (Grand Rapids: Eerdmans, 2000); Saba Mahmood, *The Politics of Piety: The Islamic Revival and the Feminist Subject* (Princeton: Princeton University Press, 2004); Donald E. Miller and Tetsunao Yamamori, *Global Pentecostalism: The New Face of Christian Social Engagement* (Berkeley: University of California Press, 2007).

BIBLIOGRAPHY

Buckley, James J., and David S. Yeago, eds. *Knowing the Triune God: The Work of the Spirit in the Practice of the Church.* Grand Rapids: Eerdmans, 2001.

Cocksworth, Christopher. *Holding Together: Gospel, Church and Spirit the Essentials of Christian Identity.* London: SCM Canterbury Press, 2008.

Gillet, David K. *Trust and Obey: Explorations in Evangelical Spirituality.* London: DLT, 1993.

Grenz, Stanley. *Renewing the Center: Evangelical Theology in a Post-theological Era.* Grand Rapids: Baker, 2000.

Guroian, Vigen. *Incarnate Love: Essay in Orthodox Ethics.* 2nd ed. Notre Dame: University of Notre Dame Press, 2002.

Harmon, Steven R. *Towards Baptist Catholicity: Essays on Tradition and the Baptist Vision* Eugene, Ore.: Wipf and Stock, 2006.

Miller, Donald E., and Tetsunao Yamamori. *Global Pentecostalism: The New Face of Christian Social Engagement* (Berkeley: University of California Press, 2007).

Sugden, Christopher, *Radical Discipleship*, Basingstoke, Hants: Marshall, Morgan and Scott, 1981.

Leithart, Peter J. *The Kingdom and the Power: Rediscovering the Centrality of the Church.* Phillipsburg, N.J.: P and R Publishing, 1993.

Willard, Dallas. *The Spirit of the Disciplines.* San Francisco: HarperCollins, 1991.

Wuthnow, Robert. *After Heaven: Spirituality in America since the 1950s.* Berkeley: University of California Press, 1998.

CHAPTER 17

ESCHATOLOGY

TREVOR HART

Eschatology in the Wider Scheme of Things

True to its name, eschatology often comes last in compendiums or "systems" of Christian doctrine. From the Greek adjective *eschatos* (last), it is generally understood as that part of Christian theology whose proper concern is with *ta eschata*, "the last things," the things that will come last—not just in our theological manuals but in God's dealings with his creation. This, though, is at best only a half-truth (albeit an important one), and failure to appreciate this has sometimes produced unfortunate theological consequences. Too often eschatology has been last not just in our mapping of the content of the faith but in terms of theological significance, being relegated to a detachable appendix without any apparent purchase on most of what precedes it. The extent to which this is so is an index of our failure to grasp the sense in which Christian faith and theology are, or should properly be, eschatological from first to last. Eschatology concerns the fact that, just as God spoke the primordial word which called the world into being, so too he will have the final say about its future, a word that he has already uttered under the form of promise. While, therefore, eschatological doctrine certainly has to do with final destinies—of individual people, human history, and the cosmos as a whole—beyond the threshold of finitude and death, in a vital sense it is not just about the "end" (the final few pages) of the world's story, but about the story as a whole (past, present, and future) and individual parts of it read now consistently in the light of that promised end.

As Daniel Migliore notes, apart from this eschatological orientation "every Christian doctrine becomes distorted."[1] Christian faith is fundamentally expectant, forward looking and forward moving, and theology in all its departments therefore is and must always be *spes quaerens intellectum*—hope seeking understanding.[2]

None of this means, of course, that theology should lose sight or fail to speak of the final things themselves and as such; but in eschatology these can never be the focus of a wholly "other-worldly" esotericism, because our imaginative grasp on the promise quickly discovers it to be pregnant with meaning for faith's present, and constantly threatening to break in and transform that present through the Holy Spirit's action.

Eschatology, Revelation, and Imagination

Faith's grasp on eschatological realities is, we should note from the outset, inherently and inevitably of a highly imaginative sort, having to do with some state of affairs more or less remote from our experience of the given present. Evangelical eschatology has often shown a particular interest in what might be called "penultimate" matters: that is, "last things" which are nonetheless believed to arise within the framework of this present world and its history and immediately before it is drawn to a close. Such beliefs, drawing on Revelation 20, have looked for a "millennium," a transitional period of one thousand years either immediately preceding or immediately following the second coming of Christ, and during which the conditions of this-worldly existence will approximate more completely to those of the new creation itself.[3] Quite apart from disputed exegetical issues, such beliefs are important in their acknowledgment of the vital this-worldly significance of Christian belief in another, more ultimate, and transcendent future.

The larger part of eschatological belief, though, concerns "ultimate" rather than penultimate matters, having to do precisely with another world lying beyond the limits of this one and its history. Here the systematic theologian faces a particular challenge, albeit not a unique one.[4] For in dealing with the final things, we are dealing with what lies in principle beyond the range of any historical human experience, and thus beyond the normal working reach of the words and concepts we use to make sense of that experience. Here, in other words, we run up against the problem of a reality that transcends the given limits of our knowing and speaking in an absolute rather than merely a relative way, and we are therefore driven to acknowledge two very basic things about any knowledge that we may claim to have about it.

First, the accounts we may offer of such realities may never legitimately aspire to the status of a "literal" description[5] of future states of affairs but are bound to be and to remain self-consciously figurative in a way that is not quite true of human speech in most other contexts. In eschatology, as in our wider talk about God, there are dangers involved in failure to adopt a stance of appropriate epistemic humility. Too often, works of "licensed religious imagination"[6] have been mistaken for or replaced by something much more ambitious and damaging in its epistemic claims. If our eschatology is to be theologically responsible, though, we must resist any literalizing tendency while yet refusing to underestimate the epistemic status of the imaginative as a respectable form of "knowledge" in the broader sense.

Second, given that the "final things" transcend the range of general patterns of human speaking and knowing in this radical way, any genuine knowledge that we have of them must be given to us from beyond the sphere of human capacity. In other words, it must have its origin in an act of revelation. Only God is in a position actually to know of those things lying beyond the horizons of human history, and therefore only by an act of divine revealing could historical beings ever come to know of them. Again, to insist upon the imaginative form such knowing takes is not in any way to undercut or contradict this claim, unless we suppose that all divine revealing occurs in and through epistemic forms of one particular (unimaginative) type. But here, as so often elsewhere, God makes himself and his purposes and promises known not by downloading a body of digitised factual data, but by taking our imagination captive, lifting us up through Spirit-filled reading to "see" and "taste" the substance of things lying way beyond our natural purview, and calling us responsibly to imagine further.

The trajectories along which such eschatological imagining travels are set in Scripture itself, which encourages extrapolation both positively and negatively from features of life in the here-and-now. We cannot *know* what life in God's new creation will look like; but the vision of the prophets urges us to imagine a world in which all that is good and worthwhile and fulfilling in human life will be taken up and transfigured and handed back to us with unprecedented, unimaginable value added, while all that is evil and distorts or destroys human life in this world will be conspicuous only by its absence.[7] Concomitantly, images of what it might mean to be excluded from God's presence for eternity are ones drawn from the very darkest of human experiences—images of misery, pain, decay, and destruction. Again, we cannot *know* what such a state of Godforsakenness would be like; but we are encouraged to imagine it as something terrible and final.

Eschatology, Immanence, and Optimism

The intellectual climate of modernity has presented significant challenges to religious belief, and eschatology has duly borne its share of the criticism. If, though, certain elements of traditional eschatology have simply been rejected by the secular culture emanating from the Enlightenment, the broad pattern of eschatological hope as such has suffered a rather different fate, having been appropriated and forced into service in various secularized versions. Modernity, too, in other words, has its stories to tell about the meaningfulness of human history, and about bright future toward which history as a whole is moving. Torn out of its proper biblical and theological context, though, such secular eschatology has a tone radically different from that of its Christian parent.

Typically, having abandoned any notion of a God whose reality transcends that of the spheres of nature and history as such, secularism is compelled to seek meaning and grounds for hope *within* these spheres. The most familiar version of this is what we may term the modern "dogma" or "myth" of progress,[8] a secularist metaphysics which understands natural and historical processes themselves as possessed of an inbuilt capacity for and tendency toward perfection. From the empirical observation that with the passage of time something identifiable as "progress" in human understanding and behavior occurs, we witness a shift to the dogmatic (one might almost say "religious") claim that process and progress are themselves inseparable, and that things are thus bound to get better as each day dawns and we move "onward and upward." Such thoroughgoing immanentalism, replacing Christian faith in divine providence with a conviction that historical process contains the seeds of its own meaning and eventual fulfilment, places a huge burden on human shoulders. For faith in natural and historical forces is also faith in human nature (Enlightened humans are a key part of the "process") and thus faith in us to exercise freedom responsibly and intelligently and bring the utopian future into existence. The absence of God from the picture also means the absence of grace, and the return to a vision of "salvation" by good works. Unfortunately, the works in question seem to lie beyond our moral and spiritual resources.

That modern science and technology represent huge strides forward in human understanding of the world and have rendered equally significant improvements to the qualify of life for large portions of the human race cannot be gainsaid and ought not to be underestimated. What must be acknowledged with equal force, though, is that the basic moral and spiritual disposition of human beings appears not to have changed, and shows no prospect of doing so. Against genuine advances in Western society, such as the abolition of slavery, the establishment of universal suffrage, and the promotion and protection of human rights we must set those inhuman atrocities that human beings are still perfectly capable of perpetrating upon one another. Indeed, the technological mastery of nature itself, wedded to this abiding fundamental moral flaw, has enhanced and extended both the repertoire of humanity's self-destructive options and the set of precision tools available with which to commit them. When we add to this the statistics of deaths still caused by wholly preventable starvation and curable disease (the fruits of technological advance withheld by human greed and selfishness), the fact that "modern" lifestyles appear to render us more susceptible to some fatal illnesses just as science has learned to alleviate the symptoms of many others, and the serious threat to our natural habitat itself caused in large measure by patterns of human exploitation and misuse of natural resources, it all paints a picture that fits ill with narratives of inevitable or unalloyed progress. And over all this, of course, there looms the shadow of one uncomfortable reality that calls even such progress as has been made into serious question: death eventually robs us of it, and brings it all to nothing. The cruel fact of transience, and scientific predictions of our planet's own end in some cosmic conflagration, challenge all attempts to locate the meaning and value of existence within the limits and patterns of historical existence as such.

For many, the challenges have been insurmountable, and postmodern cynicism and nihilism have already taken up residence in many of the myth's former intellectual haunts.

Transcendent Eschatology and Christian Activism

The Christian gospel remains good news amidst all this precisely insofar as faith recovers its grasp on transcendence as something essential to the structure of its own eschatological vision. For Christian faith, that is to say, the "end" and meaning of history can only come from beyond it, from an act of the God who himself transcends all creaturely reality and whose promised redemptive act always comes as grace, rescue, redemption, something which history and nature alike are incapable of providing or producing for themselves. According to Jürgen Moltmann (whose theology has done more than any other to spearhead the renaissance of concern with eschatology in the past fifty years), this is what differentiates hope from modernist optimism most clearly.

The ultimate future of the world (and of human beings as part of the world), Moltmann insists, lies beyond the temporal "end" of history and comes to us as a promised gift of God. Meanwhile the penultimate future (the period between the present and history's end-point) is the time of anticipation, a time when human life must be lived in the light of the promise, and in the power of the Spirit of the promise. Thus, alongside eschatological transcendence, Moltmann's theology sets the claim that what has still to come in its fullness nonetheless already exercises a powerful draw on the shape of the present through the transforming power of God's Spirit at work in the lives of believers and elsewhere.[9] This motif of dynamic anticipation, of "the power of the future over every historical time," as Moltmann puts it,[10] helps to redress an imbalance to which traditional eschatologies have sometimes been prone, and of which they have regularly been accused.

An eschatology concerned entirely with the depiction and expectation of "other-worldly" realities can generate an ethically, politically, and ecologically deficient "demobilising ideology,"[11] fundamentally irresponsible in its attitudes to and treatment of the here and now. This can take the form of "quietism," an effective withdrawal from practical, social, and political concerns, content to tolerate conditions of injustice, oppression, and worse without protest, because the present state of affairs is recognized to be temporary and penultimate, to be replaced duly by enjoyment of a kingdom of peace and justice and unimaginable bliss. This was the thrust of Karl Marx's notorious description of religious hopes as the "opiate of the masses," an analgesic numbing the pain of history's victims, and thereby debilitating the urge for political reform in the real world. More damaging still are those forms of "end time" apocalypticism which take the biblical promise that God will fashion a new heaven and a new earth as notice served from on high that this current world is already marked for destruction, and tacit license to treat it and its resources carelessly or even in an ruthlessly exploitative manner.[12] In an age of north-south economic imbalance, nuclear weapons, and global climate change, such attitudes offer scant theological resources to underwrite political initiatives of a hopeful and responsible sort.

Thus, as Migliore notes, it is a matter of urgency today that the proper link between Christian hope and Christian ethics be recovered and proclaimed loudly and clearly.[13] Commitment to the biblical conviction that God's kingdom will finally be established by a sovereign act of God at the end of history (transcendent eschatology) must not result in an unbiblical devaluing or diminution of our commitment to this world.[14] It is important to note that the "new creation" of which Christian Scripture speaks does not entail the replacement of this world but precisely its redemption. What faith hopes for is no second *creatio ex nihilo*, but a sovereign divine act which lays hold of and renews that same world which God made in the beginning. This means, of course, that as the object of God's creative and redemptive purpose and promise, this present world and our existence in it have supreme value for God (a value gauged finally by the radical commitment revealed in the incarnation and death of the Son), and we must value it too, not just in theory, but in the way we treat it. And, even though no historical initiative or action can ever establish the kingdom or advance the ultimate redemption of God's world, we are nonetheless called to act in ways that correspond to the shape of the promise, to fashion (in the Spirit's power) concrete parables of the new creation in the midst and under the conditions of the old.

Furthermore, the biblical vision of the end times does not lend itself naturally or easily to spiritualizing interpretations in which immortal souls survive the perishing of material and historical existence to enjoy a private disembodied vision of God. The prominence of such notions in Christian eschatology owes much to its historical engagement with Platonism and has been reinforced by more recent versions of philosophical idealism. But it loses sight of the witness of Scripture to a redemption cosmic as well as personal in its scope and its nature.[15] The bodily resurrection of Jesus (finally the touchstone of Christian eschatology) reminds us that material as well as immaterial realities await their transformation and glorification at God's hands, while expectation of a heavenly kingdom characterized by justice and peace compels us to imagine redeemed existence in common rather than merely individual terms, and the core image of a new creation envisages the salvation of humans only as part of a hope that extends to the nonhuman creation, too. Here, too, we might note the significance of Moltmann's suggestion that it will be the pattern of human history and particular human lives *as a whole* that will be raised up and regenerated in the new creation, and not just their condition at their temporal end point.[16] Since, therefore, we are encouraged to imagine not just "the world" in some abstract sense, but many of the particular things and sorts of things that we know and have known in this world being taken up and restored to us in eternity in a redeemed but recognizable form, our disposition toward them in the here-and-now must be one which cherishes and respects them, and takes due responsibility for their well-being. To do any less is not merely socially, politically, and ecologically irresponsible; it is a sinful affront to the God who made and values them and has trusted us with their interim welfare.

Nor is a politically passive quietism an option for eschatologically oriented faith. Christians are called to struggle against the forces of death and corruption that damage God's good creation, wherever and in whatever form they may be found; and hope, far from dulling our sensibilities to the pain and injustice of the present, actually serves to heighten those sensibilities and to provoke resistance. In Moltmann's words, "Those who hope in Christ can no longer put up with reality as it is, but begin to suffer under it, to contradict it. Peace with God means conflict with the world, for the goad of the promised future stabs inexorably into the flesh of every unfulfilled present."[17]

Final Destinations

Christian eschatology over the centuries has often been focused primarily on a cluster of four biblical images depicting the "final things." The images are those of resurrection, judgment, heaven, and hell. In broad narrative form, it was traditionally maintained that at the point of death human beings enter an "interim state." This is an area of some ambiguity, but was widely understood either to involve an immediate particular judgment and conscious disembodied existence (sometimes entailing a purgation to fit the faithful soul for eternity) or some form of "sleep." This intermediate condition continues until the second advent or *Parousia* of Christ, when all the dead will be raised up and judged before being dispatched to an eternity in the presence of God (heaven) or in eternal separation from him (hell).[18] True to its biblical concentration, modern evangelical theology has been faithful in maintaining the force of such imagery in an age where it has too often been permitted to fall into abeyance.

The modern world has an odd and uneasy relationship with death. In part it is fascinated by death's mechanics and cannot leave it alone, making it the gruesome subject of myriad film and video-game simulations. But this is a fascination born of fear, and the dying which is, as it were, an inevitable part of everyday life in communities of finite human beings is largely banished from public gaze, hidden away in hospital wards, with the processes of dealing with the dead more or less industrialized.[19] When we are forced to face the fact of death publicly in rituals of grieving, the adopted tone is often a sentimentalizing one, denying death's tragic and destructive force to rob us of something good, and turning it into a friendly release from the sufferings of life. Christian faith, though, never understands death as a friend but always as an enemy, something unnatural that tears away from us the gift of life that

God has granted. In biblical terms "death" does not refer simply to a biological process, but to the additional power of sin to interrupt our spiritual relationship with the God of life. Death robs us of God; this, and not its robbing us of the many other admittedly good things of life in the world, is its full and final horror. That faith can look death in the eye without blinking (and even picture it as a mere "falling asleep")[20] has nothing to do with sentimental denial of this horror. It rests securely on the promise of resurrection, the gift of immortality that will restore to us in all its fullness not just the best of what creation has to offer, but that new quality of living which faith already tastes and enjoys in the here and now.[21] Death's sting must not be trivialized, but it has been drawn and need hold no fear for us.

The central Christian creeds follow the pattern of Scripture in their expectation of a glorious return of Christ at the end of history to judge "both the living and the dead." This image of a final judgment has suffered neglect in the modern period, but it is an essential part of the promised future to which faith looks forward expectantly. Despite the way in which it has sometimes been presented and deployed, it must be understood fundamentally as an image of hope and good news rather than a mechanism for generating guilt and fear. To insist that God will exercise judgment at the end is an essential part of hope's conviction that God "will set the world right once and for all."[22] Judgment means both an acknowledgment of realities and a dispelling of all illusions, and the destruction of evil by a holy God in whose presence it cannot finally exist. Nothing that does not correspond to God's own holy character can be taken up into the new creation, but will be identified and purged, whether instantaneously or via some process entailing the passage of time.[23] Furthermore, while the cosmic assize is pictured as involving the judgment of individual human lives in terms of their complicity in good and bad actions,[24] it must be related theologically to the atonement in which God has borne the penalty of sin "once and for all." Thus the last judgment cannot be a new judgment introducing some further ground for fixing the eternal destiny of God's creatures than that which faith discovers in its crucified and risen Savior, but must be understood as the divine confirmation and final implementation of a verdict already reached.[25] The significance of the symbol of *Parousia* is precisely to stress this essential continuity; the God into whose hands our final judgment will fall is the very same one who, in an act of holy love, has first permitted himself to be judged in our place. Therefore the place of "punishment" and exclusion from God is described as "prepared for the devil and his angels";[26] it was never intended for God's human creatures, and by entering it himself God has robbed it of any legitimate hold on them. Those pictured as entering it must thus be reckoned to be those who, despite the destiny created and secured for them in Christ, have made an irrevocable and final choice for evil and thus can have no possible place in the coming kingdom of holiness. Again, "God's final judgment is not understood as a legalistic implementation of distributive and retributive justice. What is judged is the appropriateness of a life for entry into eternity,"[27] its fundamental alignment toward God and the good, or its fundamental rejection of them.

Unlike modern sensibility, which tends to favor the thought of a quick and painless death, traditional Christian attitudes often placed an emphasis on the importance of "dying well," and some feared the prospect of sudden death without opportunity for due preparation. This was largely because death was seen as the decisive point at which a person's alignment toward or against God was fixed, the period between death and final judgment being deemed soteriologically insignificant.[28] Other voices, emphasizing that only the last judgment will seal questions of eternal destiny, have envisaged a continuing personal development and relation with Christ straddling the gap between death and general resurrection, what follows death being salutary for some in the unfolding of redemption in a way that what preceded death was and could not be. Only this, they insist, can do justice to the God who offers the gift of eternal life to all and without condition, and whose holy love for us burns eternally and not only for a time. Peremptory withdrawal of the offer, or opportunity bounded by the accidents of life in this world (which is uneven in the distribution of its shortness, and nasty and brutish into the bargain for many) is, this view would argue, inconsistent with the revealed character and purposes of such a God.[29]

As regards the final destiny of human beings at God's hands, Christian tradition across the centuries has virtually always envisaged some form of eschatological dualism in which the restoration of those found in Christ to indwell a new creation is paralleled by the consignment of the impenitent to a place of punishment and eternal loss. Some such vision has certainly formed the backdrop to the eschatological imagining of the vast majority of Christian believers.[30] Furthermore, despite the fact that most of the major ecumenical creeds leave matters of eschatology rather underdetermined (being much more concerned with issues of Christology), numerous creeds and confessions do include clear reference to a dualistic eschatological scenario,[31] and as Richard Bauckham notes, "until the nineteenth century almost all Christian theologians taught the reality of eternal torment in hell."[32]

Despite its prominence in biblical teaching (including that of Jesus himself), the theme of the final consignment of any to an eternity of "punishment" rather than joyful participation in God's promised new creation has been vigorously challenged in the modern era. Such challenges sometimes arise from a simple failure to grant appropriate authority to Scripture as a theological source and norm. Others, though, are born of a deep and sustained engagement with the mind of Scripture, and may safely claim their place among interpretations about which biblically authorized theologies may and do legitimately disagree. The notion of "hell" as a place of eternal and conscious torment has frequently been treated to lurid and theologically irresponsible elaboration, straying way beyond the boundaries of biblical warrant, often to the point of sadism. J. H. Leckie refers to the "crude vulgarity" of medieval depictions of this sort which "revealed often a singular acquaintance with the worst horrors of human life. They depicted the future state of the masses of men as one of a torture like that of the rack or the vivisection table, protracted to all eternity. It was a state of every nameless outrage, of every agony and shame, of every unendurable wrong."[33] But the idea of an abiding state of pain and evil of any sort (even one which, as many advocates of the doctrine of hell would insist, is effectively self-imposed, a matter of God's respect for the dignity of human freedom) has been rejected by many theologians (including numerous evangelicals) as inconsistent in principle with God's holy love. Thus, for instance, John Wenham concludes that "unending torment speaks... of sadism, not justice,"[34] while P. T. Forsyth suggests that God's holiness could never coexist with evil eternally (even chastised evil), but must see it either purged or destroyed at the last.[35] Some have therefore favored exegetical arguments for the doctrine of "conditional immortality," according to which God will finally permit evil (and those who identify themselves with evil) to slip back into that state of nonexistence out of which the creation was called in the beginning.[36]

The most popular eschatological perspective in modern times, though, has undoubtedly been some form of the doctrine of *apokatastasis* or universal restoration, the claim that God will ultimately redeem all from their sin and draw them into the new creation. Unsurprisingly (given the prima facie pattern of biblical teaching on the subject), this doctrine has typically been treated as a Shibboleth among evangelicals. Despite the impression sometimes given, though, the doctrine is not always the symptom of liberal attitudes to biblical teaching and creedal orthodoxy. Universalism has, to be sure, enjoyed a less prominent and secure place in the Christian tradition than alternative scenarios, but there are versions of and arguments for it which are based confidently on exegetical grounds and based upon rather than corrosive of such core doctrines as the redemptive uniqueness of Christ, the holy judgment of God upon sin, and justification by grace through faith alone.[37] If it is to be true to its own avowed commitment to the priority of Scripture over theological tradition as a theological norm, Evangelicalism must certainly continue to wrestle afresh with the biblical text and deal seriously and generously with such arguments where they are to be found, rather than dismissing them out of hand.[38]

In closing, we should note again the inherent vulnerability of all attempts to systematize what are imaginative expressions rather than literal descriptions of what will occur at the end, and the need for appropriate levels of exegetical and theological confidence to be balanced by caution in a doctrinal territory which, biblically speaking at least, is often characterised by the note of surprise.

NOTES

1. Daniel Migliore, *Faith Seeking Understanding: An Introduction to Christian Theology* (Grand Rapids: Eerdmans, 1991), 231.

2. See Jürgen Moltmann, *Theology of Hope*, trans. James W. Leitch (London: SCM Press, 1965), 33.

3. On so-called pre- and post-millennial beliefs in evangelicalism, see David Bebbington, "Eschatology in Evangelical History," in *What Are We Waiting For? Christian Hope and Contemporary Culture*, ed. Stephen Holmes and Russell Rook (Milton Keynes: Paternoster, 2008). On the wider importance of millennial belief, see Richard Bauckham and Trevor Hart, *Hope against Hope: Christian Eschatology at the Turn of the Millennium* (Grand Rapids: Eerdmans, 1999), 132–139.

4. Parallel problems arise in the doctrine of creation and most familiarly in our talk about the reality of God himself, who, being "other" than the world, lies beyond the range of functioning of a language and cognition fitted to deal with it. For a discussion of this, see Bauckham and Hart, *Hope against Hope*, 72–108. See also Karl Rahner, "The Hermeneutics of Eschatological Assertions," in *Theological Investigations Iv* (New York: Crossroad, 1982).

5. On the distinction between literal and metaphorical ways of using words see, briefly and helpfully, Colin Gunton, *The Actuality of Atonement: A Study of Metaphor, Rationality and the Christian Tradition* (Edinburgh: T & T Clark, 1988), 27–52.

6. John Baillie, *And the Life Everlasting* (London: Oxford University Press, 1934), 200.

7. See Bauckham and Hart, *Hope against Hope*, 96–100. See also Hendrikus Berkhof's appeal to the twin principles of "exclusion" and "extrapolation" from Christian existence in the framing of eschatological statements. See Hendrikus Berkhof, *Christian Faith: An Introduction to the Study of the Faith*, trans. Sierd Woudstra, revised ed. (Grand Rapids: Eerdmans, 2000), 540.

8. On this see, for example, Baillie, *And the Life Everlasting*, 28f.; Bauckham and Hart, *Hope against Hope*, 10–20.

9. This idea is central to Moltmann's pneumatology. See Jürgen Moltmann, *The Spirit of Life: A Universal Affirmation*, trans. Margaret Kohl (London: SCM Press, 1992).

10. Jürgen Moltmann, *The Coming of God: Christian Eschatology*, trans. Margaret Kohl (London: SCM Press, 1996), 23. Alternatively, the "presence of eternity" in the midst of history. See Moltmann, *The Spirit of Life*, 153.

11. See David Fergusson, "Eschatology," in *The Cambridge Companion to Christian Doctrine*, ed. Colin Gunton (Cambridge: Cambridge University Press, 1997), 228.

12. See on this Tom Wright, *Surprised by Hope* (London: SPCK, 2007), 130–131.

13. Migliore, *Faith Seeking Understanding*, 247.

14. Fergusson, "Eschatology," 239.

15. See the structure adopted in Moltmann's *The Coming of God*.

16. What Moltmann envisages is the simultaneous existence of human pasts, presents, and futures in a redeemed state. See, for example, Moltmann, *The Coming of God*, 70. See also Trevor Hart, "The Sense of an Ending: Finitude and the Authentic Performance of Life," in *Faithful Performances: Enacting Christian Tradition*, ed. Steven R Guthrie and Trevor Hart (Aldershot: Ashgate, 2007).

17. Moltmann, *Theology of Hope*, 21. See further Trevor Hart, "Imagination for the Kingdom of God? Hope, Promise and the Transformative Power of an Imagined Future," in *God Will Be All in All: The Eschatology of Jürgen Moltmann*, ed. Richard Bauckham (Edinburgh: T & T Clark, 1999), 62f.

18. For more detail on this classic eschatological pattern see, helpfully, Brian Hebblethwaite, *The Christian Hope* (London: Marshall, Morgan & Scott, 1984), 43–90.

19. See Moltmann, *The Coming of God*, 54f.

20. See, for example, 1 Cor. 15:6, 1 Thess. 4:13.

21. See Baillie, *And the Life Everlasting*, 204f.; P. T. Forsyth, *This Life and the Next: The Effect on This Life of Faith in Another* (London: Macmillan, 1918), 73f.

22. Wright, *Surprised by Hope*, 150.

23. Tom Wright has recently argued against notions of a purgatorial interim state, while Moltmann urges the need for something analogous to the passage of time for meaningful transformation of personal and social realities to occur. See Moltmann, *The Coming of God*, 96ff.; Wright, *Surprised by Hope*, 178–183. So, too, P. T. Forsyth insists that "We threw away too much when we threw Purgatory clean out of doors" (Forsyth, *This Life*

and the Next, 34.) See further on the issues, Hart, "The Sense of an Ending: Finitude and the Authentic Performance of Life."

24. It is a judgment "according to deeds," as Tom Wright argues. See Wright, *Surprised by Hope*, 152. See also Bauckham and Hart, *Hope against Hope*, 142–143.

25. See Bauckham and Hart, *Hope against Hope*, 144.

26. Matt. 25:41.

27. Bauckham and Hart, *Hope against Hope*, 142.

28. See, for example, Hebblethwaite, *The Christian Hope*, 62f.; John Polkinghorne, *The God of Hope and the End of the World* (London: SPCK, 2002), 126–127.

29. See, for example, Forsyth, *This Life and the Next*, 34f.; Hart, "The Sense of an Ending"; Moltmann, *The Coming of God*, 49–118; Polkinghorne, *The God of Hope and the End of the World*, 127–128.

30. See J. H. Leckie, *The World to Come and Final Destiny* (Edinburgh: T & T. Clark, 1918), 188.

31. The so-called Athanasian Creed, for instance, refers to "everlasting perdition," and the Westminster Confession of Faith (1647) to the "eternal torments" and "everlasting destruction" suffered by the wicked (chapter 33).

32. Richard Bauckham, "Universalism: A Historical Survey," *Themelios* (new series) 4, no. 2 (1979): 48. Among patristic theologians, for example, Irenaeus and Tertullian allude to "eternal fire" (see Leckie, *The World to Come*, 353.) and Augustine (*City of God* 21.9) to "the eternal punishment of the damned." The major Reformers, too, were unequivocal on the matter (see, for example, Luther's *Commentary on Galatians* 3:10, and Calvin's *Institutes of the Christian Religion* 3.21.5), while in the dawn of modernity the New England theologian Jonathan Edwards could present a dualistic patterning of eschatological events not simply as the demand of clear exegesis of relevant biblical texts, but as essential to the aesthetics of the *ordo salutis*, a glorious manifestation of divine justice (see, for example, his famous sermon "Sinners in the hands of an angry God").

33. Leckie, *The World to Come*, 118–119.

34. John Wenham, "The Case for Conditional Immortality," in *Universalism and the Doctrine of Hell*, ed. Nigel M. de S. Cameron (Grand Rapids: Baker, 1992), 187.

35. See, for example, P. T. Forsyth, *The Justification of God: Lectures for War-Time on a Christian Theodicy* (London: Duckworth, 1916), 152.

36. On arguments for and against "conditionalism," see Edward William Fudge, *The Fire That Consumes* (Houston: Providential Press, 1982); Kendall S. Harmon, "The Case against Conditionalism: A Response to Edward William Fudge," in *Universalism and the Doctrine of Hell*, ed. Nigel M. de S. Cameron (Grand Rapids: Baker, 1992); P. E. Hughes, *The True Image* (Leicester: IVP, 1989); Leckie, *The World to Come*; Robin Parry, "'Hell,'" in *What Are We Waiting For? Christian Hope and Contemporary Culture*, ed. Stephen Holmes and Russell Rook (Milton Keynes: Paternoster, 2008); Wenham, "The Case for Conditional Immortality."

37. See further Trevor Hart, "Universalism: Two Distinct Types," in *Universalism and the Doctrine of Hell*, ed. Nigel M. de S. Cameron (Grand Rapids: Baker, 1992). For advocates of a "Christian universalism" see, for example, Leckie, *The World to Come*; J.A.T. Robinson, *In the End God* (London: Fontana, 1968).

38. In this sense, the recent appearance of a publication and Web-based forum exploring the possibility of an "evangelical universalism" is a welcome one. See Gregory MacDonald, *The Evangelical Universalist* (London: SPCK, 2008). The relevant Web site may be found at www.evangelicaluniversalist.com. "Gregory MacDonald" is a pseudonym drawing on the names of two mainstream Christian universalists, Gregory of Nyssa and George MacDonald.

REFERENCES

Baillie, John. *And the Life Everlasting*. London: Oxford University Press, 1934.

Bauckham, Richard. "Universalism: A Historical Survey." *Themelios* (new series) 4, no. 2 (1979): 48–54.

Bauckham, Richard, and Trevor Hart. *Hope against Hope: Christian Eschatology at the Turn of the Millennium*. Grand Rapids: Eerdmans, 1999.

Bebbington, David. "Eschatology in Evangelical History." In *What Are We Waiting For? Christian Hope and Contemporary Culture*, ed. Stephen Holmes and Russell Rook, 75–86. Milton Keynes: Paternoster, 2008.

Berkhof, Hendrikus. *Christian Faith: An Introduction to the Study of the Faith*. Translated by Sierd Woudstra. Revised ed. Grand Rapids: Eerdmans, 2000.

Fergusson, David. "Eschatology." In *The Cambridge Companion to Christian Doctrine*, ed. Colin Gunton, 226–244. Cambridge: Cambridge University Press, 1997.

Forsyth, P. T. *The Justification of God: Lectures for War-Time on a Christian Theodicy*. London: Duckworth, 1916.

———. *This Life and the Next: The Effect on This Life of Faith in Another*. London: Macmillan, 1918.

Fudge, Edward William. *The Fire That Consumes*. Houston: Providential Press, 1982.

Gunton, Colin. *The Actuality of Atonement: A Study of Metaphor, Rationality and the Christian Tradition*. Edinburgh: T & T Clark, 1988.

Harmon, Kendall S. "The Case against Conditionalism: A Response to Edward William Fudge." In *Universalism and the Doctrine of Hell*, ed. Nigel M. de S. Cameron, 193–224. Grand Rapids: Baker, 1992.

Hart, Trevor. "Imagination for the Kingdom of God? Hope, Promise and the Transformative Power of an Imagined Future." In *God Will Be All in All: The Eschatology of Jürgen Moltmann*, ed. Richard Bauckham, 49–76. Edinburgh: T & T Clark, 1999.

———. "The Sense of an Ending: Finitude and the Authentic Performance of Life." In *Faithful Performances: Enacting Christian Tradition*, ed. Steven R Guthrie and Trevor Hart, 167–198. Aldershot: Ashgate, 2007.

Hart, Trevor "Universalism: Two Distinct Types." In *Universalism and the Doctrine of Hell*, ed. Nigel M. de S. Cameron, 1–34. Grand Rapids: Baker, 1992.

Hebblethwaite, Brian. *The Christian Hope* Foundations for Faith, ed. Peter Toon. London: Marshall, Morgan & Scott, 1984.

Hughes, P. E. *The True Image*. Leicester: IVP, 1989.

Leckie, J. H. *The World to Come and Final Destiny*. Edinburgh: T. & T. Clark, 1918.

MacDonald, Gregory. *The Evangelical Universalist*. London: SPCK, 2008.

Migliore, Daniel. *Faith Seeking Understanding: An Introduction to Christian Theology*. Grand Rapids: Eerdmans, 1991.

Moltmann, Jürgen. *Theology of Hope*. Translated by James W. Leitch. London: SCM Press, 1965.

———. *The Spirit of Life: A Universal Affirmation*. Translated by Margaret Kohl. London: SCM Press, 1992.

———. *The Coming of God: Christian Eschatology*. Translated by Margaret Kohl. London: SCM Press, 1996.

Parry, Robin. "'Hell.'" In *What Are We Waiting For? Christian Hope and Contemporary Culture*, ed. Stephen Holmes and Russell Rook, 98–111. Milton Keynes: Paternoster, 2008.

Polkinghorne, John. *The God of Hope and the End of the World*. London: SPCK, 2002.
Rahner, Karl. "The Hermeneutics of Eschatological Assertions." In *Theological Investigations Iv*. New York: Crossroad, 1982.
Robinson, J.A.T. *In the End God*. London: Fontana, 1968.
Wenham, John. "The Case for Conditional Immortality." In *Universalism and the Doctrine of Hell*, ed. Nigel M. de S. Cameron, 161–191. Grand Rapids: Baker, 1992.
Wright, Tom. *Surprised by Hope*. London: SPCK, 2007.

PART IV

THEOLOGY OF CHURCH

CHAPTER 18

CHURCH AND SACRAMENTS

EPHRAIM RADNER

The basic judgment adopted in this chapter is that evangelical ecclesiology is congregationalist in form, and ultimately "free church" in its associative motives and meanings. This is not merely a sociological evaluation. It derives from a consideration of evangelicalism's theological impulses and commitments. To be sure, the structural and theological elements outlined here are not a consistent part of evangelicalism's patrimony. That is part of the tension that lies at the heart of evangelical ecclesiology. The bequests of Luther, Calvin, and some Anglican actors, along with evangelicalism's successful but diverse missionary expansion, all point to variety and nuance as proper descriptors of evangelical ecclesiology. "Most evangelical bodies have essentially a Lutheran, Reformed, and Wesleyan theology into which are blended or grafted Anabaptist ecclesiological elements," as one scholar has written.[1] Nonetheless, the congregationalist framework has inexorably triumphed within evangelicalism, even in traditions ostensibly upholding episcopal polity, like Anglicanism.

This chapter will first trace historically some of the theological building blocks, initiated in the Reformation, that lay behind what became a full-blown evangelical ecclesial atomism. An outline of John Owen's late seventeenth-century Congregationalist ecclesiology will provide an exemplar for later evangelical ecclesial presuppositions. Finally, certain evangelical ecclesiological distinctions and challenges will be enumerated.

Within this essay, sacramentology is not treated separately, largely because such a separate character for Baptism and Eucharist is generally not identifiable in evangelical theology, or (as in evangelical Anglicanism) has had its historical foundations and theological rationales diluted. Furthermore, we should recognize that what evangelical scholars say, for example, about the sacraments, and what evangelical Christians do are often very different, given the lack of common teaching structures within most evangelical churches.

The Origins of Discrete Ecclesial Bodies

How did the indubitably "catholic" ordering of the early church—bishops, councils, systems of sacramental authorization—manage to be theologically dismissed in the Reformation and post-Reformation? Behind this watershed lay a long development in how oppositional reform within the Church was understood, one that overtook its visible structures. The development and implications of this reform dynamic were formally explicated by the end of the seventeenth century on the basis of a refocused appeal to New Testament ecclesiological representations, which gave rise to innovative modern notions of the ecclesial "body."

Sixteenth-century reforming piety had already returned to the New Testament and seen there the image of the "congregation" as the central form of the Church. William Tyndale's translation of *ekklesia* by the word "congregation" (following Luther's change from the previously normal *kirche* to *gemeine*)[2] was deliberate and debated. It was a central feature of the Geneva Bible's profile, and its rhetoric shaped the ecclesiological imaginations of Puritan reformers and their successors.

Tyndale himself recast the shape of the Christian leader into individualist rather than re-presentative sacerdotal terms. Even pope and bishop were equivalent to other Christian individuals (except the monarch!) and should not be obeyed when in error.[3] John Owen would later signal the nature of this shift to reading the New Testament "church" in terms of a congregation made up of individual believers with his discussion of the ecclesial "body" language in the New Testament.[4] If an individual is (hypothetically) utterly isolated from other Christians, he becomes a member of the Church by virtue of believing in Christ, though separated from all community.[5] Visible "bodies," in Owen's exemplary taxonomy, refer to *individuals*, and individual congregations are aggregates of individuals; they do not refer to anything larger. Hence "the Body of Christ" cannot be described in practical terms as subject to religious connections founded upon anything greater than individual belief, animated by one Holy Spirit. In the New Testament, according to this exegesis, "church" refers only to individual church*es*, or conversely, the invisible gathering of the elect, that is, of individual "true" Christians. But, so Owen argued on Reformation exegetical principles, there is no single visible Church in Paul's writing that encompasses all particular congregations.

What became the evangelical definition of the Christian "body" in local terms, whether a return to New Testament understanding or an innovative interpretation, nonetheless stood in contrast to hundreds of years of Western ecclesial self-understanding. Already Augustine had established the claim that the Christian Church was a visible and single "body" embracing multiple congregations. The visible Church, he argued, was a *corpus permixtum*, a "mixed body" of the elect and the nonelect, saints and sinners, though not always visibly distinguishable. And with this notion came the idealistic conception of a true "invisible" Church, which is not coincident with visible members. Augustine himself, however, limited the applicability of the visible/invisible distinction in favor of a borrowed distinction between two "bodies," Christ's and the Devil's.[6] These two conflicting bodies maintain their concrete stature within history. Christ's Body, the Catholic Church, while it does indeed contain within it sinners and those ultimately destined to damnation, nonetheless is a visible Body of visible individual bodies. Its spanning of the temporal-eternal spheres of reality is itself instanced in the sharing of the Eucharist, which is both a "participation" (1 Cor. 10:16; 11:29) in the actual Body of Christ and an enactment of the charity between individual Christians that constitutes the life of that Body as Christ's own graceful agency at work through his Spirit.[7]

Ecclesial and Eucharistic unity for the Western pre-Reformation tradition represent aspects of a single participatory reality "in Christ." This understanding founds all catholic sacramentology in a way that is later set aside by most Protestant and certainly evangelical theology.[8] The Catholic vision involves ecclesial fellowship in and through time as constitutive of the Church's participation in Christ's being. The comprehensive Body of Christ that is the Church struggles within history against the Devil's Body of unbelievers, heretics, and schismatics, a struggle that can be observed and described, and is expressed and supported by sacramental participation in Christ's life. While Augustine's ecclesiology therefore crystallizes the Catholic claim to a visible, historical, and geographically connected Church as Christ's single Body, bound by concrete authoritative structures and sacramental communion, it does so by asserting alternative bodies of religious opposition that vie with one another throughout history and sometimes even infiltrate the one Body of Christ.

Sociologists of religion have theorized a vital religious organization's need for such concrete opposition.[9] But the increasing integration of Christian life within Western Christianity through the mid-fourteenth century, along with its geographic isolation, meant that renewal within the Latin Church was generally carried out through a focus upon "reform" *interior* to the single body of the Church.[10] Often this was understood in terms of a return to the primitive New Testament character of apostolic life. Sometimes it was understood as a transformation of hearts and structures, preceding such a return. The Franciscan renewal of the thirteenth and fourteenth centuries followed both these related trajectories, finding their oppositional energies initially in the general character of human history, but increasingly from within the Church's own ranks. Augustine's Two Bodies were intertwining, and the *corpus permixtum* was becoming, in the eyes of renewal movements, less a limited burden to be borne by the visible Church than a battle being waged within the bare container of the visible Church: ecclesial structures were increasingly being seen as independent of the Two-Body struggle, sometimes aligned with one or the other, but in themselves at best indifferent in their virtue.

The Character of Protestant Ecclesiology

Modern reforming evangelicalism emerges as a religious response to this late medieval sense of the Two Bodies' confusion. John Wycliffe's late fourteenth-century century call to cleanse the Church drew explicitly from the Two Bodies' oppositional ecclesiology, now intimately located within the visible structures of the Church.[11] Wycliffe's desire to see the Church cleansed of corruptions was based on a primitivist New Testament vision. But it included elements that are new to medieval reform movements: along with virtues of simplicity and moral purity, Wycliffe established his reform, and the Church's very constitution, on the foundation of an exclusive scripturalism. His role in the translation of the Bible into the vernacular was one vitally important aspect of this. And with this project, propagated through itinerant "poor" preachers, he ordered the Church's reform according to the free exercise of hearing, receiving, choosing, and finally distinguishing association with the "true" Church.

Luther himself adopted the Two Bodies theology in ways parallel to Wycliffe's. The pope's church was not really the "Church," but the Devil's Body, he claimed, in distinction from the true Church of the Reformers. But as his own understanding of the gospel became more pointed amid increasing ecclesial conflict, Luther also turned more thoroughly to Augustine's view of the *corpus permixtum* as invisible differentiation *within* the visible Body of the true church. From a reformist vision like Wycliffe's that depended on visible moral purity, Luther developed by contrast his characteristic theology of justification by faith that depended on the interior grasp, through the Holy Spirit's agency, of God's promised forgiveness and salvation in Christ. Such faith, he argued, is not accessible to the judgment of other Christians, because it is located in the "heart." It is known only to God, and is in this sense "invisible."[12]

The Church for Luther is thus a gathering of individuals who freely hear, receive, and choose the message of the Gospel. But an important tension is built into this conception. On the one hand, the key "marks" of the Church for Luther are the preaching of the Word and the right administration of the sacraments. These are visibly defined and individually discerned. Furthermore, they are subject to the ordering forces of human structure and modes of authorization, forces that became important for Luther, especially in the wake of ecclesial and social disruption in the latter 1520s. But on the other hand, the marks of the church suffice only for the Church's visible functioning; they are not enough to indicate her invisible integrity and actual truth, which are constituted by the collection of elect individuals whose faith, though genuine, may be hidden to human eyes. The true Church, then, is more properly a "spiritual" reality, still constituted by individuals, but ones who are joined invisibly by a common faith.[13] This emphasis upon individual faith pressed toward an interiorization of religious reality and retreat from material assertions of the Gospel.

Luther himself stoutly resisted this movement in certain key sacramental aspects, stressing, for instance (against more radical reformers like Zwingli), the reality of Christ's offer of his body and blood in the eucharistic elements. Still, even here Luther emphasized the individual believer's need to receive that body on the basis of a divine *promise* humanly embraced, rather than on blunt assertion of an (irrationally convoluted) metaphysical reality, such as the doctrine of Transubstantiation seemed to represent.[14] The logic was now in place to locate the Christian truth apart from bodily realities, and instead within the processes of subjective appropriation. As the reform movement spread, especially in Switzerland and then into other parts of northern Europe, this logic imposed itself on large areas of theological discernment: interior judgment was thought to prevail over external vehicles of authority; the image or sign indicated the interior and invisible *res* or reality, an interpretation that informed sacramental, liturgical, and devotional life; finally, the essential quality of formal and material participatory visions of the Christian life softened and disappeared.[15] In their place, we see associative notions of the Church gather force, as voluntary choices—bound to an interior faith in the Scriptural promises—are seen increasingly to govern the shape of Christian existence and the church's consequent formal meaning.

This logical trajectory moved unevenly in different locales and traditions, from Zwinglian and Anabaptist churches to Calvinist and even Anglican. Calvin himself retained and more fully captured the inherent tension between visible order and the freedom of the individual's interior faith. "Order," as ministerial structure and discipline, were matters of divine "ordinance" for Calvin. Though particular forms might not be unchangeably laid out in the New Testament, both the need and the obligation to submit to some order, "lawfully" imposed within the church, was divinely mandated. An individual's separation from such a lawfully ordered church constituted sinful schism.[16] Calvin could justify separation from Rome, conversely, on the basis that the papal church was no "real" Church but rather a counterfeit body, whose "fundamental" commitments in Word and Sacrament—the two major marks of the Church, as with Luther[17]—were so self-evidently corrupt as to demand ecclesial self-distancing.

But Calvin also claimed, more insistently than Luther, that invisibly marked election, which establishes the gift of faith, locates the sign of Christian identity within the materially inaccessible interior of the individual. Election will coincide (though not exhaustively) with the visible church body, as Augustine argued, yet that body is distinct from it and acts mainly as a forum for the elect's practice of obedience. Calvin's vital sacramental theology, confined to Baptism and the Lord's Supper, maintains a similar tension: obligated Scriptural form (hence the language of "ordinance"), bound to the ethical demand of obedience, is very real, but it serves an invisible and spiritual reality of pneumatically wrought and "heavenly" participation in Christ. The important action of Christian existence takes place in this spiritual realm where the individual is brought close to Christ.[18] Later Reformed devotion around Holy Communion could be as rigorously sublime as Catholic piety (cf. the poetic meditations of the American Puritan Edward Taylor).[19] But by the late seventeenth century, such focus had become so inwardly and subjectively oriented as to become unsustainable ecclesially. This logic will eventually lead to the attenuation of sacramental reality altogether in developed Protestantism and evangelicalism: spiritual intimacy will come to demand the elimination of all form.

Practically, for most Protestants, Luther's anti-Pelagian evangelical center was transformed into various standards of ecclesial and sacramental purity, and the Church's authority was grounded in these. Lutherans moved toward a strict confessional standard, Calvinists toward a complex interplay of moral and penitential standards, and Anabaptists toward a related interplay of moral and public testimonial.[20] These visible standards provided the oppositional force necessary for the maintenance of distinct ecclesial bodies in an era of still often violent Christian mutual encounters. We can see in retrospect the tension of these practical standards with the interiorized character of the Protestant Gospel's effective essence. But this is only because the passage of time and the development of the right social permissions were necessary for a truly evangelical ecclesiology to emerge, one that could disentangle the discrete bodies of the Church's individual believers from larger somatic entities and all their confusing metaphysical and scriptural denominators.

Evangelical Congregationalism: The Example of John Owen

Such resolution emerged with the gradual establishment of social and religious pluralism, especially in England, in the later seventeenth and eighteenth centuries. Here finally a permitted congregationalism could flourish. Political protections granted the free space for individual belief and apprehension of the Scriptures within various transient local communities, ordered by voluntary association. Such Congregationalist polity could nonetheless maintain practical purity, however construed, through the free and constant regeneration of these localities. The primary notion of the Christian "body" was now decidedly individual and denominated: it had to do with particular persons or with particular congregations. The resolution of the tension between external order and interior faith, especially among hostile ecclesial realities, was given in what one might call "evangelical atomism": oppositions are always either internal or local, never global or exhaustive.

The Congregationalist John Owen offered an exemplary exposition of this fully formed ecclesiology. Contemporary theologians have shown new interest in Owen's possible Trinitarian ecclesial vision.[21] More concretely, Owen's peculiar location as an apologist for toleration within the new context of Christian pluralism provided him with the spur to delineate the elements of a modern ecclesiology that remains regnant within contemporary evangelicalism. Owen provides us with a lucid paradigm for what became a shared modern evangelical ecclesiology.

Owen articulates his fundamental ecclesiology in his discussions of schism, for here he attempts to grapple with the tension between the Christian integrity of individual faith and the ambiguous reality of corporate identities.[22] Owen noted that there are three main senses of the Church deployed in the Scriptures: the "mystical body" of the elect; the visible aggregation of those who profess Christ; and finally, particular churches that are localized.[23] Although the notion of the "mystical body" is both traditional and continuous with a range of Catholic and magisterial Reformed senses, Owen was less interested in this entity in large part because it had little historical traction, and could not be applied in a way that brings or directs historical knowledge. To be sure, the "notes" of the Church—for example, perpetuity, infallibility, catholicity, holiness—pertain to the elect of this mystical Body. Such notes may even pertain to the visible church or churches insofar as they contain some of the elect. But the point for Owen was that the "nature" of the Church, according to which we can refer to its particular "notes," is formalized only within individual believers: the Church is "catholic" insofar as she is formed of the elect, but the elect are identified only as individuals.

Practical ecclesiology in this light will be governed by the history of individuals. The elect are "visible," not as parts of a chosen collective, but only as they are identifiable members of particular churches, ordered by individual choices and interactions. What is a Christian? Owen replied: a voluntary member of a particular church.[24] This answer undercuts the overriding significance of election as a category of practical self-understanding, since now individual choice—the exercise of individual will and faith in relation to particular groups of other individual Christians—determines ecclesial order and locates the "true" Christian. Indeed, we see election's general disappearance as a fundamental principle in later evangelicalism. The Roman Catholic idea of the "local church" representing the "fullness" of the Church Catholic is not pertinent here:[25] the local church, rightly conforming to New Testament usage, represents nothing other than its individual members.

This does not, however, humanize a divine reality. The individual Christian is joined to Christ the "head" of the true Church, through the work of the Holy Spirit. Like the American Puritan Edward Taylor, Owen's approach to the Lord's Supper demands an intensity of focus upon this spiritual connection. But it is *spiritual*, in that, following Calvin, Owen insisted on distinguishing the "local body" of Christ, confined to his ascended presence in "heaven," from tangible Christians and their aggregate as the local church. Spiritual "union" is always ordered individually and locally and its fullness is exhausted in such ordering.

One of Owen's distinctive Christological positions is founded on this understanding of individual pneumatic direction, for it describes, more originally, the human life of Jesus.[26] Jesus represents the perfect Individual Believer, whose own life is shaped socially by chosen associations, not by intrinsic memberships. There is no room here for notions of representative ecclesial office (Owen accepts the Reformation principle of the "priesthood of all believers"),[27] or of the Holy Spirit as the "soul" of the Church, or of the Church therefore as having a personality and consequent authority that extends beyond the aggregate of individual relations.

When Owen speaks of "unity" in faith or love, he is not describing some entity that exists independently of the individual believers who hold particularly their faith in Christ and exercise love one to another in particular circumstances. The elect *in fact* believe in common and love one another. But there is no external testimony or structure of love that can prove a criterion for such faith and love apart from the individual acts that embody them. (Hence Owen was willing to accept an established least-common-denominator Anglican statement of faith, if it left individual conscience free to determine particulars.)[28] Furthermore, since no individual can "prove" another individual's lack of the Holy Spirit's directive work in the heart, pneumatic proof remains self-authenticating in purely individual terms. It is just this practical conclusion that someone like Jonathan Edwards mightily struggled to resist, with the result that his own more specifically Puritan ecclesiology became marginalized in evangelicalism's evolution.[29]

Owen's notion of schism is notoriously neat: schism cannot exist among believers by definition, and it cannot be defined according to criteria independent of individual believers and their free choices. One might make bad decisions. But one cannot prove the Spirit's absence in any particular case. To be sure, it is possible to make coherent claims regarding another individual's or another particular church's failure to evidence "truth," for one can and must measure the lives of professing Christians and their churches according to scriptural standards as one understands them. (So, it is possible to conclude that the Roman Catholic Church is reprobate, just as Calvin argued.)[30] But such judgments can only be made by individuals, followed by individual choices for association. Therefore the existence of plural particular churches, ordered by the choices of individual believers, rightly or wrongly, is simply a given within the context of the Christian's historical existence[31] and embodies the exhaustive character of the visible Church. Owen's well-known acceptance of a "protestant" general church—the basis of all future evangelical ecumenical visions—even embracing different forms of polity (like "bishops"), relies on this fundamental ecclesiology of historic plurality, where somatic oppositionalism and the ordered sanctions that express it can now be transfigured into permissive voluntarism.

Owen's resolution of the tension between individual faith and ecclesial structural authority lies, therefore, in affirming ecclesial atomism as the only historic means and form through which Christian faith is exercised. There are continuities between modern evangelicalism and the Reformation. But the discontinuities are fundamental, and their conditions were given in Britain's late seventeenth-century expanding social space for religious and sectarian pluralism.[32] The key distinctive features of evangelicalism vis-à-vis earlier Protestantism, according to David Bebbington—biblicism, crucicentrism, conversionism, and activism—should be viewed as critically shaped by this new political environment that permitted the embodiment of ecclesial atomism as the logical extension of Reformation reconstruals of the Christian faith. The flourishing of evangelicalism within the United States in particular is undergirded by the fruit of this political-ecclesial reordering.

Theologians like Gunton have worried about the "voluntarism" central to this reordering, and have sought to avoid a crude individualistic autonomy by drawing on ecumenical efforts to found ecclesiology upon Trinitarian premises.[33] But although Augustinian soteriology is built upon the transformed human *voluntas* or "will," this has not historically required Augustine's own communion-oriented ecclesiology to sustain or limit it. The Holy Spirit can act individually, and the notion of human election can work itself out individualistically without falling into a necessary Pelagianism. A particular church of individuals, some of whom are efficaciously moved toward salvation through the deployment of their will in faith and faithful works is not problematic, except in social contexts where wills might be coerced. But where love can be freely given and received according to the commands of Christ, no more is required to define the church than the actual historical embodiment of such actions. This is not to say that a catholic Trinitarian ecclesiology of communion poses no challenges to evangelical understandings of the Church—only that the latter's final distillation into a vision of nonoppositional ecclesial atomism has proven internally consistent. Indeed, evangelicalism can function with a consistent ecclesiological focus even when the Trinity is jettisoned altogether as a central theological concept, as in Pentecostal developments that have adopted "oneness" theologies or affirmed a universal pneumaticism across cultures.[34]

Aspects of Evangelical Ecclesial Atomism

Common features of evangelical ecclesiological atomism, manifested in various historical and denominational forms, are as follows.

It Is Scripture-Oriented

Locating the oppositional structure of Christian existence according to scriptural reference, in the Augustinian tradition, meant that the spiritual discernment of the Church was bound to scriptural discipline. As Wycliffe taught, reading the Scripture and associating with the truth were two aspects of the same Christian vocation. They focused in the individual imperative to read, understand, and believe the Word of God written. From such scriptural reading, which can parse true from false, including true Christianity from its counterfeit, the individual Christian is directed to the choice of association with the right ecclesial "body."

To be sure, for Luther as for all Protestants and certainly evangelicals, the central issue of Bible-reading is the discovery of the saving promise of salvation given by God in Christ Jesus, and the individual's eager reception of this promise. But the original Reformation standard for the Church—true preaching of this Word and right administration of the sacraments according to its ordinance—binds this kind of faith to a locality, and orders the hearing of Scripture to its associative direction. Although faith is individual, it is not idealist. It demands a context—that is, a church—that is expressive of the Scripture's own formal distinctions.

It Is Scripture–Based

To some extent, this is why Luther's focus upon the gospel as prior to the Scripture has always proven (even in Lutheranism!) something of a minority position among Protestants. The Reformation originally, and then in its embrace as a social-political legacy within liberal democracy, has had as its logical consequence the demand that individual faith choose its associations. For this, the Bible's comprehensive directive scope has taken center stage in evangelicalism: the church not only "preaches" the Bible so that the core of its message can bring about faith but the church also *reads* and *studies* Scripture as the center of its life. As a "mark" of the Church, Bible-reading by individual believers becomes primary in evangelicalism.

It Requires Internal Assent and Confession (Testimony)

The choice of association is central to the individual act of faith in God's forgiveness in Christ. "Choose this day whom you will serve" (Josh. 24:15) becomes also "Who is on the Lord's side, let him come to me" (Exod. 32:26). Faith takes upon itself the form of the scriptural directive, which is enacted in a series of choices. The evangelical character of "testimony" on the basis of this—analogous to the original Anabaptist public confession of faith—means that the church is constituted by the activity of individual choosing. The "conversionary" character rightly identified as a mark of evangelicalism has its ecclesiological expression in associative choice.

It Features Believer Baptism

Although some evangelical circles (for example, Anglicans and other Reformed churches) accept infant baptism, generally the formal character of choice has determined that baptism represent an active decision-making before the calling of the Word. This has practically precluded baptism of the very young, although there is a range of (often socially influenced) measures among evangelicals as to what constitutes an acceptable maturity of scripturally founded discernment and commitment. More crucially, baptism's meaning is tied to the associative choice—to Christ and to the place where the following of Christ is rightly ordered—it embodies. Evangelicals differ in how they understand the exact nature of the liturgical act of baptism. But there is a general tendency to view baptism's sign-referring character as initiating a life of *repeated* choosing amid obstacles, rather than as a once-for-all choice that ends all choosing. Hence, baptism does not tie one to the Church, but rather founds the ongoing imperative of individual church association according to Scripture.

It Regards the Lord's Supper as Faith-Reminding

If baptism initiates an individual's relationship with Scriptural ecclesial association, the Lord's Supper (by various names) represents a repetitive reminder of its call. More recently the participatory character of the sacrament has been rediscovered by some younger evangelicals, drawing on both Catholic and Calvinist traditions. Still, it is the Zwinglian memorializing view of the Lord's Supper that predominates, even in Anglican circles.[35] Performed with increasing rarity within Protestantism in the nineteenth century, the liturgical act of Holy Communion was generally oriented to Scripture's witness to the work of God in Christ on our behalf in his sacrifice—in Owen's terms, to Jesus' *particular* body broken. This acted to reestablish a focus upon integrity of faith each individual was called to engage. It was logical that "closed communion" proved to be the general evangelical approach, restricting the Supper to those whose lives were somehow recognized as framed by right belief and conduct, that is, by faithful choices. Although closed communion itself has waned as a common discipline over the past decades, this is less because the character of the Supper has become less obvious than because the nature of associative choice has become more ramified, and settled communities are less and less the outcome to faithful decision making. Already in the eighteenth century, we see this pressure mounting in something like the conflict Jonathan Edwards set loose in trying to reassert visible Eucharistic discipline, a battle Edwards himself largely lost. At the same time, liberal (and, to some extent, Methodist) notions of Holy Communion as a "converting" ordinance, that represents a form of teaching to all who come even prior to their choices, have also influenced evangelical thinking, especially among the young.

It Supports Evangelism

The energetic practice of evangelism as a particular ministry within the larger world was a late-comer to Protestantism, historically. But when social conditions permitted its embrace, evangelicals engaged evangelism with unparalleled vigor. At least two important aspects of ecclesiology proved crucial in this development. In the first instance, the oppositionalist decision-making imperative that lies at the root of Protestant existence engages the Christian in a constant restlessness of discernment, association, and finally testimony. This restlessness inevitably engendered the ecclesial mobility that Catholics noted from the start of the Reformation. But this mobility was given an empowering energy that was finally harnessed by developing evangelicalism in the eighteenth and nineteenth centuries, as political freedoms (sometimes imposed by force, as in China at the hands of the British) tore down previous restraints upon the religious search for voluntary associative life. What had begun as local individual regeneration and the search for related communities within Anglo-European churches was politically facilitated so as to include whole societies, and even the world.[36] From Henry Venn's Anglican evangelical missionary principles of autonomous indigenous churches, later taken up by the Church Missionary Society, to the Chinese Inland Mission principles of the "three selves," the evangelistic expansion of evangelical Christianity had a consistent thread: it proved an extension of a peculiar way of viewing the Christian's ecclesial vocation, which was overlaid upon, but then integrated with, the more basic missionary impulse of disseminating the gospel, understood in ways that evangelicalism shared, ironically, with an equally evangelistic Roman Catholicism.[37]

Just this evangelistic ecclesial impulse within evangelical Christianity may prove to be a link back to a faith shared with Catholic Christianity. Especially as martyrdom in the cause of mission has become a centrally noted feature of modern evangelicalism,[38] the common martyrdom of different traditions' servants has proven an ecumenical gift, building a bridge of witness that has been recognized as led by the same Holy Spirit.[39] Not insignificantly, the offering of individual *bodies* by evangelical Christians, through the act of conscious faith, has demonstrated the reality of the Church of Christ as lying beyond denominated spheres. This is one area where the modern obscuring of crucicentrism, in Christianity as a whole, has been checked and perhaps even reversed, as the cross of Christ has been reasserted as the basis for the world's life.

It Embraces Eschatology and Pre-Millennialism

Although the visible church is fundamentally a local congregation, evangelicals can apply the term "Church" more broadly. This larger sense, however, will refer to something outside of historical description and denoted individual choices. The visible character of the "mystical" or "true" Church is revealed only at the end of time. Evangelical ecclesiology in its modern form, as in much Protestant thought, relies heavily on an eschatological orientation when examining the statements of the New Testament regarding the Church "as a whole."

This eschatological orientation informs contemporary evangelical ecclesial developments, as individual associative choices are increasingly geared less to specific congregations and more to the work that will lead into the End Times. Pre-millennialism, which asserts the second coming of Christ Jesus *before* the restoration of all creation, in a time of decay and cataclysm, arose as a theological vision mostly in modern Protestant sectarian contexts. But the vision has been widely disseminated within worldwide evangelical circles partly because of its fit with the broader ecclesial presuppositions of the movement.[40] The full nexus of individual decisions of faith is not historically demonstrable within history as we know it; and these decisions have appeared, over time, less and less measured by congregational contours. Para-church, movement-oriented, and fissiparous affiliative commitments have come increasingly to define evangelical ecclesial life, as individual Christians have chosen to align themselves, in their scriptural discernment, with certain kinds of *ministry support* that is geared toward the eschatological "hastening of the day" (2 Pet. 3:12).[41] Transient congregational membership has increased, even while there has been a search for mission-oriented commitments that sustain God's historical purposes. "Church-shopping" is, on this score, only partly related to consumerist spirituality.[42]

The rise within evangelical churches of the small group or "cell," is another example of this.[43] The small-group movement grew out of eighteenth-century Anglican and Methodist religious societies and "classes," and has responded to needs felt within a secularizing and fragmenting society. More recently, it has partly offset the breakdown of local congregational life, long a mainstay of evangelical practice. But the sharpening of millennial expectation over the past fifty years, especially within that context, has had the ironic consequence of weakening the very means of engaging the scriptural directives of mutual engagement that first grew out of, for example, Wycliffe's renewal, and provided the basis for the congregationalist vigor that impelled evangelical development in the eighteenth century. As commitments to particular congregations become more transient, it has become less possible to choose to love concretely because one is less consistently bound to others. In this way, the Augustinian paradox of the visible Church as a *corpus permixtum* yet also true Body of Christ, to which the Christian is committed *over time*, has reemerged as a specifically Christian challenge to evangelical congregationalism's weakening possibilities for persistent mutual engagement.

Ecclesiological Difficulties

This last observation points to certain challenges to evangelical ecclesiology. Evangelicals have always asserted the primacy of individual faith. They have also sought, and even argued for, visible confirmations and tests for this faith. Nonetheless individual faith has always remained, in theory, inaccessible to others. This leaves to communal view only the concrete decisions that derive from faith, not faith itself. Church life is founded upon and shaped by the reality of such decisions. These can either wholly determine, in their variation, the order and direction of congregational life at any given time, or they can become the objects of contestation or manipulation. Evangelical churches, in their evolved life, have often become arenas for the "test of wills," rather than communities of accountability. An engagement with something like *Baptism, Eucharist, and Ministry* and its ecumenical outline of ecclesial commonality is now due.[44]

Second, the rootedness, continuity, and hence integrity of discipleship, however important, has come under assault. As the larger Western and global culture has appropriated religious life within its consumerist economy, individual choice for scriptural directive has only weakly resisted, falling victim to rapidly changing tastes and even commodified styles. The lack of integrated ecclesial structures within evangelicalism, which might otherwise uphold such resistance, has not been met with alternative individualist habits of consistency. Many rightly wonder if evangelical ecclesiology can weather the demise of a sustaining Christian culture that, at least in early modernity, may have permitted the liberal freedoms of congregational atomism to flourish without disintegrating into religious subjectivism.[45]

The third challenge to evangelical ecclesiology, then, lies precisely in the disappearance of a coherent Christian context in which confession or testimony can prove compelling beyond idiosyncratic assertion.

Some of these challenges are currently being tested in areas of the world where evangelical growth has been wedded to more catholic ecclesial forms, and conversely, where more traditionalist Catholicism has adopted many aspects of evangelical self-understanding (for example, in versions of African Anglicanism and Catholicism). These are areas where cultural patterns have been less open to Western adversarial individualism. These are also areas where the somatic oppositionalism that has fueled evangelical ecclesiology is already built into a social life of endemic economic, political, and cultural dislocation, and where churches themselves, by contrast, still have retained traditional local forms of social solidarity. How this develops, and especially how such alternatives affect evangelical projects and theological self-understandings, remains uncertain. There are signs that even in places like Africa, social change is encouraging versions of evangelical ecclesial life that resemble the West far more closely than in the past.

The rapid spread of evangelical Christianity around the non-Anglo-European world, however, and its flourishing in the face of hostile forces that have occasioned widespread martyrdom in the twentieth and early twenty-first centuries, may well encourage evangelicalism to reappropriate some of its lost catholic ecclesial sensibilities. For, as John Paul II noted, it is just the rediscovery of the Body of Christ as disclosed through sacrificial witness for the faith that is reestablishing a sense of experienced participation in a unified divine life given historically in the Communion of Saints.[46] The retrieval of a fuller Augustinian sacramentology may well lie here, a gift given in a difficult time for the world Church.

In this respect, although all of this suggests that evangelicalism has indeed come to constitute the most adaptive Christian ecclesiology for the modern pluralistic world, its future, along with that of its burgeoning Pentecostal progeny,[47] may well depend on a readaptation of ecclesiology to the form of its catholic roots. For evangelicalism's very success at dissemination may now call again for a Church more vitally understood to be a single Body, capable of integrating individuals into a global communion that is constituted by Christ's own life.

NOTES

1. Howard A. Snyder, "The Marks of Evangelical Ecclesiology," in John G. Stackhouse, Jr., ed., *Evangelical Ecclesiology: Reality or Illusion?* (Grand Rapids: Baker Academic, 2003), 94.

2. See Tyndale's translation (publ. 1526) of Matthew 16:18: "upon this rocke I wyll bylde my congregation"; see the modern edition of W. R. Cooper and David Daniell, for the Tyndale Society (London: British Library, 2000). See also Luther's *Large Catechism*, a. 3.

3. Tyndale, *The Obedience of a Christian Man* (1528).

4. Owen, for instance, sought insistently to restrict the referent of "body of Christ" to Jesus' physical body, and its apprehended representation. See his *Sacramental Discourses* (1669), especially discourses 2 and 9.

5. John Owen, *Of Schism. The True Nature of It, Discovered and Considered* (1657), ch. 4.

6. Augustine, *On Christian Doctrine*, III. 42–55. The two-body distinction has roots in the North African Christian tradition, and here Augustine follows the hermeneutic rules of his compatriot, the Donatist Tyconius.

7. Augustine, *City of God*, 15.1–6; 22.17–18; *Sermons* 227–229 (Augustinian Historical Institute numbering).

8. In terms of baptism's engagement with Christ's death and resurrection, and the Eucharist's engagement with his self-offering (Rom. 6:3f.; 1 Cor. 10:16).

9. See Rodney Stark and William Sims Bainbridge's theory of "high tension" religious movements, in Stark and Bainbridge, *A Theory of Religion* (New Brunswick: Rutgers University Press, 1996).

10. See Gerhart B. Ladner's classic, *The Idea of Reform: Its Impact on Christian Thought and Action in the Age of the Fathers*, rev. ed. (New York: Harper and Row, 1967), esp. part 3.

11. See Wycliffe's, or at least the Wycliffite, summary of the master's ecclesiology, *The Church and Her Members*, in Herbert E. Winn, ed., *Wyclif: Select English Writings* (Oxford: Oxford University Press, 1929).

12. Martin Luther, *Werke: Kritische Gesamtausgabe*, ed. J.K.F. Knaake et al. (Weimar: H. Böhlaus 1883–) 21: 332f.; 46: 11 (hereafter cited as *W.*). *Large Catechism*, a. 3.

13. Luther, *W.* 6: 292, 301.

14. Luther, *The Babylonian Captivity of the Church* (1520), part 1.

15. See Sergiusz Michalski, *The Reformation and the Visual Arts: The Protestant Image Question in Western and Eastern Europe* (London: Routledge, 1993), which is profoundly illuminating on the question of the evaporation of Protestant sacramentology.

16. Calvin, *Institutes*, IV.1.5–8.

17. Though discipline was centrally important for Calvin (see *Institutes* IV.12:1–13), it did not become a "third mark" of the Church until later, among Scottish and English Puritans.

18. Calvin, *Institutes*, IV.17.31.

19. Edward Taylor, *The Poems of Edward Taylor* (New Haven: Yale University Press, 1960).

20. See Balthasar Hubmaier's *A Christian Catechism* (1526), in Denis R. Janz, *Three Reformation Catechisms: Catholic, Anabaptist, Lutheran* (Toronto: Edwin Mellen Press, 1982), 147–156.

21. See Colin E. Gunton, *The Promise of Trinitarian Theology* (Edinburgh: T & T Clark, 2003).

22. Owen, *Of Schism* (1657).

23. Ibid., ch. 4.

24. Ibid., ch. 3.

25. See the Vatican II *Decree on the Pastoral Office of the Bishop* ("Christus Dominus," 1965), 11.

26. Cf. Alan Spence, *Incarnation and Inspiration: John Owen and the Coherence of Christology* (London: T and T Clark, 2007).

27. Owen, *An Exposition of the Epistle to the Hebrews*, ch. 7. The lineage is from Luther and Calvin.

28. John Owen, *Some Considerations about Union among Protestants and the Preservation of the Interest of the Protestant Religion in This Nation* (1680).

29. Jonathan Edwards, *An Humble Inquiry* (1749).

30. Calvin, *The Necessity of Reforming the Church* (1543), and *Institutes*, IV.2.

31. Owen, *Of Schism*, ch. 4.

32. David Bebbington, *Evangelicalism in Modern Britain: A History from the 1730s to the 1980s* (London: Unwin Hyman, 1989); see Michael A. G. Haykin and Kenneth J. Stewart, eds., *The Emergence of Evangelicalism: Exploring Historical Continuities* (Nottingham: Apollos/Inter-Varsity Press, 2008).

33. See also the free church apologist Miroslav Volf, *After Our Likeness: The Church as The Image of the Trinity* (Grand Rapids: Eerdmans, 1997).

34. Amos Yong, *Beyond the Impasse: Toward a Pneumatological Theology of Religions* (Grand Rapids: Baker Academic, 2003); David K. Bernard, *The Oneness of God* (Hazelwood, Mo.: Word Aflame, 1986).

35. For a full discussion of the historical logic at work in this development, see Ephraim Radner, *The End of the Church* (Grand Rapids: Eerdmans, 1998), ch. 4.

36. Andrew Walls, *The Missionary Movement in Christian History* (Maryknoll, N.Y.: Orbis, 1996), ch. 12; and *The Cross-Cultural Process in Christian History* (Maryknoll, N.Y.: 2002), 11–12.

37. In fact, this gives rise to some problems culturally with respect to individual choice, when conversion in some societies cannot support Western versions of autonomous decision making. See J. Waskom Pickett, *Christian Mass Movements in India* (Lucknow: Lucknow Publishing House, 1933).

38. See David B. Barrett's groundbreaking statistical work in publications like the *World Christian Encyclopedia*, 2nd ed. (New York: Oxford University Press, 2001), and more popular works like Paul Marshall's *Their Blood Cries Out* (Nashville: Thomas Nelson, 1997).

39. John Paul II's encyclical on Christian unity, *Ut Unum Sint* (1995), 84–85; also his homily at the May 7, 2000, "Commemoration of Witnesses of Faith."

40. Timothy P. Weber, *Living in the Shadow of the Second Coming: American Premillennialism 1875–1982* (Chicago: University of Chicago Press, 1987).

41. Note the nineteenth-century YMCA work of evangelization in India, for example, that was no longer oriented to building congregations, let alone denominations.

42. The dynamic is visible in nonevangelical churches, too, of course; but probably in part because of the informing power of evangelicalism on the larger religious culture. See the 2008 Pew Forum on Religion and Public Life's *U.S. Religious Landscape Survey*, which confirms earlier work by people such as Robert Wuthnow.

43. Robert Wuthnow, *Sharing the Journey: Support Groups and the Quest for a New Community* (New York: Free Press, 1994); Rad Zdero, ed., *Nexus: The World House Church Movement Reader* (Pasadena, Cal.: William Carey Library Publishers, 2007).

44. *Baptism, Eucharist, and Ministry* is the World Council of Churches' Faith and Order Paper 111 (1982), which remains the most widely embraced statement of ecclesial fundamentals.

45. See the essays in John G. Stackhouse, Jr., *Evangelical Ecclesiology: Reality or Illusion?* (Grand Rapids: Baker Academic, 2003).

46. Cf. "The Communion of Saints: A Statement of Evangelicals and Catholics Together" (2003), published in *First Things*, March 2003. A new appreciation of Bonhoeffer by evangelicals is related to this. Cf. the Baptist appreciation by Mark DeVine, *Bonheoffer Speaks Today: Following Jesus at All Costs* (Nashville, Tenn.: Broadman & Holman, 2005).

47. David Martin, *Tongues of Fire: The Explosion of Protestantism in Latin America* (Oxford: Blackwell, 1990), gave one of the first clear outlines of this evolution.

BIBLIOGRAPHY

Avis, Paul. *The Church in the Theology of the Reformers.* Eugene, Ore.: Wipf and Stock, 2001.

Haykin, Michael A. G., and Kenneth J. Stewart, eds. *The Emergence of Evangelicalism: Exploring Historical Continuities.* Nottingham: Apollos/Inter-Varsity Press, 2008.

Husbands, Mark, and Daniel J. Treier, eds. *The Community of the Word: Towards an Evangelical Ecclesiology.* Downers Grove, Ill.: InterVarsity Press, 2005.

Michalski, Sergiusz. *The Reformation and the Visual Arts: The Protestant Image Question in Western and Eastern Europe.* London: Routledge, 1993.
Owen, John. *The Works of John Owen*, ed. William Goold. Edinburgh: T & T Clark, 1862.
Radner, Ephraim. *The End of the Church: A Pneumatology of Christian Division in the West.* Grand Rapids: Eerdmans, 1998.
Stackhouse, John G., ed. *Evangelical Ecclesiology: Reality or Illusion?* Grand Rapids: Baker Academic, 2003.
Sommerville, C. John. *The Secularization of Early Modern England: From Religious Culture to Religious Faith.* New York: Oxford University Press, 1992.
Utzinger, J. Michael. *Yet Saints Their Watch Are Keeping: Fundamentalists, Modernists, and the Development of Evangelical Ecclesiology, 1887–1937.* Macon, Ga.: Mercer University Press, 2006.
Walls, Andrew. *The Missionary Movement in Christian History.* Maryknoll, N.Y.: Orbis, 1996.
Williams, Daniel H. *Retrieving the Tradition and Renewing Evangelicalism: A Primer for Suspicious Protestants* (Grand Rapids: Eerdmans, 1999).

CHAPTER 19

CHURCH AND CHURCHES: ECUMENISM

WILLIAM J. ABRAHAM

OCTOBER 18, 1966, was a watershed day for evangelicals in Britain. The occasion was the Second National Assembly of the Evangelical Alliance. The crucial players were John Stott, a leading Anglican evangelical from All Souls, Langham Place, and Martyn Lloyd-Jones, a leading independent evangelical from Westminster Chapel. The issue at hand was the relationship between evangelicals and the diverse denominations to which they belonged. After the previous National Assembly, a Commission on Church Unity had been set up to discuss ecumenism, denominationalism, and the possibility of a future United Evangelical Church. At a commission meeting Lloyd-Jones had already indicated that the future for evangelicals lay in leaving their denominations and building a future together. He intimated that he would pursue this line in his upcoming address at the next Annual Assembly. So no one should have been surprised when he pressed home his views with characteristic logic and rhetorical skill.

The audience was astonished when John Stott, breaking convention as chairman, made it clear that he disagreed radically with the call to evangelicals to separate and form a United Evangelical Church.[1] Such was the consternation at the meeting that there is no agreed account of what happened on that momentous occasion.[2] The National Assembly had to be canceled the following year as a direct consequence. Around this public episode one can detect the ecclesiological fissures that continue to lie beneath the surface of evangelical agreement and goodwill.

The dispute was no mere parochial episode in the history of evangelicalism. Stott and Lloyd-Jones are towering figures in modern evangelicalism. Both of them are household names across the world of evangelicalism. As preachers, they were unsurpassed; as organizers, they assembled networks of followers across the globe; as theological teachers, they have left a legacy that can readily stand with earlier leaders within the tradition. Both men exhibited the hallmarks of evangelical piety: a commitment to scripture, a thirst for holiness, a passion for evangelism, a focus on the cross of Christ, and a love for the people of God. Both were also deeply committed to a Reformed version of evangelicalism. In the end they went their separate ways.

Their differences ran deep. Stott stood for staying within the Church of England, working for renewal and reform. Lloyd-Jones rejected this, arguing for separation. Their disagreement makes manifest a turmoil at the heart of evangelical ecclesiology that spills over into radically diverse understandings of evangelicalism itself. In this chapter I shall explore the contours of this turmoil, identify its wider implications for the understanding of evangelicalism, and make some modest suggestions for the future.

Evangelicalism as a movement within Protestantism is best understood as an essentially contested tradition that is instantiated in at least three significantly diverse embodiments over its long historical pilgrimage. It is embodied in the magisterial Protestantism of the Reformation, in the evangelical awakenings of the eighteenth and nineteenth centuries, and in twentieth-century conservative evangelicalism. The differences in ecclesiology that appear in these diverse articulations of the tradition are vital to understanding the recent tensions evoked by ecumenism. The first embodiment of evangelicalism (Magisterial Protestantism) represents the drive to establish a true church according to the scriptures; the second (the evangelical awakenings) represents the drive to transcend the divisions of the Reformation and find unity in a common experience of conversion centered on faith in Christ as Savior and Lord and in common evangelistic ministry; the third (conservative evangelicalism) represents the divided mind of evangelicals as heirs of the earlier embodiments of the tradition and as a reiteration of the tradition in a new context.

The public dispute between Stott and Lloyd-Jones brings to the surface the ecclesial ambivalence within the tradition across its long and tangled history. The position of Lloyd-Jones rearticulated one strain of the Reformed tradition in its quest for a true church marked by discipline and opposed to Roman Catholicism; the position of Stott reaffirmed the reaction against this as seen in the ecumenical and renewalist tendencies of revivalism. My schema is overly simplistic; but this initial summary can help focus sharply what is at stake. Working through the history will enable us to fill out the more complex story that needs to be told.

Contrary to first impressions, evangelicalism is pivotal in the development of ecumenism. By ecumenism I mean here the quest for organic, visible unity of all Christians. It has long been recognized that one expression of ecumenism was the founding of the Evangelical Alliance in England in 1846. Eight hundred evangelical leaders belonging to fifty-two Protestant denominations in the West were in attendance. The aim was to make the invisible church visible. They came together on the basis of a shared experience of faith in Jesus Christ. Although the Alliance faced serious challenges in its first decades due to differences over slavery, it continues to flourish. It began the tradition of a week of Christian prayer, it made plans for the first International Missionary Conference, and it conducted surveys of missionary work throughout the world. All of these were harbingers of the ecumenical movement to come. More important, the Evangelical Alliance provided significant impetus for the establishment of national and regional evangelical fellowships. A century later, in 1951, many of these flourishing fellowships teamed up to form the World Evangelical Fellowship (WEF). Today WEF claims to represent four hundred and fifty million evangelical Christians across the world. Many of those involved in WEF are also heavily involved in the World Council of Churches (WCC), the flagship instrument of the ecumenical movement in the twentieth century. The commitment to ecumenism on the part of WEF is further exhibited in an ongoing consultation with the Roman Catholic Church and in various dialogues with the Orthodox tradition. In this instance, there is no contradiction between being evangelical and being ecumenical.

The relationship between evangelicalism and ecumenism, however, goes deeper than this kind of institutional testimony would suggest. Far from being at odds with ecumenism, evangelicals spearheaded the drive to ecumenism in the early twentieth century. In fact, the evangelical awakenings fostered two developments that led to ecumenism: the discovery of a deep unity across the denominations that developed after the Reformation, and the pioneering of the missionary work that was the driving force behind ecumenism in the twentieth century.

The evangelical awakenings are best seen as a spiritual response to the dead orthodoxy that bedeviled the churches of the Reformation. This is clearly visible in the eighteenth century in the Pietist Movement in Germany, in Methodism in Great Britain, and in the Great Awakenings on the American frontier. The primary focus in the developments was soteriological, the quest for salvation. This is not to say that there was no interest in the great slogans of the Reformation (*sola scriptura, sola fide, solus Christus, sola gratia*), but it is to claim that there was change of key. These slogans and other features of the Reformation (like the quest to build a truly scriptural church) are best seen as background music. The primary concern was the drive toward the deep personal appropriation of the faith as identified in the experience of justification, new birth, assurance, and sanctification. It was not enough to believe in a nominal fashion; it was vital to know inwardly the great truths of the gospel. The experience of salvation could be encountered even where there were significant differences in the faith itself. Thus early Methodism had both a Calvinistic and an Arminian wing; and John Wesley would have loved to have seen a united front among the leaders of the evangelical awakening in England. Common spiritual experience provided a genuine sense of unity across denominational, national, and cultural differences. Ecclesiological differences about worship, polity, and theology were not buried; they were marginalized. The unity experienced in conversion and in working together in evangelism melted the hard edges and fostered a radical change of attitude.

The ecclesiological ambivalence at issue shows up in John Wesley's vision of the church. On the one hand, he is drawn to a true believer's conception of the church, where the church is simply all the true Christians in one place; on the other hand, he remains a loyal son of the Church of England and models Methodism in North America on a revised version of its doctrines, polity, and practices. On the one hand, he founded a movement that in places quickly became one more triumphalist, biblicist effort to establish true Christianity; on the other hand, his heart and mind were set on the renewal and reform of the existing church to which he belonged. It is as if he represents Lloyd-Jones on two days of the week and John Stott the other five. Yet, the ambivalence was really a marginal issue for Wesley; it was not resolved in part precisely because his first priority was the fostering of spiritual experience and the igniting of evangelistic zeal. In these endeavors he was the paradigm for the evangelical awakenings and the form of evangelicalism they embody. The continuation of the awakenings in the revivalism of the nineteenth century did not alter the landscape dramatically. There was an intensification of the drive to social reform that led to new divisions over slavery, but the underlying sense of unity rooted in common experience of the gospel remained intact. The ecumenical undercurrents remained as strong as ever.

If the evangelical experience of grace was one vital source of the drive to unity in the evangelical awakenings, the other was the impetus toward missionary work. The mode of causation in this instance is both direct and indirect. When the London Missionary Society was founded in 1795, it began as a union of Congregationalists, Presbyterians, Methodists, and Anglicans. Some saw in it the funeral of bigotry, for Christians seemed able to bury their denominational and party affiliations in order to win the lost to faith. The founding of the Young Men's Christian Association (Y.M.C.A.) in 1840 and of the Student Christian Movement (SCM) in 1895, represented later expressions of the same spirit. When George Williams was discussing the creation of the Y.M.C.A. with three other young men, he exclaimed: "Here we are, an Episcopalian, a Methodist, a Baptist, and a Congregationalist—four believers but a single faith in Christ. Forward together!"[3] The globalization of the Student Christian Moment in the form of the World's Student Christian Federation was a critical harbinger of the ecumenism.

John R. Mott, who helped form the federation, provided an unintended prophecy of what was to come: "The Federation will... unite in spirit the students of the world and in doing this it will be achieving a yet more significant result—the hastening of the answer to our Lord's prayer, 'that they all may be one.'... Surely there has been no more hopeful development towards a real spiritual union of Christendom than the... Federation, which unites in common purpose and work the coming leaders of the Church and State in all lands."[4] Mott, an American Methodist layman, saw no tension between evangelism and ecumenism. *The Evangelization of the World in This Generation*, the title of one of his books, became a slogan of the Student Volunteer Movement for Foreign Missions. He was tireless in his efforts in mission. He was equally tireless in ecumenical work. In 1913 he chaired the conference on reunion among the different branches of the Syrian

Church in India. By means of his extensive travel in Greece, the Balkans, and Russia, he played a central role in bringing the Orthodox Church into the ecumenical movement. Moreover, he saw in the student organizations a model for ecumenical relations. He saw there "the idea of a new type of Christian organization, a new conception of the basis on which Christians belonging to different Churches might unite to win the world for Christ—on an 'interdenominational' rather than 'undenominational' basis."[5]

From this brief sketch we can see how the missionary movement spawned within evangelicalism in the Great Awakenings had a direct impact on the drive to ecumenism. It drew Christians together across denominational boundaries; it reinforced the vital evangelical experience of grace that marginalized barriers to unity; it moved them beyond mere pragmatism to initial theological convergence; it supplied models for future forms of ecumenism; and it made available a host of future leaders. John R. Mott was, in fact, just one of a host of figures in the SCM who become pivotal leaders of ecumenism. The more dramatic role played by the missionary movement within evangelicalism, however, was indirect. The experience of the missionary movement on the field drove its leaders to intensify the quest for unity in order to further the cause of the Gospel throughout the world. Whereas in the early period divisions were tolerated, they were now excoriated as an impediment to the spread of Christianity. Many missionaries saw the disunity of the church as a deep hindrance to evangelization; host cultures were put off by the divisions among Christians; unity itself was seen as a vital step toward more effective missionary activity.

The turning point in the emergence of ecumenism was the famous World Missionary Conference held in Edinburgh in 1910. As Kenneth Scott Latourette noted, "Edinburgh 1910 summed up and focused much of the previous century's movement for uniting Christians in giving the Gospel to the world. Its membership and leaders were predominantly from the societies which had arisen from the religious awakenings within Protestantism in the preceding century and a quarter."[6] Edinburgh 1910 not only built on past achievements in evangelism and unity, it also "prepared for the turbulent years which lay ahead, blazed new trails in Christian fellowship and co-operation, and enlisted and inspired men who were to become outstanding in the ecumenical movement in later years."[7] In time, Edinburgh 1910 spawned the International Missionary Council, the World Conference on Life and Work, and the World Conference on Faith and Order. The latter two groups came together to form the World Council of Churches that was established in its first Assembly in Amsterdam in 1948. The International Missionary Council joined later in 1961. The crucial point to register is now clear: right up to and including the creation of the World Council of Churches, the flagship institution of the ecumenical movement, evangelicals had a central role in ecumenism.

This is not to say that evangelicals had no misgivings or that some were not resolutely opposed to ecumenism. There is a strong divisive and sectarian streak within evangelicalism across its history; the proliferation of evangelical churches across the world is ample testimony to this.[8] In fact, the very success of the ecumenical movement as represented by World Council of Churches awakened some from their ecclesiological, if not sectarian, slumbers. Another factor causing alarm was increasing openness to the Roman Catholic Church. When it was clear that a massive change of spirit was also afoot with respect to unity within Vatican II, then the worries were bound to intensify. Opponents were given their chance to counterattack when the World Council faltered in its commitment to evangelism. The Uppsala Assembly of the WCC, in the words of Donald McGavran, was in danger of forgetting the two billion who had never heard the name of Christ. "By the 'two billions' I mean the great number of persons, at least two billion, who either have never heard of Jesus Christ or have no real chance to believe on Him as Lord and Saviour. These inconceivable multitudes live and die in a famine of the word of God, more terrible by far than the sporadic physical famines which occur in unfortunate lands."[9] McGavran's criticism was actually aimed at changing the direction of the WCC. When his comments did not have the desired effect, and it looked to many as if the WCC had settled for a leftist sociopolitical missionary agenda, the stage was set for evangelicals to develop their own world conferences on evangelism.[10] They had already begun this process in Berlin 1966; they followed up with Lausanne 1974 and a host of local Lausanne Consultations thereafter across the continents.

Given the perceived loss of commitment to evangelism within ecumenism, it was only to be expected that many evangelicals would in time turn against ecumenism itself. Thus since the nineteen sixties it has been common to see evangelicals and ecumenists as opposing groups. To be evangelical is to be anti-ecumenical; to be ecumenical is to be anti-evangelical. It meant very little that the WCC made significant efforts to engage its evangelical critics. John Stott was, in fact, given a prominent role at the Nairobi Assembly in 1975. He was also heavily involved in a round of formal dialogues with Roman Catholicism on mission.[11] Nor did it seem to matter that the Lausanne 1974 Conference refused to endorse all the criticisms of the WCC; a vocal minority from the Third World insisted that issues of justice and oppression be incorporated into the mission of the church. A combination of historical amnesia, polemical politics, sensational press coverage, and genuine rejection of ecumenism on the part of influential evangelical leaders ensured that the split between ecumenism and evangelicalism would remain the stereotype for most observers.

We can approach the challenge from another angle. In their theology of the church, evangelicals have long agonized over how best to handle the balance between personal evangelism and social action. The debate can easily become a sterile affair. When it flared up in the context of ecumenism, however, it became a trip wire for deeper questions about the nature and not just the mission of the church. To change metaphors, we might say that there was an accident waiting to happen. When it did happen in the confrontation between Stott and Lloyd-Jones in 1966, some did not want to leave the scene of the accident.

In his own way, Lloyd-Jones was utterly committed to the unity of the church. The problem was that Stott and many other evangelicals rejected his vision of unity. Despite a host of shared theological commitments on the authority of scripture, on doctrine, on conversion, on mission, and even on the privileging of Reformed theology, they could not agree on the nature of the church. Lloyd-Jones was committed to a congregationalist, disestablished, and more purist conception of the church. Stott was committed to an episcopal, established, and mixed conception of the church. Hence they could not agree on a strategy of action for renewal. Lloyd-Jones felt that the time had come to abandon the way of internal reform and ecumenism, and for evangelicals to come together in a fellowship of local churches that would reject the apostasy of the mainline traditions. Stott was convinced that the future lay in patient, resilient renewal and reform from within; and as a loyal Anglican he did not accept the charge of apostasy; so long as the Church of England had not repudiated its canonical doctrine, charges of apostasy were misplaced. Lloyd-Jones had his own canon of heroes who vindicated his vision; Stott had an alternative canon. Lloyd-Jones had his own reading of the Reformation and the evangelical awakenings; Stott had a very different reading. Lloyd-Jones had carefully worked out his own exegetical grounds for his judgments; Stott had done exactly the same. It certainly did not help that Lloyd-Jones was Welsh and Presbyterian to his finger tips, and that Stott was the quintessential Englishman and Anglican; however, the deeper fissure lay in the opposing visions of the nature of the church. Both leaders had long pondered the challenge of ecclesiology; both had reached a point in theory and practice where reconciliation was impossible.

In the short term, Stott was more than vindicated on the English scene. At the time he challenged Lloyd-Jones, he had been at work preparing for the National Evangelical Congress at Keele in 1967 for Anglican evangelicals. David Bebbington sums up the impact of Keele in dramatic fashion: "The place of Keele in the development of evangelicalism in the Church of England has been compared to that of the Second Vatican Council in the Roman Catholic Church."[12] At Keele, Anglican evangelicals set their face toward an agenda of openness and engagement; they rejected a strategy of withdrawal and isolation. Since then, they have multiplied and diversified into broad, mainstream, and charismatic streams of evangelicalism. They have produced a raft of scholars and bishops; they have taken up a vigorous agenda of social action without compromising the gospel; they have sustained a network of significant theological colleges and institutions; and they have stayed the course on the commitment to evangelism. Even in the midst of divisive turmoil over homosexuality, they continue the bedrock work of Christian ministry in a host of effective parishes anchored in Scripture and the rich evangelical tradition of the church since the Reformation.

The division within mainline Protestantism over homosexuality vindicates prima facie those critics who say that the strategy of the evangelical Anglicans and its correlative ecclesiology has failed. Iain Murray has made the case afresh for the ecclesiology of Lloyd-Jones.[13] He rejects comprehensiveness, reading it as a fatal compromise with heresy and apostasy; he catalogues the failure to bring about significant reform from within; he highlights how openness has led to novelty and passing fashion; he reiterates the classical Protestant objections to Roman Catholicism; and he laments the slippage from the inspiration and inerrancy of scripture among evangelical scholars and theologians. The initial and perhaps primary worry is that evangelicals are once more going the way of Schleiermacher and nineteenth-century liberal Protestantism. What is at issue now is not just the nature of the church but the very meaning of what it is to be a Christian. The stakes have been raised as high as they could be.

The deep divisions I have charted within English evangelicalism are multiplied beyond number throughout the wider evangelical community across the world.[14] This is true diachronically as well as synchronically, historically as well as geographically. Historically, evangelicals have never agreed on the kind of comprehensive theology that would permit consensus on the nature of the church and a correlative vision of unity. The attempt to develop some kind of pure evangelical line that runs from Paul through Augustine, Luther, Calvin, Wesley, Finney, and Warfield to Billy Graham is a fantasy. The expansion and diversification of evangelicalism across the globe in radically different contexts make it abundantly clear that consensus is even less likely in the near future than in the past. The evangelical tradition never has been a monolithic movement; it is even less so once we factor in ethnic and racial diversity and the emergence of Pentecostalism. Moreover, there is no *magisterium* to settle controversies or impose order and discipline; many evangelicals would be the first to be skeptical of the creation of hierarchies possessing epistemic or executive authority. Even consensus on the essentials of evangelicalism is always short-lived.

At times the internal disagreements run so deep that it is tempting to dismiss evangelicalism as hopelessly chaotic and unstable. Furthermore, disputes about definition, identity, and continuity can readily become occasions for ugly power politics over the ownership and control of various constituencies. It would be a mistake, however, to dismiss evangelicalism as a useless category for understanding Christianity; without it we would have to invent a functional equivalent immediately. Evangelicalism represents a network of Christians bound together by a loose but identifiable cluster of convictions and practices that have been and continue to be a potent religious force. It cannot be defined out of history by verbal fiat. As we have seen, evangelicals have played a pivotal role in the search for church unity; we can expect that many will continue to do so in the future. Even the intense and long-standing disagreements about the nature of the church itself can have a salutary role in the quest for the unity of the church. If nothing else, they shatter any utopian fantasy about the quest of unity; ecumenical pessimists can be forgiven for saying that they show that visible unity is simply not attainable.

We have also seen heretofore that two considerations drove evangelicals toward visible church unity in the past. On the one hand, there was a shared sense of believing and experiencing the same gospel, despite differences in what was at stake in being fully formed in the Christian faith. On the other, there was a common passion to work together to take the gospel to the world. Future developments in ecumenism could well be built afresh on these twin commitments. However, before we look at the future, it is important to get our bearings on the current state of play in ecumenism.

At one level, ecumenical work would appear to be on life support, if not brain dead. The enthusiasm that marked ecumenism in the 1960s has evaporated. Ecumenism no longer arouses interest among students; mainline church leaders are preoccupied with survival and growth; and the standard instruments of unity (the World Council of Churches and the various national councils of churches) have become marginalized. Truth be told, we are likely to see further division within the churches, as is exemplified in the case of the Anglican Communion. In these circumstances we are more likely to see a fresh quest for denominational identity, as continuing and breakaway groups hammer out the doctrines and practices that will secure their identity. The United Methodist Church, for example, is currently in search of a new identity as a global, mainline Protestant denomination. Over against this, a new generation of evangelicals has gone postmodern and revels in the fragmentation involved; they are happy to get together and simply see what emerges. Yet others are preoccupied with postcolonial developments and are drawn into identifying new sources of division along sociopolitical lines. So those who have given up on ecumenism have our sympathy.

However, this catalogue of woe from an ecumenical standpoint is not the whole story. For one thing, the ecumenical movement has totally changed the landscape within Christianity. The old divisions, animus, and triumphalism that kept Christians apart have not disappeared, but they are no longer fully operative. Christians are thrown together in civil society; they are constantly absorbing the resources of each other's traditions with delight and gratitude; they are internalizing the criticisms of each other; they collaborate in a host of ad hoc and formal cooperative ventures. While the drive to engage in official dialogues may have dried up, the theological fruits of a century of discussion are significant. The Joint Declaration on Justification, to take one example, is an extraordinary achievement despite the misgivings that rumble around it. Equally important, the Roman Catholic Church has committed itself irrevocably to the work of ecumenism. On this front, Pope John Paul II's encyclical *Ut Unum Sint* represents a major shift, in that the Vatican genuinely and humbly opened its doors to substantial dialogue about how it might best serve the cause of Christian unity.[15]

Many evangelicals have criticized the ecumenical movement on the grounds that it sacrificed doctrine to experience or common service. In truth, the ecumenical movement has invested incredible amounts of energy in attempting to reach doctrinal agreement. One of the deepest challenges in ecumenism has been the quest for appropriate doctrinal consensus; and there is no end to this challenge in sight. Evangelicals should have no difficulty in understanding this. The challenge to find doctrinal agreement within the ecumenical movement has been as difficult as it has turned out to be within evangelicalism across its history. Even when there is considerable basic agreement, the differences seem neuralgic and nonnegotiable. The lesson to be learned from this is obvious. Persistent disagreement does not undermine the unity that clearly exists among Christians; nor does it prove that visible unity should not be pursued; it shows what many knew from the beginning, namely, that the quest for unity is extraordinarily difficult. It is natural to become exhausted in the effort to achieve unity; but this represents a natural turning point in the process; it need not signal the end of the quest. At this point we need to make a virtue of necessity and look upon the retreat to foundational definitions and identity-conferring, nonnegotiable commitments as the starting point of fresh exploration. What we have discovered is that both evangelicalism and Christianity are essentially contested realities whose unity is much more difficult to secure than even the most ardent pessimist believed. We need a deeper and more historically grounded realism.

Essential to this realism is the recognition that from the beginning of the ecumenical movement it was obvious that radical differences in doctrine, ecclesial structures, and practices would sooner or later take center stage in the quest for unity. The danger of losing sight of evangelism and the concomitant temptation to substitute secular conceptions of mission were waiting in the wings to seduce unwary ecumenists who had forgotten the birth pains of ecumenism. The problem was neatly captured by one of the great evangelical leaders of the twentieth century, Bishop Stephen Neil. In the epilogue to *A History of the Ecumenical Movement, 1517–1948*, he wrote:

> One of the chief problems of the ecumenical movement in the mid-20th century is that occasioned by the separation between its essential components. This *History* has shown at point after point the intimate connection between the missionary work of the Church and the ecumenical ideal. Throughout, the word "ecumenical" has been used to designate the efforts of Christians to seek and promote unity; but it should now be plain to the reader that these efforts are not ends in themselves: the aim of Christian union is *that the world may believe.* The world includes the non-Christian world as well as Christendom. Evangelism, missionary work, the proclamation of the Gospel to earth's remotest end, are not extras or fringes on the ecumenical movement; they are essentials without which its true nature cannot be grasped. Unhappily, in the thought of the Churches the two aspects have not always been held together.[16]

This measured assessment can serve as the cue for ruminating afresh on the role of evangelicals in the future of ecumenism.

At the outset, evangelicals need to come to terms with their important role in the origins of ecumenism. Positively, evangelicals need to recognize that they were very important but not exclusive agents in the creation of the ecumenical movement in the first place; they were, at the very least, midwives in the delivery room. It is to their credit that they were often ahead of the times in recognizing the imperative of the quest for unity among Christians. They should be delighted that their wisdom has been shared by mainline Protestantism, Roman Catholicism, and Eastern Orthodoxy. Negatively, evangelicals should shed their defensiveness with respect to the ecumenical movement. This means they need to suppress their gloomy conservative instincts and refuse to be intimidated by those within evangelicalism who have used the challenge of ecumenism to further their own sectarian and divisive goals. Evangelicals have no need to apologize for a hearty commitment to ecumenism. They should see the ecumenical movement as a crucial renewal movement in the contemporary church; they should look upon it as the work of the Holy Spirit. Given their own tangled and volatile history, they should be alert to the dangers of institutionalism in the second and third generations. Rather than engage in one more despairing jeremiad, they should help reignite the engines of the ecumenical train.[17]

Furthermore, evangelicals should boldly develop ways to reconnect ecumenism to evangelism and mission. At this stage in the journey, we need to give serious attention to working together in mission rather than simply develop more position papers. This is not to say that the demanding work of dialogue and consensus building should not continue. The whole raft of church-dividing issues—both old and new—requires painstaking theological investigation and resolution. Evangelicals have come sufficiently of age as biblical scholars, historians, theologians, and missiologists to give leadership rather than sit pouting on the sidelines. Engaging in this work can be a catalyst for intellectual work that reconnects the academy with the church. It can also inhibit the functional atheism that so readily becomes the hallmark of reductionist forms of scholarship. However, we are now at the point where we need to go beyond intellectual endeavor and work together as one in evangelism and mission. On this front we need bold new initiatives.

Consider, for example, the creation of a new ecumenical order of evangelists who could work together across the churches. Let's call it the Order of St. Patrick and St. Nina. Imagine a network of evangelists committed to the same gospel, formed together in the canonical faith of the church, trained in the practices of evangelism, following a common rule of life, and intoxicated with the energy of the Holy Spirit. Imagine an Order endorsed at the highest levels by the churches. Imagine members of the Order working in prisons, rebuilding dying, dysfunctional congregations in changing neighborhoods, holding special evangelistic missions in healthy congregations, reaching into the youth culture, and working among the hard-to-reach. The Order would be committed to a robust conception of evangelism, that is, the proclamation of the gospel and initial formation in the canonical faith of the church. Converts would be sent into appropriate local congregations. The converts formed would, it could be hoped, be sufficiently strong to survive the hostility of contemporary culture, and sufficiently sensitized to the *adiaphora* of the Christian faith to help Christians come to terms with the complexity of ecumenism.

Such work could well enable the churches to develop a whole new angle of vision on the content and nature of doctrine, a thorny site of ecumenical discussion. The great creeds of the church were not developed by professional theologians trying to get tenure in the academy; nor were they doctorates in the epistemology of theology. They were hammered out by hard-pressed evangelists and teachers who needed to provide a meaty summary of the faith for those coming to Christ for the first time. Facing up to this could lead to the recovery of the soteriological and salutary character of Christian teaching. In turn, this could revolutionize systematic theology by recapturing the original purpose of systematic theology as a further critical exploration of the faith beyond initial Christian initiation. Equally important, it could lead to appropriate work in apologetics and cultural contextualization that would keep in mind the need to be faithful to the gospel and the deep faith of the church; this would undercut the temptation to develop hasty forms of translation into the cognitive categories of the host culture.

We might even hope that this kind of work could get the churches beyond some of the current impasses in ecumenism that have caused so much despair about the prospects for the visible unity of Christians. One such impasse is the requirement that Christians agree to a particular vision of authority as a condition of visible unity. Consider the extraordinary attention that has been given to resolving disputes about the foundations of Christian belief. Two assumptions have governed this procedure. First, it has been assumed that agreement on epistemology is constitutive of Christian and ecclesial identity.[18] Second, it has been posited that agreement on epistemology would enable us to resolve other outstanding disagreements in theology and practice. Both of these assumptions are highly questionable. The first posits agreement in the epistemology of theology as essential to unity; on the contrary, this is a sure recipe for continued disunity. The truth is that historically the church reached agreement in the early centuries on the essentials of the faith without reaching agreement on authority, the relation between faith and reason, or the epistemology of theology. The second assumption rests on a highly dubious thesis, namely, that agreement on method or epistemology will lead to the resolution of particular disputes. On the contrary, this is an illusion fostered by modern projects in epistemology; it is more often the case that agreement on method or epistemology only arises on the other side of agreement on particular judgments.

The history of evangelicalism and the divisions from which it suffers amply bear out this analysis. Agreement on authority has not at all led to the resolution of disputed questions; it has simply multiplied the disputes and fostered internal division. Indeed, granting primacy to the epistemology of theology as enshrined in various debates about the authority of scripture has caused many evangelicals to defect from the movement, and, in a host of cases, to abandon the faith entirely. Reflecting on such phenomena should lead evangelicals to engage in the kind of metalevel inquiry that can reframe the debate about ecclesial differences, about what is constitutive of the church, and about what is essential to Christian initiation. This is painful work intellectually, spiritually, and theologically; yet it is essential if we are to pursue the quest for unity among evangelicals, not to speak of the quest for unity among Christians more generally.

None of this suggests that Christians should abandon their current identities; nor should they cease to engage in work of the highest order in the epistemology of theology. All ecumenical work rests on transparency about identity and in following wherever the conversation leads. Moreover, many evangelicals have become aware of the revolutions in epistemology that have emerged after the collapse of classical foundationalism. They are well placed to provide critical leadership in this domain. Within this work, they have rightly recovered the critical place of the Holy Spirit in coming to knowledge of God.[19] In this regard they have not just stumbled into a neglected topic in the epistemology of theology; they have stumbled into what may be the key to all our ecumenical endeavors.

It is no accident that it was the evangelicals of the Great Awakenings who became pioneers of the ecumenical movement. The hallmark of these awakenings was the rediscovery of the work of the Holy Spirit in the human heart under the proclamation of the Gospel. Ecumenism will flourish again when we attend to the fullness of the work of the Holy Spirit in the aftermath of the Incarnation. This makes immediate room in the life of the church for scripture, for the quest for holiness, for guidance and power in ministry, and for the standard practices of piety that have been so central to all forms of evangelicalism. However, it also creates space for openness to those institutional instruments of unity that have all too readily been dismissed in the manner of a functional atheism as a terrible fall into institutionalism and early Catholicism. In the long run there can be no visible, organic unity without ecclesial structures furnished by the Holy Spirit. Securing these structures without abandoning the other inimitable gifts of the Spirit we already possess is a desideratum of future ecumenical work. It will take much waiting upon the Holy Spirit, a hallmark of all forms of authentic evangelicalism, to gain this highly disputed goal.

NOTES

1. D. M. Lloyd-Jones, "Evangelical Unity: An Appeal," in *Knowing the Times* (Edinburgh: Banner of Truth Trust, 1989), 246–257.

2. For contrasting accounts, see Iain H. Murray, *Evangelicalism Divided* (Edinburgh: Banner of Truth Trust, 2000), 45–50, and Timothy Dudley Edwards, *John Stott, A Global Ministry* (Downers Grove, Ill.: InterVarsity Press, 2001), 65–71.

3. Ruth Rouse and Stephen Charles Neill, eds., *A History of the Ecumenical Movement, 1517–1948* (Philadelphia: Westminster Press, 1954), 327.

4. Ibid., 341.

5. Ibid., 342.

6. Kenneth Scott Latourette, quoted in Rouse and Neill, eds., *A History of the Ecumenical Movement, 1517–1948*, 341.

7. Ibid., 356–357.

8. For this tendency within Anglicanism, see Grayson Carter, *Anglican Evangelicals, Protestant Secession from the* Via Media, *c1800–1850* (Oxford: Oxford University Press, 2001).

9. Quoted in T. V. Philip, *Edinburgh to Salvador, Twentieth Century Ecumenical Missiology* (New Delhi: CSS & ISPCK, 1999), 103.

10. In reality what was at issue was the contested place of commitment to justice in ecumenical work.

11. See Basil Meeking and John Stott, eds., *The Evangelical-Roman Catholic Dialogue on Mission, 1977–1984* (Grand Rapids: Eerdmans, 1986).

12. Quoted in Peter Baron, "The Case against REFORM," in Charles Yeats, ed., *Has Keele Failed? Reform in the Church of England* (London: Hodder and Stoughton, 1995), 67.

13. Murray, *Evangelicalism Divided.*

14. It would be difficult to overestimate the negative role played by dispensational theology (a hallmark of much North American evangelicalism) on the very idea of church unity.

15. Ironically, this openness is accompanied by a tendency to shut down critical voices inside Roman Catholicism. See Michael Fahey, S.J., "Magisterium," in Gerard Mannion and

Lewis S. Mudge, eds., *The Routledge Companion to the Christian Church* (New York : Routledge, 2008), 529–532.

16. Rouse and Neill, eds., *A History of the Ecumenical Movement, 1517–1948*, 730. Emphasis in the original.

17. The creation of the Global Christian Forum represents an important new innovation in developing instruments of unity. See http://www.globalchristianforum.org.

18. The constant reference to a problem of "authority" masks the issue as epistemological in nature.

19. See, for example, Paul K. Moser, *The Elusive God: Reorienting Religious Epistemology* (Cambridge: Cambridge University Press, 2008).

BIBLIOGRAPHY

Abraham, William J. *Canon and Criterion in Christian Theology.* Oxford: Clarendon Press, 1998.

———. *The Logic of Evangelism.* Grand Rapids: Eerdmans, 1989.

Dayton, Donald W. *Discovering an Evangelical Heritage.* New York: Harper and Row, 1976.

Gillies, Donald. *Unity in the Dark.* London: Banner of Truth Trust, 1964.

Lloyd-Jones, D. M. *Knowing the Times.* Edinburgh: Banner of Truth Trust, 1989.

Manwaring, Randle. *From Controversy to Co-existence: Evangelicals in the Church of England, 1914–1980.* Cambridge: Cambridge University Press, 1985.

McGrath, Alister. *Evangelicalism and the Future of Christianity.* Downers Grove, Ill.: InterVarsity Press, 1995).

Murray, Iain. *Evangelicalism Divided.* Edinburgh: Banner of Truth Trust, 2000.

O'Gara, Margaret. *The Ecumenical Gift Exchange.* Collegeville, Minn.: Liturgical Press, 1998.

Rouse, Ruth, and Stephen Charles Neill, eds. *A History of the Ecumenical Movement, 1517–1948.* Philadelphia: Westminster Press, 1954.

Stott, John. *Evangelical Truth: A Personal Plea for Unity, Integrity, and Faithfulness* (Downers Grove, Ill.: InterVarsity Press, 1999).

CHAPTER 20

WORSHIP

JOHN D. WITVLIET

Interrelated Meanings of the Term "Worship"

In evangelical usage, the English term "worship" conveys multiple, interrelated meanings, each reinforced by their use in English translations of the Bible and in the history of evangelical sermons, hymns, theological treatises, and devotional guides.[1]

First, the term is used to refer to a God-pleasing and God-focused way of life. Rom. 12:1–2 calls believers to "present your bodies as a living sacrifice" which is "spiritual worship." Used in this broad sense, worship involves loving God "with heart, soul, mind and strength," resisting evil, and obeying God's will through the power of the Holy Spirit. In contemporary writings, this sense of the term is sometimes conveyed through the phrases "24/7 worship" or "worship in all of life."

Second, the term is used to refer to specific actions that intentionally adore, magnify, and praise God, both inside and outside public worship services. This sense of the term closely matches the etymology of "worship," from the Middle English *weorthscipe*, which refers to an act which "ascribes worth" to someone or something. Acts of explicit adoration are modeled in many Psalms, in various theophanies (e.g., Ex. 3, 33, Is. 6, Ez. 1), and in the grand canticles of Revelation (Rev. 4, 5, 7). This adoring affirmation of God arises not merely from human beings but also from all creation (Ps. 98, 148).

Third, the term is used to refer to a public assembly, liturgy, or ritual event, as in a "worship service." Most English Bibles use the term "worship" to translate the words of the Samaritan woman "our ancestors worshiped on this mountain" (John 4:20), a reference to a particular ritual event. The Bible includes several texts that describe liturgical actions, or reflect on their nature and purpose, including descriptions of the individual sacrifices of Abel, Noah, Abraham, Isaac, and Jacob, the sacrificial rituals of the tabernacle and temple, and the covenant renewal liturgies led by Moses, Joshua, and Nehemiah. The New Testament features references to synagogue prayers and sermons, as well as explicit instructions for the liturgical actions of the Lord's Supper, speaking in tongues, prayer, and song. Also significant are biblical descriptions of false worship represented by Cain, the worship of the golden calf, the prophets of Baal, and those who participate in idol feasts.

The history of evangelical worship can be understood as a series of repeated attempts to reintegrate each of these three meanings as part of the Christian life. If there is anything that unites the astonishingly wide range of evangelical worship practices, it is evangelicalism's deep resistance to ritualism, ceremonialism, or anything else that disengages corporate ritual action (the third meaning) from either an all-pervasive orientation to God's service (the first meaning) or heartfelt acts of adoration (the second meaning). Although evangelical corporate worship practices range widely from the informal to formal, from "high church" to "low church," evangelicals are unified in insisting that external acts of worship be "from the heart" and connected with integrity to all of life.

At times, this emphasis has led evangelicals to downplay the significance of worship assemblies. This in turn has generated a series of responses, well represented by A. W. Tozer's famous complaint that "worship is the missing jewel of the evangelical church," and Robert E. Webber's resistance to passive or merely cognitive worship with the claim that "worship is a verb."[2]

Biblical Motifs in Evangelical Theologies of Worship

Throughout the history of evangelicalism, preachers, theologians, and poets have drawn on a wide range of scriptural teaching about worship. One distinctive feature of evangelical approaches is sustained attention to the wide range of worship-related biblical texts.[3] While some streams of evangelicalism have downplayed the value of historical interpretations of scripture, several recent streams of thought insist that faithful interpretation requires learning from both the history of interpretation as well as from readings of the texts from many cultures.[4]

Old Testament descriptions of worship at altars, the tabernacle, and the temple introduce the central motif of holiness, and depict practices mandated by God in which certain holy places, persons, actions, and festivals would restore holiness to the life of God's people—who in turn were called to embody holiness for the nations. The first four commandments (Ex. 20:1–4) offer a succinct foundation for a theology of worship: worship is due to God alone (first commandment), without superstitiously linking God with any object (second commandment), with attention to the character of God, without any flippant or disrespectful language (third commandment), and through Sabbath observance that sanctifies the marking of time (fourth commandment). The Psalms model an approach to worship that is not an act of self-achievement or an act of obeisance to placate a deity. Instead, Psalmic poetry offers scripts for a personal covenantal encounter between the people and their Lord, including both God-humanward actions which announce and confirm covenantal promises, and human-Godward covenantal actions of adoration, intercession, dedication, confession, and lament. The Psalms also offer testimonies about the compelling beauty of divine worship (Psalm 84), and the life-giving, corrective perspective that worship offers (Psalm 73:13). The prophets offer both a stern critique of false worship (e.g., Is. 1, Amos 6) and eschatological vision of true worship (e.g., Zech. 14:16–21, Is. 25:6–9).

The New Testament gospels offer Jesus' teaching about prayer, Jesus' mandates about baptism and the Lord's Supper, and exemplary canticles (e.g., the songs of Zechariah, Mary, the angels, and Simeon). The gospel of John offers rich, proto-Trinitarian descriptions of mutual glorification among persons of the Trinity (e.g., John 5:23, 20:28). The book of Acts offers descriptions of liturgical events (e.g., Acts 2:42), a sampling of liturgical actions (e.g., the prayer in Acts 4), and references to the ongoing use of synagogue practices. The epistles present specific instructions about worship practices, including singing, speaking in tongues, the Lord's Supper, as well as examples of early Christian hymnody (e.g., Phil. 2:6–11). The book of Hebrews is an especially important book for an evangelical theology of worship, with its vivid portrayal of the ongoing priesthood of Christ. The book of Revelation offers vivid visions of worship in which all of creation offers praise to God (Rev. 4, 5, and 7). It suggests that worship is a deeply political act, as the worship of God is also the refusal to worship any other power or authority. And it depicts the future of worship in which no temple will be needed because of the pervasive and intimate fellowship of God and God's people (Rev. 21:22).

Despite all of this, the New Testament offers relatively few explicit liturgical mandates. The varied responses to this apparent lacuna offer some of the most revealing displays of evangelical theological reasoning. Working out their anti-ritualism, many evangelicals have insisted that this lacuna should erode any dogmatic adherence to particular set forms and give believers great freedom in developing worship practices ("as long as they are from the heart, celebrate Jesus, and are connected with a life of praise," the typical argument might go). This is a line of critique frequently applied to the Roman Catholic Church and other liturgical traditions that require the use of particular forms or texts.

Puritans, Presbyterian evangelicals, and some Baptists have responded by invoking the "regulative principle of worship" (the claim articulated in the 1647 Westminster Confession that every specific action in worship should arise out of an explicit biblical command), resulting in worship services that feature the relatively few actions explicitly warranted in scripture (for example, acts of praise, preaching, intercessory prayer, baptism, and the Lord's Supper). Restorationist movements within evangelicalism have also focused on these central biblical actions, in an explicit effort to peel away historic practices and return to the simplicity and purity of biblical faith.[5]

More recently, some evangelicals have noted that while Jesus and the apostles may not have offered many explicit liturgical mandates, they did participate in highly ritualized actions, including the Passover. This perspective commends the use of regular patterns, rituals, and disciplines in both private and public worship, and is sometimes used to defend the use of disciplines that derive from ancient practice (for example, the Christian year as an adaptation of the Jewish calendar of feasts, patterns of Eucharistic prayers that emerged from Jewish table prayer practices, and practices of daily prayer at set times).[6]

Another line of reasoning insists that even if the Bible leaves us with great freedom to develop culturally appropriate worship forms, it also offers extensive resources for judging those forms. This view is based on the claim that worship practices must cohere with all biblical convictions about God, the church, salvation, and a Christian way of life. This desire for coherence fits the frequently cited patristic maxim *lex orandi, lex credendi* (the rule of prayer [fits] the rule of belief), which evangelicals typically invoke to claim that scriptural teachings should ground worship practices.[7]

Among recent theological work, an especially compelling approach to "biblical worship" is offered by both Kevin Vanhoozer and Michael Horton, who each develop the provocative metaphor of corporate worship as a dramatic enactment or improvisation of the scriptural script. This metaphor affirms the deeply embodied nature of worship practices, and probes how scripture not only gives warrant for certain practices but also conveys the spirit, character, and patterns by which those practices are enacted.[8]

Christian Doctrine and the Practice of Worship

Although biblical theology is the starting place for an evangelical theology of worship, systematic theology has often been crucial for integrating various biblical motifs and articulating how they respond to pastoral needs and opportunities. Nearly every major area or locus of Christian doctrine has direct implications for both the understanding and practice of worship.[9]

The doctrine of God clarifies the nature of the deity Christians address in worship. The doctrine of the Trinity articulates the fundamental grammar of worship in which God is the One who simultaneously receives, perfects, and prompts human worship, making worship a sharing or participation in divine action and not merely an act of human achievement—a central concern for Basil in the fourth century and Calvin in the sixteenth. The doctrinal explication of divine attributes explores how God is described in worship, questioning any practices which speak of some divine attributes to the exclusion of others, or which unwittingly portray a given divine attribute in a way that does not cohere with others (for example, depictions of divine mercy and justice that slip into sentimental substitutes).

The doctrine of revelation grounds the centrality of the Bible as the source of knowledge of God—and warrants the prominence of scripture readings in the practice of both private and public worship. It also insists on the centrality of Jesus Christ as the "perfect image" of God, as thus the focal point for the evangelical contemplation of God, and on the creation (general revelation) as a source of the knowledge of God which complements rather than competes with the knowledge of God revealed in the Bible.

The doctrine of humanity clarifies that worship involves the whole self: body, mind, and soul. This balanced perspective resists both intellectualism and anti-intellectualism in worship, as well as any kind of dualism that disparages embodied actions, gestures, and postures.

Theological reflection on human sinfulness clarifies multiple distortions of worship, including idolatry (misdirecting worship to someone or something other than the triune God), superstition (thinking that human action can manipulate divine favor), hypocrisy (practicing holy actions without holy intention), and disobedience (ignoring explicit scriptural commands about worship). It also clarifies the subtle and insidious ways that pride and narcissism distort otherwise beautiful acts of worship.

The doctrine of salvation clarifies that worship participates in something much larger than merely the redress of sin, something that encompasses the healing and redemptive development of the entire creation—a concern addressed already by Irenaeus and expressed in several patristic liturgical prayers. The doctrine further stresses that worship is truly based on an economy of covenantal promises rather than contractual obligation, an economy of grace and gifting, not onerous obligation. And it calls attention to the death and resurrection of Jesus as the decisive, atoning, life-giving action which inspires and enables worship.

The doctrine of the Christ clarifies that Jesus Christ as the fully divine Son of God is the right recipient of worship alongside of the Father, as well as the fully human Lord who is the true worshiper of the Father (Heb. 2:12, 4:14), scriptural motifs that Athanasius and other patristic writers articulated with a particular interest in their liturgical significance. The doctrine also explains how Christ fulfills Old Testament worship practices, and points to the multiple roles that Christ plays in the economy of redemption (as prophet, priest, and king), each of which should be celebrated in both private and public acts of worship.

The doctrine of the Holy Spirit clarifies that the Holy Spirit is the One who both illumines the hearts of believers to receive God's promises (1 Cor. 1) and enables God's people to cry "Abba Father" (Rom. 8:15–17, Gal. 4:6–7) in worship. The doctrine explores how the Spirit works through both order and spontaneity, through both dramatic intervention and long-term formation, in both dramatic conversions and lifelong growth—all by probing how the Spirit is depicted in scripture as the One who inspired both powerful spontaneous sermons in Acts and carefully planned, acrostic poems in the Psalms, and the One who generated charismatic ardor on Pentecost, but also brought order out of chaos in Genesis 1.

The doctrine of the church calls attention to the communal nature of Christian worship, stressing that we offer worship in continuity with believers in all times and places. It gathers up the scriptural insistence that Christians work together in unity and holiness to carry out the apostolic mission to proclaim the gospel and make disciples through baptism and teaching, each of which become key criteria for evaluating the strength of both private and corporate worship practices.

Christian missiology clarifies the inseparability of worship and mission: mission leads to worship, worship motivates mission, and worship is an occasion for mission as God works in and through worship practices to form and sustain faith. Missiology also clarifies the complex relationship of the practice of worship to local cultures—how faithful worship is simultaneously transcultural, contextual, countercultural, cross-cultural, and how Christians might both value indigenous worship practices and resist syncretism that dilutes or distorts Christian witness.

Theological reflection on Baptism and the Lord's Supper often become discrete topics in systematic teaching of the Christian faith, whether they are called "ordinances" (a term that highlights how these actions are explicitly mandated by scripture) or "sacraments" (a term that highlights how these actions are means by which God acts to nourish and sustain faith). This reflection highlights the vivid metaphors and images which Scripture offers for understanding baptism as a sign of washing (Acts 2:38), of new birth (Tit. 3:5), of dying and rising with Christ (Rom. 6:4), of incorporation into the church (1 Cor. 12:13), and of church unity (Eph. 4:5); and for understanding the Lord's Supper as a sign of covenant renewal, remembrance, thanksgiving, anticipation of the heavenly feast, spiritual nourishment, "participation in the body and blood of Christ," unity of the church, and proclamation (motifs that are clustered in Matt. 26:26–30, Mark 14:12–25, Luke 22:14–23, and 1 Cor. 10: 14–22 and 11:17–34). This area of reflection also probes how these actions can be not only occasions for human testimony, gratitude, and faith, but also means of grace by which God works to sustain and strengthen faith.

Eschatology explores how present day-worship is a harbinger of the coming kingdom of God and why feasting at the Lord's Supper not only celebrates Christ's life-giving death and resurrection in the past for the present, but also looks forward to the wedding feast of the lamb. Christian eschatology challenges any worship practices which unwittingly suggest that the fullness of the kingdom has already come, as well as those which unwittingly cast doubt on the decisive victory already accomplished in Christ. Several different eschatologies persist within evangelicalism, including amillennial, postmillennial, and premillennial perspectives. Each has implications for worship, including how the end times are spoken about in sermons, hymns, and prayers, as well as the overall spirit of worship practices, and the attitude toward engagement with contemporary culture that worship conveys.

In each area of doctrinal reflection, the history of the church offers rich resources for helping contemporary Christians engage in faithful theologizing and worship. Contemporary evangelical students have much to learn from the catechetical sermons of Ambrose and Cyril of Jerusalem, the liturgies of Chrysostom and Cranmer, the hymns of Ambrose and Wesley. Additional wisdom is crystallized in ancient lectionaries, Bible commentaries, church orders, visual iconography, and architectural design.[10]

Theological Dimensions of Common Evangelical Worship Practices

Any attempt to offer a comprehensive analysis of evangelical worship practices is fraught with difficulty. A complete account would need to include various types of private, family, and public services, various elements of these services, and various art forms by which these elements occur. Further, each of these events, elements, and art forms features complex patterns of leadership, community interaction, economic support, historical roots and precedents, and sensibilities about time and space. And each is practiced by hundreds of evangelical congregations on each continent, now that evangelical Christianity is as prominent in Asia, Latin America, and Africa, as in Europe, North America, and Australia. Despite this diversity, the following five core Christian practices have been especially important for evangelicals.

Preaching

First, evangelicals have nearly universally valued the preaching of the gospel. For many, evangelical worship calls to mind a picture, first of all, of a dynamic (or aspiring) preacher expounding a facet of biblical teaching, highlighting the unmerited grace of God offered uniquely in Christ, and calling the congregation to renewed faith and obedience. This emphasis draws on Scripture's own insistence on the importance of preaching (Rom. 10:14), and accounts of the vigorous preaching of Jesus, Peter, and Paul. So important is this emphasis that many accounts of evangelicalism are essentially a history of evangelical preachers, including Jonathan Edwards, Charles Finney, Charles Spurgeon, D. L. Moody, John Stott, and Billy Graham (a list of notables that is likely to become increasingly global in emerging histories).

In evangelical congregations in the Anglican and other liturgically structured traditions, this emphasis on preaching typically means that the sermon is longer and more explicitly tied to scripture than are sermons in other congregations in the tradition. In evangelical congregations in other traditions, the sermon has often dominated the liturgy, even relegating other songs, prayers, and testimonies to what have sometimes been called the "preliminaries."

The practice of preaching raises several provocative theological questions. How should preachers be called, trained, and confirmed? What risks attend high-profile preachers? How should preaching be like or unlike teaching? How does preaching, often called a "means of grace," relate to other means of grace, including baptism and the Lord's Supper? How should preaching balance concern for both individual and corporate faith, both personal piety and cultural engagement, both divine grace and human obedience?

Congregational Song

Second, evangelicals have nearly always placed great emphasis on musical expression, and especially congregational song. Mark Noll concludes that "evangelicalism at its best is the religion displayed in the classic evangelical hymns"—a thesis that explains the emphasis on hymnology among evangelical scholars.[11] In contrast to the Orthodox, Roman Catholic, and some other Protestant traditions, music has at times even overshadowed the Lord's Supper, being described in sacramental language as something which "ushers worshipers into the presence of God."[12]

Over the centuries, each of evangelicalism's defining features has been reflected in prominent hymnody, including its concern for the centrality of the cross ("When I Survey the Wondrous Cross") and the importance of conversion ("Amazing Grace"). Several landmark evangelical hymns had their origin in high-profile revivals, from Charles Wesley's famous hymns about conversion ("And Can It Be" and "O For Thousand Tongues"), to Thomas Hastings singing "Come You Disconsolate" for a Charles Finney revival, Charles Tindley leading "Stand by Me" in worship among Philadelphia Methodists, Ira Sankey singing "There were ninety and nine" for a D.L. Moody crusade, George Beverly Shea singing "How Great Thou Art" at a Billy Graham crusade, and the Maranatha Praise Band leading songs and choruses at Promise Keepers rallies in the 1990s. In the twentieth century, evangelical radio programs were a significant formative influence on evangelical worship, from the gospel hymns that were broadcast in the 1950s and 1960s to the contemporary praise choruses and ballads of the 1980s and 1990s.

A complete history of evangelical music would need to include discussions of Southern gospel quartets, evangelical college glee clubs, shape note singing, African-American spirituals and gospel songs, and explorations of how evangelical congregations influenced and were influenced by classical, folk, blues, jazz, country Western, and hip hop musical traditions. Emerging histories will increasingly feature discussions of how African drumming circles, Southeast Asian gamelans, and Latin American dance rhythms have reshaped musical practices, as well as analysis of how Western Christians exported or imposed not only nineteenth-century gospel hymns but also late twentieth-century praise choruses and pop music ballads on non-Western congregations. Both traditional and emerging histories will continue to rehearse how all of these musical expressions reflect the persistent populism and pietism in evangelical experience.[13]

Personal and Private Devotion

Third, nearly all evangelicals insist on the importance of personal and family devotional practices to complement participation in public worship.[14] This emphasis has also long been focused on home life, with eighteenth- and nineteenth-century women often taking leading roles in cultivating practices of daily prayer and Bible reading. In some parts of evangelicalism, this insistence on personal piety has been so strong that it might be more apt to speak of private prayer or devotional acts as the "real liturgy" that public assemblies are designed to complement and strengthen. Thus, some of the most important worship-related texts for evangelicals are devotional books, such as Oswald Chambers's perennial bestseller *My Utmost for His Highest.* Similarly, evangelical hymnals have long been used not only in a public worship services but also in homes where singing is accompanied by pianos, fiddles, accordions, and guitars—a practice now partially displaced by CDs, iPods, YouTube, and Internet downloads.

This emphasis on personal engagement also carries over into public worship practices. In many congregations, evangelicals are challenged to bring their own Bibles to worship, take notes during sermons, publicly identify prayer requests, or offer personal testimonies of God's work in their life. Other historically noteworthy practices include weekly prayer meetings, healing prayer, centering prayer, "concerts of prayer," and other worship events that emphasize heartfelt personal participation in prayer. This emphasis also shapes the piety of preachers, musicians, and other worship leaders, who frequently gather for prayer prior to worship and challenge each other to ensure that their "heart is right" before leading worship.

Practices of Evangelism and Conversion: Revivals, Altar Calls, Testimonies, Baptism

Fourth, the evangelical emphasis on evangelism and conversion has long been reflected in a prominent set of worship practices. For one, many evangelical communities, both historically and today, are known for prominent public assemblies whose primary purpose is to present the gospel and seek new converts. From the eighteenth to the twentieth centuries, these assemblies have evolved from "sacramental seasons," to camp meetings, revivals, crusades, and seeker services. While there are great differences between eighteenth-century urban revivals and camp meetings, between open-air crusades at huge athletic stadiums and annual revivals at small rural congregations, these events share several common features: preaching of the gospel which calls for personal conversion, music which expresses the gospel in a culturally contextual way, prayers for the conversion of seekers, and an explanation of a simple process by which new converts could express their faith and seek baptism.[15]

So important is this evangelistic impulse that it has tended to become the most important criterion for designing public assemblies. In nineteenth-century revivals, this meant praying for unconverted people publicly by name, inviting seekers to sit in a prominent "anxious bench" near the preacher, and planning "protracted" meetings over the space of several days. For late twentieth-century megachurches, in contrast, this pragmatism was expressed by creating spaces for anonymity, hosting carefully timed meetings without explicit Christian symbols, using brief dramatic enactments of ordinary life scenes to depict the need for the gospel, and multimedia presentations to convey themes of the gospel. In each of the past three centuries, this approach has engendered the criticism that evangelical worship is too pragmatic—either too confident in human means for bringing about salvation or too prone to avoid aspects of the gospel that are not appealing in a given cultural context.[16]

These evangelistic events, in turn, have long influenced the weekly worship of many congregations. Many nineteenth- and twentieth-century evangelical services looked like mini-weekly revivals, complete with weekly altar calls for those making new commitments to Christ. In turn, many late twentieth-century evangelical congregations reshaped their weekly worship to resemble "seeker services." In many parts of the world, missionaries who established evangelical churches functioned not only as evangelists but also as the first liturgists of a part of the global church, shaping patterns of prayer, preaching, singing, public scripture reading, and baptism and Lord's Supper practices. It is nearly axiomatic that the worship practices that are in place when an individual or community become Christian end up defining their approach to worship throughout their Christian life.[17]

Even apart from these controversies, the emphasis on evangelism is also reflected in several practices in weekly worship: the inclusion of testimonies by individual believers, reports about local and global missions, offerings and intercessory prayer for missionaries and for mission organizations, and the use of mission hymns.

The altar call—a practice of inviting worshipers to the front of the assembly near the end of a service as part of the process of making a decision for Christ—has long been a particularly significant practice in some streams of evangelical worship, especially in streams influenced by Arminian theology. Some commentators have perceptively suggested that the altar call (in some places called "invitation hymn") is the most "sacramental" moment in some evangelical communities, the moment understood to be most fraught with divine presence and activity.[18]

The drama of the altar call is matched only by the drama of baptism. Evangelical baptism practices have varied widely, depending largely on the denominational identity of a given evangelical congregation. Reformed, Methodist, and Anglican evangelicals tend to baptize both believers and their children, including infants, by sprinkling or pouring, often at prominent fonts, but not always in the context of regular weekly worship inside church buildings. Baptist and many nondenominational evangelicals tend to baptize believers only by immersion, either in large baptismal pools built into church buildings or in nearby rivers or lakes. Uniting all evangelical baptism practices is a deep concern that it not be approached as mere ritual, but rather celebrated, in the context of genuine faith.

The Lord's Supper

Fifth, the Lord's Supper has long been an element of central importance in many evangelical communities, though its theology and practice often varies widely across denominations. Evangelical practice is influenced by two competing theological impulses: one shaped by Zwingli, which sees the Lord's Supper as an occasion at which the worshiper recalls the work of Jesus on the cross, and the other shaped by Luther, Calvin, Wesley, and others who add to this a conviction that the meal is an occasion for participation in the body and blood of Jesus, through which God is at work to nourish the faith of the congregation.

In general, the combination of persistent anti-Catholicism and an Enlightenment preference for cognitive understanding has made the Zwinglian strand most prominent in many evangelical communities. Several recent reform movements have begun to challenge this tendency, often by focusing on the multiple scriptural images for the Lord's Supper as a feast of covenant renewal, eschatological anticipation, holy remembrance, participation in the real presence, church unity, and ethical dedication.[19]

The place to look for unique evangelical contributions to the broad landscape of Christian Eucharistic practice is, not surprisingly, in the area of personal piety and personal experience of the Lord's Supper. Evangelical Christians have kept alive many of Charles Wesley's famous Eucharistic hymns and have produced a long stream of personal devotional meditations and sermons (from Charles Spurgeon, John Stott, and others) that address the individual experience of believers' participation in the Lord's Supper.

Recent Movements, Current Scholarship, Prospects for the Future

Contemporary worship practices among evangelicals remain as difficult to describe as ever. Many evangelicals claim a denominational identity in an Anglican, Reformed/Presbyterian, Holiness, Methodist, Baptist, or independent church tradition, as well as identities in a variety of socioeconomic, ethnic, and cultural contexts throughout the world. This complexity is enhanced by the array of charismatic leaders, publishing companies, educational institutions, Internet sites, renewal movements, parachurch organizations, denominations, global networks, and television, radio, and Internet broadcasts that both represent and shape parts of the evangelical world.

Still further complexity arises from the multiplicity of recent renewal movements, including the charismatic movement, the church growth movement, the liturgical movement, the emerging church movement, varieties of neo-confessionalism, and the rise of Western awareness of the churches of global South and East. In fact, there arguably has never been a time when evangelicals have been reforming their worship in so many directions at the same time.[20] These movements have given rise to a number of remarkable leaders, congregations, and pockets of renewal that feature such countercultural forces as congregations aggressively pursuing cross-cultural hospitality, hymns and songs that recover doctrinal orthodoxy, renewed practices of corporate Eucharistic spirituality, and new approaches to interweaving worship and pastoral care and discipleship.

At the same time, recent evangelical worship has also been the subject of many criticisms and even satire, especially focused on the slippage of populist, pragmatist, and pietist tendencies into sentimentality and consumerism.[21] Particularly trenchant are critiques that accuse evangelical Christians of inconsistency related to their own criticisms of others: for example, that a tradition with such a high view of Scripture would have so little of it read in public worship, that a tradition which nurtured opposition to set forms often gave way to extemporaneous expressions that soon developed very strict patterns, that traditions so concerned with a theocentric theology would harbor worship practices that seemed so narcissistic, that traditions so opposed to deism would have such a modest vocabulary for describing God's activity in and through liturgical assemblies, that traditions so opposed to the experience-oriented theology of Protestant liberalism would themselves become so "experiential," and that traditions so eager to embrace the biblical claim that the citizenship of believers is in heaven (Phil. 3:20) would so readily embrace nationalistic expressions in worship (for example, the use of patriotic hymns and national flags, and the celebration of national holidays), especially in the United States.

Given its breadth and diversity, it is not surprising that evangelicalism could at once give rise to luminous examples of vitality and orthodoxy as well as to excesses that generate these critiques, and that charges of intellectualism and anti-intellectualism could each be apt critiques of part of the evangelical world.

Taken together, these dynamics of ferment and complexity offer a clarion call for thoughtful, poised theological reflection. Especially important topics in emerging literature include:

1. Discerning the opportunities for and threats to vibrant, orthodox worship in the context of modern and postmodern thought.[22]
2. Discerning the shape and texture of faithful worship in diverse cultural contexts, particularly in light of changing patterns of immigration, multicultural expression, and global Christianity in a postcolonial age.[23]
3. Discerning faithful practices of artistic expression and reception in all artistic forms, including music, multimedia, architecture, visual arts, and language, in light of historic evangelical iconoclasm, and continuing reflections on the specific capacities and limitations of each art-form for worship.[24]

4. Discerning the shape of faithful ecclesiology in light of tenacious cultural individualism and pluralism.[25]
5. Discerning the nature of healthy ritual practices, disciplines, and patterns of liturgical action—a particularly challenging assignment given evangelicalism's traditional aversion to ritual.[26] Work in this area includes reflections on ways of marking time and arranging space, on the nature of the Holy Spirit's agency in both extemporaneous expressions and patterned action, on the virtues and capacities that various worship practices form, and on the ways that worship practices implicitly reinforce attitudes toward government, the environment, gender roles, technology, and other societal practices.
6. Discerning healthy ways of integrating worship practices with practices of pastoral care, evangelism, discipleship, and social witness, in times of growth and plenty, but also in times of crisis, controversy, and transition.[27] Particular attention is needed on the nature of healthy worship practices in campus ministries, youth organizations, nursing homes, military bases, and in intergenerational worshiping communities that offer hospitality to persons with disabilities, to former prisoners, and others who have often felt unwelcome.
7. Discerning the most fruitful approaches to teaching Christian worship to worshipers; to pastors, musicians, and those who will lead worship; and to historians, theologians, and other professional students of the Christian tradition.[28]

At their best, these recent lines of inquiry seek to recapitulate historic evangelical concern for proclaiming the scandal of the cross, the glory of God in Jesus Christ, and for integrating personal piety, communal worship, and lifelong service in society.

NOTES

1. For a summary of the Hebrew and Greek scriptural terms behind these English uses, see "Worship," *Dictionary of Biblical Imagery*, ed. Leland Ryken et al. (Downer's Grove: InterVarsity Press Academic, 1998), 969–973.

2. A. W. Tozer, *Worship: The Missing Jewel of the Evangelical Church* (Harrisburg, Pa.: Christian Publications, n.d. [early 1960s]), and Robert E. Webber, *Worship Is a Verb* (Peabody, Mass.: Hendrickson, 1995).

3. Orthodox, Roman Catholic, and mainline Protestant scholars have given much more attention to the way the Bible is used in worship (including the shape and use of lectionaries), while evangelicals have focused more on discerning the significance of biblical texts about worship.

4. See John Thompson, *Reading the Bible with the Dead* (Grand Rapids: Eerdmans, 2007).

5. See Richard T. Hughes, ed., *The American Quest for the Primitive Church* (Urbana: University of Illinois Press, 1988).

6. See, for example, Robert E. Webber, *Ancient-Future Worship* (Grand Rapids: Bakers, 2008).

7. This is in contrast to both the original use of the phrase by Prosper of Aquitaine and many current uses of the phrase by Orthodox, Catholic, and Anglican scholars in which the established tradition of the church (*lex orandi*) is also a source and norm for forming, but also for judging belief (*lex credendi*).

8. Kevin Vanhoozer, *The Drama of Doctrine* (Louisville, Ky.: Westminster John Knox Press, 2005), 409; Michael S. Horton, *Covenant and Eschatology: The Divine Drama* (Louisville, Ky: Westminster John Knox Press, 2002), 265–271.

9. For works on worship and doctrine, see, for example, Leanne Van Dyk, ed., *A More Profound Alleluia: Worship and Theology in Harmony* (Grand Rapids: Eerdmans, 2004).

10. See the various sources studied in Hughes Oliphant Old, *The Reading and Preaching of the Scriptures in the Worship of the Christian Church*, 8 vols. (Grand Rapids: Eerdmans, 1999–2009); James F. White, *Documents of Christian Worship* (Louisville, Ky.: Westminster John Knox, 1992); and Geoffrey Wainwright and Karen Westerfield Tucker, *The Oxford History of Christian Worship* (New York: Oxford University Press, 2006).

11. Mark Noll, *Where Shall My Wond'ring Soul Begin? The Landscape of Evangelical Piety and Thought*, ed. Mark A. Noll and Ronald F. Thiemann (Grand Rapids: Eerdmans, 2000), 1.

12. Sarah Koenig, "This Is My Daily Bread: Toward a Sacramental Theology of Evangelical Praise and Worship," *Worship* 82.2 (March 2008): 141–161.

13. See, for example, Nathan O. Hatch, *The Democratization of American Christianity* (New Haven: Yale University Press, 1989).

14. See, for example, David K. Gillett, *Trust and Obey: Explorations in Evangelical Spirituality* (London: Darton, Longman, and Todd, 1993).

15. See Leigh Eric Schmidt, *Holy Fairs: Scottish Communions and American Revivals in the Early Modern Period* (Princeton: Princeton University Press, 1989), and Lester Ruth, *A Little Heaven Below: Worship at Early Methodist Quarterly Meetings* (Nashville, Tenn.: Kingswood Books/Abingdon, 2000).

16. See, for example, James Bratt, *Antirevivalism in Antebellum America* (New Brunswick: Rutgers University Press, 2006).

17. Todd E. Johnson, "Disconnected Rituals: The Origins of the Seeker Service Movement," in *The Conviction of Things Not Seen* (Grand Rapids: Brazos, 2002), 53–66.

18. David Bennett, *The Altar Call* (Lanham, Md.: University Press of America, 2000).

19. See, for example, Leonard J. VanderZee, *Christ, Baptism and the Lord's Supper* (Downers Grove, Ill.: InterVarsity Press, 2004), and Anthony R. Cross and Philip E. Thompson, eds., *Baptist Sacramentalism* (Milton Keynes: Paternoster, 2003).

20. On the recent history of these movements, see David W. Bebbington, "Evangelicals and Public Worship, 1965–2005," *Evangelical Quarterly* 79.1 (2007): 3–22; Robb Redman, *The Great Worship Awakening* (San Francisco: Jossey-Bass, 2002); and Robert E. Webber, *The Younger Evangelicals* (Grand Rapids: Baker, 2002).

21. See D. G. Hart, *Deconstructing Evangelicalism: Conservative Protestantism in the Age of Billy Graham* (Grand Rapids: Baker Academic, 2004), and David Wells, *Above All Earthly Powers: Christ in a Postmodern World* (Grand Rapids: Eerdmans, 2003).

22. See James K. A. Smith, *Who's Afraid of Postmodernism?* (Grand Rapids: Baker Academic, 2006).

23. See, for example, Pedrito U. Maynard-Reid, *Diverse Worship: African-American, Caribbean, and Hispanic Perspectives* (Downers Grove, Ill.: InterVarsity Press, 2000), and Charles Farhadian, *Christian Worship Worldwide* (Grand Rapids: Eerdmans, 2007).

24. See, for example, Jeremy Begbie, *Resounding Truth: Christian Wisdom in the World of Music* (Grand Rapids: Baker Academic, 2007); Debra Rienstra and Ron Rienstra, *Worship Words* (Grand Rapids: Baker Academic, 2009); Quentin Schultze, *High-Tech Worship? Using Presentational Technologies Wisely* (Grand Rapids: Baker, 2003); and William Dyrness, *Senses of the Soul: Art and the Visual in Christian Worship* (Eugene, Ore.: Cascade Books, 2008).

25. See, for example, John Stackhouse, ed., *Evangelical Ecclesiology* (Grand Rapids: Baker Academic, 2003).

26. See John D. Witvliet, "The Cumulative Power of Transformation in Public Worship: Cultivating Gratitude and Expectancy for the Many Ways the Spirit Works," in *Worship and Transformation*, ed. Alexis Abernethy (Grand Rapids: Baker Books, 2008), 41–60.

27. See, for example, Kathy Smith, *Stilling the Storm: Worship and Congregational Leadership in Difficult Times* (Herndon, Va.: Alban Institute, 2006).

28. See, for example, John D. Witvliet, "Teaching Worship as a Christian Practice," in Dorothy Bass and Craig Dykstra, eds., *For Life Abundant: Practical Theology, Theological Education, and Christian Ministry* (Grand Rapids: Eerdmans, 2008), 117–149.

REFERENCES

Chan, Simon. *Liturgical Theology*. Downers Grove, Ill.: InterVarsity Press Academic, 2006.

Ellis, Christopher. *Gathering: A Theology and Spirituality of Worship in Free Church Tradition*. London: SCM Press, 2004.

Farhadian, Charles. *Christian Worship Worldwide: Expanding Horizons, Deepening Practice*. Grand Rapids: Eerdmans, 2007.

Kilde, Jeanne Halgren. *When Church Became Theatre: The Transformation of Evangelical Architecture and Worship in Nineteenth-Century America*. New York: Oxford University Press, 2002.

Plantinga, Cornelius, and Sue R. Rozeboom. *Discerning the Spirits: A Guide to Thinking about Christian Worship Today*. Grand Rapids: Eerdmans, 2003.

Torrance, James A. *Worship, Community, and the Triune God of Grace*. Downers Grove, Ill.: InterVarsity Press, 1997.

Van Dyk, Leanne. *A More Profound Alleluia: Worship and Theology in Harmony*. Grand Rapids: Eerdmans, 2004.

Wainwright, Geoffrey, and Karen Westerfield Tucker, eds. *The Oxford History of Chrsitian Worship*. New York: Oxford University Press, 2006.

Webber, Robert E. *Ancient-Future Worship*. Grand Rapids: Baker, 2008.

Woods, Robert, and Brian Walrath, eds. *The Message in the Music: Studying Contemporary Praise and Worship*. Nashville, Tenn.: Abingdon, 2007.

CHAPTER 21

SPIRITUAL GIFTS

HOWARD SNYDER

THE New Testament refers to spiritual gifts in several passages, and the Old Testament provides important background to the NT teaching. In church history, spiritual gifts have at times been controversial and at other times largely ignored. Evangelicals showed growing interest in gifts in the twentieth century, in large measure due to the impact of Pentecostal and charismatic movements.

The church inhabits the space between the unity of "one Lord, one faith, one baptism" of Ephesians 4:5 and the diversity of the "great multitude o from every nation" of Revelation 7:9. Spiritual gifts are best understood within these wide parameters of unity and diversity, and in light of the historic Christian doctrine of the Trinity.

BIBLICAL BASIS

Terminology

The characteristic New Testament Greek word for "spiritual gift" is *charisma* (pl., *charismata*), the basis for the English terms "charism" and "charismatic." Since the Greek word for "grace" is *charis, charisma* may properly be translated "gift of grace" and specifically, in the New Testament, "gift of God's grace." The word *charisma* occurs in several NT passages, in particular 1 Corinthians 12, Romans 12:6, and 1 Peter 4:10.

Occasionally in the NT other words are used with the same general sense of *charisma*. For example, in Ephesians 3:7–8 Paul speaks of "the gift of grace" (*dorean tes charitos*) God had given him, and then refers simply to "this grace" (*charis*), meaning in both cases his charismatic calling as an apostle. Thus "grace" (*charis*) and "gift of grace" (*charisma*) are closely related. Other word combinations may also carry the same meaning as *charisma*. In 1 Corinthians 12:1 and 14:1, Paul uses the term "spiritual matters" (*pneumatika*) with the evident sense of "spiritual gifts." Hebrews 2:4 speaks of "distributions" (*merismois*) of the Holy Spirit in the early church, clearly with the meaning of spiritual gifts. Thus the NRSV translation: "gifts of the Holy Spirit, distributed according to his will." (As in English, Greek has several synonyms for "gift," and the specific meaning has to be determined by the context.)

These examples illustrate a central theme of biblical teachings about the church: The church is the result of God's grace through Jesus Christ by the Holy Spirit, and the Spirit continues to work graciously in the church to build it up, to glorify God, and to extend the church's mission in the world. 1 Peter 4:10–11 exhorts, "Like good stewards of the manifold grace of God, serve one another with whatever gift [*charisma*] you have received... so that God may be glorified in all things through Jesus Christ." Romans 12:6 tells us, "We have gifts [*charismata*] that differ according to the grace [*charis*] given to us."

Old Testament Background

Spiritual gifts are a particularly NT emphasis because they have to do with the fullness of grace in Jesus Christ working in and through the church, Christ's body. However, important Old Testament material illuminates and enriches the NT teaching.

The OT reveals God's Spirit at work in varied ways. At times the Spirit is described as coming upon or filling various prophets or servants of God (e.g., Num. 24:2; Jdg. 3:10, 11:29; 1 Sam. 11:6; 2 Chr. 15:1; Isa. 61:1). The Spirit was occasionally poured out on particular people for specific tasks for a limited period of time. In the NT, by contrast, God's Spirit is poured out on all believers, as prophesied (Acts 2:16–21), and Christ gives gifts to all (Eph. 4:7–10). Thus both continuity and discontinuity mark the relationship between the Old and New Testaments: The continuity of the Spirit's work; the discontinuity introduced by Christ's coming and the pouring out of the Holy Spirit at Pentecost.

The OT speaks of God working at times through "signs and wonders" (Ex. 7:3; Dt. 4:34, 6:22, 26:8, 34:11; Neh. 9:12; Ps. 135:9; Jer. 32:20–21; Dan. 4:2, 6:27). This also forms part of the background of NT teaching. Although Jesus warned of an over-reliance on signs and wonders (John 4:48), authentic signs and wonders were a distinctive part of the earliest church's life and witness (Acts 4:30, 5:12, 14:3, 15:12; Rom. 15:19; Heb. 2:4). Paul speaks of "signs and wonders and mighty works" as "signs of a true apostle" (2 Cor. 12:12). When the gospel was first proclaimed, "God added his testimony by signs and wonders and various miracles, and by gifts of the Holy Spirit, distributed according to his will" (Heb. 2:4).

Such references to "signs and wonders" show that they are not to be equated with spiritual gifts; the *charismata* are not always or even primarily manifested through signs and wonders. However, spiritual gifts and signs and wonders appear in Scripture as somewhat overlapping categories, both referring to the grace and power of God's Spirit working through his people.

The fullest OT foreshadowing of the NT *charismata* is found in the book of Exodus. God chose two Israelites, Bezalel and Oholiab, "to devise artistic designs, to work in gold, silver, and bronze" and to engage "in every kind of craft" in constructing the tabernacle and its furnishings (Ex. 31:1–11). Oholiab was an "engraver, designer, and embroiderer in blue, purple, and crimson yarns, and in fine linen" (Ex. 38:23). God filled Bezalel with his Spirit to do this artistic work (Ex. 31:3, 35:31) and gave both these craftsmen the ability to teach others as well (Ex. 35:34), so that the whole Israelite community would be productively and creatively engaged in building the tabernacle.

This account is instructive both historically and prophetically. Historically, it shows how God used a diversity of persons and gifts—and specifically artistic gifts—to construct the central symbol and locus of God's covenantal dwelling among his people. Exodus emphasizes that God used many gifts of both men and women to make the tabernacle. Bezalel and Oholiab were important in transforming these gifts into works of art so that God could be worshiped by all Israel in ways specifically revealed to Moses at Sinai. Exodus 36:5 notes that the people brought "much more than enough" for building the tabernacle and its furnishings. All the people were involved, people with special Spirit-inspired skills and gifts played key roles, and the result was the appropriate worship of God.

This OT example takes on added meaning when viewed through the lens of the NT *charismata*. In Exodus, diverse people from diverse tribes employed diverse artistic and leadership gifts to make a variety of specific objects and to teach others as they worked together. Yet this was confined to a particular time and project: building the tabernacle. Now in the NT age, through the resurrection of Jesus Christ and the pouring out of the Spirit, a wider, ongoing diversity of grace-gifts functions in the church to glorify God and equip God's people. In this sense the diversity of gifts and crafts in Exodus foreshadows 1 Peter 4:10–11, "Like good stewards of the manifold [or many-colored] grace of God, serve one another with whatever gift each of you has received... so that God may be glorified in all things through Jesus Christ."

Gifts in the New Testament and Early Church

The principal NT passages dealing with spiritual gifts are Romans 12:4–8, 1 Corinthians 12–14, Ephesians 4:7–16, Hebrews 2:4, and 1 Peter 4:10–11. (Romans 1:11, 1 Corinthians 1:7, 7:7, 1 Timothy 4:14, and 2 Timothy 1:6 also refer to spiritual gifts.) Together these passages teach several things about spiritual gifts:

1. *Spiritual gifts are an expression of God's grace at work in the church.* Spiritual gifts refer not to "natural" talents or inherent abilities but to the gracious work of the Holy Spirit in the body of Christ. On the other hand, it is clear that God's Spirit

may use native capacities and acquired knowledge and skills as part of the exercise of spiritual gifts, as evident in the ministry of Paul. Writing to the Corinthian church Paul asks, "What do you have that you did not receive?" (1 Cor. 4:7). In the broadest sense, both inherent capacities and acquired learning are gifts from God; they should not be set in opposition or apposition to the *charismata*.

Spiritual gifts are, literally, gifts of the Spirit. The various *charismata* in the church operate within the larger sphere of God's gracious self-giving and the comprehensive work of the Holy Spirit in creation, redemption, and new creation.

2. *Spiritual gifts are integral to the nature, function, and mission of the church as body of Christ.* The *charismata* are woven into the fabric of NT teachings about the church, rather than being something peripheral or secondary. Thus the church is essentially charismatic, constituted by God's grace (*charis*) and equipped for ministry through a variety of gifts (*charismata*).[1]

In Ephesians 4:4–6, after speaking of the unity of the church Paul says, "But each of us was given grace according to the measure of Christ's gift" (Eph. 4:7). Similarly, 1 Corinthians 12:7 says, "To each [Christian] is given the manifestation of the Spirit for the common good," referring to the *charismata*. The church as body of Christ and community of the Spirit is enriched by gifts given to the church generally and to each member specifically. In Paul's exposition of the church in both 1 Corinthians 12 and Ephesians 4, as well as in Romans 12, the *charismata* are integral to the meaning and function of the body of Christ.

Paul makes extensive use of body imagery in 1 Corinthians 12 to show how God intends gifts to function in the church. The church is one body with many members (1 Cor. 12:12–14). To be whole and function properly the body needs all its members—that is, all its limbs and organs—functioning together organically "for the common good" (1 Cor. 12:7), or "so that the church may be built up" (1 Cor. 14:5). It is through the diversity of gifts, Paul says, that God's Spirit works to build up and grow the church.

The organic, rather than institutional, language of "body" is notable here. All the NT passages relating to gifts use organic imagery, and particularly the image of "body," to explain the nature and function of gifts. This underscores the relational nature of the church, of gifts, and of the Spirit's work in the church. In this sense we can speak of the *ecology* of the church as a charismatic organism. In Ephesians 1:10 and elsewhere Paul speaks of God's "plan" or "economy" (*oikonomia*) to bring reconciliation through Jesus Christ. That plan includes the church as living organism with an interdependent ecology of gifts all working interdependently for the health and witness of the whole body.

God's Spirit endows the church with a variety of spiritual gifts out of the "fullness of Christ" (Eph. 4:13) so that the church may "grow up…into Christ" (Eph. 4:15). The goal is that the church should actually be Christ's body in the world, continuing his works and shining "like stars in the world" (Phil. 2:15). Although specific gifts imply specific ministries, the larger dynamic is that Jesus Christ, the head of the church, distributes a diversity of gifts so that the church may fully be Jesus' body and Jesus' mission in the world. In this sense gifts are inherently related to the mission of God (*missio Dei*) and the mission of the church. Gifts are given so that the church may be the visible ministering body of Christ in the world (1 Cor. 12–14).

3. *Spiritual gifts show the diverse ways God's grace operates in and through the church.* In the NT vision, the church's unity, diversity, and mutuality constitute an organic wholeness in which the church's oneness is enriched by its diversity and its diversity in persons and gifts contributes to its integral dynamism. This charismatic unity-in-diversity is itself a gift of the Spirit. Due to sinful self-centeredness, however, gifts may at times become divisive and competitive—the precise problem addressed in 1 Corinthians.

Paul teaches that the diversity of spiritual gifts contributes to the vitality and wholeness of the body. "Now there are varieties of gifts, but the same Spirit; and there are varieties of services, but the same Lord; and there are varieties of activities, but it is the same God who activates all of them in everyone. To each is given the manifestation of the Spirit for the common good.... All these [gifts] are activated by one and the same Spirit, who allots to each one individually just as the Spirit chooses" (1 Cor. 12:4–11). Paul adds, "For in the one Spirit we were all baptized into one body—Jews or Greeks, slaves or free—and we were all made to drink of one Spirit" (1 Cor. 12:13), showing that the diversity of gifts operates synergistically with the church's cultural and social diversity. Through the Holy Spirit, within the one body the diversity of gifts and the diversity of persons and cultures together contribute to the church's vitality and witness.

Specific gifts are to be understood within this larger picture of diversity. The lists of gifts in Romans 12, 1 Corinthians 12, and Ephesians 4 themselves differ. It is fruitless therefore to try to enumerate a precise number of specific gifts. The number and diversity of gifts are in God's hands.

Rather than a predetermined list, the gifts mentioned in the NT are examples or instances of how God's grace works in the church. The NT writers interpret what God was graciously doing in granting a wide distribution of gifts. These teachings helped the earliest Christians (and the church through history) to understand that the diverse ministries arising in the church were part of God's intent and economy for the church.

In 1 Corinthians 12 Paul mentions several specific gifts. Presumably the particular gifts listed mirror the conflicted situation in the Corinthian church. Paul mentions "utterance of wisdom," "utterance of knowledge," faith, healing, "working of miracles," prophecy, discernment of spirits, "various kinds of tongues," and the interpretation of tongues (12:8–10). Later, in verse 28, he mentions apostles, prophets, teachers, "deeds of power" (presumably equivalent to "working of miracles" in verse 10), healing, "forms of assistance," "forms of leadership," and tongue-speaking.

Clearly, Paul's intent here is not a narrowly defined comprehensive list but an affirmation of the variety of gifts and how they all are to function jointly in an orderly fashion in the one body. Thus Paul's reference to "first apostles, second prophets, third teachers" in verse 28 does not indicate a hierarchy of office or authority but rather describes the orderly way God worked in establishing the church—first sending apostles and prophets to found the church, then teachers to guide and build it up, then the full diversity of other gifts. The church's principle of operation is that of the mutually interdependent charismatic body functioning under the headship of Jesus Christ, animated by the Holy Spirit.

In writing to the church in Rome, where gifts were less a matter of controversy and conflict, Paul gives a more generalized list: prophecy, "ministry" or service (*diakonia*), teaching, exhortation, generosity, leading, and mercy (Rom. 12:6–7). Ephesians 4:11–12 mentions apostles, prophets, evangelists, shepherds and teachers—leadership gifts Christ has given "to equip the saints [i.e., the church] for the work of ministry [*diakonia*], for building up the body of Christ." The perspective in both passages is the same: The church is Christ's Spirit-animated body, endowed with a diversity of gifts so that it may truly be Christ's body in the world.

Since the gifts and gift-ministries mentioned in the NT are examples, not comprehensive lists, the church may benefit from other gifts not specifically listed. In fact, some passages imply other gifts not indicated in 1 Corinthians 12, Romans 12, and Ephesians 4. Paul in 1 Corinthians 7:7 implies that celibacy may be a spiritual gift: "I wish that all were as I myself am. But each has a particular gift [*charisma*] from God, one having one kind and another a different kind."

1 Peter 4:10–11 speaks of the *charismata* in two general categories: speaking and serving (*diakonia*). All Christians should be "good stewards of the manifold [or many-colored] grace of God" manifested in the *charismata*, serving one another and glorifying God "in all things through Jesus Christ." The basic perspective is the same as that of the Pauline passages, though 1 Peter 4:10 adds the important note of the *stewardship* of gifts. Christians are to be good stewards of the precious gifts they have received, as Jesus taught in his parables.

4. *God provides gifts of general leadership in order to equip the whole church for ministry.* This teaching is most explicit in Ephesians 4:11–12, "The gifts he gave were that some would be apostles, some prophets, some evangelists, some pastors and teachers, to equip the saints for the work of ministry, for building up the body of Christ." The same is implied in 1 Corinthians 12:28, which highlights the roles of apostles, prophets, and teachers among the range of gifts. The emphasis is not on office (the word "office" does not occur in these passages) but on gifted persons and their function.

These passages highlight the important role of leaders in equipping the whole church for ministry through the diversity of persons and gifts. The passages do not indicate a clergy-laity distinction, since in the NT "laity" refers to all the people (*laos*) of God and all Christians have areas of giftedness and ministry. Rather, in the divine economy, Jesus has gifted some people specifically to teach and nurture so that the whole church functions as Christ's ministering body. The key function of pastors, teachers, and other leaders is to equip the whole church for ministry. Ministry (*diakonia*) is a gift to, and the work of, the whole body of Christ, not just of leaders. The key role of apostles, prophets, evangelists, and pastors is to nourish and guide a wide range of gift-ministries in the church.

Ephesians 4 and 1 Corinthians 12 thus show how God's economy of gifts and graces works. Early Christians were aware of the various apostles, prophets, evangelists, and teachers that were appearing in the church. Paul points out that such leaders arise by God's grace (through a charismatic process, so to speak) and that their function is to assist the church truly to be Christ's body. Apostles, prophets, and some evangelists (cf. Acts 21:8) were having a general and largely itinerant ministry throughout the church, whereas pastors and teachers (also called elders) exercised leadership within local churches. The NT teaching shows the charismatic logic at work as God's Spirit distributed varieties of gifts "for the common good" (1 Cor. 12:7), "so that the church may be built up" (1 Cor. 14:5) as Christ's ministering body.

5. *NT teaching on spiritual gifts makes no distinctions on the basis of gender, social status, or ethnicity.* All members of Christ's body receive gifts, irrespective of gender or social location. This is consistent with the fact that in the church "there is no longer Jew or Greek, ... slave or free, ... male or female; for all of you are one in Christ Jesus" (Gal. 3:28; cf. 1 Cor. 12:13). Evangelicals vary considerably, however, in their interpretation of leadership gifts in relation to the issue of gender.

The wide distribution of spiritual gifts has both theological and sociological implications. Theologically, it affirms the value of every human being created in God's image and born into the family of God through faith in Jesus Christ. Sociologically, this teaching is revolutionary because it opens the door to participation, initiative, ministry, and leadership to every believer, irrespective of the world's systems and values (cf. Mt. 20:24–28). Every believer thus has some avenue of gift ministry. Any believer may potentially, by God's grace, become a leader in the church. Much of the dynamic of early Christianity as a movement is due to this fact.

The church has often permitted men only to exercise some gifts, particularly those of leadership such as pastors, apostles, and bishops. Since the NT teachings on gifts do not restrict the *charismata* in this way, such limitation has to be justified on some other basis than NT teachings on the *charismata.*

6. *Nowhere does the NT specifically define "spiritual gift."* Taken together, however, the NT material suggest this definition: Spiritual gifts are instances of God's grace working through the personalities of Christian believers, equipping them for particular ministry so that the church may be strengthened in worship, community, and witness, the kingdom of God advanced, and God glorified in all things.

More broadly, gifts may be viewed as reflecting the mystery of the Trinity. Just as God the Father sends Jesus Christ the Son in the power of the Spirit to accomplish salvation and bring the kingdom of God in fullness, so the Trinity distributes gifts to the church out of the divine fullness. Gifts assist the church to truly function as Christ's body. As the initiative of the Holy Spirit, gifts are one of the ways the Holy Spirit "testifies" to Jesus Christ (John 15:26), thus revealing the Father, and reminding us of Jesus' words about the Spirit in John 16:14, "He will glorify me, because he will take what is mine and declare it to you." It is all of grace.

Spiritual Gifts throughout Church History

After the New Testament age, the understanding and function of spiritual gifts in the church gradually shifted. There was a lessening of emphasis on gifts and a growing tendency to identify particular gifts with ecclesiastical offices. However, from time to time throughout history a renewed emphasis on charismatic gifts emerged, especially in movements of renewal or in various marginal groups.

The Protestant Reformation placed relatively little emphasis on spiritual gifts. Martin Luther tended to associate gifts with the priesthood of believers. John Calvin maintained that supernatural gifts ceased with the end of the apostolic age, but identified the ministry gifts of Ephesians 4:11 with church offices.

Historically speaking, the most dramatic new emphasis on the *charismata* came in the twentieth century, with the birth of modern Pentecostalism and then a range of charismatic movements.

The "Cessation" of Spiritual Gifts

Since the NT discusses spiritual gifts, the seeming disappearance of gifts in later church life required some explanation. In general, three different answers have been given to the question: Why do gifts not function today as they did in the early church?

1. *The* charismata *were a special endowment for the NT church only.* This view holds that the Holy Spirit gave the *charismata* to help establish the church during the early period when the canon of Scripture was being finalized. Such gifts were no longer needed once the Bible was generally available. In this view, the role of the first apostles is central. The Twelve Apostles (including Paul, seen as replacing Judas Iscariot) were the foundation upon which Jesus Christ built the church (Eph. 2:20, Rev. 21:14). With the death of these founding apostles and the availability of the NT writings, the church now had the apostolic witness embodied in Scripture. Thus by God's design the original apostleship and other charismatic gifts disappeared or were withdrawn from the church.

This is a dispensational argument in the sense that it holds that the *charismata* were intended for the NT dispensation only. This view has been called "cessationism." Cessationists appeal to 1 Corinthians 13:8–10, "But as for prophecies, they will come to an end; as for tongues, they will cease; as for knowledge, it will come to an end. For we know only in part, and we prophesy only in part; but when the complete comes, the partial will come to an end." Cessationists argue that God intended tongues and other gifts to "cease" after the apostolic age. Some argue that the statement "when the complete [or perfect] comes" refers to Scripture, meaning that once the Bible was available in the church, it superseded the operation of the *charismata.*

The cessationist argument has taken various forms. Some hold that while gifts have ceased generally in the church, God's Spirit may use them in mission situations as an aid to evangelism, in a manner somewhat parallel to the situation of the early church. Others argue that the more dramatic gifts such as prophecy, healings, and tongues-speaking were "sign gifts" for the early church only, but that God still may work in the church through miracles or other gifts, though only occasionally and not in a way that adds anything to Scripture. The most extreme view holds that God no longer works through spiritual gifts at all.[2]

The rise of Pentecostalism in the twentieth century provoked a renewal of cessationist arguments, particularly among fundamentalists who saw the Pentecostal emphasis on tongues-speaking, prophecy, and healing as theologically aberrant and as compromising the unique authority of Scripture.

2. *The* charismata *now operate primarily or exclusively through ecclesiastical office.* This view is similar to cessationism in that it sees the NT *charismata* as having been given uniquely for the initial establishment of the church. However, this view holds that the *charismata* do in fact continue, but now through officially recognized offices. Charismatic authority is conferred through ecclesiastical ordination. As the Holy Spirit initially endowed the church with charismatic gifts, so he subsequently guided the development of the church's official structures through which the *charismata* continue to function. (As a sociological phenomenon, this development was famously labeled "the routinization of charisma" by German sociologist Max Weber [1864–1920].)[3]

Although this view is associated especially with the church's theological and institutional development in the third, fourth, and fifth centuries, and later with official medieval Roman Catholic teaching, in a more informal way it is often found among evangelicals and other Protestants. Versions of this argument hold that God's Spirit works in the church today primarily through ordained clergy as they teach and apply the Scriptures to the church's life. Functionally, *charisma* and office are conflated into one, whether or not the terms "charisma" and "office" are employed.

3. *The* charismata *ceased to be manifested because of the church's spiritual decline.* Throughout church history, many have argued that the "cessation" of the *charismata* in the church was never God's intent. God's design was that gifts should function in the church throughout its history. Decline in practice of gifts, or the prohibition or restriction of gifts, shows the church's defection from God's plan, its spiritual decline and unfaithfulness.

John Wesley (1703–1791) is one example of those who have held this view. Wesley noted that although from the time of the Emperor Constantine "extraordinary gifts... almost totally ceased" in the church, the reason was not that they were no longer needed. Rather, the "real cause was, 'the love of many'—almost of all Christians, so called," had grown cold.[4] Perhaps the *charismata* "were designed to remain in the church throughout all ages," Wesley reflected, and would "be restored at the nearer approach" of the restoration of all things.[5]

If gifts disappeared in the church due to its spiritual decline, then renewed manifestations of gifts should accompany its renewal. This argument has often been found in church renewal movements. God wills to renew the church by his Spirit, and a part of that renewing work is a fresh outpouring of *charismata*—the restoration of gifts to their intended normative place in church life.

This view naturally raises the question of discerning the genuineness of fresh effusions of gifts. Since various kinds of spiritual manifestations are found in non-Christian religions, and since the Bible itself warns of false prophets and teachers and the deceptive work of Satan, how is the church to discern the genuine from the counterfeit? The discernment question has been a contentious one throughout church history; it is a major reason the *charismata* often prove controversial. At times of renewed emphasis on gifts, the question of discerning authentic gifts becomes a key consideration.

Renewed Emphasis on Gifts

Spiritual gifts have functioned in the church throughout history in varying degree, whether or not the actual language of gifts was used. Even when the church did not teach about gifts, or even denied them, devout Christians often ministered God's grace to others simply as an expression of Christian love. Gifts operated—even if not specifically recognized or emphasized.

The more dramatic gifts, such as prophecy, ecstatic speech, or miracles, appeared from time to time especially in marginal or heretical groups. Where the church lacked a robust biblical understanding of gifts, it tended to view such manifestations as extreme, subversive, or even as evidence of heresy. Charismatic gifts came to be associated with millenarian, apocalyptic, or heretical groups and movements.

The birth and growth of Pentecostal and charismatic Christianity in the twentieth century prompted a reconsideration of gifts in both Roman Catholic and Protestant Christianity. Pentecostalism raised the question of the *charismata* as never before since the second and third centuries. Most early Pentecostals viewed glossolalia (tongues-speaking) as an authenticating sign of baptism in the Holy Spirit. This was especially true in the remarkable Azusa Street Revival in Los Angeles in 1906–1907. Debates about the *charismata* in the early twentieth century thus centered especially on glossolalia, and to a lesser degree other "sign" gifts such as prophecy and miracles. Tongues-speaking and other charismatic gifts proved divisive, sometimes provoking schism in denominations and local churches. This was especially true in the case of several U.S. denominations that traced their origins to the Holiness Movement which emerged within Methodism in the 1800s. Those groups that accepted the Pentecostal teaching became Pentecostal denominations; those that rejected it maintained a theology of the work of the Holy Spirit that viewed glossolalia as inauthentic or even demonic.

More generally, charismatic gifts provoked controversy in many Protestant denominations in the early to mid-1900s. However, by the 1970s and 1980s many of the older denominations had come to tolerate or even welcome the charismatic emphasis, viewing it as a potentially renewing force in the church. When the Catholic charismatic renewal arose in the United States in the 1960s, the Roman Catholic Church accommodated the new movement, largely preserving its energy within the church by establishing links between the church's hierarchy and charismatic leaders.

By the early twenty-first century, much of worldwide Christianity viewed spiritual gifts as an integral part of church life, whatever their particular interpretation of glossolalia or other gifts. A kind of "charismatic leavening" occurred due to the growth and influence of Pentecostal and charismatic Christianity, and due also to new Christian churches and movements throughout the world, where spiritual gifts often seemed to flourish spontaneously.

The Practical Meaning of Spiritual Gifts

An inherent affinity exists between evangelical theology and spiritual gifts because of the normative role of Scripture in the church and the evangelical emphasis on salvation by grace (*charis*). Though views regarding the *charismata* vary widely within evangelicalism, most evangelical churches now recognize and attempt to take seriously the biblical teachings regarding gifts.

Several general points and distinctions are helpful in understanding the practical role of gifts in the church today:

1. God's Spirit endows the church with a range of spiritual gifts out of the fullness of Christ so that the church may truly function as Christ's body. The *charismata* are gracious, continuing endowments to the church for the sake of the church's wholeness, growth, and maturity ("edification"), and authentic witness.

2. All believers receive one or more spiritual gifts by virtue of their membership in the body of Christ and participation in Christ through the Holy Spirit. No believer has all the gifts, for the fullness of gifts is found only in Jesus Christ. The point of gifts is gracious diversity for the sake of the church's health and witness.

3. No one particular gift is necessary or required of all believers, since gifts vary and their distribution is determined by the Spirit, not by personal choice or ecclesiastical authority.

4. Since false or counterfeit gifts may appear from time to time, the church faces the task of discerning between the authentic and the inauthentic. Paul makes clear in 1 Corinthians that gifts are not self-authenticating but are to be evaluated on the basis of whether they build up the church and extend its witness.

5. Gifts of the Spirit are to be understood in relation to the fruit of the Spirit (Gal. 5:22–23). In the NT, the gifts and the fruit of the Spirit are correlative ways the Spirit enriches Christ's body. The point of gifts is diversity—not all have the same gifts—but the point of the fruit of the Spirit is the manifestation of the character of Jesus Christ, something to be expected of all believers. Gifts function in a healthy way in the church when they are accompanied by the Spirit's fruit—love, joy, peace,

patience, kindness, generosity, faithfulness, gentleness, and self-control. In each believer, particular gifts become effective channels through which the fruit of the Spirit is manifested, both within and beyond the church.

6. Faithfulness in exercising gifts leads to greater fruitfulness. God's will is that Christians "abound" and are fruitful through God's grace in their lives (cf. Rom. 15:13; 1 Thess. 3:12; John 15:1–8), "bearing fruit in every good work" (Col. 1:10). This is true regarding gifts as well as in other respects, and is reinforced by Jesus' stewardship parables.

7. In order that gifts may flourish and function healthily, the Spirit endows the church with charismatically gifted leaders whose primary task is "to equip the saints for the work of ministry" so that the church may grow up into Christ and become an agent of God's grace in the world. Ministry is given to the whole church, not just to its leaders, and the role of gifted leaders (the "apostles, prophets, evangelists, shepherds and teachers" mentioned in Ephesians 4:11) is principally one of "equipping" through encouraging and guiding the diversity of gifts and in general supervising and building up the church (Eph. 4:11–16).

Though evangelicals and other Christians vary in their interpretation of different gifts and their function, evangelicals increasingly recognize the practical role of gifts in building up the church and extending its witness. The NT makes little explicit connection between spiritual gifts and the church's mission in the world, but an implicit logic is clear. Gifts are given so that the church may fully be Christ's body, and as the authentic body of Christ, fulfill its witness in the world. Jesus said, "As the Father has sent me, so I send you" (John 20:21). Spiritual gifts take on added meaning when understood as the Spirit's endowment through which the church truly becomes Jesus' body sent into the world.

Gifts and Culture

The church always lives within a particular cultural context—even as Jesus in his incarnation came into a particular social context. Culture therefore plays a part in the church's life and witness, and thus in the exercise of spiritual gifts. Three observations are useful here.

First, the church will manifest a diversity of spiritual gifts, whatever the cultural context. Gifts transcend culture in the same way that the gospel does. However, the manifestation of gifts may vary somewhat according to the cultural context. For example, the gifts of women may function more freely and openly in societies that grant greater freedom for women, and in more hidden or limited ways in societies where women's roles are restricted.

Second, the terminology and understanding of gifts may vary from one culture to another. The specific NT terminology of gifts need not be considered normative everywhere, since the terms used in the NT are partly a function of cultural context and vary even in the NT. It is not required, for instance, that churches everywhere must use the terms "apostles," "evangelists," or "pastors." In different cultures varying terms and somewhat differing understandings may be employed as the church allows the Spirit sovereignly to distribute gifts "as the Spirit chooses" (1 Cor. 12:11).

Third, spiritual gifts are a key means by which the church engages its culture. By God's grace, gifts help the church actually live in the world as he did, as salt and light (Matt. 5:14), showing forth God's love and truth and exposing society's "works of darkness" (Eph. 5:11). Spiritual gifts are important ways by which Christians practice the priesthood of believers and act in the world as redemptive servants of Jesus Christ. In principle, gifts may be seen as part of the way God equips the church to engage its culture in all dimensions.

Spiritual Gifts and Eschatology

Since spiritual gifts are God's ongoing provision for the church, they have no special connection to the end times. However, gifts and eschatology are in fact linked.

Acts 2:16–21 makes clear that the pouring out of the Spirit at Pentecost came in fulfillment of the OT prophecy of Joel. Gifts are eschatological in the sense that they are given so Christ's body may be equipped to walk and witness in the power of the Holy Spirit, testifying to the fulfillment of God's promises and demonstrating the good news of the kingdom of God now present and still coming. In this sense, gifts foreshadow the restoration of all things in Jesus Christ by the Spirit.

Spiritual gifts are the operation of the Holy Spirit in the church so that the church may truly and visibly be Jesus' ministering body in the world, a redemptive community that visibly embodies now the kingdom of God. The larger purpose is "that God may be glorified in all things through Jesus Christ" (1 Pt. 4:11).

NOTES

1. Hans Küng, "The Charismatic Structure of the Church," *The Church and Ecumenism*, Vol. 4 of *Concilium* (New York: Paulist Press, 1965), 41–61.

2. Jon Ruthven, *On the Cessation of the Charismata: The Protestant Polemic on Postbiblical Miracles* (Sheffield, England: Sheffield Academic Press, 1993).

3. Max Weber, *The Theory of Social and Economic Organization*, trans. A. M. Henderson and Talcott Parsons (New York: Free Press, 1964), 363–373.

4. John Wesley, Sermon 89, "The More Excellent Way," *The Works of John Wesley*, Vol. 4, ed. Albert C. Outler (Nashville, Tenn.: Abingdon, 1986), 263–264.

5. John Wesley, Sermon 4, "Scriptural Christianity," *The Works of John Wesley*, Vol. 1, ed. Albert C. Outler (Nashville, Tenn.: Abingdon Press, 1984), 160.

BIBLIOGRAPHY

Crehan, J. H., S.J. "Charisms." *Catholic Dictionary of Theology*. London: Thomas Nelson, 1967, 2:19–22.

Davis, Kenneth R. "Charismata." In J. D. Douglas, ed., *New International Dictionary of the Christian Church*, rev. ed. Grand Rapids: Zondervan, 1978, 211–212.

Dorries, David. "Azusa Street Revival." In Michael McClymond, ed., *Encyclopedia of Religious Revivals in America*. Westport, Conn.: Greenwood, 2007, 2:37–42.

Kinghorn, Kenneth Cain. *Gifts of the Spirit*. Nashville, Tenn.: Abingdon, 1976.

Küng, Hans. "The Charismatic Structure of the Church." In *The Church and Ecumenism*, Vol. 4 of *Concilium*. New York: Paulist Press, 1965, 41–61.

Michaels, J. R. "Gifts of the Spirit." In Stanley M. Burgess, ed., *New International Dictionary of Pentecostal and Charismatic Movements*, rev. and expanded ed. Grand Rapids: Zondervan, 2002, 664–667.

Robeck, Cecil M., Jr., ed. *Charismatic Experiences in History*. Peabody, Mass.: Hendrickson, 1985.

Ruthven, Jon. *On the Cessation of the Charismata: The Protestant Polemic on Postbiblical Miracles*. Sheffield, U.K.: Sheffield Academic Press, 1993.

Snyder, Howard A. *The Community of the King*, rev. ed. Downers Grove, Ill: InterVarsity Press, 2004.

Snyder, Howard A., with Daniel V. Runyon. *The Divided Flame: Wesleyans and the Charismatic Renewal*. Grand Rapids: Francis Asbury Press, 1986.

Suenens, Léon Joseph. *A New Pentecost?* Trans. Francis Martin. New York: Seabury, 1975.

Sullivan, Francis A., S.J. *Charisms and Charismatic Renewal: A Biblical and Theological Study*. Ann Arbor, Mich.: Servant Books, 1982.

Synan, Vinson. *The Holiness-Pentecostal Tradition: Charismatic Movements in the Twentieth Century*. Grand Rapids: Eerdmans, 1997.

PART V

THEOLOGY OF MISSION

CHAPTER 22

MISSION AND EVANGELISM

MICHAEL J. MCCLYMOND

THE term "mission"—derived from the Latin verb, *missio*, meaning "send"—came into general use in its specifically Christian and theological sense only in the sixteenth century, when the Roman Catholic Jesuit order used the term to refer to the sending of its members to preach, instruct, serve, and win converts.[1] The term "evangelism," by contrast, is based on biblical vocabulary, specifically the Greek terms *euanggelion* ("gospel"), *euanggelizo* ("preach good news"), and *euanggelistes* ("one who preaches good news" or "evangelist"). In its Old Testament sense (as in the Septuagint version of Isaiah 52:7–10) *euanggelizo* evokes a powerful and dramatic image. The city of Jerusalem is at war. The people eagerly await news from the army fighting on their behalf. Sentries stand on the city walls, scanning the horizon for signs of an approaching messenger. At last the long-awaited messenger (the *euanggelistes*) appears on the hills surrounding the city and bears good news. The army has won and their victory is also God's victory: "Your God reigns!" The entire city erupts into celebration.[2] The word "evangelism," despite its varied use over time, in its original sense refers to a joyful message of God's gracious and peaceable reign.

It was not until the latter half of the twentieth century that reflection on mission and evangelism became a major focus within the broader field of Christian theology. Since the early 1800s, when most Protestant and Catholic seminaries established a standard fourfold curriculum in biblical studies, systematic or dogmatic theology, church history, and practical theology, there had been a question as to how the study of mission and evangelism might fit (or not fit) into the curriculum. Most held that mission study fell under practical theology, though some insisted that it could function as a component within all four major disciplines.[3] Since practical theology received less scholarly attention and carried less prestige than the other three seminary disciplines, the study of mission was not a priority during the 1800s. Though New College at Edinburgh University appointed Alexander Duff in 1867 to teach mission studies, Duff's teaching position was phased out upon his retirement.[4]

At the start of the twentieth century, pioneering scholars like Gustav Warneck (1834–1919) sought to make a place for the study of Christian mission (*Missionslehre)* in academic life. Nonetheless, the theology of mission and theology of evangelism did not truly come into its own until after World War II. During this time of soul-searching, there was a reaction against the glib optimism and self-confidence that characterized many European and American missionary-sending churches of the early 1900s. Moreover, there was also a realization of the growing importance of the "younger churches" of Africa, Asia, and Latin America. The new theme that emerged at the 1952 missionary conference in Willingen, West Germany, became known as *missio Dei* ("mission of God"). The Christian church is missionary by its very nature, it was said, because the Christian God is a missionary God.

Like a photographic image coming into focus, the outlines of mission theology became increasingly clear from the 1950s to the 1990s. By the century's end one could speak, with David Bosch, of an "emerging ecumenical paradigm" in the theology of mission.[5] While there were differences of emphasis among Protestant evangelicals, Roman Catholics, and participants in the World Council of Churches (WCC), there was also a remarkable convergence among the three groups on the foundational theology of Christian mission. One finds notable commonalities in comparing such Catholic documents as *Ad Gentes* (1965), *Evangelii Nuntiandi* (1975), and *Redemptoris Missio* (1990), with the WCC's declaration on *Mission and Evangelism* (1982), and the evangelical *Lausanne Covenant* (1974), *Manila Manifesto* (1989), and sixty-plus Lausanne Occasional Papers (1974 to 2004).

Outline of a General Theology of Mission

Today's shared theology of mission may be described as *trinitarian, christological, eschatological, pneumatological,* and *ecclesiological.* The word *trinitarian* points toward eternal distinctions within the being of God as foundational for understanding Christian mission. According to the Nicene Creed, God as Father shares with or transmits his essence to the Son: "Jesus Christ . . . eternally begotten of the Father, God from God, Light from Light, true God from true God, begotten not made." This means that God's self-giving is primordial. For God, to be is to give and to love. To invoke Augustine's analogy, the Father is the eternal Lover, the Son is the eternal Beloved, and the Spirit is the eternal bond of Love between Father and Son. This trinitarian understanding implies that God's very nature is to communicate and impart his own being, blessedness, and glory. That is, God is missional. Or, as Jonathan Edwards stated, "God is a communicating being"—a theme for describing both the internal life of the triune God and the external work of God in creating the world.[6]

Such a trinitarian rendering of the theology of mission is also *christological.* Horst Bürkle writes: "Christian mission, as a life expression of the church, is grounded in the salvific event of the divine Logos."[7] God's decision to give his Son as a gift to and for the world undergirds the church's mission. Jesus Christ is himself the pattern for mission. The words and deeds of Jesus as recorded in the gospels are the mission paradigm. When Jesus sends out the twelve apostles (Matthew 10:1–42) and the seventy evangelists (Luke 10:1–24), he bids them to go and do as he has done. "Cure the sick, raise the dead, cleanse the lepers, cast out demons. You received without payment, give without payment" (Matthew 10:8).[8] Their sending is based on Jesus' sending: "As the Father has sent me, so I send you" (John 20:21). All mission has a *representative* character: "Whoever welcomes you welcomes me, and whoever welcomes me welcomes the one who sent me" (Matthew 10:40). The Apostle Paul describes himself as among the "ambassadors for Christ, since God is making his appeal through us" (2 Corinthians 5:20). The idea of representation, at its deepest level, merges into the notion of incarnation. Rodger Bassham points to Christ's Incarnation as a model for understanding the task of Christian mission: "The principle of the incarnation points to an involvement in the world by Jesus Christ which the church seeks to emulate as it strives to penetrate into the very life and existence of those to whom it ministers and serves."[9] Furthermore, the church's mission is *christological* in that it is based on Jesus' resurrection from the dead—the event whereby Jesus' claim of authority was vindicated (Matthew 12:38–40; John 2:18–22; Romans 1:4)—followed by Jesus' ascension and God's conferral of ultimate authority upon him and "the name that is above every name" (Acts 1:9–11; Philippians 2:5–11; Ephesians 1:19–23). The commissioning of the disciples in Matthew 28:19–20 is preceded by Jesus' declaration: "All authority in heaven and on earth has been given to me" (Matthew 28:18). In light of a commission received from Jesus, the disciples have both the privilege and responsibility to "make disciples." The command to the disciples to preach among the nations occurs in the Gospel of Matthew only in a post-resurrection context. The Christian mission makes sense only if viewed in light of the risen and ascended Christ.

The theology of Christian mission is *eschatological.* God's promises to Abraham in Genesis and to the nation of Israel in the latter part of Isaiah (chapters 40–66) set the context for the New Testament mission. According to the Hebrew Scriptures, the Gentile nations belong to the Messiah as an "inheritance" or "heritage" given to him upon his entrance into his kingly reign: "Ask of me, and I will make the nations your heritage, and the ends of the earth your possession" (Psalm 2:8). The promise given by God to his Servant has application to all peoples of the world: "It is too light a thing that you should be my servant to raise up the tribes of Jacob... I will give you as a light to the nations, that my salvation may reach to the ends of the earth" (Isaiah 49:6). This universal dimension was already suggested when God promised Abraham that "in you all the families of the earth shall be blessed" (Genesis 12:3). God's intention in choosing Abraham and his descendents was never to abandon the Gentile peoples. Instead God sought to bring Israel into the fullness of blessing so that other nations might be drawn to Israel and thus to Israel's God (Psalm 67:1–2). When Israel receives God's full blessing, then the Gentile nations will seek to obtain the blessing themselves through joining themselves to the Israelites (Zechariah 8:23). Johannes Blauw referred to the Old Testament pattern as a centripetal movement—a coming of the nations toward Israel—to distinguish it from a centrifugal movement—a going forth with good news—such as we find in the New Testament texts.[10] The coming of the Messiah and the messianic mission are eschatological in that they represent the culmination of God's ancient promises to Israel.

The Christian mission is *eschatological* in another sense. The present-day missional church looks toward the Messiah's return. The German missiologist Walter Freytag commented: "If we know of the coming Kingdom, we cannot rejoice in the promise without proclaiming it."[11] The Christian church lives between the times of Christ's first and second comings—the "already" and the "not yet" of God's kingdom. The Gospel of Matthew connects the preaching of the gospel among the nations with the Second Coming of Christ: "And this good news of the kingdom will be proclaimed throughout the world, as a testimony to all the nations, and then the end will come" (Matthew 24:14). The so-called Great Commission passage at the end of Matthew concludes with Jesus' eschatological promise that "I am with you always, to the end of the age" (Matthew 28:20). Similarly, in Acts of the Apostles, Jesus responds to the disciples' query regarding the end-times, "Lord, is this the time when you will restore the kingdom to Israel?" (Acts 1:6), with an answer linking mission, the end-times, and the coming of the Holy Spirit (Acts 1:7–8). In Acts, as in Matthew, the preaching of the good news of salvation through Christ is an eschatological activity—a sign of the end-times.

With particular clarity, Luke-Acts makes the preaching of the good news of Christ a *pneumatological* sign and activity. When the Spirit comes upon the disciples on the day of Pentecost, they speak in many languages and bear witness to "God's deeds of power" (Acts 2:11). The promise of Acts 1 is thus fulfilled in Acts 2 as the disciples, "filled with the Holy Spirit," become Christ's "witnesses" in Jerusalem and thereafter among the nations. The stress lies on the free and spontaneous character of this witness. Mission is less a task than a privilege. As Lesslie Newbigin has noted, the statement of Acts 1:8 that "you will be my witnesses" is not given as a command but rather as a promise. Moreover, this promise is tied to the coming of the Spirit, understood as the empowerer and enabler of the church's witness. Newbigin writes: "Mission, in other words, is gospel and not law; it is the overflow of a great gift, not the carrying of a great burden."[12] This insight serves as a corrective to the understanding of mission exclusively or primarily in terms of obedience to a command.

The eschatological and pneumatological dimensions of the biblical mission intertwine with *ecclesiology*. Emil Brunner famously declared that "the church exists by mission, just as fire exists by burning."[13] Mission, that is, is not just one among many activities of the church. Instead the church is missional or missionary by nature, since the church is a sign of God's mission in the world and an anticipation of the fulfillment of God's final purposes. The disciples are made "witnesses" to

Christ (Acts 1:8). Just as the Spirit bears witness to Christ (John 15:26–27, 16:13–15), so also does the Spirit-filled church. The preaching of Christ to many peoples and nations is an anticipatory sign of Christ's coming reign. As the Book of Revelation shows, the heavenly congregation includes some "from every nation, from all tribes and peoples and languages" (Revelation 7:9; cf. 5:9)—thus fulfilling the hope prefigured on the day of Pentecost. The Christian church, as a community of Jews and Gentiles in one body, represents a "mystery" hidden for ages but revealed in the last days (Ephesians 3:1–13). As a "mystery," the church is a sign that is not obvious to all. Nonetheless, the church exerts a hidden influence in the world that may be compared to "salt," "light," "yeast," or the growth of a "mustard seed" (Matthew 5:13–16, 13:31–33). Late twentieth-century mission theology recovered the *ecclesiological* dimension of mission—that is, a sense that mission is not only something the church *does* but also something corresponding to what the church *is*.

Historical Patterns in the Practice of Mission and Evangelism

Having delineated a general theology of mission, we turn now to a number of historical paradigms of Christian witness. Much may be learned from the early church. Adolf von Harnack in *The Mission and Expansion of Christianity* (1902) observed that non-Christians converted for multiple reasons during the church's first three centuries:

> We must eschew the error of imagining that everyone who came over to Christianity was won by a missionary propaganda of dogmatic completeness. So far as our sources throw light on this point, they reveal a very different state of things, and this applies even to the entire period preceding Constantine. In countless instances, it was but one ray of light that wrought the change. One person would be brought over by means of the Old Testament, another by the exorcising of demons, a third by the purity of Christian life; others, again, by the monotheism of Christianity, above all by the prospect of complete expiation, or by the prospect which it held out of immortality, or by the profundity of its speculations, or by the social standing which it conferred.[14]

Harnack challenged the idea that theological argumentation and intellectual persuasion were the primary means of conversion in most cases. Most believers had little or no formal education. Tertullian noted that "the uneducated are always the majority with us," and thus most would not have responded to elaborate or philosophical argumentation.[15]

What Greco-Romans responded to was the Christian way of life. The perceived moral excellence of early Christians, their deeds of mercy toward those in need, and their reputation as healers of the sick and exorcisers of demons combined to make the gospel plausible in a cultural context seemingly inimical to the message. Paradoxically, it was the early Christians' fierce renunciation of Greco-Roman lifestyles and values that gave them credibility and esteem, as Harnack comments:

> This resolute renunciation of the world was really the first thing which made the church competent and strong to tell upon the world. Then, if ever, was the saying true: "He who would do anything for the world must have nothing to do with it." Primitive Christianity has been upbraided for being too unworldly and ascetic. But revolutions are not effected with rosewater, and it was a veritable revolution to overthrow polytheism and establish the majesty of God and goodness in the world.... This could never have happened, in the first instance, had not men asserted the vanity of the present world, and practically severed themselves from it.[16]

Without romanticizing the early Christians, one can see among them a wholeness of missionary witness that was rarely matched in later history. Also impressive is the fact that the missionary successes of the early church were largely due to informal or lay missionaries.[17] Witness to Christ was a characteristic of the early Christians' way of life rather than a deliberate, rationalized activity assigned to specialists or plotted out by means of formal plans and strategies.

Speaking broadly, one might identify four major historical patterns in the practice of Christian witness—*catholic, charismatic, social-ethical*, and *evangelical*. These patterns are not chronologically sequential, inasmuch as the early church exhibited all four patterns and there seems to be in our day a growing convergence of the four.

The *catholic* tradition of mission lays stress on the messenger as much or more than the message. The missionary functions as a personal embodiment of Christ. He or she must be saintly.[18] The catholic tradition thus fosters an incarnational approach to ministry. The missionary must completely identify with the people and share in their way of life and their daily concerns. Such an approach to mission is self-sacrificial—like Christ's own mission and ministry. In the teeth of opposition, the missionary must be willing to endure martyrdom—to suffer harm rather than doing harm. The catholic paradigm finds literary expression in the classic hagiographic tradition, including such early accounts as Sulpicius Severus, *The Life of St. Martin* (ca. 396), describing the ascetic and self-denying life of Martin of Tours, the missionary bishop and evangelist in Gaul. Also in this genre is Bede's *Ecclesiastical History of the English Nation* (731)—a crucial witness to the early spread of Christianity in the British Isles. Of great importance for the spread of Christianity in the early Middle Ages were the Celtic monastic communities in Ireland and Scotland, from which many missionaries went forth to found new monastic communities and to evangelize continental Europe. The monastic virtues of self-discipline, orderliness, patience, and service to others were directly pertinent to the tasks of evangelization in the early medieval context. The same may be said of the men's and women's missionary orders of modern Catholicism. In Roman Catholic thought, past and present, there is no conversion to Christ that does not include conversion to the church. Indeed, the Vatican II documents refer to the church itself as "the universal sacrament of salvation."[19] The sacramentality of the church lies at the center of the catholic model for mission. This means that Christians witness by its nature is corporate rather than individualistic.

The *charismatic* tradition of mission was conspicuous during the church's first two centuries and has been revived during the last 150 years in the global evangelical missionary movement and among Pentecostal and Charismatic Christians. A key idea is that the verbal presentation of the good news should be accompanied by tangible signs of God's presence and power. The Epistle to the Hebrews states that "God added his testimony [to the gospel preaching] by signs and wonders and by various miracles, and by gifts of the Holy Spirit, distributed according to his will" (Hebrews 2:3–4). Proponents argue that there is no reason to believe that charismatic manifestations abruptly ceased with the passing of the first apostles. Indeed, even those holding the cessationist position (that is, that miracles ceased in the first century) must admit that as late as the second and third centuries such authors as Irenaeus and Origen reported the healing of the sick and the casting out of demons as regular phenomena among ordinary Christians.[20] Their importance for the growth of the early church is underscored not only by Adolf von Harnack but also more recently by Ramsey McMullen in *Christianizing the Roman Empire* (1984). McMullan asserted that the reputation of the early Christians for healing and exorcising demons was a primary motive for conversion among the ancient pagans.[21] Moreover, the later Catholic missionary literature is replete with the miraculous.

In contrast, many conservative, Bible-oriented Protestants—as well as liberal Protestants influenced by Enlightenment rationalism—have difficulty accepting the possibility of supernatural signs of grace. Nonetheless, attitudes among evangelicals began to shift during the 1800s. William Arthur's *The Tongue of Fire* (1856) argued that the Christian church needed to experience a "new Pentecost" and receive a fresh infusion of spiritual power to fulfill its global missionary mandate. Evangelical missionaries in various parts of the world during the 1800s and early 1900s recounted episodes of the miraculous. Among indigenous peoples, tangible manifestations of spiritual power were often far more convincing than intellectual arguments and sometimes resulted in the conversion of an entire tribe. By the 1880s and 1890s more books were being written about the Holy Spirit than at any previous point in the history of the church. When Christian revival struck just after 1900 in various regions of the world—Topeka (1901), Wales (1904–1905), India (1905), Los Angeles (1906), Korea (1907), Chile (1909)—a Pentecostal movement gradually took shape that incorporated healing, exorcism, and charismatic gifts as part of its ordinary functioning. During the 1980s, John Wimber used the term "power evangelism" to describe the combination of verbal evangelism with supernatural manifestations. By the century's end, expectant prayer for the healing of the sick was more a mainstream phenomenon—even in mainline Protestant and Catholic circles—than it had been just a generation earlier.

Christian mission throughout its history has involved deeds of love and mercy. A stress on good works is thus not a defining quality of any one tradition of mission. Yet the *social-ethical* tradition has been preoccupied with social transformation and issues of justice. Adherents believe that mission should aim at changing the structures of society. Genuine Christian compassion will not merely tell people about Jesus and then leave them in circumstances of exploitation and mistreatment. Where injustice and oppression exist, the church must side with those who suffer. Advocates of this view have often been inspired by Old Testament exhortations to show mercy to the widow and orphan, to deal fairly with foreigners and other vulnerable people, and to uphold justice under law. The biblical story of the Exodus shows that God hears the cry of the oppressed and intervenes to rescue them. The social-ethical tradition has been influential in evangelical Protestantism, liberal Protestantism, and Roman Catholicism. Nineteenth-century social reformers such as William Wilberforce and the Clapham sect in England, and the abolitionist followers of Charles Finney in America, were ardent evangelicals. Social Gospel proponents such as Washington Gladden, Walter Rauschenbusch, and more recent figures like Martin Luther King, Jr., had a more liberal theological basis. The Wesleyan-Methodist movement has been in the vanguard of the social-ethical tradition. A Roman Catholic tradition of social engagement began with Pope Leo XIII's encyclical *Rerum Novarum* (1893), and continued in later documents, such as *Gaudium et Spes* (1965), and more than a dozen other official Catholic documents.[22] An intensification of this Catholic social-ethical tradition began with the Medellíin, Colombia, bishops' conference of 1966, followed by the emergence of Latin American liberation theology as developed by Gustavo Gutierrez, Jon Sobrino, Juan Luis Segundo, Leonardo Boff, and others. Though the liberationists' occasional appeals to Marxist concepts proved controversial, liberation theology had a powerful effect by thrusting the world's poor into the spotlight and bringing them to the attention of the churches of the wealthier nations.

The *evangelical* tradition of mission (discussed more fully below) may be traced back to the Evangelical Awakening in the British Isles and the Great Awakening in the North American colonies during the 1730s and 1740s. The history-making surge of international Protestant mission interest in the late 1700s and early 1800s was a fruit of these mid-1700s revivals. Evangelical missionary churches and agencies stressed the authority of the Bible, the gospel's doctrinal content (including the divinity of Jesus, his atoning death, and bodily resurrection), the necessity of conversion and the "new birth," the "lostness" of unevangelized people, and the urgency of preaching Christ to all nations before Jesus' Second Coming. Evangelicals identified the goal of mission as church planting, and laid emphasis on taking the Christian message to those who had never before heard of Christ. They often specified the Great Commission passage (Matthew 28:18–20) as the "biblical basis" of Christian mission and searched for "biblical methods" for church-planting. John Nevius and other nineteenth-century missionaries proposed the "three-self principles"—self-governing, self-supporting, self-propagating—which, when applied to newly established churches around the world, dictated that they could and should be freed from permanent dependence on mother churches in Europe or North America. Where three-self principles were implemented—as in Korea—one found culturally indigenous congregations led by native pastors and laypersons. Though critics have charged evangelical missionaries with doctrinal precisionism, sociopolitical passivity, and triumphalistic attitudes (for example, in speaking of "conquering the world for Christ"), the tangible results of evangelicals' efforts around the globe are evident today in the vibrant churches of Africa, Asia, and Latin America. Moreover, the Lausanne Congress (1974) and its ongoing conversations and reflections have addressed many long-standing criticisms of evangelical missions.[23]

The Lausanne Movement and Contemporary Evangelical Mission Theology

In the early 1900s the international Protestant missionary movement included conservative and liberal wings that collaborated and shared in the epochal 1910 Edinburgh Conference on world evangelism. Yet by the 1920s the fundamentalist-modernist rift had emerged and much of the controversy centered on foreign missions. The suspicions of conservatives that modernist missionaries were engaged in humanitarian service and no longer sought conversion were confirmed with the publication of W. E. Hocking's *Re-Thinking Missions* (1933), which redefined the goal of mission as "preparation for world unity in civilization." The proposal was for Christians to join with non-Christians and affirm a common religiosity in the face of secularism. From the 1930s, evangelicals were often at odds with conciliarists—that is, mainline Protestants (later joined by Catholics) who affiliated with such ecumenical bodies as the World Council of Churches (WCC) and, in the eyes of evangelicals gave scant attention to the issue of eternal salvation. The 1960s saw the gap grow wider, when a new secularity emerged and some in WCC circles claimed that "the world sets the agenda for the church"—that is, that God guides the church not through scripture or church tradition but through secular trends.[24] Theologian J. Hoekendijk urged European students "to begin radically to desacralize the church" and insisted that Christianity was "a secular movement" and not "some sort of religion." The WCC's 1968 Assembly at Uppsala, Sweden, reflected the secular mood. Some spoke of "humanization" instead of salvation.[25] The pièce de résistance for many evangelicals came with the call for a moratorium on missions from certain ecumenical leaders in the early 1970s.

By this stage evangelical leaders were generally opposed to ecumenical theologies of mission. Arthur Glasser spoke of a "secularized gospel and reduction of the mission of the Church to social and political activism."[26] Pope John Paul II later made analogous statements critical of secularizing trends in mission theology.[27] Under the aegis of the Billy Graham organization, evangelicals held conferences on evangelism first in Wheaton, Illinois (1966), and then Berlin (1966). In retrospect, the chief significance of these was to prepare for the 1974 Lausanne Consultation. Given the evangelical-conciliar contentions during the 1970s, the surprising thing about Lausanne is that evangelicals embraced many ideas and themes of ecumenical missiology from the 1950s through the 1960s. Lausanne made it acceptable for evangelicals to embrace social action as one aspect of a biblically based theology of mission. Lausanne shifted evangelical approaches to mission much as Vatican II had changed the Catholic Church. James Scherer wrote that "the Lausanne movement appeared to be giving evangelicalism a new spirit—a fresh blend of evangelical tradition with modernity.... Evangelicalism was demonstrating that it could adapt to the modern world without surrendering biblical principles or forsaking the missionary mandate."[28]

The presence of numerous delegates at Lausanne from the developing world—about 1,200 of the 2,473 officially registered participants—seems to be a key reason that the consultation embraced a broader, holistic theology of mission.[29] Non-Western evangelicals had largely avoided the fundamentalist-modernist split of the early 1900s, with its divorce between biblical evangelism and the "social gospel." For them there was no trade-off between doctrinal fidelity and social compassion. At Lausanne, a subset known as the Radical Discipleship Group pressed fellow delegates to reject a spiritualized, otherworldly idea of mission and to sanction Christian involvement in sociopolitical issues. Two leading voices—C. René Padilla and Samuel Escobar—were Latin American. British evangelical John Stott, in his plenary address at Lausanne, signaled a paradigm shift in evangelical mission theology, admitting that his own thinking had altered since the Berlin gathering in 1966. "The mission of the church," said Stott, "arises from the mission of God and is to be modeled on it." For Stott, "mission" includes "everything the church is sent into the world to do," and "a proper understanding of loving service includes both evangelism and social action as authentic." Social action is thus "a partner of evangelism." Nonetheless "evangelism"—a narrower concept than mission—"may and must be defined only in terms of the message."[30] Stott's address thus enlarged the evangelical mission agenda without relinquishing the traditional evangelical focus on presenting a biblically based and doctrinally correct message.

Despite debates subsequent to Lausanne on whether there were "two mandates" (that is, evangelism and social action) or just "one mandate" with differing aspects, and what some perceived as retrenchment after Lausanne, it was Padilla, Escobar, and Stott who won out and reshaped the global evangelical mission agenda during the 1980s and 1990s. Later collaborations resulted in no fewer than sixty Lausanne Occasional Papers from 1974 to 2004, with some recent documents ranging up to one hundred pages in length and offering a sophisticated analysis of church, culture, and society.[31] The Lausanne documents reaffirmed many points previously made by conciliarists. Lausanne documents have stressed the trinitarian foundation of mission, the church's missionary character, the local church, the laity's role, the need for partnership, and the role of women in global mission. The "holistic" character of mission—as including verbal evangelism, deeds of love and mercy, and action on behalf of justice—has been a special focus. Another stress is the local community with its worship, service, and proclamation as the locus of Christian witness.[32] Since the 1980s, the term "transformation" has been used to describe a gospel-centered process of social, political, cultural change that is led by the churches of a given city or region.[33] Recently both Lausanne and the WCC have highlighted reconciliation between conflicting groups as a crucial aspect of the church's missionary mandate.

In addition to these areas of evangelical-conciliar-catholic agreement, there are topics of continuing discussion and debate. With their commitment to verbal evangelism, evangelicals have been concerned that a postmodern and relativistic worldview might undercut the claims of the gospel and its call for decision. Many secular people no longer believe in any "truth" that transcends the culture or the biases of individuals.[34] Evangelicals and conciliars—though calling for sociopolitical involvement—have disagreed as to the appropriate level and nature of such involvement. Specific criticisms of political policies—for example, WCC documents taking issue with United States foreign policy in Central America in the 1980s—were poorly received by evangelicals who were anti-Communist and pro-Ronald Reagan. Moreover, conciliar support for revolutionary movements in developing nations became intensely controversial. With few exceptions (such as Orlando Costas), self-described evangelical thinkers have not adopted liberationist models for understanding Christian mission or for criticizing capitalistic societies.[35] Another area of disagreement relates to the status of non-Christian religions. During the 1960s, Karl Rahner's theology of the "anonymous Christian," Karl Barth's doctrine of universal election in Christ, and statements by WCC leader D. T. Niles raised the specter of universalism for evangelicals—that is, the teaching that all persons will achieve final salvation. While there are some recent signs of a softening of views among evangelicals, most have stuck to the biblical emphasis on the necessity of preaching Christ (Romans 10:13–17) and the statement that "there is no other name [besides that of Jesus] . . . by which we must be saved" (Acts 4:12). Not all paths lead to God. Scripture and tradition speak of damnation as well as salvation.

Perhaps the greatest unresolved issue for the evangelical theology of mission lies in the sphere of ecclesiology—often noted as a weak point. There are concerns related to proselytism, inter-mission rivalries, and partnership. Proselytism has been disavowed in conciliar documents and is a special concern for Orthodox and Catholic leaders whose members are lured away by freewheeling evangelical church or parachurch ministries that do not cooperate with one another, let alone with traditional churches. One might speak of a "wild West" ecclesiology, where everyone straps on a gun and goes out shooting, heedless of striking down Christian co-workers with "friendly fire"! Partnership in mission has been a focus in Lausanne documents, and yet the concept is not rigorously defined. Who establishes a partnership? Who sets the terms? Can individuals, churches, or parachurch ministries simply leave a partnership whenever they so desire? Is there any binding authority above the level of the partnering parties that may adjudicate their disputes? Substantive, long-term collaboration in Christian mission requires that greater attention be paid to such issues. In what some call the city-reaching movement, local evangelical leaders since the 1990s in various parts of the world have pursued new ways of establishing oversight and coordination for all ministries in their regions. Yet the new ways are old ways. The bishop (Greek, *episkopos*) of the first centuries was assigned precisely this function of coordinating the otherwise haphazard growth and expansion of the early Christian communities. The recent evangelical engagement with missional ecclesiology is but one sign of convergence—drawing together diverse historical traditions (catholic, charismatic, social-ethical, and evangelical), and distinct parties in today's church (conciliar, Roman Catholic, evangelical, and so on)—to produce a more complete and convincing witness to the Lord and Savior, Jesus Christ.

NOTES

1. "Mission" in the modern sense was first used in the 1500s by the Jesuits in northern Germany to refer to their work of reconverting Protestants to Catholicism; David J. Bosch, *Believing in the Future: Toward a Missiology of Western Culture* (Valley Forge, Pa.: Trinity Press International, 1995), 29.

2. See Gerhard Friedrich, "euanggelizomai . . .," in Gerhard Kittel, ed., *Theological Dictionary of the New Testament* (Grand Rapids: Eerdmans, 1964), 2:707–737, esp. 708.

3. Friedrich Schleiermacher spoke of a "practical theology" in the situation when "religious strangers . . . live in the vicinity or region of a church," and adds that "possibly a theory of missions which for all intents and purposes still does not exist could be added at this point"; cited in Johannes Verkuyl, *Contemporary Missiology: An Introduction*, translated by Dale Cooper (Grand Rapids: Eerdmans, 1978), 6–7.

4. Verkuyl, *Contemporary Missiology*, 12–13.

5. See David J. Bosch, *Transforming Mission: Paradigm Shifts in the Theology of Mission* (Maryknoll, N.Y.: Orbis, 1991).

6. Not discussed here is the universal salvific will of God (see 1 Timothy 2:3–4), as it ties into the intricate issue of divine election, understood as conditional (as held in Arminianism) or as unconditional (as held in Calvinism). Catholic theology has been on both sides, as noted in André Seumois, *Théologie Missionaire*, 3 vols. (Rome: Bureau de Presse OMI, 1973–1974), 3:37–49.

7. Horst Bürkle, "Mission VII: Systematisch-theologisch," in Horst Balz et al., eds., *Theologische Realenzyklopädie* (Berlin: Walter de Gruyter, 1994), 23:59–68, citing 59 (translation mine). The paragraphs that follow are indebted to Bürkle's discussion on 59–61.

8. This biblical quotation, and all that follow, are from the New Revised Standard Version.

9. Rodger C. Bassham, *Mission Theology, 1948–1975; Years of Worldwide Creative Tension; Ecumenical, Evangelical, and Roman Catholic* (Pasadena, Cal.: William Carey Library, 1979), 334.

10. Johannes Blauw, in *The Missionary Nature of the Church: A Survey of the Biblical Theology of Mission* (New York: McGraw-Hill, 1962).

11. Walter Freytag, *Von Sinn der Weltmission* (1950), 75; cited in Blauw, *Missionary Nature*, 109.

12. Lessie Newbigin, *Mission in Christ's Way* (Geneva: WCC, 1987), 60–61.

13. Brunner, cited in Bosch, *Believing in the Future*, 32.

14. Adolf von Harnack, *The Mission and Expansion of Christianity in the First Three Centuries*, translated and edited by James Moffatt (New York: Harper Brothers, 1961), 86–87.

15. Ibid.

16. Ibid., 98.

17. Margaret A. Schatkin, "Laity," in Everett Ferguson, ed., *Encyclopedia of Early Christianity*, 2nd ed. (New York: Routledge, 1999), 661.

18. See Pope John Paul II's encyclical *Redemptoris Missio* (1990), par. 90–91, "The True Missionary Is the Saint."

19. *Lumen Gentium*, 48, 59, cf. *Ad Gentes*, 1, 5.

20. See B. B. Warfield, *Counterfeit Miracles* (New York: Scribner's, 1918), esp. 5–31. Cf. John Ruthven, *On the Cessation of the Charismata: The Protestant Polemic on Postbiblical Miracles* (Sheffield, UK: Sheffield Academic Press, 1993).

21. Ramsey McMullen, *Christianizing the Roman Empire, A.D. 100–400* (New Haven, Conn.: Yale University Press, 1984), 1–43, esp. 36–41.

22. See David J. O'Brien and Thomas A. Shannon, eds., *Catholic Social Thought: The Documentary Heritage* (Maryknoll, N.Y: Orbis, 1992).

23. An oft-criticized evangelical tendency is the focus on statistics and the assumption that numerical growth is always to be expected, as in the following: "Churches should always be growing. We should never be content with churches which are static or even receding" (*The Thailand Report on Muslims;* Pattaya, Thailand: Lausanne Committee on World Evangelization, 1980), 5.

24. See Ludwig Rütti, *Zur Theologie der Mission: Kritische Analysen und neue Orientierungen* (München: Kaiser Verlag, 1972), esp. the section "Welt als Horizont der Sendung," 136–252.

25. Bosch, *Transforming Mission*, 326–327. Cf. Bassham, *Mission Theology*, 332–336.

26. Arthur Glasser, "Salvation Today and the Kingdom," in Donald A. McGavran, ed., *Crucial Issues in Mission Tomorrow* (Chicago: Moody Press, 1972), 33. Cf. Arthur F. Glasser and Donald A. McGavran in *Contemporary Theologies of Mission* (Grand Rapids: Baker Books, 1983), 47–99; James Scherer, *Gospel, Church, and Kingdom: Comparative Studies in World Mission Theology* (Minneapolis: Augsburg, 1987), 108–128; M. M. Thomas and Lesslie Newbigin, "Salvation and Humanization," in Gerald A. Anderson and Thomas F. Stransky, *Mission Trends No. 1: Crucial Issues in Mission Today* (New York: Paulist Press, 1974), 217–229.

27. See Pope John Paul II's encyclical *Redemptoris Missio* (1990), esp. 11, 33–36.

28. Scherer, *Gospel*, 191.

29. Bassham, *Mission Theology*, 231.

30. John Stott, "The Biblical Basis for Evangelism," in J. D. Douglas, ed., *Let the Earth Hear His Voice: International Congress on World Evangelization, Lausanne, Switzerland* (Minneapolis: World Wide Publications, 1975), 66–69.

31. The Lausanne documents are available online at www.lausanne.org. See also: C. René Padilla, ed. *The New Face of Evangelicalism: An International Symposium on the Lausanne Covenant* (Downers Grove, Ill.: InterVarsity Press, 1976); and David Claydon, ed., *A New Vision, a New Heart, a Renewed Call: Lausanne Occasional Papers from the 2004 Forum on World Evangelization*, 2 vols. (Pasadena, Cal.: William Carey Library, 2005).

32. Cf. Bryan P. Stone, *Evangelism after Christendom: The Theology and Practice of Christian Witness* (Grand Rapids: Brazos, 2007), and Paul W. Chilcote and Laceye C. Warner, eds., *The Study of Evangelism: Exploring a Missional Practice of the Church* (Grand Rapids: Eerdmans, 2008).

33. See Al Tizon, *Transformation after Lausanne: Radical Evangelical Mission in Global-Local Perspective, Regnum Studies in Mission* (Eugene, Ore.: Wipf and Stock, 2008).

34. See J. Andrew Kirk and Kevin J. Vanhoozer, eds., *To Stake a Claim: Mission and the Western Crisis of Knowledge* (Maryknoll, N.Y.: Orbis, 1999).

35. In common with other liberationist thinkers, Orlando E. Costas was sharply critical of the form of Christianity adopted in nations with a strong capitalistic orientation, such as the United States: "The content of this gospel is a conscience-soothing Jesus, with an unscandalous cross, an otherworldly kingdom . . . a pocket God, a spiritualized Bible, and an escapist church. Its goal is a happy, comfortable, and successful life"; *Christ Outside the Gate* (Maryknoll, N.Y.: Orbis, 1982), 80.

BIBLIOGRAPHY

Bassham, Rodger C. *Mission Theology, 1948–1975; Years of Worldwide Creative Tension; Ecumenical, Evangelical, and Roman Catholic*. Pasadena, Cal.: William Carey Library, 1979.

Blauw, Johannes. *The Missionary Nature of the Church: A Survey of the Biblical Theology of Mission*. New York: McGraw-Hill, 1962.

Bosch, David J. *Believing in the Future: Toward a Missiology of Western Culture* (Valley Forge, Pa.: Trinity Press International, 1995.

———. *Transforming Mission: Paradigm Shifts in the Theology of Mission* (Maryknoll, N.Y.: Orbis, 1991.

Bürkle, Horst. "Mission VII: Systematisch-theologisch," in Horst Balz, et al., eds., *Theologische Realenzyklopädie*, 23: 59–68. Berlin: Walter de Gruyter, 1994.

Claydon, David, ed. *A New Vision, a New Heart, a Renewed Call: Lausanne Occasional Papers from the 2004 Forum on World Evangelization*. 2 vols. Pasadena, Cal.: William Carey Library, 2005.

Harnack, Adolf von. *The Mission and Expansion of Christianity in the First Three Centuries*. New York: Harper Brothers, 1961.

Padilla, C. René, ed. *The New Face of Evangelicalism: An International Symposium on the Lausanne Covenant*. Downers Grove, Ill.: InterVarsity Press, 1976.

Pope Paul VI. *Evangelii Nuntiandi* (1975).

Scherer, James. *Gospel, Church, and Kingdom: Comparative Studies in World Mission Theology*. Minneapolis: Augsburg, 1987.

Seumois, André. *Théologie Missionaire*. 3 vols. Rome: Bureau de Presse OMI, 1973–1974.

Verkuyl, Johannes. *Contemporary Missiology: An Introduction*. Translated by Dale Cooper. Grand Rapids: Eerdmans, 1978.

Weston, Paul, ed. *Lesslie Newbigin: Missionary Theologian; A Reader*. Grand Rapids: Eerdmans, 2006.

CHAPTER 23

OTHER RELIGIONS

SUNG WOOK CHUNG

Evangelicals are living in an increasingly pluralistic age, when major world religions are competing to attract adherents in all places of the world. North America and Europe can no longer be regarded as Christian societies, but have become post-Christian and religiously pluralistic. For example, Islam has been increasingly attracting British and French citizens to the worship of Allah. Buddhism has drawn greater numbers of Americans and Canadians to the practice of Zen. Hinduism has been popularized by the spread of Yoga practice all over North America. As a result, it is not difficult to find in most neighborhoods a Buddhist temple, Islamic mosque, and Hindu sanctuary.

In this context of religious pluralism, evangelical Christians should ask several questions. What attitude should evangelicals maintain toward other religions? How should we engage the adherents of other religions? How can we affirm the absolute uniqueness of Christ without being separated from and condemning those who have other faiths? How can we engage Muslims, Buddhists, Hindus, and Confucians without compromising the integrity of the gospel of Jesus Christ?

This chapter aims to provide biblical answers to the above questions by exploring an evangelical theology of other religions. First I will explain current options for Christian thinking about other religions, focusing on their inadequacy. Then I will propose a creatively evangelical approach that is grounded in biblical teaching, classical tradition, and evangelical theology. Finally, I will apply this new approach to real situations of engagement with other religions.

Christian Attitude toward Other Religions: Currently Available Options

The first option currently available is the so-called exclusivist[1] approach which is connected with a claim that Christianity is the absolute truth and thus has nothing to do with other religions. According to this view, other religions are the products of devilish endeavors to oppose the Christian claim of absolute uniqueness. The truth claims of other religions are completely contradictory to the truth claims of Christianity. In addition, other religions are thought to be the results of idolatry, which God condemns as eternally damnable. Karl Barth has long been viewed as one of the most outspoken representatives of this approach.[2] The implication of this approach is that Christians should separate themselves from other religionists and condemn their beliefs. Christian theologians should expose the demonic character of other religions and debunk their truth claims. In this way they rightly express Christian antipathy toward what is damned by God.

Evangelicals cannot endorse this fundamentalist approach. It conflicts with the biblical teaching that we should love our neighbors, and especially our enemies, as ourselves. This means that the Lord Jesus Christ has commanded us to love our Muslim, Hindu, Buddhist, Daoist, and Confucian neighbors as ourselves. Rather than separating ourselves from and condemning other religionists, we should make every effort to develop biblical strategies to love them, thus honoring the Lord's authority and obeying his command.

The exclusivist and separatist approach also contradicts the Lord's command to make disciples of all nations. If we are to pray and work toward making Muslims, Buddhists, Hindus, and others the disciples of the Lord Jesus Christ, we must strive to engage them wisely and faithfully. While the exclusivist and separatist approach rightly affirms the absolute uniqueness and truthfulness of Christ, the Lord also wants us to engage other religionists by loving them as ourselves and praying for and seeking their conversion to disciples.

The second option is the so-called inclusivist approach, which is closely connected with Karl Rahner's notion of "anonymous Christian."[3] According to Rahner, most other religions share a Christlike character with Christianity. In other words, most religious traditions are repositories of God's self-revelation, mixed with error, while we have the ultimate and final self-revelation of God in Jesus Christ alone. Therefore, we can call faithful Buddhists and Hindus "anonymous Christians" because they are already implicitly Christian, insofar as they taste the essence of God's self-revelation available in and through their own religious traditions. Some inclusivists insist, however, that God's revelation comes despite, not through, religions outside the Judeo-Christian tradition.

Such an inclusivist approach is inadequate for a number of reasons, not least because it is impossible to prevent the Buddhists from calling Christians "anonymous

Buddhists." Hindus could do the same. Furthermore, the inclusivist approach seems to miss the fact that the truth claims of other religions contradict the central truth claims of Christianity. For example, the Theravada Buddhist claim that there is no personal God who creates and rules the universe according to his own purposes contradicts the biblical teachings that the triune God is the Creator and Ruler of the universe. The Islamic claim that human beings can make a significant contribution to their salvation is inconsistent with the Christian claim that human beings are saved by grace alone. Most versions of the inclusivist approach dismiss too easily the foundational differences between Christianity and other religious traditions.

We need to acknowledge that most inclusivists, like Rahner, say non-Christians can be saved only through Jesus. The difference comes between those who insist on personal knowledge of Jesus and the gospel for salvation, and those who do not. The former typically speak of a revelation of Jesus and the gospel at death or after death, or in a time and manner only God knows. The latter usually say the good Buddhist can be saved if he realizes he needs the grace of some god to be saved, and that this god is really Jesus Christ, though the Buddhist doesn't know the name.

The third approach currently available is the pluralist approach, whose central claim is that all religions including Christianity have equal access to ultimate truth and salvation. According to this approach, every religious tradition teaches basically the same thing. So the apparent differences among diverse religious traditions are only on the surface. At deeper levels every religion shares the same fundamental commitment to the same ultimate reality. One of the most outspoken representatives of this approach is John Hick.[4]

This pluralist approach is problematic because its central claim is antithetical to the explicit declaration of the Lord Jesus Christ that he is the Truth, Way, and Life, and that only through him can anyone have access to final truth and salvation. According to the apostolic witness, "Salvation is found in no one else, for there is no other name under heaven given to men by which we must be saved" (Acts 4:12). In this context, it is important to appreciate that Christianity loses its identity and integrity when it abandons its claim for absolute uniqueness—which is embedded in the very nature of the Christian faith. When one confesses Jesus Christ as one's Lord and Savior, one confesses at the same time that Jesus Christ is the only and unique way, truth, and life for salvation. This affirmation of the uniqueness of Jesus Christ leads Christians to reject the pluralist option as inimical to the finality of Jesus Christ.

The Missional Approach

I have discussed so far why currently available options in approach to other religions are inadequate. Now I want to propose an evangelical, biblical, and more creative approach. While maintaining the uniqueness of Christian faith without endorsing the options above, the key question is how to share the gospel without separating ourselves from and condemning those who are committed to other religions.

I call this model a "missional" approach. The word "missional" comes from Darrell L. Guder's seminal work, *Missional Church: A Vision for the Sending of the Church in North America.*[5] Although one can define the word "missional" in various ways, I use it to mean "ontologically mission-oriented," which means the very *being* of the church is oriented toward mission. According to missional theology, the triune God is a missional God in that he is mission-oriented in his very being. God the Father sends God the Son to the world and both God the Father and God the Son send God the Spirit to the church and the world. Furthermore, the triune God sends the churches and Christians to the ends of the earth to witness to the grace of the triune God revealed in Jesus Christ. In other words, mission is not merely a function of the church, but rather the central character of the church's being.

With this definition, we can define the missional approach to other religions as that which allows Christians to explore and identify the possible points of contact between Christianity and other religious traditions, and to employ these points of contact in efforts to share the gospel with adherents of other religions. This approach is indebted to Alister McGrath, who emphasizes the significance of points of contact between Christian faith and secular religious and philosophical traditions, and urges Christians to use them in apologetic and missional endeavors.[6]

Points of Contact: Theological Rationale

On what theological basis can we acknowledge points of contact between Christianity and other religious traditions? What theological rationale do we have for the reality of commonalities[7] between Christian faith and other religions?

First, the idea of general revelation is one way to explain the existence of points of contact. According to an evangelical notion of general or universal revelation, natural order and beauty in creation, natural law, human history, human conscience, and divine judgments in history are the vehicles for God's self-revelation to all humanity. Because of their sinfulness, however, human beings cannot obtain genuinely saving knowledge of the triune God from this general revelation. But general revelation nevertheless can provide all human beings with a basic, albeit confused, knowledge of the existence and works of God the Trinity. If we apply this truth to the adherents of other religions, it is undeniable that they have some confused but basic awareness of God.

Second, according to the Genesis account, the triune God created human beings in his own image, making them the bearers of *Imago Dei*. The Bible teaches that even after the fall of our first parents, the image of God has never been obliterated completely but remains in a defaced and marred condition. This means that all human beings, despite their fallenness and sinfulness, remain the bearers of this obscured image of the triune God. In other words, all human beings, regardless of their religious commitment, possess the remnants of the image of God. If we apply this truth to those who are committed to other religious traditions, we should acknowledge that all Buddhists, Muslims, Daoists, and Hindus are the bearers of the image of God, like Christians. Therefore, it is undeniable that we can find some fundamental commonalities between Christians and people committed to other world religions as the co-bearers of the *Imago Dei*.

Third, evangelical tradition has affirmed unanimously that all human beings are in a predicament which possesses several distinct dimensions. First, the human predicament has a spiritual character, which means that all human beings are spiritually dead because their relationship with the triune God is broken by their sinful rebellion. Second, the human predicament has a psychological character, which means it involves shame, agony, fear, anxiety, and suffering. Third, the human predicament has a physical dimension, in that it suffers disease and biological death. Although no other major religions acknowledge that human beings are sinners before the triune God, they all recognize a psychological and physical predicament from which humans strive to be freed. In other words, every world religion agrees that human lives and their environments have been distorted and corrupted.

Another theological rationale for the existence of points of contact between Christian faith and other religions is the moral consciousness that pervades all human cultures. Of course, there are significant differences among human cultures and their consciousness of right and wrong. But moral and cultural relativism can be exaggerated. For example, no culture commends and rewards those who betray and murder their parents. No society or culture encourages its members to betray their wives or considers adultery to be moral. Even polygamous societies condemn adultery. Every society condemns selfishness and praises those who live for the benefit of others. Therefore it is undeniable that there are instances of universal moral consciousness that unite Christians and non-Christians.[8]

Case Study: Application of the Missional Approach to Islam

We can identify several substantial points of contact between Christianity and Islam. First, for Muslims there is no god but God. Islamic religion is essentially monotheistic.[9] Similarly, Christianity affirms the oneness of God in strong terms. This is a significant point of contact. Second, the Islamic idea of God shares much with the Christian idea of God. Both religions identify God as the creator, sustainer, and ultimate judge of the world.

Furthermore, Muslims worship Allah as the God of mercy and compassion, while Christians worship the triune God as the God of grace and mercy. This is another significant point of contact. By stressing common ground rather than fundamental differences, but without sacrificing doctrinal clarity, Christians can help Muslims become more open to hearing the gospel.

Second, both Christianity and Islam believe in the concept of divine revelation. According to Islamic tradition, the God of Muslims revealed himself and his will to the prophet Muhammad through the angel Gabriel. Muhammad wrote down what he had received from Gabriel. Muslims say this became the Qur'an.[10] Importantly, Christian orthodoxy teaches a similar idea of divine revelation—that the triune God revealed himself and his will to a plurality of prophets and apostles and they wrote down what they had received, the sum total of which became the Bible. Of course, the orthodox tradition has for the most part rejected the dictation theory of revelation, which most Muslims hold, and Christians say the Holy Spirit inspired the minds of the biblical authors. For this reason, most evangelical Christians believe the Bible is infallible in what it affirms and has divine and absolute authority for their belief and practice. This means that the idea of divine self-revelation can be another point of contact between Christianity and Islam.

Third, Christianity shares with Islam the ideas of divine commands and human sin. According to Islamic tradition, God the Creator commanded human beings to obey his will. However, human beings failed to keep God's commands by rebelling deliberately against God's authority. Most Muslims believe that this willful rebellion against God is essential to the notion of sin, and that the result of sin is broken relationship between God and human beings.[11] Likewise, Christian faith teaches that human beings commit sins against God by disobeying God's clear commands. And the wages of sin is death, which means spiritual and eternal separation from God. On the basis of this commonality between Christianity and Islam, we can conclude that the idea of sin as personal offense against God's authority can be a significant point of contact between the two religions. When Christians begin to converse with Muslims, we can use this point of contact in an effort to open Muslims' minds to listen to what Christians believe about sin.

Fourth, both Christianity and Islam emphasize the necessity of redemption and forgiveness of sins. This is because both religions believe that sin incurs divine punishment. According to Islamic tradition, sin deserves punishment, and our final destiny is determined by God's judgment. Therefore Muslims feel keenly the need for redemption and forgiveness. They know that if their sins are not forgiven, they will pay the penalty both in time and eternity.[12] Christians should recognize that they agree with Muslims on the necessity of redemption and forgiveness of sins. Most evangelicals also believe that that if sinners remain unredeemed, they will pay penalties which Scripture compares to a "lake of fire." Their destiny will be decided by God at the final judgment.

We see here yet another point of contact—the idea of the necessity of redemption and forgiveness of sins. Christians can take the initiative to engage with Muslims on this shared belief. When Christians confess their own sinfulness and moral failures to Muslim friends, Muslim friends may be more open to jump the wall of distrust and begin to listen to a Christian perspective on redemption and forgiveness of sins.

Limitations of the Points of Contact

Although Christians can make use of these points of contact between Christianity and Islam at the first stage of dialogical engagement with Muslims, it must also be said that that these points of contact have limitations. They must be supplemented by a clear presentation of the explicit message of the Christian gospel, which will highlight differences as well as similarities. Only after understanding both continuity and discontinuity will most Muslims be ready to receive Jesus Christ as Lord and Savior.

Among the many fundamental differences between the Christian and Muslim faiths is, first, the identity of God. The God of Islam is a one-personed Being while the God of Christianity is a three-personed Being. The God of Muslims is a monad, while the God of Christians is a God of community, or more precisely a communion of Father, Son, and Holy Spirit.

Second, while both Christianity and Islam uphold the ideas of divine revelation and divine scripture, the ultimate mediator of revelation is different for each. In Islam, the prophet Muhammad received divine revelation from Gabriel sent by Allah, but for Christianity Jesus the Son of God is the ultimate mediator of divine revelation. Furthermore, the Holy Spirit is the ultimate author of the Bible, the divinely inspired Word of God. The God of Islam cannot or does not have a Son, while the Christian God is the Father of Jesus Christ, the Son of God.

Third, although Christianity and Islam share the idea of sin, they disagree on the means of redemption and forgiveness of sins. While Muslims believe their moral merit can make a significant contribution to their redemption, evangelical Christians believe that their own moral merit has no place in their redemption. Instead, evangelical Christians say, our sins are forgiven by the merit won through the blood of Jesus Christ. Furthermore, we are saved from eternal punishment by Christ's grace alone and by our faith in the Lord Jesus Christ who paid all the penalties for our sins by laying down his life and being raised again on the third day.

After opening the hearts of Muslim friends by making use of points of contact between Christianity and Islam, Christians can share the good news of Christ's unconditional love and forgiveness. Then there may be one of two results.[13] With the help of the Holy Spirit, Muslim friends might begin to realize the deficiencies and inconsistencies of Islam, and open their hearts to the attractiveness of Jesus Christ. Or Muslim friends might remain unconvinced. That could be because they do not understand the full implications of the gospel, or because they simply refuse to open their minds and hearts. In either case, however, the use of points of contact may leave them with a more positive view of Christian faith. A seed has been planted.

For these reasons, the missional approach, which uses points of contact between Christianity and Islam at the first stage of dialogical engagement, seems the best option for evangelical Christians. It is especially concerned to express concern, love and respect for Muslims. Its effort to identify common grounds between Christianity and Islam stems from authentic appreciation for the dignity of Muslims as co-bearers of the image of God.

Case Study: Application of the Missional Approach to Buddhism

There are several significant pints of contact between Christianity and Buddhism. First, Buddhist insight into human reality. According to Buddhist tradition, after his enlightenment the Buddha began to teach about the tragic reality of human life, namely suffering (*dukha*). The Four Noble Truths summarizes Buddha's teaching about dukha.[14] According to the first Truth, human life is characterized by suffering, inevitably chained by frustration and despair. Human experience is full of grief, unfulfilled desires, sickness, old age, physical pain, mental anguish, unsatisfactoriness and frustration. Moreover, we are said to be bound to a vicious and endless cycle of birth, death, and rebirth (*samsara*). This Buddhist picture of human life, then, is pessimistic and tragic.

In this context, it is important to appreciate that the Christian ideas of fall, sin, curse, and corruption have commonalities with the Buddhist description of human life. According to the Bible, human life is filled with vanity, suffering, and frustration (Eccl. 1:2; Ps. 90:10; Rom. 8:20–21). The Christian scriptures teach plainly that human sin has brought human beings the curses of suffering, vanity, despair, and eternal condemnation.

Because of these parallel teachings, we can conclude that both Christianity and Buddhism describe the reality of human life in a pessimistic and negative manner. Both traditions affirm that human beings are enslaved to decay, suffering, and meaninglessness. Therefore when Christians enter a dialogue with Buddhists, they can make use of suffering as a starting point. We can tell Buddhists that the Christian view of human reality is similar to theirs. This may lead some Buddhists to suspend their distrust and explore what Christians believe about the tragic reality of human life.

Second, according to the second Noble Truth, suffering and frustration result from human desires and attachment—desires for sensory pleasures and fame and fortune, and attachment to impermanent things. The Buddha condemned human desires and attachment to the world because those, he said, bring suffering and frustration, and bind us to the cycle of reincarnation. Furthermore, according to Buddhism, the world is impermanent and passing away (*anicca*). Because of their ignorance of the true reality of the world, human beings have craving and thirst for a separate and permanent self to be attained through attachment to the various processes of existence. Like Buddhism, the Christian faith also condemns evil and selfish desires because they separate us from God and bring God's punishment (1 John 2:15–17).

We can conclude here that the Buddhist condemnation of desire for and attachment to the world can be a significant point of contact between Christianity and Buddhism. At the same time, we must recognize how these two religions differ on why humans should avoid desire and attachment. However, it is still true that both Christianity and Buddhism condemn selfish attachment to the world. Therefore,

Christians can make use of this commonality when we begin a dialogical engagement with the Buddhists. Third, according to the third Noble Truth, suffering will cease if all desires cease. Then illusion ends and ultimate reality is revealed. As a result, nirvana is achieved. Buddhism not only condemns desire but also claims to be able to remove desire. This is the way to the Buddhist "salvation" of nirvana.[15]

Here is a point of contact between Christianity and Buddhism. Christian faith also teaches that we should put off evil desires in order to put on the righteousness of Christ. We should remove the old garment of evil and the desires of the flesh so as to put on the new self in Jesus Christ. When Christians approach Buddhists who are struggling with the task of eliminating their selfish desires, they can sympathize.

Fourth, Mahayana Buddhism's concept of the *bodhisattva* is another point of contact. This is a being who is dedicated to attaining enlightenment but also helping other people gain their own. Bodhisattvas are usually viewed as mature Buddhists who have accumulated sufficient merits to enter nirvana. They can help other people achieve enlightenment either by transferring them some of their own merit or by taking on themselves the burden of their suffering. In addition to these earthly bodhisattvas, according to Mahayanan tradition, there are numerous heavenly bodhisattvas who hear the pleas of those who are suffering. Worshipers can pray to them for help.[16] Among especially popular bodhisattvas are Avalokiteshvara (the Buddha of mercy) and Maitreya (the messianic Buddha).

The Buddhist idea of heavenly bodhisattvas bears some similarity to Christian ideas of Christ as mediator. Just as a heavenly bodhisattva can transfer his or her own merit to the seekers of enlightenment and take on himself or herself the burden of their suffering, Christians say Jesus Christ takes on himself the burden of their sin and death.

Fifth, in the tradition of Pure Land Buddhism, people trust in Amida Buddha (in Japan; in China it is Amitabha Buddha), the Buddha of Boundless Light, for their salvation. Amida Buddha is viewed as an ancient prince who vowed to attain enlightenment. It is believed that he created a paradise called the Pure Land. Everyone who invokes his name even once in faith will be reborn there. When people get to the Pure Land, it will be much easier to reach nirvana from there. In Pure Land Buddhism, Amida Buddha is a savior figure. It is not moral behavior but faith in Amida Buddha that leads Pure Land Buddhists to paradise.[17] This idea of faith in a savior has obvious overlap with Christian views.

Finally, the Buddhist idea of karma is significant. The word *karma* means "act or action" and stands for the consequences of human actions that are accumulated as time passes. In the Buddhist context, the consequences of human beings' negative actions make an impact upon not only this life but also lives to come. Karma is understood to be the energy that drives the wheel of samsara, the vicious and endless cycle of birth, death, and rebirth. Because human beings accumulate bad karma through their bad conduct, they are enslaved to the cycle of samsara. In order to achieve nirvana, people must be liberated from samsara by removing bad karma and building up good karma.

Christianity also teaches that human sins result in bad consequences. Sin brings us corruption, punishment, and curse; there is a causal relationship between iniquity and its bad effects. It seems undeniable that there is a significant similarity between the Christian idea of sin and the Buddhist idea of karma.

Limitations of the Points of Contact

As we saw for Islam, points of contact between Christianity and Buddhism have both merits and limitations. For example, Christians can agree with the Buddhists at many points, including to some degree the fundamental human problem, but they insist that the Christian solution is fundamentally different.

This can be seen most clearly in a Christian response to the Buddha's fourth Noble Truth. It asserts that the way to liberation from suffering is a life of morality, concentration, and wisdom. This way is spelled out by the Noble Eightfold Path, which involves right understanding, right thought, right speech, right action, right livelihood, right effort, right mindfulness, and right meditation. Buddhists believe that by practicing this Noble Path, people can eliminate their desires and attachment, and realize nirvana. Although Pure Land Buddhism believes the Amida Buddha of Pure Land Buddhism to be a savior figure, Amida Buddha does not offer an atoning sacrifice for the forgiveness of sins. In addition, Theravada Buddhists are urged to accumulate merits by performing moral actions if they want to remove karma and its effects. Buddhism has no parallel to the Christian idea of free justification of sinners on the basis of atoning sacrifice.

At this point, similarities between Christianity and Buddhism eventually come to an end. Although evangelical Christians can appreciate the sincerity of those Buddhists who are practicing this style of moral life, they do not endorse it as a way of salvation. For Buddhism, despite its good intentions and insights, remains a self-salvific scheme which elevates human power and ability. In contrast, Christians believe that human beings are saved by grace alone and the goal of our life is not dissolution of the self but union with the triune God.

Those Who Have Never Heard of the Gospel

Recent discussions of evangelical theology of religions have focused on the question of salvation for those who have never heard the gospel. We have three major evangelical options. First, traditionalist and conservative evangelical theologians argue that those who have never heard of the gospel will not be saved because they are already condemned sinners; they are born into the world as sinners.[18] According to this approach, human beings are condemned because they are sinners, not because they have not responded to the gospel. Second, there are evangelical theologians who are more open to the question of the eternal destiny of those who have never heard of the gospel.[19] According to this approach, there may be a limited possibility of salvation for those who have never heard of the gospel. They believe that God will remain fair and just to them—but how God will do this is a hidden mystery. For these theologians, agnostic reverence is the best attitude toward this question. They do not claim there is salvation apart from Christ's work and person, but that people who do not know Christ's name and work might be nevertheless saved by Him. They believe that some who have not heard while on earth will hear the gospel and confess and surrender to Jesus in a time and manner only God knows. As Gerald McDermott has argued in his *God's Rivals*, this is similar to the approach of the early Greek theologians such as Justin Martyr, Irenaeus, Clement, and perhaps Origen.[20]

Third, evangelical inclusivists argue that God is at work redemptively among all cultures and religions of the world in various times.[21] Clark Pinnock, for example, argues that people cannot be held responsible for not responding to revelation they never received. People will be judged on the basis of revelation they have received and how they have responded to that revelation.[22]

I believe the missional approach is compatible with both the first and second options, and that biblical revelation supports them. The first option stresses the biblical declaration that all human beings are already dead in their sins and trespasses (Eph. 2:1). Whether they have heard of the gospel or not, they are already under condemnation and destined to eternal death. The second option is also appropriate in that Old Testament believers were saved without hearing the gospel of Jesus Christ directly and explicitly. But it also seems certain that God's way of saving those who have never heard the gospel will remain hidden in divine mystery, and that it will be consistent with the revealed way of salvation in and through Jesus Christ alone.

The missional approach cannot endorse the third option. This evangelical inclusivist approach, which affirms salvation apart from Jesus Christ, contradicts explicit biblical declarations that Jesus Christ is the one and only Lord and Savior

When considering people committed to other religions, evangelicals should not take a separationist approach, for we are commanded to love those outside the church and to share the gospel with them. Therefore we should explore how to engage them in a loving and respectful manner. We should try to understand their beliefs by analyzing their worldviews and identifying significant points of contact between Christianity and their religions. Although points of contact can help begin dialogue, they also have limitations. Therefore differences with Christian doctrine must be identified, and the gospel of grace clearly articulated. The missional approach does not guarantee success, but with sensitivity and prayer, it can serve the *missio dei*.

NOTES

1. Veli-Matti Kärkkäinen prefers the term "particularism" to "exclusivism" because of the latter's pejorative connotations; see *An Introduction to the Theology of Religions: Biblical, Historical and Contemporary Perspectives* (Downers Grove, Ill.: InterVarsity, 2003). However, I believe that the term "exclusivism" communicates better what the fundamentalist attitude toward other religions implies.

2. Karl Barth, *Church Dogmatics*, ed. G. W. Bromiley and T. F. Torrance; tr. G. W. Bromiley. 2nd edition. (Edinburgh : T & T Clark, 1975), I/2, 297–325. In contrast, J. Augustine Di Noia has recently argued that Barth's theology of religions should be interpreted in a different direction; see "Religion and the Religions," in John Webster, ed., *The Cambridge Companion to Karl Barth* (Cambridge: Cambridge University Press, 2000), 243–257.

3. Karl Rahner, "Anonymous Christian," in *Theological Investigations*, vol. 6 (London: Darton, Longman and Todd, 1969), 390–391, 393–395.

4. See John Hick, *A Christian Theology of Religions* (Louisville, Ky.: Westminster/John Knox, 1995); Hick, *God Has Many Names* (Louisville, Ky.: Westminster/John Knox, 1982).

5. Grand Rapids: Eerdmans, 1998.

6. McGrath calls this position the "creative" approach; see *Intellectuals Don't Need God & Other Modern Myths: Building Bridges to Faith through Apologetics* (Grand Rapids: Zondervan, 1993), 30–47, 56–65.

7. Mainstream evangelical theologians have recently paid considerable attention to such points of contacts, while also acknowledging fundamental differences. See Gerald R. McDermott, *Can Evangelicals Learn from World Religions? Jesus, Revelation and Religious Traditions* (Downers Grove, Ill.: InterVarsity, 2000); Winfried Corduan, *A Tapestry of Faiths: The Common Threads between Christianity and World Religions* (Downers Grove, Ill.: InterVarsity, 2002); Timothy C. Tennent, *Christianity at the Religious Roundtable: Evangelicalism in Conversation with Hinduism, Buddhism, and Islam* (Grand Rapids: Baker Academic, 2002).

8. C. S. Lewis did a marvelous job defending the notion of universal moral consciousness, which he called the "Tao," in his appendix to *Mere Christianity* (New York: Macmillan, 1952).

9. John L. Esposito, *Islam: The Straight Path* (New York: Oxford University Press, 1988), 68–71.

10. Ibid., 20–23.

11. Ibid., 31–32.

12. Ibid., 34–35.

13. Of course, there are other possible results such as that we did not share our message in a culturally sensitive way, with the result there is no real understanding by our Muslim friend, or even if we were sensitive, there still may be a failure to understand, for any one of a host of reasons—perhaps linguistic or past hurts by Christians that have made it impossible for them to hear objectively what is being said.

14. Donald W. Mitchell, *Buddhism: Introducing the Buddhist Experience* (New York: Oxford University Press, 2002), 45–60.

15. Ibid., 60–62.

16. Ibid., 96–125.

17. Ibid.

18. John Piper, *Let the Nations Be Glad!* (Grand Rapids: Baker, 1993); D. A. Carson, *The Gagging of God: Christianity Confronts Pluralism* (Grand Rapids: Zondervan, 1996).

19. John Stott, *The Authentic Jesus* (London: Marshall Morgan and Scott, 1985); Klaas Runia, "The Gospel and Religious Pluralism," *Evangelical Review of Theology* 14 (October 1990): 341–379; Alister McGrath, "A Particularist View: A Post-Enlightenment Approach," in Dennis K. Okholm and Timothy R. Phillips, eds., *More Than One Way? Four Views on Salvation in a Pluralistic World* (Grand Rapids: Zondervan, 1995), 149–180.

20. Gerald McDermott, *God's Rivals: Why Has God Allowed Different Religions? Insights from the Bible and the Early Church* (Downers Grove, Ill.: InterVarsity, 2007).

21. Clark Pinnock, *A Wideness in God's Mercy: The Finality of Jesus Christ in a World of Religions* (Grand Rapids: Zondervan, 1992).

22. Ibid., 157–158.

BIBLIOGRAPHY

Corduan, Winfried. *A Tapestry of Faiths: The Common Threads between Christianity and World Religions*. Downers Grove, Ill.: InterVarsity, 2002.

Di Noia, J. Augustine. "Religion and the Religions." In John Webster, ed., *The Cambridge Companion to Karl Barth*. Cambridge: Cambridge University Press, 2000.

Kärkkäinen, Veli-Matti. *An Introduction to the Theology of Religions: Biblical, Historical and Contemporary Perspectives*. Downers Grove, Ill.: InterVarsity, 2003.

———. *Trinity and Religious Pluralism: The Doctrine of the Trinity in Christian Theology of Religions*. Aldershot: Ashgate, 2004.

McGrath, Alister. *Intellectuals Don't Need God and Other Modern Myths: Building Bridges to Faith through Apologetics*. Grand Rapids: Zondervan, 1993.

———. "A Particularist View: A Post-Enlightenment Approach." In Dennis K. Okholm and Timothy R. Phillips, eds., *More Than One Way? Four Views on Salvation in a Pluralistic World*. Grand Rapids: Zondervan, 1995), 149–180.

McDermott, Gerald R. *Can Evangelicals Learn from World Religions? Jesus, Revelation and Religious Traditions*. Downers Grove, Ill.: InterVarsity, 2000.

———. *God's Rivals: Why Has God Allowed Different Religions? Insights from the Bible and the Early Church*. Downers Grove, Ill.: InterVarsity, 2007.

Pinnock, Clark. *A Wideness in God's Mercy: The Finality of Jesus Christ in a World of Religions*. Grand Rapids: Zondervan, 1992.

Piper, John. *Let the Nations Be Glad!* Grand Rapids: Baker, 1993; D. A. Carson, *The Gagging of God: Christianity Confronts Pluralism*. Grand Rapids: Zondervan, 1996.

Runia, Klaas. "The Gospel and Religious Pluralism." *Evangelical Review of Theology* 14 (October 1990): 341–379.

Stott, John. *The Authentic Jesus*. London: Marshall Morgan and Scott, 1985.

Tennent, Timothy C. *Christianity at the Religious Roundtable: Evangelicalism in Conversation with Hinduism, Buddhism, and Islam*. Grand Rapids: Baker Academic, 2002).

PART VI

THEOLOGICAL APPROACHES TO CONTEMPORARY LIFE

CHAPTER 24

THE BIBLE AND ETHICS

M. DANIEL CARROLL R. AND
DARRELL L. BOCK

Many different kinds of issues arise—theological, hermeneutical, exegetical, and historical—when we use the Bible to help answer ethical questions. Those who appeal to the biblical text must make informed choices on these matters.[1] The goal of this chapter is to provide an overview of the most salient topics that are foundational for a proper appropriation of the Bible, both those of a more general sort and those most significant for the Old and New Testaments.

Introduction

The Authority of the Bible for Ethics

Christians have always believed that the Bible is the most important resource for thinking about the moral life of individual believers and their communities. For two millennia, in discussions on ethical issues a strong view of the Bible's authority was a given. The Church Fathers, medieval theologians and ethicists, the Reformers, and their heirs well into the nineteenth century all presupposed that the Bible was the Word of God. Disagreements concerned the interpretation of texts and the particular theological and philosophical framing of ethical positions, but all grounded their views in the settled conviction that the Bible was divine revelation and trustworthy.

Today, however, the authority of the Bible is a flashpoint of deliberation and dispute. The formulation of the meaning of this authority varies, and depends largely on the definitions of particular theological traditions and decisions on text-critical and higher-critical matters. Those of conservative persuasion hold that the authority of the Bible is an inherent property of the text as the Word of God, and ground this in a doctrine of inspiration that emphasizes the Bible's divine origin.[2] Others are less at ease with the notion of divine inspiration as classically understood, and argue instead that the Bible has earned its authority by proving its worth. They contend that the Bible's authority is based on its proven value over time in providing guidance and shaping moral imagination. Authority, from this perspective, arises from the recognition by believers of the Bible's value as Scripture, even though it contains elements that do not commend themselves for application today.[3] A third approach arises from what is called a "theological interpretation" of the Bible. It looks to precritical perspectives and incorporates into the articulation of biblical authority the role of the Spirit and liturgical practices, the interpreter's character, and the importance of reading in community.[4]

The Bible and the Moral Life

The Bible, from beginning to end, is permeated with moral considerations. In a technical sense, ethics is the articulation of the framework, motivations, and standards for right conduct, whereas morality refers to that behavior itself. The Bible contains both. That is, the Bible demonstrates a broad sensitivity to moral life.

There are three classical schools of philosophical ethics. These are deontology (considering rules and duty), utilitarianism (weighing consequences—whether probable or actual), and cultivation of the virtues (or, character ethics). Each focus surfaces in Scripture. First, deontology corresponds to the demand to obey God's statutes. This divine claim on humanity is evident even before the giving of the law codes at Sinai (Exodus-Numbers) and at the shores of the Jordan River (Deuteronomy), and is grounded in the creation order and mandates.[5] Jesus continues that theme, saying that obedience testifies to love for God (Jn 14:15, 23–24, 31). Second, submission to God and rebellion matter. There are consequences, both at individual and community levels. Note, for instance, the blessings and curses of Leviticus 26 and Deuteronomy 28, throughout Proverbs, and in the New Testament (Matt 7:24–27; 2 Jn 6–11). Third, in both testaments, God seeks a virtuous people, who should exemplify his character within the believing community and before the world (e.g., Exod 19:3–6; 1 Pet 2:9). Other elements of virtue ethics, such as practices, exemplars, and tradition, also appear in the biblical material. That the various ways of approaching ethical matters all appear within the Bible's treatment of issues confirms its supreme value as an ethical resource.

Another important consideration is attentiveness to the Bible's presentation of moral reality. The four levels of moral discourse are helpful at this point. These are the expressive, the moral (concerning rules), the ethical (concerning principles), and the post-ethical.[6] The expressive is a spontaneous reaction to a given situation. The Bible is full of these, both good and bad (for example, explosive anger, the desire for revenge, sexual lust). The text sometimes explicitly condemns these responses (e.g., 2 Sam 11:27; Acts 23:1–5); at other times, the criticism is subtle and appears in narrative denouements or asides. Moral rules are widely accepted sociocultural norms of behavior. In the Bible, we find the mores of the ancient Near East, first-century Palestine, and the Greco-Roman world. Of course, these may or may not be aligned with God's values. Note, for example, the expectations to which Tamar appeals (2 Sam 13:11–19), or the ways in which the ideals of the Israelite monarchy contradict the ancient ideology of kingship (Deut 17:14–20). New Testament examples include Martha's assumptions concerning Mary in Jesus' presence (Lk 10:38–42) and Jesus' treatment of women (Jn 4). Ethical principles, the third level, are the conscious reasoning that informs ethical actions. Scripture shows people processing matters of moral import and receiving moral instruction (e.g., 1 Sam 12; Neh 8; Prov 1–9; Matt 5–7, 15). The post-ethical level concerns the most basic justification and authorization for ethics. In the Bible, God's person is the ultimate grounds for being ethical (e.g., Lev 19:2, 20:26; Deut 10:17–19; 1 Pet 1:16).

Awareness of these four levels allows the Bible to be used with greater discrimination. What is presented in a given passage—that is, what moral level is operative? Is there an assessment of moral actions or ethical thinking in the passage or broader context? How is this communicated to the reader? Scripture does not condone or commend everything it records, even those who are presented as pillars of faith (note, for example, the David—Bathsheba incident, 2 Sam 11:27–12:13). The presence of certain behaviors and attitudes is not automatic endorsement; portrayal is not the same as prescription (one could mention, for example, polygamy in the Old Testament and slavery in the Pauline epistles).

Our focus on contemporary biblical ethics in no way suggests that earlier voices appealed to the Bible in naïve fashion and, therefore, are of little value. In fact, the history of Christian ethics is a testimony to sophisticated deliberation on matters related to textual method and the hermeneutical process. Helpful research has chronicled these developments—both in general fashion[7] and in more focused studies of great thinkers (such as Augustine, Martin Luther, and John Calvin)[8] and important events (such as the English Civil War and the American Civil War).[9] These ethical reflections remain a rich resource for the Christian church.

Furthermore, to emphasize biblical scholarship in ethics does not diminish the importance of the work of theologians and ethicists, who appeal to the Scriptures in creative and relevant ways. Among the theologians within the last hundred years whose attention to biblical ethics has been important and influential are Dietrich Bonhoffer, the German martyr to the Nazis who exposited the Sermon on the Mount and wrote a more academic treatment of ethics; Karl Barth, a pioneer in the theological interpretation of the Bible in an age of skeptical biblical criticism; Helmut Thielicke, who moves beyond the Lutheran doctrine of justification by faith to sanctification; and Oliver O'Donovan, a philosopher in the Augustinian tradition.[10] Ethicists such as John Howard Yoder, Stanley Hauerwas, and Lisa Cahill, and others of earlier generations, have gone to the Scripture to establish their views.[11] Much can be gleaned from these and others who take the Bible seriously as the

Word of God for the church and the world. It must be recognized, however, that some of the perspectives and particular concerns of biblical ethicists differ from those of philosophical and theological ethicists. This chapter focuses on the work of biblical ethicists.

Finally, to look at recent work by certain Western biblical scholars does not mean that ethical reflection on the Bible by non-Westerners is not worthy of consideration. It is clear that the center of gravity of the Christian church is shifting to the Global South—to Asia, Africa, and Latin America, and minorities in developed countries. Philip Jenkins has brought this new reality to the consciousness of the West.[12] A fuller treatment of the Bible and ethics would incorporate these contributions as well.

The Old Testament and Ethics

The study of ethics as it pertains to the Old Testament can be divided into two categories: the ethics *of* the Old Testament and the ethics that can be drawn *from* the Old Testament.

Research into the ethics *of* the Old Testament is a descriptive exercise. Its object is the moral life of ancient Israel as presented in the biblical text. Such an historical focus has several components. A descriptive approach attempts to reconstruct the social world of ancient Israel in order to better understand the context within which God's ethical demands were fleshed out. In addition, it tries to trace the possible historical development of Israel's moral life and views. There is also the comparative interest in ascertaining how the laws and values of Israel overlapped with or differed from those of the surrounding cultures.

To glean ethical instruction *from* the Old Testament involves another set of issues. This emphasis certainly can use descriptive studies, but its driving questions are different. First, what in the text is context-bound and what continues to be relevant? Second, what is the best way to appropriate that material? These discussions are inescapably methodological: How do we engage the Old Testament for ethics? In what follows, four approaches are surveyed: social and textual reconstruction, interaction with the context, virtue ethics, and the privileging of one part of the Old Testament. This categorization is not as neat in practice, but it demonstrates the principal ways of utilizing the Old Testament for ethics.

Social and Textual Reconstruction

This approach bases its work in a recreation of the sociohistorical contexts of ancient Israel and the hypothetical stages of production of the text. It does not stay, however, at this purely descriptive level. An example is David Pleins's *The Social Visions of the Hebrew Bible.*[13]

Pleins contends that there is a plurality of ethical voices in the Old Testament, each of which reflects the perspective of a particular social group and setting. These varied and competing ethical stances do not allow for a uniform perspective to be imposed onto the text. This complicated mix is the Bible's enduring legacy, because it reflects the different dimensions of human existence and the kinds of moral thinking these elicit. Dialogue today with this diversity allows for richer ethical reflection on complex modern dilemmas.

Another example is a recent study by Walter Houston, which is informed especially by sociological studies.[14] He argues that the Old Testament reflects the views and mores of an ancient patronage system characterized by hierarchy and mutual obligations. Understanding the text requires awareness of this cultural dynamic and of the nature of peasant life, the symbiotic relationships between rural and urban environments, and the changing political realities of Israel. The Old Testament's views are contextually determined and, consequently, in some ways are limited. However, the concern for justice is transcendent and continues to be relevant. The text reveals how that value was defined and lived out in that world; today, this is done differently.

These efforts at reconstruction call attention to an important issue. They correctly emphasize the variety of ethical voices within the Old Testament.[15] This variety reveals that the Old Testament has different perspectives on the same topic, as well as the fact that different parts of the Old Testament can highlight diverse ethical matters. Some specific examples of this variety in the Old and New Testaments will illustrate that fact. The emphasis on diversity, however, suggests to some that there is little coherence in the ethics of the Old Testament, something with which evangelicals would strongly disagree. At the same time, the potential weakness of any of these approaches is that any reconstruction is only as viable as the presuppositions and data that undergird it. New information or a more comprehensive theory might reconfigure the reconstruction.[16]

Interaction with the Context

Another way of looking toward modern application draws lessons from how the people of God may have interacted with the moral life and thinking of their own context. These approaches can appeal to reconstructions of the sort just mentioned, but their interest lies more in a comparative direction.

John Rogerson explores the relationship between Israel's ethics at any given moment and what he calls the "natural morality" of that time and place.[17] Moral absolutes exist, he explains, but are situated within a context that has an ethical consensus (that all consider "natural"). The ethics of the people of God have always engaged these consensuses, with which they have had points of agreement and disagreement. The moral motivations and actions of God's people, however, are distinct at deeper levels because of what Rogerson labels the "imperatives of redemption." These are the ethical demands generated by God's gracious acts. In the Old Testament, Israel's redemption from slavery in Egypt is a key motivation for moral life (e.g., Exod 22:21 [Heb 22:22]; 23:9). These took concrete expression in "structures of grace"—that is, the legislation and tangible social measures designed to embody that redemption. These are context specific. For instance, laws for alleviating the suffering of the poor (such as the Sabbath and gleaning laws) fit the agrarian economy of ancient Israel.

Today, believers live in a different situation, and the imperative of redemption has changed because of the redemption at the cross of Christ. They, too, engage their context, but the structures of grace appropriate to the twenty-first century would look quite unlike those needed long ago. Rogerson's approach expects some affinity with the moral thinking of others, even as there are dissimilarities. It allows for Christians to think through where these may lie and why, and allows for consideration of cooperation with that broader context. For instance, Christians could participate in government programs for the poor, even if their prime motivation for such efforts (God's love for the vulnerable, the example of Jesus, and the example of the early church) does not match those of the state or of secular colleagues (or those of other religious persuasions). Developing initiatives suitable for the situation that are reflective of Christian redemption and discerning the best level of collaboration with non-Christians are challenges for believers in any age.

Concentrating mostly on the book of Isaiah, John Barton argues that one source for ethics in ancient Israel is what today is labeled "natural law."[18] This is the notion of a divine moral order built into creation. This order should govern behavior in every sphere, and to ignore or violate it inevitably brings negative consequences. This appreciation of the moral life was shared by the surrounding cultures of that time, even if they described it differently. Other scholars compare the legal material of the Old Testament with other ancient law codes to try to specify its unique perspectives.[19] For instance, some of the laws regarding slavery are more humane than those of Israel's neighbors, and the Old Testament does not tie penalties to social class—all stand equal before God. Obviously, the basis of the Law and the divine demands (such as the redemption from Egypt) are different from those of any other people.

These approaches to Old Testament ethics are a reminder that ethical thinking and moral actions do not occur in a vacuum. Nor are biblical principles necessarily distinct from the values and commitments of others. Christians live in the world, even as they are not to be of the world. This need to be relevant to the context, while holding to the unique features of the faith, requires discernment, graciousness, and steadfastness.

Virtue Ethics

Virtue ethics is more inward-focused than the previous approaches, which emphasize ethical decisions and actions. It is concerned with character as it is shaped within the believing community—about the kind of people who will make the proper choices to live in ways pleasing to God. Virtue ethics emphasizes the role of tradition in shaping the moral imagination. So it notes the ways the Old Testament calls for training children in its heritage (e.g., Deut 6:4–9; 31:9–13). Virtue ethicists who use the Old Testament look at how characters work through personal and social issues and extrapolate to similar situations today, suggesting to readers the consequences of those kinds of decisions. Recent studies use literary theory to show how narratives engage the world and change readers in the reading process.[20]

Wisdom and prophetic literature also contribute to the evaluation of character. Job and the person-types in Proverbs (the wise person, the fool, the scoffer, the sluggard) serve as mirrors for self-examination. The Prophets indict the behavior and attitudes of individuals and groups who remain anonymous (for example, "woe to those who . . .") and single out leaders as negative examples (e.g., Jer 22; Mic 3). The prophets themselves become models in their enduring all manner of opposition.[21] These texts offer examples to follow or pitfalls to avoid, as one grows in a life pleasing to God and edifying for others.

A Privileged Framework: The Law

Finally, it is possible to favor one part of the canon as the fundamental framework for Old Testament ethics. This is not the same as concentrating on one part, like the prophets, for ethical reflection.[22] Instead, one section serves as the primary basis for determining the Christian appropriation of the entire Old Testament. Historically, this prerogative has been assigned to the Law—that is, the law codes of the Pentateuch.

Exemplary is Christopher Wright's paradigmatic approach.[23] By searching for paradigms, Wright does not mean extracting universal moral principles from the Law.[24] A paradigm is a substantive, transcendent set of beliefs and values that ground a life and worldview. He argues that the critical aspects of the Old Testament's paradigm for ethics are God (the theological angle), Israel (the social angle), and the land (the economic angle). These three form a triangular configuration that can be extrapolated paradigmatically to all of humanity and creation, typologically to New Testament parallels, and eschatologically to the hope for a redeemed world.[25]

Wright takes very seriously the shape of Israel's laws, social structures, and contextual realities, and avoids the vagueness of a disembodied set of supposed eternal principles. The move to the contemporary world is neither direct nor simplistic. This is the usefulness of the three components (two of which—people and land—are very concrete), and the interlocking triangles. Divine values took one shape in Old Testament times, whereas their projection and application to the broader society of the early church and today, and ultimately in the eschaton, are different. At the same time, there is continuity in these iterations: God's demands remain the same. For example, community measures for the poor are different in each context, but concern for the vulnerable is a constant requirement of God.

Another contribution of Wright's paradigm is that it extends to the New Testament. Approaches to Old Testament ethics often move to the modern world without assessing the potential impact of the New on the topic or moral quandary at hand. While the Old Testament indeed has its own contribution to moral life today, the New Testament vision of issues should inform more comprehensive ethical reflection.[26] We will return to this point in the examples offered at the end of the chapter.

The New Testament and Ethics

Discussion of New Testament ethics is also complex and in several ways parallel to Old Testament concerns. Some of the issues have to do with the composite nature of the documents; others with the diverse contexts these texts treat. Key issues include: first, the centrality of Jesus, second, the diverse ways in which themes are treated, and third, basic hermeneutical concerns about the move from an ancient context to the modern world.

Because what is known about Jesus is mediated through the Bible or secondary means, scholars hold different views concerning the importance of Jesus for New Testament ethics. The challenge involves establishing both the nature and value of our sources about Jesus and the content of his ethics. The Sermon on the Mount is a case in point. It is viewed either as idealistic (and therefore not realistic for the modern world) or as a key feature of the New Testament ethics.[27] Most treatments consider Jesus and his larger teaching as vital and note the consensus that his principal concern was the kingdom of God and the community that emerges from it.

The second issue concerns the diversity of perspectives on morality and ethics in the New Testament. A careful reading quickly brings this reality to the surface. For example, Romans 13:1–7 urges submission to the state as an instrument of God (cf. 1 Pet 2:13–17; 1 Tim 2:10–2), while Revelation presents a world power moved by satanic influence and headed toward judgment (Rev 18–19).[28] Jesus' call to be sensitive to the poor (Lk 4:16–21; 14:12–14) can be contrasted with Paul's challenge to ignore the lazy (2 Thess 3:10–12). Galatians 3:28 might stand in tension with Paul's instructions about gender distinctions in 1 Corinthians 11:2–16.[29] Such differences underscore the hermeneutical challenge of postulating a single New Testament view on key topics. Most works wrestle with how to assess these multiple treatments of themes, eschewing approaches that pick and choose among options or that look for unqualified, timeless principles. Such balancing or weighing of the whole collection of passages on a theme can yield qualifications about the universal applicability of certain specific texts, with attention given to the specific context of each passage. At the same time, evangelicals can assert that the various angles of a given text cohere within a broader, and thus richer, framework on a topic drawing on the full range of biblical texts applied to the theme. The result is that passages can present complementary perspectives, with the nuances of a given situation being a part of the total perspective that can be gained when all the relevant passages on a topic are placed side by side. Once more, convictions concerning biblical authority come into play. How this approach works is presented in our final summary section, which discusses different kinds of textual grouping.

The third challenge focuses on differences between the first-century context and the modern world. For instance, in the New Testament, spiritual forces and principalities are a given, whereas now attention is given to analyzing the social forces at work in people's lives. An example drawn from the realm of sexuality perhaps makes this point most powerfully. In ancient Jewish and Christian circles, homosexuality was widely considered a distortion of the created order.[30] Some segments of Roman society, such as those standards which the family of Augustus supported, also questioned such practices.[31] Today debate rages about whether people are born with a particular sexual orientation that may not be heterosexual. Many accept this as a given, confirmed by scientific inquiry—despite the fact that to this date there is no scientific consensus on this.[32] Biblically rooted ethics has to wrestle with how to deal with the significant differences in perspective between those who claim sexual preference is natural and those who see it as morally defective. The topic of homosexual relationships is one of the examples treated below.

These three fundamental concerns have generated diverse approaches. A representative survey of models can help the reader appreciate the complexity of the task of appealing to the Bible for ethics.[33]

Models for Ethics in the New Testament

The Imitation of Jesus

A recent approach is the narrative-biographical approach of Richard Burridge that argues that ethics in the New Testament should start and end with the gospel presentations of Jesus.[34] The gospels, Burridge emphasizes, are ancient biographies. They can be compared to stained glass, where the image in the glass (the gospels) is more crucial than whatever lies behind it (a reconstructed historical Jesus). The gospels depict what is most important about Jesus and offer his teaching and actions as guides. The modern reader is called to imitate this Jesus and live according to his instruction and example.

Burridge investigates how Jesus is presented by the authors and through the various genres of the New Testament. He discusses themes, such as the kingdom, discipleship, and love. Burridge looks at how key ethical issues are handled by the gospel writers in light of such themes. At times it is hard to discern whether Burridge is searching for a way to proceed through the hard decisions of life (ethics) or if he is more intent on the presentation of a New Testament theology out of which ethics can be addressed. A theological basis is important to ethics, but it seems that much energy is spent on formulating that foundation and not on working toward a solution of the usefulness of the material for ethics. Nonetheless, Burridge's dominant idea is that Jesus consistently showed an inclusive approach to various oft-rejected groups. It is this inclusiveness that needs to be imitated today. The treatment of apartheid by South African Christians is the author's exemplary case study.

Herein lies an issue concomitant with the prioritization of Jesus for New Testament ethics. That is, what about the life and/or teaching of Jesus is to be highlighted, and is this emphasis exaggerated at the expense of other matters? Burridge's emphasis on inclusivity is certainly an important New Testament theme, but not in the selective way he seems to present it. He appears to severely understate the idea of accountability in the pursuit of a genuine righteousness and the emphasis Jesus brought to the consequences of unrepentant sin with his affirmation of divine judgment (that is, exclusion). Burridge's summary of Matthew's ethical message shows the tension.[35] He treats the ways the new righteousness is to work itself out in the movement from forgiveness to practiced righteousness, but he does not give sufficient weight to the responsibility for righteousness, which is present in the key discourse of Matthew 23, or to the consequences for failing to respond.[36] These are significant omissions and result in an imbalance.

Jesus—Centered Character Ethics

Like Burridge, Stassen and Gushee begin with Jesus, but, unlike him, their approach focuses especially on a specific slice of gospel material (the Sermon on the Mount) and adheres to the emphases of virtue or character ethics as the window into authentic discipleship.[37]

Stassen and Gushee argue that the essence of kingdom ethics is following Jesus. Crucial to their proposal is a threefold structure employed throughout the Sermon on the Mount: a statement of traditionally defined righteousness for an area of life, the destructive cycle that prevents true righteousness, and Jesus' transforming initiative that reorients the topic.[38] For instance, the command not to murder is coupled with a warning that anger can be tantamount to that crime. The transforming initiative is the call to be reconciled (Matt 5:21–26). From this starting point, Stassen and Gushee work through a series of issues including war, the penalties for homicide, biotechnology, marriage and divorce, gender roles, love and justice, race, economics, creation care, and politics.

Their presentation of the ethical orientation of Jesus is more directive and presents more specifics than the call to imitate Jesus argued by Burridge. Stassen and Guchee do not proceed by presenting one central overriding theme (like Burridge's inclusiveness), but cover a greater breadth of gospel material while using a particular ethical tradition (the virtues). This is both a strength and weakness. The study of the Sermon on the Mount is sustained throughout, allowing for thorough reflection on its meaning and implications, and is enriched by attempting to trace the background to Jesus' thinking in Isaiah. The appeal to the Old Testament should be applauded, as few New Testament ethicists look to prior revelation to inform their work.[39]

Nevertheless, *Kingdom Ethics* appears to fall prey in some measure to the individualized focus of virtue ethics, even as it trumpets the importance of community. There is little discussion of how to assess a biblical role for corporate structures like the state. Corporate issues not directly addressed by the text are informed by principles of proper character. For example, in regards to economics, they underscore Jesus' principle that it is impossible to serve both God and mammon. The transforming initiative is to store up treasure in heaven, a reorientation that should be distinguished by a grace-based, simple lifestyle, whose munificent manner seeks justice for the poor. Other communal concerns such as property rights, work, ownership, economic systems, and business ethics are treated through the filter of these observations. This can leave the impression that Stassen and Gushee's model, though helpful in many ways, fails to reach into corporate arenas with principles that utilize corporate concerns.

The Biblical Jesus in Combination with a Theological Matrix

The most elaborate presentation of New Testament ethics is set forth by Richard Hays. He is very self-aware methodologically, carefully explaining his procedures and convictions and contrasting his way with other studies of New Testament ethics.[40]

Hays does not believe that the historical Jesus can be the starting point for New Testament ethics. This reconstruction would require immensely detailed and difficult textual and social data. Consequently, it is the impression or portrait left by Jesus in the gospels that must be examined.[41] But Hays does not limit his ethics to this material, and therein lies his contribution to the concerns of this chapter. His approach is a good example of using diverse lenses through which to read the New Testament. Hays combines synthesizing themes across the New Testament such as love and justice with the contributions of three "prisms' through which to investigate the principal elements of these themes. These prisms are community, cross, and new creation. Hays also works with the theological quadrilateral of Scripture, tradition, reason, and experience.

Hays examines the primary units of the New Testament, starting with Paul and the tradition tied to him, followed in order by Mark, Matthew, Luke-Acts, John, and Revelation. From this biblical-theological base, Hays makes the case for his three prisms through which to treat ethical themes. He dedicates a chapter each to several ethical issues and relates them to the central foci. That is, how should these topics to be processed in the community of faith and the world, in light of the cross, and as a reflection of new creation? Is their treatment consistent across the New Testament?

While Hays's work is a wide-ranging and thought-provoking treatise, questions do arise. For example, it appears that his theological approach does not adequately handle the virtues rooted in a kingdom perspective that normally are significant in ethical discussion. This contrasts with Stassen and Gushee, who concentrate on character and highlight the development of specific traits as the key to New Testament ethics. His dismissal of the historical Jesus (or even an overall impression of Jesus) as largely irrelevant also is a point of disagreement with many New Testament ethicists. It limits the impact of the one whose presence drove the movement.

More problematic, Hays's treatment of ethical issues has limitations. For example, he presents a largely pacifist take on the Christian calling but sidesteps discussion of the state as authorized by God to protect its citizens and ignores the topic of the Christian as citizen. There also is no engagement with the just war tradition, introduced by Augustine and elaborated by Aquinas and others. And while he argues that homosexuality should be treated as other sins in the church, and the church should not affirm homosexual unions, he also supports civil rights for homosexuals (which is commendable) but without explaining how Christians should negotiate their dual citizenships in church and society.

Biblical Theological Focus

The most straightforward presentation of New Testament ethics simply utilizes biblical theology as the grid by which to engage the topic. Frank Matera undertakes such an approach in a recent work that concentrates on Jesus and Paul.[42] His, however, is not a study of the historical Jesus or Paul; rather, it is a literary reading of their "ethical legacy" left to the church in the pages of Scripture. Matera sees the task of New Testament ethics as primarily descriptive—that is, presenting the theological emphases of its authors. The moral teaching of the New Testament is an "account of how the kingdom of God (Jesus' ethical horizon) and the saving justice of God (Paul's ethical horizon) released the ethical forces of freedom, love, and faith."[43] Jesus advocated these values to the disciples. He also taught them to view the law with an eye to love and mercy, while Paul called for the "imitation of himself and Christ in a community for whom Christ had put an end to the law."[44]

Matera moves through each Gospel writer before turning to Paul and his communities. Mark points to life lived in light of the kingship of God. There is a call to surrender life to service, while awaiting the kingdom's manifestation in power. This requires dependence and faithfulness. Matthew calls disciples to a greater righteousness, which stands in contrast to the religious leadership of the time and reckons with the judgment and reward to come. Luke points to a time of salvation that reverses the fortunes of the poor and oppressed. Humility and repentance are central to the life of the disciple, as is the call to love one's neighbor. Discipleship is demanding and possessions can be an obstacle, so their use calls for a generous lifestyle. John emphasizes Christology. Ethics means responding to the One God has sent, while loving one another as Jesus loved. John and the Synoptic Gospels share the themes of the kingdom, repentance, faith, love, discipleship, and judgment.

The apostle Paul emphasizes election into a sanctified community that is to walk by the gift of the Spirit. They are to imitate Paul, even as he seeks to imitate Christ in an obedience of faith, which reflects life in the new creation that this new community is becoming. God's gracious work requires that followers respond with a life of faith lived among others and conducted in light of his coming salvation. All of this should find expression in love for God, neighbor, and one's enemy.

This descriptive approach involves little more than highlighting the values that emerge from biblical theology. Hermeneutical complexities are not tackled directly. The benefit of this study is its close reading of the text and its attempt to define parameters for how theological concepts and ethical responses relate; the limitation is not addressing clearly how to move from the New Testament text to our world.

Ethics and the Canon: A Taxonomy

The discussion of approaches to each testament has raised a series of issues that require consideration. One that needs to be explored a bit further in this survey is the role of Scripture as canon in establishing coherence vis-à-vis the rich and diverse ethical voices found in its pages. The following taxonomy is a brief introduction to a difficult topic.

Variety with Complementarity

The multiple perspectives on an ethical problem can all be parts of a larger vision. A good example is poverty. In the Old Testament, Proverbs points at individual failures as the cause of poverty (even as it calls for individuals, wise persons, to be charitable), whereas the prophetic literature denounces systemic exploitation of the poor by unjust legal, economic, and political practices. On the other hand, the Law contains legislation, which today might be called a series of safety nets, to insure the provision of food and a just wage. The same kind of sensitivity to New Testament material can enhance these observations by looking at parallels with the practices of Jesus and within the early church. In other words, the canon's treatment of poverty is multileveled, the components of its various strands complementing one another to form a wide and very realistic perspective. The danger for the Christian is to opt for one emphasis to the exclusion of the others.

Tension between Absolutes and Progressive Revelation

It is generally agreed that the Bible's word on a topic might develop in emphasis as one moves across the Old Testament and into the New. Christians must decide how to define the relationship between the testaments and factor in the eschatological breaking-in of the kingdom of God into their ethical stances—without seeing New Testament ethics as simply trumping Old Testament ethics.

Slavery comes to mind: from the acceptance of the institution, but always attempting to reduce its severity in the Old Testament, to the declaration in the New that slave and master are family in Christ. In the case of other topics, the implications of such shifts can be debated. One example is the role of women: Is there any change with the coming of Jesus and the Spirit (progression) or are the words of God in Genesis 3 still binding (absolute)? Might this way of posing the question, as it often is posed, be a false dichotomy? Might the OT emphases on roles be tempered and even reconfigured by how the NT teaching points to the service quality of relationships, whether in marriage or in communities at large?

Another example is the case of armed conflict. Just war theorists tend to look at the realities of war in the Old Testament, the ongoing need to defend the weak with force in a fallen world, and Paul's statement that the state has the authority to carry the sword (absolute), whereas pacifists prioritize the peaceableness of Jesus, his teaching to love the enemy, and the call to leave vengeance to God (progression). The debate concerns how to relate the two principles to each other. Is Jesus giving individual ethics, while Paul points to the corporate right of the state? Or, is Jesus' emphasis the decisive key? The just war position has a long tradition, from Augustine and Aquinas to more recent times in the work of Paul Ramsey and James Turner Johnson. The pacifist position recently has gained impetus through spokespersons, such as John Howard Yoder, Stanley Hauerwas, and Ron Sider. Both options seek to reflect the message of the breadth of Scripture.

Consistency across Testaments

There is also the case where the canon has an unchanging view of an ethical matter. Here there is no progression of revelation along the lines explained in the preceding category of texts. Two examples are the invariable support for the sacredness of life and the unwavering condemnation of homosexual acts. That life is inviolable, a gift from God, is upheld whenever the topic is directly addressed. In the same way, the rebuke of same-sex relationships as a violation of God's design for sexuality and family is unwavering. Even the recognition that a person may be inclined in a given direction is no warrant for committing certain sexual acts.

In sum, the Bible handles ethical topics with a depth that reflects their complexity. What some see as cacophony, hopelessly confused, and confusing for modern appropriation is in fact inspired appreciation for the intricacy of some issues, which are sorted out best when these three ways of coordinating texts are understood. Ultimately, treatment of these issues must be located within the entire canon, the divinely authoritative Scripture. Biblical ethics must take into account all that God says on a topic, not playing books and texts against one another or arbitrarily choosing one over another. The interpreter must judiciously weigh the range of contributions made by the Bible on an ethical matter to ascertain the full breadth of its teaching.

Conclusion

This chapter has aimed to introduce readers to the multiple factors to consider in order to use the Old and New Testaments for ethics and the moral life. As stressed at the beginning of our discussion, fundamental convictions concerning the nature of biblical authority require careful articulation. In addition, biblical ethics can embrace in beneficial ways the insights of philosophical ethics.

The challenges in appealing to the biblical text itself are many, however, and some basic issues pertain to both testaments. The interpreter must decide how to utilize descriptive studies in formulating the prescriptive teaching that arises from the biblical text. In addition, are there elements that deserve pride of place, such as the Law or the life and teaching of Jesus (or Paul)? Is any one approach to ethics best, to the exclusion of other alternatives, or is an eclectic method advisable? If so, what would such a configuration look like? Finally, the interpreter must know the Bible well enough and possess the hermeneutical skills to discern how to coordinate relevant texts across the Bible (the three options of complementarity, progressive revelation, and universal application) in any given ethical discussion.

The challenges that lay ahead are many and complex. There is no definitive method that Christians are mandated to follow in the use of the Bible for ethics, but a carefully crafted methodology is what is needed today as individual believers and Christian communities strive to be faithful to their mission in and for the world. What remains as the constant evangelical nonnegotiable is the commitment to the Bible as the prime source for ethical life.

NOTES

1. See the helpful surveys of Brevard S. Childs, *Biblical Theology of the Old and New Testaments: Theological Reflection on the Christian Bible* (Minneapolis: Fortress, 1992), 658–673; Charles H. Cosgrove, *Appealing to Scripture in Moral Debate: Five Hermeneutical Rules* (Grand Rapids: Eerdmans, 2002); cf. David H. Kelsey, *The Uses of Scripture in Recent Theology* (Philadelphia: Fortress, 1975).

2. A careful articulation of an evangelical persuasion is found in Christopher J. H. Wright, *Old Testament Ethics for the People of God* (Downers Grove, Ill.: InterVarsity, 2004), 441–471.

3. Bruce C. Birch and Larry L. Rasmussen, *Bible and Ethics in the Christian Life*, rev. ed. (Minneapolis: Augsburg, 1989), 141–188; Bruce C. Birch, *Let Justice Roll Down: The Old Testament, Ethics, and Christian Life* (Louisville, Ky.: Westminster John Knox, 1991), 29–50.

4. Stephen Fowl, *Engaging Scripture: A Model for Theological Interpretation* (Challenges in Contemporary Theology; Malden, Mass.: Blackwell, 1998); *The Blackwell Companion to Christian Ethics*, ed. S. Hauerwas and S. Wells (Malden, Mass.: Blackwell, 2004), 139–221.

5. Wright, *Old Testament Ethics for the People of God*, 103–129; James K. Bruckner, *Implied Law in the Abrahamic Narrative: A Literary and Theological Analysis* (London: Sheffield Academic Press, 2001).

6. H. D. Aiken, "Levels of Moral Discourse," in Aiken, *Reason and Conduct: New Bearings in Moral Philosophy* (New York: Alfred A. Knopf, 1962), 65–87.

7. Note the helpful study by John Rogerson, Christopher Roland, and Barnabas Lindars, *The Study and Use of the Bible* (Basingstoke: Marshall Pickering; Grand Rapids: Eerdmans, 1988).

8. For example, Pamela Bright, ed., *Augustine and the Bible* (Notre Dame: University of Notre Dame Press, 1986); William H. Lazareth, *Christians in Society: Luther, the Bible, and Social Ethics* (Minneapolis: Fortress, 2001); Donald K. McKim, ed., *The Cambridge Companion to John Calvin* (New York: Cambridge University Press, 2004).

9. Henning Graf Reventlow, *The Authority of the Bible and the Rise of the Modern World*, trans. J. Bowden (London: SCM, 1984); Christopher Hill, *The English Bible and the*

Sixteenth-Century Revolution (London: Penguin, 1993); Mark A. Noll, *The Civil War as a Theological Crisis* (Chapel Hill: University of North Carolina Press, 2006); cf. Ernest R. Sandeen, ed., *The Bible and Social Reform* (Philadelphia: Fortress; Chico: Scholars Press, 1982).

10. Dietrich Bonhoeffer, *Discipleship*, in *Dietrich Bonhoeffer Works*, vol. 4, trans. M. Kuske and I. Tödt (Minneapolis: Fortress, 2003); Bonhoeffer, *Ethics*, in *Dietrich Bonhoeffer Works*, vol. 6, trans. R. Krauss, C. C. West, and D. W. Scott (Minneapolis: Fortress, 2005); Karl Barth, *Ethics*, trans. G. W. Bromiley (Edinburgh: T & T Clark, 1981); Helmut Thielicke, *Theological Ethics*, 3 vols. (Grand Rapids: Eerdmans, 1966, 1969, 1964); Oliver O'Donovan, *Resurrection and Moral Order: An Outline for Evangelical Ethics* (Leicester: Inter-Varsity; Grand Rapids: Eerdmans, 1986).

11. See, for example, John Howard Yoder, *The Politics of Jesus: vicit, Agnus noster*, 2nd ed. (Grand Rapids: Eerdmans, 1994); Stanley Hauerwas, *The Peaceable Kingdom: A Primer in Christian Ethics* (London: SCM, 1983); Lisa Sowle Cahill and James F. Childress, eds., *Christian Ethics: Problems and Prospects* (Cleveland: Pilgrim, 1996).

12. Philip Jenkins, *The Next Christendom: The Coming of Global Christianity* (New York: Oxford University Press, 2002); *The New Faces of Christianity: Believing the Bible in the Global South* (New York: Oxford University Press, 2006).

13. J. David Pleins, *The Social Visions of the Hebrew Bible: A Theological Introduction* (Louisville, Ky.: Westminster John Knox, 2001).

14. Walter J. Houston, *Contending for Justice: Ideologies and Theologies of Social Justice in the Old Testament* (London: T & T Clark, 2008).

15. Cf. Childs, *Biblical Theology of the Old and New Testaments*, 678–685; Birch, *Let Justice Roll Down*.

16. For example, scholars have tried to reconstruct what specific socioeconomic and cultural framework that the prophets condemned. In arguing for the patronage system, Houston points out the weaknesses of other suggestions, such as the "rent capitalism" and the "tributary state" models; Houston, *Contending for Justice*, 18–51.

17. John Rogerson, *Theory and Practice in Old Testament Ethics*, ed. M. D. Carroll R. (London: T & T Clark, 2004).

18. John Barton, *Understanding Old Testament Ethics* (Louisville, Ky.: Westminster John Knox, 2003), 45–54, 130–153.

19. Bruce V. Malchow, *Social Justice in the Hebrew Bible* (Collegeville, Minn.: Michael Glazier, 1996); Eckart Otto, *Theologische Ethik des Alten Testaments* (Stuttgart: Kohlhammer, 1994).

20. For example, Robin Perry, *Old Testament Story and Christian Ethics? The Rape of Dinah as a Case Study* (Milton Keynes: Paternoster, 2004); cf. supra, notes 3, 4.

21. William P. Brown, *Character in Crisis: A Fresh Approach to the Wisdom Literature of the Old Testament* (Grand Rapids: Eerdmans, 1996); Brown, ed., *Character & Scripture: Moral Formation, Community, and Biblical Interpretation* (Grand Rapids: Eerdmans, 2002); Gordon J. Wenham, *Story as Torah: Reading the Old Testament Ethically* (Edinburgh: T & T Clark, 2000); Barton, *Understanding Old Testament Ethics*, 55–64; M. Daniel Carroll R. and Jacqueline Lapsley, eds., *Character Ethics and the Old Testament: Moral Dimensions of Scripture* (Louisville, Ky.: Westminster John Knox, 2007).

22. For example, Carol Dempsey, *Hope amid the Ruins: The Ethics of Israel's Prophets* (St. Louis: Chalice, 2000); Johanna W. H. van Wijk-Bos, *Making Wise the Simple: The Torah in Christian Faith and Practice* (Grand Rapids: Eerdmans, 2005).

23. Wright, *Old Testament Ethics for the People of God*; cf. Waldemar Janzen, *Old Testament Ethics: A Paradigmatic Approach* (Louisville, Ky.: Westminster John Knox, 1994).

24. See Walter C. Kaiser, Jr., *Toward Old Testament Ethics* (Grand Rapids: Zondervan, 1983); Joe M. Sprinkle, *Biblical Law and Its Relevance: A Christian Understanding and Ethical Application for Today of the Mosaic Regulations* (Lanham, Md.: University Press of America, 2006).

25. Richard Hays's three foci from the New Testament (community, cross, new creation) work similarly. See his *The Moral Vision of the New Testament: A Contemporary Introduction to New Testament Ethics* (San Francisco: HarperSanFrancisco, 1996).

26. From a different perspective, see Childs, *Biblical Theology of the Old and New Testaments*, 686–716.

27. Contrast Glen H. Stassen and David P. Gushee, *Kingdom Ethics: Following Jesus in a Contemporary Context* (Downers Grove, Ill.: InterVarsity, 2003), 32–54, for whom the Sermon is essential, with Reinhold Niebuhr, *Moral Man and Immoral Society* (New York: Scribners, 1932) and *An Interpretation of Christian Ethics* (New York: Harper, 1935). Niebuhr believes the Sermon to be an impossible ethical ideal.

28. One sees a reference to the state of Rome here but, in fact, the challenge is broader than a single state. It is a rebuke of an entire world structure abusing resources and power.

29. So controversial are these contrasts in the treatment of gender that 1 Cor 14:33–36 is often said not to come from Paul, while 1 Tim 2:11–15 is handled in a myriad of ways.

30. Rom 1:18–32 is a critique most see as rooted in a Jewish critique of such practices, as well; cf. *Letter of Aristeas* 152; *Sybilline Oracles* 3.184–187; *Pseudo-Phocylides* 190–192.

31. Earlier, Plato spoke of laws to curb sex that was "against nature" (*Laws* 838E–839A). Also against such relationships was the first-century Stoic philosopher Musonius Rufus, who speaks against homosexuality with the same rigor he challenges adultery (chap. 12).

32. Stanton L. Jones and Alex W. Kwee, "Scientific Research, Homosexuality, and the Church's Moral Debate: An Update," in *Journal of Psychology and Christianity* 24 (2005), 304–316. Jones and Kwee say that "findings of biological causation of homosexuality are not unequivocal, while there is suggestive but similarly inconclusive evidence of environmental causation"; Ibid., 304. See also Stanton L. Jones and Mark A. Yarhouse, *Homosexuality: The Use of Scientific Research in the Church's Moral Debate* (Downer's Grove, Ill.: InterVarsity, 2000).

33. For a wider-ranging study, see Brian Brock, *Singing the Ethos of God: On the Place of Christian Ethics in Scripture* (Grand Rapids: Eerdmans, 2007), 3–95. He discusses approaches that center on hermeneutics (Schüssler-Fiorenza, Patte), community (Birch and Rasmussen, Fowl and Jones), biblical ethics (Matera, Hays, Yoder), biblical theology (Childs, Watson, Webster), and exegetical theology (Bonhoffer).

34. Richard A. Burridge, *Imitating Jesus: An Inclusive Approach to New Testament Ethics* (Grand Rapids: Eerdmans, 2007); Stassen and Gushee's *Kingdom Ethics* would agree with Burridge.

35. Similar emphases are made for Mark (the open acceptance of others; Ibid., 184), Paul (an open and mixed community; Ibid., 154), Luke (love for the marginalized; Ibid., 283), and John (the mixed, inclusive nature of the community; Ibid., 346).

36. The lack of appeal to accountability to God is also shown by Burridge's failure to deal in any detail with the ethical implications of Revelation.

37. Stassen and Gushee, *Kingdom Ethics*; cf. Robert L. Brawley, *Character Ethics and the New Testament: Moral Dimensions of Scripture* (Louisville, Ky.: Westminster John Knox, 2007).

38. Stassen and Gushee, *Kingdom Ethics*, 125–145.

39. Hays explicitly addresses the issue in *The Moral Vision of the New Testament*, 306–309.

40. Ibid., 207–312.

41. Ibid., 158–168.

42. Frank Matera, *New Testament Ethics: The Legacies of Jesus and Paul* (Louisville: Westminster John Knox, 1996).

43. Ibid., 6.

44. Ibid.

BIBLIOGRAPHY

Barton, John. *Understanding Old Testament Ethics*. Louisville, Ky: Westminster John Knox, 2003.

Brock, Brian. *Singing the Ethos of God: On the Place of Christian Ethics in Scripture*. Grand Rapids: Eerdmans, 2007.

Burridge, Richard A. *Imitating Jesus: An Inclusive Approach to New Testament Ethics*. Grand Rapids: Eerdmans, 2007.

Carroll R., M. Daniel, and Jacqueline Lapsley, eds. *Character Ethics and the Old Testament: Moral Dimensions of Scripture*. Louisville, Ky.: Westminster John Knox, 2007.

Gushee, David P., and Glen H. Stassen. *Kingdom Ethics: Following Jesus in a Contemporary Context*. Downers Grove, Ill.: InterVarsity, 2003.

Hays, Richard. *The Moral Vision of the New Testament: A Contemporary Introduction to New Testament Ethics*. San Francisco: HarperSanFrancisco, 1996.

Houston, Walter J. *Contending for Justice: Ideologies and Theologies of Social Justice in the Old Testament*. London: T & T Clark, 2008.

Matera, Frank. *New Testament Ethics: The Legacies of Jesus and Paul*. Louisville, Ky.: Westminster John Knox, 1996.

Pleins, J. David. *The Social Visions of the Hebrew Bible: A Theological Introduction*. Louisville, Ky.: Westminster John Knox, 2001.

Perry, Robin. *Old Testament Story and Christian Ethics: The Rape of Dinah as a Case Study*. Milton Keynes: Paternoster, 2004.

Rogerson, John. *Theory and Practice in Old Testament Ethics*, ed. M. D. Carroll R. London: T. & T. Clark, 2004.

Wright, Christopher J. H. *Old Testament Ethics for the People of God* (Downers Grove, Ill.: InterVarsity, 2004.

CHAPTER 25

POLITICS

ERIC GREGORY

SUSTAINED theological reflection on the nature and purposes of politics is not a hallmark of evangelical thought. For systemic and contingent reasons, evangelical theology lacks dogmatic focus on the politics of a people who confess "Jesus is Lord" (Romans 10:9). This intellectual neglect stands in stark contrast to polarizing debates about politics and Christian mission that characterize evangelical life.[1] Despite numerous calls for a distinctive approach to politics, and an evangelical renaissance in related fields such as philosophy, history, and political science, *political theology*—which involves thinking theologically about our common life together—remains implicit or peripheral in most evangelical scholarship. Some celebrate this apparent rejection of the so-called captivity of liberal theologies beholden to "secular humanism" or the theocratic ambitions of Christendom and fundamentalism. They seek true religion, not theological fads or political opinion. They defend orthodoxy and spiritual authenticity by establishing a safe distance from the rough and tumble world of earthly politics, its penultimate concerns, moral compromises, and passing authority. Doctrine and ethics are linked by appeal to moral reformation, but political theology is a rabbit hole down which the distinctiveness and clarity of Christian proclamation are lost. So it is thought.

By my lights, however, an appropriate evangelical wariness of political accommodation too often yields an anxious and ahistorical rejection of political theology as such. This vacuum leaves evangelical theology vulnerable to the seductive cooptation by ideologies it seeks to avoid. But it is foremost a theological failure that undermines the particularity and fullness of Christian confession. Evangelicals of different stripes reveal modern prejudices in their ironic complicity with the separation of theology from politics. In this essay, I argue that the future of evangelical political theology demands a reconstruction of older models of Christian political thought rather than an application of evangelical convictions to existing politics.

Given a high view of the authority of Scripture, exegetical efforts to apply biblical principles to concrete political issues populate a crowded landscape of monographs, sermons, occasional pamphlets, and declarations. These often supply biblical proof-texts for preferred public policies across the political spectrum: from "evangelical left" to "Christian right." Certain passages (2 Chronicles 7:14, Jeremiah 29, Matthew 5 and 25, Galatians 3, Ephesians 6, 1 Peter 2, Romans 13) and whole books (Genesis, Exodus, Daniel, Luke, Revelation) stand out for regular commentary. At the same time, scattered attention to concepts like the Kingdom of God, Israel, messiah, covenant and election, love and justice, common good, and Christian liberty inform numerous accounts of politics and discipleship. With the rise of neo-evangelicalism, these formulations typically elicit a "worldview" or "social ethics" that draws heavily from an Augustinian account of politics mediated by Reformation theologies broadly in support of constitutional and democratic political arrangements (for example, Carl Henry). They typically highlight the dangers of political idolatry and secularized modernity even as they call individual Christians to exercise political responsibility, joining both evangelism and social action (for example, John Stott and Francis Schaeffer). Related projects in biblical theology promote civic engagement by critical interaction with the influential typologies of H. Richard Niebuhr's classic work, *Christ and Culture.* Still others propose norms and principles that might inform a Christian political theory, with increasingly sophisticated attention to the structural and institutional analysis of social ills. These commendable efforts, however, fall short of a genuinely political theology informed by the rich tradition of Christian theopolitical reflection.

Recent developments in political theory, theology, biblical studies, and cultural theory have led to a revived interest in political theology in both the academy and the wider public. Many of these developments emerge from thinkers without traditional evangelical convictions (postliberal theology) or constructive theological interests (postsecular political theory). But they have gained an appreciative audience in some evangelical circles. This chapter briefly examines these developments in relation to classical and evangelical traditions as well as more conventional approaches to "religion and politics." I consider these projects, and their critics, in the context of contemporary global politics and propose future directions for evangelical thinking on the subject.

A Theological Approach: What Is Political Theology?

Most normative discussions of evangelical politics focus on the appropriate role of religion in politics, especially with regard to controversial moral issues. This approach, which dominates the social sciences, philosophy, and jurisprudence, concentrates on "church-state" issues regarding religious liberty, toleration, and secularization. Its popularity relies on the dominant influence of theories of liberal democracy that seek to constrain religious privilege or comprehensive visions of the good by appeal to notions of rights, neutrality, and a distinction between public and private. Many secularists see religion, especially conservative Protestantism, as a self-righteous absolutism incompatible with political cooperation, equality, and freedom. Evangelicals often are portrayed as theocratic threats to Enlightenment ideals of rationality and democratic progress. This approach tends to treat religion as a generic phenomenon of human culture, but it relies heavily on a Christian background in differentiating "religious" and "secular" spheres of human activity. A prominent aspect of these debates has been the ethics of citizenship under conditions of pluralism, especially proposals that place moral restrictions on reasoning from religious convictions to political commitments. Such epistemic restrictions, it is claimed, are necessary for the social stability and mutual respect demanded by societies faced with conflicting beliefs. While some evangelical leaders tacitly adopt these restrictions in practice, evangelical scholars rightly have challenged this claim as antidemocratic and incompatible with moral, intellectual, and religious integrity.

The primary burden of this chapter for a volume on evangelical theology lies elsewhere. Here the effort concentrates on political theology *as theology*, attentive to familiar theological concerns (that is, God, Christ, salvation, revelation, the church, Trinity, providence, creation, and eschatology). But they are not isolated from politics. The basic theological question, for example, is not how or whether Christians or the church should be involved in politics. Such a question may be a subset of political theology so long as it does not assume the normative priority of any given structure (such as nation-states, democracy, or capitalism). Politics itself is to be interpreted theologically rather than placed as an epilogue or addendum to doctrinal or biblical exposition. Definitions of a more robust style of political theology invite controversy, especially given modern associations of the term with the controversial writings of Catholic jurist Carl Schmitt, liberation theology, or various experiments in civil religion. In general, we can begin with a helpful recent statement: "What distinguishes all political theology from other types of theology or political discourse is the explicit attempt to relate discourse about God to the organization of bodies in space and time."[2] For my purposes, I see two models as live options of this kind.

First, political theology can identify shared concepts between political philosophy and theology proper, and then make simultaneous inferences about both politics and theology. This approach compares and contrasts notions such as community, obligation, law, virtue, and human nature. It often takes the form of intellectual history in the service of conceptual analysis, tracing how theological beliefs, practices, and innovations illuminate changes in political ideals and arrangements (or the other way around). For example, it might relate Christian beliefs about the "image of God" or "original sin" to democratic language about the dignity of persons or the limits of politics. It might also examine ways in which theological discourse about sovereignty and authority, or legality and morality, finds concrete expression in politics. Renewed interest in the history of political philosophy displays increased sensitivity to the significance of religious thought for understanding the structure of these debates.

Second, a more ambitious kind of political theology reflects an original sense of the term. Like most Christian authors from the patristic age through the early modern period, it is unapologetically theological in its appeal to divine revelation rather than transcendental ideals. It risks theological interpretation of politics based upon God's action in revealing the Word of God. As one leading Anglican evangelical puts it, political theology seeks a "unifying conceptual structure" that connects "political themes with the history of salvation as a whole."[3] For Oliver O'Donovan, this exegetical task furnishes a charitable interpretation of both the idea of Christendom and classical liberalism as responses to Christian mission. Other powerful examples of this type emerge from critical reactions to liberal Protestantism and messianic nationalism in Germany and America: Karl Barth's Christological conception of the state and Stanley Hauerwas's conception of the church as an alternative *polis*. I do not wish to separate these two models, but here initially highlight them as alternatives to the dominant ways of thinking about evangelicals and politics.

Evangelicals have a long and varied history of bearing witness to God through political action, moral reform, and social criticism. Since the 1970s, there has been no shortage of empirical attention to the political mobilization of evangelicals and their global influence. For much of the twentieth century, liberal Protestants and secular reformers criticized evangelicals for their individualistic "otherworldly piety" and apolitical focus on "saving souls and winning hearts." Today, across the globe, many wish evangelicals would conform to this stereotype of sectarian piety. Over the past several decades, however, historians have labored to uncover the complex role of evangelicals in crucial periods of American and British politics. More recently, scholars have noted the importance of evangelicals for democratization in Africa, Asia, and Latin America.[4] Still others identify a broadening social agenda among younger evangelicals energized by renewed evangelical concern for global justice, racial reconciliation, and human rights. Like most Christian traditions, especially populist ones, evangelicalism is diverse enough to claim its progressives, moderates, and conservatives. What curiously unites their heated internal debates over politics is the absence of theology.

Classical Sources: Two Cities, One World

While not alone in their neglect of classical sources of political theology, evangelicals often imagine church history in terms of an authentic early Christian identity that was lost or distorted until the spiritual renewal movements of the Protestant Reformation, the Great Awakenings, or the Holiness movements of the nineteenth century. Nevertheless, figures like Augustine and Aquinas, and their medieval heirs, cast a massive shadow over Western thought in ways that unwittingly give shape to evangelical theology. Augustine's influence on evangelical piety and theology through the writings of Calvin, Luther, and Edwards is more pronounced, but recent Protestant readings of Aquinas on law and virtue are salient. In fact, evangelical interest in Thomism (especially treatments of natural law) is a notable feature of the contemporary period.[5]

Augustine's influence on Western political thought and its diffuse streams, including Aquinas, owes much to his pregnant biblical image of "two cities." In fact, current debates about modern liberalism in both theology and political theory can be seen as variations on Augustinian themes and critical response to them (for example, Reinhold Niebuhr, John Rawls, Martin Luther King, Jr., and John Milbank). Augustine himself does not offer a systematic account of church and state, much less a proposal for the best form of government or legal design. But, in addition to his much discussed comments on just war, slavery, and coercion, his theology is saturated with politics and its deep undercurrents. This section offers one reading of his eschatological theology of the "two cities" as a principal guide to his theological interpretation of politics.

It should be noted that evangelical suspicion of political theology finds a potential ally in many textbook readings of Augustine as a God-intoxicated, otherworldly critic of sinful politics on the edge of chaos. Augustine's polemical rhetoric and his accent on the inward journey of the soul encourage this dualistic claim. For him, the present age is "so miserable that it is like a hell on earth; and there is no escape from it other than through the grace of Christ, our Saviour, God and Lord."[6] His great work, *City of God*, is a devastating assault on the pretensions of the Roman Empire, its cultural ideals, and Christian enthusiasm for them. Augustine was initially attracted to the imperial theology of the Constantinian establishment, but he came to reject the sacralization of earthly politics as a vehicle of salvation. This rejection inspires diverse strands in modern, and now postmodern, theology. It is a sober vision of a politics of imperfection that frustrates more worldly utopian traditions. Yet it can also support anxiety for any theological politics, especially when paired with individualistic readings of the intense conversion narrative of *Confessions.* Theology is about God, Christ, and the wondrous rebirth of the soul; all else is ephemeral. Mixing politics with theology, it seems, is essentially a pagan exercise in vanity. Sin finds its ground in excessive attachment to the finite goods of this world, including earthly justice and even human institutions like the church. There will never be true justice until God is praised rightly in heaven. What really matters is not the surface political drama of civilizations which come and go, or even making the world a better place, but the restless heart on pilgrimage. Christians are resident aliens in a foreign land.

This hyper-spiritualized reading of Augustine's Platonism, of course, is a caricature. For example, it neglects Augustine's strong affirmation of the goodness of creation, resolutely Christological reading of the two love commandments, and pastoral vision of Christian life as training in virtue. But it is a popular one, sponsored by secular critics and evangelical defenders of Christianity alike.[7] Is there another way to read Augustine? One promising route begins by recognizing Augustine's contribution to framing theology as a kind of sociology:

> Two cities, then, have been created by two loves: that is, the earthly city by love of self extending even to contempt of God, and the heavenly city by love of God extending to contempt of self. The one, therefore, glories in itself, the other in the Lord; the one seeks glory from men, the other finds it highest glory in God, the Witness of our conscience. (14:28)

These two cities have different origins, histories, and destinies. It is Augustine's complex interrogation of their inner dynamics—and their historical unfolding from Adam to Christ, Babylon to Jerusalem—that continues to fascinate readers and would fund later Christian defenses of the separation of church and state. Augustine suggests that human beings are best understood as bundles of loves in community. We are fundamentally social creatures. The heavenly city will be a transparent community of wills, constituted by loving, and being loved, by others and God. In this life, however, Augustine is impressed by the opacity and cruelty of human relations. Rome's lust for domination (*libido dominandi*) reveals its claims to justice and mercy are a parody of the heavenly city. The history of the earthly city is, in fact, the history of empire—a point recently amplified by some progressive evangelicals in relation to the United States.

Augustine's harsh unmasking of Roman vice, however, is not a thorough deconstruction. Sin is not that spectacular for him. It is parasitic on a genuine good. The desire for justice and peace is inescapable, even if it will not be fully realized in this life, and can be wrongly desired even in this one. The fall, so to speak, does not go as deep as creation and the goodness of our embodied existence. As such, political communities, intent on their own perverted kind of peace, admit diverse historical expressions in response to the witness of the Gospel. They display both surprising virtue and demonic vice. It was this move that led to his famous transformation of Cicero's definition of a commonwealth: "A 'people' is an assembled multitude of rational creatures bound together by a common agreement as to the objects of their love ... the better the objects of this agreement, the better the people; and the worse the objects, the worse the people" (19.24). For Augustine, our loves are misdirected unless they are ordered toward God and neighbor. Pride fundamentally disorders proper loving and sociality. Humility gives birth to proper loving as humanity is graciously taken up into the Body of Christ and bends toward the love of others as God does in the Incarnation. The objects of our love, and our ways of loving, are central to Augustine's exegesis of biblical and secular history. One defines the earthly city, sometimes identified with Babylon and Rome; the other defines the heavenly city, sometimes identified with Israel and the church. But a related claim is salient.

For Augustine, there are not two orders of reality, one spiritual and the other natural. In this mortal age, according to the mature Augustine, the two cities are inextricably mixed: "Both cities alike make use of the good things, or are afflicted with the evils, of this temporal state; but they do so with a different faith, a different hope, a different love, until they are separated by the final judgment, and each receives its own end, to which there is no end" (18.54). Earthly peace is governed by the providence of God in a fallen world, and Christians are commanded to "endure this earthly commonwealth, however depraved and wholly vile it may be" (2.19). They are to make use of earthly peace which at least offers remedial constraint on wickedness: "The earthly city, which does not live by faith, desires an earthly peace, and it establishes an ordered concord of civic obedience and rule in order to secure a kind of co-operation of men's wills for the sake of attaining the things which belong to this mortal life" (19.17). There is no unity of ethics and politics for Augustine; at least no unity short of the heavenly, eternal city. But there also is no neutral *tertium quid*. Our souls are always being shaped by one of the two cities in agonistic struggle. Given the eschatological division of human wills and our shared mortality, this temporal state remains ambivalent as a site of ongoing penitential discernment and constant hope. Such a complicated picture vexed medieval Christendom, tempting it to close in on itself by fusing sacred and secular powers, but it could also encourage a stance of patient attention to the plurality of creation and the need for deliberation on communal matters. Here many find a nascent Christian conception of secularity which affirms the shared time in this present age of the common grace of God.

Lutheran, Calvinist, and Anabaptist diverse restatements of Augustine's "two cities" theology were fundamental to the political, legal, and ecclesiological shockwaves of the Protestant Reformation. Luther's famous attack on the medieval sacramental system and celebration of the priesthood of all believers were rooted in his radicalized Augustinian notions of conscience, spiritual inwardness, neighbor-love, and "two kingdoms." Calvin's vigorous defense of constitutional political order and law—which later gave rise to theories of resistance and rights—also reveal an Augustinian heritage in its concern for injustice and the social presence of the church. Anabaptist models of apostolic community lay claim to Augustine's legacy of monastic rule and rejection of a Christian "state." The complex history of these different developments in the early modern period is a notable strength of evangelical scholarship. But their contested normative legacy, alongside the influential writings of Karl Barth, Dietrich Bonhoeffer, and John Howard Yoder, is the focus of much contemporary political theology.

Resourcement: Evangelical Political Theologies and Future Directions

Stanley Hauerwas and Oliver O'Donovan agree that all theology is political. Both resist the stories that modern secularists tell about religion and politics as well as vague abstractions about Christianity and culture found in many volumes of

Christian social ethics. Their prolific work has made signal contributions to emerging evangelical interest in mending the conversational breakdown between classical and contemporary political theology. Their political ethics are not deductive conclusions from systematic theology; rather, they emerge from sustained reflection on the biblical revelation of God's saving work through Israel and the life and ministry of Jesus. While perhaps best known for their disagreements over pacifism and political liberalism, their parallel visions reflect divergent receptions of the Augustinian tradition via the magisterial Reformation and Anabaptist theology. One emphasizes the Christological character of eschatology, the other emphasizes ecclesiology. Echoing Barth, though with notable qualification, O'Donovan posits a dialectical relation between church (which gives witness to the Gospel) and political society (which exercises judgment). Secular political order is humbled by the witness of the church through the Spirit of Christ, yet it shares a joint responsibility under the Lordship of Christ. For O'Donovan, the democratic ethos under the rule of law is the "prodigal son" of Christian thought. For Hauerwas, even such cautious defenses betray a triumphalism at odds with the properly ecclesial focus of Christian proclamation. Evangelical theology will continue to benefit from critical interaction with these authors, especially by focusing on the dogmatic, liturgical, and exegetical issues at hand rather than ciphering their claims through general categories of "liberal and anti-liberal" or "church and world."

Another important tradition with widespread evangelical appeal should be noted because it avoids traditional dichotomies between personal salvation and political reform. "Christian Pluralism," which borrows heavily from Dutch neo-Calvinism and the writings of Abraham Kuyper, prominently emphasizes the doctrine of creation in defense of a Christian conception of democracy in a pluralist society. Kuyper argued that the animating principle of Calvinism is not "justification by faith" but "in the widest sense cosmologically, *the Sovereignty of the Triune God over the whole cosmos*, in all its spheres and kingdoms, visible and invisible."[8] Followers of this tradition typically hold that political institutions are not so much a remedial "order of providence" but an aspect of God's creation with their own normative integrity to pursue the public common good and establish justice. The state, in this view, is not responsible for all aspects of human flourishing. But it has limited responsibility according to its own differentiated authority ("sphere sovereignty"). Prominent exponents of this tradition, including Richard Mouw, Timothy Sherratt, Nicholas Wolterstorff, James Skillen, and Jonathan Chaplin, offer trenchant analysis of the other proposals I have mentioned and will continue to inform evangelical political reflection.

I have indicated how and why evangelical theology needs to abandon its neglect of political theology. Attention to political theology need not imply a wholesale theological innovation. On the contrary, evangelical theology is well suited to become self-consciously political by attending to its central concerns. But areas of future work include already identified weaknesses in evangelical theology:

1. Critics of evangelicalism have long argued that weak ecclesiology renders it susceptible to political manipulation and reduces its theopolitical imagination

to individual conversionism. Given the significance of ecclesiology for political theology, continued evangelical discussions of Christian worship and diverse ecclesial patterns will be of significance (including "New Monasticism," "emerging church," and the vast interlocking network of evangelical ministries). Moreover, while this chapter emphasizes "big ideas," a growing evangelical model of "lived theology" focuses explicitly on the piety of local Christian communities and their situated social practices. It draws more from ethnography, social history, and cultural anthropology than traditional evangelical theology. Future political theology should profit from these empirical studies, especially with regard to global Christianity, Pentecostalism, gender issues, and faith-based social movements.

2. Another promising but largely unexplored area for political theology is the effort in biblical studies to rethink the significance of Israel and Judaism for early Christianity. For example, the "new perspective" on Paul is a central aspect of recent evangelical theology, especially in response to the influential writings of N. T. Wright. But these debates typically focus narrowly on the doctrine of justification and the historical character of Jewish messianism and responses to Roman rule. They have been rather silent on its normative implications for politics and Christian self-understanding of synagogue and church today—despite Wright's interventions on these questions. More generally, Jewish-Christian schism and Christian supercessionism (as a theological rather than simply ethical issue) remains a neglected topic in contemporary theology and should be a priority for evangelicals. Here the question is not so much that of evangelical attitudes toward the modern state of Israel, anti-Semitism, or even inter-religious dialogue. These remain important issues with theological dimensions. As a central task in political theology, however, what seems needed is further attention to the broadly political dimensions of Pauline soteriology and ecclesiology in order for evangelicals to best maintain their commitment to the high Christology of classical Trinitarian traditions and the biblical witness to God's covenant with the Jews.

3. Evangelical rapprochement with Roman Catholic social teaching primarily has focused on topics in bioethics, sexuality and marriage, and war (especially through the influence of Richard John Neuhaus and George Weigel). Wide-ranging Roman Catholic discussions of political economy, however, are another vast resource for evangelical thought in age of globalization. They might inspire more theological attention to economics beyond moral criticism of consumerism.

4. Evangelical political imagination was forged within the crucible of modernity and democratic faith. Today, most challenges to democracy, if an alternative is proposed, bear the marks of central features of democratic traditions. Indeed, the Catholic Church has moved from being one of the strongest critics of democracy to one of its great defenders. Fights about democratic political arrangements are often proxies for other debates, like relativism, value pluralism, or views of morality as mere social agreement. Most evangelical thinkers support democratic institutions even if they are critical of democratic culture or secularist theories of liberalism. Perennial questions about the status of politics as created or postlapsarian will

remain on the theological agenda. But a related avenue for future evangelical work is the analogical relation between discipleship and citizenship. This turn would focus less on structures of politics or public policy and more on the formation of character through civic engagement. Can such engagement, for example, serve as an ascetic practice which cultivates virtues of faith, hope, and love?

Conclusion

Evangelicalism is a notoriously complex tradition that often reflects its diverse cultural contexts as much as it shapes them. The Spirit-filled world of evangelicalism casts up prophets and martyrs, patriots and cosmopolitans, pacifists and soldiers, culture warriors and dissenting separatists, coalition builders and apocalyptic mystics, realists and idealists, court theologians and revolutionaries. In Augustinian terms, it produces its share of Pelagians, Manicheans, and Donatists. It also includes many defenders of the status quo who confuse theological orthodoxy with traditionalist conservatism—a strange irony given evangelical origins as a renewal movement with an ambivalent relation to the concept of tradition. In addition to its most celebrated or lamented public moments, evangelicalism also offers a history of ordinary men and women performing extraordinary works of love and justice in the everyday life of local churches and communities.

Evangelical political theology seems an unlikely candidate for a fresh interdisciplinary theological focus which might join otherwise disparate concerns of the many varieties of confessional and nonconfessional evangelicalism. It may exacerbate the fragmentation of evangelical theological identity and perpetuate a tendency to define itself negatively only by way of what it opposes (and often with caricature). However, I have argued that the neglect of political theology is a theological failure that may partially explain—and contribute to—the schizophrenic character of evangelical politics. Evangelical theology will remain in intellectual isolation, and fail as a genuinely *evangelical* theology, unless it is political in a new way. This does not mean that evangelicals must share a political theory or political judgment, without regard to particular circumstance. But my hope is that critical engagement with the broader tradition of Christian political thought, and contemporary political theology, will promote a more confident, ecumenical, and humble orthodoxy. Prophetic critique is an important mode of theology with strong New Testament origins. It dominates most theological discussions of politics, and finds evangelical sympathy in both its radical and conservative wings. But constructive theology, attentive to historical traditions and committed to justice, is also needed if sectarian and theocratic temptations are to be avoided. Fortunately, given its scholarly strengths and renewed intellectual vibrancy in other disciplines, such a future for evangelical theology is not entirely bleak.

NOTES

1. The historical dissonance between high-energy politics and embryonic political theology was an important feature of Mark Noll's much discussed book, *The Scandal of the Evangelical Mind* (1994), especially 149–175. Noll argued that "activistic, intuitive, populist, and biblicistic" approaches to politics hamper a theologically informed evangelical politics (161).

2. Peter Scott and William T. Cavanaugh, eds., "Introduction," in *The Blackwell Companion to Political Theology* (2004), 2.

3. Oliver O'Donovan, *The Desire of the Nations: Rediscovering the Roots of Political Theology* (1996), 22. According to O'Donovan, political theology "postulates an analogy—not a rhetorical metaphor only, or a poetic image, but an analogy grounded in reality—between the acts of God and human acts, both of them taking place within the one public history which is the theatre of God's saving purposes and mankind's social undertakings" (2).

4. A review of an important series on democracy and global evangelicalism updates Noll's previous assessment: "Evangelicals are inventive, resourceful, and opportunistic. But their proclivity for ad hoc creativity and activism often works against their valuing intellectual work, engaging traditions of Christian social and political thought, and developing principle-driven, long term strategies. Personally being good and doing good, and expecting that God will bring sweeping social change by means of the next revival, are not promising ingredients for a sustained approach to social reform... if ever there was a time that evangelical Christians needed to develop lines of social and political thought, it is now," in Joel Carpenter, "Now What? Revivalist Christianity and Global South Politics," *Books & Culture* 15.2 (March/April 2009): 37.

5. J. Budziszewski argues that "the problem for evangelical political thinkers is not that the Bible contains no political teaching (for it does) but that the Bible does not provide enough *by itself* for an adequate political theory" (Budziszewski 2006, 23). To trade on this helpful formula, this essay argues that Christian political theory does not provide enough *by itself* for an adequate political theology. For an evangelical defense of natural law, see J. Daryl Charles, *Retrieving the Natural Law: A Return to Moral First Things* (Grand Rapids: Eerdmans, 2008).

6. Augustine, *City of God*, translated by R.W. Dyson (1998), 22.22. Future references in the text refer to this edition.

7. Evangelical opposition to abolitionism and civil rights movements often claim a pseudo-Augustinian justification by radically distinguishing spiritual and temporal matters and rejecting notions of "social sin." For a lucid account of the diversity of evangelical politics in antebellum America, see Richard Cawardine, *Evangelicals and Politics in Antebellum America* (1993).

8. Abraham Kuyper, *Lectures on Calvinism* (1970), 79.

BIBLIOGRAPHY

Augustine. *City of God*, translated by R.W. Dyson. Cambridge: Cambridge University Press, 1998.

———. *Augustine: Political Writings*, edited by E. M. Atkins and R. J. Dodaro. Cambridge: Cambridge University Press, 2001.

Barth, Karl. *Community, State, and Church*, with a new introduction by David Haddorff. [c. 1960] Eugene, Ore.: Wipf and Stock, 2004.

Bebbington, David. *Evangelicalism in Modern Britain: A History from the 1730s to the 1980s.* London: Unwin Hyman, 1989.

Benson, Bruce Ellis, and Peter Goodwin Heltzel, eds. *Evangelicals and Empire: Christian Alternatives to the Political Status Quo.* Grand Rapids: Brazos, 2008.

Budziszewski, J. *Evangelicals in the Public Square: Four Formative Voices on Political Thought and Action.* Grand Rapids: Baker, 2006.

Carson, D. A. *Christ and Culture Revisited.* Grand Rapids: Eerdmans, 2008.

Carwardine, Richard J. *Evangelicals and Politics in Antebellum America.* New Haven: Yale University Press, 1993.

Davis, Creston, John Milbank, and Slavoj Žižek, eds. *Theology and the Political: The New Debate.* Durham: Duke University Press, 2005.

Eberle, Christopher. *Religious Convictions in Liberal Politics.* Cambridge: Cambridge University Press, 2002.

Emerson, Michael O., and Christian Smith, eds. *Divided by Faith: Evangelical Religion and the Problem of Race in America.* Oxford: Oxford University Press, 2001.

Freston, Paul, ed. *Evangelical Christianity and Democracy in Latin America.* Oxford: Oxford University Press, 2008.

Grabill, Stephen J. *Rediscovering the Natural Law in Reformed Theological Ethics.* Grand Rapids: Eerdmans, 2006.

Gregory, Eric. *Politics and the Order of Love: An Augustinian Ethic of Democratic Citizenship.* Chicago: University of Chicago Press, 2008.

Gushee, David. *The Future of Faith in American Politics: The Public Witness of the Evangelical Center.* Waco: Baylor University Press, 2009.

Hatch, Nathan. *The Democratization of American Christianity.* New Haven: Yale University Press, 1989.

Hauerwas, Stanley. *The Stanley Hauerwas Reader.* Durham: Duke University Press, 2001.

Henry, Carl F. H. *Aspects of Christian Social Ethics.* Grand Rapids: Eerdmans, 1964.

Hertzke, Allen D. *Freeing God's Children: The Unlikely Alliances for Global Human Rights.* New York: Rowman and Littlefield, 2006.

Husbands, Mark, and Daniel J. Treier, eds. *The Community of the Word: Toward an Evangelical Ecclesiology.* Downers Grove, Ill.: InterVarsity Press, 2005.

Johnson, Kristen Deede. *Theology, Political Theory, and Pluralism: Beyond Tolerance and Difference.* Cambridge: Cambridge University Press, 2007.

Kerr, Nathan. *Christ, History, and Apocalyptic: The Politics of Christian Confession.* Eugene, Ore.: Cascade Books, 2009.

Kuyper, Abraham. *Lectures on Calvinism.* [c. 1931] Grand Rapids: Eerdmans, 1970.

Lumsdaine, David H., ed. *Evangelical Christianity and Democracy in Asia.* Oxford: Oxford University Press, 2008.

Marsh, Charles. *The Beloved Community: How Faith Shapes Social Justice from the Civil Rights Movement to Today.* New York: Basic Books, 2006.

Mathewes, Charles. *A Theology of Public Life.* Cambridge: Cambridge University Press, 2007.

McDermott, Gerald R. *One Holy and Happy Society: The Public Theology of Jonathan Edwards.* University Park: Pennsylvania State University Press, 1992.

Milbank, John. *Theology and Social Theory: Beyond Secular Reason.* Oxford: Blackwell, 1990.

Mott, Stephen Charles. *A Christian Perspective on Political Thought.* Oxford: Oxford University Press, 1993.

Niebuhr, H. Richard. *Christ and Culture.* [c. 1951] New York: Harper & Row, 2001.
Noll, Mark. *The Scandal of the Evangelical Mind.* Grand Rapids: Eerdmans, 1994.
O'Donovan, Oliver. *The Desire of the Nations: Rediscovering the Roots of Political Theology.* Cambridge: Cambridge University Press, 1996.
O'Donovan, Oliver, and Joan Lockwood O'Donovan, eds. *From Irenaeus to Grotius: A Sourcebook in Christian Political Thought.* Grand Rapids: Eerdmans, 1999.
Ranger, Terence O., ed. *Evangelical Christianity and Democracy in Africa.* Oxford: Oxford University Press, 2008.
Rawls, John. *Political Liberalism.* New York: Columbia University Press, 1996.
Scott, Peter, and William T. Cavanaugh. *The Blackwell Companion to Political Theology.* Oxford: Blackwell, 2004.
Smith, James K. *Radical Orthodoxy and the Reformed Tradition: Creation, Covenant, and Participation.* Grand Rapids: Baker Books, 2005.
Smith, Ted A. *The New Measures: A Theological History of Democratic Practice.* Cambridge: Cambridge University Press, 2007.
Stott, John *Christian Mission in the Modern World.* [c. 1975] Downers Grove, Ill.: InterVarsity Press, 2008.
Stout, Jeffrey. *Democracy and Tradition.* Princeton: Princeton University Press, 2003.
Taubes, Jacob. *The Political Theology of Paul*, translated by Dana Hollander. Stanford: Stanford University Press, 2004.
Wannenwetsch, Bernd. *Political Worship: Ethics for Christian Citizens.* Oxford: Oxford University Press, 2004.
Witte, John, Jr. *Law and Protestantism: The Legal Teachings of the Lutheran Reformation.* Cambridge: Cambridge University Press, 2002.
———. *The Reformation of Rights: Law, Religion, and Human Rights in Early Modern Calvinism.* Cambridge: Cambridge University Press, 2007.
Wolterstorff, Nicholas. *Until Justice and Peace Embrace.* Grand Rapids: Eerdmans, 1983.
Wright, N. T. *Paul: In Fresh Perspective.* Minneapolis: Fortress, 2009.
Yoder, John Howard. *The Politics of Jesus: Vicit Agnus Noster.* Grand Rapids: Eerdmans, 1972.

CHAPTER 26

ECONOMICS

JOHN LUNN

CHRISTIANS living in modern industrial or postindustrial societies live differently from almost all Christians over the previous millennia. Most Christians participate in the capitalistic, or market, economies in which they live. Churches often borrow business models in administering and marketing the church. Christian publishing houses, radio stations, and products are significant entities in the economy. Some Christians wonder whether the material success of modern Christians who live in the wealthy nations is something about which to be concerned. The New Testament seems to presume that Christians will be persecuted rather than prosperous, as do many of the writings of Christians from the early church onward. As John Schneider writes, "It is widely presumed in Christian theology today that the economic condition of affluence is not a very good one for Christians to be in. It is widely presumed that this condition is almost inherently a bad one for hearing and responding with faith and integrity to the Gospel of Jesus Christ."[1] The concern over the condition of affluence that exists today also includes concern over the economic system that exists today—capitalism or, the term I will use more often in this chapter, market systems.

In this chapter, I examine the differences between the economic systems that prevailed in ancient Israel, including Palestine at the time of Christ, with modern market systems. I will also examine some of the traditional Christian views of wealth and poverty in light of the economic conditions that prevailed then as compared to today. I will then look at the problem of poverty, both global and within the wealthy nations. Finally, I will discuss greed and materialism.

The Economy of Israel and Scripture

The Old Testament pictures Israel as a theocracy, with God graciously giving the land of Canaan to the Israelites after they were liberated from Egypt. While in the wilderness, Israel received God's law, and this law included economic provisions. Among the provisions of the Torah were the distribution of the land among tribes and clans, laws that protected the poor and marginalized such as gleaning and the Jubilee (when debts were canceled and agricultural land returned to the original owners), and a call to love one's neighbor as oneself. David Stubbs contrasts Israel's experience at Sinai with the Promised Land saying, "The Promised Land was the place where the intentions of God for all humanity were to be lived out by Israel before the face of the nations."[2] The promises to Israel for faithfulness to Yahweh and keeping the Torah involved both peace and prosperity.

The economic regulations in the Torah primarily dealt with issues related to land. A key concept is that the land belongs to Yahweh, and the families of Israel are stewards of the land. Yahweh dispensed the land to families, and the land was to stay in the family. Property, with the exception of property within a walled city, could not be sold in perpetuity. The tithe was on agricultural products, and the poor laws generally related to agricultural production—for example, leaving the corners of the fields unharvested for the poor to glean. The Jubilee referred to both land and debt, but most of the debts were related to the land as well.

In general, the economic regulations were designed to prevent some bad fortune on the part of a family or clan from leading to permanent poverty. Kinsmen were important as well, with kinsmen obligated to redeem a relative who had lost land or fallen into slavery. Other laws were for those who were not connected to a family unit with land—the widows, orphans, and strangers. For most families, though, the ideal was to farm land that was part of the family's patrimony from the distribution of land to the tribes and families.

It is clear from the complaints of prophets such as Amos that Israel did not always live in accordance with the Torah. Some landholders came to acquire additional land when other families fell on difficult times. It appears from the prophetic books that the Year of Jubilee was not practiced and many families ended up landless. The government and the wealthy manipulated the system to enrich some and impoverish others.

The economy of Israel was agrarian but not static, and there is evidence of increasing affluence in Israel from the days of the judges to the eighth and seventh centuries B.C.E.[3] Morris Silver cites evidence that Judah and Israel controlled important trade routes during the eighth century.[4] After this period, Israel was under the influence of several empires—Assyria, Babylon, Persia, and Greece. During most of this time, the land was not owned by the families designated as landholders in the early years of Israel.

Palestine was part of the Roman Empire when Jesus lived and taught. The patron-client relationship predominated in the Roman Empire, including Judah and Galilee. Sean Freyne argues that while there were still some small landholdings, there were also large estates that utilized tenant farmers.[5] Freyne outlines the evidence that Galilee was undergoing economic growth and change during the time of Jesus' ministry, and that the changes brought about by this growth clashed with the values of those connected to the temple in Jerusalem and on the focus on purity laws.[6] He argues that Jesus offered "another set of values in addition to the competing ones which we have seen within the social world of Antipas' Galilee."[7]

The gospels' picture of Galilee reflects social tensions, as would be expected in the presence of both Roman control through Herod Antipas and the widespread use of tenant farming and absentee ownership. But we must be careful not to interpret things in light of modern ideas concerning liberty or economics. The Context Group, a collection of theologians who use anthropology and sociology in biblical interpretation, argue that the way people viewed themselves in relation to other people differed greatly from biblical times to today. Sociologists and anthropologists identify four primary social domains—kinship, politics, religion, and economics.[8] Bruce Malina argues that there were only two explicit social systems in antiquity—kinship and politics—with economics and religion embedded in one or both of these two explicit domains.[9] Kinship groups include the family and the extended family or clan, and can also include fictive kin groups "in the form of a range of associations, generally marked by the central kinship activity of eating a common meal."[10]

Malina claims that most people in biblical times perceived all goods to be limited in supply, including land, wealth, prestige, power, status, honor, and security.[11] There was a zero-sum mentality concerning any of these goods. So, if someone was accumulating more, it had to come at the expense of others. Malina writes, "Any apparent relative improvement in someone's position with respect to any good in life is viewed as a threat to the entire community. Obviously, others are being deprived and denied something that is theirs, whether they know it or not."[12]

Malina draws out some implications from this concept of limited goods, noting that "by and large, only the dishonorable rich, the dishonorable non-elites, and those beyond the pale of public opinion (such as city elites, governors, and regional kings) could accumulate wealth with impunity."[13] The status of "the poor," on the other hand, was not determined by economic standing per se, but by an inability to maintain their inherited status. Poor persons seem to be those who cannot maintain their inherited status due to circumstances that befall them and their families, such as debt, being in a foreign land, sickness, death of a husband, or some personal physical accident. Consequently, the poor would not have a permanent social standing but be a sort of revolving category of people who unfortunately could not maintain their inherited position. And "poor" would most certainly not be an economic designation. Thus day laborers, landless peasants, and beggars born into their situation were not poor persons in first-century society. Furthermore, the opposite of rich would not necessarily be poor. To repeat, in the perception of people in limited-good society, the majority of people are neither rich nor poor, but equal in that each has a status to maintain in some honorable way. Personal assessment is not economic but a matter of lineage. In this context, the designations rich and poor really refer to the greedy and the socially ill-fated. The terms do not characterize two poles of society as much as two minority categories, the one based on the shameless desire to expand one's wealth, the other based on the inability to maintain one's inherited status of any rank.[14]

If Malina is correct, then we have to be careful in taking New Testament statements about the wealthy and the poor and using modern connotations of those terms. It is inappropriate to take comments made about the wealthy in the New Testament and apply them anachronistically to modern market societies. In the biblical era, the wealthy were exploiters virtually by definition. Today, "rich" and "poor" are economic descriptions and not descriptors of attitudes or behavior (greedy and exploitative for "rich") and plights (changes in inherited status for "poor").

Market Economies

Beginning in the early part of the nineteenth century, the world changed greatly. Prior to about 1820, economic growth was very slow and sporadic; after 1820, economic growth was extraordinarily rapid. Angus Maddison estimates that between 1820 and 1992, world population increased fivefold, per capita product increased about eightfold, world Gross Domestic Product (GDP) increased about fortyfold, and world trade increased about 540-fold.[15] For the United States, per capita GDP increased 1,575 percent between 1820 and 1992.[16] The economist Deirdre McCloskey writes about this figure, "If you do not find this figure impressive, I suggest you are not grasping it. It is utterly unprecedented."[17] Or, as stated by other economists, "The most astonishing thing about the extraordinary outpouring of growth and innovation that the United States and other economies have achieved over the past two centuries is that it does not astonish us."[18]

If we examine the countries and regions where the growth was the greatest, we see that they also were places that developed capitalist, or market, institutions. As McCloskey notes: "Modern economic growth did not depend on central planning, nor corporate welfare, nor, again, any sort of theft from the poor. Modern economic growth was not a result of trade unions or government regulation or the welfare state. It was a result of letting markets work."[19]

Economic historians have tried to identify the causes of this seismic change. Since the industrial revolution was an important part of the change, it is easy to focus on industrialization, technological change, and the growth of scientific knowledge. Technological change is one of the four causal factors in Maddison's explanation.[20] Joel Mokyr emphasizes "useful knowledge."[21] Douglass North and Robert Thomas argue for institutional arrangements: "Our arguments central to this book are straightforward. Efficient economic organization is the key to growth."[22] This view has become more central in the profession. "There is now a general consensus that differences in economic institutions are the primary cause of differences in income per capita across countries."[23]

Although the foundations for growth may have been laid and slowly accumulated over several centuries, there was a takeoff around 1820. Technological change in power, transportation, and communication led to expanding markets and economies of scale which led to lower prices, so that even poor people could benefit from the changes. Labor productivity increased, leading to higher wages and higher real incomes. Life expectancy increased, which encouraged more saving and more investment in education and skills, which in turn resulted in increased productivity and incomes. In each of these areas there were feedback mechanisms reinforcing the overall effect. For example, with higher incomes it became possible to improve sanitation and quality of water, which led to better health and longer lives. Compared to the early 1800s, current income differences in Great Britain are narrower today by a little, but life expectancy differences have narrowed considerably. The life expectancy of the lower classes in Britain in 1875 was 41 years, while it was 58 years for the upper classes. Today these numbers are 74 and 78. There is still a gap, but the gap has narrowed by about three-quarters in 125 years.[24]

An important difference between modern market economies and the economies of antiquity is the degree to which impersonal exchange has replaced personal exchange. Frederick Hayek describes the market economy as a type of spontaneous order.[25] By this he means that the market economy has evolved over time and has not been the deliberate creation of anyone, yet functions in such a way that there is order rather than chaos. The market economy is one type of social order, but is not the only social order in modern society.[26] Hayek focuses on two different types of social order. The first is dominated by personal relationships, involving families, friends, churches, and communities, and is referred to by Hayek as the microcosmos.[27] Within the micro-cosmos, exchange tends to be performed face-to-face and involves long-term relationships with people who know a great deal about each other. The family is the prime example. The second type of order is the extended order or macrocosmos. This is the world of impersonal exchange. If I buy a pencil, it is unlikely that I know the person selling the pencil in a personal way. It is certain that I do not know the myriad of people who were needed to produce the pencil and ship it to the store where the purchase is made.[28] Information about the personal characteristics of other market participants is difficult to obtain, and often irrelevant to the participants.[29]

It is the evolution of market systems and the increase of impersonal exchange that has allowed the enormous increases in production over the last two hundred years. North argues that in order to grow, a society must "develop institutions that permit anonymous, impersonal exchange across time and space."[30] For people to obtain the benefits of highly specialized labor and production processes, they must participate in an economic system that is impersonal. The impersonal market system also relies upon people adhering to the "rules of the game" rather than upon good intentions by market participants.

The economy is embedded in society. For an economy to operate efficiently and to provide people a high and rising standard of living, the existence of numerous institutions that support the economy is required. North offers a definition of institutions: they are the rules of the game in a society or, more formally, are the humanly devised constraints that shape human interaction. In consequence, they structure incentives in human exchange, whether political, social, or economic. Institutional change shapes the way societies evolve through time, and hence is the key to understanding historical change.[31] Examples include formal institutions such as the courts and contract law, and informal institutions such as etiquette when greeting people and tipping.

John Kay notes, "We are usually more productive when we work in cooperative teams."[32] Cooperation is needed to take advantage of the productiveness of specialization of labor. We cooperate with others when we buy and sell rather than steal, and when we work in a team. Business firms can be thought of as teams or groups of teams,[33] but there are numerous other teams the typical American is a part of-churches, clubs, political groups, unions, school boards, investment clubs, and so on. The higher incomes in developed countries are due to the existence of these teams and institutions. Through these, people are able to better "manage information, pool risks, achieve cooperation and coordination, generate knowledge, and to do so within an extensive and elaborately developed set of conventions and rules."[34]

Scripture, Ethics, and Market Economies

In the previous two sections, we have examined briefly the agrarian economy of Palestine in the time of Jesus and modern market economies. The differences are immense. In Palestine, exchange was usually personal, often involving kinsmen; today, exchange is usually impersonal, seldom involving someone we know well. The modern economy requires that people abide by the "rules of the game" rather than focus on intentions. Much of the ethical treatment of economic exchange in Scripture is based on a society in which relationships are primarily personal.

Another important difference between the economy of first-century Palestine and today involves differences in attitudes and basic beliefs of people. To the extent people viewed most of life as a zero-sum game, it is easy to see why the view would develop that the rich are rich at the expense of the poor. The OT prophets condemn Israel's repeated turns to idolatry, oppression of the poor, perverting justice, and reliance on foreign alliances rather than on Yahweh. Amos, more than any other prophet, focuses on economic injustice.[35] He charges Israel with violating the law for the poor (2:8), exploiting the poor through improper influence of government (5:11), selling people into slavery over a small debt (2:6), and bribery (5:12). Many of these accusations are examples of the rich oppressing the poor.

Who were the rich in biblical times? The majority of the wealthy were large landholders. As noted above, some people managed to obtain the land of other families, perhaps through government influence and bribery. At the very least, there were those who failed to follow Torah's regulations concerning lending to other Israelites without interest, returning land to original families, and releasing slaves after a period of time. Other wealthy individuals included the royal family, the priests who controlled the temple, and probably some merchants. In the minds of most people in that period, the wealthy were exploiters by definition.

Economists do not see the modern economic world as a zero-sum game; instead, it is a positive-sum game in which all sides to an exchange benefit. Wealth does not necessarily come at the expense of the poor. In fact, many people who have created businesses and have obtained wealth have also provided jobs for numerous other people. It is not necessarily the case that the rich oppress the poor. If we examine the last two hundred years of Western history, hundreds of millions of people moved out of poverty by means of employment in the business sector of the economy. While the owners of the firms and large stockholders grew wealthy, they did so by providing opportunities for many others to improve their material well-being.

The nature of wealth also differs today, at least for the majority of people who live in the wealthier countries of the world. In the past, land was the primary source of wealth. Today, with the exception of the wealthiest who have substantial holdings of real estate and hold large portfolios of stocks, bonds, and other financial assets, wealth tends to be human capital.[36] This takes the form of the skills and education people have acquired that enable them to earn a relatively high income. The key difference between human capital as a source of wealth and either landholdings or portfolios is that the owner of human capital must work in order to receive the income. In modern economies, exploitation is not inherent in obtaining or using wealth.

Given the differences in the economy from biblical times to today, what are the appropriate responses to economic issues by Christians who take the Bible seriously? Hill and Lunn suggest that there are three.[37] First, the development of an appropriate ethic for the world of impersonal exchange should be developed. An emphasis on the "rules of the game" might be appropriate here. These rules include the laws and regulations established regarding property rights and liability, honoring contracts, and accounting norms. Second, another ethic for the world of personal relationships should be articulated. It is likely to be similar to the ethic emphasized by biblical ethicists today. Third, effort should be made to define the boundaries between the world of personal relationships and the world of impersonal relationships. To the three mentioned in Hill and Lunn, a fourth response may be appropriate—to recognize that Christians have an obligation to identify with the poor and to help them. I examine the question of the poor in the next section.

Preferential Option for the Poor in a Global Economy

We have discussed the fact that the rise of market economies has been associated with the movement of billions of people out of poverty. However, it is obvious that not all people in the world, or even in the wealthier countries, have escaped poverty.

In fact, the material well-being of billions of people remains dismal. Many economists see the best hope of bringing more people out of poverty to be expansion of market systems to more countries. Rapid economic growth has taken place in the last couple of decades for many countries that had been less developed for many years. Included among these countries are China, India, and many other nations in Asia, as well as countries in South America.[38] A key factor in the growth of these countries was opening their markets and participating in the globalization process. However, there are still numerous countries, mostly in sub-Saharan Africa, which are still very poor. Paul Collier refers to the people of these lands as the "bottom billion."[39]

Collier argues that there are four important factors that "trap" countries in poverty. The bottom billion live in countries that experience one or more of these traps. The traps he identifies are the conflict trap, the resource trap, being landlocked with bad neighbors, and bad governance. Many of the countries experience more than one of these traps. "Seventy-three percent of people in the societies of the bottom billion have recently been through a civil war or are still in one."[40] Sometimes the wars are related to the second trap—natural resources such as oil or diamonds. Collier notes that "about 29 percent of the people in the bottom billion live in countries in which resource wealth dominates the economy. Thus resource wealth is an important part of the story of the poverty of the bottom billion."[41]

Even when the resource wealth is not the cause of civil war, it can be a trap—in fact, economists often refer to the "oil curse." It is related to the "Dutch disease," which refers to the effects of North Sea oil on the Dutch economy. Collier explains: "The resource exports cause the country's currency to rise in value against other currencies. This makes the country's other export activities uncompetitive. Yet these other activities might have been the best vehicles for technological progress."[42] Nigeria in the 1970s illustrates the phenomenon. Oil revenues increased and the currency appreciated, causing the country's other exports (peanuts and cocoa) to be overpriced in world markets and unprofitable. As production fell, the farmers who produced them were harmed. It also prevented the development of export activities that helped other countries experience growth at that time—such as the labor-intensive manufacturing China has developed. "A low-income country with abundant natural resources is unlikely to be able to break into these markets because the foreign exchange they generate is not sufficiently valuable within the society."[43]

The third trap has to do with being landlocked, which makes trade more difficult. Africa and Central Asia have a disproportionate share of the world's countries that lack access to the sea. Further, these countries' neighbors are not like Switzerland's neighbors—rich with good infrastructure in place. Instead, they are poor themselves, cannot provide markets for the country's goods, and are lacking in infrastructure.

Bad governance is the final trap. Probably the worst example in recent years is Robert Mugabe's regime in Zimbabwe. Good governance by itself will not generate growth, given the other problems that can exist. But bad governance makes economic development almost impossible.

Collier offers some solutions, but they are not easily implemented. He takes a middle-of-the-road position to foreign aid. While William Easterly argues that aid has not been effective, and Jeffrey Sachs urges massive increases in aid,[44] Collier argues that aid can speed up the development process, but that the larger the amount of aid, the greater the chance that the Dutch disease will affect the recipient country. His proposals for aiding the bottom billion require that the G-8 nations work together to provide aid, military support, legal initiatives, and changes in trade policies of the developed nations. He writes: "But we will need not just a more intelligent approach to aid but complementary actions using instruments that have not conventionally been part of the development armory: trade policies, security strategies, changes in our laws, and new international charters."[45]

Collier, along with many other economists, argues that changes are needed in the trade policy of the developed nations. In particular, developed nations tend to protect domestic agriculture at the expense of farmers in poor countries, and tend to apply tariffs to labor-intensive manufacturing goods such as textiles. These policies harm the poor in many poor countries. As Albino Barrera writes:

> Industrialized countries have an obligation to reform their agricultural support policies as they currently stand. As part of general justice and their contribution to the global common good, OECD nations should not impose such unnecessary adverse pecuniary externalities on others, especially since there are other ways of delivering public assistance to their distressed farmers. They should not protect their own agricultural sectors from economic compulsion by inflicting the same on the less developed countries' rural populations.[46]

The focus has been on government actions that can help the poor in the developing world. There are also many Christian (and other) organizations that offer aid and support to the poor. The cumulative effect of these actions can be significant. However, economic growth is needed if the billions remaining in poverty are to escape poverty. Still, as Claar and Klay note: "In part because global markets do not simultaneously lift all ships, Christians and others who care about the poorest of the poor are called to supplement market forces. Loving and well-targeted assistance can create sustained increases in labor productivity and incomes for those who have fallen behind. They too can have their day in the sun."[47]

The Poor in the Rich Countries

Two issues with respect to income in the rich countries are important to many people, including many Christians. The first has to do with poverty in rich nations—how can rich nations have relatively large numbers of people living in poverty? The second has to do with income distribution, especially the increasing inequality of income in the United States over the last several decades.

Measuring income inequality is difficult, and interpreting the data can be more so. For example, there is a typical life-cycle pattern to income—a person usually makes more when he or she is forty-five than twenty-five. Graduate students often have incomes at "poverty level," but their long-term prospects differ markedly from those of a single mother who never graduated from high school. Other things being equal, when the baby-boom generation was relatively young, the size of the group tended to lower median income figures. Now that they are in their prime earning years, they tend to raise median income figures. These larger incomes for baby boomers in their fifties cause incomes to be more unequally distributed. Another factor is family composition. Suppose a married couple makes $100,000 a year, with $50,000 provided by each spouse. A divorce creates two households of $50,000 income each, instead of one household of $100,000. Families in which both spouses work make more, on average, than families in which one spouse works. To the extent that the composition of families changes over time, the data can show increasing or decreasing inequality over time. Immigration also affects income distribution. If immigrants tend to be relatively young and less educated, there is a continuous influx of low-income families that keeps the numbers of households in the low-income brackets larger. Robert J. Samuelson, a columnist for *Newsweek*, wrote: "The median household was once imagined as a family of Mom, Dad and two kids. But 'typical' no longer exists. There are more singles, childless couples and retirees. Smaller households tend to have lower incomes. They drag down the overall median. So do more poor immigrant households."[48]

Most of the developed countries have progressive tax systems and welfare programs (or transfers) that lower poverty rates. In a study that compared Canada, Germany, Netherlands, Sweden, the United States, and the United Kingdom, each had lower poverty rates (defined as an income whose income is less than 50 percent of the whole population's median income) posttax and transfers than pretax and transfers.[49] In the case of the United States, the poverty rate fell from 19.5 percent to 14.2 percent.[50] The posttax and transfer percentage of the population that had been poor during the entire time period under study (1988–1993 for the United States) was 4.6 percent.[51]

Many Christians support a minimum wage or, perhaps, a living wage. Economists place considerable focus on the "unintended consequences" of policy prescriptions, and minimum wage laws are an example of the production of unintended consequences. Many studies have tried to estimate the size of the effect of an increase in the minimum wage. Basic economic theory says that if a wage is mandated above the market wage, there will be increased unemployment. In the 1990s, however, the Clinton administration used the results reported in a book, *Myth and Measurement: The New Economics of the Minimum Wage*,[52] to support passage of an increase in the minimum wage. The book generated a lot of publicity in the popular press because it argued that a minimum wage increase could raise incomes without increasing unemployment. However, additional studies have shown that increases in the minimum wage do increase unemployment, although most conclude that the impact on unemployment is fairly small.

The latter result leads some to argue that the minimum wage should be increased because the unemployment effects are small. There are several problems with this argument. First, many people who receive minimum wage are not in poor households.

This includes high school and college students of middle- and upper-middle-class families working in part-time jobs or summer jobs. Second, increases in the minimum wage tend to create and increase unemployment among the least productive workers the most—primarily minority youth in our society. Even if the increase in unemployment is not large, those who are unemployed because of the minimum wage are people in need of employment experience to be able to create job skills that can lead to higher incomes in the future.

Calls for living wages, which really can be thought of as higher minimum wages, are more problematic. Obviously, there are the concerns over unemployment. In addition, would living wage legislation also have to restrict the use of part-time employment? Suppose we have a law that says that a wage must be high enough to support a family of four. Would we then have to limit families to one wage-earner unless there are enough jobs to provide all heads of households with a job at the living wage? Klay and Lunn argue:

> workers may be best served by some jobs whose earnings are relatively low because the jobs provide attractive nonmonetary benefits. Not every job must provide remuneration sufficient to support a family for a labor market to be considered just. In fact, in a dynamic economic setting, it is probable that a society in which every job provides remuneration sufficient to support a family would be grossly inferior to a society in which many jobs were low paying, temporary, or part-time. The key is to focus on what job seekers desire from a job.[53]

An important nonmonetary benefit of many low-paying jobs is training that increases the person's productivity over time, also increasing the earnings capacity of the individual. A living wage could freeze some people out of the job market permanently, while the current system provides opportunities for people to obtain jobs even when they have few skills, and the jobs allow them to develop more marketable skills for the future. Klay and Lunn conclude: "Modern economies are dynamic. Thus, a more dynamic approach to economic justice is needed to prevent well-intentioned proposals from harming many of the people whom the proposals are meant to help."[54] They argue that Christians need to reflect on a dynamic focus on poverty relief when trying to find ways to help the poor.

There have been attempts by some Christian economists to draw out principles from Scripture and identify ways in which modern societies could implement programs that would meet the goal of reducing poverty. John Mason writes:

> Reciprocal obligations existed between the poorer members of society, in need of assistance, and the larger community.... Those receiving assistance were obligated to the community to work when possible, even in the actual receiving of assistance (e.g., gleanings) and to live modestly; idleness was condemned strongly. The community was responsible to assist all of those who were poor due to arbitrary circumstances—including the able-bodied as well as the dependent.[55]

Kurt Schaefer and Edd Noell illustrate how the sabbatical and Jubilee laws provided a floor that prevented the poor from falling into chattel slavery.[56]

Gleaning is an example of a practice that could still be recommended, although it would not have the same impact as it did in biblical times because we have an industrial or postindustrial rather than an agricultural economy. But there is another important difference—the economy is now impersonal rather than personal. When Boaz saw Ruth gleaning in his fields, he did not know who she was and had to ask about her. There were other gleaners whom he presumably knew personally, or knew their families. A modern farmer would not know many of the people who might show up if he allowed gleaning. If some gleaners did not take proper care and ended up damaging crops or equipment, the farmer might not know who was responsible. If such damage becomes common or likely, the farmer would probably stop people from coming on his land. However, there are nonprofit organizations that fulfill a similar function today. They use volunteers to pick up crops where permitted. The organization can be held responsible if people damage crops or equipment. The practice of gleaning has been altered to account for changes in farming practices and technology, and the more impersonal nature of economic interactions.[57]

Greed and Materialism

I argued above that wealth is not necessarily associated with exploitation in modern market economies. But a Christian concern for wealth involves not just how one obtains wealth, but also what one does with it and how one looks at it. Greed is often associated in people's minds with capitalism, but greed is equivalent to idolatry, according to Paul (Col. 3:5). Is greed necessary for the functioning of market systems? I believe the answer is no.

Markets are a way of organizing economic activity that economizes on the information needed to make decisions. A higher price for a good encourages people acting in their self-interest to use less of it. They do not have to know why the price increased in order to make the appropriate decision. Greed and self-interest are not the same thing. For some people, greed and self-interest may go together, but that is not always the case. Deirdre McCloskey writes:

> Many non-economists imagine that, on the contrary, avarice is necessary to keep the wheels of commerce turning, "creating jobs" or "keeping the money circulating"; that people must buy, buy, buy or else capitalism will collapse and all of us will be impoverished. It's a bubble theory of capitalism.... I say as an economist that it is mistaken. Nothing would befall the market economy in the long run if we tempered our desires down to one car and a small house and healthy foods from the Co-op.
>
> The mistake is to think that the relevant mental experiment is that tomorrow, suddenly, without warning, we all begin to follow Jesus in what we buy.... People following Jesus would... make the plain pottery that an economy of moderation would demand and spend more time with their children. But the point is that the pottery would still be produced most efficiently in a marketing,

free-trade, private property, enterprising, and energetic economy. We would be richer, not poorer, in the things and deeds we value.[58]

Markets require virtue for their operation. In particular, trust is required. Without it, a market economy will not function well. Contracts are enforced by the courts, but the percentage of contracts that are litigated is a miniscule fraction of all the formal and informal contracts people enter into. If people had to constantly consult with their lawyers to enforce every contract, little would be accomplished in business. McCloskey argues that markets make us both richer and better.[59] Perhaps it would be better to say that markets *can* make us better. As people are more affluent and have more choices, they can become either greedy and materialistic—or generous and caring.

Conclusions

Market systems are good at creating wealth. Given the negative associations with wealth in the New Testament, it is tempting to conclude that market systems are problematic for the Christian. We have seen that wealth was associated with exploitation by those who lived in the society in which Jesus lived. Wealth can be associated with exploitation today, but it also can be used to create a better life for oneself and others. At the same time, wealth can be an idol that separates us from God. The Christian must live with tension and temptation.

But markets have enabled many in the world to escape from poverty—or at least from the deeper poverty of their forbears. As a system of organizing production, distribution, and consumption, markets are unsurpassed in effectiveness. In less than two hundred years markets have helped pull billions of people out of poverty. It can be hoped that we will see billions more pulled out of poverty in a shorter time period in the future.

NOTES

I wish to thank P. J. Hill, Kristin Johnson, Robin Klay, Todd Steen, Kent Van Til, and Gerald McDermott for helpful comments on an earlier draft. Any remaining errors or omissions are my responsibility alone.

1. John R. Schneider, *The Good of Affluence: Seeking God in a Culture of Wealth.* (Grand Rapids: Eerdmans, 2002), 3.

2. Personal (e-mail) correspondance, September 18, 2008.

3. See Morris Silver, *Prophets and Markets: The Political Economy of Ancient Israel* (Boston: Kluwer-Nijhoff, 1983), 13ff.

4. Ibid., 50. Note that the New Revised Standard Version has Ammonites in verse 8 instead of Meunites. Unless otherwise noted, scriptural references will use the NRSV.

5. Sean Freyne, "The Geography, Politics, and Economics of Galilee and the Quest for the Historical Jesus," in Bruce Chilton and Craig A. Evans, eds., *Studying the Historical Jesus: Evaluations of the State of Current Research* (Leiden: Brill, 1998), 107.

6. Ibid., 116–121.

7. Ibid., 120–121.

8. K. C. Hanson and Douglas E. Oakman, *Palestine in the Time of Jesus: Social Structures and Social Conflicts* (Minneapolis: Fortress, 1998), 8–9.

9. Bruce J. Malina, "Embedded Economics: The Irrelevance of Fictive Christian Domestic Economy," *Forum for Social Economics* 26 (Spring 1997): 8–9.

10. Ibid., 8.

11. Bruce J. Malina, *The New Testament World: Insights from Cultural Anthropology* (Louisville, Ky.: Westminster John Knox, 2001), 81ff. See also George M. Foster, "Peasant Society and the Image of Limited Good," *American Anthropologist* 68 (1965): 293–315.

12. Malina, *New Testament World*, 89.

13. Ibid., 98.

14. Ibid., 100.

15. Angus Maddison, *Monitoring the World Economy 1820–1992* (Washington, D.C.: Paris Development Centre of the Organisation for Economic Co-operation and Development, 1995), 19.

16. Calculation based on tables in Maddison, *Monitoring the World Economy.*

17. Deirdre McCloskey, "Avarice, Prudence, and the Bourgeois Virtues," in *Having: Property and Possession in Religious and Social Life*, ed. William Schweiker and Charles Mathewes (Grand Rapids: Eerdmans, 2004), 327.

18. William J. Baumol, Robert E. Litan, and Carl J. Schramm, *Good Capitalism, Bad Capitalism, and the Economics of Growth and Prosperity* (New Haven: Yale University Press, 2007), 1.

19. McCloskey, "Avarice," 326. McCloskey's statement may be too strong, since governments have seldom let markets work without some form of regulation. Further, tariffs and other trade distortions have been ubiquitous.

20. Maddison, *Monitoring the World Economy*, 19.

21. Joel Mokyr, *The Gifts of Athena: Historical Origins of the Knowledge Economy* (Princeton: Princeton University Press, 2002), 1–15.

22. Douglass C. North and Robert Paul Thomas, *The Rise of the Western World: A New Economic History* (Cambridge: Cambridge University Press, 1973), 1.

23. Daron Acemoglu and James A. Robinson, "The Persistence and Change of Institutions in the Americas," *Southern Economic Journal* 75 (October 2008): 282.

24. Robert William Fogel, *The Escape from Hunger and Premature Death, 1700–2100: Europe, America, and the Third World* (Cambridge: Cambridge University Press, 2004), 40.

25. Frederick A. Hayek, *Law, Legislation and Liberty*, Volume 1, *Rules and Order* (Chicago: University of Chicago Press, 1973), 35–54.

26. There are other orders as well, besides the social—law, language, science are examples.

27. Frederick A. Hayek, *The Fatal Conceit: The Errors of Socialism* (Chicago: University of Chicago Press, 1988), 18.

28. The production of a pencil requires materials from various countries and numerous production processes. For a history of the pencil and its production process, see Henry Petroski, *The Pencil: A History of Design and Circumstance* (New York: Knopf, 2004), especially 343–345. A more complete discussion of this with respect to market economies is

found in John Lunn and Vicki TenHaken, "Human Finitude and Specialized Production: A Christian-Realist Rationale for Business Enterprise," *Journal of Markets and Morality* 11 (2008): 255–273.

29. Further discussion of personal versus impersonal exchange is found in Peter J. Hill and John Lunn, "Markets and Morality: Things Ethicists Should Consider When Evaluating Market Exchange," *Journal of Religious Ethics* 35 (December 2007): 630–639.

30. Douglass North, "Economic Performance through Time," *American Economic Review* 84 (June 1994): 363.

31. Douglass North, *Institutions, Institutional Change and Economic Performance* (Cambridge: Cambridge University Press, 1990), 3.

32. John Kay, *Culture and Prosperity*: The Truth about Markets—Why Some Nations Are Rich but Most Remain Poor (New York: HarperBusiness, 2004), 252.

33. The idea of teamwork as essential to the firm is found in Armen A. Alchian and Harold Demsetz, "Production, Information Costs, and Economic Organization," *American Economic Review* 62 (December 1972): 777–795.

34. Kay, *Culture and Prosperity*, 301.

35. Note, though, that a contemporary, Hosea, focused on Israel's unfaithfulness to Yahweh.

36. John Lunn, "On Riches in the Bible and the West Today," *Faith and Economics* 39 (Spring 2002): 16–17.

37. Hill and Lunn, "Markets and Morality, 648–649.

38. for the case of China, see Angus Maddison and Harry X. Wu, "Measuring China's Economic Performance," World Economics 9 (April-June 2008): 13–44.

39. Paul Collier, The Bottom Billion: Why the Poorest Countries Are Failing and What Can Be Done about It (Oxford: Oxford University Press, 2007).

40. Ibid., 17.

41. Ibid., 39.

42. Ibid.

43. Ibid., 40.

44. William Easterly, *The White Man's Burden: Why the West's Efforts to Aid the Rest Have Done So Much Ill and So Little Good* (New York: Penguin, 2007); and Jeffrey Sachs, *The End of Poverty: Economic Possibilities for Our Time* (New York: Penguin, 2005). Sachs also refers to the bottom billion in his book.

45. Collier, *The Bottom Billion*, 192.

46. Abino Barrera, *Economic Compulsion and Christian Ethics* (Cambridge: Cambridge University Press, 2005), 211.

47. Victor V. Claar and Robin J. Klay, Economcs in Christian Perspective: Theory, Policy and Life Choices (Downers Grove, Ill.: IVP Academic, 2007), 162. This is an excellent resource for Christians who want to learn more about economic policy from a Christian perspective.

48. Robert J. Samuelson, "The Changing Face of Poverty," *Newsweek*, October 18, 2004. Available at http://www.newsweek.com/id/55278.

49. Transfers refer to payments from the government to households such as welfare, unemployment, housing subsidies, and so on.

50. Howard Oxley, Thai Thanh Dang, and Pablo Antolin, "Poverty Dynamics in Six OECD Countries," *OECD Economic Studies* 30 (2001): 14.

51. Ibid.

52. David Card and Alan B. Krueger, *Myth and Measurement: The New Economics of the Minimum Wage* (Princeton: Princeton University Press, 1995).

53. Robin Klay and John Lunn, "'Just Remuneration' Over a Worker's Lifetime," Journal of Markets and Morality 6 (Spring 2003): 181.

54. Ibid., 196.

55. John D. Mason, "Biblical Teaching and Assisting the Poor," *Transformation* 4 (April-June 1987): 2.

56. Kurt C. Schaefer and Edd S. Noell, "Contract Theory, Distributive Justice, and the Hebrew Sabbatical," *Faith and Economics* 45 (Spring 2005): 3–7.

57. The example comes from Hill and Lunn, "Markets and Morality," 645–646.

58. McCloskey, "Avarice," 321–322.

59. See Deirdre N. McCloskey, The Bourgeois Virtues: Ethics for an Age of Commerce (Chicago: University of Chicago Press, 2006). She has plans for three more volumes on the theme.

BIBLIOGRAPHY

Baumol, William J., Robert E. Litan, and Carl J. Schramm. *Good Capitalism, Bad Capitalism, and the Economics of Growth and Prosperity*. New Haven: Yale University Press, 2007.

Claar, Victor V., and Robin J. Klay. *Economics in Christian Perspective: Theory, Policy and Life Choices*. Downers Grove, Ill.: IVP Academic, 2007.

Collier, Paul. *The Bottom Billion: Why the Poorest Countries Are Failing and What Can Be Done about It*. Oxford: Oxford University Press, 2007.

Fogel, Robert William. *The Escape from Hunger and Premature Death, 1700–2100: Europe, America, and the Third World* Cambridge: Cambridge University Press, 2004.

Hayek, Frederick A. *The Fatal Conceit: The Errors of Socialism*. (Chicago: The University of Chicago Press, 1988).

———. *Law, Legislation and Liberty*. Volume 1, *Rules and Order*. Chicago: University of Chicago Press, 1973.

Hill, Peter J., and John Lunn. "Markets and Morality: Things Ethicists Should Consider When Evaluating Market Exchange." *Journal of Religious Ethics* 35 (December 2007): 627–653.

Kay, John. *Culture and Prosperity: The Truth about Markets—Why Some Nations Are Rich but Most Remain Poor*. New York: HarperBusiness, 2004.

Klay, Robin, and John Lunn. "Just Remuneration over a Worker's Lifetime." *Journal of Markets and Morality* 6 (Spring 2003), 177–199.

Maddison, Angus. *Monitoring the World Economy 1820–1992*. Washington, D.C.: Paris Development Centre of the Organisation for Economic Co-operation and Development, 1995.

McCloskey, Deirdre N. *The Bourgeois Virtues: Ethics for an Age of Commerce*. Chicago: University of Chicago Press, 2006.

North, Douglass. *Institutions, Institutional Change and Economic Performance*. Cambridge: Cambridge University Press, 1990.

Schneider, John R. *The Good of Affluence: Seeking God in a Culture of Wealth*. Grand Rapids: Eerdmans, 2002.

Silver, Morris. *Prophets and Markets: The Political Economy of Ancient Israel*. Boston: Kluwer-Nijhoff, 1983.

CHAPTER 27

THE ARTS

ROGER LUNDIN

WHETHER we are trying to judge issues of immediate interest or fathom matters of long-standing concern, history gives us the key for understanding the complex and often tangled relationship of evangelicalism to the arts.

We need the help of that history for two reasons, the first of which is that the story of the evangelical engagement with the arts has largely been one of action and adaptation rather than one of theory and reflection. As Mark Noll notes in his introduction to this volume, from its inception the evangelical movement has been an extraordinarily complex, diverse, and multiform phenomenon. Because the term "evangelical" has long been defined primarily in terms of a series of commitments and stances that can and do cross denominational lines, we discover evangelicals distributed across the full expanse of the Protestant landscape.

There are, for example, numerous evangelicals to be found in churches from the Anabaptist tradition and from the Lutheran heritage, from the Swedish Covenant movement and from the black Baptist tradition, as well. Lutheran theology offers rich resources for thinking about the arts, but a Lutheran aesthetic will differ sharply from a Mennonite theory of the arts, and an evangelical cultural understanding from the African American perspective will be quite distinct from one that has emerged from the free church experience of immigrant Swedes. There are countless evangelical traditions of aesthetic reflection and artistic practice, but no single or dominant one.

There is a second reason why an understanding of history is essential for approaching this subject. It has to do with the fact that evangelical Christianity and the contemporary arts are fluid realities rather than fixed entities, and even though each has grown and flourished in a strikingly different fashion in the modern age, they have common roots that reach back to the Protestant Reformation.

The claim of kinship might seem peculiar to evangelicals and artists alike, because for good reason we commonly think of these two groups as foes locked in adversarial conflict. As a case in point, in the nineteenth century a story of disenchantment with the evangelical faith played itself out repeatedly in the lives of such figures as George Eliot, Vincent van Gogh, and Emily Dickinson. At the same time, even as these dramas were unfolding among the artists of the Victorian age, evangelical suspicions about the arts were beginning to spring up, and those doubts came to full bloom with the rise of fundamentalism at the century's close.

Still, however strong the disagreements may have been at times, the conflicts of the past two centuries have the feel of a family drama, with evangelicalism and the arts cast as siblings arguing over the family inheritance. For these two movements are descendants of the Reformation, and they are the offspring of the prodigious growth and dizzying fragmentation of Protestantism in the modern age. Only when we begin to comprehend the kinship of modern evangelicalism and the arts, can we begin to understand the points of division that have come between them.

Reforming Culture

To gauge the central importance of the Reformation for evangelicalism as well as the arts, we need to travel back to the late medieval world into which Martin Luther, John Calvin, and the other Reformers were born. These were men of action, but they came into a world where an ideal of contemplation held sway. Through its strong emphasis upon the monastic orders, its standard of priestly celibacy, and its elevation of the religious vocations, late medieval Catholicism placed a premium upon the life of contemplative devotion. This ideal, which was grounded in the practices of ancient Greece, held that a life given to contemplation was superior to one driven by the needs of production and reproduction, the endless cycle of work and family. In this vision, the highest good was to contemplate the harmony of the cosmos and the connections that bound nature, the human soul, and the heavens one to another. For medieval Catholicism, the earth and the human body served as microcosms that mirrored the macrocosmic beauty of the heavens and the God who ruled them. In Dante's *Divine Comedy*, the whole of the created universe is pictured as a book bound together by love, and the poet's beatific vision ends with his praise of that "Love that moves the sun and the other stars."

The medieval stress upon contemplation strengthened the grip that the *mimetic* view of the arts had long held on Western thought. If the soul, the earth, and the heavens all manifest an elaborate pattern of beauty and order, the highest calling art can fulfill is to re-present that harmony. In the words of Hamlet, the "purpose of all playing"—the goal of all art—is to hold a "mirror up to nature."

For many medieval thinkers, order and symmetry were not only spatial categories but temporal ones as well. Both literature and the visual arts developed under the influence of a *figural* theory of interpretation in the Middle Ages. In this vision of reality, the Bible is seen as encompassing the whole of human time and experience within its narrative framework. For the figural interpreter, the Old Testament is packed with *types* that find their eventual completion in the *antitypes* of the New Testament; for example, the priest Melchizedek is the type who anticipates Christ, the antitype and High Priest of God (Hebrews 5).

Typological interpretation sees the Old and New Testaments as including within their scope the centuries of human experience that stretch between us and the time of Christ. Through the use of types and antitypes, the medieval imagination uncovered a seemingly infinite series of links connecting the contemporary world to that of the Bible. With the support of the typological model, the mystery plays of England could present biblical events and contemporary settings side by side as elements of a seamless drama, and painters and sculptors were free to set their contemporaries in the midst of scenes lifted straight from the biblical story.

These settled practices were to be scuttled in the wake of the Reformation. Along with other powerful forces at work in early modernity—including the Copernican revolution in science, the emergence of capitalism, the nascent development of democratic political theory, and the invention of the printing press—the Reformation served to level the medieval hierarchies and to place ordinary life and the religious vocations on the same plane. The skies of Copernicus, Galileo, and Newton no longer set the earth at the center of the universe, and over the course of the sixteenth and seventeenth centuries, the medieval mysteries of the spirit turned into the modern laws of matter. Francis Bacon and others argued that it was "vain and misguided" for human beings to idle away their time in contemplation, when there was so much to learn about how things work in the mechanisms that lie before our eyes and in our hands.

The attack on the contemplative ideal dealt a crippling blow to the concept of mimesis. Why would we wish to hold a mirror up to a mechanism or search for beauty and harmony where they cannot be found? The scientific dismissal of contemplation also dovetailed neatly with questions the Reformers were raising about the role of the church and the sacraments. Luther and others rejected the Catholic belief that those sacraments had an efficacy independent of the spiritual state of the recipient. According to the Reformers, the sacramental host could not in itself embody the presence of God or convey his grace. Instead, the miracle of faith was required, and the human soul became the center of heavenly activity in an increasingly mechanistic world.

To be sure, the shift to human inwardness took place gradually at first, and the likes of Luther and Calvin struggled to counter its more radical outworkings. Yet the inward momentum proved hard to resist. To an ever-increasing degree, motives supplanted actions and consequences as the standard for religious experience, and human inwardness became the earthly dwelling place of a God who had been banished from the cosmos. "The homeliest service that we do in an honest calling," wrote Anglican divine Joseph Hall in the early seventeenth century, "if done in obedience, and conscience of God's commandment, is crowned with an ample reward; whereas the best works for their kind (preaching, praying, offering evangelical sacrifices) if without respect of God's injunction and glory, are loaded with curses. God loveth adverbs; and cares not how good, but how well."[1]

In ways that the Reformers could never have anticipated, the adverbial culture of Protestantism hastened the displacement of the center of spiritual activity from the cosmos arrayed outside the self to the labyrinthine world layered within it. The further we travel into the Protestant experience and into the modern era, the less likely we are to find God spinning the heavenly wheel, and the more likely we are to come upon him sounding the depths of the human soul. Between the Reformation at the start of the sixteenth century and the rise of Romanticism at the close of the eighteenth, intensity and authenticity came to replace fidelity and authority as the supreme spiritual ideals, and the idea of originality overtook the practice of imitation in the arts.

The Paths of Inwardness

These developments stretched over several centuries, but for evangelicalism and the arts the events of a few decades made all the difference. During those decades–in the mid-eighteenth century—both evangelicalism and Romanticism were born. These two movements drew from the same Protestant well of inspiration, but as soon as they emerged in the eighteenth century, they set off down separate paths in their pursuit of distinctly different goals.

The poet and essayist W. H. Auden often made note of the crucial consequences of the Reformation, both for piety of the evangelical kind and art of the modern variety. The Reformers' view of the sacraments, he suggested, led to "*the loss of belief in the significance and reality of sensory phenomena.*" Auden traces the origins of this "loss of belief" to Luther's sixteenth-century denial of "any intelligible relation between subjective Faith and objective Works" and to Descartes's seventeenth-century distinction between primary qualities (length, width, depth, duration) and secondary qualities (sound, light, color, taste, and touch).[2]

Auden argues that by the eighteenth century, these new views of the relationship of mind (or spirit) to matter had led to the collapse of the medieval system of "sacramental analogies." To Dante and Thomas Aquinas, "what the senses perceived was an outward and visible sign of the inward and invisible." Both were taken to be real, and both were seen as valuable. "Modern science," however, "has destroyed our faith in the naïve observation of our senses." It tells us we can never know what the universe is "*really* like," and we can only cling to whatever subjective notions may be appropriate to our particular needs.[3]

"This destroys the traditional conception of *art* as *mimesis*," for there is no longer a moral or spiritual order of nature "out there" that can be either "truly or falsely imitated." The artist can only attempt to be true to his or her "subjective sensations and feelings." To highlight this point, Auden cites William Blake's "remark that some people see the sun as a round golden disc the size of a guinea but that he sees it as a host crying Holy, Holy, Holy." Blake may have abhorred Newton's science, but he accepted its division "between the physical and the spiritual." The poet simply turned the tables on the physicist, as he lauded the spiritual imagination, labeled the material universe "the abode of Satan," and refused to attach any "value to what his physical eye" looked upon.[4]

Auden's reference to Blake provides a useful historical marker, because the great poet and painter reached the peak of his output in a period (1785–1810) when the Romantic poets and idealist philosophers were swiftly rewriting the rules of art for the modern world. In turn, at the same time, American culture in particular was witnessing an "unprecedented expansion of evangelical Protestant Christianity." In the early decades of the Republic, "Protestantism boomed," Mark Noll observes, "and the Protestant bodies that led the way were the most militantly evangelical churches."[5]

With the simultaneous rise of Romantic aesthetics and evangelical religion at the close of the eighteenth century, the split in the tradition of Protestant inwardness became complete. For evangelical Christianity the key would be to combine the intensity of inner piety with a commitment to outward purity and to the centrality of the cross; for the modern arts, the Protestant impulse broke free of sacrament and scripture alike to form the expressive self of a therapeutic age. Both the Romantic impulse in the arts and the evangelical principle in religion would go on to wield considerable influence in modern culture, and despite their common origin, they were to work independently of one another in a state of mutual ignorance and occasional hostility.

For its part, from the beginning the Romantic tradition pressed an essentially religious argument for the arts, and it did so by promoting a sharp distinction between the fine arts and the useful ones. The Romantics made this move in an effort to secure a refuge for beauty and the spirit in a world that had come under the rule of mechanistic necessity. By the mid-eighteenth century, the separation of spirit and nature—and of art and reason—had become a commonplace in Western thought. To use the terminology of Immanuel Kant, the quintessential theorist of the modern arts, both reason and art worked with the sensory manifold, that array of disparate particulars furnished by the experience of the senses to the workings of the mind. With its synthesizing powers, reason unified these phenomena and made them available to scientific description and technological control.

Meanwhile, as reason catalogued the flow of data in the realm of necessity, art was at work constructing an alternative sphere of freedom. Kant defined art as being "distinguished from nature as doing is from acting or producing in general." Art produces works, while nature can only come up with effects. To Kant, the products of the fine arts differ sharply from the works of craft produced in the useful ones. Fine art can be successful "only as play, i.e., an occupation that is agreeable in itself; the second [useful art] is regarded as labor, i.e., an occupation that is disagreeable (burdensome) in itself" and is attractive only because it brings payment. We have the domain of freedom—the playful world of art that refuses to look beyond itself for a ground or purpose—and the province of necessity—the realm of the crafts in which we work toward practical ends with the tools of our trade.[6]

For Kant and for many who came after him, beauty became the central category for judging authentic art. "Only that which has the end of its existence in itself," he wrote, "[that is,] the human being, who determines his ends himself through reason...: this human being alone is capable of an ideal of beauty." Animals may enjoy objects, but only human beings can appreciate their beauty, which is an end in itself. "Beauty is the form of the purposiveness of an object, insofar as it is perceived in it without representation of an end."[7] For Kant the "experience of the beautiful is... an experience of 'purposiveness without purpose,' a sense that things fit together according to a purpose that we cannot state."[8]

By the end of the eighteenth century, then, a powerful new understanding of the arts had planted its flag on the Western intellectual landscape and staked its claim to a sizable plot of cultural ground. The aesthetic realm was governed by the belief that while science disclosed a cosmos governed by law, the drama of the spirit played itself out in an imagined world of oppositional freedom. Yet as highly as modernity prized this inner realm, it worried about its epistemological status and struggled to reaffirm the "significance and reality of sensory phenomena." The creation of a domain of the fine arts was meant to establish the epistemological authority of sensory perception and to secure the spiritual rights of beauty.

While the theorists of the nineteenth century labored to build the kingdom of the arts, evangelical Christians were busying themselves with the task of "storming heaven by the back door."[9] As they swept across the religious landscape of early nineteenth-century America, the evangelicals were all about moving people to repentance and teaching them about the grace of God. For the evangelicals of that era, the useful arts were the ones that mattered. When a man teetered on the brink of hell, he had little time for the fine art of contemplating the beautiful; instead, he needed to grab the lifeline that would lead him from the edge of the pit to the foot of the cross. As one convert described the verbal powers of a prominent Methodist preacher: "He never indulged in metaphysical discussions and rarely in doctrinal expositions. His themes were repentance, salvation by faith in Jesus Christ, and the witness of the Spirit.... He was full of his subject, and intent only upon the rescue of sinners from impending wrath."[10]

Artists and evangelicals alike flourished over the course of the nineteenth century, but they had few common interests and carried on few conversations. Indeed, in England and the United States, the most accomplished writers often proved to be those who sought in their art a surrogate for a faith they no longer professed. The brilliant George Eliot, for example, was representative on this score. She became an evangelical Christian in her adolescence but turned from the faith in early adulthood. Her disdain for evangelical excess and hypocrisy is on brilliant display in an essay written early in her career. This work offers a scathing indictment of a prominent evangelical minister, Dr. John Cumming, and does so with a withering clarity that sets the perceptive artist sharply at odds with the fatuous evangelical. "Given, a man with moderate intellect," an average moral standard, "some rhetorical affluence and great glibness of speech, what is the career in which" such a mediocre man "may most easily attain power and reputation" in Victorian society? "Where is that Goshen of mediocrity in which a smattering of science and learning" can pass for profound understanding? Where are platitudes treated as wisdom, "bigoted narrowness" taken to be "holy zeal," and "unctuous egoism" seen as "God-given piety? Let such a man become an evangelical preacher; he will then find it possible to reconcile small ability with great ambition, superficial knowledge with the prestige of erudition, a middling morale with a high reputation for sanctity."[11]

On the evangelical side, in the nineteenth century, fervent Protestants generally felt no deep aversion to the works that the novelists, painters, and composers of the day were producing. They were simply too busy to cultivate their aesthetic tastes or to develop theories promoting the fine arts. Instead, the useful arts touched evangelical hearts and served evangelical ends. Hymn singing had become a central element of the evangelical experience, so the composition of tunes and the writing of verses became highly prized as a practical skill. Novels could also fit into this vision as long as they brought the moral force of faith to bear upon the issues of the day, as Harriet Beecher Stowe did with astonishing success in *Uncle Tom's Cabin*. Nineteenth-century evangelicals prized the arts, but they did so on their own terms and in their own forms.

Fundamentalism, Modernism, and the Manichean Impulse

In a matter of years at the close of the nineteenth century, the divide between evangelicals and artists became an unbridgeable chasm. What hastened this split was the rapid ascendancy of the naturalist consensus. Spurred in part by the enormous impact of Charles Darwin, this naturalistic view saw human life as a product of impersonal forces at work within a closed system governed by physical laws and packed with adaptive organisms.

In the arts, naturalism was to have a powerful shaping influence upon the modernist movement of the twentieth century. Faced with the banalities of bourgeois culture and the indifference of nature and nature's God, modernism seized upon the aesthetic isolationism at the heart of the Kantian aesthetic and pressed it into the service of artistic resistance. At the same time, evangelical Christianity assumed its own hostile stance vis-à-vis naturalism, as it changed from a broadly based, mainstream movement into a narrowly focused, subcultural force.

On the surface of things, religious fundamentalism and aesthetic modernism appeared so irreconcilably opposed that it was hard to conceive that there were deep underlying ties between them. To the painters, novelists, and poets who led the modernist movement, fundamentalism seemed at best an irrelevance and at worst a menace to clear thought. From Theodore Dreiser's *An American Tragedy* to Sinclair Lewis's *Elmer Gantry* to the stage and film productions of *Inherit the Wind*, fundamentalists were routinely depicted either as rubes or charlatans.

In like manner, the fundamentalists viewed the writers, actors, and moviemakers of their day as purveyors of devilish diversions. In 1912, Charles Blanchard, the president of Wheaton College and a leading fundamentalist, praised those Christians who "knew that greed and pleasure loving never could construct a glorious civilization.... They did not play cards, nor go to dances, nor tolerate liquor shops, nor attend theaters, nor raise their sons for gamblers and libertines."[12] He might well have added, "nor waste their time with novels, nor fritter way their hours with poetry." Symphonic music and the literary classics, from Sophocles to Shakespeare, would have received a pass from Blanchard, but for more than half a century, fundamentalists generally shunned the arts that were being practiced and produced in their day.

An irony underlies the tension between evangelicalism and the arts in the period from 1880 to 1960. It is that for all their differences, modernists and fundamentalists did share a fundamental antagonism toward nature and, to a degree, toward culture. As we have seen, both evangelicalism and the modern arts were, at least in part, reactions to a rising view of nature as an intricate mechanism governed by impersonal laws. In a stinging critique of the "Christ against culture" position, H. Richard Niebuhr argues that the fundamentalist reaction in particular led to "an ontological bifurcation of reality." Its suspicion of "nature and nature's God" readily gave way to the temptation "to divide the material world into the material realm governed by a principle opposed to Christ and a spiritual realm guided by the spiritual God." We always discover the Manichean heresy developing "at the edges" of the "Christ against culture" position, Niebuhr concludes, as it denies or obscures the "relation of Jesus Christ to nature and to the Author of nature."[13]

One might argue that in both fundamentalism and the arts, the response to naturalism was a story of the emergence of a sophisticated, thoroughly modern Manicheanism. In the end, the fundamentalist suspicion of nature and nature's God is but a few steps removed from an attitude expressed repeatedly in the letters of Gustave Flaubert, the French novelist and patron saint of modernism. "Life," he wrote, "is such a hideous business that the only method of bearing it is to avoid it. And one does avoid it by living in Art, in the ceaseless quest for Truth presented by Beauty."[14] Substitute "Christ" for "Art," and a fundamentalist might nod his or her head in agreement.

The Evangelical Resurgence

The relationship between evangelicalism and the modern arts began to change in the mid-twentieth century, when conservative Protestant thinkers started issuing calls for fundamentalism to break free of its isolation and reclaim the broader cultural heritage of the West. More often than not, such calls came from the men and women who were teaching in the newly flourishing network of evangelical liberal arts colleges and seminaries. Faced with an enormous influx of new students, the postwar teachers of literature, music, and art felt compelled to explain the novels of Virginia Woolf and the poetry of W. H. Auden, to make sense of the paintings of Pablo Picasso and Jackson Pollock, and to discover pertinent categories for interpreting the music of Igor Stravinsky and the theories of Arnold Schoenberg.

Even as these professors were beginning to promote modernist arts and attitudes in their classrooms, some of them also undertook to write about the arts in the evangelical magazines and journals springing up across the American landscape. Some evangelicals founded professional organizations to promote Christian activity in the arts, while others dedicated themselves to the training of aspiring writers, musicians, actors, and artists. The fundamentalist parents may have abandoned the arts, but their evangelical children seemed eager to adopt them as their own.

Nevertheless, for all the enthusiasm of the postwar evangelicals, their cultural efforts were often hindered by the shallowness of evangelical theology and the poverty of evangelical cultural understanding. For almost a century, fundamentalism had turned its back on the arts and on popular culture, just as it had neglected the task of sustained theological and historical reflection. Such failures of engagement meant that the first generation of evangelicals had a vast amount of ground to cover in a short amount of time. Their task was further complicated by the fact that like almost all other middle-class movements, evangelical Christianity has often led a largely derivative cultural existence. To this day, the evangelical church remains content to allow other institutions in American life to set the parameters and provide the content for the culture. Lacking a vigorous theory of culture, evangelicals have often responded to innovations with fear and then waited for the bizarre to become, through time, domesticated.

This has proven to be true as well for much of the evangelical intellectual engagement with the arts. In literary theory and art criticism, the pattern has been for new theories to surface and circulate for a decade or more before evangelical scholars begin to appropriate them. In the past half century of literary studies, for example, this cycle has played itself out repeatedly in the evangelical response to one new theoretical movement after another—from the New Criticism to archetypal criticism to poststructural theory, postcolonial theory, and globalization studies. Highly adept at the art of delayed appropriation, evangelical theorists have been masters of adaptation rather than agents of creation. Evangelicals have made few original contributions to the theoretical debates, and the theological offerings of evangelical artists and critics have been slender, as well.

There have been exceptions to this rule. In some cases, we discover them in the efforts of bands of scholars from confessional traditions that share evangelicalism's commitment to orthodoxy but not its fundamentalist history of cultural suspicion. On this front, a key source has been the Reformed tradition as mediated by the Dutch Calvinist churches and schools of North America. The central figure here is Abraham Kuyper, the late nineteenth-century statesman and theologian from the

Netherlands. Kuyper's vision coupled a strong emphasis on the doctrine of creation with a commitment to the Christian effort to transform culture. Working within this tradition, scholars such as Nicholas Wolterstorff have developed nuanced and powerful arguments about the relationship of the Christian faith to modern culture and the arts.

Whereas the Reformed influence on evangelical thinking about the arts reached its peak in the 1970s and 1980s, from the 1990s to the present, the Anabaptist tradition has been the rising star in the evangelical cultural firmament. In this case, the influence has been less theoretical than practical. The Anabaptist emphasis has fallen upon the ethics of aesthetics, and it has entailed a critique of the myriad facets of economic, political, and cultural life. For evangelicalism this influence has led to a focus upon ecological concerns, a markedly oppositional stance toward elements of the dominant culture, and a strongly functional approach to matters of art, craft, and form.[15]

Even as these twists and turns of academic theory have been unfolding over the past half century, countless evangelical artists have continued to go about their artistic callings diligently and without great fanfare. As practitioners, evangelicals have had their greatest impact in music, where they have made their mark in the classical sector as well as in the popular arena. Some evangelicals have had distinguished operatic careers (Sylvia McNair, Wendy White), others have played in America's most prestigious orchestras, and some have become conductors of considerable renown (John Nelson).

In popular music, evangelical contributions have come either in the subcategory of gospel music or in the niche market of "Christian music." In particular, four centuries of African American experience have fed into gospel music, and the influence of spirituals, jazz, and the blues has reached into every branch of contemporary music and every corner of contemporary culture. Arguably the most significant contributions evangelical Christianity has made to the modern arts have come through the black church.

In drama, literature, and the visual arts, evangelical Christians have been active, but their contributions have been peripheral to the larger culture and have focused mainly on the evangelical subculture and its broad middle-class market. Beyond that domain, evangelical artistic efforts have left few marks. To be sure, in the past half-century there have been major writers whose work has resonated deeply with Christian themes. Yet as serious as they were about Christianity, by no plausible definition of the term could the likes of James Baldwin, John Updike, Flannery O'Connor, and Walker Percy be included within the ranks of evangelical writers.

In one area of the contemporary arts evangelicals have played a pivotal role, but here the influence has been a matter of reception rather than production. I am referring to the extraordinary passion evangelical Christians have shown for fantasy literature. When the postwar evangelical community began to search for cultural exemplars, a growing number started to turn to the fiction of C. S. Lewis, J.R.R. Tolkien, and others. Neither Lewis the Anglican nor the Roman Catholic Tolkien would have identified himself as an evangelical, but their sustained critiques of modernity and their unblinking commitment to orthodoxy made them seem to conservative evangelicals like natural allies and advocates.

Art and the Evangelical Future

In addition to writing remarkably popular fantasy literature and children's stories, C. S. Lewis was a brilliant literary historian. And in one of his works, *The Discarded Image*, he sets the context for the inward turn that set evangelicalism and the modern arts in motion. He does so by mapping the medieval world view that modernity displaced, and his analysis illumines the difficulties both evangelicals and artists face when they seek to explore religious experience in the stories they tell, the pictures they paint, or the music they play.

Lewis asks us to imagine the universe that confronted a medieval viewer of the heavens and to consider how it "affected those who believed in it." He describes the medieval cosmos as an immense spatial structure undeniably intricate in its complexity but unmistakably finite in its totality. It embodies an architectural harmony that the eye can see and the heart can delight in. To gaze at "the towering medieval universe" is like looking up "at a great building." We behold "an object in which the mind can rest, overwhelming in its greatness but satisfying in its harmony."[16]

The modern view of the universe is something else entirely. We can neither rest in the spatial dimensions of its structure nor construct a satisfying structural model to embody the whole of it. In the words of Lewis, "to look out on the night sky with modern eyes is like looking out over a sea that fades away into mist, or looking about one in a trackless forest—trees forever and no horizon." This "space" of modern astronomy can "arouse terror, or bewilderment or vague reverie," but it cannot offer a satisfying structural or visual pattern.[17]

In aesthetic terms, if we are to find something like that medieval harmony in the modern world, we must turn to other models, in which the structural intricacy of God's creative and redeeming love can be told, can be sung, and can be heard. In twentieth-century theology, the most powerful artistic models proved to be those that employed metaphors of drama or patterns of narrativity to capture the majesty of God's activity. The greatest systematic expressions of the Christian faith in the past century—Hans Urs von Balthasar's multivolume *Theo-Drama* and *The Glory of the Lord: A Theological Aesthetics*, as well as Karl Barth's *Church Dogmatics*—display an architectural brilliance of the kind Lewis attributes to the medieval picture of the cosmos. In their own way, the theologies of Barth and Balthasar, like the fantasy novels of Lewis and Tolkien, might be considered "objects in which the mind can rest, overwhelming in their greatness but satisfying in their harmony."

There are simple reasons for the turn to narrative and drama in modern theological aesthetics. As he draws his comparisons to a close, Lewis notes that the difference between the medieval and modern models explains "why all sense of the pathless, the baffling, and the utterly alien—all agoraphobia—is so markedly absent from medieval poetry when it leads us" into the heavens.[18] Such imagery abounds in the poetry and fiction of the past two hundred years, and it points to a sense of profound spiritual displacement, for as Charles Taylor observes, the shift from medieval to modern involved a move "from living in a cosmos to being included in a universe." The order of the modern universe does not involve "a hierarchy of being," nor does it require eternity as the source of its cohesion. Instead, the universe as we know it "flows on in secular time," and the rules that regulate its workings have little or nothing to do with human meaning.[19]

In contemporary theology, the pressure of "the pathless and the baffling" has led to a pronounced shift in Christian imagery away from spatial models toward temporal schemes. These changes have prompted an intense interest in the theology of history and they have led to renewed emphases upon eschatology and the incarnation. In many respects, Colin Gunton argues, the disappearance of the medieval spatial model has enabled the modern church to overcome the "false eternity" that dogged Christian thought for many centuries. Throughout much of Christian history, theology remained "ambivalent about the reality and value of time," and only after the collapse of medieval cosmology did thought reaffirm boldly the goodness of creation and its temporality. Modernity has made possible—or inevitable—a recovery of the theme of "recapitulation," which expresses "the narrative structure of the Christ-history... [as] that history... takes up into itself the whole of created reality."[20]

So it has been that time has replaced space as the central dimension of theological aesthetics. In the words of the poet Czeslaw Milosz, with the disappearance of viable spatial imagery, "what remains" for the Christian artist and thinker "is the covenant, the Word, in which man trusts."[21] This "Word" has a decidedly temporal dimension, and it frames human life within a narrative of God's creative and redemptive love. Over the past century, the covenantal theology of the Word has provided a firm foundation for Christian thought and artistic activity at a time when Catholicism's hierarchies have been eroded and the Protestant argument from design has been swept away.

As if reinforcing this point, Balthasar concludes his seven-volume *Theological Aesthetics* with a meditation that portrays transcendence temporally rather than spatially; "no innerworldly hope," he says, "has a power for transcendence like that of the Christian hope, which has the 'down-payment' of the new aeon in the midst of the old aeon, to which it gives an orientation that carries it up beyond itself in all its dimensions." All the "futility and decay of earthly existence" can become fruitful, if they are understood to be "the 'pangs' of the new aeon and a sharing in Christ's sufferings."[22] In like manner, Barth begins his massive treatment of the "doctrine of creation" by setting the theme of "creation" specifically within that of "covenant." "As God's first work," he argues, "creation stands in a series, in an indissolubly real connexion, with God's further works," and these works have at their center "the institution, preservation and execution of the covenant of grace."

As important as it is in its own right, creation simply "sets the stage" for the drama of grace, which "requires a stage corresponding to it; the existence of man and his whole world."[23]

For an evangelical theology of the arts, what might we learn from the history we have charted and the modern theological responses we have discussed? To begin, we can acknowledge that in their passion for the *useful* arts, the evangelicals of earlier centuries understood a crucial truth that Nicholas Wolterstorff has repeatedly reminded us of in recent decades. It is that "works of art are objects and instruments of action," and we can and should think of them as having myriad uses, both *fine* and otherwise.[24]

Wolterstorff's emphasis upon art as a form of action has the virtue of pointing us to the fact that like all human actions, our thinking, our making of art, and our use of art all unfold within embedded contexts. In those contexts, our actions are always both a response to the world we receive and a dream of the world that we might, through human action and the grace of God, create. "*Is music in any way grounded in or obliged to be faithful to a world that we did not make but that is in some sense given to us?*" asks Jeremy Begbie.[25] And his answer is a resounding "Yes," for he understands that an evangelical vision of the arts must balance a respect for the ordered world God has created with a hunger for the world God is recreating and reconciling to himself through Christ.

As Lewis and Taylor, along with Barth and Balthasar, have made clear to us, the universe that has been given to modern understanding looks radically different from the cosmos that greeted men and women at the dawn of the modern age. In this brave new world, the spatial and architectural categories of medieval Catholic aesthetics have given way to the temporal and historical categories that dominated the past century's most accomplished theologian efforts to explore the cultural implications of Christian orthodoxy.

The temporal dynamics of music, for example, powerfully informed Mikhail Bakhtin's theory concerning Fyodor Dostoevsky's creation of the *polyphonic* novel, just as they animated Dietrich Bonhoeffer's remarkable reflections on the *contrapuntal* themes of the love of God and earthly affection. In like manner, metaphors of drama and stagecraft deeply shaped Karl Barth's theories of election, creation, and covenant; they provided Hans Urs von Balthasar with the *theo-dramatic* framework he needed to recast Catholic aesthetics from a spatial to a temporal format; and in recent years, the evangelical theologian Kevin Vanhoozer has employed them to consider Christian doctrine as a "theo-drama [that] is nothing less than a covenant-comedy of cosmic significance."[26]

Throughout their history, evangelical Christians have faithfully borne witness to what Barth calls the "covenant of grace," and in works of mission and mercy they have brought the message of the cross into virtually every culture and corner of the world. Over the past century, the likes of Lewis, Balthasar, and Barth have demonstrated how that word of grace might be carried even into the heart of the culture of the arts. In recent years, such figures as Wolterstorff, Begbie, and Vanhoozer have taken up that task with genuine intelligence and creative élan. The next several decades will show whether they are isolated cases or crucial harbingers of a genuine renewal in the evangelical engagement with the arts.

NOTES

1. Joseph Hall, quoted in Charles Taylor, *Sources of the Self: The Making of the Modern Identity* (Cambridge: Harvard University Press, 1989), 224.

2. W. H. Auden, *The Dyer's Hand and Other Essays* ([1962] New York: Vintage, 1989), 78.

3. Ibid.

4. Ibid., 78–79.

5. Mark A. Noll, *America's God: From Jonathan Edwards to Abraham Lincoln* (New York: Oxford University Press, 2002), 165–166.

6. Immanuel Kant, *Critique of the Power of Judgment*, ed. Paul Guyer, trans. Paul Guyer and Eric Matthews (Cambridge: Cambridge University Press, 2000), 182–183.

7. Ibid., 117, 120.

8. Terry Pinkard, *German Philosophy 1760–1860: The Legacy of Idealism* (Cambridge: Cambridge University Press, 2002), 72.

9. Nathan O. Hatch, *The Democratization of American Christianity* (New Haven: Yale University Press, 1989), 49.

10. Robert Paine, *Life and Times of William McKendree, Bishop of the Methodist Episcopal Church* (Nashville: Publishing House Methodist Episcopal Church, South, 1922), 29.

11. George Eliot, "Evangelical Teaching: Dr. Cumming," *Westminster Review* 64 (October 1855): 229.

12. Martha Farnham Webster, *Seventy-Five Significant Years: The Story of Knox College, 1837–1912* (Galesburg, Ill.: Wagoner Printing, 1912), 185.

13. H. Richard Niebuhr, *Christ and Culture* (New York: Harper, 1951), 81.

14. Gustave Flaubert, "Letter to Mlle. Leroyer de Chantepie," in *The Modern Tradition: Backgrounds of Modern Literature*, ed. Richard Ellmann and Charles Feidelson, Jr. (New York: Oxford University Press, 1965), 72.

15. See John Howard Yoder, "How H. Richard Niebuhr Reasoned: A Critique of *Christ and Culture*," in Glen H. Stassen, D. M. Yeager, and John Howard Yoder, *Authentic Transformation: A New Vision of Christ and Culture* (Nashville: Abingdon, 1995), 31–90.

16. C. S. Lewis, *The Discarded Image: An Introduction to Medieval and Renaissance Literature* (Cambridge: Cambridge University Press, 1964), 98–99

17 Ibid., 99.

18. Ibid.

19. Charles Taylor, *A Secular Age* (Cambridge: Belknap Press of Harvard University Press, 2007), 59–60.

20. Colin E. Gunton, *The One, the Three and the Many: God, Creation and the Culture of Modernity* (Cambridge: Cambridge University Press, 1993), 80.

21. Czeslaw Milosz, *To Begin Where I Am: Selected Essays*, ed. Bogdana Carpenter and Madeline G. Levine (New York: Farrar, 2001), 320.

22. Hans Urs von Balthasar, *The Glory of the Lord: A Theological Aesthetics*, vol. 7, *Theology: The New Covenant*, ed. John Riches, trans. Brian McNeil C.R.V. (San Francisco: Ignatius, 1989), 519.

23. Karl Barth, *Church Dogmatics*, ed. G. W. Bromiley and T. F. Torrance (Edinburgh: T & T Clark, 1956–1962), 3.1.43–44.

24. Nicholas Wolterstorff, *Art in Action: Toward a Christian Aesthetic* (Grand Rapids: Eerdmans, 1980), 3.

25. Jeremy S. Begbie, *Resounding Truth: Christian Wisdom in the World of Music* (Grand Rapids: Baker, 2007), 307.

26. Kevin J. Vanhoozer, *The Drama of Doctrine: A Canonical-Linguistic Approach to Christian Theology* (Louisville, Ky.: Westminster John Knox, 2005), 53.

BIBLIOGRAPHY

Abrams, M. H. *The Mirror and the Lamp: Romantic Theory and the Critical Tradition*. New York: Oxford University Press, 1953.

Auden, W. H. *The Dyer's Hand and Other Essays*. [1962] New York: Vintage, 1989.

Auerbach, Erich. *Mimesis: The Representation of Reality in Western Literature*. Trans. Willard R. Trask. Princeton: Princeton University Press, 1953.

Barth, Karl. *Church Dogmatics*. 5 vols. in 13 pts. Ed. G. W. Bromiley and T. F. Torrance. Edinburgh: T & T Clark, 1956–1962.

Begbie, Jeremy. S. *Resounding Truth: Christian Wisdom in the World of Music*. Grand Rapids: Baker, 2007.

Dyrness, William A. *Reformed Theology and Visual Culture: The Protestant Imagination from Calvin to Edwards*. Cambridge: Cambridge University Press, 2004.

Genovese, Eugene D. *Roll, Jordan, Roll: The World the Slaves Made*. New York: Pantheon, 1974.

Gunton, Colin E. *The One, the Three and the Many: God, Creation and the Culture of Modernity*. Cambridge: Cambridge University Press, 1993.

Hart, David Bentley. *The Beauty of the Infinite: The Aesthetics of Christian Truth*. Grand Rapids: Eerdmans, 2003.

Hatch, Nathan O. *The Democratization of American Christianity*. New Haven: Yale University Press, 1989.

Jeffrey, David Lyle. *People of the Book: Christian Identity and Literary Culture*. Grand Rapids: Eerdmans, 1996.

Lewis, C. S. *The Discarded Image: An Introduction to Medieval and Renaissance Literature*. Cambridge: Cambridge University Press, 1964.

Lundin, Roger. *Believing Again: Doubt and Faith in a Secular Age*. Grand Rapids: Eerdmans, 2009.

Marsden, George M. *Fundamentalism and American Culture*. 2nd ed. New York: Oxford University Press, 2006.

Niebuhr, H. Richard. *Christ and Culture*. New York: Harper, 1951.

Noll, Mark A. *America's God: From Jonathan Edwards to Abraham Lincoln*. New York: Oxford University Press, 2002.

Oakes, Edward T. *Pattern of Redemption: The Theology of Hans Urs von Balthasar*. New York: Continuum, 1994.
Taylor, Charles. *A Secular Age*. Cambridge: Harvard University Press, 2007.
Vanhoozer, Kevin J. *The Drama of Doctrine: A Canonical-Linguistic Approach to Christian Theology*. Louisville, Ky.: Westminster John Knox, 2005.
Wolterstorff, Nicholas. *Art in Action: Toward a Christian Aesthetic*. Grand Rapids: Eerdmans, 1980.

CHAPTER 28

SCIENCE

ALISTER E. MCGRATH

EVANGELICALISM is characterized by an ambivalent attitude toward the natural sciences, reflecting both the lingering aftermath of difficult historical controversies and current concerns about reductionist tendencies within the sciences that seem to threaten the essence of the Christian gospel. Whereas Catholicism, Orthodoxy, and mainstream Protestantism have found conceptual space and theological strategies to accommodate the sciences, evangelicalism generally remains wary of them, particularly in the United States. Although many evangelicals adopt a positive attitude toward science, significant concerns about issues of biblical interpretation and reductionism remain widespread within the movement, especially at the grassroots level. So how has this situation developed?

Although evangelicalism mirrors general Christian attitudes toward the natural sciences, it has its own distinctive concerns. Given evangelicalism's characteristic emphasis on the authority of Scripture, it is not surprising to find that one of the major concerns within the movement concerns apparent challenges to biblical authority arising from scientific advance. This is seen most acutely in evangelical concerns about challenges to traditional interpretations of the Genesis creation accounts posed by evolutionary biology.

In this chapter, we shall explore the development of evangelical attitudes toward the natural sciences. Although many scholars regard evangelicalism as having taken its present forms in the eighteenth century, it is important to appreciate that the movement inherited both its emphasis on the authority of Scripture and its understandings of how Scripture was to be interpreted from the sixteenth-century Reformation. For this reason, it is instructive to consider the Reformation as laying the foundations of evangelicalism's complex attitude toward the natural sciences.

The Protestant Reformation

Leading early Protestant writers affirmed the centrality of the Bible to Christian thought and life, while recognizing the need for interpretive schemes which allowed its meaning to be discerned and applied. Although these approaches to biblical hermeneutics had much in common, their divergences led to a degree of diversity in early Protestant biblical interpretation. Martin Luther and Huldrych Zwingli, for example, adopted quite different hermeneutical schemes, which led to significant variations in their interpretation of some core biblical passages—for example, those relating to the "real presence" of Christ in the Eucharistic elements.

The importance of these hermeneutical schemes in shaping attitudes toward the natural sciences became obvious as a result of the heliocentric approach to the solar system, developed by Nicholas Copernicus (1473–1543). Copernicus's theory, published shortly after his death, held that the traditional view of the astronomical location and function of the earth was incorrect. The sun and planets did not revolve around the earth; rather, the earth and other planets revolved around the sun. This new theory seemed to call into question the reliability of some biblical passages—for example, those which spoke of the sun "standing still" (Joshua 10:11–13). Although some early Protestant writers regarded this divergence from Scripture as providing sufficient grounds to reject the Copernican theory, one development in particular within Protestantism lessened the importance of this point.

John Calvin's notion of "accommodation," which gained wide acceptance from about 1560 onward, held that God's self-revelation was "adapted" or "accommodated" to its audiences. Scripture regularly used vivid anthropomorphic and other figurative ways of speaking, designed to enable its audiences to relate easily to its ideas and doctrines. Biblical passages that seemed to imply a geocentric worldview were thus to be understood as "adapted" to their audiences, and were not to be taken at face value. Calvin, for example, wrote that when Moses had spoken in Genesis of the sun and the moon as "two great lights," he was simply adapting his discourse to the common usage.

These concerns about biblical interpretation might be taken to imply that early Protestantism was suspicious of scientific development. In fact, the evidence indicates that it was generally supportive, and may well have provided an intellectual context within which the scientific enterprise could flourish. In recent years, growing attention has been paid to how methods originally developed to interpret the Bible could also be applied to the natural world. This process was made easier through the widespread image of the "two books"—the book of Scripture, and the book of Nature.

Protestantism in effect stripped the "book of Nature" of any mystical or symbolic meanings, and allowed it to be studied directly without any sense of violation of religious sensibilities. Individual Protestant theologians, such as Jonathan Edwards (1703–1758), remained committed to the notion of nature as a emblazoned with signs and symbols of the glory of God. Yet as writers such as Max Weber (1864–1902) argued, the movement as a whole increasingly tended towards a "desacralized" or "disenchanted" view of nature, rendering it the legitimate object of scientific analysis.

This notion of a link between Protestantism and the development of the natural sciences has been explored in a number of ways. One of the most famous is the "Merton thesis," first set forward by the sociologist Robert Merton (1910–2003) in 1938, suggesting that English Puritanism in particular offered considerable intellectual stimulus to the natural sciences. Although Merton himself came to be critical of his own idea, it continues to generate considerable scholarly interest and attention. The extensive involvement of English Puritans in the development of the sciences in the seventeenth century—for example, through the foundation of the Royal Society—is well documented. Many English Protestants took the view that the pioneering work of Isaac Newton (1643–1726) had shown that there was a strong degree of convergence between the sciences and Christian theology. The idea of God as the divine clockmaker, creating an orderly and intelligent universe, came to be widely accepted.

Early Evangelicalism and the Sciences

By the middle of the eighteenth century, however, the "Newtonian synthesis" was in decline, and there were new tensions emerging between science and religion. Evangelicalism, which began to emerge as a distinct religious grouping at this time, thus found itself forced to engage with the sciences. Although issues of biblical interpretation raised by scientific advances remained contentious, these appear to have receded into the background as other issues came to the fore. Evangelicalism found itself confronting two major questions, which would become increasingly prominent as time progressed.

First, the Newtonian worldview seemed to have little place for the notion of divine providence. God was portrayed in essentially deistic terms, as an explanatory principle. The notion of God being active in history or nature came to be seen as increasingly problematic. This naturally led to a critique of miracles, which were seen as violations of the laws of nature. As rationalism gained headway during the eighteenth century, this criticism came to be applied increasingly to the resurrection of Jesus of Nazareth. Deist critics of Christian orthodoxy came to see this as an irrational belief. Christianity was either a republication of the laws of nature (in which case it merely replicated what could be known from free scientific inquiry), or it contradicted the laws of nature (in which case it was probably wrong).

Second, the growing successes of the natural sciences seemed to reduce religious belief and experience to natural causes. An emphasis on the natural order and rational ways of viewing nature and society were preferred to the transcendent mysteries affirmed by classical Christianity. For evangelicals, as for orthodox Christians as a whole, this both eroded the concept of the supernatural and threatened to eliminate any role for God in the natural world. This anxiety about reductionism became particularly significant for certain forms of evangelicalism such as pietism, which placed an emphasis on the importance of religious experience as a means of direct encounter with God. Yet it was also troubling for other forms of evangelicalism, in that it suggested that the Bible could be reduced to an account of essentially natural phenomena.

To glimpse some of the problems that emerged, consider the attitudes toward science of the leading English evangelical John Wesley (1703–1791), who played a pivotal role in the British "evangelical revival." Historical scholarship has made it clear that Wesley had read many of the leading scientists of his own day, and was aware of some of the questions arising from their work. It is clear from Wesley's writings that he was aware that mechanistic triumphs of seventeenth-century natural science pointed to an essentially impersonal deity who ruled through unchanging natural laws.

Wesley responded to these challenges in a number of ways. At one level, he argued that Scripture was not to be read as a scientific textbook, but as a disclosure of the nature and intentions of God. While Scripture, when correctly interpreted, is consistent with scientific truth, its focus and interests lie elsewhere. "The Scriptures were written not to gratify our curiosity but to lead us to God." While the sciences were able to offer a superficial engagement with nature, a deeper encounter with nature led to its creator, who continued to govern nature through his providence. Wesley also challenged the assumption that human reason would be able to discover all truths, insisting upon its limits and the necessity of revelation. Science gave access to one form of knowledge; the Christian faith offered a different type of knowledge.

Although the efficacy of Wesley's challenge to the growing intellectual and cultural influence of the natural sciences was limited, his engagement with the sciences of his day identifies many of the questions that would confront evangelicalism in the future.

Evangelicalism and the Crisis of Geology

As we noted earlier, evangelicalism emerged as a distinct, coherent movement too late to be significantly affected by the great astronomical controversies sparked by Copernicus, Kepler, and Galileo. It was not until the eighteenth century that evangelicalists can be considered to be a reasonably well-defined group, either in Britain or in North America. The first major challenge to evangelicalism from the natural sciences came from the field of geology, and raised certain fundamental questions about the age of the earth and the interpretation of the Genesis creation accounts.

This controversy anticipated aspects of the later debates about biological evolution, especially the issue of the age of the earth and the development of its features over time. It is, however, best to see this controversy as an episode of importance in its own right, rather than as a mere anticipation of later controversies.

The growing realization that the earth was far older than a simple literal reading of the book of Genesis suggested caused much spiritual agony for British evangelicals in the first six decades of the nineteenth century. The influential Victorian cultural critic John Ruskin (1819–1900) lost his evangelical faith while a young man, and attributed this partly to the geologists with their "dreadful hammers." Evangelicalism split into factions, in response to the new geological findings. One group was severely critical of geology, seeing it as antireligious and dedicated to the advance of secularism. Writers such as John Mellor Brown argued that geologists were "attacking the truth of God." Geology ought to be denounced as "not a subject of lawful inquiry," in that it was "dangerous and disreputable," a "dark art" which was to be avoided. Yet it must be noted that this group of writers was neither large nor representative. The growing realization during the first decades of the twentieth century that the earth was probably millions of years old raised relatively little ecclesiastical opposition or comment.

As far as can be seen, most evangelicals believed that it was possible to reconcile geology and Genesis. One of the most significant evangelicals to develop this view was put forward in 1814 by the Scottish theologian Thomas Chalmers (1780–1847). For Chalmers, the first Genesis creation account allowed for a chronological gap between the initial act of creation and the beginning of the creative acts of the six days of creation. All geological time, Chalmers argued, was to be located in that gap. This view was also developed by William Buckland and Hugh Miller. Although regarded by some as a somewhat forced interpretation of Genesis, Chalmers' approach allowed geological insights to be incorporated within a traditional Christian understanding of creation. The popular *Scofield Reference Bible*, first published in 1909, began to make reference in 1917 to the "Gap Theory" in its footnotes accompanying Genesis 1. This development is widely regarded as having given the theory a new lease of life in the twentieth century, on the eve of the great fundamentalist controversy in North America.

While the details of this controversy are not without interest, the main point to note is the anxiety that new scientific discoveries created about the reliability of traditional interpretations of the Bible, especially the first Genesis creation narrative. Evangelical responses to this challenge generally fell into three categories: the declaration that science and religion had nothing to do with each other, so that developments in one field had no impact upon the other; the rejection of science as inconsistent with traditional interpretations of Scripture; or the accommodation of Scripture to science, either through the retrieval of older ways of interpreting biblical narratives or through the adjustment of existing approaches. The same pattern of challenges and responses emerged during the evolutionary controversies, to which we may now turn.

The Great Evangelical Debate over Evolution

Recent debates over evangelical identity have sought to identify certain markers or traits that are essential to being an evangelical. It is a mark of the polarization that has developed within the movement over Darwinism in recent years that some are now suggesting that rejection of evolution is an essential characteristic of true evangelicalism. This is historically incorrect, in that evangelical hostility toward Darwinism became significant in the 1920s, partly as a result of the rise of fundamentalism. For the first fifty years of Darwinism's existence, evangelical hostility was muted, with more accommodationist approaches tending to prevail.

In his *Origin of Species* (1859), Darwin argued that the best explanation for the observable features of contemporary life forms, both plant and animal, was "natural selection." Random hereditary changes over a long period of time led to the survival and reproduction of those organisms which proved to be better adapted to their environments. This idea, often expressed in the unhelpful phrase "survival of the fittest," lies at the heart of Darwin's account of evolution. Although Darwin lacked a reliable account of how genetic changes were transmitted, he nevertheless realized how his idea of "natural selection" was able to account for some features of the natural world that caused difficulty for the doctrine of "special creation," as found in William Paley's influential work *Natural Theology* (1802).

For example, Darwin's research voyage on the *Beagle* had persuaded him of the uneven geographical distribution of life forms throughout the world. In particular, Darwin was impressed by the peculiarities of island populations, such as those found on the Galapagos Islands in the Pacific. Paley's theory required the special creation of these species; Darwin's account interpreted them as arising from the specific environments within which evolution took place. It seemed to Darwin that his account was more elegant than that offered by Paley.

What about vestigial organs, such as male nipples in mammals, or the appendix? These seemed to have no obvious biological function. Paley's approach seemed to imply that God intentionally designed and created features of the natural world that had no purpose. Why, Darwin wondered, would God design such redundancies? Darwin's own explanation was that evolutionary progress resulted in "vestiges" of earlier forms remaining, even though they had no role to play.

Today, the term "Darwinism" is generally used to mean the general approach to biological evolution set out in Darwin's canonical works, as developed and extended through clarification of the molecular basis of inheritance. Yet before proceeding further, it is important to make a clear distinction between two senses of the word "Darwinism," as it is encountered both in the writings of "scientific atheists" such as Richard Dawkins and Daniel Dennett, and creationist critics of evolution. First, the term can designate a provisional scientific theory about the biological processes which led to the origin of species, open to correction, development or even refutation over time, in the light of the available evidence. Second, it can designate an essentially naturalistic worldview, which holds that everything—including belief in God—can be accounted for by using reductionist scientific explanations. Evangelicalism has been more or less unanimous in challenging the second sense of this term. There is, however, considerable disagreement within evangelicalism over whether Darwinism, considered purely as a provisional scientific theory, entails reductionism and atheism, as some suggest.

Evangelical concerns about Darwinism began to emerge in the late nineteenth century. The main areas of concern are easily identified, and may be listed as follows.

1. Darwinism offered an account of the origins of species that appeared to many to be incompatible with a literal interpretation of the opening chapters of the book of Genesis. We have already noted how evangelical attitudes toward science are closely linked to concerns about biblical interpretation.
2. Darwin's theory seemed to undermine arguments for the existence of God which appealed to evidence of design in the natural world. The most famous of these, as Darwin himself acknowledged, was the form of natural theology developed by the celebrated English apologist William Paley (1743–1805).
3. The special place of humanity in the natural world was called into question by the theory of evolution. Darwin himself realized that this was a very sensitive matter, and held back from explicitly engaging with this question until *The Descent of Man* (1871).
4. The traditional notion of providence seems to be contradicted by Darwin's account of things, which proposed that evolution took place through random variations in the forms of living creatures.
5. The traditional popular notion of creation as the special simultaneous divine production of carefully designed living entities could only be sustained with some difficulty or awkwardness after Darwin. This called into question some traditional approaches to apologetics.

For some evangelicals, the cumulative force of these concerns was enough to make Darwinism unacceptable. Yet most evangelical writers, both in Great Britain and the United States, held back from any dismissal of Darwinism. Each of these five concerns could be addressed, in some way. To illustrate this point, we shall consider the attitude to Darwinism of perhaps the most influential American evangelical writer of the late nineteenth and early twentieth centuries, Benjamin B. Warfield (1851–1921).

Benjamin B. Warfield on Evolution

Benjamin Breckinridge Warfield served as professor of didactic and polemic theology at Princeton Theological Seminary from 1887 to 1921, and is generally regarded as a leading representative of the "Old Princeton School." He is widely revered within conservative evangelical circles for his theories of biblical inerrancy and inspiration, which have had a significant impact on contemporary evangelical thought—most notably, J. I. Packer's landmark book *"Fundamentalism" and the Word of God* (1957).

So how did Warfield approach Darwin's theory of evolution? Warfield developed a sophisticated analysis of contemporary Darwinism, making two points that deserve to continue to be central to evangelical reflection on this question. First, Warfield drew the distinction we noted earlier, between Darwinism as a scientific theory and as a grander, reductionist account of reality. No evangelical could tolerate Darwinism if it was interpreted as "supplying a complete account of the origin and state of the universe." This, for Warfield, was "tantamount to atheism." Warfield here echoed earlier concerns about Darwinism expressed by his older Princeton colleague, Charles Hodge (1797–1878). Warfield insisted that Darwinism was to be seen as a "working hypothesis" or a "conjecture as to the method of creation," which should be judged on the basis of its empirical adequacy.

Second, Warfield emphasized that the natural sciences were prone to speculation. A clear distinction had to be made between the empirical facts of nature and extravagant interpretations of these, especially when these involved inferring speculative metaphysical conclusions. It is at this point that we find Warfield making one of his most important criticisms of Darwinism—its rejection of any form of teleology within nature. For Warfield, this was metaphysical speculation, not scientific observation.

It is important to note that Warfield finds this tendency in Darwin himself, rather than Darwin's later interpreters. One of Warfield's most pointed criticisms of Darwin is that he sought to replace any notion of teleology in the biological world with those of natural selection and random variation. For Warfield, this suggested that Darwin had an anti-theistic agenda, however subtly it may have been stated. There is, he argued, no reason why the concept of a natural developmental process should be held to entail atheism. Rather, it can be interpreted and even subsumed within a Reformed view of divine providence, which holds that God creates a world with the capacity for development, and is sovereign over that subsequent process of development.

Warfield developed this point further in his analysis of the concept of divine creation. For Warfield, the term "creation" refers to God's primal act of bringing everything into being from nothing (*ex nihilo*). It describes God's initial creation of the universe, with the potential for further development under God's sovereign providential guidance. To express this developmental aspect of things, Warfield introduces the notion of "mediate creation," by which he means something intermediate between natural processes and divine providence. "Mediate creation" refers to the direct action of God on material entities, in which God brings about novelty—that is, something that was not originally present in the primary act of creation itself. Warfield does not hold that "naturalistic evolution" and "divine creation" are identical; he does, however, insist that they are consistent with each other, provided both are interpreted correctly.

The Old Princeton theology followed a traditional Reformed approach to the natural sciences, grounded in the notion that that God testified to himself through two books, the book of Scripture and the book of Nature. Although these two books were different, they nevertheless shared the same divine author. When rightly interpreted, these two sources could not be in conflict with each other. Any conflict between the actual facts revealed in nature (as opposed to extravagant scientific speculation about nature) and the biblical texts should lead the responsible exegete not to reject a scientific account of nature, nor to doubt the truth of Scripture, but to seek a better interpretation of Scripture in the light of these facts.

The assumption that a doctrine of biblical inerrancy demands a literal biblical hermeneutic was not shared by Warfield. Indeed, for Warfield, it was axiomatic that a commitment to biblical inerrancy left open the question of how any passage of Scripture was to be interpreted correctly. There was no a priori reason why an inerrantist could not adopt a nonliteralist interpretation of the early Genesis texts, if that appeared to be the manner in which that text required to be understood.

From this brief account of Warfield's theological analysis of Darwinism, it can be seen that evangelicalism has access to a very sophisticated approach to the question, which merits continuing consideration. Warfield's approach involves the rejection of any account of evolution that eliminates or disregards God's primal action or continuing involvement with the created order, or which sees evolution as a random process. Warfield offers a theological framework within which Darwinism can both be accommodated and criticized.

Contemporary Evangelical Approaches to Evolution

Evangelical hostility toward Darwinism was most marked in the United States, reaching a peak around the time of the great fundamentalist controversies of the 1920s. Perhaps the most familiar icon of these controversies is to be found in the Scopes trial of 1925. In May 1925, John T. Scopes (1900–1970), a young high school science teacher, was prosecuted under a recently adopted statute that prohibited the teaching of evolution in Tennessee's public schools. Although Scopes later suggested that he hadn't actually taught evolution, the trial attracted enormous media attention, and helped crystallize the perception that fundamentalism and anti-evolutionism were synonymous. In fact, the situation was considerably more complex than this. *The Fundamentals*—a collection of tracts issued over the period 1910–1915, which lent its name to the fundamentalist movement—included contributions that castigated Darwinism as unbiblical alongside others by James Orr (1844–1913) and George Frederick Wright (1838–1921), which held that Darwinism, if interpreted carefully and responsibly, could help illuminate our understanding of the development of species.

Evangelical hostility toward Darwinism began to decline in the late 1940s, before resurging in the 1980s. A major theme in the 1980s revival of evangelical anti-Darwinism is the perceived reductionism of the sciences in general, and evolutionary theory in particular. This revival has generally been led by influential evangelical pastors, parachurch organizations, and media activists, rather than theologians and scientists. This has often led to issues of science being reduced to the question of whether they appear to challenge the authority of the Bible, or might be argued to encourage atheism.

An excellent example of evangelical anti-evolutionism is found in the writings of Philip Johnson (born 1940), an academic lawyer at the University of California. One of Johnson's most significant arguments is that methodological naturalism inevitably implies ontological naturalism. Darwinism in particular, and the sciences in general, thus have an inherent proclivity toward eliminating the divine from any account of reality. Johnson's argument that Darwinism is inherently atheistic thus shifts the discussion from "creationism versus evolution" to the safer ground of "Christianity versus atheism," thus significantly altering the terms of the debate. Other evangelicals, however, have challenged such a viewpoint. Nancey Murphy (born 1951), for example, argued that nonreductive strategies could easily be developed, allowing evangelicals to affirm naturalist scientific explanations without in any way implying the nonexistence or inactivity of God.

In what follows, we shall offer a descriptive analysis of the wide spectrum of evangelical approaches to Darwinism encountered in the early twenty-first century. These are best grouped together using four broad categories: Young Earth Creationism; Old Earth Creationism; Intelligent Design; and Evolutionary Theism. Each of these can be regarded as consisting of a number of strands, with divergence within each school on points of significance.

Young Earth Creationism

In this view, the earth was created in its basic form between 6,000 and 10,000 years ago. Young earth creationists generally read the first two chapters of the book of Genesis in a way that allows for no living creatures of any kind before Eden, and no death before the Fall. Adam and Eve are treated as primal human beings, rather than as representative or symbolic figures. Although the notion of "the Fall" is actually best seen as an Augustinian theological construction, rather than a direct reading of the book of Genesis, most Young Earth Creationists tend to treat it as an historical event. In many ways, this position represents the continuation of the "common reading" of Genesis, which was widely encountered in popular and at least some academic writing before 1800. Most young earth creationists hold that all living things were created simultaneously, within the timeframe proposed by the Genesis creation accounts, with the Hebrew word *yom* ("day") meaning a period of twenty-four hours. The fossil records, which point to a much longer timescale and to the existence of extinct species, are often understood to date from the time of Noah's flood, which is seen as a biblical catastrophe capable of accounting for evidence of earlier forms of existence. One influential variant of this approach was developed by Philip Henry Gosse in 1857. Gosse argued that the universe was created young, but with the appearance of great age.

Old Earth Creationism

This view has a relatively long history, and is probably the majority viewpoint within conservative Protestant circles. Perhaps its most common form could be described as "Progressive Creationism," which holds that God created "kinds" or "types" of organisms sequentially, in the order seen in the fossil record, while insisting that each new type of organism is to be seen as having been specially created, rather than having evolved from older life-forms. This approach has no particular difficulty with the vast age of the world, and argues that the "young earth" approach requires correction and modification in at least two respects. First, it is held that the Hebrew word *yom* may need to be interpreted as an "indefinite time participle" (not unlike the English word "while"), signifying an indeterminate period of time which is given specificity by its context. In other words, the word "day" in the Genesis creation accounts is to be interpreted as a long period of time, not a specific period of twenty-four hours. "Day-age creationists" (as these are sometimes known) thus interpret each day of creation as a long period of time, even thousands or millions of years. This form of creationism recognizes a parallel between the order of events presented in the first Genesis creation account and the evolutionary order accepted by mainstream science. Second, it is argued by some that a large chronological gap intervenes between Genesis 1.1 and Genesis 1.2. In other words, the narrative is not understood to be continuous, but to make way for the intervention of a substantial period of time between the primordial act of creation of the universe and the emergence of life on earth. As noted earlier, this viewpoint was advocated by the influential Scofield Reference Bible, first published in 1909, although the ideas can be traced back to writers such as the earlier nineteenth-century Scottish divine Thomas Chalmers.

Intelligent Design

This movement, which has gained considerable influence in the United States in recent years, argues that the biosphere is characterized by an "irreducible complexity" which makes it impossible to explain its origins and development in any other method on than positing intelligent design. For Michael Behe, this irreducible complexity is a sure indicator of design. Intelligent design does not deny biological evolution; its most fundamental criticism of Darwinism is teleological—that evolution has no goal. The Intelligent Design movement argues that signs of intelligence may be discerned in nature, and specifically in biological systems. It further argues that standard Darwinism runs into significant explanatory difficulties. (Its critics, however, argue that these difficulties are overstated, or that they will in due course be resolved by future theoretical advances.) Although the movement avoids direct identification of God with this intelligent designer (presumably for political reasons), it is clear that this assumption is intrinsic to its working methods. The movement is particularly associated with Michael Behe, author of *Darwin's Black Box*, and William Dembski, author of *Intelligent Design: The Bridge between Science and Theology*. Both Dembski and Behe are fellows of the Discovery Institute, based in Seattle.

Evolutionary Theism

A final approach argues that evolution is to be understood as God's chosen method of bringing life into existence from inorganic materials, and creating complexity within life. "Creation" is here understood to mean both a primordial divine act and its subsequent development or unfolding under God's providential guidance. Although this view is dominant within mainstream Protestantism and Catholicism, it is a minority perspective within evangelicalism. Although this approach is widely known as "evolutionary theism," many of its proponents regard this as misleading, in that it appears to deny that they accept the divine creation of reality. While there is merit in this concern, no alternative designation for the group has yet gained widespread acceptance. Whereas Darwinism gives a significant place to random events in the evolutionary process, evolutionary theism sees the process as divinely directed. Some evolutionary theists propose that each level of complexity is to be explained on the basis of "God working within the system," perhaps at the quantum level. Others, such as Howard van Till, adopt a "fully-gifted creation" perspective, arguing that God built in the potential for the emergence and complexity of life in the initial act of creation, so that further acts of divine intervention are not required. Van Till argues that the character of divine creative action is best expressed in terms of "God's giving being to a creation fully equipped with the creaturely capabilities to organize and/or transform itself into a diversity of physical structures and life-forms."

Evangelicalism and a Scientific Culture

The evangelical debates over Darwinism cannot be separated from broader cultural agendas, especially in the United States. Science is not simply an intellectual movement; it is a competitor for cultural attention and authority, at times proposing itself as an alternative to religion. One characteristic feature of the "new atheism," found in writings such as Richard Dawkins's *God Delusion* (2006) and Daniel Dennett's *Breaking the Spell* (2006) is that science has displaced religion as a cultural and intellectual authority, demonstrating its superiority in both respects.

This is a classic example of the "warfare" model of the relationship of science and religion, favored by both scientific opponents of religion and evangelical critics of Darwinism. This strongly confrontational model continues to be deeply influential at the popular level, even if its appeal has diminished considerably at a more scholarly level. It was expounded in two widely read works published in the later part of the nineteenth century—John William Draper's *History of the Conflict between Religion and Science* (1874) and Andrew Dickson White's *History of the Warfare of Science with Theology in Christendom* (1896). Today, the best-known representative of this approach is Richard Dawkins, who argues that "faith is one of the world's great evils, comparable to the smallpox virus but harder to eradicate." Science and religion are implacably opposed. For Dawkins, science represents reason, and religion superstition.

Yet this model is not restricted to antireligious scientists. It is widespread within conservative religious groups within Christianity and Islam, who are often virulently hostile to the idea of biological evolution. The creationist Henry M. Morris (1918–2006) published a sustained critique of modern evolutionary theory with the title *The Long War against God* (1989). In an appreciative foreword to the book, a conservative Baptist pastor declares that "modern evolutionism is simply the continuation of Satan's long war against God." Morris even invites us to imagine Satan imagining the idea of evolution as a means of dethroning God.

This approach to the relation of science and religion is easily assimilated to the "culture wars" paradigm, which has been especially influential in North American fundamentalist circles. Conservative American evangelicals often present the struggle between creationism and evolutionism as a battle between Christianity and atheism or secularism. This cultural struggle is often focused on whether public schools in the United States should teach creationism as well as Darwinism, or whether Darwinism ought to be part of the national curriculum. Evangelical activists have been prominent in campaigns to persuade school boards to prohibit the teaching of evolution in schools, or to teach creationism or Intelligent Design alongside as alternative perspectives.

The most significant recent example of such a development took place in Kansas. In 2005, the Kansas State Board of Education ruled that, while evolution was to be taught in state schools, it was to be presented essentially as a *theory*, not a factual account of things. Intelligent Design should be taught as an alternative approach in science lessons. This brought evangelicals into open conflict with the United States National Academy of Sciences, which issued a policy statement saying "Creationism, intelligent design, and other claims of supernatural intervention in the origin of life or of species are not science because they are not testable by the methods of science." In 2007, following an election which reduced the number of conservative Christians on the Kansas State Board of Education, the Board revoked this position, and reverted to the position that evolution was to be taught in public schools without any challenge from Intelligent Design. Similar controversies took place in other states around this time.

These debates point to evangelicalism's growing importance as a political force, and its consequent clashes with cultural rivals. Such developments do not command universal consent within evangelicalism, in that some fear a reversion to the cultural isolationism of fundamentalism during the 1920s. It is important to appreciate that some evangelicals' hostility toward Darwinism is given added impetus through the cultural aspects of the movement, which supplement the more intellectual concerns noted in previous sections.

Conclusion

As evangelicalism develops further, the question of its relationship with the sciences will continue to be a significant topic for debate within the movement. History suggests that opposition to Darwinism is neither typical of, nor essential to the definition of, evangelicalism. As evangelicals become more involved in scientific teaching and research, it is possible that significant long-term changes in attitudes may take place within the movement. Cultural shifts in the future might therefore lessen hostility toward the sciences within the movement, or make them more pronounced. Although the movement is at the moment noted for its scepticism toward the natural sciences, especially Darwinism, the movement has a rich heritage that makes alternatives possible. It remains to be seen what the outcome of these discussions will be.

BIBLIOGRAPHY

Alexander, Denis. *Rebuilding the Matrix: Science and Faith in the 21st Century*. Oxford: Lion, 2001.

Carlson, Richard F., ed. *Science and Christianity: Four Views*. Downers Grove, Ill.: InterVarsity, 2000.

Davis, John Jefferson. *The Frontiers of Science and Faith: Examining Questions from the Big Bang to the End of the Universe*. Downers Grove, Ill.: InterVarsity, 2002.

Dembski, William A. *Darwin's Nemesis: Phillip Johnson and the Intelligent Design Movement*. Downers Grove, Ill.: InterVarsity, 2006.

———. *Intelligent Design: The Bridge between Science and Theology*. Downers Grove, Ill.: InterVarsity, 1999.

Falk, Darrel R. *Coming to Peace with Science: Bridging the Worlds between Faith and Biology*. Downers Grove, Ill.: InterVarsity, 2004.

Gillispie, Charles C. *Genesis and Geology: A Study in the Relations of Scientific Thought, Natural Theology and Social Opinion in Great Britain, 1790–1850*. Cambridge: Harvard University Press, 1996.

Haas, John W. "John Wesley's Eighteenth Century Views on Science and Christianity: An Examination of the Charge of Antiscience." *Church History* 63 (1994): 378–392.

Harrison, Peter. *The Bible, Protestantism, and the Rise of Natural Science*. Cambridge: Cambridge University Press, 1998.

Hodge, Charles. *What Is Darwinism?* Ed. Mark A. Noll and David N. Livingstone. Grand Rapids: Baker, 1994.

Howell, Kenneth J. *God's Two Books: Copernican Cosmology and Biblical Interpretation in Early Modern Science*. Notre Dame: University of Notre Dame Press, 2002.

Johnson, Phillip E. *Darwin on Trial*. 2nd ed. Downers Grove, Ill.: InterVarsity, 1993.

———. *Defeating Darwinism by Opening Minds*. Downers Grove, Ill.: InterVarsity, 1997.

Lienesch, Michael. *In the Beginning: Fundamentalism, the Scopes Trial, and the Making of the Antievolution Movement*. Chapel Hill: University of North Carolina Press, 2007.

Livingstone, David N. *Darwin's Forgotten Defenders: The Encounter between Evangelical Theology and Evolutionary Thought*. Grand Rapids: Eerdmans, 1987.

Livingstone, David N., D. G. Hart, and Mark Noll, eds. *Evangelicals and Science in Historical Perspective*. New York: Oxford University Press, 1999.

Lynch, John M., ed. *Creationism and Scriptural Geology, 1817–1857*. 7 vols. Bristol: Thoemmes Press, 2002.

Marsden, George. *Fundamentalism and American Culture: The Shaping of Twentieth Century Evangelicalism 1870–1925*. New York: Oxford University Press, 1980.

Murphy, Nancey C. *Bodies and Souls, or Spirited Bodies?* Cambridge: Cambridge University Press, 2006.

Numbers, Ronald L. *The Creationists: The Evolution of Scientific Creationism*. New York: Knopf, 1992.

Warfield, Benjamin B. *Evolution, Scripture, and Science: Selected Writings*, ed. Mark A. Noll and David N. Livingstone. Grand Rapids: Baker, 2000.

CHAPTER 29

SEXUALITY

ROBERT A. J. GAGNON

The belief that "sex matters" has always been a defining feature of evangelical theology. Indeed, a typical complaint about evangelicals on the part of the "liberal" or left wing of the church is that evangelicals are obsessed with sex. Paradoxically, this complaint is usually made when the left wing wants to foist its own radical, anti-scriptural sex agenda on the church, whatever the cost to church unity. The evangelical attention to sexual concerns at times has had its drawbacks. One thinks particularly of instances where women's voices have been suppressed, sexual offenders have been treated with excessive harshness, and sexual pleasure even within the context of marriage has been eschewed. However, with respect to a strong interest in sexual purity, the church has been generally on target over the last two millennia. This interest is fully consistent with the witness of Scripture, including the testimony of Jesus.

Learning from Jesus

Jesus gave the church at least six important principles from which to formulate a proper ethic of sexuality, principles that the apostle Paul faithfully followed.

1. A Creation-Based Sexual Ethic Overriding Mosaic Permissiveness for Men and Inequity toward Women

According to Mark 10:2–12 (par. Matt 19:3–9), Jesus declared the creation model of marriage in Genesis 1:27 ("male and female he made them") and 2:24 ("for this reason a man... shall be joined to his woman and [the two] shall become one flesh") to be normative for defining acceptable sexual behavior, with proscriptive implications. Jesus believed that the Creator had restricted sexual intercourse to marriage and had ordained marriage as a lifelong union of one man and one woman. So strongly did Jesus feel about the priority of Genesis 1:27 and 2:24 for defining normative sexual ethics that he used their stress on God's design of two complementary sexes for sexual relations as the basis for limiting the number of persons in a sexual union to two. He thereby prohibited both a revolving door of divorce and remarriage and, implicitly, polygamy. The importance of Genesis 1:27 and 2:24 for sexual morality in early Christian thought is confirmed by Paul's obvious allusion to Genesis 1:26–27 in Romans 1:23–27, where Paul critiques homosexual practice, and his citation of Genesis 2:24 in 1 Corinthians 6:16, in a context treating issues of sexual immorality (cf. 1 Cor 11:7–12).

The priority given by Jesus to Genesis 1:27 and 2:24 has two further corollaries. First, evangelicals should have no trouble acknowledging, as Jesus did, that some sexual laws in the Old Testament did not represent God's perfect will but, rather, were concessions made by Moses "in view of your hardness of heart" (Mark 10:5 par. Matt 19:8). At the same time, the direction of Jesus' efforts at making the Mosaic law internally self-consistent is not toward a more relaxed sexual ethic but rather toward a more rigorous demand. A second, related corollary is that Jesus repudiated inequities between men and women in the Mosaic law. Jesus declared, contrary to the prevailing view in Judaism, that it was possible for a man to commit adultery against his wife and not just against a woman's husband (Mark 10:11). Jesus extended this equity toward women not by granting women the same sexual license that men had as regards divorce and polygamy but rather by imposing on men and women alike the same rigorous new standard for sexual purity.

2. Adding a Strong Interior Component to Sexual Ethics

Consistent with his interiorizing ethic elsewhere,[1] Jesus extended the Mosaic demand for outward compliance in sexual purity to inward compliance. In his adultery-of-the-heart saying, Jesus closed the loophole given to one's sexual thought life by inferring that it was not enough to avoid committing the physical act of sexual immorality (Matt 5:27–28). Unlike the goal of so many today, Jesus' point in exposing hypocrisy was not to lower the bar for sexual purity but rather to raise it. Jesus' hyperbolic statement about what defiles a person in Mark 7:14–23 does not mean that the morality of an action is determined by whether a person's heart is "in the right place." Rather, it means that, unlike the relatively benign effect that food has on the body, the inward active desire for what God deems to be immoral (including "sexually immoral acts, . . . adulterous acts, . . . sexual unrestraint," 7:21–22) is already defiling, even before the act is committed. Food entering the body may not defile, but an inner desire for sexually immoral behavior certainly does. Paul makes a similar point when he argues against the Corinthians that, whatever truth there may be to the slogan "all things are within my right to do" when applied to food, it has no relevance for sexual intercourse, since sexual immorality affects the body holistically, not merely superficially (1 Cor 6:12–20, citing the specific example of sex with a prostitute).

3. Sexual Ethics as a Life-and-Death Matter

Consistent with his Jewish Scriptures,[2] Jesus considered sexual ethics to be a vitally important matter. Between Jesus' statements about adultery of the heart and divorce in the antitheses of the Sermon on the Mount (5:27–28, 31–32), Matthew has a saying of Jesus about removing an eye or cutting off a hand if the offending member threatens one's downfall. The point is that it is better to go into heaven maimed than to be thrown into hell full-bodied (5:29–30; cf. Mark 9:43–48 par. Matt 18:8–9). In context, the saying speaks to the utter seriousness of sexual offenses.

When Jesus protected the woman caught in adultery from the penalty of stoning (John 8:3–11), he was not communicating that adultery was a minor offense. Jesus was trying to prevent a worse fate from befalling the woman on the Day of Judgment by stimulating the woman's repentance through an act of kindness. Simply put, dead people don't repent. His statement, "Go, and from now on no longer be sinning," can be compared to the similar remark in John 5:14: "No longer be sinning *lest something worse happen to you.*" In the context of John 5:14 that "something worse" is clearly forfeiture of eternal life (5:24–29).

The importance of sexual ethics for Paul ought to be obvious. In his kingdom-of-God sayings Paul emphasized to believers that sexual immorality was a high risk factor for not entering that kingdom (1 Cor 6:9–10; Gal 5:19–21; Eph 5:3–5; cf. 2 Cor 12:21). We read in Paul's first extant letter that Paul began his moral exhortation to new converts by warning them to "abstain from sexual immorality (*porneia*)" because "God did not call us to sexual uncleanness (*akatharsia*) but in holiness" (1 Thess 4:3–7; cf. the Apostolic Decree in Acts 15:20). He added ominously: "Therefore the one who rejects [this instruction about sexual purity] rejects not a human being but God who gives his Holy Spirit to you" (4:8). In 1 Corinthians sexual issues occupy three successive chapters (5–7). The case of adult incest between a man and his stepmother in chapter 5 so exercises Paul's ire that, in a letter that everywhere else emphasizes unity, Paul insists that the Corinthians put the offender *out* of the community—not as a punitive measure but as a remedial one, a last-ditch effort at stimulating repentance in the offender so that he "might be saved on the day of the Lord" (5:5).

Some contend that sexual ethics could not have been an important concern for Jesus because few of his preserved sayings deal with the subject. However, counting up the number of sayings devoted to a given subject is not a reliable method for discerning significance. It ignores the cultural context of the speaker. For example, not a single transmitted saying of Jesus speaks specifically against incest and bestiality. Yet no reasonable interpreter would contend that Jesus regarded these as matters of indifference. Jesus did not need to tell people in his first-century Palestinian Jewish context to abstain from such acts (or from same-sex intercourse) for the obvious reason that Scripture's stance was already clear and strong, with the incidence of violation in Israel rare or nonexistent. The first-century Palestinian society in which Jesus operated already maintained a fairly exacting standard for sexual ethics. Since Jesus generally agreed with it, there was not much to add—except to intensify the demand for men as regards both thought life and divorce/remarriage and to reach out in love toward violators who were in danger of not inheriting the very Kingdom that he proclaimed. In Paul's letters the proportion of teaching devoted to sexual ethics increases substantially[3] because Paul shared the gospel of Jesus Christ in a Gentile context where he could no longer take for granted the relatively high standard for sexual ethics operating in Jesus' Jewish milieu.

4. A Heightened Ethical Demand Coupled with a Loving and Forgiving Outreach to Violators

Love and truth, or outreach and an intensified ethic, are not mutually exclusive but interdependent in Jesus' ministry. The church should neither dilute its ethical standards in a bid to show compassion to violators nor callously consign violators to hell in an effort to preserve standards. Jesus combined a compassionate outreach to "tax collectors and sinners," including sexual sinners, with an intensified ethic regarding money and sex.[4] Jesus demanded nothing less of his followers than that they take up their cross, deny themselves, and lose their lives (Mark 8:34–37; Matt 10:38–39; John 12:25).

In Jesus' understanding, loving outreach included reproof and correction. When he lifted up Lev 19:18b, "love your neighbor as yourself," as the second greatest commandment (Mark 12:31; cf. Luke 10:27–28), he obviously had in mind the immediate context in 19:17–18a (as we know other Jews of the period did). Loving one's neighbor included *both* "firmly reproving" one's neighbor so as not to "incur guilt because of him" (for failing to warn one's neighbor) *and* not hating, taking vengeance, or holding a grudge against one's neighbor. Jesus maintained *both* "if your brother sins, rebuke him" *and* "if he repents, forgive him," even "if he sins seven times a day" (Luke 17:3–4; cf. Matt 18:15, 21–22). This command to rebuke is not a contradiction of Jesus' words against judging others (Matt 7:1–5 par. Luke 6:37, 41–42). Context and Jesus' own repeated judgments[5] indicate that his criticism was aimed at overly punctilious, hypocritical, and loveless criticisms of others, not self-introspective and restorative rebuke of egregious sin.

We see a similar interaction in Pauline theology between grace and love, on the one hand, and an emphasis on moral transformation and the holy life, on the other. The middle term between the two poles is union with Christ by faith. In Paul's understanding there is no sin transfer to Christ apart from self-transfer; no application of Christ's death "for us" apart from our being joined to Christ through the reception of his Holy Spirit. One can see this clearly, for example, in Galatians 2:15–21, which sets up the second and third thesis statements of the letter. Paul insists that humans are justified or set right before God solely by God's grace manifested in Christ's amends-making death and received on the basis of faith in Jesus Christ; that is, *not* by doing the deeds stipulated by the law of Moses (2:15–16, 21; elaborated in 3:1–5:12). At the same time, he insists that people only leave the jurisdiction of the law when they "no longer live but Christ lives in" them through the Spirit and as they conduct their lives by faith in "the one who loved [them] and handed himself over [to death] for [their] sake" (2:17–20; elaborated in 5:13–6:10, esp. 5:18).

5. The Ends of Marriage

Given that Jesus did not view the command to procreate in Genesis 1:28 as binding on all persons (Matt 19:11–12) and was accused (albeit falsely) of being "a glutton and a drunkard" (Matt 11:19 par. Luke 7:34), he probably did not see sexual pleasure per se as sinful. His Scripture supplied a number of texts that spoke positively of conjugal love and companionship.[6] He also knew of Scripture's endearing use of the marriage metaphor to portray Israel's relationship to God, a metaphor later picked up in Christian communities to depict the church's relationship to Christ.[7] This metaphor suggests that, in a certain sense, marriage in its best moments gives us a glimpse of the joys of a consummated relationship with God in the future Kingdom.

Paul followed Jesus, and deviated from some in the Corinthian church, in recognizing that sexual passion in marriage was no sin and *must* be gratified in marriage (1 Cor 7:3, 28, 36–38). This is consistent with his general, nonascetic approach to life, where he is content with both abundance and lack (Phil 4:12). Paul is often criticized in our own day for limiting marriage's usefulness to a safety valve for "burning" sexual desire (1 Cor 7:2, 5, 9, 36–37). However, the tenor of his remarks was conditioned by the claim of the Corinthian "strong" that they were impervious to sexual temptation (7:1). Accordingly, it is not likely that Paul said everything that he believed about the purposes of marriage in 1 Corinthians 7.

Although the Bible has a generally positive view of sexual relations in the context of marriage, sexual gratification with or without procreation is not the highest end of marriage. Nor is the highest objective companionship as an antidote to human aloneness (Gen 2:18), since close but asexual friendships can go a long way toward fulfilling that purpose. Jesus' insistence on marriage's indissolubility, buttressed by appeal to Genesis 1:27 and 2:24, hints at the highest purpose of marriage. Marriage is God's instrument for *re*uniting male and female into an integrated sexual whole. This purpose is symbolized by the copulative act (and partly effected by it) and illustrated by the story of woman's creation from Adam's "side" (a better translation than "rib"). God designed marriage primarily for the purpose of shaping two into one—an aim more important than the satisfaction of the individual wants of husbands and wives. Sexual activity sets in motion a reality beyond the individual's control, thereby imposing obligations that transcend whatever meaning the participants wish to impute to their activity.[8] Procreation is also an important purpose of marriage (Gen 1:28) but not an indispensable component. A marriage in which one partner is infertile does not for that reason cease to be a marriage. The New Testament, including Jesus, gives no indication that infertility was a valid grounds for divorce. Both Jesus' and Paul's sense of the nearness of God's kingdom appears to have reduced the significance of procreation (cf. 1 Cor 7).

It is a human tendency to respond to marital conflict by fleeing, or at least disengaging emotionally, from one's spouse. God, however, wants husbands and wives to view even conflict as a means to a great end: conforming each partner more closely to the very "image of God" into which "male and female" were created as angled expressions of a two-faceted sexual whole (Gen 1:27). Because marriage is about reuniting two into "one flesh," what one does to one's spouse one does to one's own self. To love one's spouse is to love "oneself" or "one's own body" but to hate one's spouse is to hate "one's own flesh" (Eph 5:28–29). Retaliation in marriage produces a self-inflicted wound; in effect, cutting off one's nose to spite one's face.

Marriage is an important venue for learning to love another as oneself, even in, and perhaps especially in, moments when one is deeply hurt by the behavior of one's spouse. When we fail to respond in a Christ-like manner to our spouse, even a highly disagreeable spouse, we discover areas of our life that need to be surrendered to God. This discovery, in turn, opens up the prospect of learning more fully how to "deny oneself and take up one's cross" and "lose one's life" (Mark 8:34–35).

Paul viewed all of life's deprivations and difficulties as ideal moments when we learn that God's grace "is sufficient" for us, that God's "power is brought to completion in weakness," and that "the life of Jesus [is] manifested in our body" as we "carry around in the body the death of Jesus" (2 Cor 12:9–10; 4:10–11). Life's difficulties can feel like "a sentence of death" but they serve the useful purpose in God's sovereign plan of making us "rely not on ourselves but on the God who raises the dead" (2 Cor 2:9). As we die to ourselves, Christ more fully lives in us (Gal 2:19–20). Difficult marriages are no exception to this rule, but rather a great laboratory where we see this rule played out. In good times and in bad, God uses one's spouse—one's sexual "other half"—as the greatest daily human influence for forming Christ in one's self. Marriage's ultimate purpose follows from the ultimate purpose of all Christian life: namely, to be shaped into Christ's image.[9]

6. The Penultimate Significance of Sexual Intercourse and Marriage

The upshot of the previous point is that marriage serves a vital purpose, not merely for procreation and childrearing, sexual gratification and intimate companionship, but also for being reshaped, through reintegration with one's sexual complement, into the human being that God intends. However, this does not mean that one *must* be in a sexual relationship in order to be formed into God's image, for God has other means at his disposal to shape his human creation, including the difficulties of sexual abstinence (note Jesus' and Paul's own celibacy). Nevertheless, if a sexual relationship is to be had, it must be had in such a way that the image of God is enhanced, not effaced. The requirements for sexual purity always take precedence over longings for a sexual relationship, where the two are in conflict.

Consequently, Jesus could make strong demands for sexual purity as regards divorce and remarriage (Mark 10:2–12 par.; Matt 5:31–32 par.; 1 Cor 7: 10–11). For this reason, too, Jesus' and Paul's reference to celibacy as a gift (Matt 19:11; 1 Cor 7:7) cannot be used as a crowbar for prying loose prerequisites for sexual behavior (an argument often used to justify committed homosexual unions for persons not attracted to the other sex). There is a difference between imposing a celibacy requirement and maintaining prerequisites for a valid sexual relationship (cf. 1 Cor 5; 6:9). Persons who desire a sexual relationship but are unable to form one that meets the prerequisites can assume God's empowerment to abstain from sexual immorality.

Jesus believed that marriage, for all its benefits, had its drawbacks. When the disciples concluded, given Jesus' near-prohibition of divorce as a means to escaping a difficult marriage, that "it is not expedient to marry," Jesus merely qualified their conclusion by noting that "not all have the capacity" to carry out this conclusion by remaining single. He added that those who are capable of doing so have "made themselves eunuchs because of the kingdom of heaven" (Matt 19:10–12). Marriage involves a trade-off. On the one hand, it allows one to satisfy intense sexual urges, fulfill the command to procreate, experience a holistic reintegration with one's sexual complement, and undergo a rigorous reshaping of a self-centered character. On the other hand, this concentrated, daily, and lifelong remerging with one's sexual counterpart is hard, particularly in circumstances of recurring marital conflict and without divorce as an option. Moreover, it imposes special obligations and commitments that constrict one's flexibility, time, resources, and risk-taking for the kingdom of God. Had marriage been a better alternative to singleness, Jesus would have chosen it, especially considering the rarity of celibacy among Jewish men in Jesus' day and the religious pressure to marry and procreate.

Paul, also single by choice, is often blamed for selling marriage short with his remarks about wanting to spare those contemplating marriage the "difficult times" and the anxiety that comes from being focused on "the things of the world" (1 Cor 7:28–35). Yet his position was not materially different from the one stated by Jesus in Matthew 19:10–12.

Given the nature of the earthly body, sexual intimacy in the context of marriage is a good. However, according to Jesus, in their resurrected state people "neither marry, nor are given in marriage but are like the angels in heaven" (Mark 12:25 par. Luke 20:34–36; cf. 1 Cor 7:29, 31, 38). Earthly marriage in the flesh will be superseded by the heavenly marriage of the people of God to Christ. To say this is not to denigrate marriage, for Jesus obviously had the highest possible estimate of the importance of maintaining the marital bond, once entered. Yet it does give a sober evaluation of marriage's penultimate significance in this life, both encouraging the option of singleness to permit undivided service of God and insisting on prerequisites and standards for acceptable sexual activity.

A Challenge to Christian Sexual Ethics: Homosexual Practice

There are, of course, a number of issues that could be treated under the rubric of sexual ethics. Because of space limitations and its continuing relevance to the church and wider society, I have chosen to address the issue of homosexual practice. The issue is a vast one that cannot be covered comprehensively here. Instead I will focus on three important matters in the debate:

1. Jesus on the importance of a male-female prerequisite for sexual relations
2. The question of whether Scripture's indictment includes committed relationships
3. What constitutes the best analogies to Scripture's stance on homosexual practice

1. Jesus on the Importance of a Male-Female Prerequisite for Sexual Relations

Advocates of a homosexualist reading of Scripture often claim that Jesus had a favorable, or at least neutral, opinion of homosexual relationships. What the evidence really shows is that Jesus believed that a male-female requirement for sexual relations was foundational, a core value of Scripture's sexual ethics on which other sexual standards should be based.

Jesus predicated marital twoness—the restriction of the number of persons in a sexual union to two, whether concurrently (no polygamy) or serially (no cycle of divorce and remarriage)—on the fact that "from the beginning of creation, 'male and female He made them' [Gen 1:27] and 'for this reason a man...will be joined to his wife and the two will become one flesh' [Gen 2:24]" (Mark 10:2–12; Matt 19:3–9). In other words, the fact that God had designed two (and only two) primary sexes for complementary sexual pairing was Jesus' basis for a rigorous monogamy position. He reasoned that, since the union of the two sexual halves creates an integrated, self-contained sexual whole, a third sexual partner was neither necessary nor desirable. We know that this was Jesus' reasoning because the only other first-century Jews who shared Jesus' opposition to polygyny were the Essenes, who likewise rejected "taking two wives in their lives" because "the foundation of creation is 'male and female he created them'" (Gen 1:27) and because "those who entered [Noah's] ark went in two by two into the ark" (Gen 7:9; *Damascus Covenant* 4.20–5.1). The appeal to the "two by two" statement in the story of Noah's ark is significant because, apart from the repetition of Genesis 1:27 in 5:1, the ark narrative is the only other place where the precise Hebrew phrase *zākār ûnĕqēvāh* ("male and female") appears, and there it is strongly linked with the emphasis on a natural pair. The twoness of the sexes is the foundation for the twoness of the sexual bond. There is no other logical or nature-based argument for an absolute rejection of all polyamorous unions—even those unions that are adult-committed and show no scientifically measurable harm—than that the fundamental duality or twoness of the sexes precludes sexual unions involving three or more persons concurrently. In short, if society thinks that limiting the number of partners in a sexual union to two persons at any one time is an important requirement for sexual unions, then society should regard a male-female requirement as even more important.

There are many other arguments that one can cite as evidence of Jesus' rejection of homosexual practice, including the fact that the Old Testament that Jesus accepted as Scripture was strongly opposed; that the man who baptized Jesus (John the Baptist) was beheaded for criticizing Herod Antipas for violating Levitical sex laws (the incest prohibitions, even in adult-consensual relationships); that the entirety of early Judaism out of which Jesus emerged believed all homosexual practice to be a gross violation of foundational sexual ethics;[10] and that the early church that knew Jesus best was united in its belief that a male-female prerequisite for sexual unions was essential. The supposition of a Jesus supportive of, or even neutral toward, committed homosexual unions is without historical analogue in Jesus' immediate cultural environment. It is revisionist history at its worst. Moreover, although we have no extant saying of Jesus that loosened the Law's demand for sexual purity, we do have sayings where Jesus closed remaining loopholes in the Law's sexual commands by further intensifying God's demand (adultery of the heart; divorce and remarriage) and warning people that sexual impurity could get one thrown into hell full-bodied (Matt 5:27–32). The trend of Jesus' teaching on sexual ethics is not toward greater license but toward fewer loopholes. As already noted, that trend is not contradicted by his outreach to sinners but rather confirmed by it.

2. The Question of Whether Scripture's Indictment Includes Committed Relationships

Christians who support homosexual unions usually claim that the Bible's prohibition of homosexual practice applies only to exploitative and hedonistic forms of homosexual practice such as sex with slaves, prostitutes, and adolescents. What the evidence really shows is that the Bible's prohibition of homosexual practice, like its prohibition of adult incestuous unions, is absolute, rejecting all forms of homosexual practice regardless of consent and commitment. I will focus on five lines of evidence as they pertain to the key New Testament text that critiques homosexual practice, Romans 1:24–27.

First, Paul rejected homosexual practice because of what it was not and could never be: namely, the one model of human sexual relations ordained by God at creation according to Genesis 1–2. In Romans 1:23–27, Paul intentionally echoed Genesis 1:26–27, making eight points of correspondence, in the same tripartite structure, between the two sets of texts (humans/image/likeness, birds/cattle/reptiles, male/female). Homosexual practice for Paul was a violation of the male-female prerequisite for sexual relations ordained by the Creator at creation, irrespective of how well or badly it was done in his cultural milieu.

Second, the kind of nature argument that Paul employs in Rom 1:18–27 is not conducive to a distinction between exploitative and nonexploitative forms of homosexual practice. For Paul contended that female-female and male-male intercourse was "contrary to nature" because it violated obvious clues given in the material structures of creation that male and female, not two males or two females, are each other's sexual "counterpart" or "complement" (to use the language of Genesis 2:18, 20) in terms of anatomy, physiology, and psychology. What Paul says regarding the vertical vice of idolatry (1:19–23) is equally true of the horizontal vice of same-sex intercourse: male-female complementarity is "clearly seen, being mentally apprehended *by means of the things made*" (1:19–20). Some have argued that the ancients had no comprehension of a complementarity argument. Yet as classicist Thomas K. Hubbard notes in his magisterial sourcebook of texts pertaining to homosexuality in Greece and Rome: "Basic to the heterosexual position [among Greek and Roman moralists in the first few centuries C.E.] is the characteristic Stoic appeal to the providence of Nature, which has matched and fitted the sexes to each other."[11]

Third, in Romans 1:27, Paul specifically indicts male homosexual relations that involve mutual, reciprocal affections—"males . . . were inflamed with their yearning *for one another*"—thus precluding any supposition that Paul is thinking only of coercive relationships.

Fourth, Paul's indictment of lesbianism in Romans 1:26 further confirms that his indictment of homosexual practice is absolute, since female homosexuality in antiquity was not primarily known, or criticized, for the exploitative practices of sex with slaves, prostitutes, or children. Despite occasional claims to the contrary by homosexualist interpreters, there can be little doubt that Paul was indicting female homosexuality, as evidenced by: (1) the parallelism of the language of 1:26 ("females exchanged the natural use") and 1:27 ("likewise also the males leaving behind the natural use *of the female*"); (2) the fact that in antiquity lesbian intercourse was the form of female intercourse most commonly labeled "contrary to nature" and most commonly paired with male homosexual practice; (3) the fact of nearly universal male opposition to lesbianism in antiquity, even by men engaged in homosexual practice; and (4) the fact that lesbian intercourse was the dominant interpretation of Romans 1:26 in the patristic period (probably Clement of Alexandria and the *Apocalypse of Peter*; certainly "Ambrosiaster" and John Chrysostom).

Fifth, contrary to the false claim that ancients could not even conceive of committed homosexual relationships, there is plenty of evidence for the conception and existence of loving homosexual relationships in the Greco-Roman world, including semi-official "marriages" between men and between women.[12] Moreover, we know of some Greco-Roman moralists who acknowledged the existence of loving homosexual relationships while rejecting even these as unnatural (e.g., Plutarch, *Dialogue on Love* 751C–E [5]; cf. Plato's *Laws* 636B–D, 836B–842A). This is also true of the Church Fathers. For example, Clement of Alexandria (late second century) referred to "women . . . contrary to nature . . . marrying women" (*Paidagogos* 3.3.21.3). Obviously marriage implies commitment (else there is no need to marry) yet commitment does not change the unnatural and sinful character of the relationship.

Given the five considerations noted above, it is hardly surprising that even Louis Crompton, a homosexual scholar, acknowledges the absolute character of Paul's indictment. "However well-intentioned," the interpretation that "Paul's words were not directed at 'bona fide' homosexuals in committed relationships" appears "strained and unhistorical," he writes. "Nowhere does Paul or any other Jewish writer of this period imply the least acceptance of same-sex relations under any circumstance. The idea that homosexuals might be redeemed by mutual devotion would have been wholly foreign to Paul or any other Jew or early Christian."[13]

Also worth noting is the falsity of claims that the ancient world knew nothing akin to our understanding of a homosexual orientation or of congenital influences on at least some homosexual development. As Hubbard notes: "Homosexuality in this era [i.e., the early Imperial Age of Rome] may have ceased to be merely another practice of personal pleasure and began to be viewed as an essential and central category of personal identity, exclusive of and antithetical to heterosexual orientation."[14] Bernadette Brooten, a lesbian New Testament scholar who has written the most important book on lesbianism in antiquity, also acknowledges this point: "Paul could have believed" that some persons attracted to members of the same sex "were born that way and yet still condemn them as unnatural and shameful. . . . I see Paul as condemning *all* forms of homoeroticism as the unnatural acts of people who had turned away from God."[15]

3. What Constitutes the Best Analogies to Scripture's Stance on Homosexual Practice

Christian proponents of homosexual relationships generally claim that the closest analogies to the Bible's opposition to homosexual practice are the Bible's support for both slavery and the oppression of women and its opposition to divorce, all positions that we now reject. What the evidence really shows is that these alleged analogies are far more remote than the analogies of the Bible's opposition to incest and the New Testament's opposition to polygamy—behaviors that would disqualify any candidate from ordained office, even when the relationships in question are adult, consensual, committed, and exhibit no scientifically measurable harm.

Homosexual practice, incest, and polyamory (sexual love for multiple persons concurrently) are all sexual behaviors proscribed absolutely in one or both Testaments of Scripture, despite the fact that all three can be conducted as caring and committed adult sexual relationships. Incest is ultimately prohibited on the grounds that it is sexual intercourse with a person who, in terms of embodied existence, is too much of a "same" or like on a kinship level (compare Leviticus 18:6: "no one shall approach any *flesh of one's flesh* to uncover nakedness"). The higher risks of procreative difficulties that attend fertile incestuous unions are merely the symptom of the root problem: too much identity between close blood relations.

Similarly, the inability of persons of the same sex to procreate is merely the symptom of the root problem: too much embodied identity, here as regards gender or sex, between persons of the same sex. If anything, the identity is more keenly felt in same-sex intercourse than incest, since sex or gender is a more integral component of sexuality than blood relatedness. As regards polygamy or polyamory, we have already seen in point 1 above that Jesus predicated his rejection of such behavior on God's creation of two sexes for complementary sexual pairing. So a two-sexes prerequisite for sexual relations and a limitation of the number of persons in a sexual union to two are related as foundation and superstructure (the latter being built on the former).

Slavery is a bad analogy to the Bible's opposition to homosexual practice because, first, the Bible shows no vested interest in preserving slavery but rather at a number of points has a critical edge against slavery (for example, having mandatory release dates, maintaining the right of kin to buy loved ones out of slavery at any time, insisting that fellow Israelites not be treated as slaves). Relative to the slave cultures of the ancient Near East and Greco-Roman Mediterranean basin, the countercultural thrust of the Scriptures is against slavery. However, as regards a male-female requirement for sexual relations, the Bible's critical edge and countercultural thrust is decidedly opposed to all homosexual practice. Second, whereas race or ethnicity is a 100 percent heritable, absolutely immutable, and primarily nonbehavioral condition, and so inherently benign, homosexual desire is an impulse and, like many impulses, it is not 100 percent heritable (there may be congenital influences but these are not deterministic), is open to some change (even if only, in some cases, a limited reduction in the intensity of impulses), is primarily behavioral (here for unnatural, that is, structurally incompatible, sexual activity), and therefore is not inherently benign. Third, the parallel with slavery lies with support for homosexual unions, not opposition to such, since those insisting that homosexual desires be affirmed by the church are promoting enslavement to impulses to do what God in Scripture expressly forbids.

The Bible's stance toward women's roles is a bad analogy for similar reasons. First, proposing an analogy between being a woman and having homoerotic impulses confuses categories. Being a woman, unlike a homosexual impulse, is a condition that is 100 percent congenital, absolutely immutable, and not a direct desire for behavior that Scripture expressly forbids. Second, there are plenty of positive views of women in Scripture (for example, the roles played by Judge Deborah and Ruth in the Old Testament, Jesus' commendation of female discipleship, and Paul's salute to women coworkers in the New Testament), but only strongly negative assessments of homosexual practice. As with the issue of slavery, the countercultural thrust of Scripture leans in the direction both of supporting egalitarian roles for women and of opposing homosexual practice more stringently and consistently than anywhere else in the ancient world.

Divorce and remarriage after divorce also have serious problems as analogues to the Bible's prohibition of homosexual practice, for three reasons. First, in Scripture divorce and remarriage is simply not viewed as bad as homosexual practice.

As already noted, Jesus predicated his opposition to divorce and remarriage on the foundation that God created us as "male and female," a self-contained sexual pair. The foundation is always more important than the superstructure built on it. Logically it is not possible to justify license in a greater matter by limited license in a lesser matter. For example, it would be illegitimate to argue that greater tolerance toward divorce and remarriage should lead to greater tolerance toward adult-committed incest or "plural" marriages, for the latter two offenses are regarded as more severe. Moreover, there is no virtue to being more consistently disobedient to the will of Christ. Second, the Bible shows a limited canonical diversity toward divorce (permitted for men in the Old Testament; in the New Testament allowed in cases of sexual immorality or marriage to an unbeliever who insists on leaving) but no diversity on the matter of homosexual practice. There are also ameliorating factors in the case of some divorce situations that simply do not apply in the case of a consensual homosexual union. For example, a spouse can be divorced against her or his will or be subject to regular and serious abuse, which creates perpetrator versus victim distinctions irrelevant to a voluntary entrance into a homosexual union. Third, and most importantly, the church's stance toward divorce/remarriage on the one hand and homosexual practice on the other are alike in this respect: the church works to end the cycle. The church would not ordain any candidate for office who expressed the view: "I've been divorced and remarried a number of times and would like to continue the cycle with the fewest negative side-effects." Such a person could not be ordained because that person has an unreformed mind. Why, then, should the church ordain someone who not only engaged in homosexual practice on multiple occasions in the past but also intends to continue in such behavior in a serial, unrepentant way?

Often church proponents of homosexual unions also cite the story in Acts 10–11, 15 about the church's inclusion of Gentiles without requiring circumcision and observance of dietary law. This too is a bad analogy, for many reasons. First, a male-female prerequisite for sexual relations is grounded in creation whereas a circumcision requirement and dietary commands are not so grounded. Second, whereas circumcision was a Jewish ritual prescription enjoined only on those Gentiles who became proselytes to Judaism, affecting the body only superficially, the Bible's prohibition of homosexual practice was regarded as a universal moral proscription enjoined on all Gentiles because sexual immorality affects the body holistically. Both Jesus (Mark 7:14–23) and Paul (1 Cor 6:12–20) forbade comparisons between food laws and prohibitions of sexual immorality, and yet proponents of homosexual unions continue to make such comparisons. Third, whereas Gentile inclusion in the first century was about welcoming Gentile believers while rejecting the sexual behaviors that Scripture categorically regards as immoral, today's efforts at normalizing homosexual practice are about accepting precisely such behaviors. Fourth, whereas Scripture only incidentally links Gentiles to sin (that is, it recognizes the category of righteous or God-fearing Gentiles), Scripture intrinsically links homosexual practice to sin. Fifth, whereas Gentile inclusion has significant Old Testament precedent (for example, the stories of Rahab, Ruth, the widow at Zarephath,

Naaman, and Jonah) and uniform New Testament support, homosexual practice is totally rejected in all parts of Scripture. It is absurd to argue for affirmation of homosexual unions as the Spirit's new work inasmuch as it puts the Spirit at odds with Scripture's core values in sexual ethics.

A principle of good analogical reasoning is: The closest, and thus best, analogies are those that share the most substantive points of correspondence with the thing being compared. Honest analogical reasoning does not prefer far analogies over close analogies. Consequently, it is inappropriate to stress the alleged analogies of slavery, women's roles, divorce, and first-century Gentile inclusion while ignoring both the enormous differences with the Bible's stance on homosexual practice and the more substantive parallels to the Bible's position on incest and polyamory.

NOTES

1. Cf. Jesus' comparison of anger toward a brother with murder (Matt 5:21–26); his saying about the defiling effect not so much of what goes in a man's stomach as what emanates from a person's heart (Mark 7:15–23); and his criticism of the Pharisees for cleaning the outside of the "cup" but not the inside (Matt 23:25–26 par. Luke 11:39–41).

2. For example, the Decalogue commandments against adultery with another man's wife (Exod 20:14, 17; Deut 5:18, 21); the fine imposed on a man who has intercourse with a virgin (Exod 22:16–17) or who falsely charges that he did not find evidence of his wife's virginity on their wedding night (Deut 22:13–19); the sex laws in Lev 18 and 20 against incest, adultery, intercourse between males, and bestiality (compare also Deut 22:30; 27:20–23); the waters-of-bitterness ordeal for women suspected of adultery (Num 5:11–31); the capital sentence imposed on men and willing women who commit adultery, along with treating as adultery intercourse with an engaged woman (Deut 22:20–29).

3. Cf. 1 Thess 4:3–8; 1 Cor 5–7; 10:8, 12; 2 Cor 12:21; Gal 5:19–21 (cf. 6:7–9); Rom 1:24–27; 6:19; 13:12–14; cf. Col 3:5–10; Eph 4:17–19; 5:3–6; 1 Tim 1:9–11; outside the Gospels and Pauline literature, see the Apostolic Decree in Acts 15:20, 29; 21:25; and Heb 12:16; 13:4; Jude 7; 1 Pet 4:2–5; 2 Pet 2:4–10, 13–16; Rev 2:14, 20–21; 9:20–21; 21:8; 22:15.

4. For his outreach to tax collectors, the biggest economic exploiters among fellow Jews in first-century Palestine, see Mark 2:15–17; Matt 11:19 par. Luke 7:34; Luke 7:37–39; 15:1–10; 18:13; 19:7. For his outreach to sexual sinners, see Matt 21:31–32; Luke 7:36–50; 15:30; John 4:16–18; 7:53–8:11.

5. For example, Matt 7:13–27 par. Luke 13:23–27; 6:43–49; Luke 10:13–15 par. Matt 11:22–24; Mark 8:34–37 par.

6. For example, Gen 2:18–24; 29:9–30; Deut 24:5; Prov 5:15–23; Eccl 9:9; Mal 2:13–16; plus the entirety of the Song of Solomon.

7. Cf. Hos 2:16–20; Jer 2:2; Ezek 16:8; Isa 54:5–8; 61:10; 62:4–5; Mark 2:19–20; Matt 22:1–14; 25:1–13; John 3:29; 2 Cor 11:2; Eph 5:27, 31–32; Rev 19:7–9; 21:2, 9.

8. Thus Paul, in making a point about the unique potency of sexual sin on the body, states that all sexual activity, even casual sexual intercourse with a prostitute, joins the participants into "one body" (1 Cor 6:15–18).

9. For being shaped into the image of Christ as a prime goal of life, see Gal 4:19; 2:19–20; Rom 8:29; 6:1–14; 2 Cor 4:7–12; Phil 3:10.

10. For example, Josephus in *Against Apion* 2:199: "The law [of Moses] recognizes only sexual intercourse that is according to nature, that which is with a woman.... But it abhors the intercourse of males with males."

11. Thomas K. Hubbard, ed., *Homosexuality in Greece and Rome: A Sourcebook of Basic Documents* (Berkeley: University of California Press, 2003), 444.

12. Cf. Plato, *Symposium* 181D, 183E, 192E; Martial 1:24; 12:42; Juvenal, *Satire* 2; Plutarch, *Dialogue on Love* 750D, 752C; Xenophon of Ephesus, *An Ephesian Tale* 3.2; Achilles Tatius, *Leucippe and Clitophon* 1.7–8, 12–14, 33–34; Lucian of Samosata, *Dialogues of the Courtesans* 5; Ptolemy of Alexandria, *Tetrabiblos* 3.14; Pseudo-Lucian, *Affairs of the Heart* 46, 48.

13. Louis Crompton, *Homosexuality and Civilization* (Cambridge: Harvard University Press, 2003), 114.

14. Hubbard, *Homosexuality in Greece and Rome*, 386.

15. Bernadette J. Brooten, *Love between Women: Early Christian Responses to Female Homoeroticism* (Chicago: University of Chicago Press, 1996), 244.

BIBLIOGRAPHY

Brooten, Bernadette J. *Love between Women: Early Christian Responses to Female Homoeroticism*. Chicago: University of Chicago Press, 1996.

Campbell, Ken M., ed. *Marriage and Family in the Biblical World*. Downers Grove, Ill.: InterVarsity, 2003.

Collins, Raymond F. *Sexual Ethics and the New Testament: Behavior and Belief*. New York: Crossroad, 2000.

Davidson, Richard M. *The Flame of Yahweh: Sexuality in the Old Testament*. Peabody, Mass.: Hendrickson, 2007.

Gagnon, Robert A. J. "Are There Universally Valid Sex Precepts?" *Horizons in Biblical Theology* 24 (2002): 72–125. Also online at www.robgagnon.net.

———. *The Bible and Homosexual Practice: Texts and Hermeneutics*. Nashville, Tenn.: Abingdon, 2001. For other materials, see www.robgagnon.net.

———. "A Book Not to Be Embraced: A Critical Appraisal of Stacy Johnson's *A Time to Embrace*." *Scottish Journal of Theology* 62 (2009): 61–80.

———. "Old Testament and Homosexuality." *Zeitschrift für die Alttestamentliche Wissenschaft* 117 (2005): 367–394.

———. "Scriptural Perspectives on Homosexuality and Sexual Identity." *Journal of Psychology and Christianity* 24 (2005): 293–303. Also at www.robgagnon.net.

———. "Why the Disagreement over the Biblical Witness on Homosexual Practice?" *Reformed Review* 59 (2005): 19–130. Online at: http://www.westernsem.edu/files/westernsem/gagnon_autm05_0.pdf.

Gagnon, Robert A. J., and Dan O. Via. *Homosexuality and the Bible: Two Views*. Minneapolis: Fortress, 2003.

Grenz, Stanley J. *Sexual Ethics: An Evangelical Perspective*. Louisville, Ky.: Westminster John Knox, 1997.

———. *Welcoming but Not Affirming: An Evangelical Response to Homosexuality*. Louisville, Ky.: Westminster John Knox, 1998.

Hubbard, Thomas K., ed. *Homosexuality in Greece and Rome: A Sourcebook of Basic Documents*. Berkeley: University of California Press, 2003.

Hugenberger, Gordon P. *Marriage as a Covenant: Biblical Law and Ethics as Developed from Malachi*. Grand Rapids: Baker, 1994.

Hays, Richard B. *The Moral Vision of the New Testament: A Contemporary Introduction to New Testament Ethics*. San Francisco: HarperCollins, 1996.

Instone-Brewer, David. *Divorce and Remarriage in the Bible: The Social and Literary Context*. Grand Rapids: Eerdmans, 2002.

Loader, William. *Sexuality and the Jesus Tradition*. Grand Rapids: Eerdmans, 2005.

Roberts, Christopher Chenault. *Creation and Covenant: The Significance of Sexual Difference in the Moral Theology of Marriage*. New York: T & T Clark, 2007.

Smedes, Lewis B. *Sex for Christians*, rev. ed. Grand Rapids: Eerdmans, 1994.

Webb, William J. *Slaves, Women, and Homosexuals: Exploring the Hermeneutics of Cultural Analysis*. Downers Grove, Ill.: InterVarsity, 2001.

Note: Owing to space limitations, Dr. Gagnon's discussion of divorce and remarriage has been moved from this chapter to his website: "Divorce and Remarriage-After-Divorce in Jesus and Paul" at http://www.robgagnon.net/articles/OHETDivorceRemarriage.pdf.

CHAPTER 30

RACE

TIMOTHY TSENG

Christianity in the twenty-first century is marked by an increasing recognition of its own globalization. The growth of Christianity in Africa, Asia, and Latin America, accompanied by its increased ethnic diversity in Europe and North America, demonstrate that Christianity can no longer be identified as the religion of "white" people in the West. Though European and North American churches are still dominant, there are clear signs that an era is coming to an end. Coinciding with this development is the diminishing scientific and moral credibility of the "racial" lens. The racial hierarchy created during Euro-America colonial expansion has been undermined in the twentieth century.[1]

Nevertheless, race persists. For instance, the eruption of religion-inspired violence and brutal acts of ethnic cleansing in the post-Cold War era has led many to suspect that the modern ideologies of race and practices of racism have morphed into something different, yet strangely familiar. The delegates at the Twenty-Third General Council of the World Alliance of Reformed Churches in Debrecen, Hungary (1997), noted that "Around the globe today we are experiencing a resurgence of what has been called a 'new tribalism'—a reaffirmation of group identities." Four years later, the Roman Catholic Pontifical Council for Justice and Peace observed that "disagreements are growing sharper, ethnic violence is increasing [and] the quest for group, ethnic or national identity is becoming more relentless as the stranger and those who are different are rejected, to such a degree that at times barbarous acts are committed against them." According to the Faith and Order Commission of the World Council of Churches (2005), the current context calls for "a re-examination of what it means to affirm the humanity of all people."

Indeed, finding appropriate theological responses to human diversity and dignity are some of the greatest challenges for Church today, for the concept of race remains at the core of human differentiation and conflict. This chapter surveys the history of the modern concept of race and various theological responses, thus making a modest contribution to theological anthropology.

One of this chapter's assumptions is that modern racial ideology and racism emerged from the contexts of European and American global dominance between the sixteenth and mid-twentieth centuries. Premodern forms of ethnocentrism are qualitatively different from the modern ideology of race. According to Alan T. Davies, "ethnocentrism is a universal instinct to identify humankind with the members of one's own tribe, community, [and] nation, and to regard outsiders as less than fully human."[2] Racism emerged when the nationalist and economic aspirations of European colonial regimes suppressed and exploited "outsiders" and justified these practices by linking the physiological features of non-Europeans to subhuman inferiority. Natural sciences, Orientalist scholarship, and Darwinism in the nineteenth century further engrained in the minds of Europeans and North Americans the belief in the racial gradation of human intelligence, morality, and value. These assumptions are, of course, not self-evident. This chapter's first section will therefore examine how twentieth-century trends in the study of race have shifted away from natural sciences and toward a social constructionist definition of race.

Evangelical theologians have given little attention to race. But this does not mean that theological engagement with race and racism has been nonexistent. Until the modern era, Western theological anthropology largely focused on topics such as election, reprobation, free will, and predestination. Most theologians acknowledged that Christ's "elect" would come from every nation and tribe, but few questioned the natural inequality of humanity—a concept rooted in ancient Greco-Roman philosophy. Slavery and servitude were not yet associated with race and went largely unquestioned until the eighteenth century. But even before the Enlightenment, theological foundations were laid that challenged attempts to enslave and render non-European people inferior on the basis of their race. These early developments can be traced to Catholic missionary encounters with non-Europeans and Renaissance humanism. Pietism, the evangelical awakenings, Enlightenment philosophy, and the Social Gospel would later be associated with the abolitionist and civil rights movements. In all these cases, theologians were challenged to incorporate human experience and ethical critique into their theological methodology. Those who did so were more responsive to modern racial ideologies and racist practices.

The Transformation of Race in the Twentieth Century

At the beginning of the century, many political and religious leaders proclaimed the Anglo-Saxon "race" the redeemer of the "dark" and "heathen" world. Standing on a century of "empirical" evidence, respected scholars and scientists placed Caucasians atop the racial hierarchy. Laws were established to maintain racial purity, segregation, and exclusion. The racial order was reinforced through media stereotypes and frequent outbreaks of violence. By the end of the twentieth century, however, racist attitudes were deemed morally bankrupt, segregation and anti-miscegenation were outlawed, and biologically based definitions of race and racial hierarchy were soundly rejected. How did this transformation happen?

In the academy, natural science definitions of racial difference were abandoned by mid-century. The early anthropological work of Franz Boas (1858–1942) and his students Ruth Benedict (1887–1948) and Ashley Montagu (1905–1999) in the late 1930s, the publication of Julian Huxley and A. C. Haddon's book, *We Europeans: A Survey of "Racial" Problems* (1936), followed by Montagu's publication of *Man's Most Dangerous Myth: The Fallacy of Race* (1942), dramatically changed the social scientific debate. The concept of race was now deemed bogus.[3] Beginning with Richard C. Lewontin's "The Apportionment of Human Diversity" in *Evolutionary Biology* (1972), scientists have accumulated enough data on human genetic variation to conclude that racial difference is not biologically significant.

In 1998 the American Anthropological Association issued the following statement: "Evidence from the analysis of genetics (e.g., DNA) indicates that most physical variation, about 94%, lies within so-called racial groups. Conventional geographic 'racial' groupings differ from one another only in about 6% of their genes. This means that there is greater variation within 'racial' groups than between them." It concludes "that present-day inequalities between so-called 'racial' groups are not consequences of their biological inheritance but products of historical and contemporary social, economic, educational, and political circumstances." In other words, race is primarily a socially constructed worldview.[4]

But many years earlier, intellectual historians such as Thomas Gossett (1916–2005) and Winthrop D. Jordan (1931–2007) had argued that race was primarily an ideology used to justify European attitudes, treatment, and control of conquered and enslaved peoples. Race exaggerated differences among Europeans, Africans, indigenous people, and Asians. It created rigid racial hierarchies and rankings and linked superior traits to Europeans and negative ones to other races. It also provided the rationale for believing that racial inequity was natural or God-given.[5]

Recent studies have further elaborated on the socioeconomic and political factors in the social construction of race and racism. Howard Winant and Michael Omi are credited with introducing an integrated concept of the process of racial construction or "racialization." They argue that, in America, the different races and the meanings assigned to each race are products of the interaction of social, economic, and political forces.[6] The social construction of race has sometimes been used to justify "color-blindness." It is argued that because race is not a biological reality, any discussion of racial difference can be construed as perpetuating an illusion. Thus, many have advocated against using race in data collection and eliminating affirmative action social policies.

But most scholars argue that the social construction of race does not render racism impotent. Race may not be scientifically grounded, but institutional or structural racism persists. Unlike racial bigotry or prejudice, there is no sole, identifiable perpetrator in institutional and structural racism. These types of racism occur when what appears to be an institutional or societal norm leads to outcomes against nonwhite people. Analyses of institutional and structural racism do not attribute these outcomes solely to race, but also take into account their complex interactions with economic and political interests. Indeed, race may not even have to be mentioned. Unpaved streets and roads in predominantly black communities or the use of outdated and used textbooks in predominantly black public schools are typical examples. Sociologist Eduardo Bonilla-Silva aptly sums up these types of racism as the allocation of "differential economic, political, social, and even psychological rewards to groups along racial lines: lines that are socially constructed."[7]

These differential outcomes fuel persistent negative stereotypes, which further perpetuate institutional and structural racism. Although there is evidence of improvement, continued patterns of racial segregation and structural racism still impact interpersonal relationships. Social construction theory may have undermined the explanations of natural science, but the edifice of race and racism leaned heavily, but not entirely, on the pillar of scientific legitimacy.

Theology and the Construction of Modern Racial Ideology

Christian theology has had an uneasy relationship with modern racial ideology. On the one hand, because Christianity so successfully ensconced itself into Western society, it absorbed European philosophical and culture worldviews—including those that reinforced racial hierarchies. On the other hand, some Christians distanced themselves from ideas about race that contradicted theological affirmations about the unity and dignity of humankind. The inhumane treatment of people of other "races" during European global expansion and dominance prompted some to reexamine socially accepted assumptions that were embedded into the theological anthropology of their day.

Theological Anthropology before Race

Christian theologians in past eras have always reflected on human nature and differentiation. Several themes in Augustine's *City of God*, for example, have had important implications for Western theological engagement with modern race and racism:

The goodness of creation: Augustine is critical of Origen's belief that human bodies are merely "houses of correction" for souls who sinned by turning away from God prior to creation. Though he affirms a tripartite division of humans into spirit, soul, and body, Augustine rejected the belief that the body is evil. As a part of the created order, the body is essentially good because the Creator God is good. (Book 6:23)

The gradation of beings. Augustine writes,

> Among those beings which exist, and which are not of God the Creator's essence, those which have life are ranked above those which have none; those that have the power of generation, or even of desiring, above those which want this faculty. And, among things that have life, the sentient are higher than those which have no sensation, as animals are ranked above trees. And, among the sentient, the intelligent are above those that have not intelligence,—men, e.g., above cattle. And, among the intelligent, the immortal such as the angels, above the mortal, such as men. These are the gradations according to the order of nature. (Book 6:16)

Here Augustine reinforces the *scala naturae* (the "Great Chain of Being"), a concept that can be traced to Greek philosophy. Gradations within humanity were sometimes asserted by others, but not by Augustine. The Great Chain of Being persisted well into the nineteenth century, when racial hierarchy became the norm for human classification.[8]

The unity and rationality of humanity. Augustine recognized gradations in creation, but did not believe that human physical differences were of the same order. All humans shared one common ancestor and "one blood." "But who could enumerate all the human births that have differed widely from their ascertained parents?" Augustine noted, "As, therefore, no one will deny that these are all descended from that one man, so all the races which are reported to have diverged in bodily appearance from the usual course which nature generally or almost universally preserves, if they are embraced in that definition of man as rational and mortal animals, unquestionably trace their pedigree to that one first father of all" (Book 16:8). Rationality is the central characteristic of the *imago dei*, which distinguishes humans from animals.

The universality of the Christian faith. Augustine is explicit about the universality of the Christian faith. Indeed, one of the purposes of the *City of God* is to question Rome's demands for the highest loyalty of Christians. Citizens of the Heavenly City come from all nations and walks of life. Those who are God's "elect" are not limited to one nationality or language group.

After Augustine, Christian theologians continued to include the study of humanity and creation in their work. In the scholastic tradition, for instance, anthropology and natural sciences were considered the "material object of theology"—subordinate to the "purer" study of God and Christian doctrine, yet worthy of the theologian's attention.

Catholic Missionaries and the Iberian Empires

Race and nationalism "are the Siamese twins of modernity," notes historian Philip Nicholson. Non-Christian Europeans and people in the New World, Africa, and Asia were "turned into races" as European nation-states extended their political hegemony. The vilification of other "races" came about "after the expropriation of their land, labor, or other forms of wealth and the conflict that followed." Finally, rationalizations about the inferiority of the dispossessed justified the "legally enforced and institutionally encoded national practices of expropriation, coercion, displacement, and death of the formally vilified people."[9]

The *reconquista* and the conquest of the New World illustrate how race was created as the Spanish crown consolidated its power. About 300,000 Jews and Moors became Christians or faced expulsion during the *reconquista*. Many descendants of the *converses* benefited from their Christian identity and advanced in the civil or ecclesial hierarchies. This led to charges of heterodoxy by those who were jealous of their growing wealth, power, and influence. The Inquisition, established to screen out heresy, soon focused on heredity. Eventually, only those of "pure" Spanish descent (i.e., *limpieza de sangre*) were permitted to seek office in the church, while those of Jewish and Moorish descent did not qualify. This introduction of "bloodline purity" opened the doors to biologically based racial differences.[10]

Shortly after their arrival to the New World, Spanish *conquistadores* imported the feudal *encomienda* labor system to the Americas and the Philippines. The Spanish Crown gave colonists restricted property rights over indigenous labor, which led to the extraction of tributes from the indigenous people in the form of goods, metals, money, and labor. In return, the *encomendero* (Spanish policy holder) was to provide protection and instruction in the Christian faith for the laborers. But the system rapidly broke down, and the indigenous people, whose population was already decimated by diseases introduced by newcomers, suffered tremendous abuse at the hands of the Spaniards. To justify the brutality, many colonists considered the "Indians" wild beasts and savages, and questioned whether they were fully human at all.

The coupling of European nation-state formation with racial ideology does not mean that suspicions about cultural or ethnic differences did not exist prior to the fifteenth century. Impressions of the "other" were already deeply embedded in the European popular imagination. Shrouded in mystery and facts, Europeans created ill-defined images and ideas about non-European people. As Iberian, Dutch, French, and English explorers, merchants, colonizers, and missionaries competed to dominate the New World, they brought these perceptions of the "other" with them. But it was the nation-state that turned such sentiments into racism.

Although complicit in European expansionism, the Catholic Church also sought to curtail the growing power of the nation-state though its missionary work and response to the exploitation of the indigenous peoples. The missionaries generated new theological reflections about the nature and appropriate treatment of the racial "other," particularly as racial perceptions hardened. Bartolomé de las Casas, O.P. (1484–1566), for example, devoted his life to abolishing the enslavement and abuse of "Indians." His first book, *The Only Way to Draw All People to a Living Faith* (1534), was a response to Fray Domingo de Betanzo's claim that it was useless to convert the Indians because they were incapable of faith and doomed to extinction for their past sins. Las Casas argued that Betanzo's doctrine of predestination was erroneous. The elect comprised all people. Furthermore, he argued, missionary work must not be accompanied by military coercion, and the Spanish must restore all that they had taken from the Indians. Later he rebutted Juan Gines de Sepulveda, who argued that the native people were inferior and should be pacified forcefully, in the *Defense of the Indian Civilization*. Here he utilized Aristotelian categories to compare Indians favorably to the ancient Greeks and Romans.

Las Casas's theological writings helped lay the foundations for the doctrine of universal human rights. Many of his ideas found their way into the works of Francisco de Vitoria (1486–1546), a defender of the Indian rights, critic of violent colonialism, and founder of international law. Furthermore, his activities led to the abolition of the *encomiendas* through passage of the New Laws (1542) and influenced the Catholic Church's support for the rights of Indians. In the face of attempts to racialize and dehumanize the Indians, Las Casas's chief contribution to theological anthropology can be summed up in Pope Paul III's bull *Sublimis Deus* (1537). The bull denounced the view that "the inhabitants of the West Indies and the southern continents...should be treated like irrational animals and used exclusively for our profit and our service." The bull affirmed that "in the desire to remedy the evil which has been caused, We hereby decide and declare that the said Indians, as well as any other peoples which Christianity will come to know in the future, must not be deprived of their freedom and their possessions—regardless of contrary allegations—even if they are not Christians and that, on the contrary, they must be left to enjoy their freedom and their possessions."

Open Hearts and Open Minds: The Impact of the Awakenings and the Enlightenment

During their initial empire-building forays, Europeans justified conflict with and exploitation of indigenous peoples and the enslavement of Africans by placing these "races" beneath Europeans in the Great Chain of Being. Prior to the Enlightenment, Catholic and Protestant theologians embraced the Great Chain but did not necessarily apply it to race. The great missionary achievement was to ensure that non-Europeans were defined as fully human and deserving of humane treatment. Historians debate the effectiveness of the missionary's theological anthropology, but this episode demonstrates a central principle. Many theological advances regarding "race" have emerged from a deeper engagement with classical doctrines of human unity and dignity, often in response to social realities on the mission field. Openness to human experience and willingness to engage the racial "other" was often an important prerequisite.

"Doctrine the rider and humanities the horse": Protestant Reformers and Humanism

Before the births of the nation-state and race, Renaissance humanism inspired a vision that elevated human status higher than scholastic theologies were willing to embrace. In retrieving classical Greek and Latin texts, humanists showed great respect for "pagan" writers without abandoning their Christian faith. "No racially disparaging art or sculpture is characteristic of this period," according to Nicholson, "indeed, many works depict African royalty or aristocracy as analogous with contemporary Europeans. The Three Wise Men of the East are most often depicted in paintings that include a darkly hued and well-dressed African, known as Balthazar, as part of the adoring Magi in attendance at the birth of Christ."[11]

Though humanism is associated with Catholic theologians such as Erasmus, it also influenced many Protestant leaders. Luther, Calvin, and Zwingli were trained in the *studia humanitatis*, a curriculum comprised by grammar, rhetoric, moral philosophy, poetry and history as studied via classical authors. They replaced scholasticism with the humanist curriculum whenever possible. However, for them "doctrine was always the rider and the humanities the horse." Steven Ozment notes that the "humanities became for Protestant theologians what Aristotelian philosophy had been to late medieval theologians—the favored handmaiden of theology; the rhetorical arts served the more basic task of communicating true doctrine." Furthermore, the Reformers favored the idea that doctrine cannot be supported by philosophical arguments and thus eroded the medieval alliance between reason and faith laid out by Thomas Aquinas. Therefore they were reluctant to subject their teaching to moral critique and did not allow ethics to "sit in judgment" on the truth of their doctrine. "It became the hallmark of the Anabaptist, Spiritualist, and rational critics of the Reformation, almost all of whom were deeply influenced by Erasmus, to make moral results the test of doctrinal truth and to criticize the followers of Luther, Zwingli, and Calvin for failing to improve the moral quality of life."[12]

Such criticism of Calvin and his followers may have been exaggerated, but if it is true that Calvinism at some points refused moral critique, then was possible for theology to detach itself from issues such as slavery, human rights, and race. Furthermore, many high Calvinists believed that predestination allowed them to ignore the fate of those outside the Church. During the Puritan era, these theological assumptions commingled with the idea of a pure Anglo-Saxon church and helped create an exclusivist national identity. This national identity was gradually reshaped along racial lines in the British North American colonies as settlers interacted with Native Americans and enslaved Africans. But at this point, belief in the natural inferiority of non-Europeans was not fully embraced by leading Christian theologians.[13] Nor did it garner the weight of scientific authority until the Enlightenment.

Scientific Racism and the Abolitionist Legacy

During the Enlightenment, human dignity was again elevated to new heights as rights and rationality were privileged. Disgusted by religious warfare, Enlightenment thinkers challenged the rationality of Christian doctrine and dismissed many religious rituals as mere superstition. Many now portrayed Asians and indigenous people as exemplars of freedom, democracy, and reason, to accentuate the foibles of

European society. American independence, the French Revolution, and early abolitionist and feminist movements were direct outgrowths of these Enlightenment ideas.

Respect for human equality was short-lived, however. Recoiling from the excesses of the French Revolution, many intellectuals reconstituted a hierarchical framework of reality that privileged scientific rationality. Because of its claims to objective knowledge, scientific authority increased tremendously in the nineteenth century. Nevertheless, scientists and other intellectuals often depicted non-Europeans, women, and the religious as less rational. Race, in particular, became the preferred lens to view humanity. Most eighteenth-century scientists believed humanity to be a single species, yet Swedish botanist and founder of scientific taxonomy, Carulous Linnaeus, was compelled to classify human difference. He introduced four races of the genus *Homo: Europeaus, Americanus, Asiaticus*, and *Africanus* in *Systemae Naturae* (1735). By the nineteenth century this system was transformed into a racial hierarchy that explained human difference and justified European global dominance. The introduction of evolutionary biology and social Darwinism further reinforced belief in innate white superiority.

Theology during this period did not directly challenge the ascendant racial ideology. But some Christians, usually missionaries and social reformers, rejected the inhumane treatment of the marginalized. They planted theological kernels that would eventually challenge the exploitative institutions that existed symbiotically with the emerging racial worldview. First, Anglo-American Reformed theology, as a result of the trans-Atlantic evangelical awakenings in the eighteenth century, shifted toward a more optimistic view of human agency and provided greater space for personal and social transformation. Whether they embraced Arminianism (John Wesley) or a modified Calvinism (George Whitefield), evangelicals argued against those who believed that enslaved Africans, Native Americans, and "heathen" Asians did not have the capacity to respond to the gospel. High Calvinists agreed that God's elect included a people from every nation, but would have resisted the use of missions or other means to transmit the gospel. Consequently, evangelicals provided both the theoretical and practical justification to cross the racial barriers that were erected at the time.

Second, influenced by continental Pietism, trans-Atlantic evangelicalism began to value overt demonstrations of spiritual awakenings. Religious expressiveness often bridged cultural chasms and diversified the Church. African Americans converted *en masse*, in part, because of the heart-felt religion of the evangelicals. This would repeat itself again with the multicultural and global growth of Pentecostalism in the twentieth century. The interracial relationships forged by common religious expressions engendered empathy for those who were different, especially the exploited and enslaved. This was particularly true for Quakers, who became strong advocates for the abolition of slavery. Evangelical missionaries also became advocates for racial minorities (many protested Andrew Jackson's Cherokee removal policy and defended Chinese and Japanese against racial discrimination and immigration exclusion). The embrace of religious experience transformed theological engagement with human experience. The evangelical awakenings and Pentecostal movement helped the Church see with greater clarity the transracial implications of the gospel, which in turn dispelled the mythical nature of "race."

Despite these developments, trans-Atlantic evangelicalism was not able to articulate a theological challenge to race. Unitarians and deists might have issued such a challenge, since they embraced Enlightenment rationalism more fully than evangelicals. They, too, were generally supportive of abolition and other nineteenth century social reforms. As scientific "evidence" for a racial hierarchy mounted, however, it became increasingly difficult for religious "liberals" to challenge racial worldviews and practices. Initially, evangelicals resisted the scientific theories of "polygenism" and evolution by appealing to biblical authority. "One-bloodism," they argued, was derived from a literal reading of the Bible. But by the end of the century, biblical literalism was overshadowed by the authority of science and higher criticism. Furthermore, biblical literalism (more accurately, a Baconian approach to the Bible) could not bring about consensus with regard to slavery and colonial practices. Abolitionists and slaveholders may have read the same Bible, but they came to very different conclusions about slavery. In the end, save for a few vocal leaders, the weight of scientific racism muted theology's ability to engage race and racism. Nevertheless, the abolitionist legacy that was rooted in evangelicalism successfully shifted the focus of theology toward antiracist activism even though it was not able to challenge the dominant racial ideology and worldview.

Critiquing Race, Confronting Racism

At the beginning of the twentieth century, racial ideology reached new heights as the regulation and segregation of nonwhites and other minorities in the United States, South Africa, and European colonies were legally inscribed. Although the Civil War ended slavery in the United States, Jim and Jane Crow practices reinforced white racial domination in the South through lynching and social intimidation. In the West, violence directed towards Chinese and Japanese functioned in the same manner. Waves of immigration from southern and eastern Europe in northern cities engendered a nativist reaction that narrowed racial privilege to those with Anglo-Saxon or Teutonic blood. Educational and political institutions, religious organizations, the media, and industry reproduced a racial hierarchy that was presumed to be natural. The power of racial ideology can be seen in the eventual segregation of interracial urban and Pentecostal revivals.

Until the social and biological sciences debunked race in mid-century, Christians with abolitionist, social reform, and missionary sentiments struggled to challenge the racial ideology and racist practices of their day. Mainline Protestants continued in their efforts to influence public life under the Social Gospel banner of the "Fatherhood of God and the brotherhood of man." Thus, in response to the race question, some mainline Protestant leaders drew from lessons learned in the urban and international mission fields. In the urban centers, mainline Protestants had become aware of socioeconomic forces and corporate structures that reinforced immigrant poverty and powerlessness. As African Americans migrated north in the 1920s and racial conflicts ensued, these insights were applied to race relations, albeit inconsistently. In the mission fields, anticolonial nationalists, unhappy with their second-class status, fueled tensions with Euro-American missionaries. International church leaders, such as Joseph H. Oldham, were compelled to rebut the reigning "scientific" racism. The "fundamental issues in racial relations are not ethnological or biological but ethical," Oldham argued presciently. Nevertheless, the recommended solution to the race problem was limited to developing cross-racial understanding and friendships, not utilizing power to change the racial system, as Reinhold Niebuhr had suggested.[14]

At mid-century, the horror of the Holocaust, the cold war, anti-colonial movements, the civil rights movement in the United States, and rejection of biologically based definitions of race seemed to converge at once. International sentiment sought to tear down the edifice of the racial ideology that sanctified Western global dominance. In the United States, mainline Protestants joined African Americans, Catholics, and Jews in cautious support of racial integration. African American denominations that had consolidated at the turn of the century now discovered the power of mobilizing along racial and religious lines to effect change. Evangelical and Pentecostal participation was not distinguished during this period, due to their self-imposed separation from mainstream social issues that dated back to the modernist-fundamentalist and Methodist-Holiness controversies earlier in the century. Nevertheless, there were many interracial "evangelical counterculture" groups in the South that "challenged the theologically grounded racism pervasive among white southerners" and helped to end Jim Crow.[15]

Racial integration could mean interracial harmony, assimilation, or colorblindness. Theologians of the period did not usually grapple with its precise meaning. Most of their efforts went toward ending public segregation and encouraging interracial friendships. But African Americans and other racial minorities were more careful. Inspired by anti-colonial liberation movements, many cautioned against assimilation or the erasure of racial or cultural identities in the name of integration. The blurring of racial lines, they argued, merely disguised structural racism. In the late 1960s and 1970s, race-based caucuses were formed within most mainline denominations to advocate for racial representation and empowerment as evidence of integration. They urged denominational agencies and theological curricula to carve out space for racial groups to have their concerns addressed. Liberation, black, and other contextualized theologies proliferated as terms like "multiculturalism," "pluralism," and "diversity" entered the mainstream of American society.

Few evangelical theologians have engaged ethnicity and race. Many are concerned that the employment of "racial oppression" and "liberation" categories reduces theological reflection to the politics of identity. As Miroslav Volf notes, the "categories of oppression and liberation provide combat gear, not a pin-striped suit or a dinner dress; they are good for fighting, but not for negotiating or celebrating—at least not until the oppressors have been conquered and the prisoners set free."[16] But some evangelical theologians, such as Volf, understand that these biblically rooted categories provide criteria to adjudicate between parties in conflict. They are also reminders of the legacy of Western colonialism and the persistence of racial inequity. Without them, theological reflection about race may be limited to promoting interracial toleration and friendships; issues of institutional and structural racism may be ignored. The future direction of evangelical theology as it relates to race will be the focus of the last section.

Theological Reflection on Race Today

Until recently, theological reflection on race has been largely a mainline Protestant and Roman Catholic endeavor. Within these settings, contextualized and liberation theologies have arisen to challenge racism and colonialism. But these perspectives are not common in evangelical theology that was shaped by the modernist-fundamentalist controversies of the early twentieth century. Nevertheless, evangelicalism has become increasingly sophisticated and is becoming cognizant of the growing racial diversity within American evangelicalism today.

Evangelical theology, in general, shares a common view of humanity with the wider Christian community. All humans, regardless of race, are descendents of Adam and Eve. They are created in God's image, united with Adam in sin and the fall, and can be united in Christ's redemption of humanity and creation. These affirmations are the core theological defenses against racial ideologies. Evangelical theological reflection on the issue of race, however, will require attention to biblical hermeneutics, contextualization, and the question of the church role in society.

Evangelical affirmation of a high view of biblical authority often leads to methodological debates regarding the use of extrabiblical sources for theological reflection. For example, both abolitionists and plantation owners appealed to human and property rights, in addition to Scripture, to support their respective views about slavery. In the case of an issue as emotional as race, bringing to the surface hidden assumptions would help evangelical biblical scholars and theologians address race and racism more effectively while retaining a high view of biblical authority.

One particular area is the question of racial diversity and particularity. Even while defending the unity of humanity, Roman Catholic theologian P. Bonaventura Hinwood has appealed to Thomistic theology and papal encyclicals to conclude "that the Church recognizes a real diversity among the races of men, in virtue of which each race has something which is peculiar and native to it."[17] By appealing strictly to the Bible, however, evangelical theology can find arguments for racial diversity challenging. For instance, the New Testament trajectory appears to move toward a unity in Christ that dissolves all particularities or promotes multiculturalism (Eph. 2:14–15). Volf defends some retention of particularity because he is sensitive to how "calls to unity" and "multiculturalism" were used as tools for cultural conformity and political repression.[18] But this sensitivity is not always present in American evangelicalism. Smith and Emerson have argued that white evangelicals lean toward color-blindness and individualism, and do not see how structural racism operates in the United States.[19] Bringing this to the surface of evangelical theological reflection on race would be an important first step. Including a biblical hermeneutic that consciously views scripture from a racialized lens would go even further and give pause to imposing a unreflective universalism into the Bible.

Bringing to the surface one's assumptions about race requires a positive view of general revelation and sociocultural contexts. These forms of knowledge allow the theologian to read the Bible with "new eyes." Indeed, evangelicals are already analyzing cultural contexts in order to facilitate church growth among postmodern people, so contextualization is not a new development. Engaging unfamiliar disciplines such as ethnic studies, critical race theory, and the sociology and politics of race will be new. Evangelical theologians who understand the power dynamics of race and the reasons why racialized peoples often demand contextualized theologies are likely to be in a stronger position to reflect theologically on race. But the extent to which other disciplines are brought into an evangelical theological conversation around race will remain a methodological challenge.

Evangelical theological reflection on race will also require renewed attention to the church's role in society. Shall the church speak as a flawed prophetic witness against racism? Shall it be a countercultural community that models multiracialism? Can it do both? Should it even engage social issues? In recent years, evangelical engagement in American public life has become more visible. But its voice on issues of concern to people of color (such as affirmative action and comprehensive immigration reform) has been muted. On the other hand, multiracial congregations have garnered much attention from evangelicals and have been promoted as a solution to the problem of race.[20] African American, Hispanic, and Asian American congregations have been given much less attention, even though they represent the majority of racialized evangelicals.[21] Evangelical theology must address some of the gaps in these trends if it is to adequately discuss the church's role in a racialized society.

Throughout history, Christian theological anthropology has had a symbiotic relationship with Euro-American interactions with the wider world. For the most part, it accommodated the dominant views of human nature, whether the Great Chain of Being rooted in Aristotelian thought or the emancipated self rooted in the Enlightenment. Nevertheless, its core affirmations about the *imago dei*, "one blood" origins of humanity, the universality of sin, the universal availability of salvation through Jesus Christ, and eschatological vision of the nations before the throne of God often challenged the racism that accompanied European expansionism. Though it struggled to overcome "scientific" racism as an intellectual discourse in the modern era, theological engagement on the mission field and in social activism produced powerful ethical critiques of racist practices. As evangelicalism continues to grow around the globe and among racialized groups in the United States, evangelical theology will have many opportunities to engage race and racism in new ways.

NOTES

1. In this chapter, *race* is the term used to categorize humans into groups or populations on the basis of various sets of characteristics that are inherited. The most widely used racial categories are based on physical traits such as skin color, cranial or facial features, hair texture, heredity, and self-identification.

2. Alan T. Davies, *Infected Christianity: A Study of Modern Racism* (Toronto: McGill-Queen's University Press, 1988), 3.

3. Philip Yale Nicholson, *Who Do We Think We Are?: Race and Nation in the Modern World* (New York: M.E. Sharpe, 1999), 6.

4. The Social Science Research Council posted a series of articles online in response to new biologically based challenges to the social construction theory of race: "Is Race 'Real'"? http://raceandgenomics.ssrc.org/.

5. Winthrop D. Jordan, *White over Black: American Attitudes toward the Negro 1550–1812* (Chapel Hill: University of North Carolina Press, 1968); and Thomas F. Gossett, *Race: The History of an Idea in America*, 2nd edition ([1963] New York: Oxford University Press, 1997). See also Edmund Sears Morgan, *American Slavery, American Freedom: The Ordeal of Colonial Virginia* (New York: Norton, 1975); and Audrey Smedley, *Race in North America: Origin and Evolution of a Worldview* (Boulder, Col.: Westview Press, 1993).

6. Michael Omi and Howard Winant, *Racial Formation in the United States: From the 1960s to the 1990s* ([1986] New York: Routledge, 1994).

7. Quoted in Michael O. Emerson and Christian Smith, *Divided by Faith: Evangelical Religion and the Problem of Race in America* (New York: Oxford University Press, 2000), 7. See also Eduardo Bonilla-Silva, *Racism without Racists: Color-Blind Racism and the Persistence of Racial Inequality in the United States*, 2nd edition (Rowman & Littlefield, 2006).

8. Jordan, *White over Black*, 482–511.

9. Nicholson, *Who Do We Think We Are?*, 7–8.

10. Davies, *Infected Christianity*, 10.

11. Nicholson, *Who Do We Think We Are?*, 33.

12. Steven Ozment, *The Age of Reform 1250–1550: An Intellectual and Religious History of Late Medieval and Reformation Europe* (New Haven: Yale University Press, 1980), 315.

13. Reginald Horsman, *Race and Manifest Destiny: The Origins of American Racial Anglo-Saxonism*. Cambridge: Harvard University Press, 1981.

14. Joseph Houldsworth Oldham, *Christianity and the Race Problem* (New York: Council of Christian Associations, 1924), 80; and Oldham, *Christian Principles and Race Relations: A Discussion Course for College Groups* (New York: Council of Christian Associations, 1926).

15. Paul L. Harvey, *Freedom's Coming: Religious Culture and the Shaping of the South from the Civil War through the Civil Rights Era* (Chapel Hill: University of North Carolina Press, 2005).

16. Miroslav Volf, *Exclusion and Embrace: A Theological Exploration of Identity, Otherness, and Reconciliation* (Nashville, Tenn.: Abingdon, 1996), 103.

17. P. Bonaventura Hinwood, *Race: The Reflections of a Theologian* (Rome: Herder, 1964), 107.

18. Miroslav Volf, *Exclusion and Embrace*, 43–50.

19. Emerson and Smith, *Divided by Faith*, 69–91.

20. Curtiss Paul DeYoung, et al., *United by Faith: The Multiracial Congregation as an Answer to the Problem of Race* (New York: Oxford University Press, 2003).

21. With the possible exception of Soong-Chan Rah, *The Next Evangelicalism: Freeing the Church from Western Cultural Captivity* (Downers Grove, Ill.: InterVarsity Press, 2009).

BIBLIOGRAPHY

Statement on "Race" (American Anthropological Association, 1998). http://www.aaanet.org/stmts/racepp.htm.

Bynum, William F. "The Great Chain of Being after Forty Years: An Appraisal," *History of Science* 13 (1975): 1–28.

Davies, Alan T. *Infected Christianity: A Study of Modern Racism*. Toronto: McGill-Queen's University Press, 1988.

DeYoung, Curtiss Paul, et al. *United by Faith: The Multiracial Congregation as an Answer to the Problem of Race*. New York: Oxford University Press, 2003.

Emerson, Michael O., and Christian Smith. *Divided by Faith: Evangelical Religion and the Problem of Race in America*. New York: Oxford University Press, 2000.

Findley, James E., Jr. *Church People in the Struggle: The National Council of Churches and the Black Freedom Movement, 1950–1970*. New York: Oxford University Press, 1993.

Jordan, Winthrop D. *White over Black: American Attitudes toward the Negro 1550–1812*. Chapel Hill: University of North Carolina Press, 1968.

Gossett, Thomas F. *Race: The History of an Idea in America*. 2nd edition. [1963] New York: Oxford University Press, 1997.

Harvey, Paul L. *Freedom's Coming: Religious Culture and the Shaping of the South from the Civil War through the Civil Rights Era*. Chapel Hill: University of North Carolina Press, 2005.

Hinwood, P. Bonaventura. *Race: The Reflections of a Theologian*. Rome: Herder, 1964.

Horsman, Reginald. *Race and Manifest Destiny: The Origins of American Racial Anglo-Saxonism*. Cambridge: Harvard University Press, 1981.

Lovejoy, Arthur O. *The Great Chain of Being: A Study of the History of an Idea*. Cambridge: Harvard University Press, 1936.

Luker, Ralph E. *The Social Gospel in Black and White: American Racial Reform, 1885–1912*. Chapel Hill: University of North Carolina Press, 1991.

Nicholson, Philip Yale. *Who Do We Think We Are?: Race and Nation in the Modern World*. Armonk, N.Y.: M. E. Sharpe, 1999.

Noll, Mark. *God and Race in American Politics: A Short History*. (Princeton: Princeton University Press, 2008).

Omi, Michael, and Howard Winant. *Racial Formation in the United States: From the 1960s to the 1990s*. [1986] New York: Routledge, 1994.

Ozment, Steven. *The Age of Reform 1250–1550: An Intellectual and Religious History of Late Medieval and Reformation Europe*. New Haven: Yale University Press, 1980.

Parish, Helen Rand, ed. *Bartolomé de las Casas: The Only Way*, translated by Francis Patrick Sullivan. Mahwah, N.J.: Paulist Press, 1992.

Pontifical Council for Justice and Peace. "The Church and Racism: An Introductory Update." *L'Osservatore Romano* page 8 (5 September 2001). http://www.ewtn.com/library/curia/pcjpchra.htm.

———. "The Church and Racism: Toward a More Fraternal Society" (1998). http://www.ewtn.com/library/curia/pcjpraci.htm.

Rah, Soong-Chan. *The Next Evangelicalism: Freeing the Church from Western Cultural Captivity*. Downers Grove, Ill.: InterVarsity Press, 2009.

Smedley, Audrey. *Race in North America: Origin and Evolution of a Worldview*. Boulder, Col.: Westview Press, 1993.

Volf, Miroslav. *Exclusion and Embrace: A Theological Exploration of Identity, Otherness, and Reconciliation*. Nashville, Tenn.: Abingdon, 1996.

World Alliance of Reformed Churches. "National and Ethnic Identity." Subsection 2.3. *Study Texts of the 23rd General Council of the World Alliance of Reformed Churches* (1997). http://www.warc.ch/where/23gc/study/stud23.html#txt6.

World Council of Churches. *Christian Perspectives on Theological Anthropology. A Faith and Order Study Document*. Geneva: World Council of Churches, 2005.

CHAPTER 31

THE VULNERABLE: ABORTION AND DISABILITY

C. BEN MITCHELL

The history of the Christian church is rich with examples of ministry to the vulnerable. Hospitals, orphanages, rescue missions, and senior citizen centers have been nearly ubiquitous expressions of Christian concern. For instance, from the time of Saint Basil of Caesarea, who founded one of the first hospitals (c. 369) until today, a vast network of hospitals bears names that broadcast their legacy: St. Vincent's, Methodist, St. Luke's, Presbyterian, Mercy, and Baptist. These began, of course, as charitable hospitals, including foundling hospitals to care for abandoned children. In 1864, the symbol of the Red Cross was codified in the Geneva Convention as the emblem of an organization founded to care for the wartime wounded. In Britain, Dame Cicely Saunders founded the hospice movement by establishing St. Christopher's Hospice in south London in 1967.

In addition, Christian theologians, church leaders, denominations, and congregations have been at the forefront of ministry to those who are vulnerable—both mothers and their unborn children— because of the availability of abortion, as well as those who are vulnerable because of societal attitudes toward disability. This chapter attempts to introduce these two areas of concern as focal examples of evangelical applied theology.

The Vulnerable Unborn

No moral issue has done more to galvanize the evangelical movement than abortion. Unquestionably, the United States Supreme Court's decision in *Roe v. Wade* (1973) and its companion ruling in *Doe v. Bolton* (1973) became the loci of the abortion debate in America. Combined, the decisions made it unlawful for the government to interfere in an abortion decision where the "health" (very broadly defined) of the mother was at risk. The result has been that, as former Harvard law professor Ambassador Mary Ann Glendon has observed, the United States has the most permissive abortion laws in the Western world.[1] The consequences of that fact for evangelical identity and activism are difficult to overstate.

Evangelical distinctives shape the way the movement engages social and moral concerns. Historians George Marsden and David Bebbington have both proposed that one of the formative planks of evangelical affirmation is the authority of the Bible in matters of faith and practice. Methodologically, then, the discussion of evangelical engagement with the needs of the vulnerable, including the unborn and the disabled, should begin with the biblical witness. While evangelicals have not been entirely univocal on their view of abortion, a general consensus has prevailed that abortion should be avoided, not least because the unborn are considered vulnerable members of the human community.

The Value of Every Human Life

Contemporary debates about abortion invoke terms such as "the right to life" and "the sanctity of human life." Admittedly, neither of these expressions is found per se in the Bible. Rather, the biblical witness testifies to the uniqueness of human life among other living things. Specifically, the Bible maintains that only human beings are made in the image of God (the *imago Dei*). Carl F. H. Henry, one of the leading theologians of the evangelical movement in the twentieth century, believed that "the importance of a proper understanding of the *imago Dei* can hardly be overstated. The answer given to the *imago*-inquiry soon becomes determinative for the entire gamut of doctrinal affirmation. The ramifications are not only theological, but [for] every phase of the...cultural enterprise as a whole."[2] Thus the image of God is a good place to begin this discussion.

The *imago Dei*

Genesis 1 declares that at the zenith of God's creative activity he made Adam a "living soul" (Genesis 1:24) in God's own "image" and "likeness" (Genesis 1:27). While other animals have souls as well, only humankind is made in God's image. The image of God, then, is the source of human exceptionalism, the notion that human beings occupy a unique place in the created order.

Furthermore, the creation covenant between God and his human handiwork included the mandate, "Be fruitful and multiply, and fill the earth and subdue it; and have dominion over the fish of the sea and over the birds of the air and over every living thing that moves upon the earth" (Genesis 1:28). One could hardly imagine the other animals needing an imperative to reproduce. Fecundity comes naturally, as it were. Humans, on the other hand, can choose sexual abstinence and potentially forego populating the earth. The divine imperative to multiply establishes a presumption in favor of procreation. Subsequently, the Bible makes it very clear that offspring are a reward from God. Children are seen as a spiritual and economic blessing (e.g., Psalm 127:3–5), pregnancies are welcomed with great joy and singing (e.g., Genesis 21:6–7; 1 Samuel 1–2; Luke 1), and infertility is seen as a terrible plight (e.g., Genesis 25:21; 30:1). So from the opening of the biblical narrative, human beings are singled out as sui generis and instructed to procreate.

The locus classicus for human exceptionalism is the prohibition against murdering humans (i.e., homicide) found in Genesis 9:1–6. After the devastating flood, God renewed the creation covenant with Noah and his children:

> God blessed Noah and his sons, and said to them, "Be fruitful and multiply, and fill the earth. The fear and dread of you shall rest on every animal of the earth, and on every bird of the air, on everything that creeps on the ground, and on all the fish of the sea; into your hand they are delivered. Every moving thing that lives shall be food for you; and just as I gave you the green plants, I give you everything. Only, you shall not eat flesh with its life, that is, its blood. For your own lifeblood I will surely require a reckoning: from every animal I will require it and from human beings, each one for the blood of another, I will require a reckoning for human life. Whoever sheds the blood of a human, by a human shall that person's blood be shed; for in his own image God made humankind. And you, be fruitful and multiply, abound on the earth and multiply in it." (NRSV)

Several features of the covenant renewal are notable. First, the covenant is identical to the creation covenant with respect to the positive commands to be fruitful, reproduce, and be good stewards over the earth and its resources. Second, permission to kill animals for sustenance is added to the Noahic covenant. Third, animal life is thereby tacitly distinguished from human life by the prohibition of homicide. Finally, the rationale given for this prohibition is that humankind is made in God's own image. The conclusion seems to follow that since only members of the species *Homo sapiens* are imagers of God, human life deserves greater, or a different kind of, respect than animal life.[3]

Interpreters have varied widely in their opinions about what exactly constitutes the *imago Dei*. Numerous options have been offered: (1) humankind's erect bodily form, (2) human dominion over nature, (3) human reason, (4) human pre-fallen righteousness, (5) human capacities, (6) the juxtaposition between man and woman, (7) responsible creaturehood and moral conformity to God, and (8) various composite views.[4] Nevertheless, one thing seems clear even from the history of interpretation; namely, that the *imago Dei* is attributed solely to human beings, notably including Jesus Christ—fully divine and fully human—who is "the image of the invisible God" (Colossians 1:15), the prototypical image of what it means to be one of us.[5] Thus, what it means to be human is to image God, and what it means to image God is to be human, as Jesus Christ is human.

Early Jewish and Christian Witnesses on Abortion

From the vantage point of biblical anthropology informed by the doctrine of the image of God, the rationale for the early Jewish community's views on abortion becomes clearer. As Michael J. Gorman has shown, despite the lack of a specific prohibition against abortion in the Hebrew Bible, the Jewish witness against the practice is fairly consistent. "Though rare cases of abortion may have occurred in Judaism," observes Gorman, "the witness of antiquity is that Jews, unlike pagans, did not practice deliberate abortion."[6] Philo of Alexandria (25 B.C.E.– 41C.E.), for example, included a brief discussion of abortion under the heading of the commandment "Thou shalt not kill." He concluded that if a man should strike a pregnant woman causing her to miscarry, and the offspring was unshaped or undeveloped, a fine should accrue, but if the offspring was already shaped—with identifiable limbs—the man should be put to death.[7]

Similarly, the *Sentences of Pseudo-Phocylides* (c. 50 B.C.E.–50 C.E.), an early Jewish text based on the Septuagint, says that "a woman should not destroy the unborn in her belly, nor after its birth throw it before the dogs and vultures as a prey."[8] The Jewish apocalyptic *Sibylline Oracle* (c. second century C.E.) included among the "wicked" women who "produce abortions and unlawfully cast their offspring away" and sorcerers who dispense abortion-causing drugs.[9] Likewise, the apocryphal book *1 Enoch* (first or second century B.C.E.) declared that an evil angel taught humans how to "smash the embryo in the womb." Finally, the first-century historian and apologist for Judaism Josephus wrote in *Against Apion* that "The law orders all the offspring to be brought up, and forbids women either to cause abortion or to make away with the foetus; a woman convicted of this is regarded as an infanticide, because she destroys a soul and diminishes the race."[10] Contrast these injunctions with the barbarism of Roman culture. Cicero (106–43 B.C.E.) indicated that according to the Twelve Tables of Roman Law, "deformed infants shall be killed."[11] Plutarch (c. 46–120 C.E.) spoke of those whom he said "offered up their own children [for sacrifice], and those who had no children would buy little ones from poor people and cut their throats as if they were so many lambs or young birds; meanwhile the mother stood by without a tear or moan."[12] According to an inscription at Delphi, because of the infanticide of female newborns only 1 percent of six hundred families had raised two daughters. European historian W.E.H. Lecky called infanticide "one of the deepest stains of the ancient civilizations."[13]

Against this bleak backdrop, the Hebrew tradition provided a robust moral framework for early Christian condemnation of both abortion and infanticide. For instance, the *Didache* (c. 85–110) commanded, "Thou shalt not murder a child by abortion nor kill them when born." The *Epistle of Barnabas* (c. 130 C.E.), commanded, "You shall not abort a child nor, again, commit infanticide." Additional examples of Christian condemnation of both infanticide and abortion can be cited. In fact, some biblical scholars have argued that the New Testament's silence on abortion per se is due to the fact that it was simply beyond the pale of early Christian practice.

The Christian Apologists

The Christian apologists of the second and third centuries also spoke on the subject of abortion. Among them, Athenagoras and Tertullian stand out. Formerly a Greek philosopher who converted to Christianity, Athenagoras addressed his *Plea for Christians* (c. 177) to Roman Emperor Marcus Aurelius to defend followers of Christ against the charge that they were atheists (because they would not worship Caesar), incestuous (because they called one another "brother" and "sister" and then married one another), and cannibals (because they ate the body and drank the blood of Christ in the Eucharist). As evidence that Christians were not cannibals, Athenagoras maintained that Christians could not bear to watch the death of another human being, even at the gladiatorial games. His illustration of Christian respect for human life was telling: "What reason would we have to commit murder when we say that women who induce abortions are murderers, and will have to give account of it to God?"[14]

Raised in Carthage and trained as a lawyer, Tertullian offered a similar defense against the charge that Christians sacrificed their children in his *Apology* to Emperor Septimus Severus (197 C.E.): "In our case, murder being once for all forbidden, we may not destroy even the fetus in the womb, while as yet the human being derives blood from other parts of the body for its sustenance. To hinder a birth is merely a speedier man-killing."[15] The disapproval of abortion was clearly used as a sign of the virtue of the Christian community.

The Fathers and Augustine

Among the Church Fathers, Basil, Jerome, Ambrose, Augustine, and Chrysostom commented on abortion. Although there were clearly nuanced distinctions among them, they were univocal in their condemnation of the practice. Basil of Caesarea (c. 330–379) called abortion "murder," but just as clearly pointed out that it was not an unforgiveable sin and prescribed penance for the sin.[16] The rhetorician and Bishop of Milan, Ambrose (c. 339–397), repudiated the use of "parricidal mixtures" because they "snuff out the fruit" of the womb.[17] Jerome (c. 342–420) lamented that "some, when they learn they are with child through sin, practice abortion by the use of drugs. Frequently they die themselves and are brought before the rulers of the lower world guilty of three crimes: suicide, adultery against Christ, and murder of an unborn child."[18]

More than merely proscribing abortion and infanticide, however, early Christian communities provided alternatives, adopting children who were destined to be abandoned. For instance, Callistus (d. c. 223) provided refuge to abandoned children by placing them in Christian homes; Benignus of Dijon (third century) offered nourishment and protection to abandoned children, including some with disabilities caused by failed abortions.

Like his predecessors, Augustine of Hippo (354–430) was an ardent opponent of deliberate abortion. Gorman points out that no Church Father gave more attention to the subject than Augustine, not least because much of his own theologizing was about the origin and transmission of the soul, the doctrine of original sin, and the role of sex within marriage. For instance, in his discussion of the resurrection, Augustine asked whether an unborn fetus would be raised from the dead. He reasoned that in order for a person to be raised from the dead, he or she must first have lived. Can a fetus be reckoned to have lived? While his answer was somewhat modest about the nature of unborn human life, he preferred erring on the side of life. "On this score, a corollary question may be most carefully discussed by the most learned men, and still I do not know that any man can answer it, namely: When does a human being begin to live in the womb? Is there some form of hidden life, not yet apparent in the motions of a living thing? To deny, for example, that those fetuses ever lived at all which are cut away limb by limb and cast out of the wombs of pregnant women, lest the mothers die also if the fetuses were left there dead, would seem much too rash."[19]

In sum, the witness of Scripture and the consensus of the early church is that every human being, from conception through natural death is to be respected as an imager of God whose life has special dignity in virtue of his or her relationship to the Creator. The community of faithful Christians was marked by its rejection of abortion because it was seen as a violation of the command not to murder.

The Reformers

Although the topic of abortion did not result in a significant body of writing among the Reformers, Luther and Calvin had some pointed things to say about it. Luther, for instance, saw a correlation between contraception and abortion: "How great, therefore, the wickedness of [fallen] human nature is! How many girls there are who prevent conception and kill and expel tender fetuses, although procreation is the work of God! Indeed, some spouses who marry and live together... have various ends in mind, but rarely children."[20] Calvin decried abortion as a "monstrous crime to rob [the preborn child] of the life which it has not yet begun to enjoy. If it seems more horrible to kill a man in his own house than in a field, because a man's house is his place of most secure refuge, it ought surely to be deemed more atrocious to destroy a fetus in the womb before it has come to light."[21]

Contemporary Evangelical Witness

Early twentieth-century evangelicals were largely silent on the abortion question, despite the history of the larger Christian witness on the subject. In part, this was probably due to the emphasis on evangelism and revivalism among mid-century evangelicals.[22] Among other things, this emphasis led to myopia on the great social issues of the day. Carl Henry, one of the architects of contemporary evangelicalism and founding editor of *Christianity Today*, lamented in 1947 that "for the first protracted period in its history, evangelical Christianity stands divorced from the great social reform movements."[23] For the remainder of his life he called on evangelicals not to divorce prophetic witness to the veracity of the Bible from engaging the social ills of the hour. "The cries of suffering humanity today are many. No evangelicalism which ignores the totality of man's condition dares respond in the name of Christianity."[24]

Despite the fact that prior to 1973 abortion was by no means rare on American soil,[25] evangelicals did not address the issue until a physician collaborated with a theologian in 1976 to galvanize evangelicals on the topic. That year Francis Schaeffer and C. Everett Koop, M.D., later the Surgeon General of the United States, combined forces to produce the book and movie series, *Whatever Happened to the Human Race?* According to Koop, the book sold 50,000 copies and 45,000 people attended the seminars he and Schaeffer conducted after the movie premiered.[26] Over time, the films and the companion book brought millions of evangelicals and other Christians into the prolife movement. By their own admission, prior to that time both Schaeffer and Koop thought the movement was largely a Roman Catholic initiative. But together they "determined to awaken the evangelical world—and anyone else who would listen—to the Christian imperative to do something to reverse the perilous realignment of American values on these life-and-death issues."[27]

One piece of evidence of the success of their strategy is the turn-around by the nation's largest Protestant religious denomination, the Southern Baptist Convention (SBC). Two years prior to *Roe v. Wade* (1973), the convention passed a resolution in its annual meeting supporting the liberalization and legalization of abortion—permitting abortion in cases of "rape, incest, clear evidence of severe fetal deformity, and carefully ascertained evidence of the likelihood of damage to the emotional, mental, and physical health of the mother."[28] The resolution was reaffirmed in 1974. By 1976, however, sentiments within the denomination had changed. In a June 1976 resolution, the convention voted to "reaffirm the biblical sacredness and dignity of all human life, including fetal life," called on Southern Baptists and other citizens "to work to change those attitudes and conditions which encourage many people to turn to abortion as a means of birth control," and supported the "right of expectant mothers to the full range of medical services and personal counseling for the preservation of life and health." From that time forward SBC resolutions were decidedly prolife. In fact, on the thirtieth anniversary of *Roe v. Wade*, the convention passed a resolution confessing the sinful moral blindness of the 1971 and 1974 statements.[29]

Recent Developments

Evangelical engagement in the debate about abortion continues. The political debate, of course, garners the most attention in the media. Yet other strategies continue to develop among those who are concerned about the vulnerability of the unborn and women who feel they have no alternative but to abort. Evangelicals are at the forefront of education to prevent unplanned pregnancies. True Love Waits, The Silver Ring Thing, and other ministries have aimed at helping reduce teen pregnancies by promoting sexual abstinence until marriage. On the other side of pregnancy, Care Net represents over 1,100 pregancy care centers that offer practical and emotional support to pregnant women. Care Net was inspired by the work of Schaeffer, Koop, and the late Harold O. J. Brown, former professor at Trinity Evangelical Divinity School. Beyond that, countless evangelical families volunteer their homes to host women who need support during their pregnancies.

In 1974, the first International Congress on World Evangelization was held in Lausanne, Switzerland, under the auspices of the Billy Graham Evangelistic Association and *Christianity Today* magazine. The meeting brought together 2,700 participants from over 150 nations. International evangelical leaders such as Samuel Escobar, Francis Malcolm Muggeridge, and John Stott participated in the congress. Dozens of global meetings and consultations have followed, spawning a global movement.

In 2004 the Lausanne movement convened the Forum on World Evangelization in Pattaya, Thailand. For the first time in its history, a team was established to take up issues in bioethics. The subject covered by Issue Group 29, as they were called, was "Bioethics: Opportunity or Obstacle for the Gospel?" Abortion was included in the report. The group of ten participants, representing eight countries, affirmed that "in the womb, the foetus is already an *I* who is addressed by God and according to Christian tradition the incarnation did not take place when the baby Jesus was born, but in the virgin's womb."[30] Moreover, the authors appealed to the churches to participate in abstinence-based sex education, pregnancy care, adoption, and counseling for women and men who experience trauma following a decision to abort. Finally, they maintained: "When Christians engage in political action against abortion, it is important they are consistent in affirming the value of human life. There is no place for violence or hatred, even against those who promote abortions and perform them. In all its activities and liturgy, the church should aim to celebrate human life in all its diversity."[31]

The Vulnerable Disabled

Evangelicals have also realized that celebration of life in all its diversity is now threatened by implicit attacks on the disabled. Evangelical theology of disability is neither as robust nor as mature as the theological reflection on abortion, but there is a theological tradition to draw upon, as well as a recognition of the need for deeper thinking on the issue.

Like the terms "abortion" and "the sanctity of human life," the Bible does not use the language of "disability" or the "disabled." The other problem is that "as a contested category, there is no single agreed-on definition of disability in disability studies"[32] But the Bible repeatedly acknowledges the physical conditions we now call disabilities. The blind, the deaf, the mute, and the lame are often invoked in one way or another. The Holiness Code, for instance, prohibited cursing the deaf or putting a stumbling block before the blind (Leviticus 19:4). Mephibosheth was "crippled in his feet" and "lame" after being dropped accidentally by his nurse (2 Samuel 4:4; 9:3, 13). Although those with physical disabilities were not to perform the ritual duties of the priesthood (Leviticus 21:18–20), Isaiah indicates that despite any impairment, the faithful would receive everlasting blessings (Isaiah 56:3–5). In Jesus' parable of the Great Banquet, those who invite "the poor, the crippled, the lame, and the blind" to the feast are told they will be rewarded at the resurrection (Luke 14:11–14).

As in the abortion debate, evangelical theology of disability has started with the anthropological affirmation that every human being—that is, every member of the human species *Homo sapiens*—is made in God's image and likeness, regardless of age, abilities, or location.

Gary B. Ferngren has shown that among the classical Greek and Roman writers dignity or human worth was ascribed to virtuous persons. "Human worth, then, was not regarded in the classical world as intrinsic."[33] Nor were human rights intrinsic. They were defined judicially based on social, familial, or class membership. Slaves, foreigners, and foundlings might be granted certain privileges, but they were not regarded as rights holders.

> There was, for example, little sympathy in early Greek literature for the physically impaired or oppressed, an attitude that can be demonstrated to have characterized both popular and official opinion in virtually every period of classical antiquity. Attitudes to the physically defective reflected the belief that health and physical wholeness were essential to human dignity, so much so that life without them was not thought to be worth living. Citizenship, kinship, status, merit, and virtue formed the foundation of claims to the possession of human rights or human worth. Those who lacked them (e.g., orphans, slaves, foundlings, the physically defective, prisoners) had no claim to the rights that they alone guaranteed or even to a recognition of their human worth.[34]

Unlike the classic views, early Jewish and Christian views of human worth were shaped by the theological notion that humans were created in the image of God. The worth of human life was amplified through the Incarnation, since through it God sacralized human nature, as it were. Being both divine and human, Jesus demonstrated that embodied human nature was not to be despised or evil.

As Ferngren points out, the *imago Dei* was formative in shaping Christian views of humanity, ethics, and ministry. First, the doctrine gave impetus to Christian charity and philanthropy. Just as concern for the poor was an important feature of the Hebrew scriptures, so charity and compassion were regarded as manifestations of Christian love (*agape*) and devotion to Christ. God's love for humans was to be imitated by extending love to a brother or sister made in the image of God (John 13:34–35). Religion that is pure and undefiled before God was defined, at least partially, as caring for "orphans and widows in their distress" (James 1:27), two classes of vulnerable people.

Second, the doctrine of the image of God provided the ground for the belief that every human life had intrinsic value as a bearer of God's image and the object of redemption through Christ. This was the basis for Christian repudiation of abortion, infanticide, the gladiatorial games, and suicide.

Third, Christian understanding of the *imago Dei* gave Christians a new perception of embodiment and human personality. Greek ascetics and, later, the Gnostics had no admiration or concern for the body. On the contrary, they despised it and looked forward to the day when they would be released from its prison. The image of God, especially as reflected in the Incarnation, gave rise to notions of a more integrated body and soul, Christ himself being the exemplar. "The Christian conception of Jesus as perfect man contributed," says Ferngren, "to raising the body to a status that it had never enjoyed in paganism."[35]

Finally, the doctrine of the image of God led to a redefinition of the poor. "The human body in all its parts shared in the divine image," argues Ferngren.[36] This was true of everyone's body, not merely that of Christians. The poor, sick, and disabled, were not to be shunned, but were to be seen as the objects of Christ's love. "Just as God demonstrated in the Incarnation his solidarity with those who suffer, so the members of his 'body' must demonstrate their solidarity with the suffering poor."[37] Celebration of the Eucharist allowed Christians to embrace solidarity with Christ and with all of those made in God's image. In sum, the image of God, especially as refracted through the prism of the Incarnation, was the basis for Christian compassion and care for those in need.

One of the pivotal New Testament texts related to the subject of congenital disability is John 9:1–7, where Jesus heals a man who was blind from birth:

> As he walked along, he saw a man blind from birth. His disciples asked him, "Rabbi, who sinned, this man or his parents, that he was born blind?" Jesus answered, "Neither this man nor his parents sinned; he was born blind so that God's works might be revealed in him. We must work the works of him who sent me while it is day; night is coming when no one can work. As long as I am in the world, I am the light of the world." When he had said this, he spat on the ground and made mud with the saliva and spread the mud on the man's eyes, saying to him, "Go, wash in the pool of Siloam" (which means Sent). Then he went and washed and came back able to see.

Like Job's miserable friends, Jesus' disciples raised the theodicy question: Since judgment has obviously fallen on this man, who sinned? Jesus not only repudiated the view that this disability was the result of God's judgment for the parents' sinful behavior, or the man's while a fetus in the womb, but he took on himself the mantle of healer and caregiver. After all, Luke tells us that one of the characteristics of Jesus' ministry was that "the blind receive their sight, the lame walk, the lepers are cleansed, the deaf hear, the dead are raised, the poor have good news brought to them" (Luke 7:22).

The upshot of these texts is, according to Amos Yong, that a number of themes have emerged in Christian views of disability:

> First, nothing escapes God's sovereignty, not even "monstrous births." Deformities and disabilities exhibit the wide range of God's creative works. Second, while people with "disabilities" lived difficult lives, such were necessary to cultivate holiness. Physical suffering thus served the larger purposes of God. Finally, the church should enact works of charity toward and on behalf of people

> with "disabilities," but such works were only temporary measures that anticipated the miraculous power of God to heal either in this life or in the life to come.[38]

Indeed, this seems to be an accurate depiction of the traditional understanding of disability, even among some who minister within the disability community. Joni Eareckson Tada, for instance, is a well-known voice among evangelicals. Her autobiography of experience with disability has provided hope and comfort for many.[39] Her own answer to the theodicy question sees divine purpose for disability.

> Scripture indicates that not only is God sovereign to physical injuries or illness, but he is Lord over the changes and alterations that transpire within the womb.
>
> Does this mean that God wants disease and injury? The key here is how we use the word want. God doesn't want disease to exist in the sense that he *enjoys* it. He hates it just as he hates all the other results of sin—death, guilt, sorrow, and catastrophes. But God must want disease to exist in the sense that he *wills* or chooses for it to exist. If he didn't, he would wipe it out immediately.... we are not the brunt of some cruel, divine joke. God has reasons, and learning some of them can make all the difference.[40]

Some theologians have recently begun calling for a "reimagining" of a theology of disability. Nancy Eiesland, who died in 2009 after a lifelong struggle with a congenital bone condition, asked Christians to embrace a contextualized Christology that sees the primary symbol of the faith to be a "disabled God."[41] By remembering that Jesus Christ is "the disabled God who embodied both impaired hands and feet and pierced side and the imago Dei,"[42] she hoped that a new solidarity with the disabled would evolve—a communion incarnated through the Eucharist.

Amos Yong has cast a new vision of the relationship between theology and disability. Like Eiesland, Yong points to Christ as the disabled God figure. Instead of a liberationist approach, however, Yong reconstructs the doctrines of creation, Fall, and resurrection.[43] In his view, what medical geneticists would call "anomalies," such as Trisomy 21, are simply "variations." These variations are not the result of original sin, but represent merely "the extremes of species variation."[44] Adam and Eve were not historical figures created in a primordial paradise without sin. They represent the "'first self-aware hominids' who as individuals and collectively suppressed the truth as they understood it and resisted rather than responded to God."[45] Yong believes that by understanding creation, anthropology, and sin in this way, he can preserve the solidarity between the disabled and the rest of the human family. Furthermore, his view entails not viewing disabilities as conditions that will be removed in the eschaton. Because disability, especially congenital intellectual disability (for example, the Down Syndrome which he describes in his brother), so shapes a person's identity, the removal of the condition would mean changing the person's very identity. Thus for Yong, the view that there is an ideal person who will be liberated in heaven from the body of a disabled person is at best an unhealthy dualism, and at worst the "tyranny of the normal." Rather than hoping for a heaven in which the people hear who have been deaf all their lives, we must envision a heaven in which the deaf *sign* the praises of the One who made them.[46]

Thomas Reynolds has emphasized the relationship among Christian faith, disability, and hospitality.[47]

> In hospitality, the Spirit is at work creating relations of reciprocity between (*sic*) God's children. This includes persons with disabilities, not as an afterthought but as essential to the well-being of the household. For the moral measure of a community lies in the way it treats its most vulnerable members, those strangers who exist on the margins. Paradoxically, however, in the community managed by God's economy of grace, the vulnerable stranger is at the center as one in whom the presence of the divine becomes real.[48]

Practically speaking, Reynolds suggests that hospitality to those with disabilities may be demonstrated by (1) recognizing the presence of persons with disabilities, (2) making cognitive, emotional, and linguistic space for persons with disabilities to flourish, and (3) advocating for people with disabilities. He concludes that "vulnerability, then, is the fulcrum of God's creative-redemptive work in the Holy Spirit. It is the means to wholeness that comes from welcoming and being welcomed. Hospitality to people with disabilities is both a way to God and a way that God reaches us."[49]

The future of the disabled is uncertain. At the same time that theologians, ethicists, lawmakers, caregivers, and families have been writing, defending, and advocating for persons with disabilities, the disabled are being eliminated from our society through diagnostic technologies, such as chorionic villus sampling, preimplantation genetic diagnosis (PGD), and interventions such as abortion. At least among those who have access to medical technology, every pregnancy has become a "tentative pregnancy"[50]—awaiting the results from the most recent test to detect some potentially adverse outcome.

As Hans Reinders has observed, "When people no longer want to get involved in the lives of dependent people, because these lives appear to be burdened with a deficit of meaning, this signifies a cultural rather than a political problem."[51] Just as Christians both ancient and modern established charitable hospitals, orphanages, and took into their homes the vulnerable poor, sick, and impaired, so the church must rise to the need of the suffering in what Pope John Paul II famously called "the culture of death."

Conclusion

Although it is certainly true that evangelicalism is not monolithic and that there is diversity among those who claim the label, evangelicals are legatees of a great tradition, so that today "evangelical" and "prolife" have become nearly synonymous. For at the heart of the evangelical ethos is dependence on the revelation of God in the scriptures of the Old and New Testaments and in the person of Jesus the Christ. Because of their biblicism, anthropology, and Christology, evangelicals seek to preserve the lives of all of those who are made in God's image.

Evangelicals admittedly have not always been the first to rally to the needs of the vulnerable. Only a relatively few evangelicals helped abolish American and British chattel slavery; but some did. Only a relatively few evangelicals stood against the eugenics movement that led to human atrocities in Nazi Germany; but some did. Only a relatively few evangelicals were among the righteous Gentiles who helped Jews escape the Holocaust; but some did. Only a relative few evangelicals stood at the vanguard of the civil rights movement to help African-Americans fight state-sponsored discrimination; but some did. Chastened by their past, evangelicals seem more sensitized to the needs of the vulnerable than at any time in their history.

Some worry, however, that evangelical ethical activism has become myopic, focused too keenly on the abortion debate. Too few are engaged with threats to the other end of life, represented by growing support for assisted suicide and euthanasia. Fewer still seem aware of concerns of the vulnerable between the beginning and end of life. For instance, the inability of evangelicals and Catholics to persuade the world that human embryos are to be valued and protected rather than aborted or used as research subjects has led to a vitriolic debate over embryonic stem cell research. More than one women's group has complained that the production and harvesting of women's ova for reproductive egg donation and stem cell research puts women, especially poor women, at risk.[52] Contraception, abortifacient drugs, and reproductive technologies have become increasingly controversial because of the potential for harming women and the unborn.

These controversies are unlikely to abate any time soon. As previously, one of more prudent tactics for evangelicals in the future will be to offer a countercultural community of care. Just as Athenagoras was able to point to the living witness of the churches to refute their detractors in the second century, so evangelical churches must cultivate a culture of life within their own congregations as an apologetic for life and protective environment for the vulnerable. Establishing church-based pregnancy care centers, hospices, and services for disabled children, adults, and their families, will be increasingly important ways to resist the culture of death.

At the same time, evangelicals must continue to work across the globe with other persons of good will in an effort to influence law and policy on life issues. As Dietrich Bonhoeffer insisted, "Life, created and preserved by God, possesses an inherent right, which is wholly independent of its social utility. The right to live is a matter of the essence and not of any values. In the sight of God there is no life that is not worth living."[53]

NOTES

1. Mary Ann Glendon, *Abortion and Divorce in Western Law: American Failures, European Challenges* (Cambridge: Harvard University Press, 1987).

2. Carl F. H. Henry, "Man," in Everett F. Harrison, Geoffrey W. Bromiley, and Carl F. H. Henry, eds., *Baker's Dictionary of Theology* (Grand Rapids: Baker, 1973), 339.

3. This does not mean, however, that animals may be abused. Stewardship of the animals entails that they not be treated cruelly nor destroyed willy-nilly. Here, for instance, God says he will require "a reckoning" for every animal that is killed. Similarly, the Fourth Commandment requires that animals be given a day of rest (Exodus 20:10), and the Deuteronomic codes make provision for the protection of straying livestock (Deuteronomy 22:1–4), young birds (Deuteronomy 22:6–7), and labor animals (Deuteronomy 25:4).

4. James Leo Garrett, *Systematic Theology: Biblical, Historical, and Evangelical*, vol. 1 (Grand Rapids: Eerdmans, 1990), 394–403. A benchmark essay on the image of God is D.J.A. Clines, "The Image of God in Man," *Tyndale Bulletin* 19 (1968), 53–103.

5. Or who, in the language of the Nicene Creed (325 C.E.), "came down and was incarnate and was made man."

6. Michael J. Gorman, *Abortion and the Early Church: Christian, Jewish and Pagan Attitudes in the Greco-Roman World* (Downers Grove, Ill.: InterVarsity Press, 1982), 34.

7. This is probably a reference to Exodus 21:22–25. For excellent treatments of this text vis-à-vis abortion, see Jack W. Cottrell, "Abortion and the Mosaic Law," *Christianity Today* 17 (March 16, 1973), 6–9, and James K. Hoffmeir, "Abortion and the Old Testament Law," James K. Hoffmeir, ed., *Abortion: A Christian Understanding and Response* (Grand Rapids: Baker, 1987), 49–63.

8. *Sentences* 184–185.

9. *The Sibylline Oracles*, Book II.345.

10. Flavius Josephus, *Against Apion* 2.202.

11. Cicero, *De Legibus* 3.8.

12. Plutarch, *Moralia* 2.171D.

13. W.E.H. Lecky, *History of European Morals: From Augustus to Charlemagne*, vol. 2 (New York: D. Appleton, 1897), 24.

14. Athenagoras, *Legatio* 35; cited in Gorman, *Abortion and the Early Church*, 54.

15. Tertullian, *Apology* 9.6, cited ibid., 55.

16. Basil, *Letter* 188, to Ampilochius, cited ibid., 67.

17. Ambrose, *Hexameron* 5.18.58 (the eighth homily, on day five); cited ibid., 68.

18. *Letter* 22.13 (to Eustochium), in T. C. Lawler, ed., *The Letters of St. Jerome*, trans. C. C. Mierow, (Westminster, Md.: Newman Press, 1963); cited ibid., 68.

19. St. Augustine, *Augustine: Confessions and Enchiridion*, trans. Albert C. Outler (Louisville, Ky.: Westminister/John Knox, 2006), 23.85.

20. Martin Luther, *Lectures on Genesis* 4.304–305.

21. John Calvin, *Commentaries on the Four Last Books of Moses*, vol. 3 (Grand Rapids: Eerdmans, 1950), 41–42.

22. Garth M. Rosell, *The Surprising Work of God: Harold John Ockenga, Billy Graham, and the Rebirth of Evangelicalism* (Grand Rapids: Baker Academic, 2008).

23. Carl F. H. Henry, *The Uneasy Conscience of Modern Fundamentalism* (Grand Rapids: Eerdmans, 1947), 36.

24. Ibid., 84.

25. See Marvin Olasky, *Abortion Rites: A Social History of Abortion in America* (Wheaton, Ill.: Crossway Books, 1992), 283, where Olasky concludes: "Essentially, I have found that pro-life forces have been wrong to assume that abortion was rare in the nineteenth century, that tough laws virtually ended the practice, that doctors and ministers led the way, and that the anti-abortion consensus remained philosophically intact until the 1960s. Pro-abortion groups have been wrong, however, in their typical assertion that abortion was widely diffused throughout the population, that abortion became illegal because regular doctors sought to drive out competitors, and that

abortion rates generally are unaffected by illegality or the development of alternatives."

26. C. Everett Koop, *Koop: The Memoirs of America's Family Doctor* (Grand Rapids: Zondervan, 1992), 340.

27. Ibid., 338. See Barry Hankins, *Francis Schaeffer and the Shaping of Evangelical America* (Grand Rapids: Eerdmans, 2008), 175.

28. Southern Baptist Convention, "Resolution on Abortion," St. Louis, Missouri, June 1971. The final clause is more than reminiscent of the language of *Doe v. Bolton* (1973) on the "health" of the mother.

29. A historical reflection on the Southern Baptist Convention's reversal on abortion can be found in Timothy George, "Southern Baptist Heritage of Life," in Richard D. Land and Louis A. Moore, *Life at Risk: The Crises in Medical Ethics* (Nashville, Tenn.: Broadman and Holman, 1995), 79–98.

30. *Bioethics: Opportunity or Obstacle for the Gospel*, Lausanne Occasional Paper 58 (Pattaya, Thailand: Lausanne Committee for World Evangelization, 2004), 31.

31. Ibid., 41.

32. Saul M. Olyan, *Disability in the Hebrew Bible: Interpreting Mental and Physical Differences* (New York: Cambridge University Press, 2008), 2.

33. Gary B. Ferngren, *Medicine and Health Care in Early Christianity* (Baltimore: Johns Hopkins University Press, 2009), 95.

34. Ibid., 95–96.

35. Ibid., 102.

36. Ibid., 103.

37. Ibid., 104.

38. Amos Yong, *Theology and Down Syndrome: Reimaging Disability in Late Modernity* (Waco: Baylor University Press, 2007), 33.

39. Joni Eareckson Tada, *Joni: An Unforgettable Story* (Grand Rapids: Zondervan, 1976).

40. Gene Newman and Joni Eareckson Tada, *All God's Children: Ministry with Disabled Persons* (Grand Rapids: Zondervan, 1993), 19. Italics in the original.

41. Nancy L. Eiesland, *The Disabled God: Toward a Liberatory Theology of Disability* (Nashville, Tenn.: Abingdon, 1994).

42. Ibid., 99.

43. As against a more classically Reformed view. For the latter, see Albert M. Wolters, *Creation Regained: Biblical Basics for a Reformational Worldview* (Grand Rapids: Eerdmans, 1985).

44. Yong, *Theology and Down Syndrome*, 164.

45. Ibid.

46. Ibid., 291.

47. Thomas E. Reynolds, *Vulnerable Communion: A Theology of Disability and Hospitality* (Grand Rapids: Brazos, 2008).

48. Ibid., 245.

49. Ibid., 247.

50. Barbara Katz Rothman, *The Tentative Pregnancy: How Amniocentesis Changes the Experience of Motherhood* (New York: W. W. Norton, 1993).

51. Hans S. Reinders, *The Future of the Disabled in Liberal Society: An Ethical Analysis* (Notre Dame: University of Notre Dame Press), 2000.

52. See Deborah Spar, *The Baby Business: How Money, Science, and Politics Drive the Commerce of Conception* (Cambridge: Harvard Business School Press, 2006). Also, "Hands Off Our Ovaries," http://handsoffourovaries.com/.

53. Dietrich Bonhoeffer, *Ethics* (New York: Macmillan, 1965), 163.

BIBLIOGRAPHY

Bachiochi, Erika. *The Cost of Choice: Women Evaluate the Impact of Abortion*. New York: Encounter Books, 2004.

Beckwith, Francis J. *Defending Life: A Moral and Legal Case against Abortion*. Cambridge: Cambridge University Press, 2007.

Brown, Harold O. J. *Death before Birth*. Nashville, Tenn.: Thomas Nelson, 1980.

Davis, John Jefferson. *Evangelical Ethics: Issues Facing the Church Today*. 3rd edition. Phillipsburg, N.J.: Presbyterian and Reformed, 2004.

Eiesland, Nancy L. *The Disabled God: Toward a Liberatory Theology of Disability*. Nashville, Tenn.: Abingdon, 1994.

Ferngren, Gary B. *Medicine and Health Care in Early Christianity*. Baltimore: Johns Hopkins University Press, 2009.

George, Robert P., and Christopher Tollefson. *Embryo: A Defense of Human Life*. New York: Doubleday, 2008.

Glendon, Mary Ann. *Abortion and Divorce in Western Law: American Failures, European Challenges*. Cambridge: Harvard University Press, 1987.

Gorman, Michael J. *Abortion and the Early Church: Christian, Jewish and Pagan Attitudes in the Greco-Roman World*, Downers Grove, Ill.: InterVarsity Press, 1982.

Hoffmeir, James F., ed., *Abortion: A Christian Understanding and Response*. Grand Rapids: Baker, 1987.

Jones, David Albert. *The Soul of the Embryo*. New York: Continuum, 2004.

Koop, C. Everett, and Francis A. Schaeffer. *Whatever Happened to the Human Race?* Revised ed. Wheaton, Ill.: Crossway Books, 1983.

Matthewes-Green, Frederica. *Real Choices: Listening to Women; Looking for Alternatives to Abortion*. Ben Lomond, Cal.: Conciliar Press, 1994.

Newman, Gene, and Joni Eareckson Tada. *All God's Children: Ministry with Disabled Persons* Revised ed. Grand Rapids: Zondervan, 1993.

Olasky, Marvin. *Abortion Rites: A Social History of Abortion in America*. Wheaton, Ill.: Crossway Books, 1992.

Reinders, Hans S. *The Future of the Disabled in Liberal Society: An Ethical Analysis*. Notre Dame: University of Notre Dame Press, 2000.

Reynolds, Thomas E. *Vulnerable Communion: A Theology of Disability and Hospitality*. Grand Rapids, Brazos, 2008.

Swinton, John, and Brian Brock, eds. *Theology, Disability and the New Genetics: Why Science Needs the Church*. London: T & T Clark, 2007.

Yong, Amos. *Theology and Down Syndome: Reimagining Disability in Late Modernity*. Waco: Baylor University Press, 2007.

CHAPTER 32

GENDER

CHERITH NORDLING

"*All* things are yours," writes Paul to the women and men of the church at Corinth, be it "the world or life or death or the present or the future—all are yours, and you are of Christ, and Christ is of God" (1 Cor 3:21b–22). Paul reminds them that because of God's self-giving generosity, there is no longer any need or place for division over leadership that would limit the gifts of the Spirit poured out equally on women and men alike. To do so would be to go backward, to live as "old creation." Rather, these diverse women and men, reconstituted by the Spirit, are "new creation." They share eschatologically in all that belongs to the Son, who has guaranteed an embodied inheritance that does not prioritize gender, class, ethnicity, or anything else.

This expansive offering of life together, grounded in the generous life of the Triune God, offers a challenge to evangelical traditions and theologies where oppositional dualisms run deep, especially in terms of being female and male image-bearers of Jesus Christ. These dualisms take multiple forms. One is that of prescribing and proscribing roles according to gender and sexuality. Authority, hierarchy, tradition, and head/leadership are biblically interpreted through a set of assumptions that essentially prioritize men's being and function over that of women.[1] In this dualism, biology is God-ordained destiny.

Another dualistic tendency is toward a disembodied, neutered piety that often discounts the call to responsibility for what happens to persons in their male and female bodies.[2] Internalizing Jesus' command to love the Lord with one's "heart, soul and mind" (Matt 22:37), this "spiritual" construal makes it easy to separate, and thus to forget, that we receive and respond to God's love for us only as embodied persons. We love God and our (sexual/gendered) neighbors as our (sexual/gendered) selves. This dualism obscures the fact that we are and ever will be male and female followers of Jesus Christ. Only as such do we live, move, and have our being. In other words, the only way to be truly human and thus to be truly conformed to the image of Jesus of Nazareth, is to be redeemed and restored as women and men. We are embodied image bearers already and not yet living out our final destiny in all our particularity.

We profess this as Christians because at the heart of the *euangelion* is the radical pronouncement of the resurrection of the body and the life everlasting. In short, through Jesus Christ's resurrected life we too get our human lives back, permanently. No souls going to heaven in this gospel—only "children of the resurrection" whose future humanity is held in promise by the still incarnate, still male, still human Son of God. The New Testament Church, and all who have come after, bear witness to the fact that God raised this brutally crucified *man* from the dead and seated *him* at the Father's right hand. Thus, we too will be embodied—and arguably, sexual and gendered—human beings forever. The question, then, is, how do we live out a gendered reality in conformity to Jesus Christ, the eschatological New Adam of a new, restored human race? Before we speak to that question, however, we will consider how the concept of gender has developed, how it plays out in evangelical theology, and how the gifting and influence of various women in Church history compare to some current evangelical proscriptions.

What Is Gender?

Attempts to speak of gender in the context of evangelical theology are often fraught with misunderstanding or intransigence. Perhaps it has to do with the concept of gender itself. As gender has become a concept used within theological anthropology (rather than emerging from it), it brings along its own set of issues that mainly derive from the sociological contexts and categories in which it developed. Elaine Storkey notes that gender has taken up theological residence along with a host of uncontested assumptions and stereotypes that pose as empirical social science, on the one hand, and modern interpretations of Scripture, on the other. This gender "baggage," states Storkey, still waits to be "reclaimed, unpacked and examined before the concept can be accorded new citizenship" in evangelical theology.[3]

In a broad, nuanced sense, *gender* refers to both one's bodily and cultural identity as male and female. Gender is often construed in distinction from "sex" or "sexuality," drawn from rather simplistic demarcations between what is considered "nature" (sex and sexuality) and "nurture" (gender). Sex, determined primarily in terms of male and female reproductive function, is a natural, biological "given" and also tends to be the first classification we make upon meeting someone. Joined to that classification, however, are assumed gender expectations regarding that person's behaviors, personality, perceptions, motives, reactions, activities, and attitudes.[4] Despite the fact that these gender expectations have differed historically and culturally around the world, certain Western gender perspectives hold sway in evangelical gender debates. These can be traced as premodern, modern, and postmodern perspectives.

The "premodern" (pre-1960) perspective considers not only sex to be a natural given, but gender as well.[5] Reinforced by accepted tradition, the premodern assumption is that there is an essential, universal fixed order to things, including a core reality about being a man or woman. This reality includes biological, sexual distinction, a divinely ordained male or female "essence" or "nature, and an" inherent set of gender characteristics, behaviors, and roles.[6]

> The *essentialist* approach presumes that gender and sexuality can be defined objectively because there is a core reality to these concepts, an essential female and male nature that is universal and constant across cultures. *Essentialists* may disagree about which aspects of gender [and sexuality] are part of this core reality, but they agree there is such a reality, which is unaltered by culture, beliefs or values.[7]

The modern (post-1960) perspective fundamentally challenges this view, believing that gender has far more to do with what is social than what is "natural" to one's sex. Rejecting the assumption that "biology is destiny," modern discourse around gender moves the emphasis from essence or creation to "construction." It assumes that what in premodern terms is deemed the "natural order" is instead a highly organized social system with underlying power structures. These structures normalize certain attitudes, assumptions, and behaviors to keep the system in place and benefit those in power. Modern gender questions are concerned with how these social norms are constructed—how do they come into existence, how do they manifest, and what are the underlying values?

> The *constructionist* approach presumes that gender (and sexuality) cannot be understood apart from the historical, social and cultural contexts in which they are being defined and observed. Gender and sexuality are linguistic constructions that attempt to describe people's observations and experiences; experiences that always occur within a particular context. The meaning of these terms changes throughout history and across cultures; they are constructed as we structure our lives and communities according to the values and beliefs of those who have the power to shape those structures. Constructionists may disagree about the extent to which gender and sexuality are socially constructed, but they focus on socially given meanings and minimize objectively given realities.[8]

Modern gender debates have attempted not only to expose hidden ideologies and given norms but also to replace them with alternative values and beliefs that promote the equal flourishing of women and men. Initial efforts went toward constructing an understanding of humanity as universally equal by emphasizing gender equity, mutuality, and reciprocity. Universal or common humanity is not equated with "sameness," however, for this idea ignores biological difference or lived bodily experience. Rather, common humanity means that sexuality and embodiment do not preordain gender *roles*.

More recent modern efforts have specifically emphasized difference and distinction between women and men without any presumed hierarchy. Postmodern gender debates press the understanding of difference even further, emphasizing diversity and plurality of cultures, relationships, values, peoples, and ideologies in a way that refuses any universal or meta-narrative, including the biblical narrative. Rather, the postmodern appeal is to local narratives and cultural contexts to provide meaning regarding human identity and difference.

Studies across cultures indicate that people in different cultures learn different ways of being masculine and feminine according to accepted attitudes and expectations. These studies also tell us certain consistent things about gender, says psychologist Heather Looey. They confirm that "gender matters; that there are two genders; and that there are particular ways that males and females think, feel and act."[9] While the first two messages about gender are virtually universal across cultures and time, the content of the last message—that females and males think, feel, and act in particular ways—"varies considerably," states Looey.[10] Research around the world continues to indicate that the degree to which men and women differ, or the extent to which they "represent two qualitatively different forms of humankind as opposed to two significantly overlapping, highly similar variants of the human species," is in fact much less clear than is commonly assumed. This is because the common "overlap" between males and females is so vast.[11] Universal humanity as is fundamental to any individual person as is their human particularity.

It is becoming increasingly apparent that clear distinctions between nature and nurture (sexual being and experience) are not viable. To think too rigidly of sex as "creational" and gender as "cultural," says Storkey, is to form another unhelpful dualism. What is given is inseparable from what is learned in human experience: "Being a man or woman is as much about *learning* to be masculine and feminine [cultural constructs] as it is about living with one's differences in chromosomes."[12] Thus one can assume that there is both an objective, universal character to gender and sexuality and a socially constructed and particular dimension, as well. These complex concepts, informed through biological, relational, developmental, historical, and cultural processes, foundationally belong to creaturely human existence as both good and broken.[13] To assume that sex ("nature") is good and gender ("nurture") is fallen is a false dichotomy that does not account for God's involvement in human existence ultimately manifested in Jesus' lived experience.

> In fact, we believe in a God who is as interested in our gender as in our biology, for the way we shape our gender is also part of our human response before God. Therefore, we need to address issues of power, discrimination, poor communication, injustice, unfaithfulness, violation, competitiveness, and stereotypes, because in all of these areas we can contravene the principles that God has given us for gender relationships.... God calls us into responsible and right relationships [that reflect God's love, justice, righteousness, faithfulness, and truth], and gender patterns call from us a response of obedience.[14]

This exhortation is an important one, since in current evangelical conversations the concept of gender continues to be framed by questions of nature or nurture and the degree to which they jointly influence what it means to be a man or woman.[15] Whether in scientific study, theological discourse, or social attitudes, there are extra-scientific values that influence the analysis or interpretation of gender. Christian (including evangelical) theology has profoundly influenced theological discourse on gender and sexuality in either exhilarating or harmful ways, depending in some cases on the degree to which it has utilized these concepts.

The "New" History of Women in Scripture and the Church

One of the great benefits of an increased focus on gender among evangelicals has been the unveiling of women often hidden in Church history. Christian and non-Christian scholars alike have retrieved histories of women in the biblical world and the Church that were obfuscated or silenced. They reaffirm that both the Old and New Testaments identify women on whom the Spirit of God rested in these ancient Near East patriarchal cultures. These women are known and remembered for their Spirit-given faith, identity, gifting, leadership, and obedience to God.

Among them are prophets such as Miriam, Deborah, Huldah, and Anna, or disciples of Jesus such as Mary Magdelene, Joanna, Susanna, Mary, Martha, and the unnamed multitude of women among whom Jesus ushered in the Kingdom of God. The Acts of the Apostles and Paul's letters give indication of numerous women in key areas of church ministry: Junia the "outstanding" apostle imprisoned with Paul (Rom 16:7), Lydia and Nympha (Acts 16:11–15; Col 4:15), leaders of church communities meeting in their households, Phoebe the deacon, Priscilla the teacher and Paul's co-worker, and other women who were fellow laborers in ministry with Paul, including Euodia and Syntyche (Acts 18:26; Phil 4:2; Rom 16:1ff.)

The next generations of women were martyrs, scholars, evangelists, preachers, prophets, mystics, and mothers. These include martyrs Blandina, Perpetua, and Felicitas; prophets Prisca and Maximilla; intercessor Monica, mother of Augustine; Paula, supporter of Jerome; theologian Marcella, who was the sister of Basil of Caesarea and Gregory of Nyssa, as well as a friend to John Chrysostom and Jerome; church leaders Hildegard of Bingen, Hilda of Witby, Julian of Norwich, Catherine of Siena, and Teresa of Avila, whose lives, preaching, and teaching were dedicated to God and to serious reform of a male-led church often regarded as biblically and morally bankrupt. If, as Tertullian stated, "the blood of the martyrs is the seed of the church," then much of the church was planted through the lives of women, literally and figuratively. Their lives and/or horrific deaths for the gospel knew no gender hierarchy.

With the Reformation came European reformers Katie Von Bora Luther (former nun and wife of Martin Luther), Argula Von Stauffer, Katherine Zell (who supported the Anabaptist movement), Quaker Margaret Fell Fox, Susanna Wesley (mother of John and Charles), Margaret Davidson, Sarah Crosby, and Mary Bosanquet Fletcher. Many of these women were best known for their enduring, powerful preaching. North America saw preachers Ann Hutchinson, Mary Dyer, and Phoebe Palmer; later preachers and evangelists in Britain and North America such as Lucretia Mott, Lucy and Angelina Grimke, Antoinette Brown, Lucy Stone, Sojouner Truth, Harriet Tubman, the Blackmore sisters; social reformers and church leaders Elizabeth Fry, Florence Nightingale, and Josephine Butler.[16] Lost to history are most of the nineteenth-century commentaries written by women whose voices (and publisher's profit margins) could not be sustained in cultures unable or unwilling to hear them.[17] Among the questions raised in present evangelical discourse is how evangelicals have managed to miss, or dismiss, these women for so long.

Gender in Current Evangelical Discourse

Does evangelical theology continue to marginalize women based on the order of old creation, or does it manifest a theology of mutual participation in God's new creation? Does it challenge and shape culture by offering a new order of relationships and identity in Christ, or is it uncritically shaped by culture and tradition, thereby perpetuating broken orders of systemic sin?

These questions stem from the fact that much evangelical culture and theology mirrors aspects of popular culture, as each remains influenced by and perpetuates forms of premodern gender essentialism. For a multitude of reasons, each has "gender myths" that emphasize sexual and gender difference to keep a certain status quo. Sometimes these myths uncritically coincide. For instance, Kristina LaCelle-Peterson finds it both notable and disturbing that cultural assumptions in some conservative Christian circles about gender roles (delivered in the church as coming straight from God) "bear striking resemblance to middle-class American gender mores." These norms have been baptized by church tradition and repackaged as "the will of God" or "what the Bible says" about who women and men are and should be. "Consequently, to challenge gender assumptions and gender roles," says Peterson, "feels as if we are rejecting Christianity, or at least parts of the Bible."[18]

The evangelical equating of premodern essentialism with biblical norms concerning gender does not originate from the full range of the New Testament and its church practices. Male and female theologians within and outside the evangelical tradition argue that it seems to reflect certain Aristotelian assumptions about sex and gender that made their way into the life of the Church early on and have remained deeply embedded there throughout the centuries. Church history is replete with androcentric theologies and hierarchical male-female dualisms that rely chiefly on Aristotle's philosophy and biology.[19] Whether reading Augustine in the West or Cyril in the East, one can pick up different aspects of Aristotle's understanding of sex identity. This influence can be seen in historical discussions concerning "sex unity" (all humans are unified at the "spiritual" level of the sexless soul), "sex polarity" (in this earthly existence, only men can adequately represent the image of God), or "sex complementarity" (in heaven we keep our sexual bodies).[20]

The significant contributions to theological anthropology made by Augustine, Athanasius, Aquinas, and other early church Fathers shine when they interpret the category of "sex complementarity" through resurrection. Here their theology stands in sharp contrast to Neo-Platonic dualisms of body and soul and gender hierarchy, as they preach the resurrection of our sexually differentiated bodies, equally redeemed, restored, and empowered for the life to come.[21] Despite the Christian hope of embodied resurrection, however, this pervasive Aristotelian essentialism found in early and medieval Church history, endured into the Protestant Reformation and influenced parts of the evangelical tradition. This enduring legacy offers some evangelicals justification for an essentialist, hierarchical view on the basis of "tradition."

For some North American evangelicals, however, "tradition" held a host of negative connotations as against "pure" readings of Scripture. This led to new terminology that emerged in the 1980s. First, the word "traditional" gave way to "biblical." Eventually, "biblical" and "hierarchical" became interchangeable terms among certain evangelicals who used these terms with regard to biblical interpretation concerning women in the church. For them the "undiluted" authority of Scripture led to only one "biblical" interpretation, that of male hierarchy. Eventually hierarchicalists such as Wayne Grudem and John Piper began to describe gender roles in terms of "biblical manhood and womanhood."[22] Eventually, this position was self-described as "complementarian." From an essentialist position, complementarians argue that biblical manhood and womanhood are biological categories that include divinely ordained gender roles.

For complementarians the determination of gender role is linked to issues of authority. The authority of biblical interpretation is linked to the authority of men over women in the church and every sphere of life. In short, aspects of leadership are reserved for men on the basis of a "plain reading" of Scripture.[23] Women's full participation as leaders in the Church who are responsible for any area of decision making is considered a disregard for Scriptural authority. Men are seen as responsible under God for the leadership of both church and family/home.

Among evangelical hierarchicalists, women are understood to be "equal in being, but unequal in role." In other words, women are considered ontologically equal in being to men, but not equal in responsibility, function, and authority. This is a variation of Aristotle's conclusion that men are by nature more fit for command than women. Aristotle argued this, however, on the basis of ontological superiority; he asserted that men are by nature morally and rationally superior to women. In short, he understood role to derive from ontology.

Evangelical hierarchicalists or complementarians who conclude with Aristotle that the subordination of women to male authority is a byproduct of "the created order" are hard pressed to explain how this is merely a matter of function and not ontology, notes Becca Merrill Groothuis. Role is directly based on ontology; men are deemed created as more "fit" for certain leadership roles than women. Thus, states Groothuis, "the 'different roles' that patriarchalists assign to women and men are not just about function but are fundamentally a matter of ontology or being."[24]

Groothuis contends that the hierarchicalist argument that women are unequal in role but otherwise equal in being is neither logical nor theologically sustainable from the Genesis narrative. "It is logically impossible for the same person to be at once spiritually and ontologically equal *and* permanently, comprehensively, and necessarily subordinate."[25] Other non-hierarchicalists point out that Genesis 3 describes hierarchy as a byproduct of the curse upon fallen humanity; it represents the loss of their holy estate and shared dominion on behalf of creation. Since Christ has become the curse and redemption for women and men alike, he equally shares his "firstborn" status and authority as Lord and firstborn over all creation with all those who have died and risen with him by the Spirit (Eph 1–2).

Of increasing concern is the fact that this ontological construct is now appearing as evangelical Trinitarian doctrine. There are some who support gender hierarchy by positing an eternal subordination of "being" and/or "function" in the Trinity. Hierarchicalist Wayne Grudem has argued for the eternal subordination of the Son to the Father in terms of function.[26] In Australia, an evangelical commission has taken this a step further away from Scripture and tradition by asserting a doctrine of the Son's eternal subordination in being. In other words, distinction between the Triune persons extends to their divine nature (Nicaea notwithstanding, the Son is no longer *homoousion* with the Father).[27] The theological implications of this argument are enormous, since historical Christian orthodoxy has deemed these views heretical.

Those are evangelicals who share a biblical understanding of complementarity without hierarchy, find this view described as "biblical equality," "egalitarianism," and "evangelical feminism." Whatever the terms, or the degree of ease with which they are used, the interpretation they represent is not concomitant with secular and liberal religious feminism, contextualized gender shifts grounded in culture, negations of gender difference, or equal-rights politics. Rather, evangelicals holding this interpretative stance simply argue that the biblical text offers support for the possibility of women's equal place in church leadership and other spheres. Leadership is not assumed as a right. Rather, leadership is a gift of the Spirit for the sake of God's people. As such, it is a matter of equal obedience for both men and women.[28]

As this debate runs along the complementarian-egalitarian continuum, it consistently affirms and clarifies the evangelical commitment to Scripture as the inspired, revelatory Word of God. Through Scripture God speaks in and for the world, allowing us to know both God and ourselves in the context of God's historical involvement and covenantal commitment to his world. While the Bible is timeless in this regard, it is also historically given, involving the human language, culture, thought forms, and literary genres. Interpretation requires a simultaneous understanding and commitment to the eternal significance, historical particularity, and contextual enactment of God's Word.

There is no objective ground from which to view Scripture, nor is that how Scripture is ever read or used. The text is heard in an interpretive world, full of given assumptions and norms that the text is often used to support. Some of these are faithful to the world of the text; many are not.[29] The task, according to Gordon Fee, is "to discover and hear that Word in terms of God's original intent and then hear that same Word again in our own historical setting, even when our particulars are quite different from those of the original setting."[30]

Some of the most controversial biblical texts being interpreted within the evangelical gender debate include 1 Tim 2:12–13, 1 Cor 11:3 and Eph 5:22–23. These are read by hierarchicalists as gender essentialist mandates concerning women's "roles" in the local church and at home. For instance, 1 Tim 2:12–13 is understood as Paul's instruction to Timothy that a woman cannot have "authority" over a man. This is based on an interpretation of the word *authentien* (used only once in the New Testament) as "authority." This term is then understood to mean "to rule" based on a reading of Genesis 3. This interpretation is challenged by egalitarian and nonegalitarian scholars alike. Among their concerns it that assigning this meaning to *authentien* disregards multiple other possible meanings and all the other New Testament contexts in which authority is discussed (where *exousiadzo* and its various forms is used).[31]

If these arguments over texts sometimes focus attention away from the full biblical narrative of God's original and final intention for his creation, there are evangelicals seeking to refocus that attention. Heather Looey proposes that as we acknowledge the limited and broken nature of our assumptions, we nonetheless assume there to be something normative about gender and sexuality as two dimensions of our human multidimensionality. She contends that the nature of God's gift of creation requires us to constantly work out what it means to be gendered and sexual beings in this time and this place.[32] Having further developed this understanding of gender as a dimension of eschatological creaturely existence, Mary Stewart Van Leeuwen argues that "the constant invention and reinvention of gender roles is an expression of our creation-based sense that women and men need each other. Thus we search for ways to symbolize that need."[33] She offers the practice of gender-role complementarity as a relational sacrament, since as co-members of God's body men and women are incomplete without each other.[34]

As Elaine Storkey identifies four underlying paradigms —*difference, similarity, complementarity* (without hierarchy) and *union*—continually at work in the biblical text, she believes that these same paradigms should influence our understanding of the relationship between men and women.[35] To focus on any one of them alone "distorts our theology and leads to vehement reactions and repudiations."[36] Together, however, these paradigms work to reveal how God deconstructs broken worldviews and encounters people in ways that both contextualize gender relations and positively transgress them. Evangelical biblical scholars Gordon Fee, Aida Spencer, David Scholer, Linda Belleville, and Craig Keener are among those whose work identifies the exegetical and hermeneutical challenges of the gendered world of the texts, the consistently radical nature of Jesus' Kingdom life and word to the Father's "children of the resurrection," and Paul's understanding of the radical, Kingdom-cultural life of the Spirit-gifted Christian community of women and men.

A host of evangelical theologians, including Stanley Grenz, Colin Gunton, Ray Anderson, and Ian McFarland, have contributed to theological anthropology and the question of human personhood in the context of Trinitarian theology.[37] Miroslov Volf, also situated among these theologians, argues that we exist in an irreducible duality of genders with equal dignity, in which both men and women experience fullness and deficiency. Each needs the other for "creation," "redemption" and identity-in-relation (symmetry in construction of gender identities and the presence of the other in the self), and all is held together through self-giving love.[38] Linda Woodhead argues for a shared gender identity in Christ that is hidden with him in terms of its full eschatological expression.[39] Alan Torrance also points us to Christ, the Logos before whom we all stand, not as an ideal but as the event of new humanity. Christ is the forgiving and commissioning telos of the entire created order. He grounds our communion in the Triune life and gives us the eschatological Spirit in our spatio-temporal bodily existence as the locus of God's reality with us. Already achieved in him, Christ's purposes for our embodied lives must be conceived eschatologically.[40]

Eschatologically Reoriented by Resurrection, Ascension, and the Outpoured Spirit

So how do we live as gendered, sexual beings in our contingent historicity and cultural location, taking full account of our eschatological identity and orientation? We must look to where the Kingdom has already been inaugurated to provide both the present and future context for our humanity. Thus the question of gender requires an eschatological frame that accounts for both the ongoing, permanent humanity of Jesus Christ as divine Lord and the outpoured, indwelling Holy Spirit.

Jesus' incarnation was and remains God's ultimate affirmation of creation, and specifically of human beings. Evangelical tradition, however, has sometimes discounted this as an eternal reality. Despite the language of Scripture and the creeds, there remain hearty forms of docetism and gnosticism in evangelical thought and behavior, supported by the invisible underpinnings of gender and soul/body dualisms. To argue that our primary identity is neither sexual nor gendered as *imago Dei* in Christ simply fails to account for who Jesus is.[41] While there is no sexuality in God's being, there is now and forever human, male particularity in the "Word made flesh."[42]

The hope of reconciled and reconstituted sexuality and gender is neither a vain hope nor a hypothetical one. It is found precisely in the person of Jesus Christ in whom God has come to be present to us in our creatureliness and brokenness, redeeming and reconstituting our human being and identity. The Incarnate Word forever bears and mediates our new humanity. Held in him, we are also on the way to becoming what we will be forever, to the praise of the glorious grace of our heavenly Father—fully restored men and women socialized in the new culture of the Kingdom of God by the life-giving Holy Spirit.

The resurrected Jesus is what happens, says Jeremy Begbie, when Genesis meets Easter. He is "new creation 'first edition.'"[43] In Jesus we see not only God's Self-revelation but we also see what it means to be truly human. The risen Jesus is "the radiance of God's glory and the exact representation of his being," the truly human "image of the invisible God and firstborn from among the dead" (resurrected human beings), in whom "all the fullness of God's deity lives in bodily form" (Heb 1:3–4; Col 1:15, 2:9). Resplendent in his renewed, transfigured body, still bearing the marks of his wounds (Rev 5:6; 1 Peter 2:24), he is seated in glory at the right hand of the Father, alight with the joy that made the cross endurable, already wearing *our* future glory (Heb 2:8–10; 12:2).

Our human identity is grounded in the divine Son, the one perfect human who functions as our High Priest until the consummation of his final glory. He is the new Adam, the firstborn of a restored human race, ushering in the final new creation in which there is no prioritizing one person over another, no first or last[44] (John 1:1, 4, 14; Rom 5:12–18; 1 Cor 15:21–22, 45–49; Luke 1:54–55, 2:4–11; Matt 1:1–17; Col 1:15, 18). As Paul attempts to describe the mystery of Christ's resurrected reality while describing ours (1 Cor 15), he speaks of the redemption of our human bodies as our final inheritance of restored glory (Rom 8:17–23).

The crucified Jesus did not resurrect as an androgynous being ontologically discontinuous with humanity. He arose a new *man;* that is, his resurrected body was transformed within the continuity of creation, even as he manifested the radical discontinuity of our future bodies equipped for the age to come, where heaven and earth intersect, as it were. People experienced him in recognizably "male" fashion after his resurrection. Resurrection is a human experience from first to last, from death to life. We do not become disembodied souls or androgynous beings who cease to be human. Rather, we are new creation, men and women reconstituted in body and in social relation to God, one another, and all of heaven and earth.

The New Testament creation/exodus/new creation motifs describe our present and future eschatological human hope in terms that are all reordered to Jesus of Nazareth (Matt 24:37; Rom 5:12–18; 2 Cor 5; 2 Peter 3:6–7). Jesus' new embodied life not only guarantees the human life that awaits us. It also conditions our Kingdom life in the present. What is true in the consummation of the age to come must be true in the eschatological age of the Spirit. In other words, what is true of the future Kingdom—its character, values, and ethics—must be true in this present age. As the old creation stands under the judgment of God and is passing away (1 Cor 7:31), we are to demonstrate the future Kingdom of God "on earth as it is in heaven" as we await its completion (Matt 6:10; Rom 8:19–25).

Our Spirit-led and empowered obedience takes only one shape in this new life together, that of cruciformity. "Those who would come after me must deny themselves, take up their cross and follow me" (Matt 16: 24). Our primary identity is given in the one whose cruciform humiliation is the prerequisite to his resurrection and exaltation, whose suffering for the sake of the other is the place where divine and human glory ultimately manifest the kingdom of God. Here no privilege or division based on difference can be held to Joined to Christ as his Body, we are equally recreated, privileged, and empowered as "children of Abraham" to live as image bearers for one another, our neighbor and creation, at the cost of our lives. For we participate in his resurrection glory exactly in that place where we are also called to participate in the fellowship of his suffering on behalf of one another (Gal 3:28; 1 Cor 12–14). Equality, then, is not a principle espoused by Jesus in terms of "fairness" or human rights, privilege or entitlement. Rather, we are equally for one another. Equality is simply equal participation in the gospel and all that that entails as a call to self-giving love and service.

Paul asserts that when we come into the fellowship of Jesus Christ, our humanity is identified with his perfect image (Col 1:15; 2:9, 10). Our human dignity, value, and status are no longer based on these distinctions and their privileged status in the old order. The significance of this affirmation lies in that it equally disadvantages all by equally advantaging all, because in Christ these distinctions do not define human personhood or position.[45] Privilege is given and exercised for the building up of the whole community, whether by men or women. This does not entitle women to roles any more than it takes them away from men. All service is cruciform, all service is a gift to be given.

Jesus demonstrated the extent to which in the New Covenant surpasses current (broken) social conventions or relational norms. He addressed women as equals, gave honor and recognition to children, and championed the poor and outcast. He mingled with persons of different class, race, status, and gender. Eating and communing with them, he "equalized" their mutual relation under God. Jesus does not address roles according to gender, but rather according to God's character and Kingdom culture. Luke sums up Jesus' final lesson to his disciples by emphatically denying anyone the role of lord and authority over anyone, since to be like God is to be for the other, as one who serves, no matter the cost (Luke 22:24–30). And then God's king and only Lord of heaven and earth offers history's supreme object lesson; he enacts his role by submitting to a Roman crucifixion. For precisely this reason, says Paul, the Father has exalted him over all things. In this supreme act of being for the other, in humiliation unto death, he manifested the true servant character of God, and thus the character of a true human image bearer. Thus he bears Yahweh's name (Phil 2:8–9).

Jesus is unashamed to call us brothers and sisters. He has freely given his "firstborn inheritor" status to every person, in our gendered, ethnic, cultural identity, through which we manifest God's life for the other. We are called into being as gift, not necessity, as beloved ones, whose meaning and destiny are given through, and contingent upon, our relation to God and one another, in complementary fullness and communion. We become who we are as we live, and die, for others, in service to and celebration of the sexual, gender, racial, ethnic, cultural, and historical distinctions that make us unique in the Kingdom of God without prizing any one over the other. By not considering "equality something to be grasped" even among ourselves, but outdoing one another in love and in response to the gift-giving, equipping Spirit, we reflect the image, character, and power of the self-giving God in whom we live and move and have our being.

NOTES

1. A helpful discussion of this gender construction can be found in Rebecca Merrill Groothuis, "'Equal in Being, Unequal in Role': Exploring the Logic of Woman's Subordination," in Ronald W. Pierce and Rebecca Merrill Groothius, eds., *Discovering Biblical Equality: Complementarity without Hierarchy* (Downer's Grove, Ill.: InterVarsity, 2004), 301–333.

2. See Beth Felker Jones, *Marks of His Wounds: Gender Politics and Bodily Resurrection* (Oxford: Oxford University Press, 2007). "A concern for Christian ethics can never be far from attempts to conceptualize the body theologically... real bodies are broken, beaten, raped, tortured, killed.... 'Dualist' accounts of bodies are rightly implicated in violence against those bodies" (11, 18).

3. "Evangelical Theology and Gender," in *The Cambridge Companion to Evangelical Theology* (Cambridge: Cambridge University Press, 2007), 161.

4. Heather Looey, "Gender and Sexuality: Constancy and Change," in S. W. VanderStoep, ed., *Science of the Soul: Christian Perspectives on Psychological Research* (Lanham, Md.: University Press of America, 2003), 308.

5. See Elaine Storkey, *Origins of Difference: The Gender Debate Revisited* (Grand Rapids: Baker Academic, 2001), who uses the categories of premodern, modern, and postmodern as given by Michel Foucault and Jean Joseph Goux.

6. Ibid., 25.

7. Looey, "Gender and Sexuality," 309.

8. Ibid.

9. Ibid., 316.

10. Ibid., 319–320.

11. Ibid., 314. See also Mary Stewart Van Leeuwen, *My Brother's Keeper: What the Social Sciences Do and Don't Tell Us about Masculinity* (Downer's Grove, Ill.: InterVarsity, 2002).

12. Storkey, *Origins*, 39; Looey, "Gender and Sexuality," 319.

13. Looey, "Gender and Sexuality," 308. Van Leeuwen, Looey, Storkey, and others have argued for decades that this neat separation between sex and gender fails the church in its life as a unified and diverse people of God, reoriented and reimaged to Jesus Christ and the purposes of his kingdom. See, for example, Mary Stewart Van Leeuwen, *Gender and Grace: Love, Work, and Parenting in a Changing World* (Downer's Grove, Ill.: InterVarsity, 1991).

14. Storkey, *Origins*, 128.

15. Ibid., 315.

16. Ibid., 108; Ruth Tucker, "The Changing Roles of Women in Ministry," in Pierce and Groothuis, eds., *Discovering Biblical Equality*, 23–38; Janette Hassey, "Evangelical Women in Ministry a Century Ago: The 19th and Early 20th Centuries," in Pierce and Groothius, eds., *Discovering Biblical Equality*, 39–57.

17. Christiana de Groot and Marion and Ann Taylor, *Recovering Nineteenth-Century Women Interpreters of the Bible* (Atlanta: Society of Biblical Literature, 2007).

18. Kristina LeCelle-Peterson, *Liberating Tradition: Women's Identity and Vocation in Christian Perspective* (Grand Rapids: Baker, 2008), 13. Peterson and Van Leeuwen both discuss how this middle-class gender orientation was nonexistent until the Industrial Revolution.

19. See Prudence, Allen R.S.M., *The Concept of Woman: The Aristotelian Revolution, 750 B.C.–A.D. 1250* (Grand Rapids: Eerdmans, 1985).

20. Ibid.

21. See Felker Jones's beautiful analysis, in *Marks of His Wounds*.

22. See John Piper and Wayne Grudem, eds., *Recovering Biblical Manhood and Womanhood* (Wheaton, Ill.: Crossway, 1991).

23. "Introduction," in Pierce and Groothius, eds., *Discovering Biblical Equality*, 15.

24. Groothius, "Equal in Being," 302–304.

25. Ibid.

26. See Piper and Grudem, eds., *Recovering Biblical Manhood and Womanhood.*

27. Kevin Giles argues this in "The Subordination of Christ and the Subordination of Women," in Pierce and Groothius, eds., *Discovering Biblical Equality*, 334–352.

28. Ibid.

29. LeCelle-Peterson, *Liberating Tradition*, 22.

30. Gordon Fee, "Hermeneutics and the Gender Debate," in Pierce and Groothius, eds., *Discovering Biblical Equality*, 368.

31. For extended treatment of this and other texts that deal with interpretation around issues of authority generally and teaching specifically (e.g., *didasko*), as well as terms such as *kephale, authentein, hypostassomai, exousia*, and *authenteo*, among others, see Piper and Grudem, eds., *Recovering Biblical Manhood and Womanhood* and Pierce and Groothius, eds., *Discovering Biblical Equality.* These volumes also provide helpful bibliographies with multiple additional sources that explicate complimentarian and egalitarian positions and scholarship.

32. Looey, "Gender and Sexuality," 331–332.

33. Van Leeuwen, *Gender and Grace*, 69.

34. Ibid.

35. Storkey, *Origins*, 129–131.

36. Ibid., 131.

37. Ian McFarland, *Difference and Identity: A Theological Anthropology* (Cleveland: Pilgrim's Press, 2001).

38. Miroslav Volf, "The Trinity and Gender Identity," in Douglas A. Campbell, ed., *Gospel and Gender: A Trinitarian Engagement with Being Male and Female in Christ* (London: T & T Clark International, 2003), 155–178.

39. Linda Woodhead, "God, Gender and Identity," in Campbell, ed., *Gospel and Gender*, 84–104.

40. Alan J. Torrance, "Person and Particularity," in Campbell, ed., *Gospel and Gender*, 134–154.

41. For an eschatological perspective that suggests this possibility, see Douglas A. Campbell, "The Logic of Eschatology: The Implications of Paul's Gospel for Gender as Suggested by Galatians 3.28a in Context," in Campbell, ed., *Gospel and Gender*, 58–83.

42. John 1, Matt 3; Col 1:15–22, 2:9–10; Heb 1:1–4, 2 cf., 1 Cor 15, Rom 5–8, Phil 2:5–11. This is simply nonnegotiable for Christian orthodoxy, East and West, from Irenaeus, Athanasius, Augustine and the early fathers, through Aquinas and the medievals, through Calvin, Luther and Barth, and countless others.

43. Jeremy Begbie, *Re sounding Truth* (Grand Rapids: Baker, 2007), 197.

44. While we do not see this fully, we do "see" the resurrected Lord Jesus. Augustine, Aquinas, and Calvin may all have been ambivalent about our bodies, but each argued for fully human embodied resurrection based on the New Testament witness. See Felker Jones, *Marks of His Wounds*.

45. Gordon D. Fee, "Male and Female in the New Creation: Galatians 3:26–29," in Pierce and Groothius, eds., *Discovering Biblical Equality*, 180. See also Judith M. Gundry-Volf, "Beyond Difference? Paul's Vision of a New Humanity," and Douglas A. Campbell, "The Logic of Eschatology," in Campbell, ed., *Gospel and Gender*.

BIBLIOGRAPHY

Anderson, Ray S. *On Being Human: Essays in Theological Anthropology.* Grand Rapids: Eerdmans, 1982.

Beck, James R., and Craig L. Blomberg, eds. *Two Views on Women in Ministry.* Grand Rapids: Zondervan, 2001.

Campbell, Douglas, A., ed. *Gospel and Gender: A Trinitarian Engagement with Being Male and Female in Christ.* London: T & T Clark International, 2003.

Felker Jones, Beth. *Marks of His Wounds: Gender Politics and Bodily Resurrection.* Oxford: Oxford University Press, 2007.

Graham, Elaine. *Making the Difference: Gender, Personhood and Theology.* Minneapolis: Fortress, 1996.

LaCelle-Peterson, Kristina. *Liberating Tradition: Women's Identity and Vocation in Christian Perspective.* Grand Rapids: Baker Academic, 2008.

McFarland, Ian. *Difference and Identity: A Theological Anthropology.* Cleveland: Pilgrim's Press, 2001.

Pierce, Ronald W., and Rebecca Merrill Groothuis, eds. *Discovering Biblical Equality: Complementarity without Hierarchy.* Downer's Grove, Ill.: InterVarsity, 2004.

Piper, John, and Wayne Grudem, eds. *Recovering Biblical Manhood and Womanhood: A Response to Evangelical Feminism.* Wheaton, Ill.: Crossway, 1991.

Storkey, Elaine. *Origins of Difference: The Gender Debate Revisited.* Grand Rapids: Baker Academic, 2001.

Schwobel, Christoph, and Colin Gunton. *Persons, Divine and Human.* Edinburgh: T & T Clark, 1991.

Van Leeuwen, Mary Stuart. *My Brother's Keeper: What the Social Sciences Do and Don't Tell Us about Masculinity* (Downer's Grove, Ill.: InterVarsity, 2002.

Index

18779180R00318

Printed in Great Britain
by Amazon